Ultimate Microsoft Power Automate Desktop

Leverage Microsoft's Robotic Process Automation Capabilities to Automate Routine Tasks for Enhanced Efficiency and Productivity

Vijayendra Rao

www.orangeava.com

First Published: November 2024

Published By: Orange Education Pvt Ltd, AVA®

Address: 9, Daryaganj, Delhi, 110002, India

275 New North Road Islington Suite 1314 London,
N1 7AA, United Kingdom

ISBN (PBK): 978-93-48107-53-4
ISBN (E-BOOK): 978-93-48107-75-6

Scan the QR code to explore our entire catalogue

www.orangeava.com

Dedicated To

The love and joy

that I experience

while working on the

Power Automate Desktop tool

About the Author

Vijayendra Rao has over 18 years of experience in the field of Automation. He began his career with VBA automation before getting into the field of RPA. He is certified in SS&C Blue Prism, Automation Anywhere, Power Platform, Power Automate, and UiPath, and has knowledge of various other technologies. He enjoys solving technical issues for others, which led to his nomination as a Super User for five consecutive seasons in the Microsoft Power Automate Desktop community. A Super User rank is a recognition from Microsoft awarded to top solution authors and the most-kudoed members, among other things. Additionally, he has written several technical articles on various "how-to scenarios" in Power Automate Desktop and curated multiple documents for the benefit of the RPA PAD community.

About the Technical Reviewer

Agnius Bartninkas has been successfully leading a process improvement and automation agency since 2018, specializing in RPA using MS Power Automate (and the suite by Softomotive prior to 2020).

Agnius is one of the top voices globally when it comes to Power Automate Desktop due to the vast experience he has accumulated over the years. He has worked across various industries, with over 100 RPA projects delivered to more than 50 clients of various shapes and sizes worldwide either personally or via a directly managed team of developers.

Agnius has personally trained over 10 RPA developers to work with the Power Platform and related software, and has also been teaching students in the Kaunas University of Technology on how to apply Microsoft Power Automate to automate business processes since 2023.

Agnius is passionate about process efficiency, as well as creating stable, robust and effective solutions. He also loves sharing his knowledge with others in various communities, including the Microsoft Power Platform community forums, where he has been acknowledged as a Super User for several seasons in a row, as well as other mediums.

Agnius has also authored several articles on Power Automate, and has been speaking at various tech events related to the Power Platform since 2023, sharing his expertise, which has earned him a Microsoft Business Applications MVP award in 2024.

Acknowledgements

I am thankful to the universe for providing me an opportunity to exhibit the knowledge that has been lingering inside of me for a long time and to share it across the world.

I am grateful to every individual who supported me throughout the journey of writing this book -from my family members and friends to the reviewers, both in the forefront and behind the scenes, as well as the editors, the publisher, and everyone who played a part in bringing this book to life. Thank you.

Preface

In recent times, Robotic Process Automation (RPA) has emerged as a game-changer for automating repetitive, rule-based, and manual tasks, helping to save time, increase efficiency, and boost productivity. Power Automate Desktop, Microsoft's RPA initiative, with its user-friendly interface and robust capabilities empowers users to automate repetitive tasks, freeing up time for innovation and creativity.

This book will guide the reader and teach them the Power Automate Desktop tool right from scratch. Due to its practical nature, readers can and should work alongside the tool while going through its chapters and topics.

Whether you are an RPA beginner or an experienced developer looking to deepen your knowledge, this book offers insights, techniques, and strategies to elevate your automation game via Power Automate Desktop.

The book is divided into 12 chapters, the details of which are as follows:

Chapter 1. Introduction to RPA and Power Automate Desktop: The opening chapter offers a foundational understanding of RPA, comparing traditional automation with RPA, and examining the evolution and current state of Power Automate Desktop (PAD). It highlights PAD's role within the Power Platform, clarifies common misconceptions about Desktop and Cloud Flows, and explores the applications and services PAD can interact with. The chapter also addresses the proper use of the term "use-cases" and provides guidance on identifying good candidates for automation.

Chapter 2. Getting into Action with PAD: This chapter will directly take you into action by focusing on getting started with Power Automate Desktop (PAD), covering the prerequisites for installation and guiding you through creating your first Desktop Flow. It accustoms you to all the sections of the PAD tool's interface, explains the different methods to run a Desktop Flow, and provides information on environments and tenants to help you manage automation effectively across different contexts.

Chapter 3. Debugging the Desktop Flows: This chapter delves into the debugging techniques of Power Automate Desktop, covering how to step through Flows efficiently. It explains the use of breakpoints, running a Flow from specific points, editing and disabling Actions, and modifying variables while debugging and testing. Additionally, it highlights how Subflows simplify the debugging process, making Flow management more effective.

Chapter 4. Essential Elements of a Desktop Flow: This chapter will cover the essential elements of a Desktop Flow by exploring the use of variables and their data types in Power Automate Desktop, providing a foundation for managing data within Flows. It covers essential programming constructs like conditional statements, loops, and Flow control, enabling dynamic decision-making and process automation in PAD.

Chapter 5. Building Blocks of a Desktop Flow: This chapter explains the Unified Recorder in Power Automate Desktop, which simplifies the process of capturing interactions for automation. It provides in-depth details on how to work with UI Elements and Selectors, including how to uniquely identify them for accurate automation. Additionally, it covers about Actions without which Flows cannot be built.

Chapter 6. Automating Common Applications: This chapter focuses on automating the commonly used applications and systems using Power Automate Desktop. It covers automating tasks in Excel and Outlook, interacting with databases, and automating actions within Windows and web environments, providing a comprehensive guide to streamlining workflows across multiple platforms.

Chapter 7. File Management and Data Manipulation: This chapter covers essential file management and data manipulation techniques in Power Automate Desktop. It includes working with files and folders, interacting with Text, CSV, and XML files, using text functions for string operations, performing datetime manipulations, and integrating scripting to extend automation capabilities.

Chapter 8. Beyond Conventional Automation Techniques and Strategies: This chapter explores advanced automation techniques in PAD, including working with PDFs and OCR, as well as using mouse and keyboard Actions for simulating user interactions. It covers automating workstation tasks, various available ways for capturing screenshots, and performing HTTP communications with web applications. The chapter also dives into image-based automation, outlines the requirements for virtual desktop automation, and gives direction and guidelines on terminal emulation, SAP automation, and integration with Active Directory, providing a broad toolkit for handling complex environments and systems.

Chapter 9. Leveling Up Your Automation Workflows: This chapter focuses on leveraging the Cloud portal and the Power Platform for managing automation workflows. It covers the use of Work Queues for workload management, explains how error handling in PAD works, and outlines practices for logging and monitoring them. Additionally, it differentiates between unattended and attended automation and the varied ways for achieving attended automation via PAD, including the use of Custom Forms.

Chapter 10. Intelligent Automation via PAD: This chapter explains the Cognitive Services available in PAD, providing step-by-step instructions on how to use them and achieve Intelligent Automation. This chapter also gives multiple GPT scenarios with live inputs and their outputs. The chapter further highlights the features of Copilot available in PAD and where and how they can be used, and discusses the feature of suggested Actions that enhance workflow efficiency by providing intelligent recommendations.

Chapter 11. Development Best Practices: This chapter will take you through a varied list of development best practices, which can be put in a spreadsheet and used as a development best practice checklist during the development, or even as a code review checklist after the development is complete, so that your workflows adhere to the best standards.

Chapter 12. Extending the Landscape of Your Desktop Flows: This chapter allows you to extend the landscape of your Desktop Flows by taking you through the concepts of Hosted RPA, Picture-in-Picture for multi-tasking, and creating Custom Actions to extend functionality. It also explains the use of Power Fx with examples, Licensing information, and finally certification options to validate your skills and expertise in automation.

Links and Resources:

The book concludes by providing various key links and resources for PAD learning modules, how to dig deeper on any topic now or in the future, where to keep a watch on the frequent PAD product updates, free training workshops from Microsoft, and the community forum where you can get help any time.

Get a Free eBook

We hope you are enjoying your recently purchased book! Your feedback is incredibly valuable to us, and to all other readers looking for great books.

If you found this book helpful or enjoyable, we would truly appreciate it, if you could take a moment to leave a short review with a 5 star rating on Amazon. It helps us grow, and lets other readers discover our books.

As a thank you, we would love to send you a free digital copy of this book, and a **30%** discount code on your next cart value on our official websites:

www.orangeava.com

www.orangeava.in (For Indian Subcontinent)

☑ **Here's how:**

Leave a review for the book on Amazon.

Take a screenshot of your review, and send an email to **info@orangeava.com** (it can be just the confirmation screen).

Once, we receive your screenshot, we will send you the digital file, within 24 hours.

Thank you so much for your support – it means a lot to us!

Downloading the code bundles and colored images

Please follow the links or scan the QR codes to download the
Code Bundles and Images of the book:

https://github.com/ava-orange-education/Ultimate-Microsoft-Power-Automate-Desktop

The code bundles and images of the book are also hosted on
https://rebrand.ly/0b95d0

In case there's an update to the code, it will be updated on the existing GitHub repository.

Errata

We take immense pride in our work at **Orange Education Pvt Ltd,** and follow best practices to ensure the accuracy of our content to provide an indulging reading experience to our subscribers. Our readers are our mirrors, and we use their inputs to reflect and improve upon human errors, if any, that may have occurred during the publishing processes involved. To let us maintain the quality and help us reach out to any readers who might be having difficulties due to any unforeseen errors, please write to us at :

errata@orangeava.com

Your support, suggestions, and feedback are highly appreciated.

DID YOU KNOW

Did you know that Orange Education Pvt Ltd offers eBook versions of every book published, with PDF and ePub files available? You can upgrade to the eBook version at **www.orangeava.com** and as a print book customer, you are entitled to a discount on the eBook copy. Get in touch with us at: **info@orangeava.com** for more details.

At **www.orangeava.com**, you can also read a collection of free technical articles, sign up for a range of free newsletters, and receive exclusive discounts and offers on AVA® Books and eBooks.

PIRACY

If you come across any illegal copies of our works in any form on the internet, we would be grateful if you would provide us with the location address or website name. Please contact us at **info@orangeava.com** with a link to the material.

ARE YOU INTERESTED IN AUTHORING WITH US?

If there is a topic that you have expertise in, and you are interested in either writing or contributing to a book, please write to us at **business@orangeava.com**. We are on a journey to help developers and tech professionals to gain insights on the present technological advancements and innovations happening across the globe and build a community that believes Knowledge is best acquired by sharing and learning with others. Please reach out to us to learn what our audience demands and how you can be part of this educational reform. We also welcome ideas from tech experts and help them build learning and development content for their domains.

REVIEWS

Please leave a review. Once you have read and used this book, why not leave a review on the site that you purchased it from? Potential readers can then see and use your unbiased opinion to make purchase decisions. We at Orange Education would love to know what you think about our products, and our authors can learn from your feedback. Thank you!

For more information about Orange Education, please visit **www.orangeava.com**.

Table of Contents

Read Me

- This book is written considering version 2.43 of the Power Automate Desktop tool.
- The terms PAD, Power Automate Desktop, Power Automate for Desktop, and Microsoft Power Automate Desktop are used interchangeably throughout the book and all refer to the same tool.
- Practically work on the PAD tool while reading alongside the topics and chapters.
- If a newer version of the tool offers a certain feature that is easier to use than that is described in the book, then feel free to use the latest features.
- Even if newer versions of the tool will be released in future, this book will equip you with the foundational knowledge on how to use PAD and its various features.
- If using this as an ebook, copy pasting any text from here into any of the PAD Actions might cause issues due to the font used here and the one PAD is expecting (for example, double quotes in the ebook might appear different than the one in the PAD Actions.) So, type it manually on the PAD tool while working on it.
- Where multiple choices are given for questions, select only 1 choice.
- Some questions are intentionally mentioned to do *or not* do a certain way for better learning of complex scenarios (for example, without looping, without regular expressions, and more).
- All content is on Desktop Flows, except only in places where Cloud Flows is referred, it will be explicitly specified.
- Refer to the GitHub folder for each chapter to find any files required for exercises or to install any application (for example, Contoso application).

  https://github.com/ava-orange-education/Ultimate-Microsoft-Power-Automate-Desktop

- There are chances that the links/URLs/website addresses used in the book may get changed at their original source. To access the correct link, each of the links mentioned in the chapters is also listed in the **Links.xlsx** file in the GitHub folder of this book: https://github.com/ava-orange-education/Ultimate-Microsoft-Power-Automate-Desktop. If a link changes at its source, the new one, if available by the originator, will be updated in the Links.xlsx file on GitHub, and you can refer to the updated link from there.

Chapter 1
Introduction to RPA and Power Automate Desktop

Introduction

The first chapter in the book will introduce you to the RPA terminology, explain the key terms used in RPA, and what the technology is used for. It further explains what Power Automate Desktop or PAD is, where does it stand in the entire ecosystem of the Microsoft Power Platform, which applications PAD can interact with, and how to select automation processes.

Structure

In this chapter, the following topics will be covered:

- Understanding RPA
- Traditional Automation vs. RPA
- The Evolution and Current Status of PAD
- The Power Platform and PAD's Place in it
- Misconceptions about Desktop and Cloud Flows
- Applications and Services PAD Can Interact With
- Problem with the Term "Use-cases"
- Good Candidates for Automation

Understanding RPA

In simple terms, RPA or Robotic Process Automation, is a technology used to automate repetitive and rule-based tasks that are typically performed by humans in their day-to-day activities. To automate these tasks, there are several tools under the RPA technology.

Some of the tools, not in any particular order are, Automation Anywhere, SS&C Blue Prism, and UiPath.

Power Automate Desktop is Microsoft's RPA initiative, which is going to be the subject of this book.

Let's look at the keywords mentioned in the definition of RPA above.

Repetitive: Anything that is done over and over

Rule-based: Anything that follows a particular set of rules or a pre-defined sequence of instructions

RPA is used across various industries and sectors to automate repetitive tasks, streamline business processes, increase efficiency, reduce errors and in-turn free up human resources for more valuable tasks.

In various manufacturing units and factories, you may have noticed that physical robots have already been doing repetitive tasks thus improving productivity and allowing humans to focus on more complex tasks.

In the case of RPA, there are *no* physical robots, but the same level of efficiency and productivity has now become possible among various organizations where humans were performing repetitive and rule-based tasks - thanks to "software robots". These software robots can interact with digital systems just like humans do, and can execute tasks across multiple systems and applications without the need for human intervention.

With the help of RPA tools, one can build such "software robots".

The various terms used to refer to a software robot or to anything that is built via RPA tools are - bots, digital workers, digital agents, robotic agents, virtual workforce, software assistants, automation agents, or an inter-combination of these words, but they all point to the same.

Applications and Usages of RPA

RPA bots are used to perform a varied list of automation tasks such as the CRUD (Create, Read, Update, Delete) operations, report generation, invoice processing, data entry, data validation, data extraction and manipulation, form filling, conduct automated testing, perform IT support and maintenance activities, assist in compliance and auditing, financial processing, inventory management, HR and payroll processing, automating customer service tasks and much more.

Thus, RPA can be - and is already - used across various industries and business functions such as supply chain, logistics, human resources, customer service and support, healthcare and life sciences, finance and accounting, insurance, manufacturing, legal, IT operations, sales and marketing, real estate, education, and the list goes on.

In short, the RPA technology can be applied anywhere and everywhere.

Traditional Automation vs. RPA

Automation is not a new concept and it has been used since decades. If we refer to these earlier methods and approaches as **Traditional automation,** then they include the established tools, methods and technologies that were developed in the past such as macros, programming and scripting languages. Most of them primarily integrated user applications with the backend systems of organizations, and others automated pre-defined tasks and activities without any backend databases. Developers needed to have good programming and scripting skills to make use of such type of automation.

It is not entirely possible to replace traditional automation with RPA as you will see in the upcoming chapters where scripting and programming languages are also used in conjunction with RPA. Having said that, let's take a look at the distinction between Traditional automation and RPA.

Aspect	**Traditional automation**	**RPA**
Approach	Typically involves scripting, coding, or custom solutions tailored for specific tasks or processes	Utilizes software robots to mimic human actions and interact with applications and systems
Technology	Relies on programming and scripting languages	Relies on RPA software tools specifically designed for creating and managing bots
Know-how	For building traditional automation solutions, developers need to know the target system inside out	To create bots, developers have to understand user behavior and replicate the steps
Complexity	May handle complex automation scenarios but often requires technical expertise for development and maintenance	Designed to be user-friendly and accessible to non-technical users, with visual interfaces and drag and drop editors
Programming skills	Developers need to have good amount of programming skills	Users can start using RPA tools without knowing any specific programming language
Expansiveness	Does not have the full flexibility to interact with multiple types of applications from within a single technology and becomes challenging	One single RPA platform can be used to interact with a wide range of applications such as Excel, Outlook, Web applications, Desktop applications, Databases, ERP systems, and so on

Implementation time	Can take a long time to build automation solutions	Provides a way for easy and quick implementation
Scalability	May become less scalable when it comes to how well a system can grow to accommodate more users, data, or transactions without experiencing degradation in performance or service quality	Typically designed for scalability, with the ability to deploy and manage large numbers of bots and handle high volume data
Pricing	Some scripting and programming options are free to use while others come with licensing	Some RPA tools come with free versions but require licensing cost for advanced automation
Provider dependency	Automation built with traditional approaches may not depend solely on a single provider	Each RPA tool has its own provider and hence automation built will depend on the RPA software provider (for example, for security)

Table 1.1: *Traditional automation vs. RPA*

The Evolution and Current Status of PAD

Back in 2020, Microsoft announced the acquisition of Softomotive, a leading RPA provider and creator of products such as WinAutomation (Robotic desktop automation tool) and ProcessRobot (enterprise RPA platform). With this acquisition, Microsoft integrated WinAutomation capabilities into its already existing Power Automate stream which didn't yet had the RPA capabilities at the time. This gradually gave rise to the Power Automate Desktop tool.

Know more about the full details of the announcement at:

https://powerautomate.microsoft.com/en-us/blog/microsoft-acquires-softomotive-to-expand-low-code-robotic-process-automation-capabilities-in-microsoft-power-automate

Since then, there has been no looking back for the RPA arm of Microsoft's Power Automate. There have been frequent releases and updates of new features every single month in the Power Automate Desktop tool. This is evident from where it has positioned itself in the leading market researcher's list, as mentioned below.

- Gartner® Magic Quadrant™ for Robotic Process Automation

  Reference: https://powerautomate.microsoft.com/en-us/blog/microsoft-named-a-leader-and-positioned-furthest-for-completeness-of-vision-in-the-2023-gartner-magic-quadrant-for-robotic-process-automation

  In the chart shown in the preceding link, if you can see the mention of "**Completeness of vision**" on the x-axis, and find Microsoft's position in the top-right "**Leaders**" quadrant, it has positioned itself the farthest.

- Everest Group's PEAK Matrix® assessment for RPA products

  Reference: https://www2.everestgrp.com/reportaction/EGR-2023-38-R-6146/Marketing

  (Right-click the Assessment image on the preceding link and open in a new browser tab to get a bigger view of the image)

  Microsoft can be seen as a Star Performer in the Leaders quadrant of the above report.

Also, you will get to know the names of other RPA tools available in the market in the preceding links along with the ones that were mentioned at the beginning of this chapter.

The charts for both the preceding references are present in the GitHub folder for this chapter in case the links get changed in future.

Thus, after the acquisition, Microsoft entered into the RPA space and has taken a giant leap in the evolution of its tool.

The tool has been referred by different names among RPA enthusiasts. The wordings, Power Automate for Desktop or Power Automate Desktop or PAD as its abbreviated form, all refer to the same RPA tool from Microsoft, and from here on, these will be interchangeably used in this book and they would all mean the same.

The Power Platform and PAD's Place In It

The Microsoft Power Platform is a suite of tools and components that allows organizations to create custom end-to-end solutions using no-code/low-code development. These tools are designed to analyze data, automate processes, create applications, build web pages, and develop conversational chatbots. Let's take a graphical look at the Power Platform.

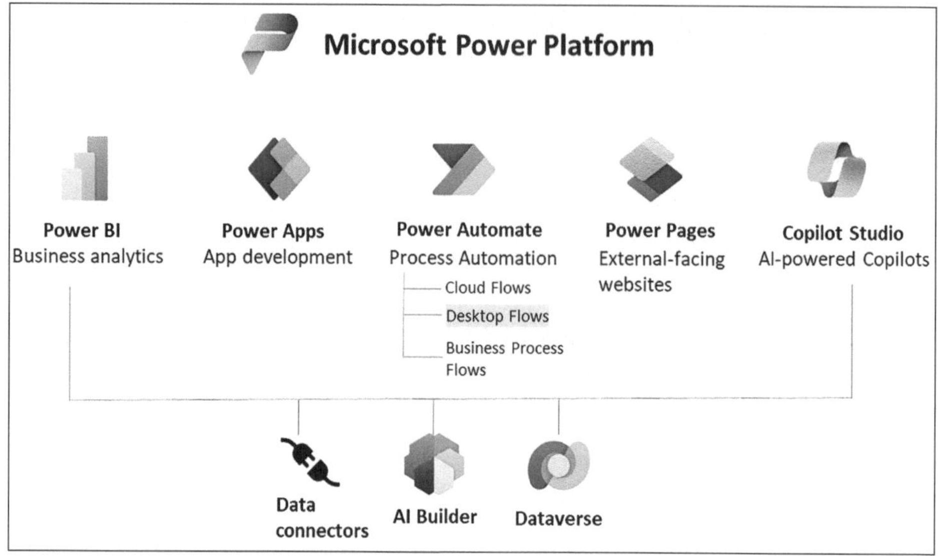

***Figure 1.1:** The Microsoft Power Platform*
(The logos used in Figure 1.1 are sourced from the official website of Microsoft.com. They are utilized here solely for illustrative purposes and do not imply endorsement or affiliation with Microsoft Corporation.)

Furthermore, let's go through each of the tools and components in a nutshell. The **tools** that comprise of the Power Platform are as follows:

- **Power BI:** Power BI needs no introduction as it (Microsoft) has been positioned as a leader in "Gartner® Magic Quadrant™ for Analytics and Business Intelligence Platforms" for 16 consecutive years as of this writing. It is an analytics tool used for business intelligence, dashboarding, interactive reporting and for generating insights that allows users to visualize and analyze data by connecting to a wide range of data sources.
- **Power Apps:** A low-code development platform that allows users to build custom applications without extensive coding knowledge. Users can develop apps for web and mobile devices for specific business needs by connecting to various data sources. Think of it as giving one or more frontend screen(s) for an underlying data at the backend and then allowing CRUD operations (Create, Read, Update, and Delete) for that data.
- **Power Automate:** Power Automate is a cloud-based service that allows users to create automated workflows across various applications and services. As shown in *Figure 1.1*, one can create several types of Flows via Power Automate.

  Simply put, *Flows* come from the word 'workflow' and so refers to a workflow automation created using Power Automate.

  - **Cloud Flows**: They are cloud-based process automation workflows that integrate with a wide array of Microsoft and several third-party services accessible via APIs, thus allowing seamless automation of business processes. A Cloud Flow automation can be triggered either automatically, or instantly, or on a set schedule. Automations built using Cloud Flows are also termed as *Digital Process Automation* (DPA). These types of Flows are created via the Cloud portal of Power Automate.

- **Desktop Flows**: **Desktop Flows** is the topic of our book and is also highlighted in the preceding figure to show its position in the entire Power Platform. Desktop Flows make use of a separate desktop application, called **Power Automate Desktop,** to create workflows that can mimic human actions such as sending keystrokes and mouse clicks, interact with databases and various desktop and web applications, call APIs and much more, which we will be learning further in this book. Desktop Flows fall under the category of *Robotic Process Automation* (RPA).
- **Business Process Flows**: These types of Flows would virtually hand-hold a user and walk them through a series of pre-defined steps in the form of visual stages. This visual representation of a sequence of steps or stages outline the path that a process should take from start to finish, guiding users so that they follow the same steps whenever they use the business process flow.

- **Power Pages:** They allow you to create, host and administer professional and modern business websites. Power Pages provides a no-code/low-code development platform with a drag-and-drop designer to build and publish websites without extensive coding experience.
- **Copilot Studio:** Formerly known as Power Virtual Agents, Copilot Studio is a low-code tool for building copilots. A copilot in this case is an AI-enabled conversational chatbot which can engage with users for various scenarios and can be incorporated in multiple channels. The studio which has a visual interface allows users to create and deploy intelligent chatbots without extensive coding or AI expertise.

The above tools of the Power Platform are closely integrated with the following **components**:

- **Data Connectors:** Data connectors are like bridges that allow Power Platform services to communicate with external applications, data sources and other services. Connectors facilitate the integration of data from various sources and applications into the Power Platform thus allowing the users to use this data and in-turn build apps, automate processes, analyze and manipulate data. There are 1000+ connectors and this number continues to increase since their inception. If there is no existing connector, then one can also create a custom connector.

- **AI Builder:** In short, add intelligence to your Power Platform tools with the help of AI Builder. They provide prebuilt models to be readily applied to common situations, or build custom AI models to cater to specific business needs. AI Builder allows to leverage the power of AI (Artificial Intelligence) to drive innovation and solve complex business challenges within the Power Platform ecosystem.
- **Dataverse:** It's a universe of data. Think of it as a database of the Power Platform. It's a cloud-based data storage service provided by Microsoft as part of the Power Platform. It serves as a secure and scalable data platform for storing, managing and leveraging business data used by Power Platform applications. It also allows businesses to build sophisticated applications, automate processes, and gain insights from this data.

Misconceptions about Desktop and Cloud Flows

Especially among new RPA enthusiasts, those transitioning from any other RPA tool or beginners who are already into Power Automate, there are certain misconceptions about the differences between Desktop and Cloud Flows.

The first one is about the term "*Desktop*" in either the name of the tool (Power Automate Desktop, Power Automate *for* Desktop) or in the wordings "Desktop Flows". It gives an incorrect idea that PAD can automate *only* "desktop" processes. It also gives rise to a misinterpretation that Desktop Flow automations can interact *only with* local resources and applications on our machines such as files, folders, desktop applications, web browsers. While this is true, PAD can *also* call a web API (facilitating data exchange *across the internet*), interact with other applications on the cloud such as SharePoint, OneDrive, Excel online, Word online, MS Teams, make use of Cognitive services, and more.

In the August 2022 product updates (https://powerautomate.microsoft.com/en-us/blog/preview-of-sharepoint-cloud-actions-in-power-automate-for-desktop-introducing-cloud-connectors-in-desktop-flows/), Microsoft announced its first cloud connector (SharePoint) into Power Automate Desktop and also mentioned that other cloud connectors will be continuously brought down to Desktop Flows, thus making the scope of automation limitless.

The PAD tool is a Desktop tool and it can automate cloud applications and services also. Even though you build the Desktop Flows via a Desktop Application (Power Automate Desktop), the Flows that you build are stored on the Cloud and therefore can be accessed from anywhere. This means if you use an account and login to PAD tool on your machine and build a Desktop Flow, the same Flow will be visible when you login to a PAD tool installed *on another machine* via the same login ID. Of course, this becomes achievable if there are no networking or login account or any other restrictions.

The second misconception is that the Cloud and the Desktop tools are two versions of the same Power Automate tool. You cannot create a Cloud Flow on the Power Automate Cloud portal and later modify it in the Desktop tool. Nor you can create a Desktop Flow in the Desktop application and later edit it on the Cloud portal. These are two different types of Flows used for different purposes. Cloud Flows cannot perform what Desktop Flows can do such as user interface-based automation of sending mouse clicks and keystrokes or screen scraping. Nor Desktop Flows have Cloud Flow capabilities such as creating Approval Flows, Business Process Flows, and so on.

However, Cloud Flows and Desktop Flows can work in conjunction with each other, for example, one can call a Desktop Flow from a Cloud Flow. You can schedule, monitor your Desktop Flow activity and view its logs from the Cloud portal of Power Automate.

It can also be noted that these two can be used individually. Meaning, Cloud Flows built using the cloud portal may not need the Desktop tool for building Desktop Flows, or the Desktop tool may not need the cloud portal.

Thirdly, the term "Power Automate" is used as a common term. You may be asked "*How to read emails from Outlook in Power Automate?*" This is a common question to both, Cloud Flows and Desktop Flows, as reading emails from Outlook can be done via both the types of Flows and both have different ways of doing it via different connectors and actions. When you come across this situation, answer by asking a question "*Are you referring to doing this using Cloud Flows or Desktop Flows?*". You may get an answer as either of the two Flow types or the questioner does not know these two types exists. Answer accordingly, now that you are aware of what these two types are and how they are accessed via different tools. A similar kind of question is "*What is the license plan for Power Automate?*". You can begin by asking "*Are you looking to have Desktop Flows in your automation, or Cloud Flows, or both?*". If needed, explain both these types. Licensing will be covered in its own section in this book.

Most of the beginners using the tool are not aware that there are two different Power Automate tools. If someone is working on the Power Automate Desktop tool, they are not aware that a cloud portal of Power Automate exists where Cloud Flows can be built, whereas anyone working on the Cloud portal is not aware that a Power Automate Desktop tool is available - that is, they are unaware of the existence of the tool other than the one they are currently using.

Since the subject of the book is Desktop Flows, the next topic will cover the applications and services PAD can interact with.

Applications and Services PAD Can Interact With

PAD can interact with a varied list of applications and services that we use in our day-to-day work and they are as follows:

- Web applications via browsers such as Edge, Chrome, Firefox, and Internet Explorer
- Database systems
- Microsoft Office applications such as Excel, Word, Outlook and so on
- Windows Desktop applications
- File interaction (for example, Text, CSV, XML, PDF) and the Windows Folder system
- APIs and web services
- Terminal Emulators
- Email clients and the use of Exchange server
- Local workstation resources
- Scripting such as VBScript, JavaScript, Python, and so on.
- Cognitive services such as Google, Microsoft, IBM
- Windows Active Directory
- Use of OCR (Optical Character Recognition)
- Cloud applications like SharePoint, Excel online, Word online, and so on.
- Citrix and RDP virtual desktop applications

And the list is ever growing. Not to mention, as specified in the earlier topic, that Desktop Flows can work in conjunction with Cloud Flows, together making the Microsoft Power Automate suite very powerful.

Problem with the Term "Use-cases"

In the RPA world, whenever automation opportunities are to be identified, the term "use-cases" is widely used. There is nothing inherently wrong with the concept, but with the way it is referred as. A use-case, by some, is generally talked about as a large or an end-to-end automation that involves several data sources and multiple applications to be automated, and this causes a lot of anxiety, unease and waiting period among RPA members. This is also because of the word "Process" in the RPA terminology that might indicate to automate an entire process. Developers and senior RPA roles spend a lot of time thinking, "*Which use-case to automate?*" using RPA automation and then do not even start due to the *analysis-paralysis* it causes. RPA individuals or groups, overanalyze an automation decision to the point of being unable to make a decision or take further action. Instead, it is suggested to try to find out which "*automation scenarios*" can be automated.

Let's go through a small example of a non-RPA kind of automation.

When using Windows 11, to shut down your computer, you would need to go to the **'Start menu'**, then look for the **'Power button'** and click **'Shut down'**. Instead, you could create a simple shortcut on your Windows Desktop that would point to the **"shutdown.exe"** file. This way, whenever you double-click the shortcut or setup a shortcut key for it, the machine would shut down immediately without going through multiple steps.

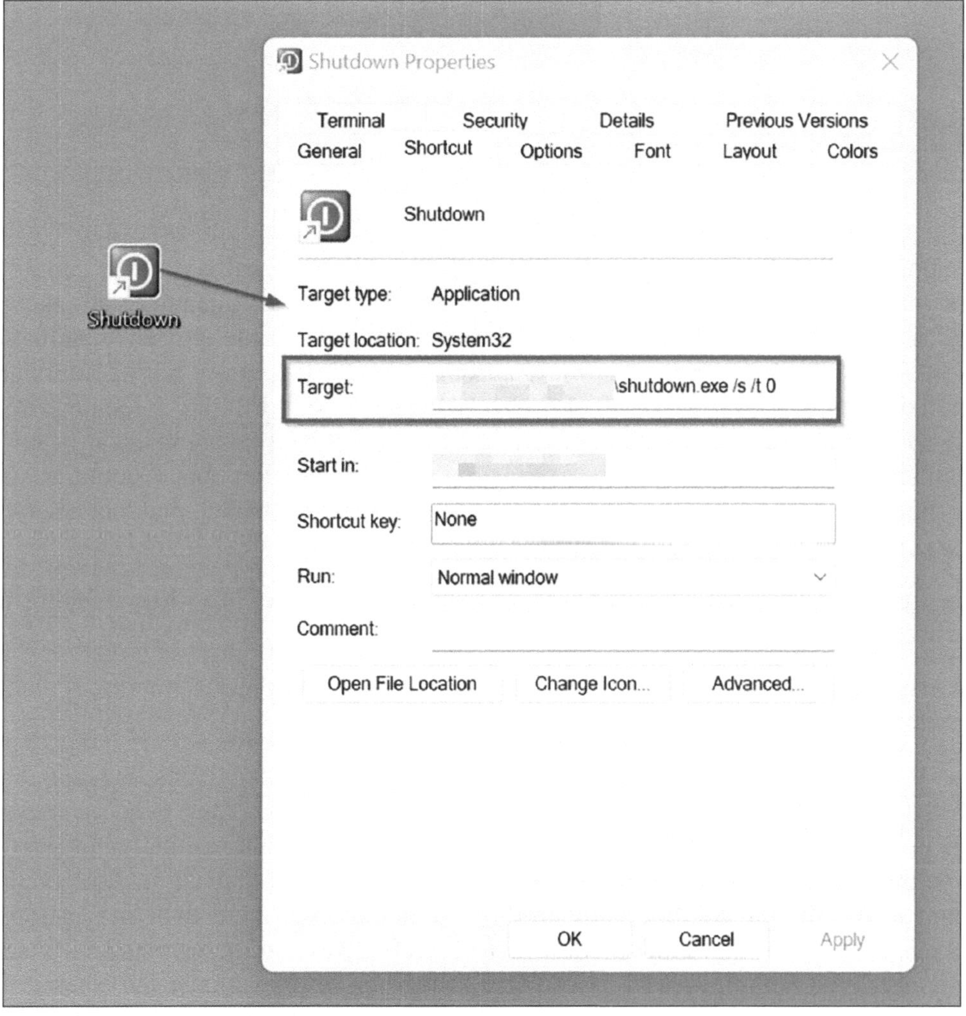

***Figure 1.2:** The Shut down shortcut properties*

Furthermore, if someone needs the **Shut Down** menu options, they can create another shortcut on the Desktop that provides these options.

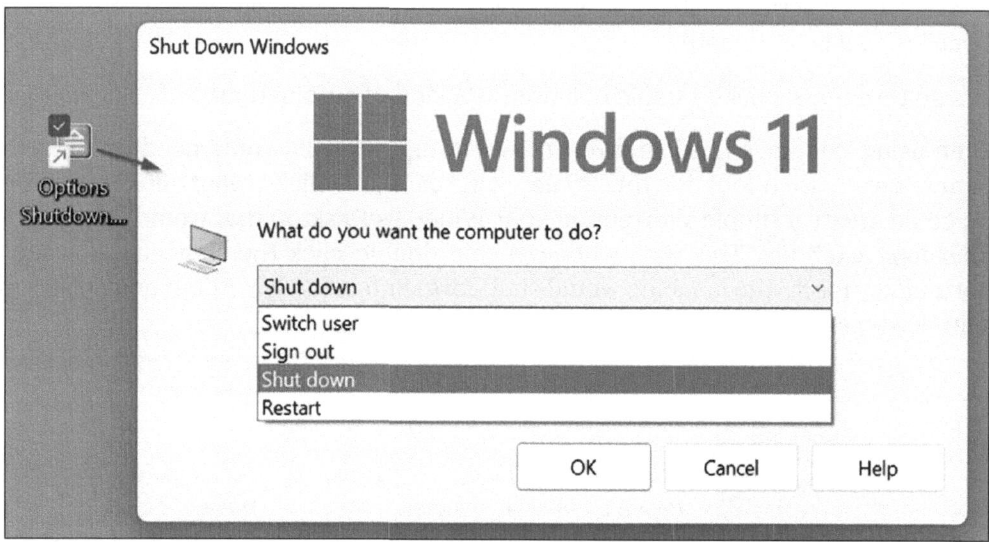

Figure 1.3: *The Shut down shortcut with menu options*

The point of the above examples is not how it is done, but what is done to simplify a task that is performed on a daily basis. As mentioned earlier, this is not an example of RPA automation. Most importantly, this is not a big "use-case" but an "automation scenario" that an individual user would automate because they are boring, mundane, time consuming, repetitive or all of them. Likewise, in RPA, instead of looking for an end-to-end project, one could begin by identifying *automation scenarios* by starting small and then scaling up versus not starting at all. Remember that RPA automation and Power Automate Desktop can be used by everyone from independent users, to small businesses, to medium and large enterprises.

Now that you understand, you can refer to the term "use-case", but without falling into the over analysis trap.

But just so that you know, from here on till the end of this book, "automation scenario" is mentioned for anything to be automated.

Yes, it's true that for certain users or organizations, since costs are spent on infrastructure, licensing and resources for RPA automation, they need to see the **ROI** in order to reap the full benefits of the automation. ROI stands for Return on Investment and, in simple terms, refers to the measure of financial benefits coming from the automation solution compared to the initial investment done in developing and maintaining the automation. There are several factors that determine an ROI such as time saved for employees who were doing the same work manually, the costs saved, reduction in errors due to the automation, if any additional costs are required for maintaining the solution after it is built, time saved due to the speed of the automation and so on.

This brings us to the next topic on identifying good candidate processes for automation without a lot of waiting and overthinking.

Good Candidates for Automation

Selecting good candidate processes for automation becomes crucial especially when there is ROI involved. The following Value/Complexity matrix will act as a good guideline in doing so:

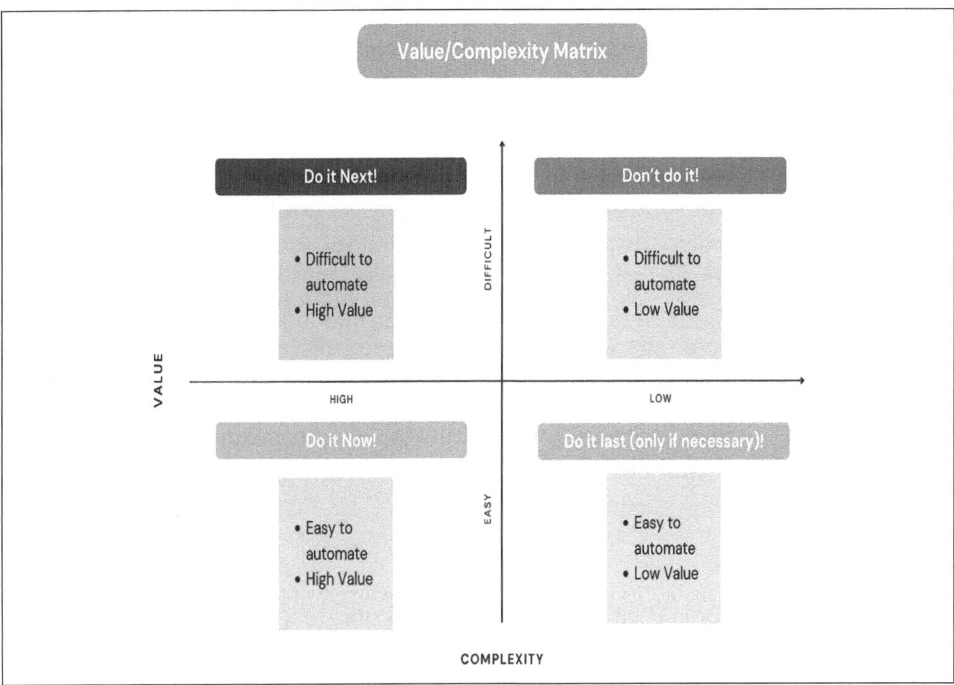

Figure 1.4: *The Value/Complexity matrix*

Before placing your processes in the above quadrants, use the following terms as a reference.

- **Complexity**: Determine the complexity by identifying if the process is rule-based, repetitive, number of screens/applications to automate, whether the RPA tool has the ability to automate what is asked, if the process has documentation or not, and if not, would it be time-consuming to create one, whether the input data is structured or not. At times, a judgment call based on *one or more* of the above parameters can be helpful to determine the same.
- **Value:** Determine the value by verifying if automating the process can reap good benefits in terms of cost or time or both, gains from a business perspective,

or is of high or low importance. This value could be for a customer or an independent end user depending on for whom the automation is being built.

It is important to note that wherever Full automation is not possible you should strive to achieve Partial automation and wherever even that is not possible then you should go for Fragmented automation (meaning, automating small portions or fragments of the manual process).

Partial or Fragmented automation can imply a hand-off from the bot to the human and back from the human to the bot. For example, a report is generated by the bot and passed over to a human, then the human will perform some operations on the report which is not possible by the bot because it requires human intelligence, and then pass back the completed report to the bot for further automation such as uploading it onto another system or send this report via an email to intended recipients, and so on. You do not have to automate 100% of the end-to-end processes all the time.

There could also be challenges such as inconsistencies in the manual process. For example, data is sent in the body of an email in an unstructured format. Since it is unstructured it would at times become difficult for the bot to read. So, the best thing to do here is to standardize the process by having the same text written in a structured format sent in an Excel file attached to the email so that the bot can easily pick up the information and proceed further. Yes, this may require approvals with necessary users to modify the incoming data format, but standardizing is the way to go for RPA automation.

Standardize the process (if necessary), document which part(s) of the process are going to be automated, start with the automation once approved.

Conclusion

In this chapter, we looked at an overview of Robotic Process Automation (RPA) and Microsoft's RPA initiative via Power Automate Desktop (PAD). We explored its evolution, place within the Power Platform, debunked misconceptions, understood the distinctions between Traditional automation and the power of RPA. By highlighting its wide range of applications, as well as knowing how to identify suitable automation candidates, you can begin to think of effectively using Power Automate Desktop as an RPA tool for automating processes.

In the upcoming chapter, we will start to look into the practical aspects of working with Microsoft Power Automate Desktop (PAD). We will be navigating from installing the tool to creating our first Desktop Flow and understanding the various components of its interface.

CHAPTER 2
Getting into Action with PAD

Introduction

This chapter will guide you through the entire process of installing PAD on your machine to building your first Desktop Flow. It will also help you understand the various components of the PAD tool's interface, preparing you to effectively use Power Automate Desktop tool.

Structure

In this chapter, we will cover the following topics:

- Pre-requisites
- Installation
- Our First Desktop Flow Using PAD
- Knowing the PAD Interface
- Ways of Running a Desktop Flow
- Environments and Tenants

Pre-requisites

Like any other software, Microsoft has provided certain pre-requisites for installing and using the Power Automate Desktop tool, and they are as follows:

- A compatible Windows Operating System version
- Hardware requirements
- Valid account to login to the PAD tool

Let us examine each of the above points in more detail.

Windows Operating System

Either of Windows 10 (Home, Pro, Enterprise) or Windows 11 (Home, Pro, Enterprise) would suffice. If you use any of the Home editions of either Windows 10 or 11, you won't be able to call a Desktop Flow from a Cloud Flow, although you would still be able to create the Desktop Flows using the PAD tool and monitor them from the Cloud portal when run from the main Console of the PAD tool. Also, note that the PAD tool is available along with the Windows Operating System in the case of Windows 11, but has to be installed as explained in the "*Installation*" topic below for Windows 10.

Hardware Requirements

Microsoft, in its minimum hardware requirements, suggests having a processor with a speed of at least 1.00 GHz, a storage capacity of 1 GB, and a minimum of 2 GB of RAM. If you plan to run multiple user sessions or involve several applications in your automation that itself would consume your machine's resources, or if you build Flows that would do an automatic login to other machines and perform the automation, then you will need hardware with higher specifications than those mentioned above.

Refer to the link provided after the section below for the minimum and recommended hardware requirements from Microsoft.

Valid Account to Login to the PAD Tool

Three types of accounts can be used to sign into the Power Automate Desktop tool.

- **Microsoft account**: This is your personal Microsoft account, such as a Hotmail.com or Outlook.com account. If you already have this as your personal account you can straight away use it to sign-in to the PAD tool. But if not, you can sign-up for a new email address on any of the above domains. Hotmail.com has transitioned to Outlook.com but you can still choose either of the domains while creating an account. Any Desktop Flows built with this type of account will be stored on the personal OneDrive account.

  Something to note here is that this account type will not have a provision for adding premium capabilities as the **"`Go Premium`"** button is not visible on the PAD tool. Also, if the Flows built with this account type ever have to be transitioned to a premium account in future, then that will have to be done manually without any export functionality for it.

- **Work or school account**: This plainly is an account created by the IT department of your organization when you become a part of it. You can use this account and sign-in to the PAD tool. The account would be without any premium capabilities and features, however to try out the premium RPA features you can start a trial from the **"`Go Premium`"** button on the main screen of the PAD tool. Desktop Flows developed using this account are stored in the Dataverse of a dedicated default environment.

- **Organization premium account**: Among the various types of Power Automate license plans, an organization purchases them for its users and ties it to this account. This would also involve making the premium features and capabilities available depending on the purchased license plan. Desktop Flows built using this account are stored in the Dataverse across the respective created environments. We will be looking at multiple environments at the end of this chapter.

Apart from the above, you would need a compatible browser such as Microsoft Edge (version 80 or later), Google Chrome, or Mozilla Firefox and an internet connection.

Keep the following link handy for extended reading on the preceding topics, for comparison between what is available in each of the above account types, and to understand any issues and limitations:

https://learn.microsoft.com/en-us/power-automate/desktop-flows/requirements

Installation

In general, you would need the right Windows version as per the mentioned pre-requisites, the right browser, a valid account and then you could proceed with the installation of the tool.

The official link from Microsoft to install the tool is as follows and there are two locations from where the tool can be installed.

Install Power Automate:

https://learn.microsoft.com/en-us/power-automate/desktop-flows/install

The two ways as explained in the link are as follows with some details to note:

- **Install using an MSI installer:** Installing via this option requires admin rights on your machine and any new updates to the PAD tool will be required to be updated manually. When a new version of the tool is released, a pop-up will show up on the PAD tool and can be updated by clicking on it.

  The installer also has an option to install a separate desktop app called as `"Power Automate Machine Runtime"` app, which is used to register a machine and connect it to the Power Automate Cloud portal further useful for triggering a Desktop Flow from a Cloud Flow. This is a recommended installation option.

- **Install from Microsoft store:** The store installation does not require admin rights and the releases are updated automatically on a regular basis as and when they are released. If you install from the store but also need the Machine

Runtime app, you can later start the installation from the MSI and select only the required check box for the Machine Runtime, as explained below.

Once you start the installation, you should see a screen as follows:

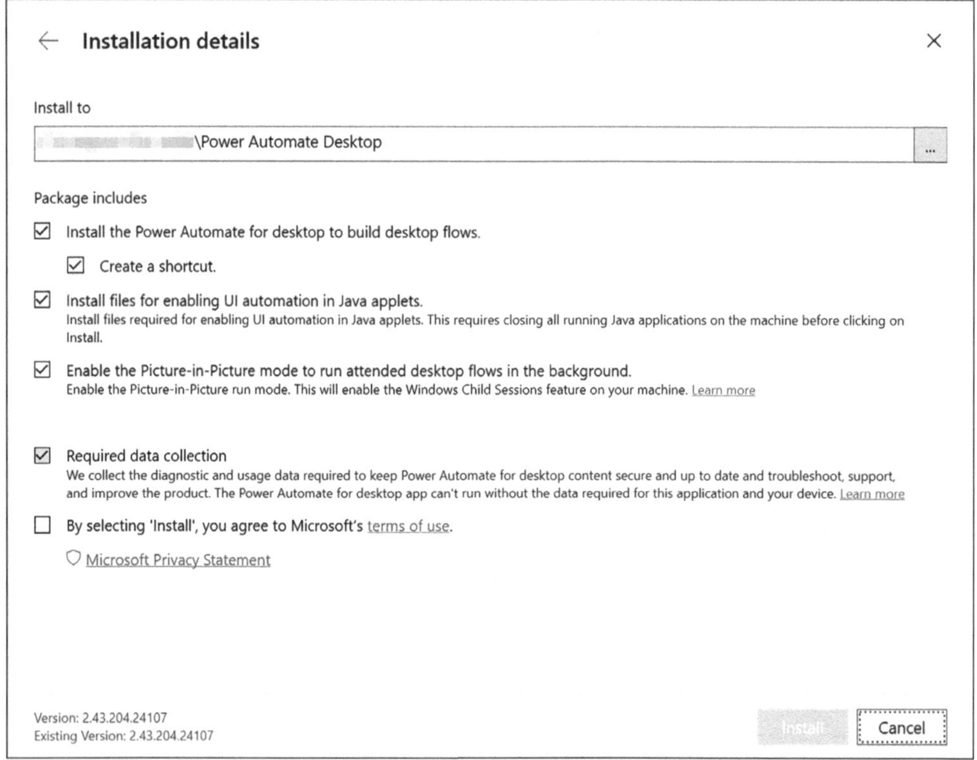

Figure 2.1: *PAD installation screen*

Along with the default check box options above, if you are using a Windows version *other than* Home edition, you will see an additional option that reads as **"Install the machine-runtime app to connect to the Power Automate cloud portal"**. Select this option and when you agree to Install, the blue **"Install"** button will be enabled, allowing you to proceed with the installation. The bottom left-hand corner shows the latest version available to be installed as well as the one that is currently installed on the machine, if any.

In the upcoming installation screens, you will have an option to install browser extensions for Chrome, Edge and Firefox. Make sure to install the one for your preferred browser as they will be needed to perform browser-based automation. Even if you miss, you will be having an option to install these from within the tool.

You will see a **"Launch app"** button on the final installation screen and clicking that will open up the PAD tool. If you selected the **"Create a shortcut"** checkbox during the installation process you will also find a shortcut to the tool on the desktop.

Another way to open up the tool is to go to the Windows Start menu and type **"Power Automate"**. Although it does not mention the word **"Desktop"** in its name, it is the same Power Automate Desktop tool we have just installed.

Once installed, you would need to sign-in with the account you have. The tool may ask you to choose certain options such as **"Region"** and once the inputs are provided you are ready to use the tool. Additionally, the tool may also ask you to take a tour through its various menus and options, which you can choose to take if you wish.

In general, the installation should proceed smoothly. However, if you encounter any issues, refer to the various sections of the provided installation link for assistance.

Our First Desktop Flow Using PAD

There are no prizes for guessing that the first process in any language or tool is the **"Hello, World!"** program.

Please follow along the steps to create our first Desktop Flow:

1. Click the **"New flow"** button on the top left corner of the main screen as marked in *Figure 2.2*

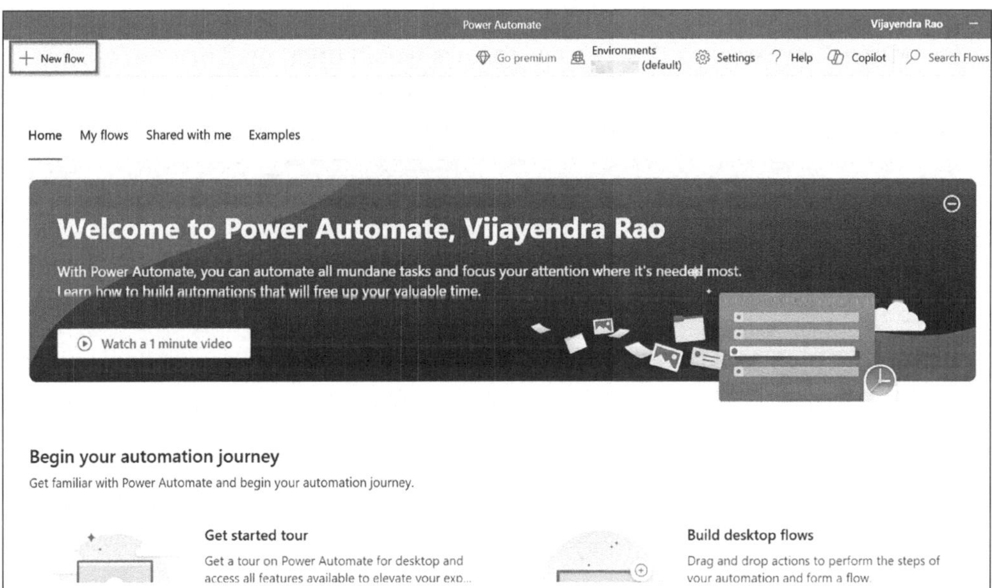

Figure 2.2: *Creating a new Desktop Flow*

2. Give a name to your Flow and click the **"Create"** button.

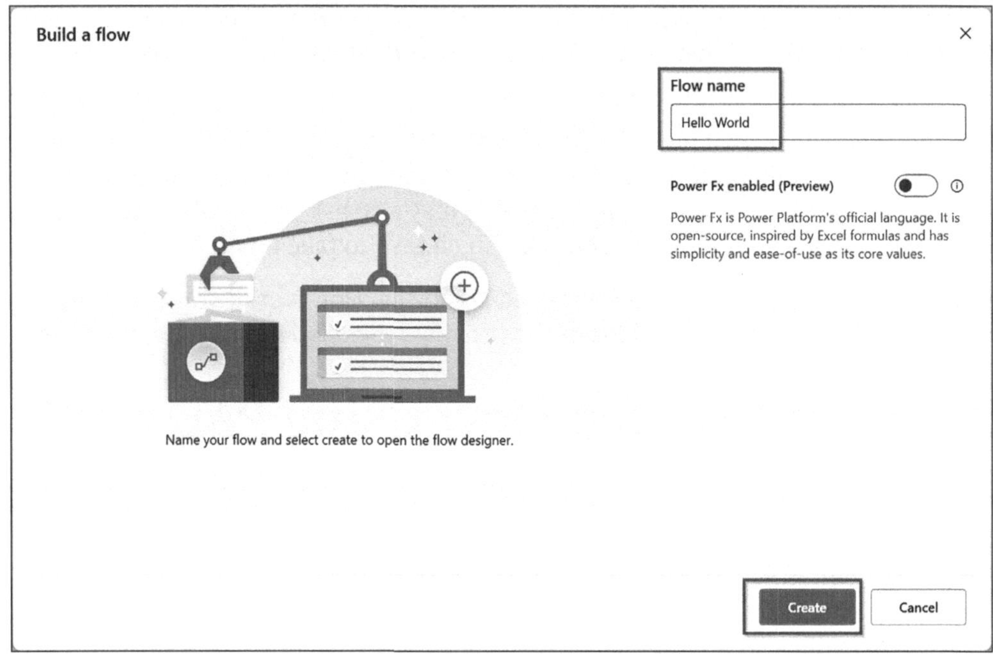

Figure 2.3: *Flow name and Create*

3. After a few seconds, a screen as follows would open up. For now, we are not referring to what each of the screens are called as they are covered in the next topic, "*Knowing the PAD Interface*".

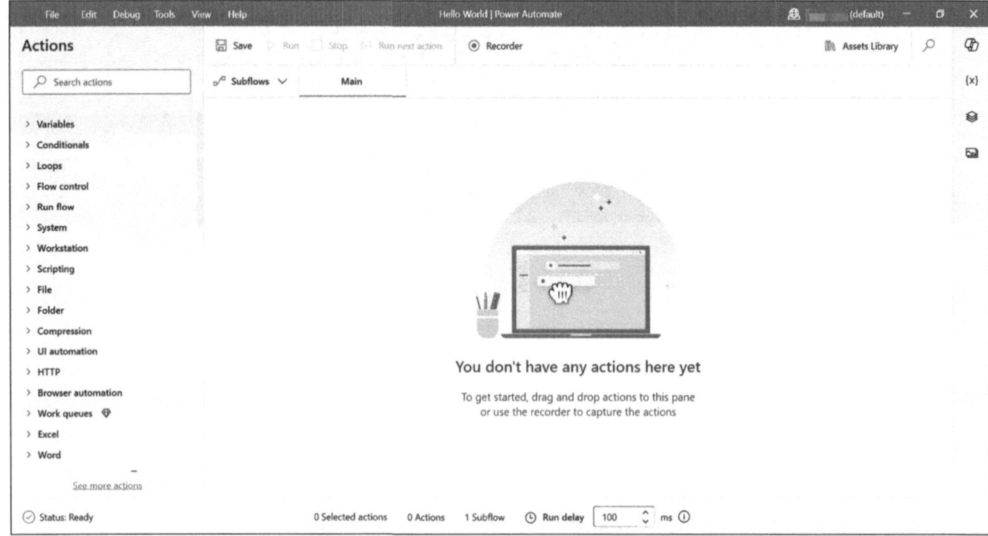

Figure 2.4: *The new Flow landing screen*

4. In the **"Actions"** section on the left-hand side, search for the word **"display"**

in the provided box, click on the **"Display message"** and drag and drop it onto the whitespace as shown. Follow the sequence as per the numbering given.

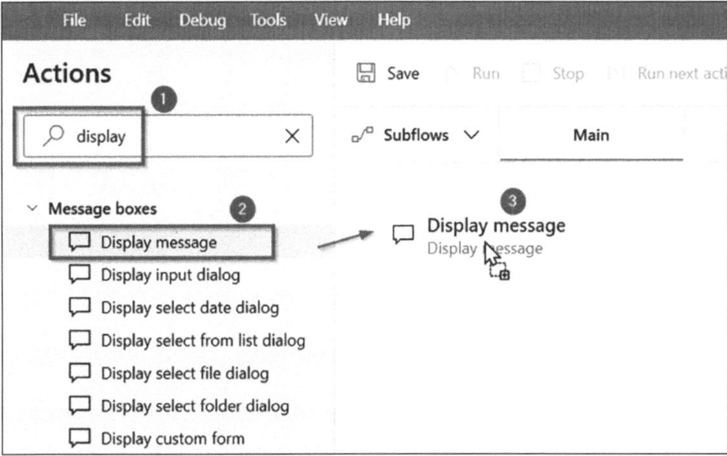

Figure 2.5: *Drag and drop Display message*

5. Once dropped, automatically a dialog box will pop-up asking you to fill up certain parameters or select some properties. Add the details as marked below and finally click the **"Save"** button.

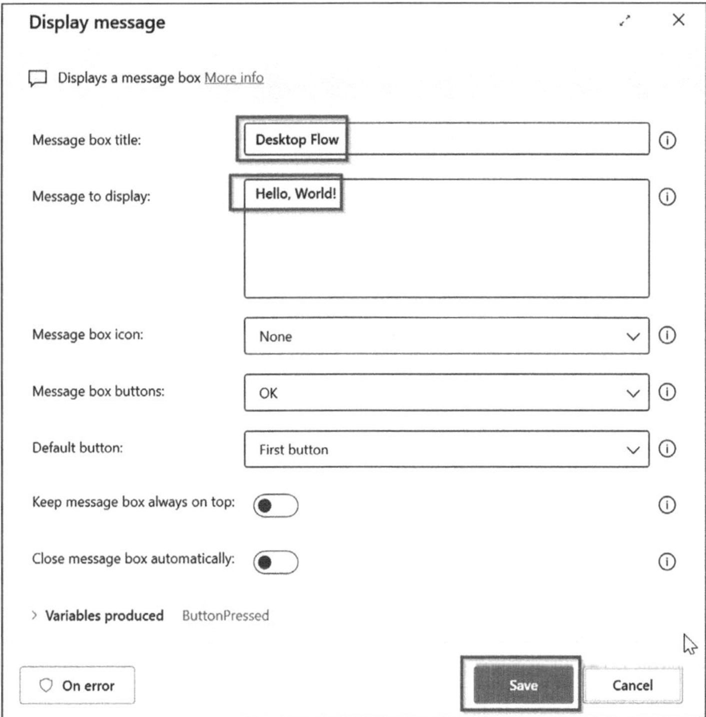

Figure 2.6: *Parameters for Display message*

6. You are now ready to run it. Click the **"Run"** button at the top, as shown.

Figure 2.7: *Run the Flow*

7. Upon executing, a message box will appear displaying the values you provided earlier. The title of the message box **`"Desktop Flow"`** as well as the message **`"Hello, World!"`**, both are seen on the resulting message box.

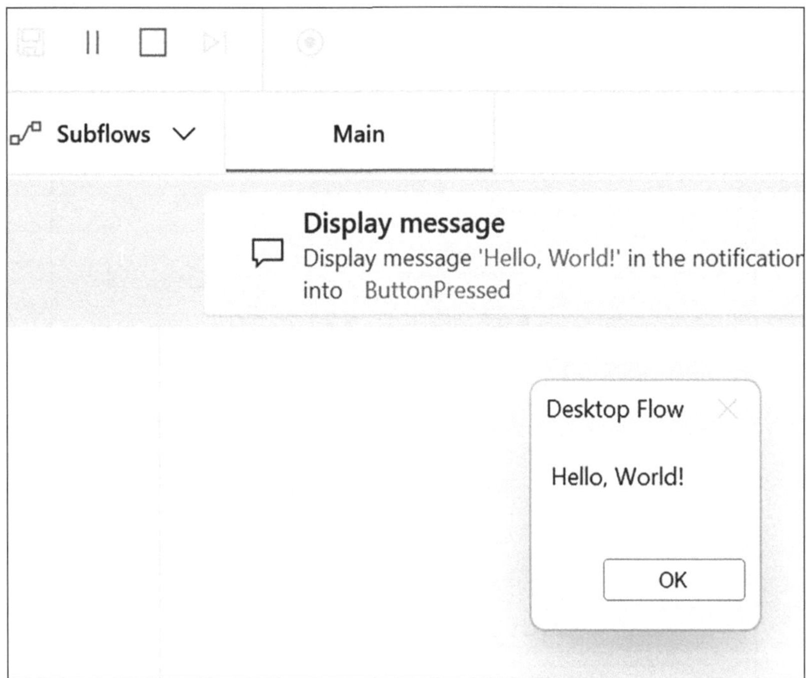

Figure 2.8: *Output of our first Flow*

With this we complete our first Flow. The nature of the Flow is intentionally simple to give you a glimpse of building a Desktop Flow and then running it. **`"Display message"`** was the *Action* that we chose and the combination of such Actions make up a Desktop Flow.

Knowing the PAD Interface

The Power Automate Desktop interface has two main components.

- The console
- Flow designer

Let's take a detailed look into each one of these.

The Console

The console is like a main control panel to the Power Automate Desktop tool from where you can open the Flow designer (second component) to create and edit Flows. The main area of the console has four tabs, as shown in *Figure* 2.9, and these tabs are **`Home`**, **`My flows`**, **`Shared with me`**, and **`Examples`**.

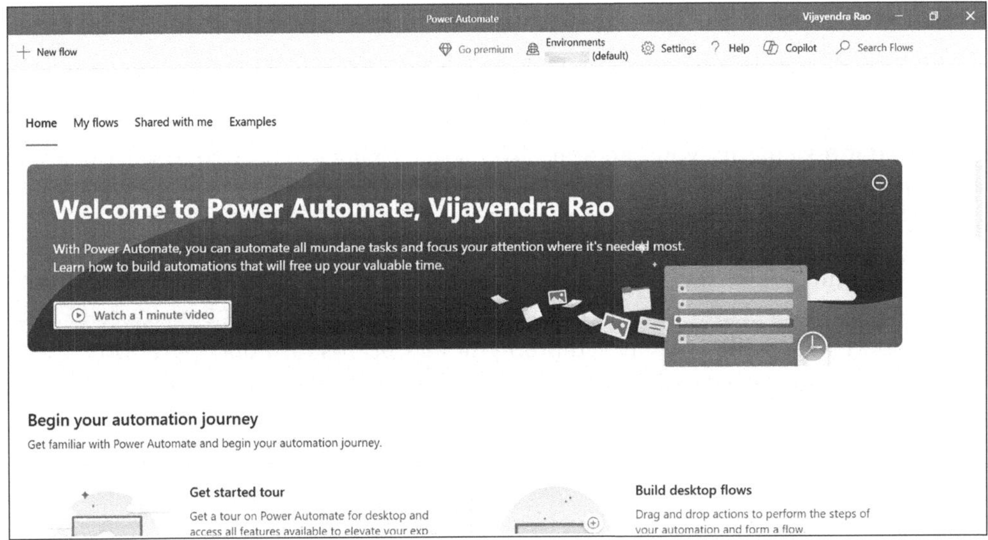

***Figure* 2.9:** *The console with four tabs*

When you launch the PAD tool, the **"`Home`"** tab opens up by default. Here you will see separate sections to take a tour through the tool, links to various examples available in the **"`Examples`"** tab, Tutorials that will take you to the Microsoft Learn page, useful links and references and an overview of the new features.

In the **"`My flows`"** tab, you will see the list of all the Desktop Flows you have built, where you can perform all the below referred operations. When you right-click a Desktop Flow that is already built or when you click the ellipsis button (indicated by the arrow), it will open the context menu as shown.

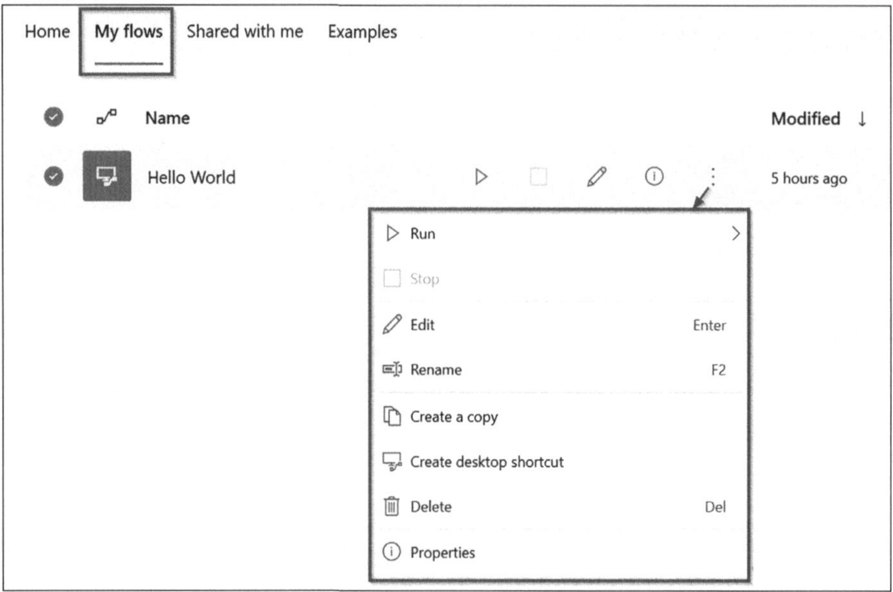

Figure 2.10: *The context menu*

From the context menu, you can start/run, edit, rename, and delete a Flow among other options, as shown in *Figure* 2.10. The **"Stop"** menu item that appears as disabled now will be enabled if the Flow is running.

The same menu will be seen on the top command bar if a Flow is selected using the tick box next to the Flow name. There is also an option to select multiple Flows at once, which will provide you with common menu options for bulk operations.

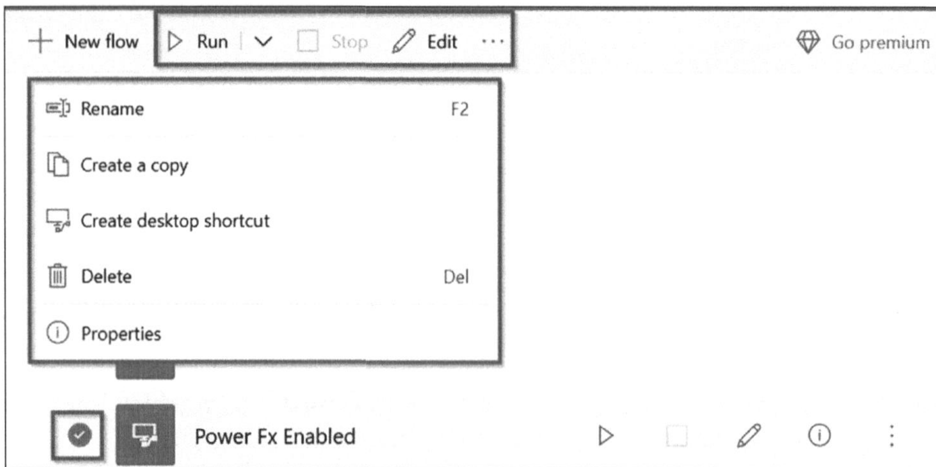

Figure 2.11: *The command bar context menu*

The third area where you have the option to **Run** or **Edit** the Flow is next to the selected Flow, where you also get to see the current status of the Flow.

Figure 2.12: *Run, Edit Flow, and Status from the selected Flow*

The **"`Shared with me`"** tab will show the list of all Desktop Flows shared by another user and this is done via the Power Automate Cloud portal. When you save a Flow from this tab, it gets added to the **"`My flows`"** tab.

Lastly, the **"`Examples`"** tab will have a list of ready-made Flows that are pre-built to get you started on a few topics such as Excel, Web and Desktop automation and so on. It is beneficial that you go through these examples for learning purposes or for using them as templates to start building your automation.

The **"`General`"** tab of the **"`Settings`"** button at the top allows you to configure the settings for Power Automate Desktop.

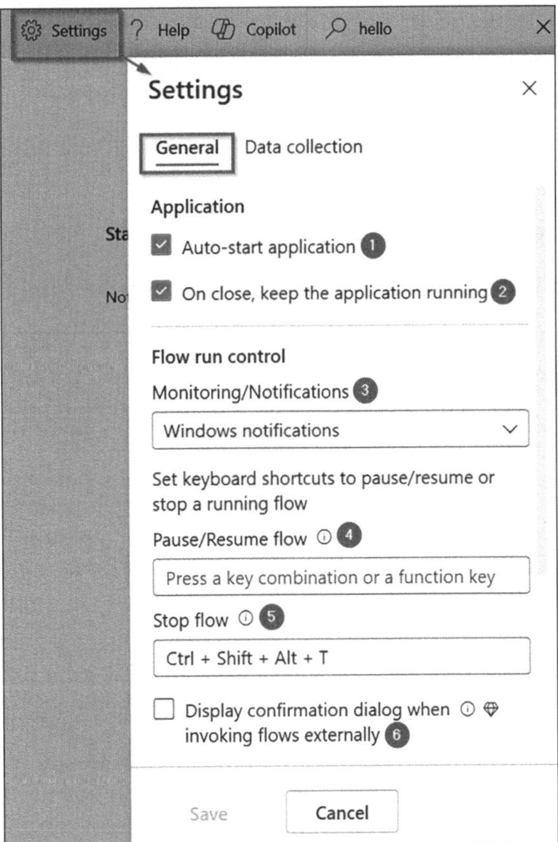

Figure 2.13: *General tab of PAD Settings*

Follow the instructions below using the numbering shown in *Figure 2.13* as a guide.

1. This setting determines whether PAD application should automatically start when the Windows operating system completes its booting.

2. The next setting, when unticked, will close the PAD application when the console is closed and will not be running in the background.

3. Through the `Monitoring/Notifications` setting, you can choose between the three options: Windows notifications, the Flow monitoring window, or disable notifications entirely.

    a. When a Desktop Flow is either running, paused in between, stopped, completed successfully, or encountered an error, the **Windows notifications** option will show a Windows notification pop-up. This pop-up will also have two buttons to either Pause or Stop the running Flow.

    b. The same features are made available via the **Flow monitoring window** option, but with some additional functionality. In place of showing separate notifications for every single Flow, this option will show the status of all running Flows in a consolidated window, along with names of which Subflow and Action are running at that time for the respective Flow and a **"`Copy error details`"** button to copy the details of an erroneous Flow.

    c. The third dropdown option **Do not display** will not display any kind of notification.

4. In label No. 4, you can configure a shortcut key to Pause or Resume a Flow.

5. Here you can set shortcut keys to instantly stop running Flows.

6. For security reasons, by default PAD will prompt you with a confirmation dialog box to verify if a Desktop Flow has been triggered via a Flow URL or through the desktop shortcut. This setting will allow you to disable that confirmation box.

At the end of the **"`General`"** tab you will also see **"`Check for updates`"** button. If a new version of PAD is released, clicking this button will notify you and provide an option to update the tool. This is the manual way of updating Power Automate Desktop. In general, Power Automate Desktop will check for updates and show a pop-up asking you to update along with an option to delay the update for a later time. Unchecking the **"`Show update notifications`"** option will not display any update notifications.

It should be noted that the updates can be controlled by your organization and you might not be allowed to update the tool whenever the notifications show up. Also, you might notice that you do not yet have an update but someone else does. This is because of the manner in which updates are released from Microsoft, but you will eventually receive the updates.

The **"Data collection"** tab of the **"Settings"** shows about required diagnostic data collection from Microsoft and these settings are handled by the admin.

As in any other software or tool, you can check the current version of PAD from the **"About"** section of the **"Help"** menu. The **"Help"** menu also has a provision to navigate to useful links such as the Power Automate Desktop community, blog for the product updates, and to provide feedback to Microsoft on the PAD tool.

Flow properties box shows up when you go into the properties of an individual Flow through the context menu or through the properties button on the selected Flow. As shown in *Figure* 2.14, the **"General"** tab allows you to provide a name or edit an existing name, and a box to describe the details of the Flow. A recent feature allows Copilot (Microsoft's AI companion) to create a description based on the Actions in the Flow. For our first Flow, it describes it as *This flow displays a message dialog with the title* "Desktop Flow" *and the message* "Hello, World!" *when triggered.*

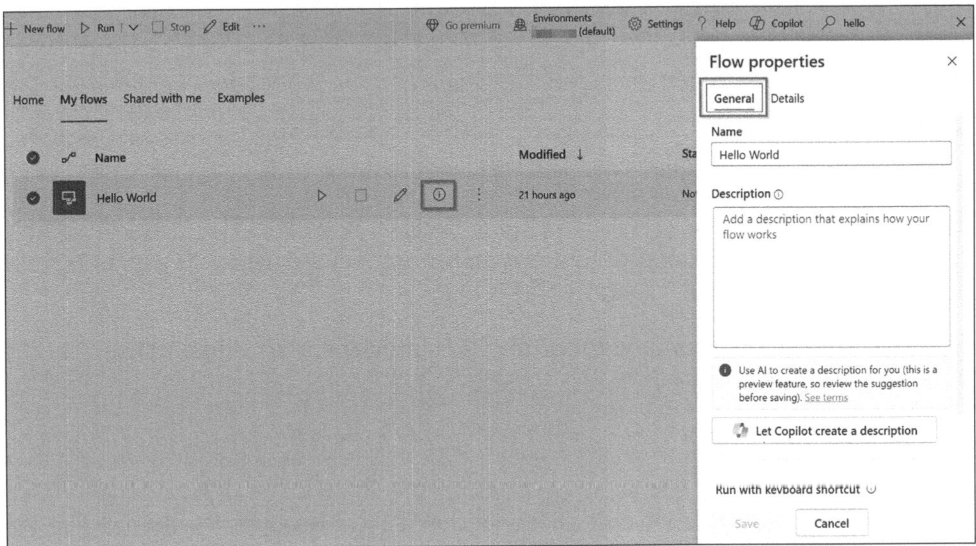

Figure 2.14: *General tab of Flow properties*

At the bottom, you can see that there is a provision to set keyboard shortcuts to start the Flow. Scrolling down further the Flow properties, there is a premium option to run the Flow in **"Picture-in-Picture"** mode, which we will be learning in the chapter named "*Extending the Landscape of Your Desktop Flows*". Anything that is a premium feature is shown with a diamond icon next to it. Also, anything that says **"Preview"** is not meant for use in the final Production environment until it comes out of Preview to become a Live feature.

Switching to the **"Details"** tab, as shown in *Figure* 2.15, will display the owner who developed the Flow along with the creation and modification date-timestamps. Next, you can see the **"Run URL"**, which is used to run the Desktop Flow from external sources and will be covered in the next topic of this chapter. The **"Flow ID"** is a unique identifier of the Flow and the storage schema version of the Flow in Dataverse.

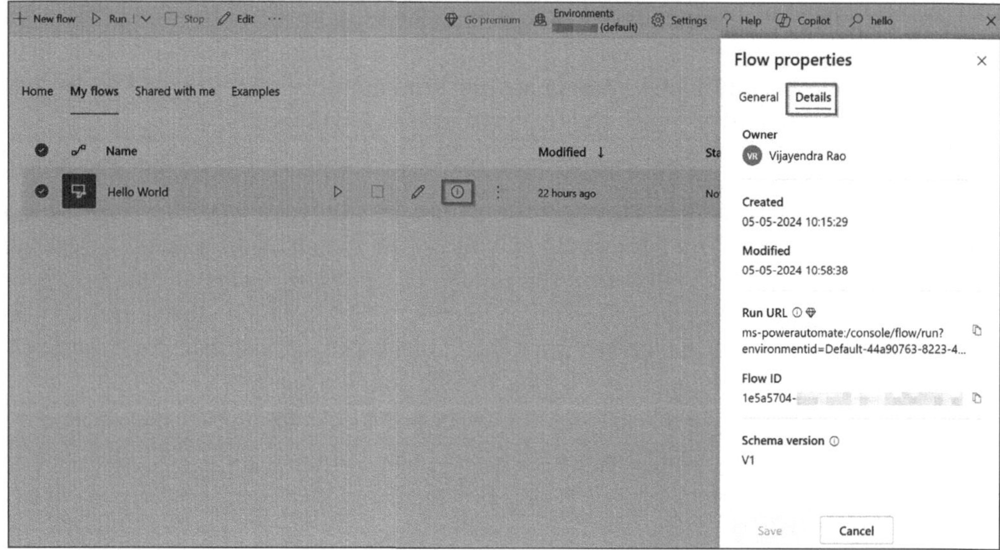

Figure 2.15: *Details tab of Flow properties*

We will learn about the **"Environments"** and **"Switch organization"** options shortly. This feature needs an explanation of what environments are, which is explained in the "*Environments and Tenants*" section of this chapter.

This concludes the first component of the PAD interface, that is, the console, and we will move on to the Flow designer.

Flow Designer

The area where you create or edit a Flow is the **"Flow designer"** window. The Flow designer further has several components. So, let us go through each one of them.

- **Workspace:** The Workspace is the main component of the Flow designer window. This is because the entire Flow development happens here. As you might have seen while building the first Flow, we dragged and dropped the **"Display message"** Action onto the Workspace. This section contains a series of such Actions that determines what the Flows does.

Figure 2.16: *The Workspace*

- **Actions pane:** The Actions pane on the left-hand side consists of a list of Actions that are categorized into different groups according to what they do. For example, the **"`Display message`"** Action that we used in our first Flow is a message box to the user, hence is categorized under the Action group called **"`Message boxes`"**. A Flow cannot be built without these Actions, hence they are the key components to any Flow.

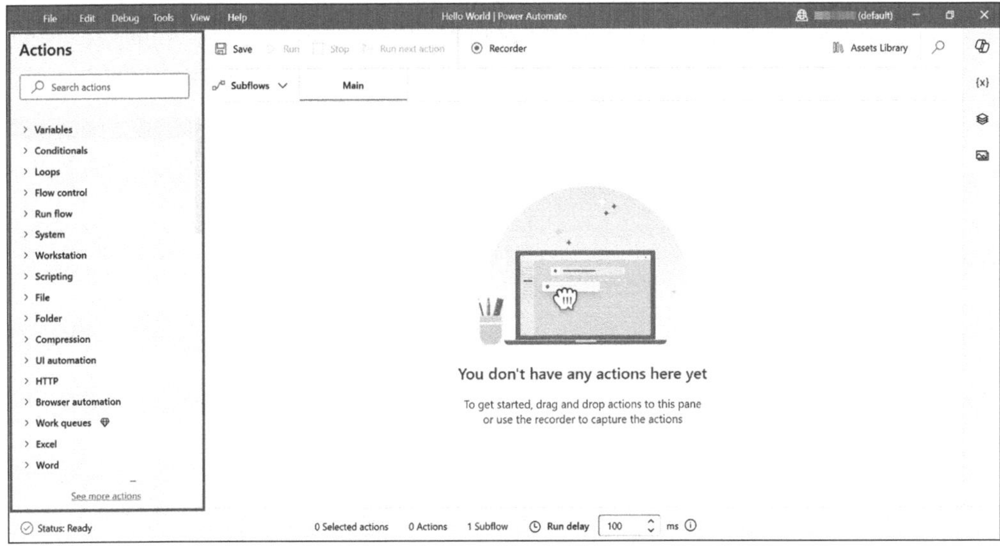

Figure 2.17: *The Actions pane*

- **Variables pane:** Variables as in any programming or scripting language act as containers that hold data. This pane lists down all the variables used in the

Flow and also gives a provision to edit their values, rename them, find where they are used in the Flow, and filter them by their type. The different types of variables and how they are used are explained in the chapter named "*Essential Elements of a Desktop Flow*".

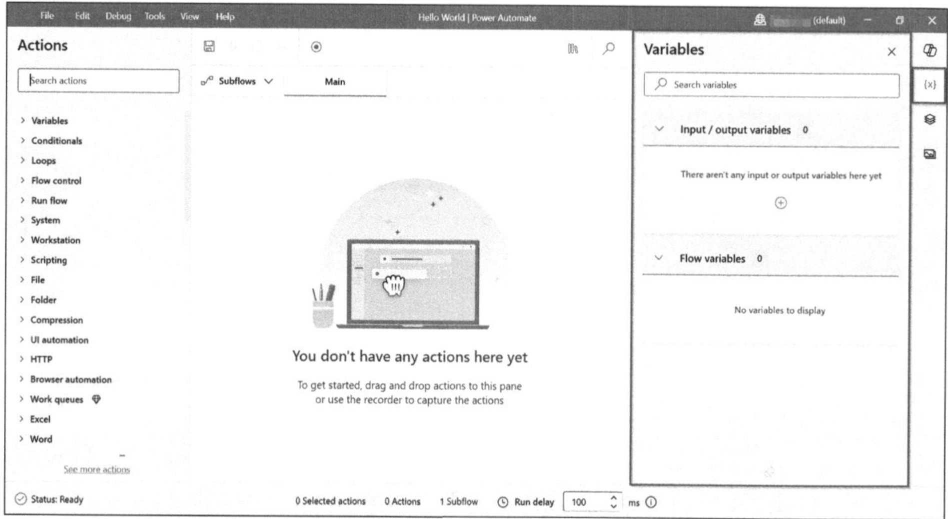

Figure 2.18: *The Variables pane*

- **UI elements pane:** UI elements or User Interface elements are used in automation scenarios where UI interaction is made using elements such as textboxes, buttons, and so on, generally for Desktop and Web automation. This pane holds all such captured UI elements and provides the ability to create new ones or manage existing ones. UI elements are explained in detail in the chapter named "*Building Blocks of a Desktop Flow*".

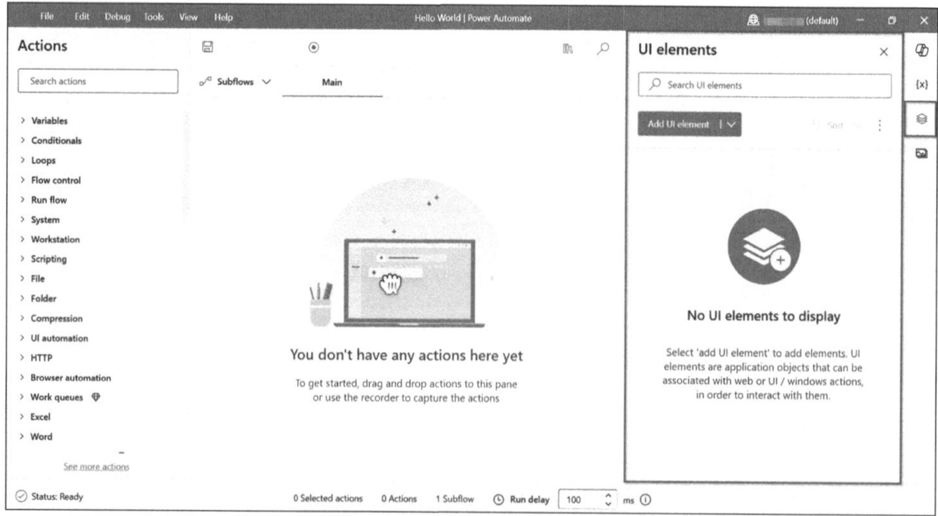

Figure 2.19: *The UI elements pane*

- **Images pane:** During automation, there arises certain scenarios where we use Flow Actions that will capture or use images. The images pane is where all such images are stored and managed.

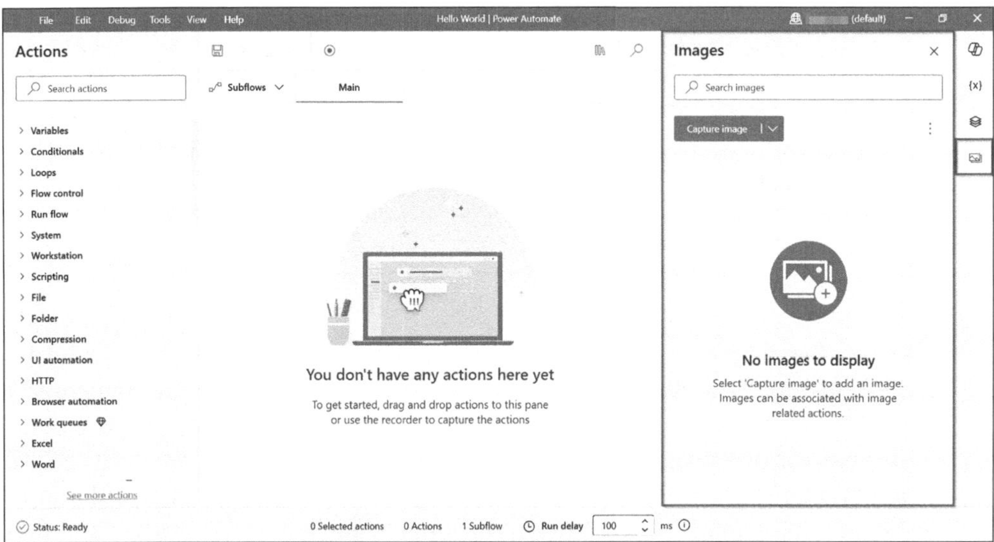

Figure 2.20: The Images pane

- **The Search boxes:** There are two search boxes, as shown in *Figure* 2.21. The first search box is to find any text, or an Action name, or a variable used anywhere in the Flow. A results pane will open up at the bottom of the Flow designer window showing the results of the search. Whereas, the second type of search box is for searching variables among a list of variables in its own pane. The second type of search box is also available in the UI elements and Image panes, which are used for searching UI elements and Image names, respectively.

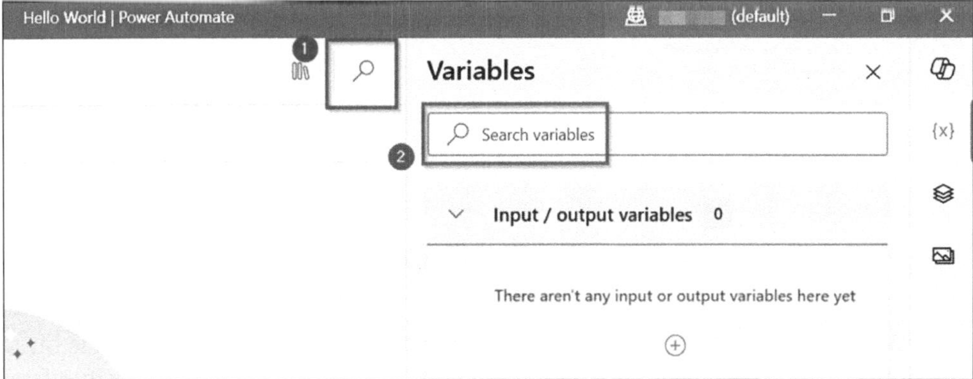

Figure 2.21: The Search boxes

- **Run delay:** The Run delay box at the bottom of the designer, which allows to enter the time in milliseconds from 1 to 10000 is used while debugging or running the Flows from the designer. Since the speed of the Flow when run from the Flow designer is different from the speed when you run it from the main console, you can manipulate the speed from the designer by giving the number of milliseconds and try to mimic the same speed as in a real automation scenario. This time in milliseconds is the time between two Actions. It can be used for troubleshooting to see why a Flow is working fine from the designer (where the speed is slower) but the same Flow is throwing errors or not behaving as expected when run from the main console (where the speed is faster).

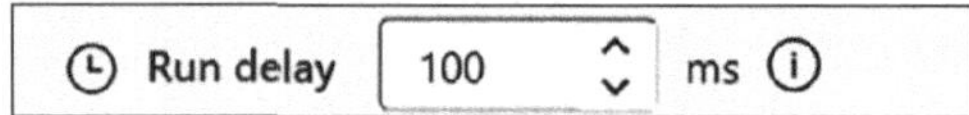

Figure 2.22: *The Run delay box*

- **Errors list:** The Errors list pane shows up any Errors or Warnings or both at the bottom of the designer window. In *Figure* 2.23, the marking indicated as No. 1 is the **"`View details`"** button, which when clicked will display the details of the error or warning such as its location and the actual error message. The button marked with No. 2 is the **"`Go to line`"**. When clicked, it will jump to the line that contains the Error or Warning, which becomes handy when there are lots of Actions within the Desktop Flow.

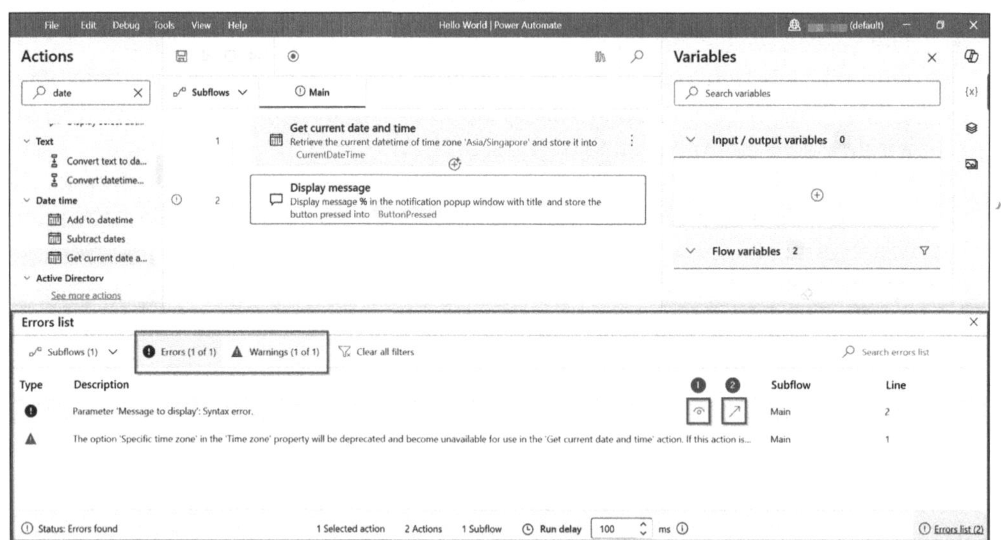

Figure 2.23: *The Errors list pane*

- **Actions context menu:** When an Action is right-clicked or the ellipsis button is used, a context menu appears showing the various options possible for an Action. You can cut, copy, paste Actions from one location of code to another or move the Actions up and down or even delete them and then undo or redo an operation performed. The same menu appears when multiple Actions are selected at once but only with the options available for bulk operations.

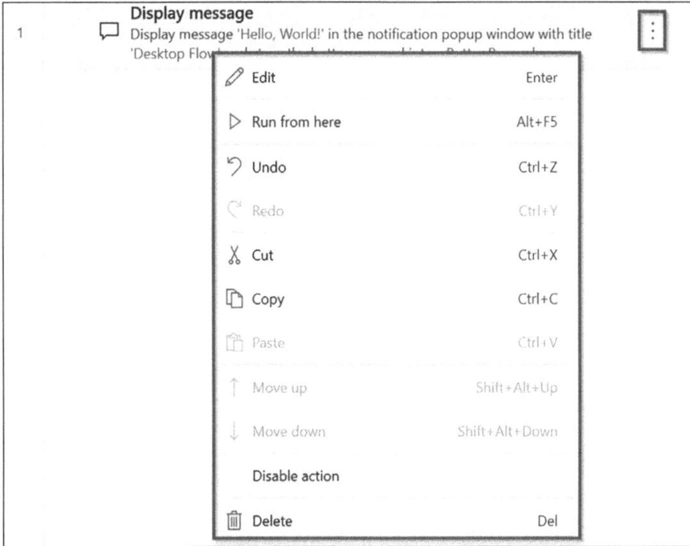

Figure 2.24: *The Actions context menu*

While building or running Flows if you start seeing messages that would indicate anything about DLP (Data Loss Prevention) policies, then you can start by looking at the **"DLP Policies"** submenu under the **"Tools"** menu of the designer. DLP policies are created and managed by the administrator. A documentation link shared by Microsoft on this topic is as follows:

https://learn.microsoft.com/en-us/power-automate/desktop-flows/data-loss-prevention

This concludes the Flow designer component and thus both the components of the PAD tool viz, The console and the Flow designer. Any key features not shown in the above sections are covered in their respective chapters where they are more relevant.

Ways of Running a Desktop Flow

We have already seen a few ways to run a Desktop Flow. Just to recap, they are as follows:

- From the main console, by using the **Run** button next to the selected Flow
- From the main console, by using the **Run** button on the top command bar
- From the main console, in the Flow properties you can set a shortcut key to run it
- From the Flow designer, using the **Run** button on the top command bar (used during development or debugging)
- From the Flow designer, using the **Run** submenu available in the **Debug** menu (used during development or debugging)

The keyboard shortcut key to run a Flow from the designer is F5.

There are a few other ways to run a Desktop Flow and they are as follows:

For the succeeding sections, you would need a **"Run URL"** available from the **"Details"** tab of the **"Flow properties"** from the main Console. You might also need the **"Flow ID"** which is also available in the same **"Flow properties"** section.

It should be noted that these ways require either a free Trial or a paid license.

Using Run URLs

Power Automate Desktop gives us a unique URL for every Desktop Flow and these URLs can be used from other external sources as follows:

- Calling from a browser
- From the Windows Run menu
- From the command prompt (or DOS prompt)
- From the in-built Windows Task Scheduler

Just to give you an idea, the procedure to use a Run URL **from a command prompt** would be as follows:

Go to the command prompt or the DOS prompt of your machine by typing the word DOS or command from the Windows Start menu and then open the Command prompt window.

Type-in the following after replacing **[workflowName]** with your actual Desktop Flow name, which is **"Hello, World"** in our case. Only if incorrect, change the path of `PAD.Console.Host.exe` file. Do not remove the double quotes and press the *Enter* key.

```
"C:\Program Files (x86)\Power Automate Desktop\PAD.Console.Host.exe"
"ms-powerautomate:/console/flow/run?workflowName=[workflowName]"
```

As soon as you hit enter, you will see at the bottom right-hand corner a notification showing that the Flow is downloading. Following that, the output of the Flow which is a message box displaying **"Hello, World!"** will appear. Finally, another notification will show that the Flow has been completed successfully. These notifications can be configured in Monitoring/Notifications setting, as we discussed earlier.

Let's look at another way which is by using the Flow ID and **via the Windows Run menu**.

This time, the syntax is a bit different as you won't have to use the path of the `PAD.`**`Console.Host.exe`**. It is as follows:

Open the Windows Start menu, type **"run"**, and select the **Run** menu. Enter the following command (including the quotes), replace **[workflowId]** with the Flow ID from the Flow properties, and press *Enter*.

```
"ms-powerautomate:/console/flow/run?workflowId=[workflowId]"
```

Before hitting enter, it would look like the following:

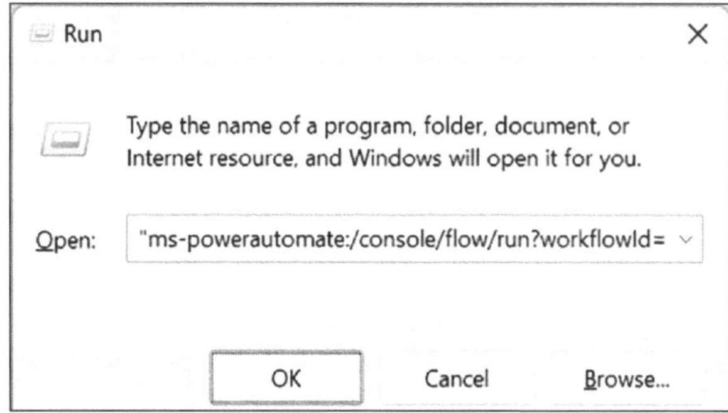

Figure 2.25: *Windows Run menu with Flow ID*

After pressing *Enter*, you would see the same set of notifications and the Flow output that you observed when running the command from the command prompt.

As specified earlier, if you see a confirmation dialog box, make sure to uncheck the PAD settings that says "**`Display confirmation dialog when invoking flows externally`**".

Using Desktop Shortcuts

The next way is through a shortcut created on the Desktop.

Note that this is different from creating a shortcut key via the Flow properties. You can create a desktop shortcut as follows from the main console via the context menu of a Flow.

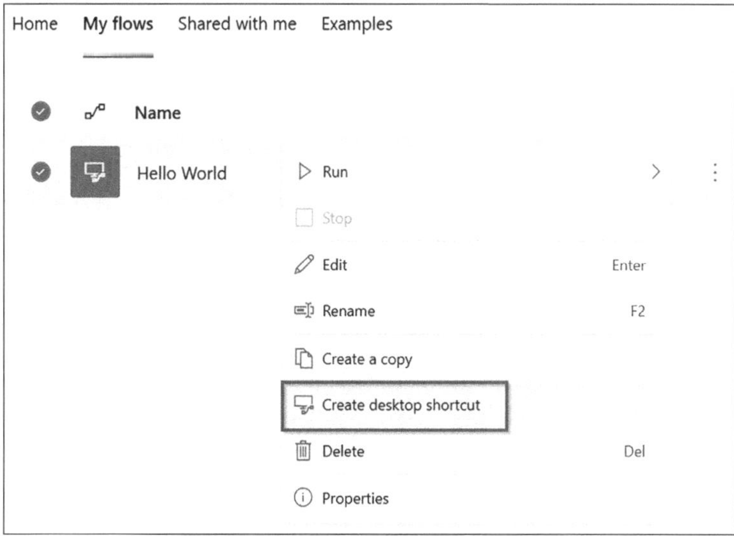

Figure 2.26: *Create desktop shortcut*

Via this option, you will be able to create a shortcut by default on your desktop and if required, it can be moved to any other folder location.

Also note that a desktop shortcut has an option to set a shortcut key to trigger configured action, in this case, our Desktop Flow. You can do so by right-clicking the desktop shortcut and then opening its properties (refer to *Figure* 2.27).

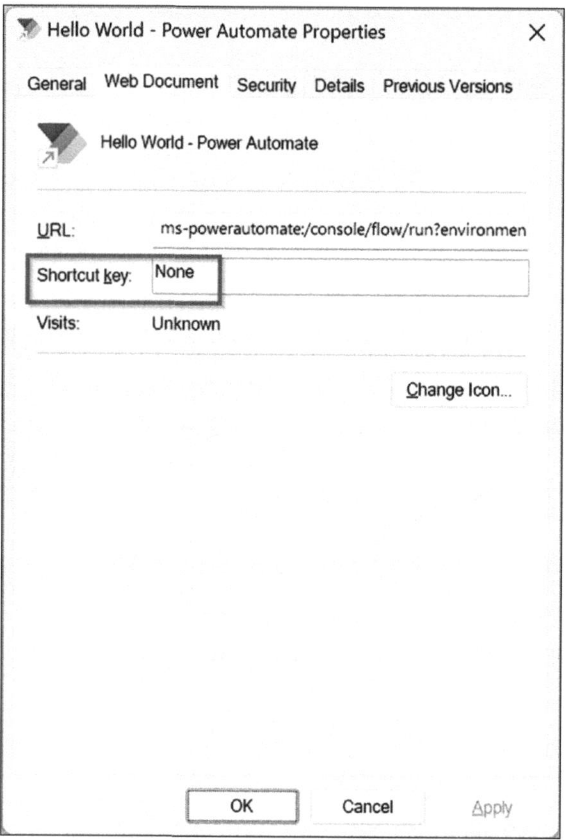

Figure 2.27: *Set shortcut key in desktop shortcut*

For a deep dive to see various syntaxes, how to use the Task Scheduler, pre-requisites, limitations, how to set parameters, refer to the following link:

https://learn.microsoft.com/en-us/power-automate/desktop-flows/run-desktop-flows-url-shortcuts

While Cloud Flows are not for the focus of this book, there are additional ways to start a Desktop Flow such as scheduling it from a Cloud Flow or running it based on an automatic trigger. These methods are touched upon in the section titled "*Making Use of the Cloud Portal and the Power Platform*" in the chapter "*Leveling Up Your Automation Workflows*".

Environments and Tenants

We have discussed Environments in the previous topics, but to fully understand them we need to look at Environments and Tenants together. So, let us explore that now.

- **Environments:**

  Environments are spaces that are configured to hold and manage the Flows you build, the apps you develop, any connections created, the data, or any other tool or component of the Power Platform. These are generally created by a Power Platform admin who can also restrict or allow permissions to use these resources within and outside the environments. An environment is also associated with a specific geographic location.

- **Tenants:**

  A tenant could be an overall organization or a dedicated instance of the Power Platform where users can create, manage, and share their business applications, workflows, dashboards, and chatbots. Tenant settings can be managed via the Power Platform Admin Center.

If tenants represent an entire organization, then environments are a separate space within that organization. A tenant is a container for all environments. This means, within a tenant you can create multiple environments.

You might have noticed that a default environment was automatically created when you logged in to the PAD tool. This is seen on the top of the main console. Some organizations rename this as "Personal Productivity" too. Likewise, one can create multiple environments either as Development, Testing and Production to go through various stages of a life cycle of a bot, or based on departments such as HR, Marketing, Operations, and so on to segregate them from one another. Users can be a member of one or more of these environments.

Let's take a look at it diagrammatically.

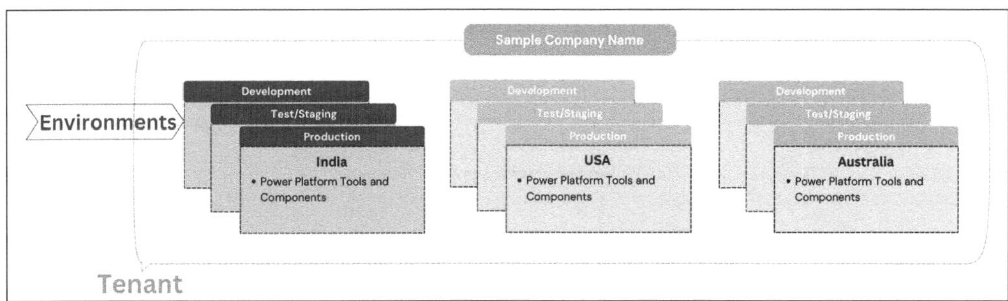

Figure 2.28: *Tenants and Environments*

For a deep dive on various combination of environment scenarios, their different types, and how they are managed in the Admin Center, refer to the following links:

https://learn.microsoft.com/en-us/power-platform/admin/environments-overview

https://learn.microsoft.com/en-us/microsoft-365/community/defining-a-power-platform-environment-strategy

From a Power Automate Desktop perspective, if you are using an environment other than the "default" environment, you can switch environments by clicking the **"Environments"** button at the top of the main console.

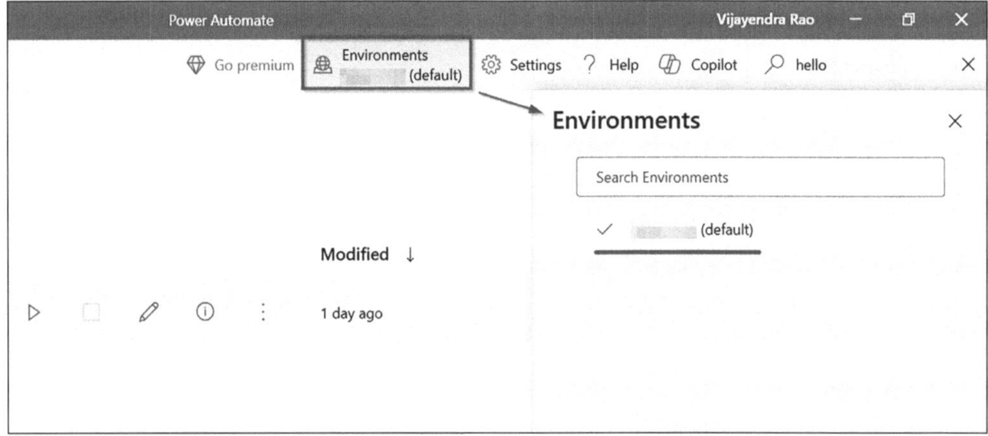

Figure 2.29: *Change Environment*

Likewise, you can switch the organization from the main console itself by clicking your name on the title bar and selecting **"Switch organization"**.

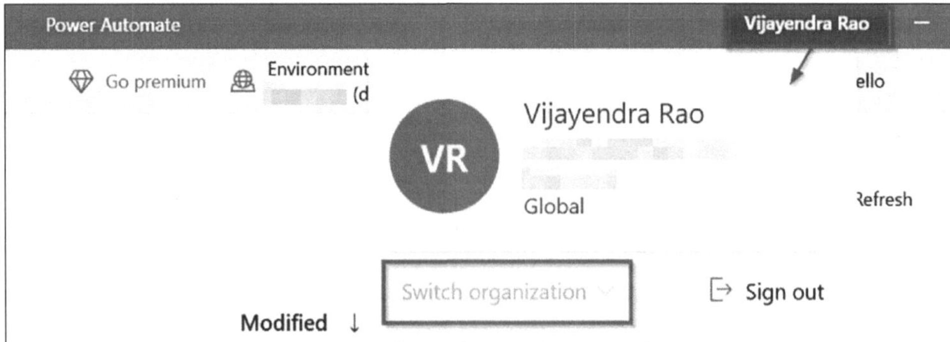

Figure 2.30: *Switch Organization*

You will see only those Desktop Flows for the selected Environment and Organization that you have access to or are a member of.

Conclusion

In this chapter, we dived into the practical aspects of working with Microsoft Power Automate Desktop. From understanding pre-requisites and installation procedures to navigating the PAD interface and creating our first Desktop Flow, we explored the essential steps to kickstart our automation journey using PAD. Additionally, we delved into different ways of running Desktop Flows and explored the concepts of Environments and Tenants within the PAD ecosystem.

Armed with this knowledge, we are ready to go a level further into the debugging process in our next installment. In the upcoming chapter, we will learn various features available to debug the Flows during troubleshooting or while building Flows to test them.

CHAPTER 3

Debugging the Desktop Flows

Introduction

Debugging has been used since the beginning of programming and implies the systematic approach of identifying and rectifying errors or bugs within a software program or system. It involves analyzing the behavior of the program, tracing the execution flow, and pinpointing the root cause of an issue. Along with identifying errors after they have occurred, debugging is also done by developers during development to verify if the program is working as designed and producing the desired output for the given inputs. In this chapter, we are going to look at how to do the same within a Flow in Power Automate Desktop.

Structure

The following topics will be covered in this chapter:

- Stepping Through
- Using Breakpoints
- Run from here
- Editing an Action
- Disabling Actions
- Modifying Variables During Debugging
- Subflows Allowing Easy Debugging of Flows

Stepping Through

Stepping through is the process of running a Desktop Flow Action by Action. On starting to step through, the execution begins from the very first Action in the Flow. Let's take a visual look at it.

Before you begin stepping through, consider your Flow looks as in *Figure* 3.1. No Actions have been run yet. At this point you need not be concerned with what Actions and variables are used in the Flow and how they are used, since we are going to look at them in *Chapter* 4 named "*Essential Elements of a Desktop Flow*". But to give you an idea, the Flow is assigning the values of first name and last name to two different variables, getting the current date and time and then displaying all of these in a message box. You will get to practice the same exercises at the end of this chapter starting from *Figure* 3.29, so at first, simply go through the below sections and then try them out practically.

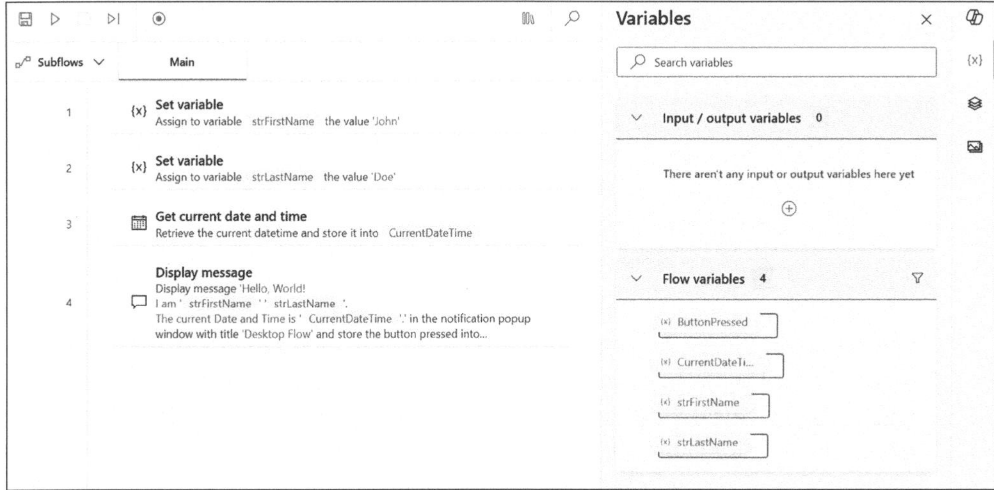

Figure 3.1: *Before stepping through*

1. We begin the step through process from the button at the top command bar of the designer that has a tooltip displaying **"`Run action by action`"**.

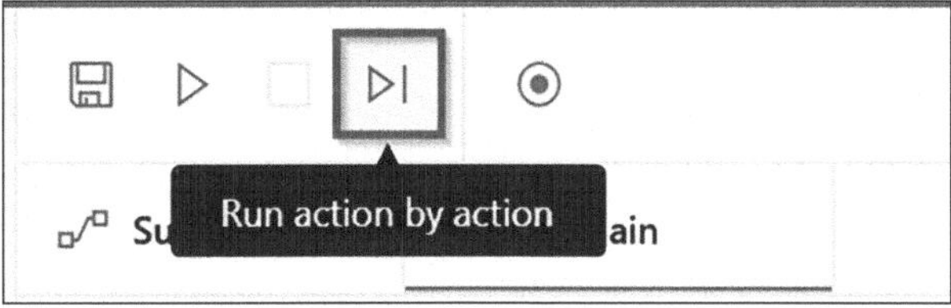

Figure 3.2: *Stepping through from command bar*

2. As soon as you click the button, an execution line becomes visible on the first line of the Desktop Flow Action (indicated by an arrow in *Figure* 3.3). Note that the first line has not been executed yet. Also, at the bottom you will see that the status of the Flow is paused.

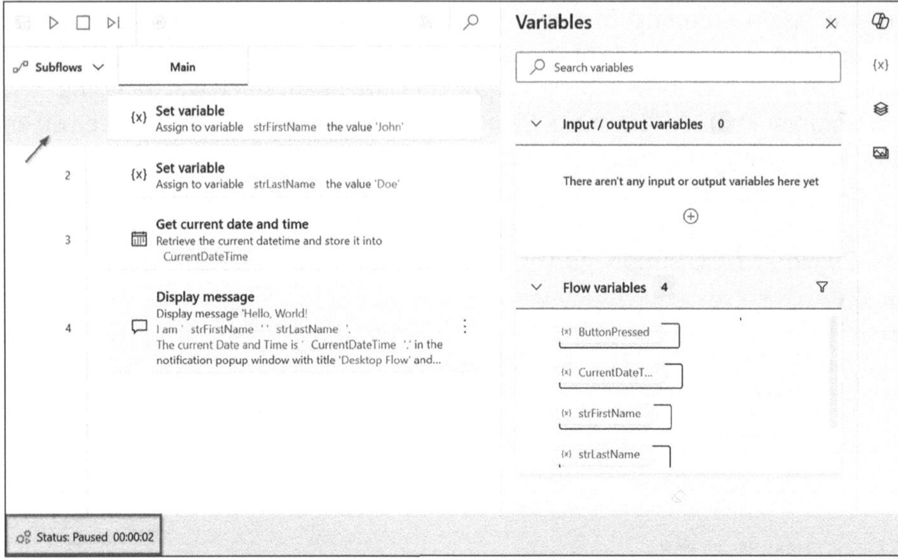

***Figure 3.3:** Started stepping through*

3. Click the same button once again and the first line of Action gets executed. This is also evident by a value assigned to the **`strFirstName`** variable in the **"`Variables`"** pane in *Figure* 3.4. Also, since **`CurrentDateTime`** is a date and time type of variable, PAD assigns a default value to it. The execution arrow is on the second line which indicates that the first line has completed its execution and moved onto the second. The Flow is paused again giving time for the developer to review the variables or for anything else that the line of Action performs, for example, opening an Excel file.

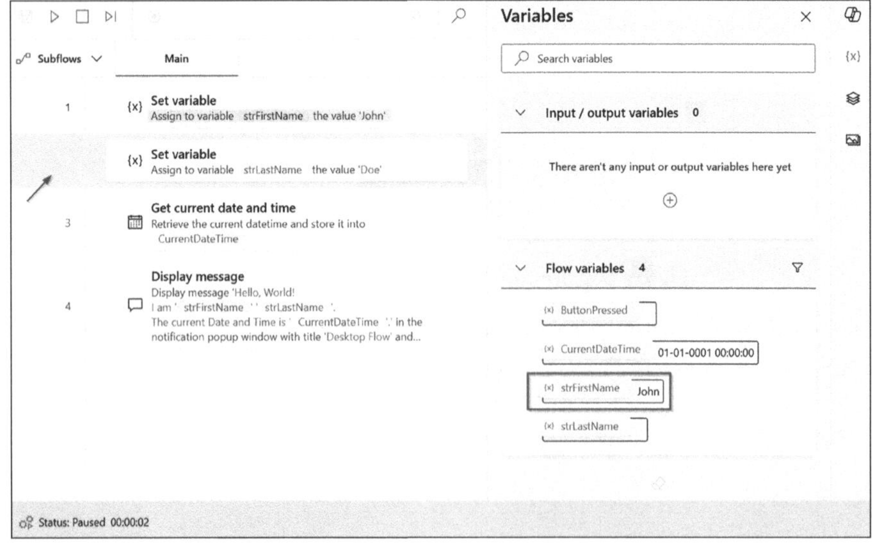

***Figure 3.4:** After stepping through first line*

4. Let's step through another line of Action but this time using a different method. Another way of running Action by Action is via the **"`Run next action`"** menu item of the **"`Debug`"** menu. On clicking it, the execution will move to the third line and the **`strLastName`** variable will be assigned a value.

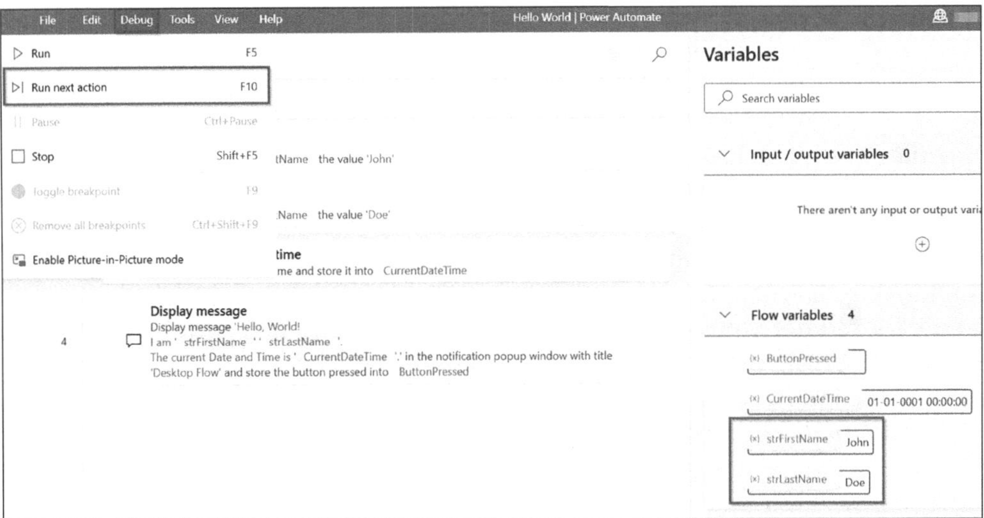

Figure 3.5: *After stepping through second line*

5. Now step through using the keyboard shortcut F10 listed next to the **"`Run next action`"** menu item in the preceding figure. Press F10 twice to execute the next two lines of Actions, which are the third and fourth lines. After the execution finishes the last line, the current date and time will be captured and a message box will appear with the text and variables configured in it.

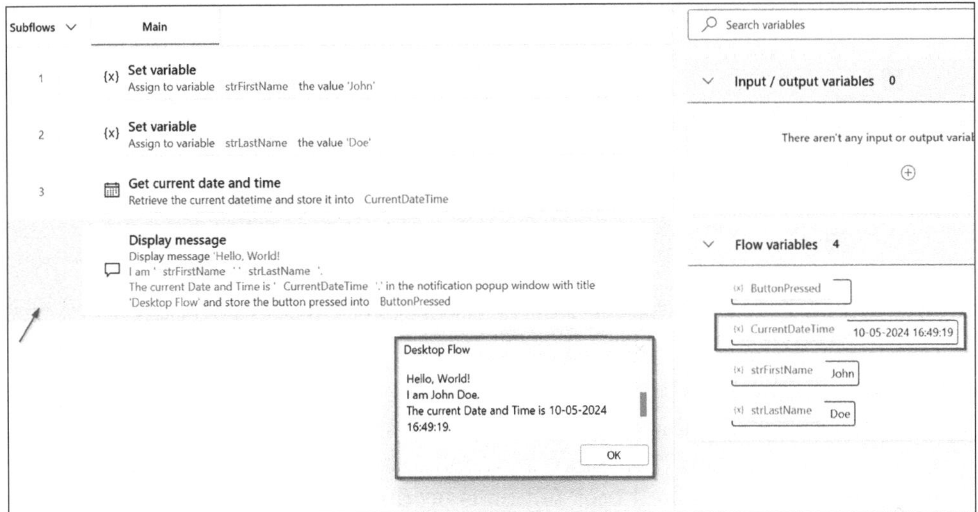

Figure 3.6: *Final stepping through output*

Thus, you step through each Action, review the output of the desired Action, and proceed further. This process helps you identify whether the Flow is behaving as expected or causing any errors.

Using Breakpoints

If there are 10 lines of Actions in your Flow and if you already know that the first 5 lines are working fine but you want to pause the Flow on the sixth line to check what's happening with the Flow, you can use a breakpoint. In our simple example, since we already know that the first name and last name are being assigned correctly, you may directly want to check if the date and time are being evaluated appropriately. For this purpose, you would add a breakpoint after the first and last names are assigned that is on the third line of Action. You add a breakpoint by clicking next to the line number and a dark red dot would appear indicating a breakpoint. Refer to *Figure* 3.7 for an example of a breakpoint on line number 3. Alternatively, you can insert a breakpoint by selecting the line of Action and choosing the **"`Toggle breakpoint`"** menu item from the **"`Debug`"** menu, or by using the F9 shortcut key.

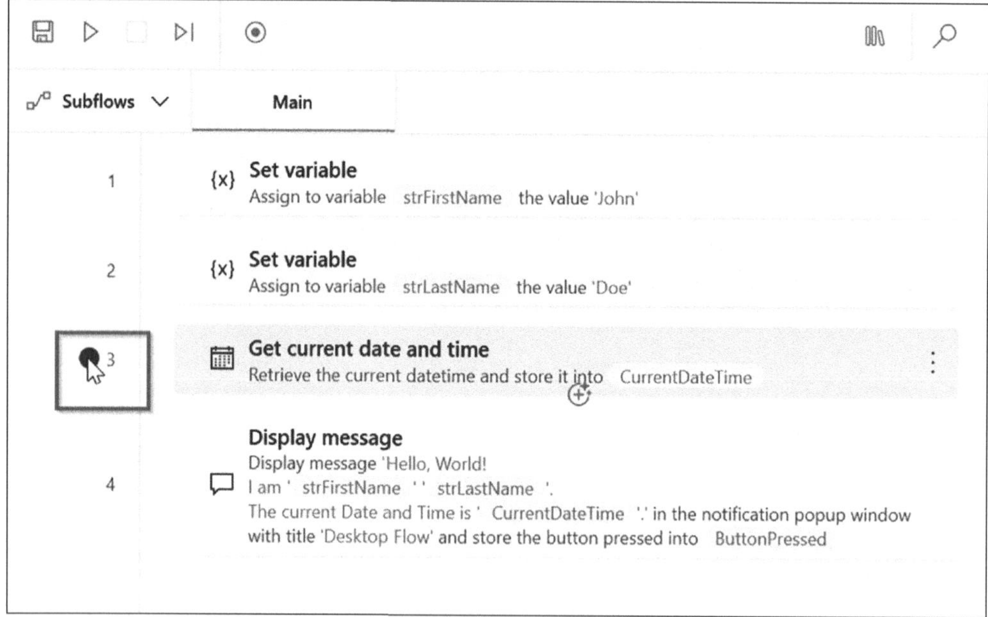

***Figure* 3.7:** *Adding a breakpoint*

Once added, run the Flow and you will see that the execution directly stops at line number 3, where the variables for first name and last name are already populated. At this point, you can use the **"`Run next action`"** to carefully step through and verify if the **"`Get current date and time`"** Action is producing the expected output. Review the variables, and then resume running the remaining Flow by using the **"`Run`"** button or pressing F5.

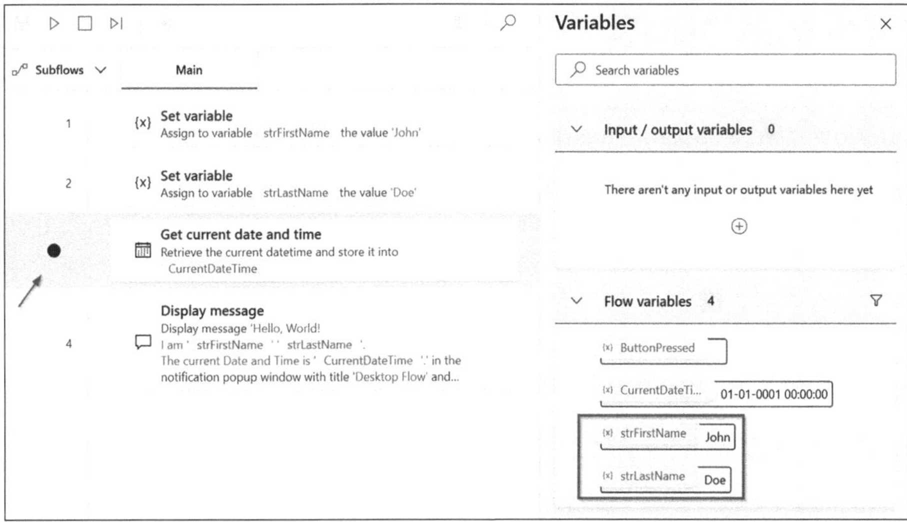

Figure 3.8: *Running till the breakpoint*

The point of this exercise is not to identify what is the error in our sample Flow, but to showcase how you can pause the execution directly at a particular line of Action with the help of breakpoints, review the outputs and then proceed further.

While the Flow is paused at the breakpoint, the **"`Pause`"** menu item becomes disabled, and the **"`Stop`"** menu item gets enabled. If you no longer need a breakpoint, you can remove it by using the **"`Toggle breakpoint`"** menu item, pressing F9 key, or clicking next to the line number as the way you did while inserting the breakpoint. If there are multiple breakpoints in your Flow and you want to remove all of them at once, use the **"`Remove all breakpoints`"** menu item or its corresponding shortcut key.

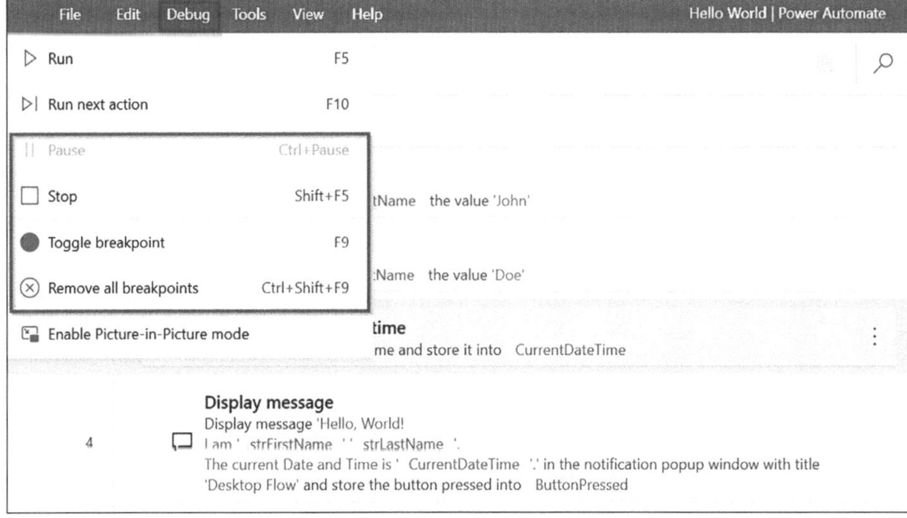

Figure 3.9: *Breakpoint options*

Run from here

The **"`Run from here`"** option is particularly useful for large Flows, as it allows you to run the Flow from a specific line of Action, ignoring all prior Actions.

In our example, let us try to run it directly from line number 3. To do so, right click the Action on that line or use the ellipsis button and select **"`Run from here`"** from the context menu.

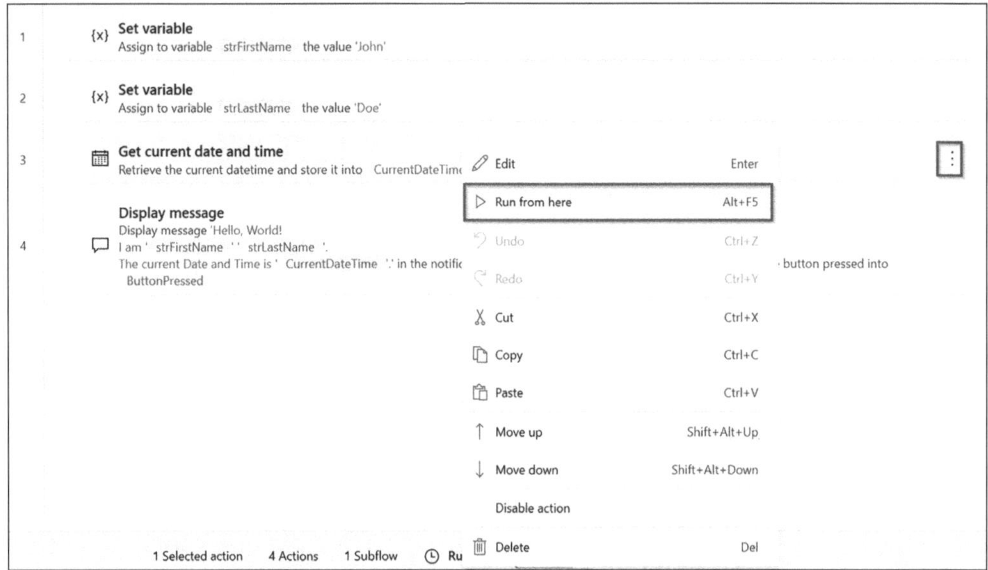

***Figure 3.10:** The "Run from here" context menu option*

As soon as you do that, the execution finishes till the last line of Action. The corresponding first name and last name variables will not be initialized as we chose to skip them. Consequently, the Flow produces the final output message box that only reflects the executed values. Our intention was to not troubleshoot the first name and last name portions, as we already know that they work fine, but rather to check the date and time segment of the Flow. Therefore, we chose the **"`Run from here`"** option from line number 3.

This approach is especially useful for large Flows, where you need to frequently run the Flow from a specific line of Action without starting over from the beginning during troubleshooting or debugging.

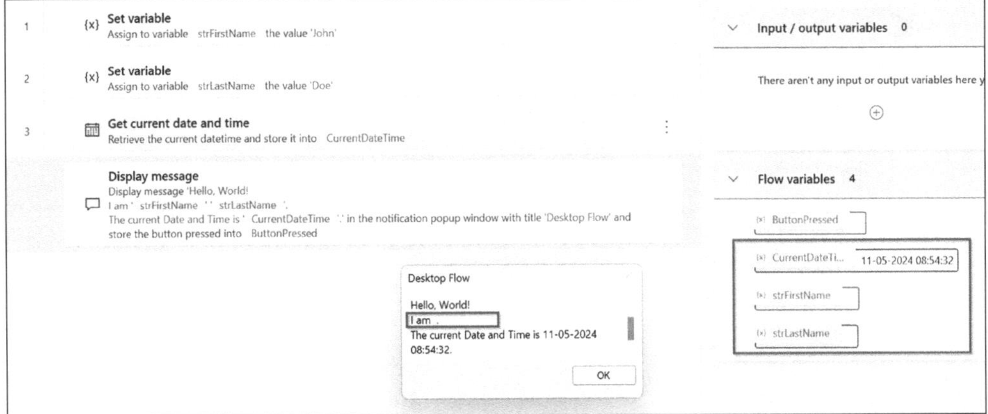

Figure 3.11: *Output after using "Run from here" option*

Please note that the **"Run from here"** option may be disabled in certain scenarios. This is because, PAD determines that it does not have the sufficient information or data to start executing from that specific line of Action. You will get to know the availability or unavailability of this option when you right-click on the Action.

A handy feature for navigating to a specific line of Action is the **"Go to line"** option. This feature asks you to enter a line number, allowing you to bring the focus on that line. This is useful if you have several lines of Actions and need to frequently visit a particular line, whether for execution or other purposes. This option can be triggered via the **"Go to line"** menu item in the **"Edit"** menu or by pressing the *Ctrl* + G shortcut key combination.

Editing an Action

There will be several situations where you would need to edit an Action after it has been dragged and dropped onto the Workspace.

Editing an Action is done via either of the following ways:

- Right-click the Action and click **"Edit"** from the context menu
- Double-click the line of Action
- Use the ellipsis button and click **"Edit"** from the context menu
- Select the line of Action and press the *Enter* key

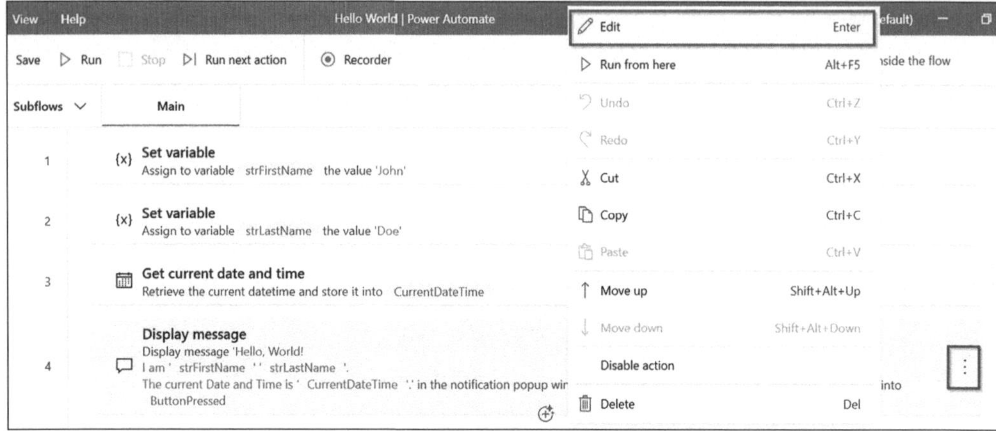

***Figure 3.12:** Edit action context menu*

Let's go ahead and edit the **"`Display message`"** Action.

Keep everything as it is from your first Desktop Flow, and only change the title of the message box as follows. You should see **"`Hello, World!`"** in the **"`Message to display:`"** box since you will be using the first Desktop Flow that you just built.

Change from this:

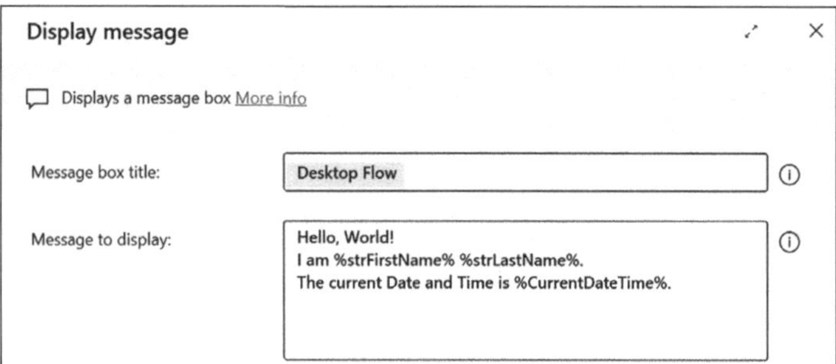

***Figure 3.13:** Edit "Display message" action from this*

Change to this:

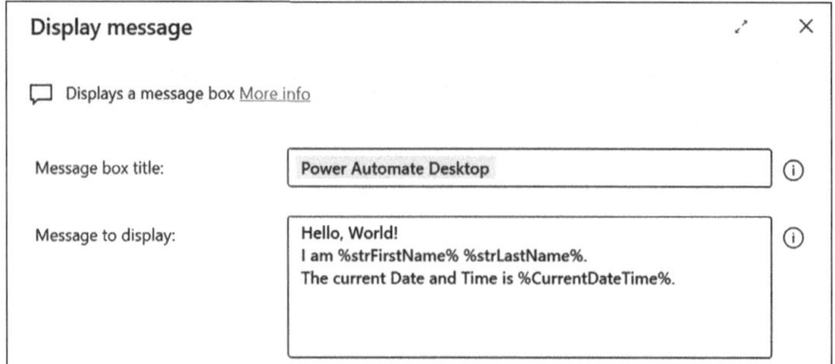

***Figure 3.14:** Edit "Display message" action to this*

On running the Flow, you will notice that the title of the message box has been changed to the new text we added. The text displayed will be **"`Hello, World!`"** in your Flow.

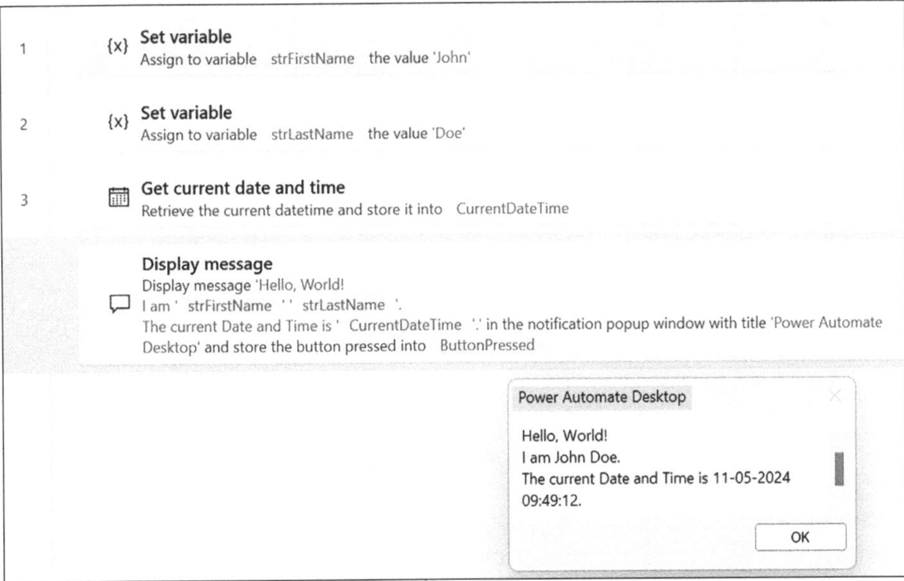

Figure 3.15: *Output after editing an action*

You can thus modify any Action during Flow development to change the parameters of that Action as needed.

Likewise, you can rearrange Actions, or cut, copy Actions from one location of your Flow and paste them onto another desired location of the Flow.

In this case, we are taking the Action on line number 3 and dragging it with the mouse to the very first line of the Flow.

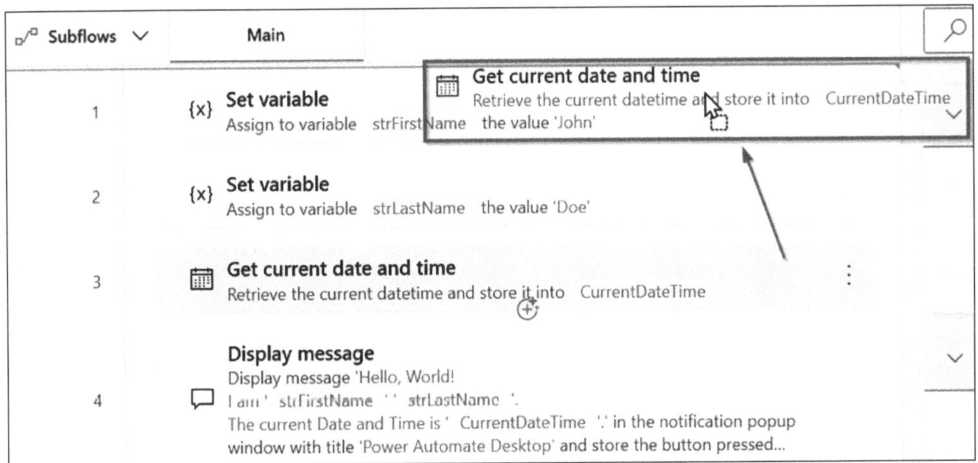

Figure 3.16: *While dragging an action*

After dragging and dropping, the Action would appear on the first line of the Flow.

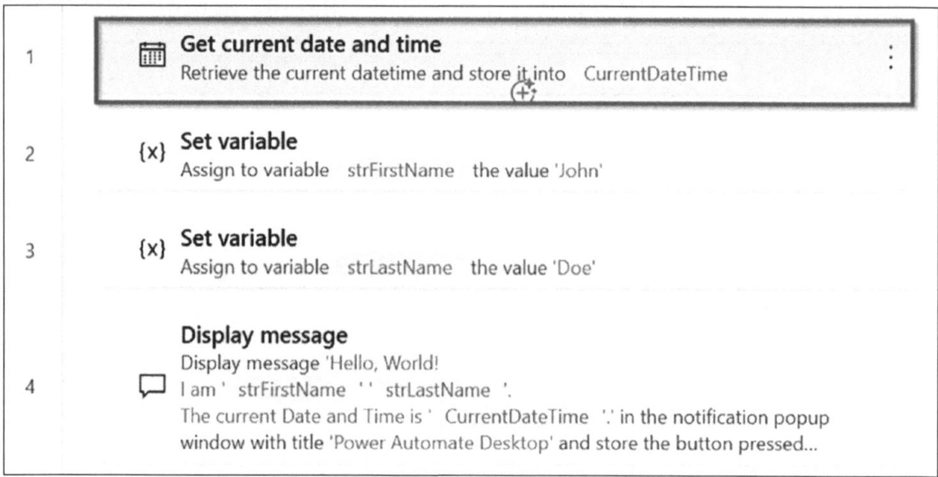

Figure 3.17: *After dragging an action*

Apart from dragging and dropping, you could also do the same via the context menu options for the relevant operations or by using the given keyboard shortcuts.

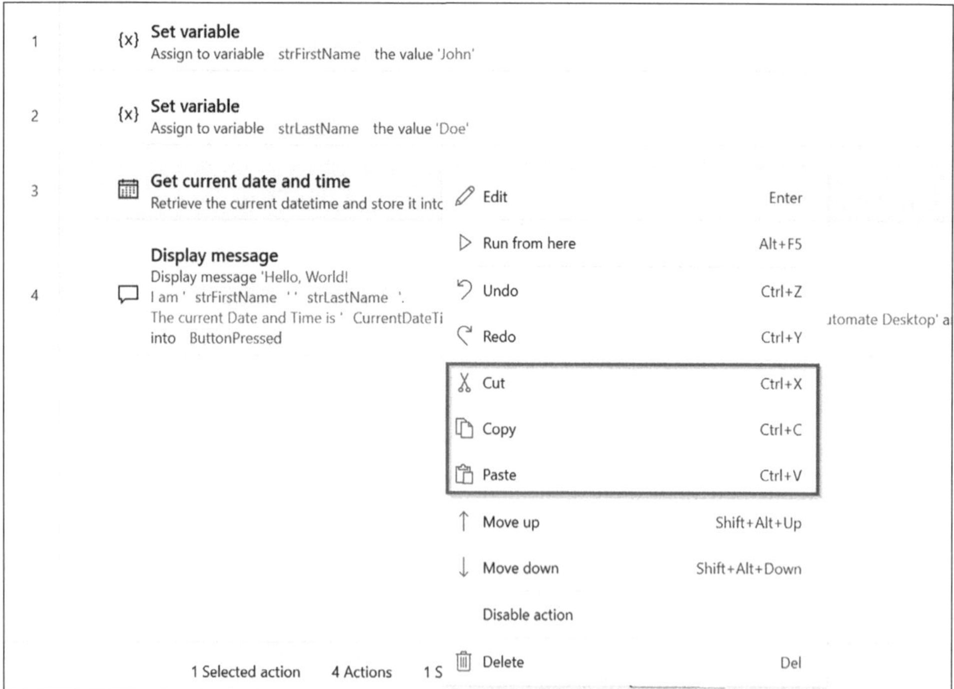

Figure 3.18: *Cut, copy, paste from context menu*

You can also cut, copy, paste or drag and drop multiple Actions at the same time. To select multiple Actions with the mouse, hold down the "*Control*" key while selecting them, which is generally used for non-consecutive Actions. To select multiple consecutive Actions, hold the "*Shift*" key. To select all Actions, use the *Ctrl* + A shortcut key combination, where *Ctrl* is the "*Control*" key.

Disabling Actions

During development or for temporary testing purposes, you may come across situations where you may not need certain Actions at that point of time, but may need it in the future. If you just want them to be temporarily excluded from the execution of the Flow, you can disable them and enable them back later.

After copying and pasting the **`"Get current date and time"`** Action from the previous topic, you now have two same Actions. If you realize that you don't need the second one at this point of time but may need it at a later stage, you can disable it from the **`"Disable action"`** option in the context menu.

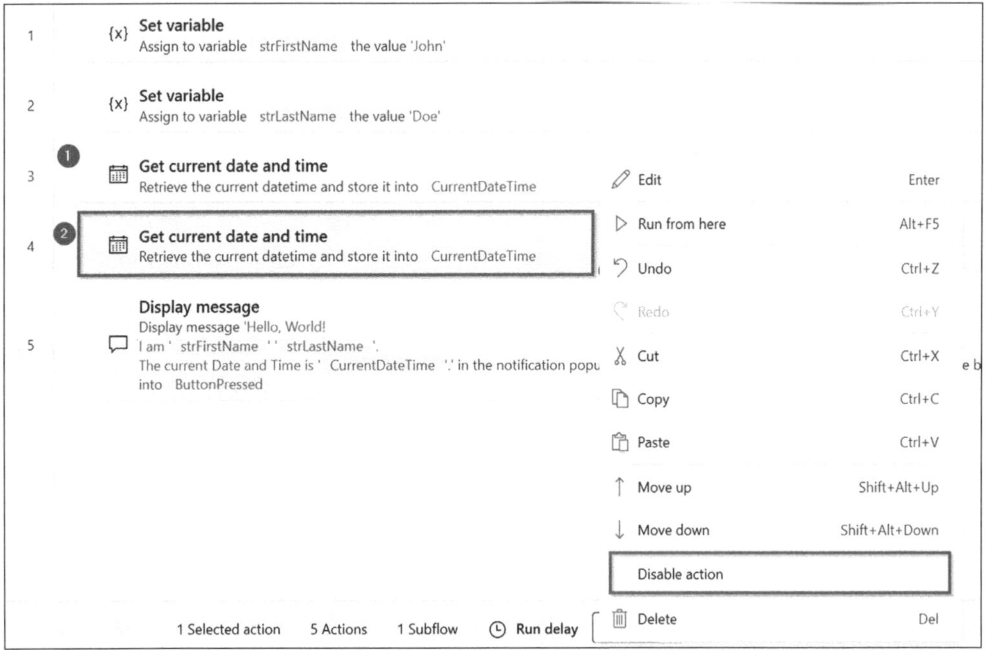

Figure 3.19: *Disable action context menu*

On disabling, the Action would be greyed out and won't be executed in the run, but will still be available to be enabled back at a later stage.

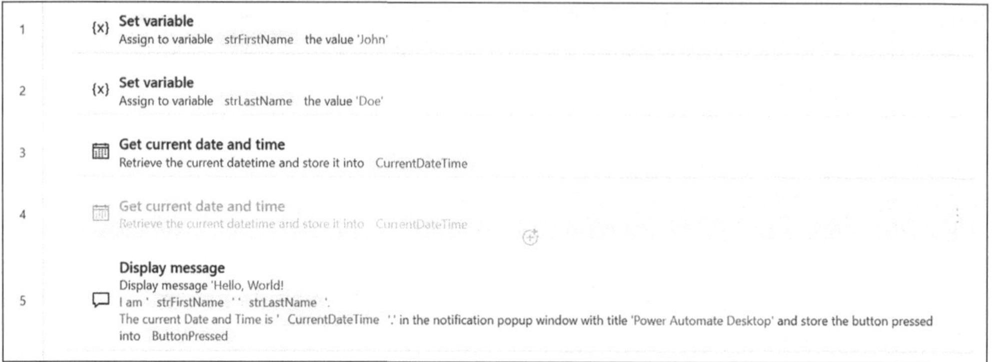

***Figure* 3.20**: *Action greyed out after disabling*

The Action can be enabled back using the same context menu. Also, one could enable and disable multiple Actions at the same time. Select multiple Actions by holding down the "*Control*" key while selecting with the mouse. Use the "*Shift*" key for non-consecutive Actions.

For permanently removing one or more Actions, you can select them and delete them via the same context menu or by using the "*Delete*" key.

Modifying Variables During Debugging

Power Automate Desktop allows modifying the values of variables while debugging the Flow. This is helpful while testing for various input scenarios.

For a simple demonstration, we will assign the first name and last name to two different variables as shown in the earlier Figures. Then, we will display the values of those two variables by changing their values during debugging.

Add a breakpoint to the third line and our Flow looks as follows. The Flow has not yet been run, hence the variable values are empty.

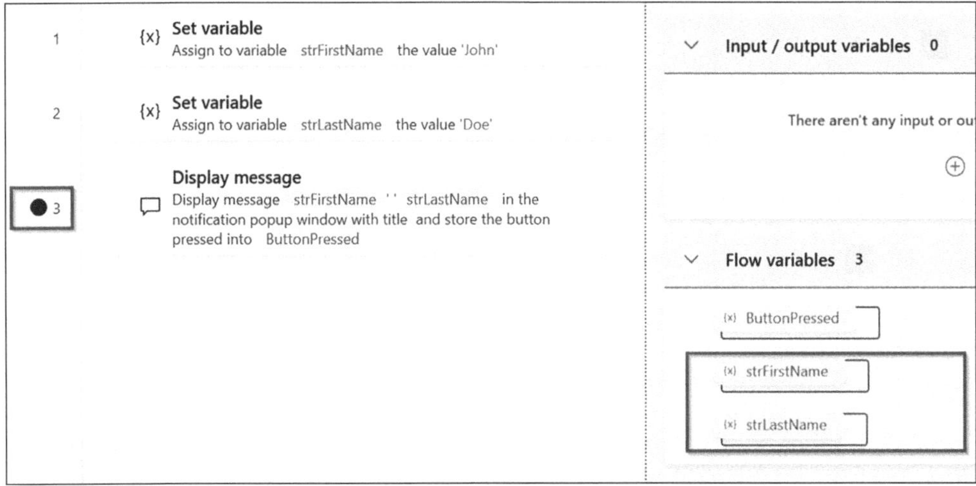

Figure 3.21: *Before starting Flow to modify variables*

On running the Flow, the execution stops on the third line due to the breakpoint you inserted and the variables now have the values that we had set.

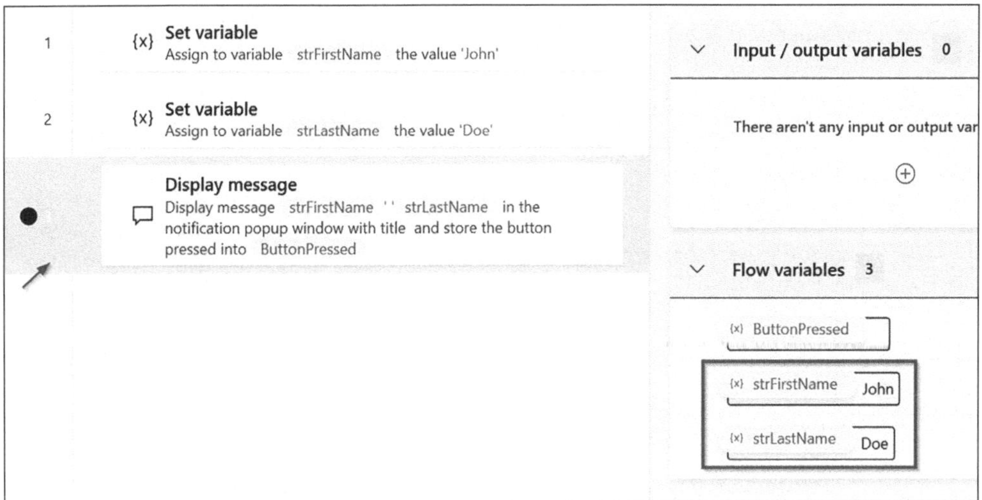

Figure 3.22: *Variable values before modifying them*

If you run the last line, a message box displaying the values you had set in the first two lines of Action would show up as follows:

Figure 3.23: *Message box without modifying variables*

But we are not going to run the last line and instead we will be modifying the value of the first name variable while the Flow is still in debugging mode. To do that, double-click the first name variable from the **"Variables"** pane and give a new name in the pop-up dialog box that shows up. For instance, if you change the name to **Jane**, you will notice the variable still shows the old name **John**. This is because we still haven't clicked the **OK** button. Click the **OK** button to update the new value and finish running the Flow from where it was earlier paused on the breakpoint.

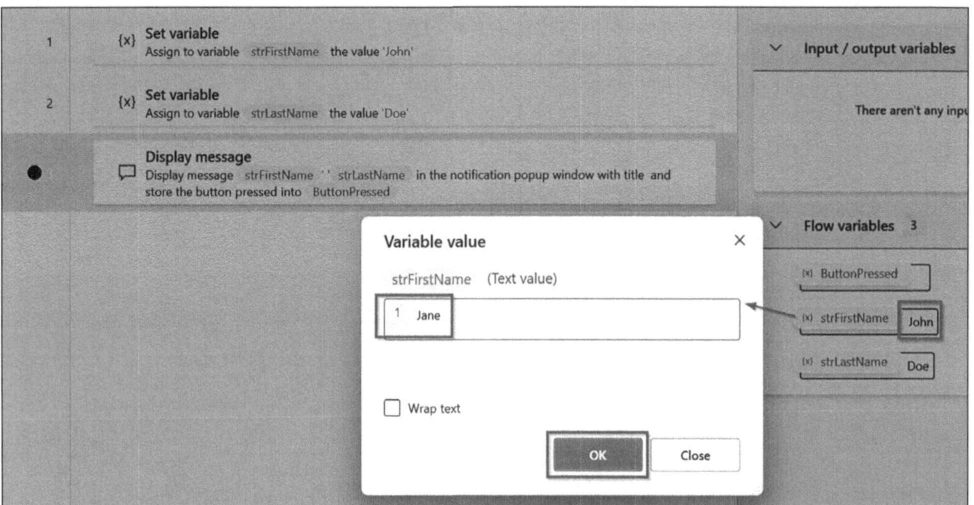

Figure 3.24: *Pop-up dialog box to modify variable while debugging*

The output with the new value is displayed as follows instead of the one in *Figure* 3.23.

Also, the variable section for the first name shows the new modified name.

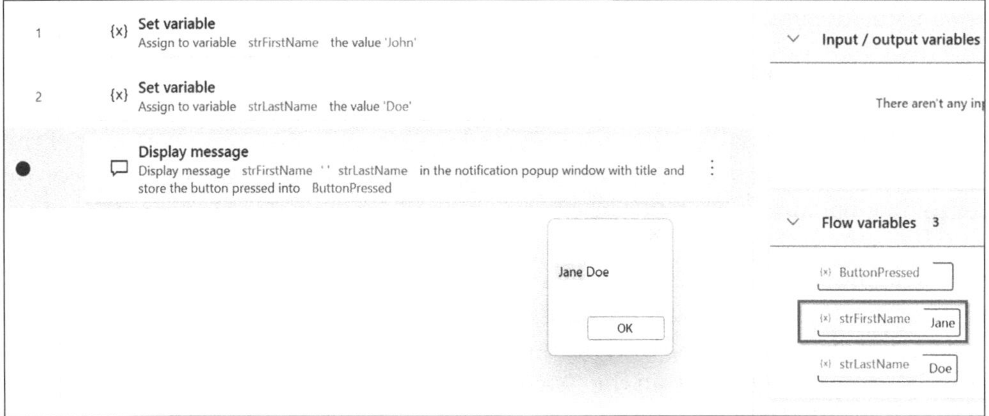

Figure 3.25: *Output after modifying the variable while debugging*

This feature is particularly useful while performing the testing for various inputs of an arithmetic calculation, or something that needs rigorous testing with multiple inputs.

Subflows Allowing Easy Debugging of Flows

Every Desktop Flow in PAD has a default **"Main"** Flow tab, which is the starting point of any Desktop Flow. All the Actions we have been adding so far were in the **"Main"** Flow tab. However, to modularize our Flow, Power Automate Desktop has provided a feature to create Subflows. Consider Subflows as nothing but another similar tab with a group of Actions. But imagine the clumsiness of developing large Flows within the same **"Main"** tab. It won't be much developer-friendly, nor will it be easy to debug. Therefore, we make use of Subflows, and we will see how to create them as well as call them.

To create a Subflow, use the **"Subflows"** downward arrow next to the **"Main"** tab and click **"New subflow"** button, which allows you to name your Subflow.

Figure 3.26: *Creating a Subflow*

Give a name depending upon the automation you are trying to develop.

Following is an example of a bot that you are building which will add and update customer details on an external system, then generate an Excel report and finally send an email. For this scenario, we have segregated our Main Flow into four parts as per their functionality. Each of these Subflows will have groups of Actions that would perform their individual functionalities. For example, the **"Generate Final Report"** Subflow would launch an Excel file, write values to it and finally save the report. The **"Send Email"** Subflow would then take this report and email it to the intended recipients. Likewise, the **"Add Customer Details"** and **"Update Customer Details"** Subflows would perform their own operations on the external system. Imagine the complexity if all of these tasks were within the **"Main"** Flow. The basic idea while designing Flows is to keep the **"Main"** Flow focused on high-level Actions and steps, which should be further divided into Subflows that would perform the detailed level steps.

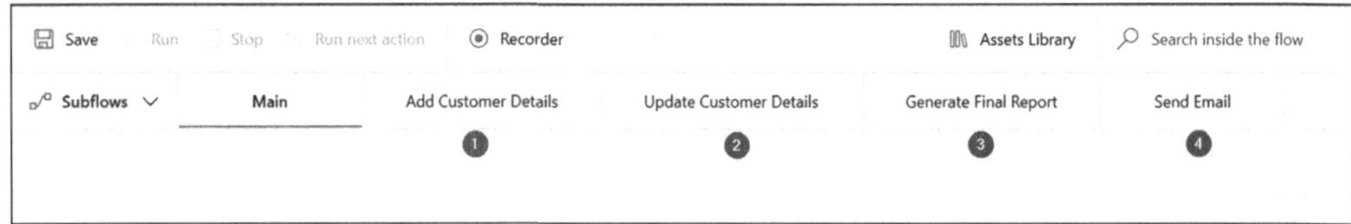

***Figure* 3.27:** *Example of Subflows*

To call a Subflow, either from the **"Main"** Flow or from another Subflow, we use the **"Run subflow"** Action. As soon as this Action is dragged and dropped from the **"Actions"** pane onto the Workspace, it opens up a dialog box showing a list of all the already existing Subflows created in *Figure* 3.27. Select the desired Subflow, click the **"Save"** button and your Flow is now ready to call the selected Subflow from the location where this Action was added.

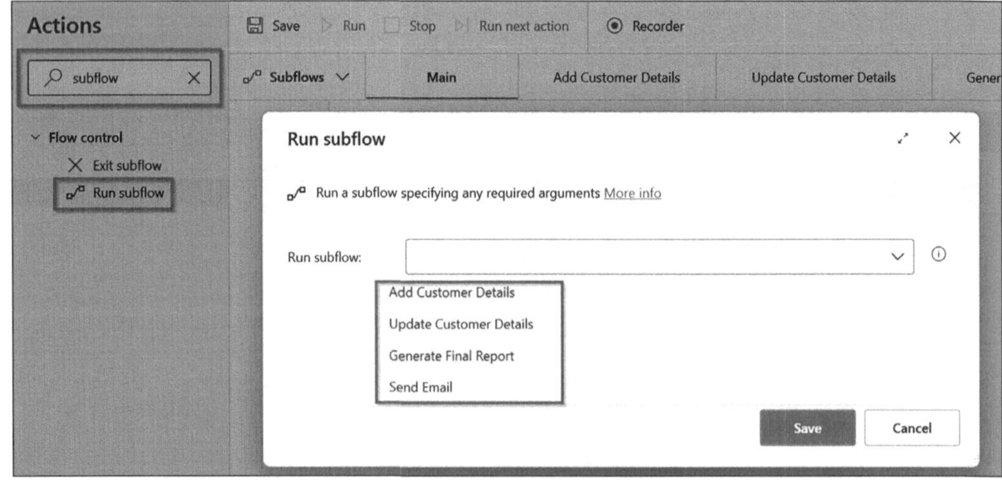

***Figure* 3.28:** *Calling a Subflow*

You can also cut or copy Actions from the **"Main"** Flow and paste them into a Subflow, just as you would do within the **"Main"** Flow itself.

Other debugging features are the **"Errors List"** pane and the **"Run delay"** box, both of which were explained in *Chapter* 2 titled "*Getting into Action with PAD*".

You may not have had the chance to practically go through the Debugging features mentioned earlier while reading about them. Following is how the Flow in *Figure* 3.1 was created, so you can create the same and practice by going through each of the above Debugging options. Again, do not worry much about understanding the variables and how they are written, as we will cover them in detail in "*Chapter* 4: *Essential Elements of a Desktop Flow*".

1. Following is the Flow we are going to develop in the subsequent steps:

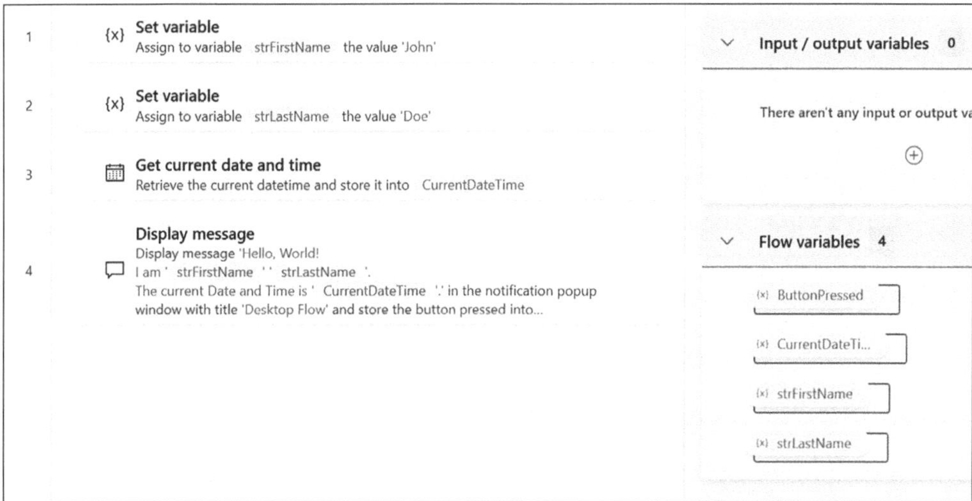

Figure 3.29: *Recreating Flow for practicing Debugging features*

2. Drag and drop the **"Set variable"** Action from the **"Actions"** pane. Name the variable as **strFirstName**, assign it a value for the first name and click **"Save"**.

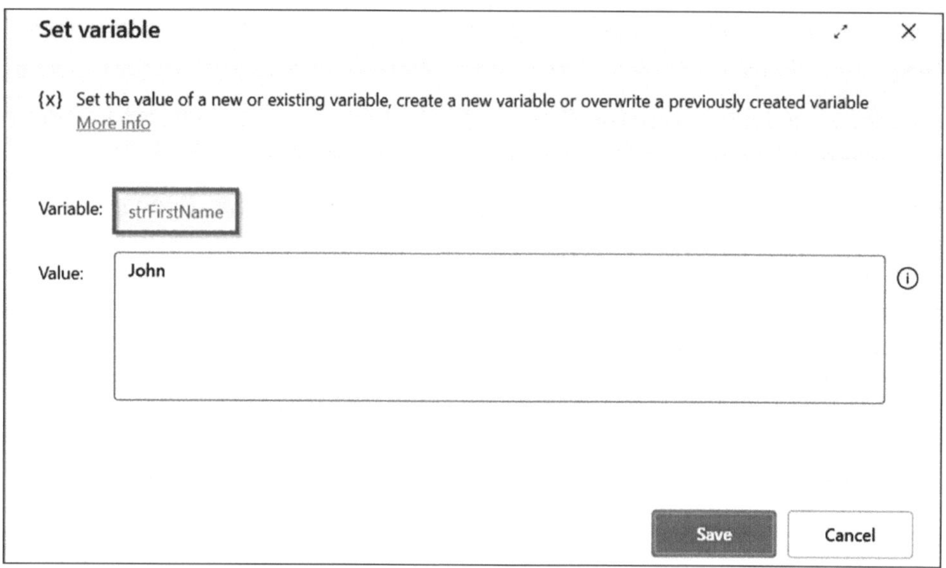

Figure 3.30: *Setting the variable for first name*

3. Repeat the same Action and set the last name variable as **`strLastName`** along with a value. Then, click **"`Save`"**.

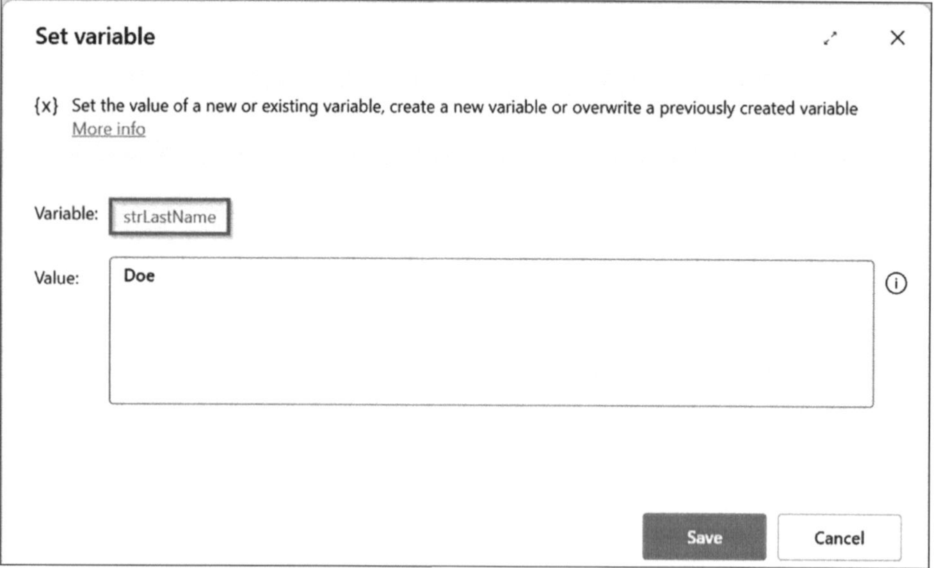

Figure 3.31: *Setting the variable for last name*

4. Drag and drop the **"`Get current date and time`"** Action. Leave its settings as it is before clicking **"`Save`"**.

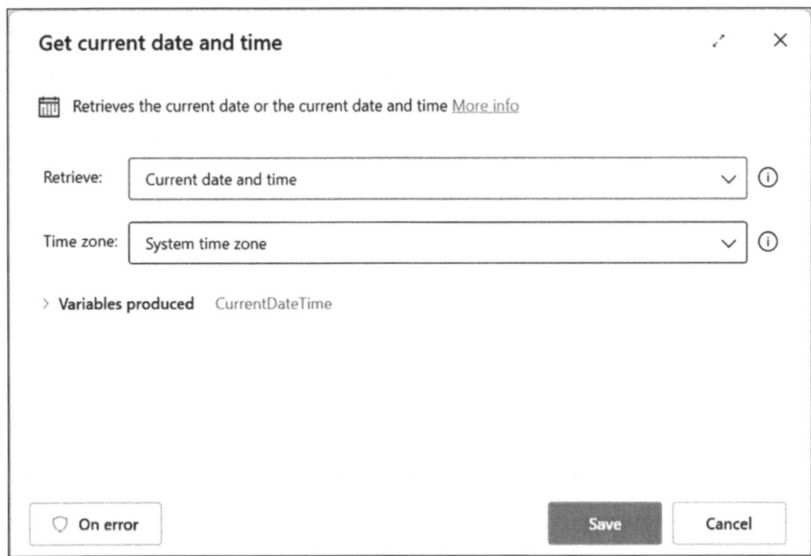

Figure 3.32: *Getting the current date and time*

5. In the **"Display message"** Action you have already specified the title and the message while creating your first Desktop Flow. Modify the **"Message to display"** box as following and click **"Save"**.

```
Hello, World!
I am %strFirstName% %strLastName%.
The current Date and Time is %CurrentDateTime%.
```

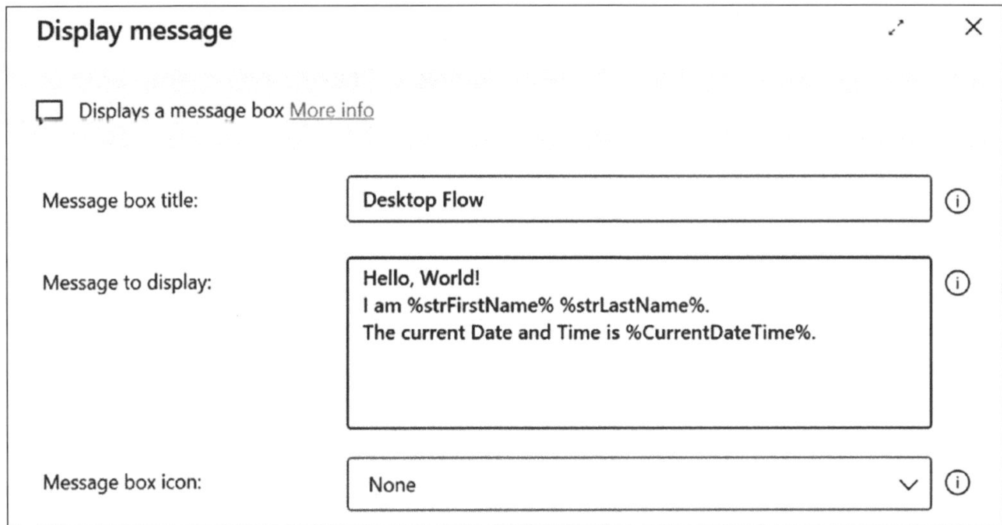

Figure 3.33: *Configuring the Display message box*

If you have used the variable names other than the ones specified in the screenshots, make sure to correct them in the **"Message to display"** box. Use the **{x}** button to select an existing variable by double-clicking on its name in the list.

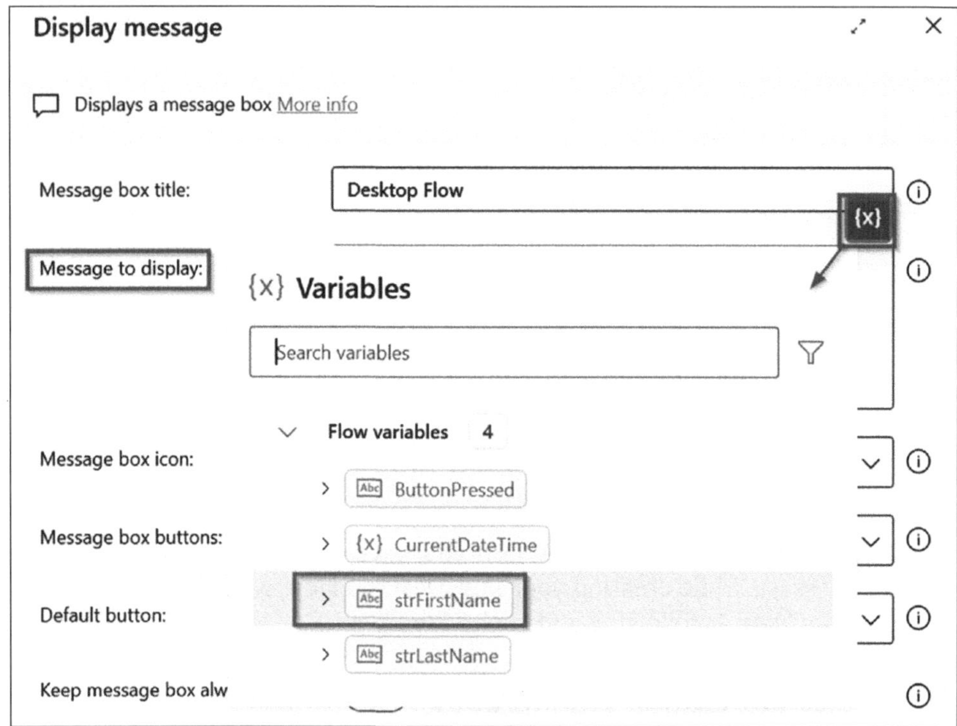

Figure 3.34: *Selecting the right variable in the Display message box*

This should complete your Flow. You are now ready to start practicing by referring to *Figure* 3.1 and trying out all the Debugging options available for a Desktop Flow.

Conclusion

In conclusion, mastering the debugging capabilities of Power Automate Desktop is necessary for streamlining automation processes. Whether stepping through the lines of Actions, utilizing breakpoints, or leveraging Subflows for efficient debugging, these techniques empower users to troubleshoot and optimize their workflows with confidence. By understanding how to edit Actions, disable or delete unwanted steps, and modify variables on the fly, users can ensure their automations run smoothly and reliably, further maximizing the debugging potential of Power Automate Desktop.

In the upcoming chapter, we delve into the necessary elements of Power Automate Desktop, exploring variables, which we have been using in this chapter. We will also look into conditional statements and loops along with Flow control for building efficient workflows within Power Automate Desktop.

CHAPTER 4
Essential Elements of a Desktop Flow

Introduction

As the name suggests, this chapter will help you uncover the necessary elements of a Desktop Flow without which building automation processes are not possible. This chapter is dedicated to discovering the essential elements of PAD where we will dig into Variables and their varied data types, decode various Conditional Statements, explore the efficiency of Loops, and understand navigating the Flows.

Structure

We will be going through the following topics in this chapter:

- Variables in PAD and Their Data Types
- Conditional Statements
- Loops
- Flow Control

Variables in PAD and Their Data Types

Variables in programming are placeholders or containers used to store and manipulate data. Each variable has a name, a data type, and a value associated with it. These values once configured are either used throughout the program for processing or can be changed during the execution of the program. Let us look at the same in Power Automate Desktop.

A variable in PAD is referred by prefixing and suffixing it with a percent sign **'%'**.

For example, **strFirstName, strLastName**, and **CurrentDateTime** are variables that we used in the previous chapter. At first, we had set or initialized a value to the **strFirstName** variable using the **"Set variable"** Action.

Set variable

{x} Set the value of a new or existing variable, create a new variable or overwrite a previously created variable
More info

Variable: strFirstName

Value: John

Save Cancel

Figure 4.1: *Setting the strFirstName variable*

Then, these three variables were referred in the **"Display message"** Action by enclosing them within a percent sign as follows:

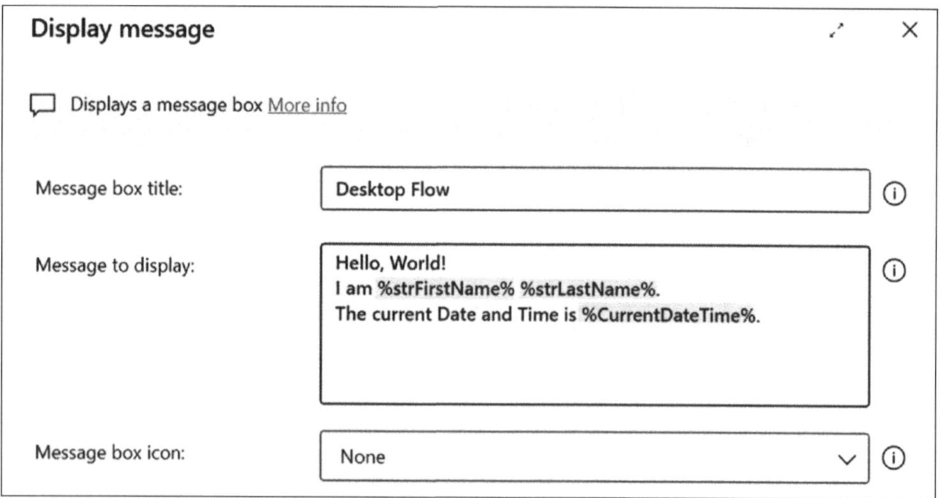

Figure 4.2: *Referring the variables*

Power Automate Desktop provides us with two types of variables:

- Input/Output variables
- Flow variables

Note that these are not data types, but types of variables. Let us look at each one of them.

Input/Output Variables

These variables are created within the Desktop Flow designer, but their values can be accessed outside the Flow designer, for example, from the Cloud Flows. In short, these variables can be used to allow the passing of data between Cloud Flows and Desktop Flows, or within two Desktop Flows too.

Input variables can be used in two different ways:

- As an example, when you call a Desktop Flow from a Cloud Flow, the Input variable from the Desktop Flow shows up as an **input** parameter in the Cloud Flow. This means you can pass a value via this variable from the Cloud to the Desktop Flow while calling it. The same is applicable when calling one Desktop Flow from another Desktop Flow (child Desktop Flows). Meaning, if Desktop Flow A is calling Desktop Flow B, and Desktop Flow B has got input variables, then these variables will be asked to be filled as input parameters in Desktop Flow A while placing the call.
- Another way is to ask the user to manually set the input values when the Desktop Flow is run from the main Console of the PAD tool. There are no Cloud Flows involved here. When a Desktop Flow is run from the main Console, the tool gives a pop-up showing all the Input variables created in the PAD Flow, thus allowing the user to set their values at the start of the run (see *Figure* 4.5).

Output variables can be used for the following:

- When a Cloud Flow calls a Desktop Flow, the Desktop Flow has the ability to pass values back to the calling Cloud Flow with the help of Output variables, and then the Cloud Flow can use the value of these variables for its own further processing. The Output variable created in the Desktop Flow shows up as an **output** parameter in the calling Cloud Flow. Again, this is also applicable when calling one Desktop Flow from another Desktop Flow. Meaning, if Desktop Flow A is calling Desktop Flow B, and Desktop Flow B has got output variables, then these will be passed as parameters back to the calling Desktop Flow A.

Input variables are created from the **"`Variables`"** pane via the **'`+`'** symbol and then by clicking the **"`Input`"** button:

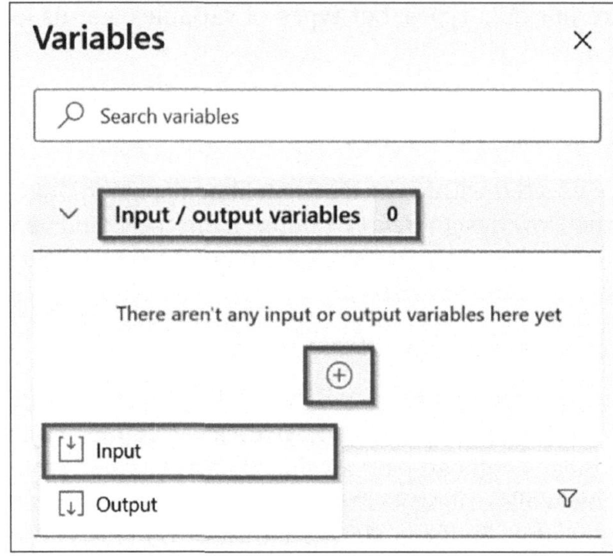

Figure 4.3: *Creating Input/Output variables*

Doing this will open up a dialog box to edit the properties of the Input variable.

Let us go through each of these configurations for an Input variable:

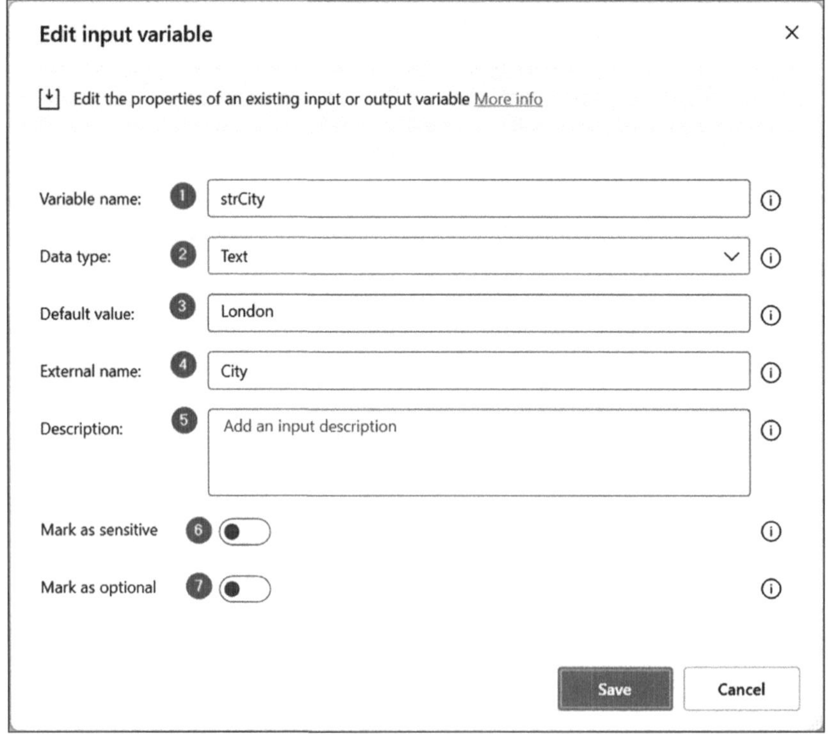

Figure 4.4: *Editing the properties of Input variables*

Follow along the below points with the help of the numbering given in *Figure* 4.4:

1. The **"`Variable name`"** box is used to provide a name for the Input variable that we are creating. **This is the variable name that is going to be referred within the Flow Designer**. In this example, we are creating a variable to store a City, which is going to hold data of type text or a string. Hence, it is given a certain convention prefixed as *str* for String type followed by what the variable is going to hold, that is, a City. At this point, we are not focusing on the exact variable naming convention, as they are discussed in detail in the "*Development Best Practices*" chapter.

2. The **"`Data type`"** box will indicate what type of data is the variable going to hold. Some examples are text, number, Boolean, and more, and we are going to look at these data types in this same chapter.

3. In some cases, you may need to have a pre-defined default value for a variable and the **"`Default value`"** box will help you to set that.

4. The **"`External name`"** box is used to give **a variable name that will be referred from outside the Flow designer**, as opposed to the **"`Variable name`"** in the first box. When you call a Desktop Flow from a Cloud Flow, the external name given here shows up as an **input** parameter while calling from the Cloud Flow.

5. A box to provide an optional description of the variable.

6. If your automation requires variables to hold any sensitive information like credit card numbers or any other PII (Personally Identifiable Information), you can mark these variables as sensitive whose values will be masked in the **"`Variables`"** pane and a sensitive icon will be shown next to it.

   There is a lot more to it in terms of how they are stored, their visibility scope, and much more. Therefore, further reading is recommended via the official documentation link on Sensitive variables:

   https://learn.microsoft.com/en-us/power-automate/desktop-flows/manage-variables#sensitive-variables

7. Determines whether to mandatorily pass a value to this variable or not. If the variable is marked as optional, you can skip passing a value, in which case it will hold a blank value.

The **Output variables** are created in the same way. The difference is that, when you call a Desktop Flow from a Cloud Flow, the given external name shows up as an **output** parameter while calling from the Cloud Flow. Other differences you will find when you create an output variable are that they cannot hold a default value or be marked as optional.

Here is the pop-up that shows up when a Flow with the **Input** variables created above is run from the main PAD Console. The user has the ability to modify the city name before clicking the **`OK`** button. Likewise, a pop-up will show up for an **Output** variable at the end of the Flow when it is run from the Console.

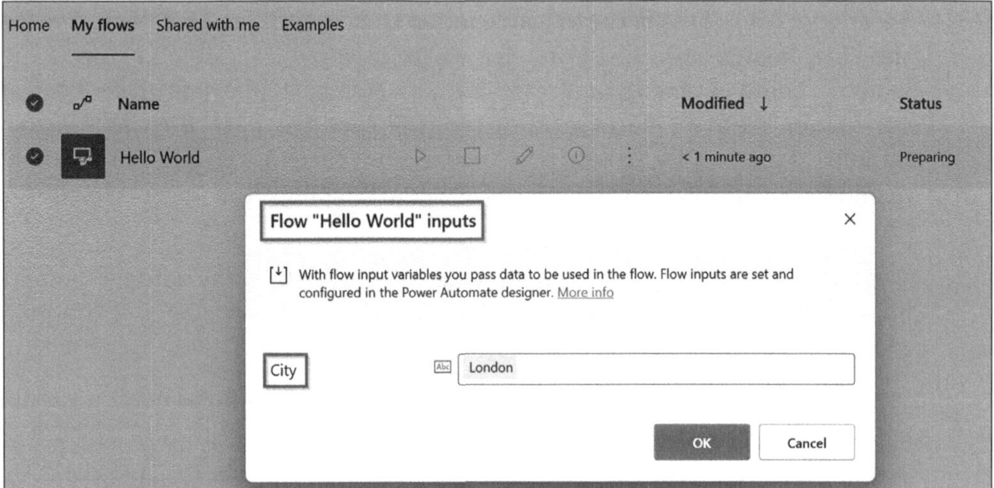

Figure 4.5: *Input variables pop-up after running from PAD console*

To use this Input variable in any of the PAD Actions, you would refer it in the same way, that is, by enclosing it with the percent sign **`%strCity%`**. PAD provides us with a variable picker button to choose from a list of available variables of our Desktop Flow.

Open up a **"`Display message`"** Action, click on the button that displays as **`{x}`**, and then select our created Input variable by double-clicking on its name.

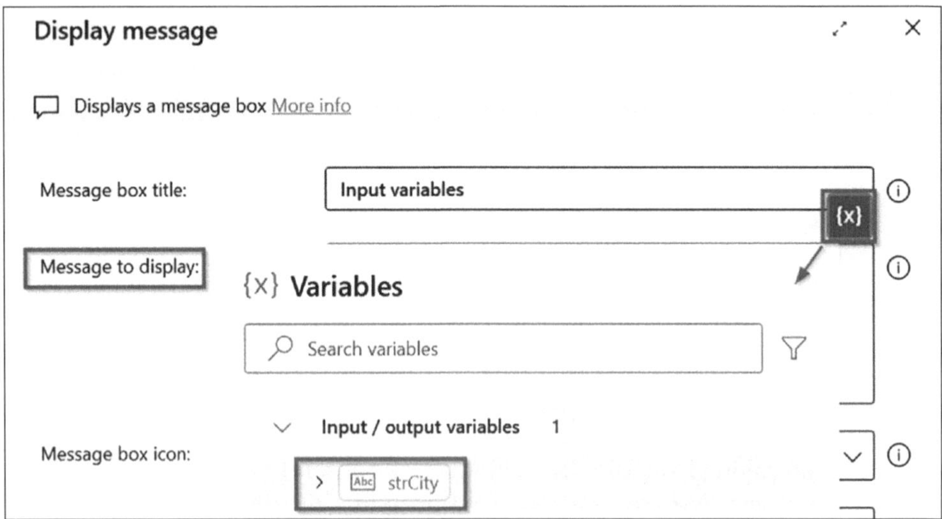

Figure 4.6: *Selecting an Input variable in an action*

The final Action would automatically contain the variable enclosed within the percent sign. After giving a text for the message box title, the Action would look like *Figure 4.7*.

The variable names are not case-sensitive. Meaning, even if you use **`%strcity%`** with all small letters in the message to display, it will show up **`'London'`** as its value.

However, it is highly recommended to always use the variable picker button **`{x}`** to select a variable instead of manually typing them to avoid human errors.

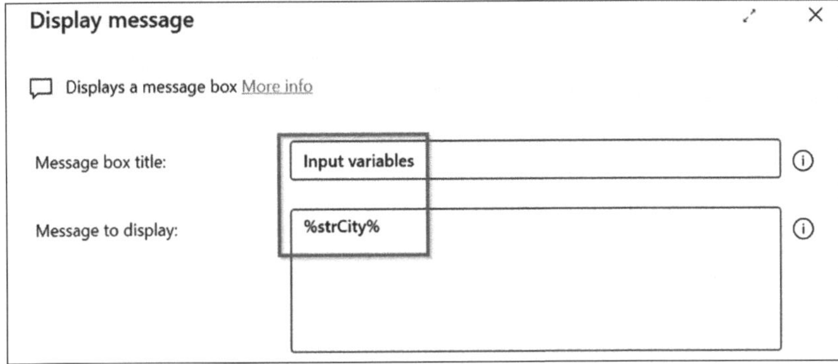

***Figure 4.7:** After selecting an Input variable in an action*

Flow Variables

Flow variables can be created and used only within the Flow designer. However, their values can also be assigned to an **Input** or **Output variable**.

They are created as follows and they show up in the **"`Flow variables`"** section of the **"`Variables`"** pane:

- They are either created by using the **"`Set variable`"** Action, for example, **`strFirstName`** in this case.

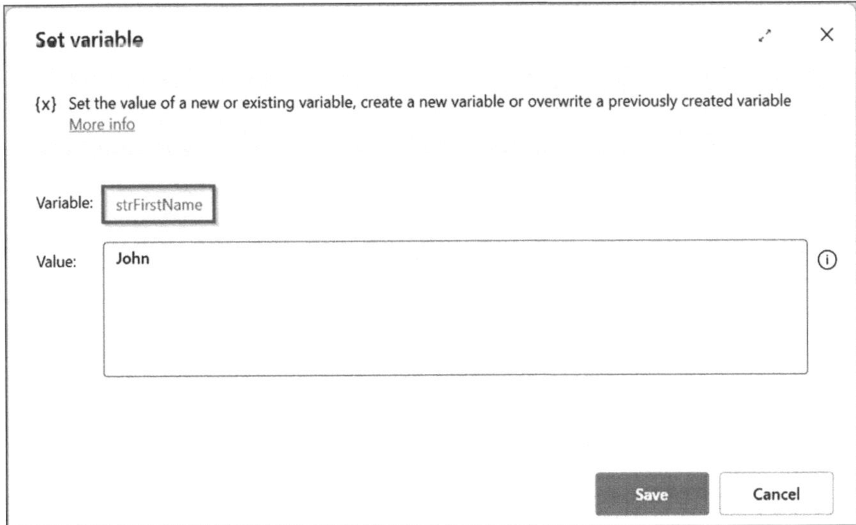

***Figure 4.8:** Flow variable from the Set variable action*

- Or they are the ones generated from any Action that shows up in the **"Variables produced"** section at the bottom of an Action, which is **CurrentDateTime** in this case.

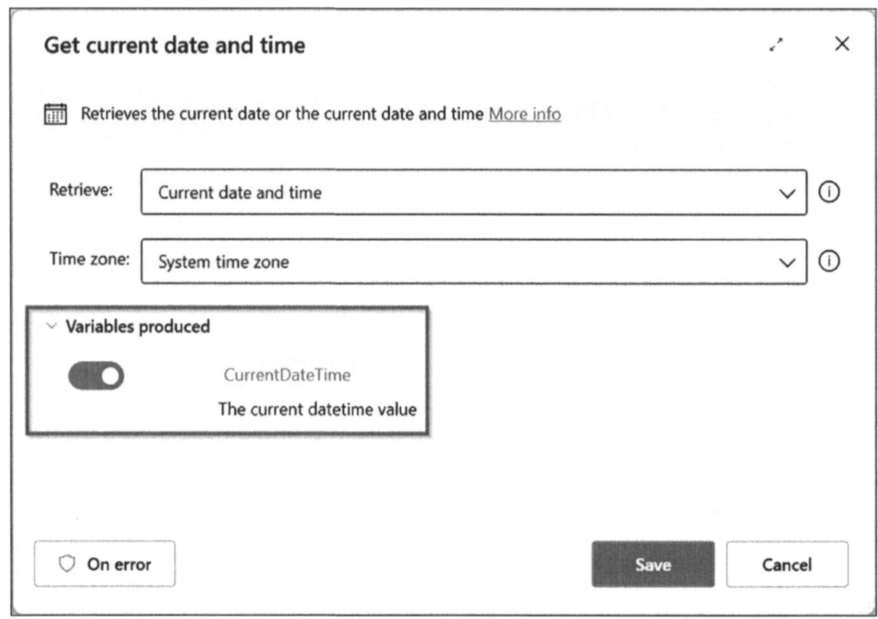

Figure 4.9: *Flow variable from the Variables produced by any action*

The developer does have the ability here to rename the variables coming from the **"Variables produced"** section.

The **"Flow variables"** are referred in an Action in the same way as the **"Input/Output variables"**, that is, by enclosing them within the percent sign.

The variable picker will categorize each of these two variable types and list them accordingly when you click on the **{x}** button.

The flask icon shown in the following figure helps to filter variables by their type and also has the ability to sort them in ascending or descending order:

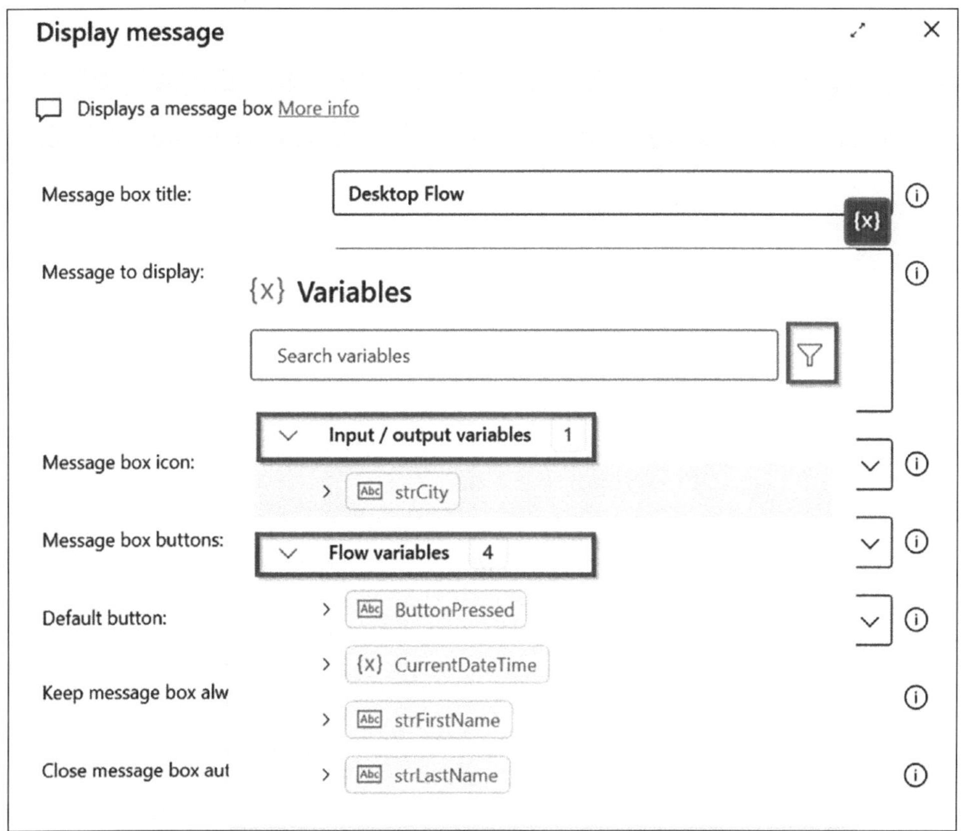

Figure 4.10: *Categorization, Filter, and Sorting of variables in the variable picker*

You can perform certain operations on the **"`Flow variables`"** from the **"`Variables`"** pane either by right-clicking the variable or by using the ellipsis button for that variable. The **"`View`"** option is disabled because the Flow hasn't been run and there is no data in the **`strFirstName`** variable as of yet. Other options include renaming a variable, finding where the variable is used within the entire Desktop Flow, marking the variable as sensitive, and pinning the variable to the top of the list if it is frequently needed to be referred.

The values of these variables can be modified while debugging, as explained in "*Chapter 3: Debugging the Desktop Flows*". If an Action that produces a **"`Flow variable`"** is deleted, the variable also gets deleted from the **"`Variables`"** pane. For example, if you delete the **"`Get current date and time`"** Action that we used in *Figure* 4.9, then its variable **`CurrentDateTime`** will be deleted from the **"`Variables`"** pane.

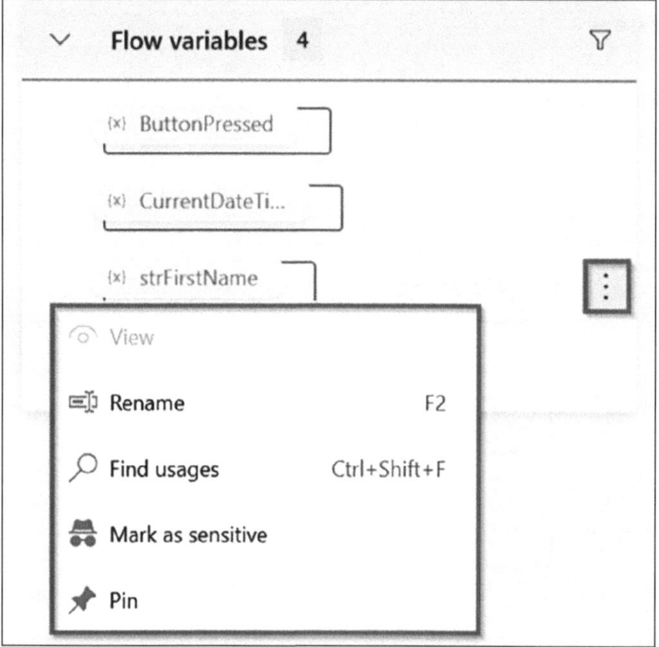

Figure 4.11: *Flow variable options*

Likewise, the **`Input/Output variables`** have the following options, as shown in *Figure* 4.12, which also have the ability to set or edit the default value before the Flow runs. An Input or Output variable does not get deleted when any of the Actions using them are deleted. If you do not need them, these have to be explicitly deleted via the delete option, as visible in *Figure* 4.12:

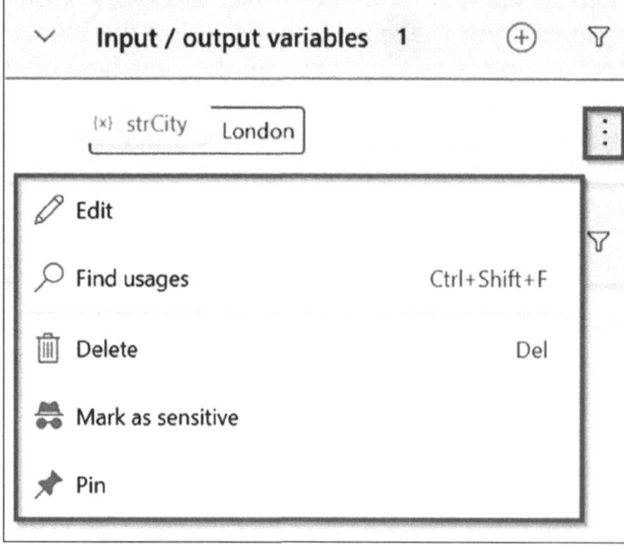

Figure 4.12: *Input/Output variable options*

Variable Data Types

When you click the **'+'** button in the **"`Input/Output variables`"** section, as shown in *Figure* 4.13, you will see the list of all available variable data types in PAD. A data type is nothing but the type of data that the variable can hold, for example, numeric or text.

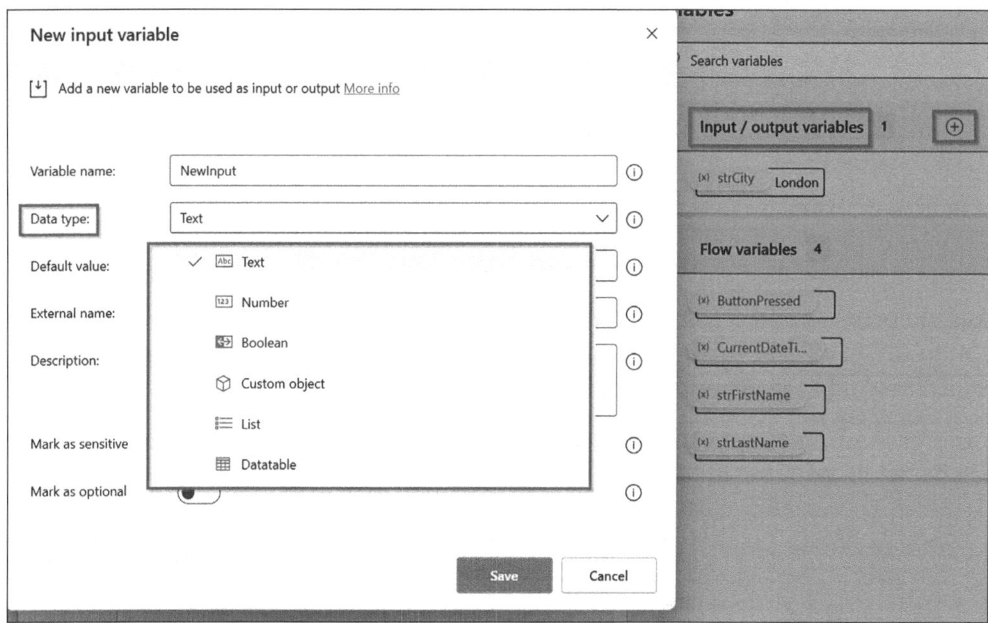

Figure 4.13: *Variable data types in PAD*

Let's take a look at each one of them in a nutshell.

Before we proceed with each of the variable data types, one important point to note is that when you create **"`Flow variables`"**, PAD automatically converts that variable to a particular type depending on the content of that variable. To exemplify this, in *Figure* 4.1, we created a variable called **`strFirstName`** with a value as *John*. Since it is a text value, the type of this variable automatically becomes a **'`Text`'** type. You can verify this by applying a breakpoint after creating the variable using the **"`Set variable`"** Action and then opening the variable. The data type of the variable is mentioned in braces as **'`Text value`'** in the following figure:

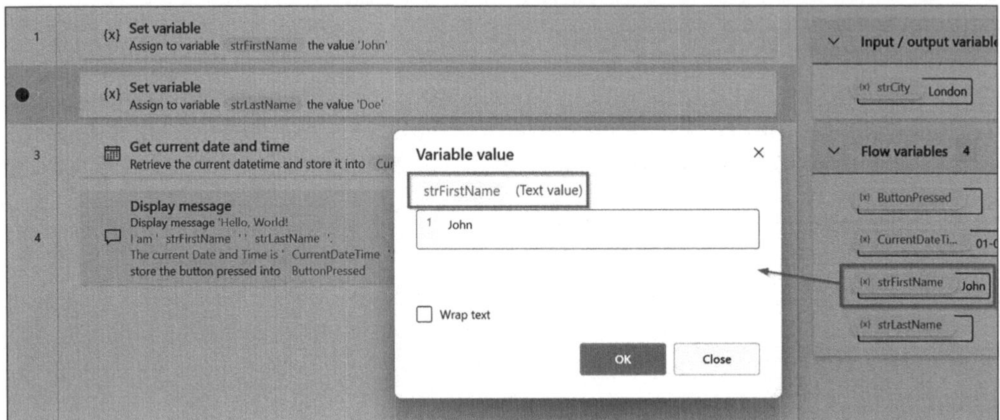

Figure 4.14: *Data type of Flow variable*

Stop the process and try re-running the Flow, but this time change the value of *John* to 10 in the **"Set variable"** Action. You will see that this time opening the variable would show up as a **'Numeric'** type because 10 is a number.

In the case of an **"Input/Output variable"**, we explicitly provide the type of the variable while creating it.

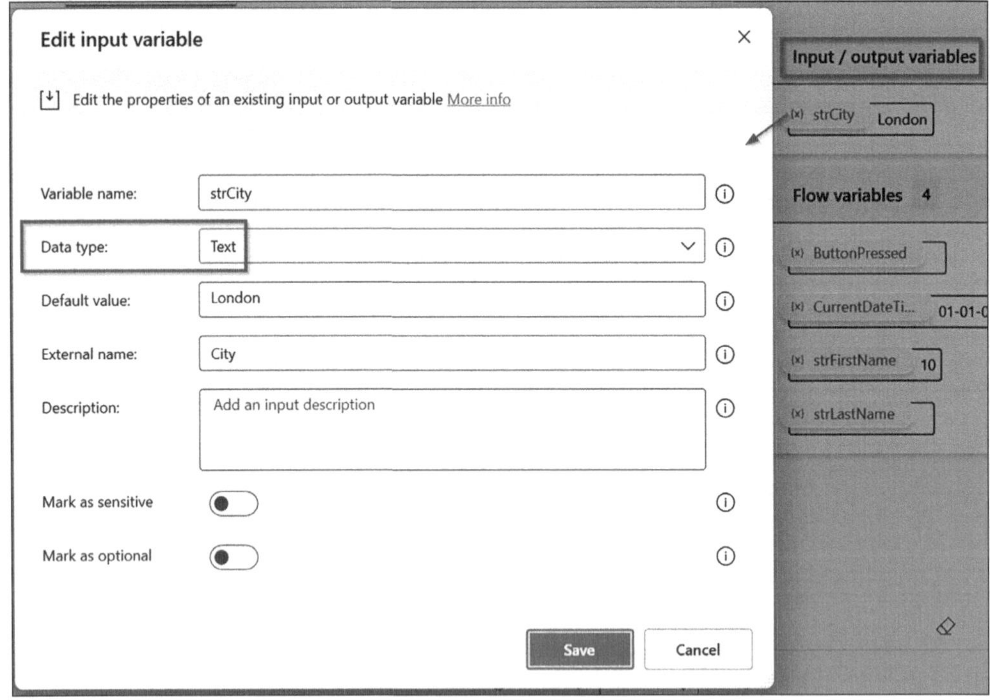

Figure 4.15: *Data type of Input/Output variable*

The first type of variable on our list, as shown in *Figure* 4.13, is the **'Text'** data type.

Text

We have already seen and used this type of variable several times in the current chapter as well as in the previous topics. Use the **"Set variable"** Action and provide any text without any quotes to make it a variable of type **'Text'**.

This time we provide a different value and give a different name to a variable.

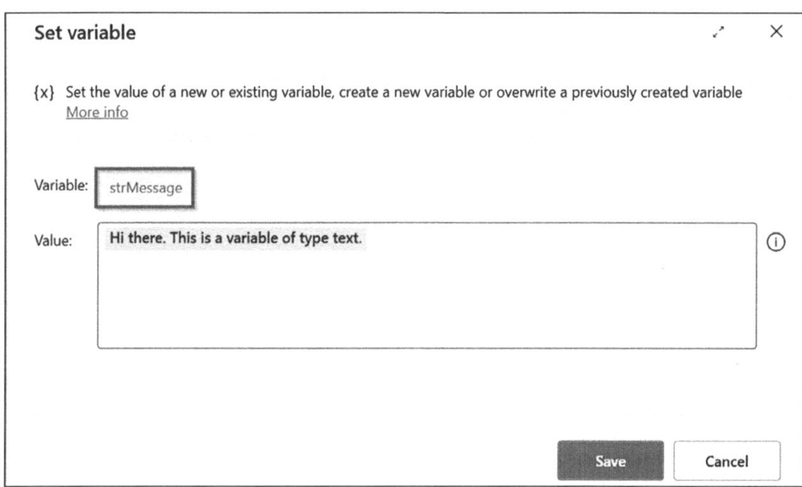

Figure 4.16: *Creating a variable of type Text*

Number

We create a numeric type of variable in the same way as that of a **'Text'** type with the only difference that the value of the variable would be a number. It is obvious that only variables of this type can be used to perform arithmetic operations, which we will be looking at in a short while.

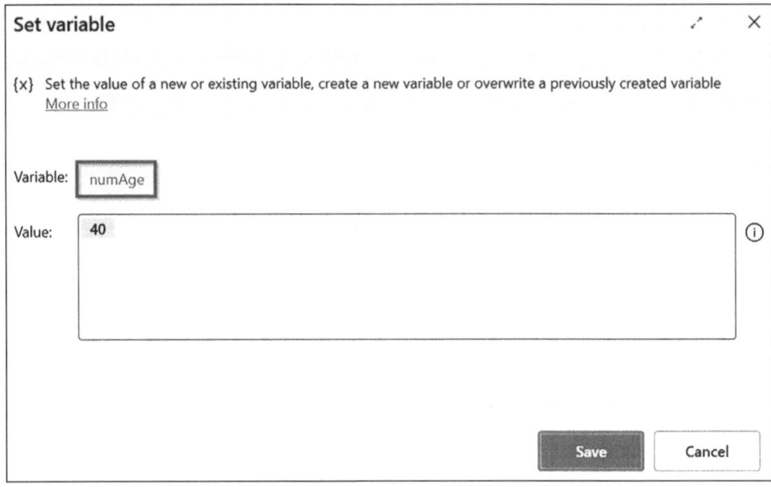

Figure 4.17: *Creating a variable of type Number*

Boolean

A **'Boolean'** type of variable that has been used since the programming ages is used to indicate a **True** or **False** type of value. This time, the value of a Boolean variable, also known as a bool or a flag variable, has to be provided as either True or False but within the percent sign. If you already guessed it why, the reason is that it would become a **'Text'** type if given without the percent sign. Try this out with the help of the aforementioned procedure by setting a variable value as True without the percent sign and then viewing the data type after the execution hits the breakpoint.

However, you can provide the value as **%True%** or **%true%**, as the case does not matter for it to be considered as a **'Boolean'** type of variable.

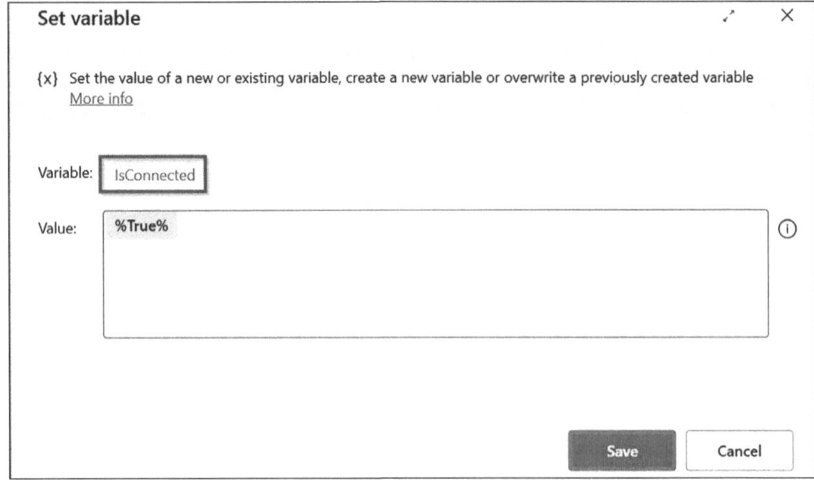

Figure 4.18: *Creating a variable of type Boolean*

You can use this type of variable where an output determines a Yes/No kind of result. Some examples are **`isFinished`**, **`isEnabled`**, **`isValid`**, **`isRunning`**, **`isActive`**, and so on.

Custom Object

They contain property-value pairs and PAD has an in-built Action to convert them to a JSON (JavaScript object notation) format for any further usage within the Flow.

Figure 4.19: *Creating a variable of type Custom object*

The value used in the preceding figure is as follows:

```
%{ 'Name': 'John', 'Age': 40, 'City': 'London' }%
```

Here is another example with a greater number of pairs that represent book details:

```
%{ 'title': 'The Power of Now', 'author': 'Eckhart Tolle', 'publicati-
onYear': 1997, 'genre': 'Self-help', 'isBestseller': True }%
```

Do not forget to prefix and suffix the percent signs. When you run the process with the above values, a **"`Custom object`"** type variable, represented in a name-value table format, will be generated.

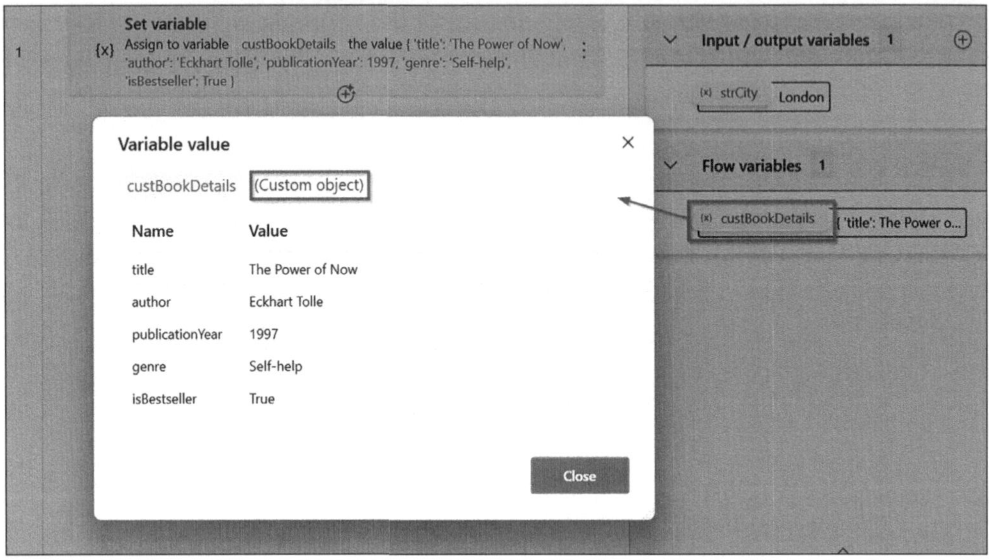

***Figure 4.20:** Running a Custom object type of variable*

The individual elements can be accessed as follows for our preceding example:

`%custBookDetails['title']%`

***Figure 4.21:** Accessing a specific item of Custom object type of variable*

Output of our Flow would show up the title of the book:

1 Set variable
{x} Assign to variable custBookDetails the value { 'title': 'The Power of Now', 'author': 'Eckhart Tolle', 'publicationYear': 1997, 'genre': 'Self-help', 'isBestseller': True }

Display message
Display message custBookDetails ['title'] in the notification popup window with title 'Message Box' and store the button pressed into ButtonPressed

Message Box
The Power of Now
OK

Figure 4.22: *Output of accessing a specific item of Custom object*

Try out the same to change the value of a specific element in a **"Custom object"**. After the first **"Set variable"** Action shown above, use another **"Set variable"** Action and give the variable name as **%custBookDetails['title']%** and configure its value to some other book name. When you check the overall **custBookDetails** variable values in the **"Variables"** pane, the title of the book will have been changed to the new one you have just set, but all other values remain the same since you have targeted to change only the title.

Actions specific to **"Custom object"** in PAD are as follows: the one to convert it into a JSON is the **"Convert custom object to JSON"** Action, while the other one is to convert a JSON to a **"Custom object"**.

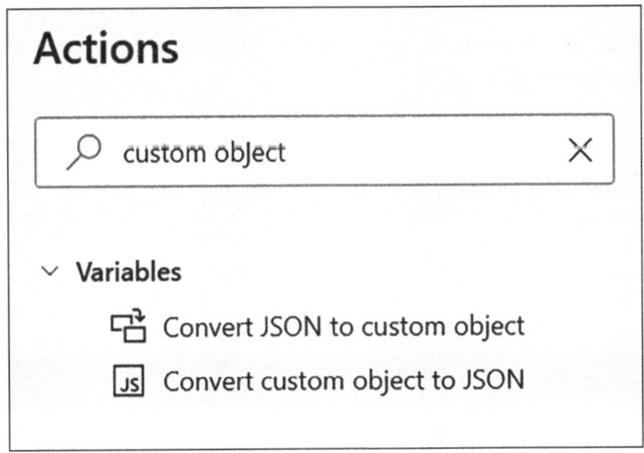

Figure 4.23: *Actions related to Custom object*

List

If you visualize an Excel spreadsheet, a List would represent a single column with multiple rows. Power Automate Desktop provides an Action to create a list as well as to add items to it.

Create a list with the help of the **"Create new list"** Action. Provide the name you would like the list to have. Then use the **"Add item to list"** Action to add items to the newly created list. If **Departments** is our list variable name, then add the name of any department to it using this Action.

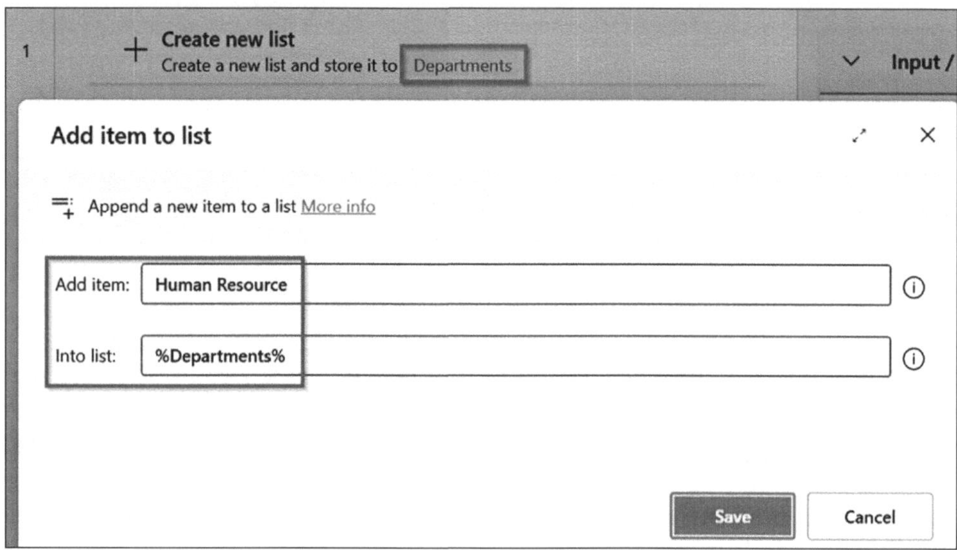

Figure 4.24: *Create and Add item to list*

Copy-paste the same Action two more times and provide different department names in each of them. When you run the Flow and open the **Departments** variable, you will see a list of three items for those added departments. Note that the indexing of the list variable starts from 0. Therefore, if you have to refer to the first item of the list, then it would be as **%Departments[0]%**.

Try displaying in a message box the third item from the list, which is **'Sales'** in the following figure, or the one you have added in your list if you have used different department names.

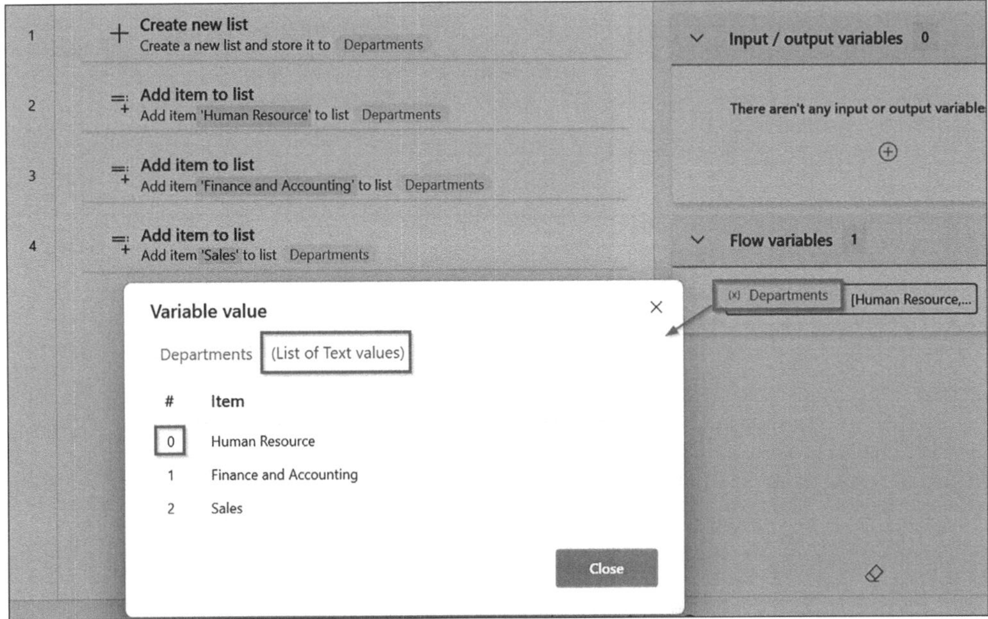

Figure 4.25: *All items after creating a List*

Since a list contains a series of items, and if we want to iterate through all of its items instead of just one item as explained above, then we make use of a looping mechanism. We will be taking a look at the various types of loops and their uses in this same chapter.

Meanwhile, practically try out the various Actions available in PAD for interacting with **"`List`"** type of variables. This is how one would gain practical knowledge and in turn mastery over building Flows in Power Automate Desktop, that is, by practically trying out the given Actions.

There is another way to create a List variable along with its items with the use of a single Action and can be especially used when multiple items have to be added to the List, all at once.

Add the following inside a **"`Set variable`"** Action and observe what happens to the variable in the **"`Variables`"** pane:

```
%['Monday', 'Tuesday', 'Wednesday', 'Thursday', 'Friday', 'Saturday',
'Sunday']%
```

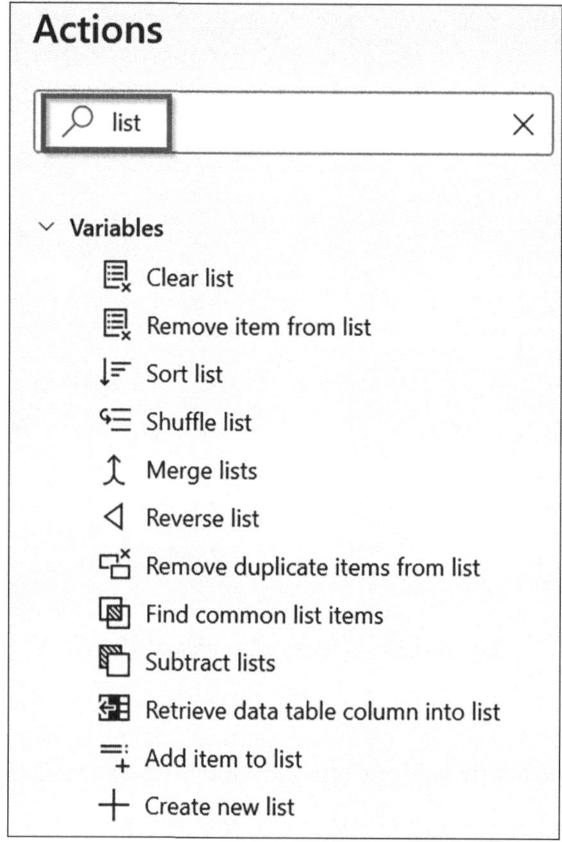

***Figure 4.26**: Different actions for List variables*

Datatable

If Lists are a single column with multiple rows, then a Datatable can have multiple columns with multiple rows. They represent a combination of rows and columns in a tabular format.

To create a Datatable, use the dedicated **"Create new data table"** Action. In its properties, hit the **"Edit"** button, which will open up a table to add the rows and columns. Add those details, including the column headers, and finally hit **"Save"** (refer to *Figure 4.27*).

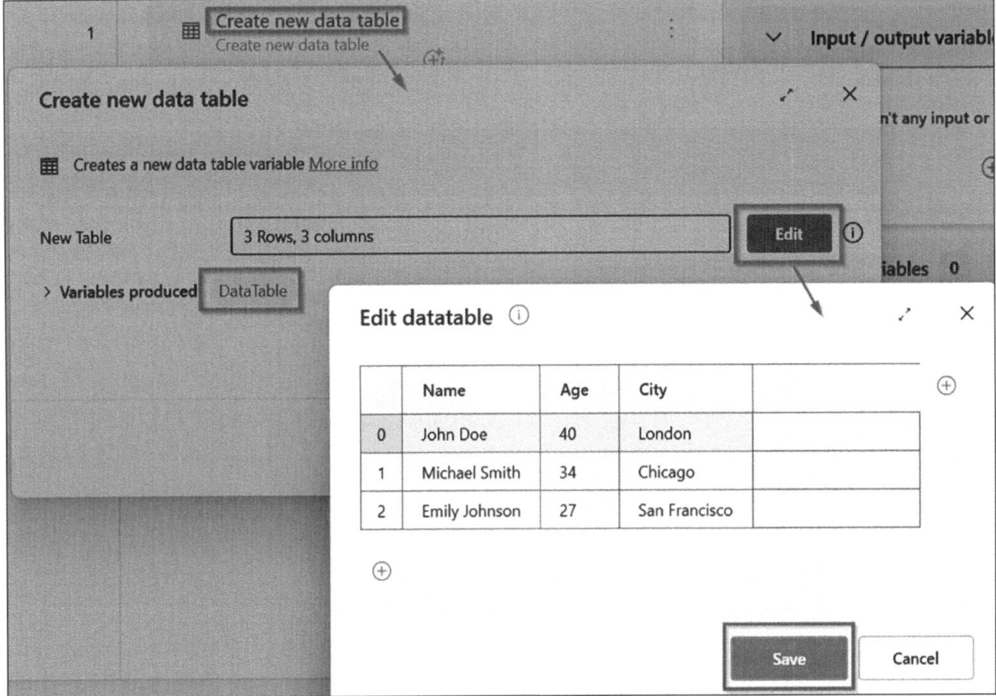

Figure 4.27: *Creating a Datatable*

Just like Lists, Datatables also start the indexing from 0. So, to access the value of **`Michael Smith`** in the above table, you would use **`%DataTable[1][0]%`**. You may also use the column header within single quotes while referring to an item, for example, **`%DataTable[1]['Name']%`**, in this case, would also point to *Michael Smith*.

So, the format could be as **`%VariableName[RowIndex][ColumnIndex]%`** or **`%VariableName[RowIndex]['ColumnName']%`**, where the latter option can be used in case you want to access it using column headers.

And again, to iterate through all items of a Datatable, we will use a looping Action, which we will look at shortly. There is one more data type specific to a Datatable called Datarow, and we will look at it in the "*Loops*" section of this chapter, where it would be much more relevant.

Just like using the **"`Set variable`"** Action for creating a List and adding items to it, you could use the same Action for Datatables too. Add the following in a **"`Set variable`"** Action and notice the created variable:

```
%{['John Doe', 40, 'London'], ['Jane Doe', 45, 'Paris']}%
```

And if you would like to add column headers to it, use the `'^'` symbol as the first entry with the column names as follows:

```
%{ ^['Name', 'Age', 'City'], ['John Doe', 40, 'London'], ['Jane Doe',
45, 'Paris'] }%
```

There are some good Actions to try out that are related to a Datatable, which can come in handy while building Flows:

Figure 4.28: *Datatable actions*

A point to note is that what we have seen above are for creating variables of specific types. However, as shown in *Figure* 4.29, there could be Actions that produce these types of variables as part of their output. For example, the **"Split text"** Action that splits a text based on a delimiter produces a variable of type List. However, the way of accessing them and using them in our Flow would still be the same as seen earlier.

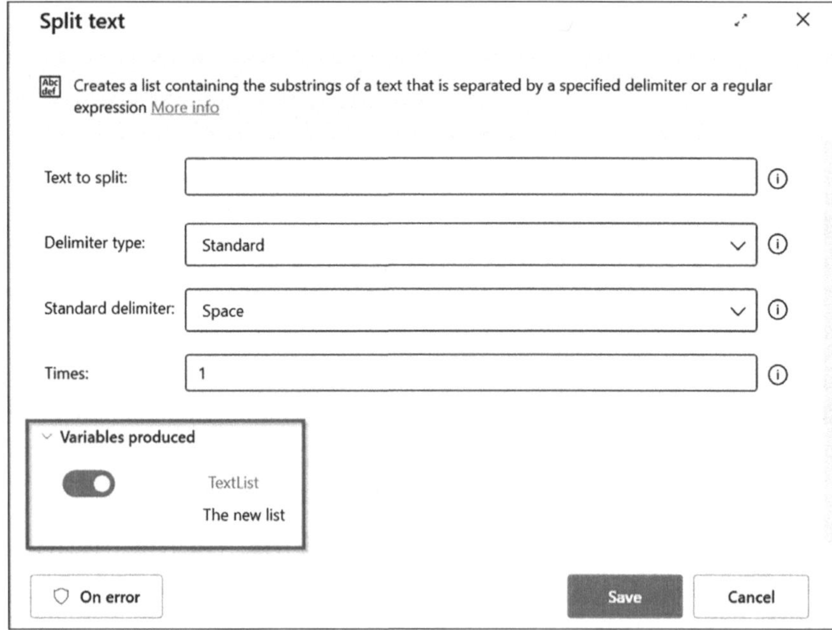

Figure 4.29: *Output variable of List type*

Certain Actions, likewise, have different types of output variables depending on the Action. The following are three examples of such different kinds of output variables:

- **`ExcelInstance`** variable produced from the **"`Launch Excel`"** Action:

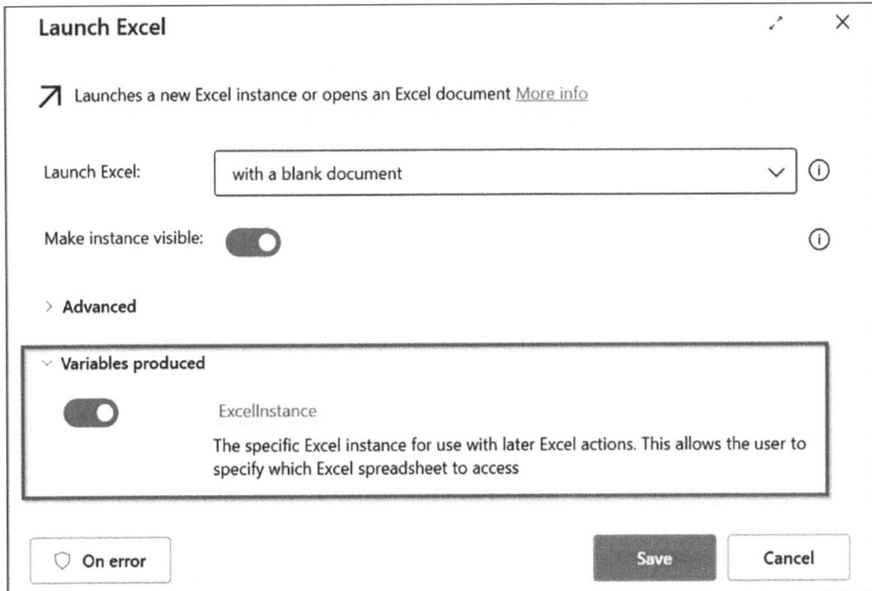

Figure 4.30: *ExcelInstance output variable type*

- Launching any browser Actions will produce a Browser instance type of output variable:

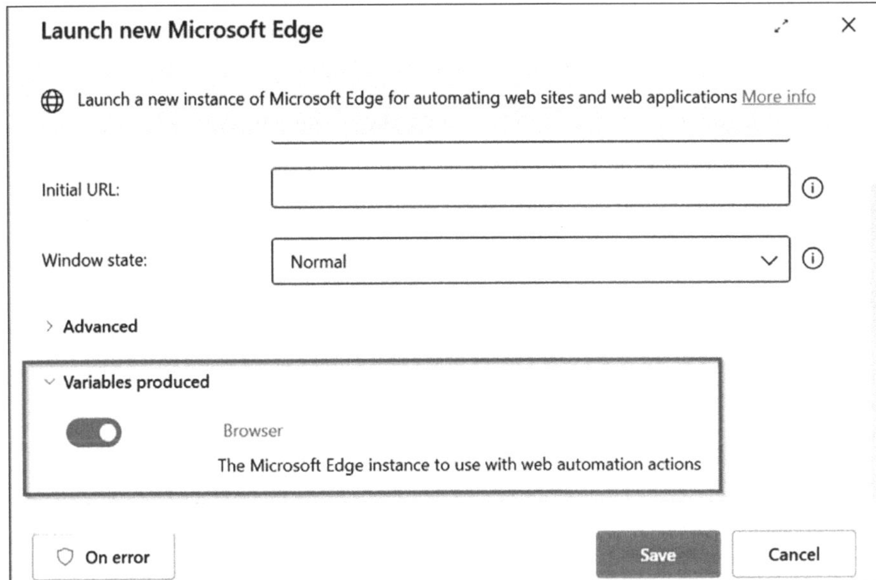

Figure 4.31: *Browser Instance output variable type*

- Creating an SQL connection will hold a reference to that connection:

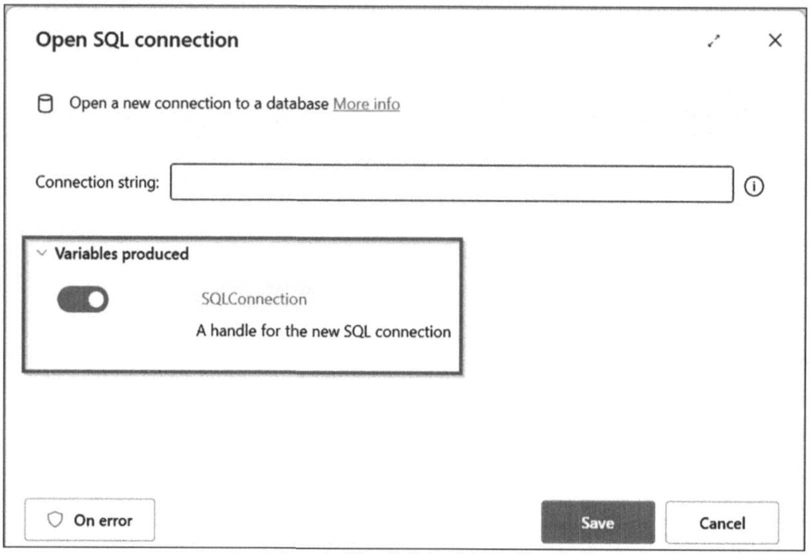

Figure 4.32: *SQLConnection output variable type*

Arithmetic Operations Using Variables

First, let us perform the arithmetic operation without variables. The numbers and operators are simply used within a relevant Action but enclosed within the percent symbol.

Here is an example that includes a combination of Addition, Subtraction, Multiplication, and Division. The expression used in the following figure is **`%8 + 5 * 3 - 6 / 2%`.**

The same can be done using the **"`Set variable`"** Action too. The outcome of the calculation is 20. The precedence of the operators would be the same as in any arithmetic calculation.

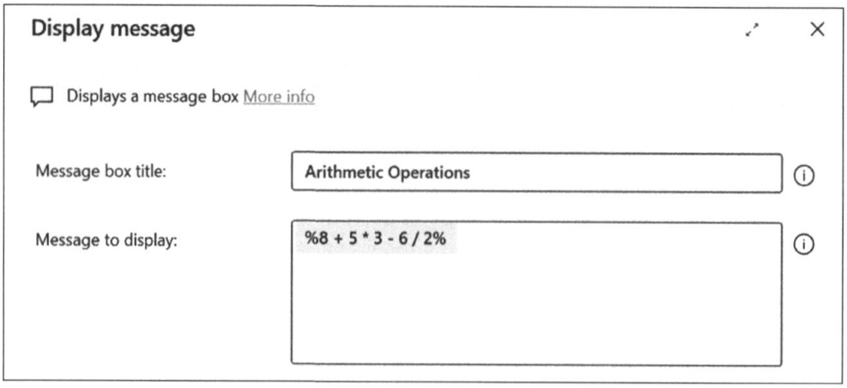

Figure 4.33: *Arithmetic operations without variables*

Following is an example using braces, which would now give a different result as compared to the above figure. The expression used is `%(8 + 5) * 3 - (6 / 2)%` and the result would be 36 with the expression in the braces performed first.

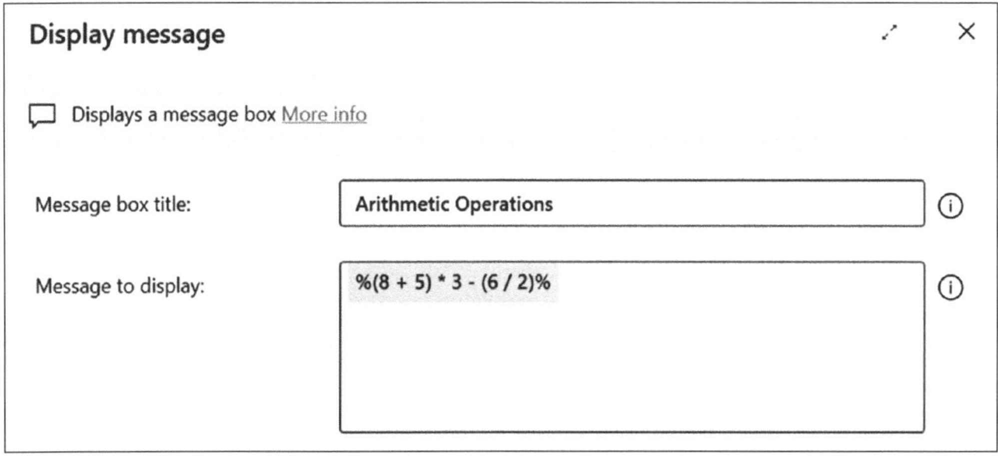

Figure 4.34: *Arithmetic operations using braces*

If **`Value1`** and **`Value2`** are two different variables that hold numeric values, then the correct way of adding those two variables is by enclosing the entire arithmetic operation within percent symbols as follows:

Correct way: `%Value1 + Value2%`

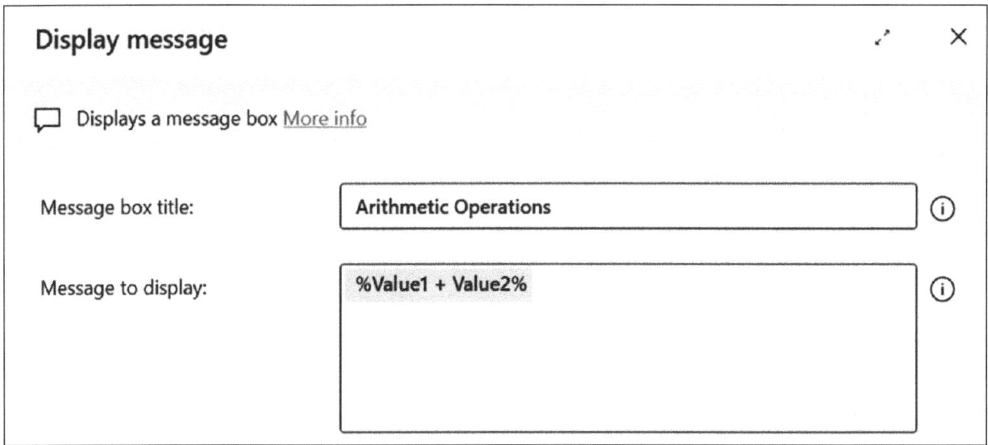

Figure 4.35: *Correct way of arithmetic operations with variables*

Here is how the entire Flow looks like along with its output after running:

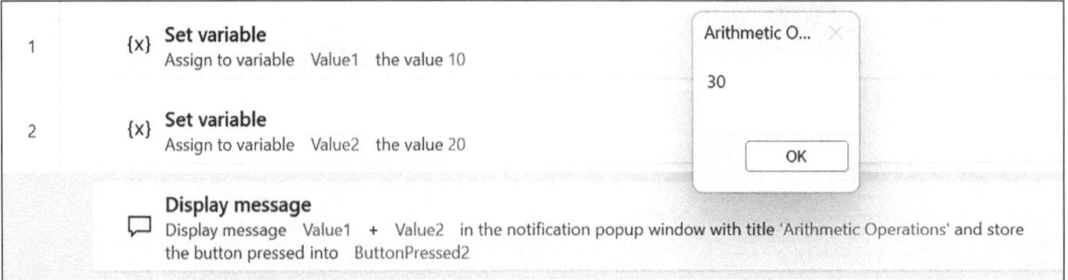

Figure 4.36: *Output after using the correct way with variables*

Incorrect way: `%Value1% + %Value2%`

If the arithmetic operation is performed in an incorrect way as in the above line by enclosing the percent sign to each variable, it would produce incorrect results and display them as follows. Only the individual variables will be evaluated but not the final calculation result:

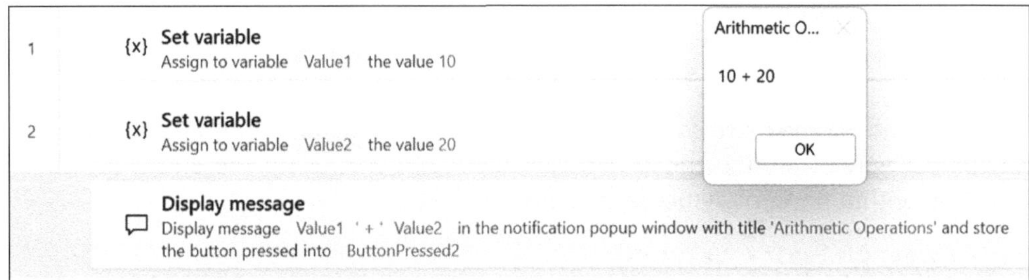

Figure 4.37: *Output after using the incorrect way with variables*

An arithmetic operation using a combination of a hard-coded number and a variable would be as follows:

Correct way: `%10 + Value2%`

Notice that a hard-coded numeric value of 10 and the variable **`Value2`**, both are inside the same starting and ending percent symbols.

Display message

Displays a message box More info

Message box title: Arithmetic Operations

Message to display: %10 + Value2%

Figure 4.38: *Correct way of using hard-coded numbers with variables*

Incorrect way: **`10 + %Value2%`**

If the syntax is used in an incorrect way as the above line, that is, the numeric value outside of the percent symbol and the **`Value2`** variable enclosed within its own percent symbols, then this would produce the same incorrect result, as shown in *Figure* 4.37.

Concatenating Text with Variables

While building Flows, there arise several scenarios where you would have to combine one or more lines of text with a variable. We have already seen this at the beginning of the chapter, and it is done by simply placing the variables in the position where they are required in that line of text (see *Figure* 4.39):

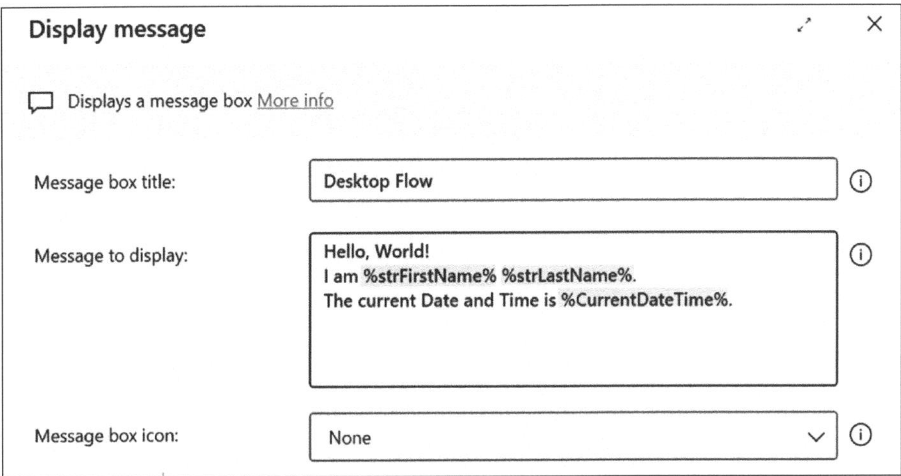

Figure 4.39: *Concatenating lines of text with variables*

In the preceding figure, each individual variables are enclosed within percent symbols and placed where they want to be appeared in the final output. Also, notice that there is a space between **`strFirstName`** and **`strLastName`** variables. Full stops are also added after the **`strLastName`** and **`CurrentDateTime`** variables, and thus the final result would also have the space and the full stops when displayed, as follows:

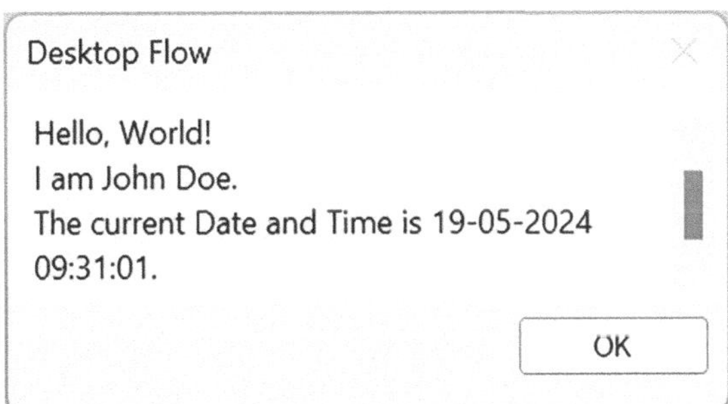

Figure 4.40: *Output after concatenating lines of text with variables*

Setting a Blank Value to a Variable

During Flow development, you might want to set a blank value to a variable, for example, to clear the values of what that variable already holds. This is done by setting the expression as `%''%` in the **"Set variable"** Action. It is a percent sign followed by two single quotes (not a double quote) and then another percent sign. There is no space used.

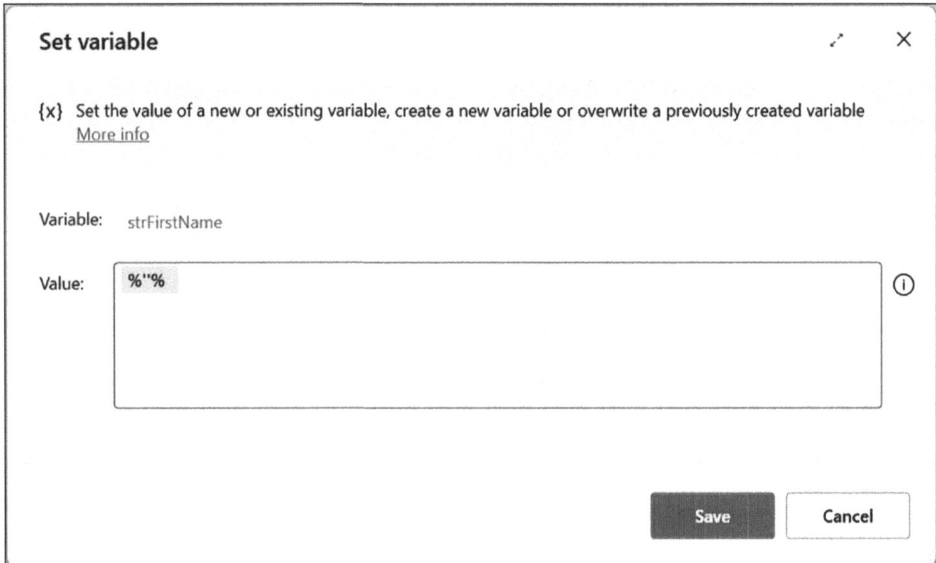

Figure 4.41: *Setting a blank value to a variable*

Setting a Percentage Value in a Variable

The notation for variables in PAD is by using the percent symbol **'%'** at the start and at the end of that variable. This causes a conflict when you want to set a variable value that has the percent symbol itself. For example, 80%. PAD indicates an error as soon as you type this.

Set variable

{x} Set the value of a new or existing variable, create a new variable or overwrite a previously created variable
More info

Variable: Percentage

Value: 80%

Invalid value

Save Cancel

***Figure 4.42:** Error while setting a percent value to a variable*

This issue is circumvented by adding one more percent sign next to the existing one as an escape character.

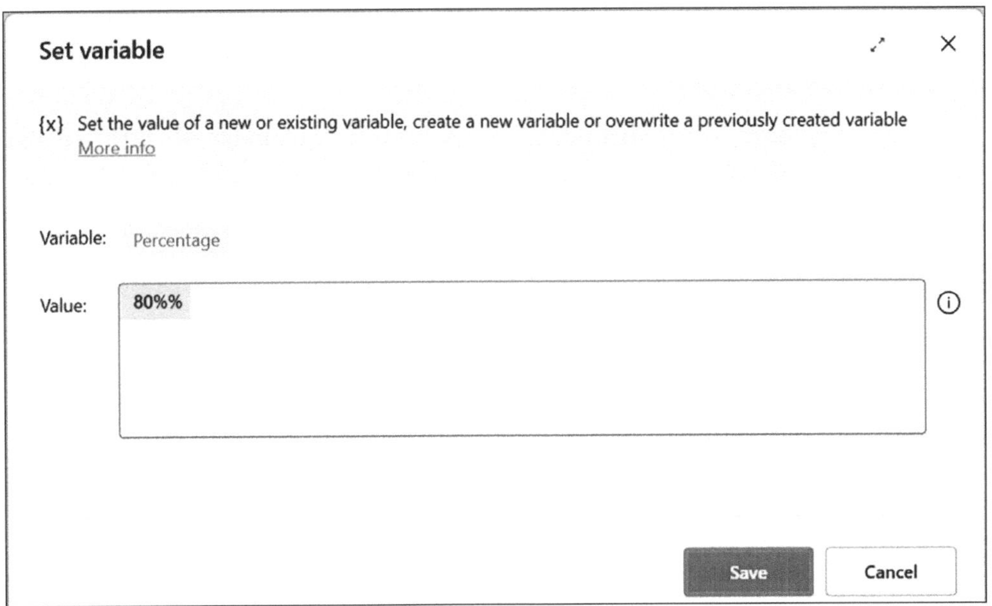

***Figure 4.43:** Adding percent sign as an escape character for percent values*

After this is done, running the Flow to display the variable value will show the correct results.

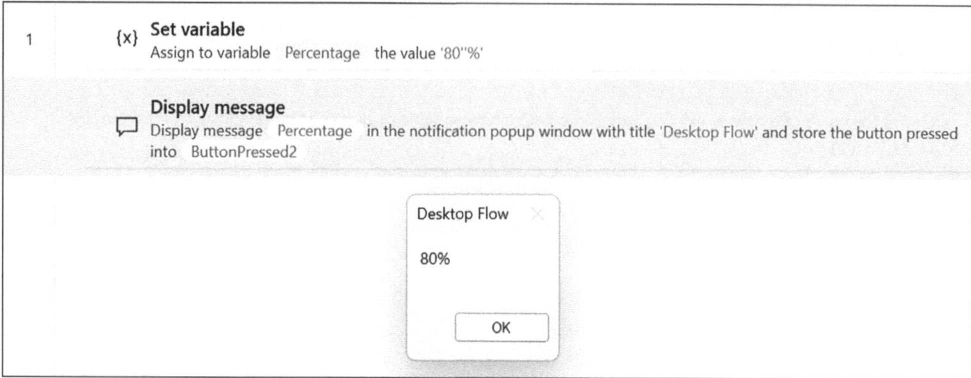

Figure 4.44: *Output after adding percent sign as an escape character*

A key point to note about variables is their scope. The scope of variables is **global** (and not **local**). Meaning, once a variable is created, the variable itself and therefore its value will be available in the entire Desktop Flow, that is, in the **"Main"** Flow and in all the Subflows.

This concludes variables and their data types, but the vastness of the **"Variables"** topic calls for a further deep dive with the help of the following links:

- **Managing variables and the variables pane:**

  https://learn.microsoft.com/en-us/power-automate/desktop-flows/manage-variables

- **Variable data types:**

  https://learn.microsoft.com/en-us/power-automate/desktop-flows/variable-data-types

- **Variable data type properties:**

  https://learn.microsoft.com/en-us/power-automate/desktop-flows/datatype-properties

- **Variable manipulation:**

  https://learn.microsoft.com/en-us/power-automate/desktop-flows/variable-manipulation

Conditional Statements

If you look at the **"Actions"** pane, you will find a dedicated group of Actions called **"Conditionals"**. These conditional statements determine which Action to run next based on the outcome of the condition set.

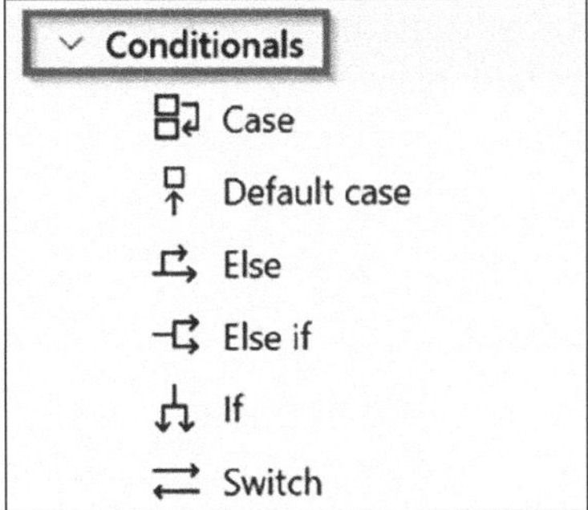

Figure 4.45: *Conditionals group of actions*

Let's take a look at each of them and how they are used.

"If" Action

It is a type of conditional statement that allows the Flow to execute certain Actions only if the condition specified inside it is true.

Using this Action, we are going to check whether a person is an Adult or not based on a particular age.

Set a new variable called **numAge** and give its value as 23. Then, drag and drop the **"If"** Action, choose the first operand as the variable created with the help of the **{x}** variable picker button, select the **>=** operator from the dropdown, and finally mention the second operand as 18. Here, we are checking if the first operand (**numAge**) is greater than or equal to the second operand (18), and if yes, then the person is an Adult.

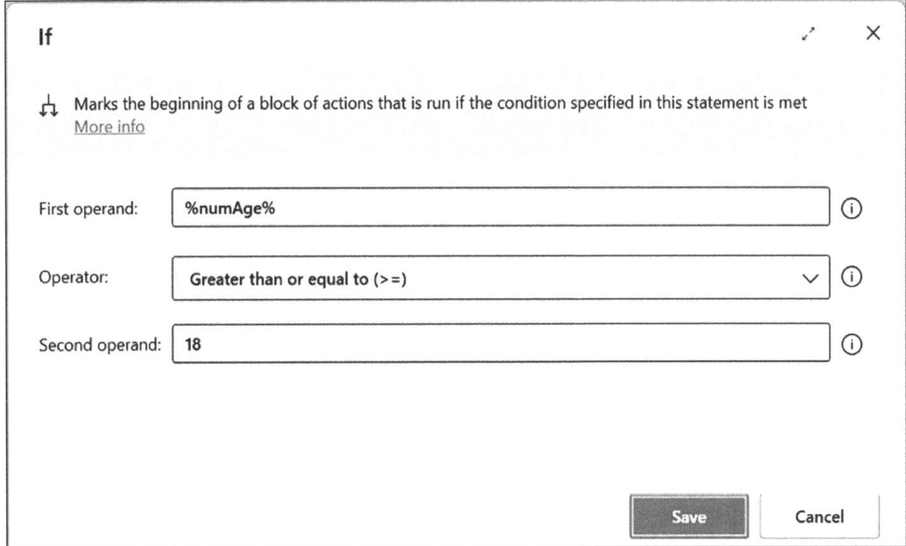

Figure 4.46: *If conditional statement*

As soon as you click the **"Save"** button, a corresponding **"End"** Action gets added below the **"If"** Action. The **"End"** is an indicator for PAD to tell where the **"If"** ends and should always be accompanied with each other. Your Flow should look as follows:

Subflows Main

1 {x} Set variable
Assign to variable numAge the value 23

2 If numAge >=18 then

3 End

Figure 4.47: *Flow after adding If conditional statement*

Any Actions to run if the condition is met will go within the **"If"** and **"End"** block. Drag and drop a message box within this block (not outside the block). In the message box Action, enter the message to display, as shown in *Figure* 4.48, with the help of the variable picker button to insert it into the right place of the entire text:

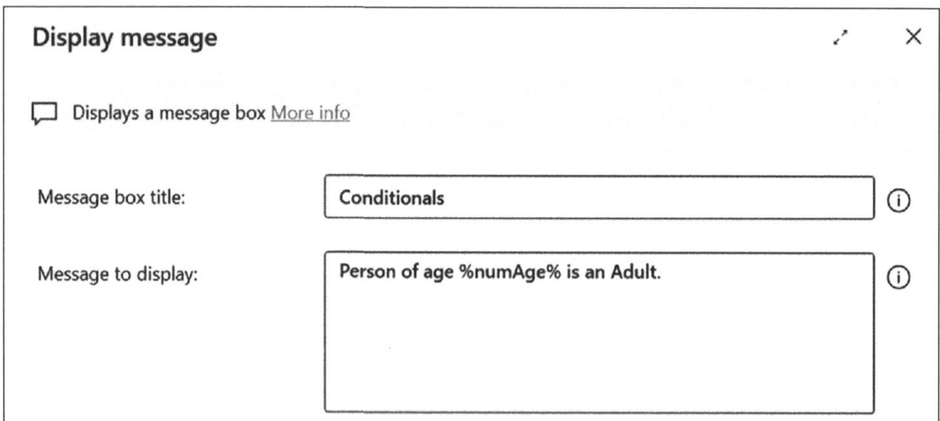

Figure 4.48: *Display message inside the If conditional statement*

The entire Flow should now look as follows:

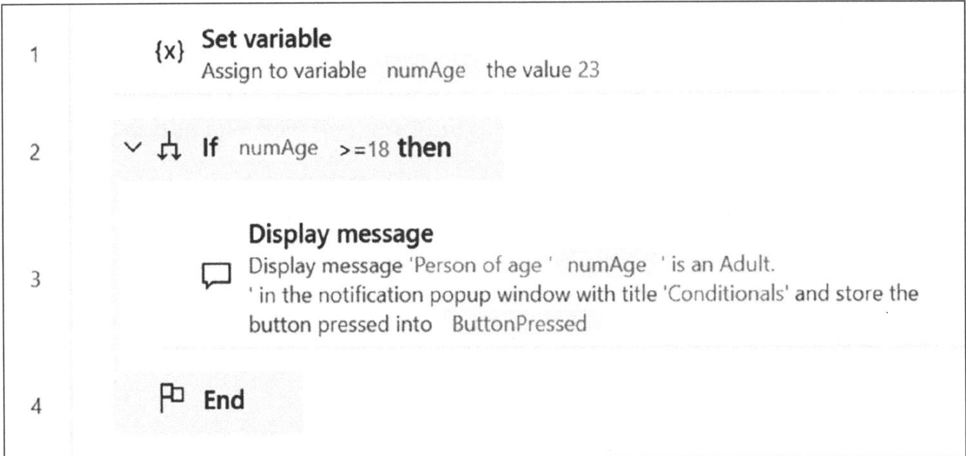

Figure 4.49: *Final Flow after Display message inside If statement*

Run the Flow to see the output for the chosen Age:

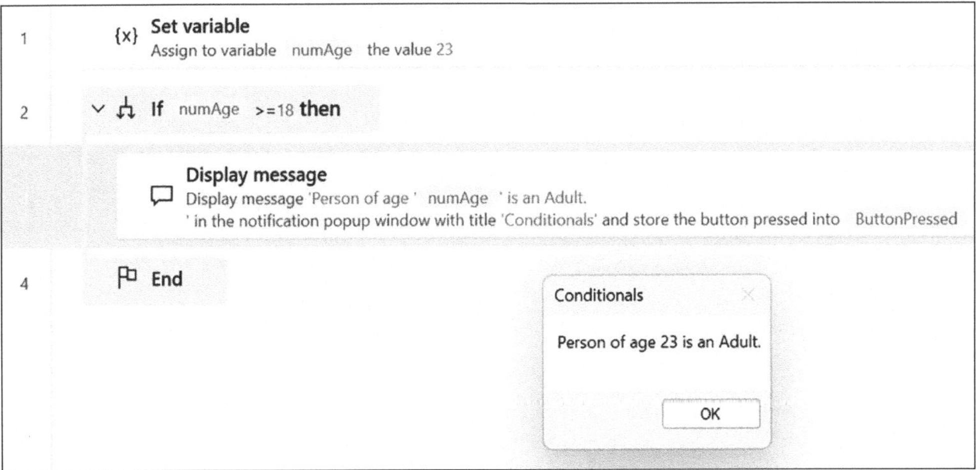

Figure 4.50: *Output on running the Flow*

The **"If"** statement was used to check whether the Age value of 23 was greater than or equal to 18, and if it was, then the message box was displayed as above. This has produced the message box as expected. Also, notice the clean message with the age variable replaced by 23 and with a full stop at the end, just as we had designed in the **"Display message"** Action.

Try out the same with two different inputs, once with **numAge** less than 18 and once equal to 18 in the **"Set variable"** Action, and review what happens. When the age variable holds the value of 18, the Flow produces the same output as above, but does not display any message if the age is below 18. This is because we haven't designed the Flow to handle ages below 18, and this is where the next Action comes into play.

"Else" Action

The **"Else"** Action has to be a part of an **"If"** statement to tell the Flow what to do if the **"If"** Action does not satisfy the given condition. Let's see it in action.

Continuing with the Flow, as shown in *Figure* 4.50, drag and drop the **"Else"** Action and place it below the **"Display message"** Action that is already present in the Flow. We are going to make a copy of this **"Display message"** Action and paste it after the **"Else"** Action to create another message box. To paste it at the right place, the procedure is to first copy the desired Action, then click on the line of Action where you want the new Action to be pasted. If you want the new Action to be on the fifth line, then click on the Action that is currently present on the fifth line and paste it over there so that the new Action now becomes your fifth line.

In our case, copy the earlier **"Display message"** Action, then left-click on the **"End"** Action to select it and paste it there. The newly pasted Action will show above the **"End"** Action and after the **"Else"** Action, as shown in *Figure* 4.51.

Configure the new message box to display that the person is *not* an Adult. Your entire Flow should look as follows:

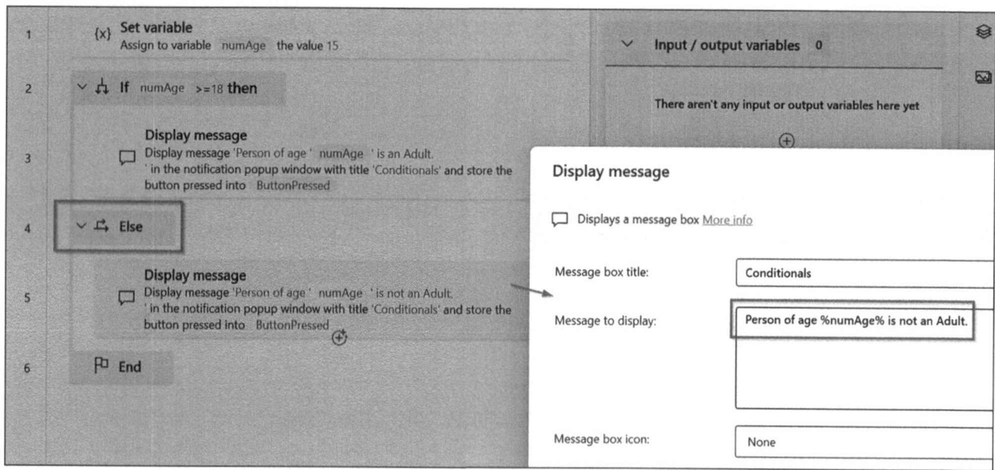

Figure 4.51: *Flow after adding Else statement and message box*

Run the Flow thrice, each with three different inputs, and observe the outputs as follows:

1. When Age is below 18 (for example, 15): Output will be **`Person of Age 15 is not an Adult.`**
2. When Age is 18: Output will be **`Person of Age 18 is an Adult.`** (This is because we have used the greater than or equal to operator.)

3. When Age is above 18 (for example, 23): Output will be **`Person of Age 23 is an Adult.`**

"`Else If`" Action

What if the age categories increase and the above **"`If`"** and **"`Else`"** Actions cannot hold them and you would like to check for more age groups? This is where the **"`Else If`"** Action comes in handy.

The age groups and their categories are different in different geographies, but as a generalized example, let us consider how to use the **"`Else If`"** Action for the following categories:

If age < 10, then consider as a **"`Child`"**

If age >= 10 and <=17, then consider as an **"`Adolescent`"**

If age >= 18 and <=59, then consider as an **"`Adult`"**

Or else consider as a **"`Senior Citizen`"**

Continue building the Flow further from the one shown in *Figure* 4.51 by changing the **"`If`"** Action in line number 2 to a **`<`** operator from the dropdown and mention the second operand as **`10`**. Modify the display message to include **`Person of age %numAge% is a Child`**. After the display message, drag and drop an **"`Else If`"** Action and modify, as shown in *Figure* 4.52:

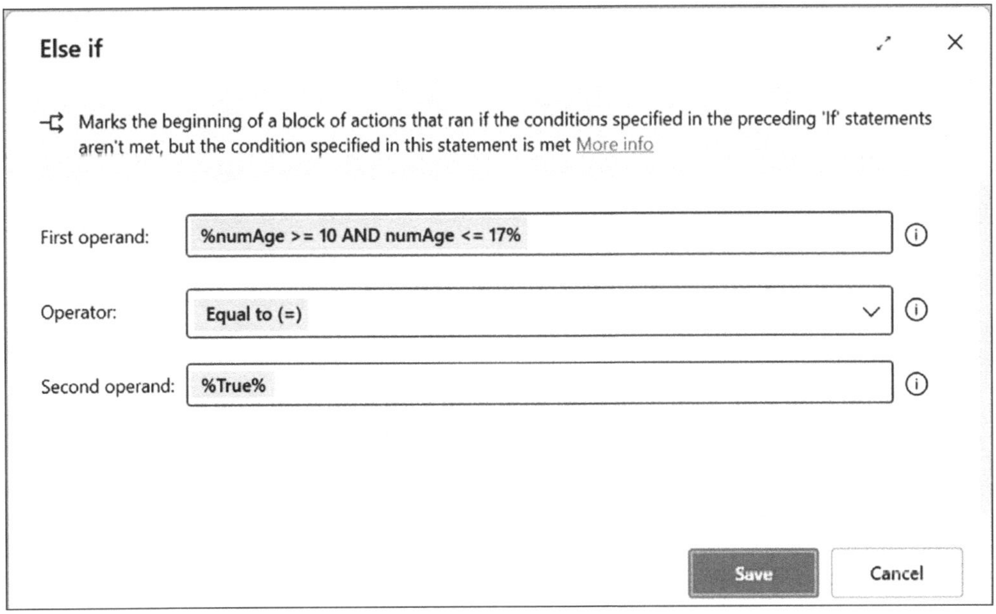

Else if

Marks the beginning of a block of actions that ran if the conditions specified in the preceding 'If' statements aren't met, but the condition specified in this statement is met More info

First operand: %numAge >= 10 AND numAge <= 17%

Operator: Equal to (=)

Second operand: %True%

Save Cancel

***Figure* 4.52:** *Else If action with multiple conditions*

What we have done here is by adding the below expression we are checking multiple age conditions against a Boolean value of True with the help of an AND operator:

```
%numAge >= 10 AND numAge <= 17%
```

This would mean if any age between 10 and 17, both inclusive, turns out to be True, then we will be considering this age group to fall under the **"Adolescent"** category. Click **"Save"** and drag and drop a message box, or preferably copy-paste the previous one, and place it after the **"Else If"** Action, with a message showing as **Person of age %numAge% is an Adolescent.**

Repeat the same but this time with the below expression to check for age groups from 18 to 59 and modify the display message to show as an Adult:

```
%numAge >= 18 AND numAge <= 59%
```

At the last, you already have an **"Else"** Action (not an **"Else If"** Action) from line number 4 of *Figure* 4.51. In the message box below the **"Else"** statement, modify the value to display as **Person of age %numAge% is a Senior Citizen**. This **"Else"** statement will take care of all the inputs that are not handled by the earlier **"If"** and **"Else If"** conditions.

Your entire Flow from line numbers 1 to 8 looks as follows:

Figure 4.53: *Final flow from line 1 to 8*

And the remaining Flow from line number 8 and onwards is as follows:

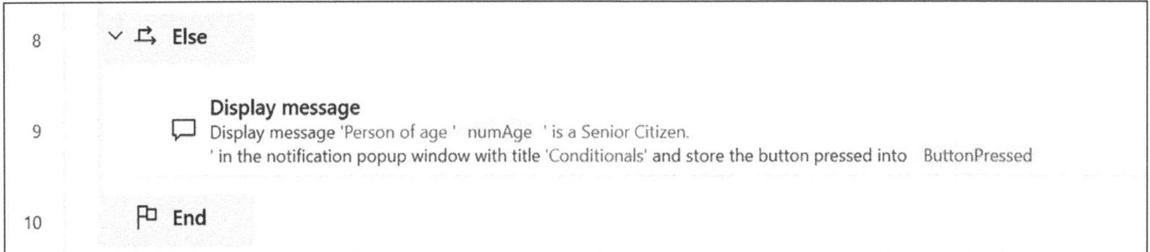

Figure 4.54: *Final flow from line 8 till end*

In line number 1, modify the age and debug the Flow with different random inputs matching the different age criteria. It is good to debug the Flow so that you can see how the execution fails for a particular condition and then goes inside the right **"Else If"** condition. The inputs and outputs will be produced as follows:

1. When Age is below 10 (for example, 9): Output will be **Person of Age 9 is a Child.**
2. When Age >= 10 and <=17 (for example, 15): Output will be **Person of Age 15 is an Adolescent.**
3. When Age >= 18 and <=59 (for example, 45): Output will be **Person of Age 45 is an Adult.**
4. When Age is anywhere between 60 and above (for example, 70): Output will be **Person of Age 70 is a Senior Citizen.**

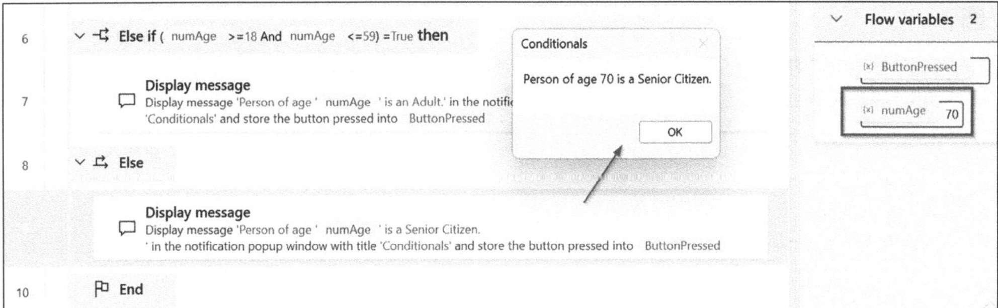

Figure 4.55: *One of the outputs of the Flow*

Of course, we haven't added any validation to handle ages that are invalid like 0, -1, and so on, but this gives a good idea as to how the **"Else If"** Action works. We have also taken the extra step of adding multiple conditions with an AND operator and also an **"Else"** condition. In applicable scenarios, you can also use an OR operator.

"Switch" Action

A **"Switch"** Action works faster than the checks performed by **"Else If"** and is used as a best practice when there are several conditions to be checked. For ease of understanding, let us use the same conditions that were used in the **"Else If"** example and build the same via a **"Switch"** Action.

Keep only the first **"Set Variable"** Action and remove all others. Drag and drop the **"Switch"** Action. Provide the **%numAge%** variable with any value to be tested. When you click **"Save"**, a corresponding **"End"** Action adds up for the **"Switch"** Action, indicating the start and end of the **"Switch"** statement. Drag and drop a **"Case"** Action in between the **"Switch"** and the **"End"** Actions. In this Action, provide the operator as **<** and value to be compared as 10. Your Flow so far should look as follows:

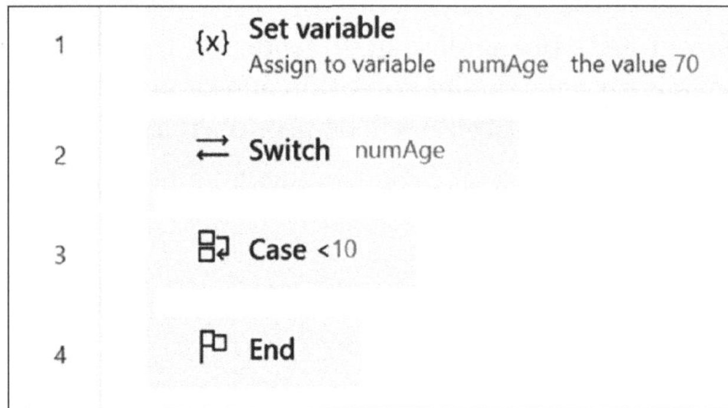

***Figure 4.56:** First-level Flow with Switch case*

Likewise, add two more **"Case"** Actions and provide the upper limits of the ages used in the **"Else If"** example, that is, 17 and 59, and use the **<=** operator in each of the **"Case"** Actions.

Then drag and drop the **"Default case"** Action, which does not require any parameters to be set. The updated Flow now looks as follows:

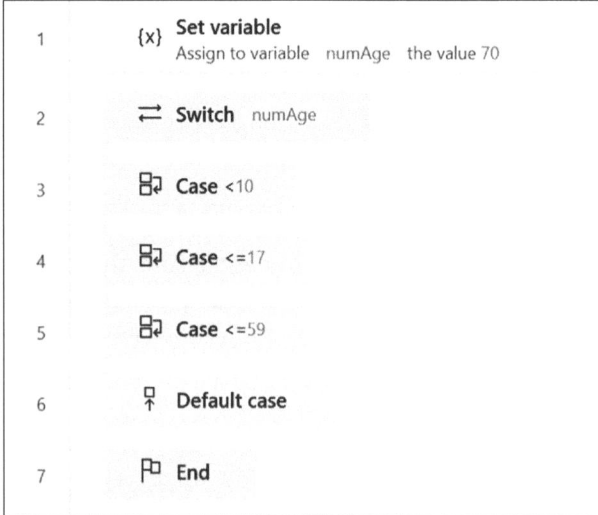

***Figure 4.57:** Second-level Flow with all Switch cases and Default case*

Be noted that the first case has a **<** operator, whereas others have a **<=** operator. If you refer to *Figure* 4.53, the operators and the upper age limits are in line with what we have used here. If you recall, the **"Else"** Action that we had used at the end to handle all the ages that are not met in the **"If"** and **"Else If"** Actions; for the **"Switch"** Action, this is handled by the **"Default case"** Action. We have now built a skeleton of the Flow, as shown in *Figure* 4.57, and now let's go ahead and add the respective message boxes as per the age limits.

On doing so, the Flow should be complete, and the entire Flow from line numbers 1 to 6 looks as follows after adding the message boxes as done in the **"Else If"** example:

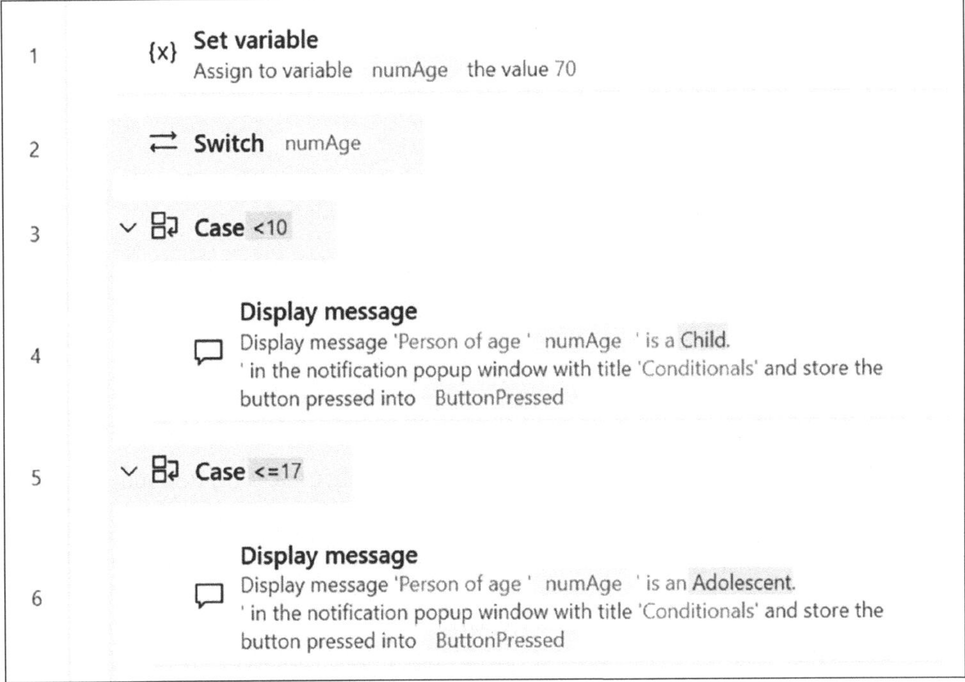

Figure 4.58: *Final Flow from line 1 to 6*

And the remaining part of the Flow is as follows:

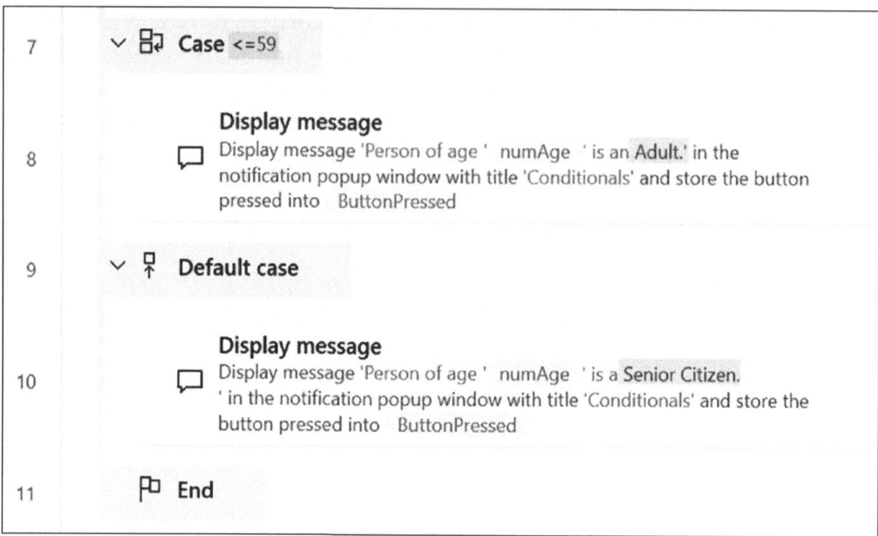

Figure 4.59: *Final Flow from line 7 till end*

Run the Flow in exactly the same way as you did in the **"Else If"** Actions by giving different inputs for different age groups, and you should see the different outputs as follows:

1. When Age is below 10 (for example, 9): Output will be **`Person of Age 9 is a Child.`**
2. When Age >= 10 and <=17 (for example, 15): Output will be **`Person of Age 15 is an Adolescent.`**
3. When Age >= 18 and <=59 (for example, 45): Output will be **`Person of Age 45 is an Adult.`**
4. When Age is anywhere between 60 and above (for example, 70): Output will be **`Person of Age 70 is a Senior Citizen.`**

Use the "*Step through*" debugging feature explained in "*Chapter 3: Debugging the Desktop Flows*" and observe how the execution goes into a specific **"Case"** statement for a specific age category including the **"Default case".**

With this, we conclude all the Actions under the **"Conditionals"** group of Actions.

Loops

Loops are also something that have been around since programming ages. During the development of Flows, they allow us to execute a block of Actions repeatedly until a specific condition is met.

Here is a list of loops in the **"Actions"** pane under the **"Loops"** category:

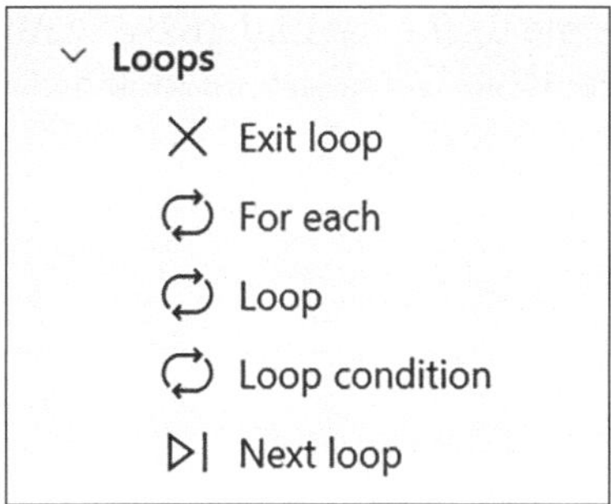

Figure 4.60: *Loops category of actions*

Let us look at each one of them in action.

"`For each`" Action

A **"`For each`"** loop iterates through a sequence of elements within a List, Datatable, or a Datarow type of variable. The number of iterations the loop will perform is already known to the loop before it even starts looping. For example, if a List variable contains 10 items, then if a **"`For each`"** is applied to run against the List, it knows that it has to run 10 times.

Let us reuse the Flow from the previous **"`Switch`"** Action. The first line of Action is the **"`Set Variable`"** Action. At the second line, drag and drop a **"`Create new list`"** Action. Give a name to the variable produced as **`ListofAges`**. We have just created a new list variable but we still haven't added items to this list. To do so, drag and drop a **"`Add item to list`"** Action. Add an item as 9, which is going to be the age that we used to review the outputs in the **"`Switch`"** Action. You can take any other random age too. Furthermore, tell the Action as to which list the value of 9 is to be added, which is **`%ListofAges%`** in our case.

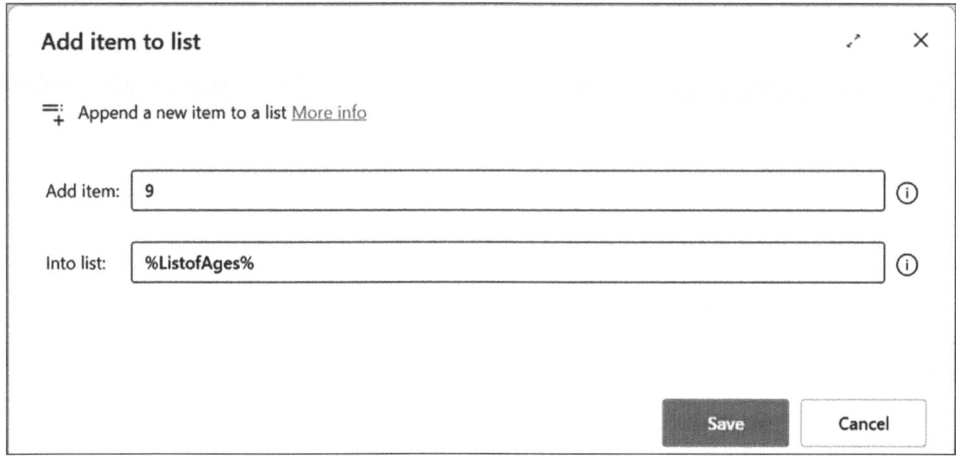

Figure 4.61: *Add a list item*

Likewise, add three more items to the list and give any random ages or **15**, **45**, and **70** as in the **"Switch"** case. Your Flow so far should look as follows:

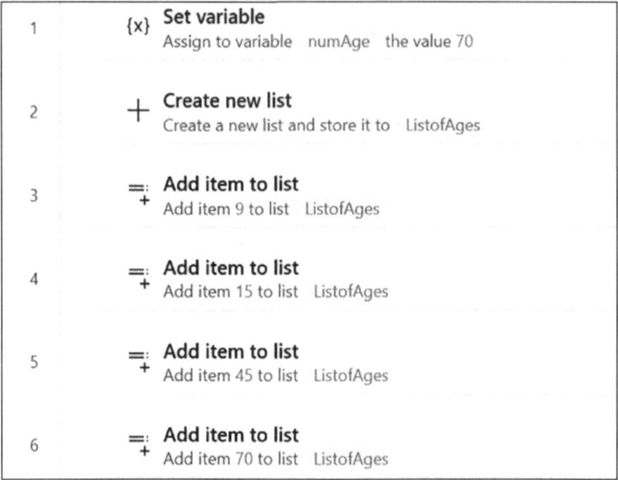

Figure 4.62: *Flow after adding list items*

After the sixth line of Action, add a **"For each"** Action with the value to iterate as our List variable. While the **"For each"** is running, we will be storing each item of the list in a variable called **numAge**, which we have been using in all our previous Flows in this topic.

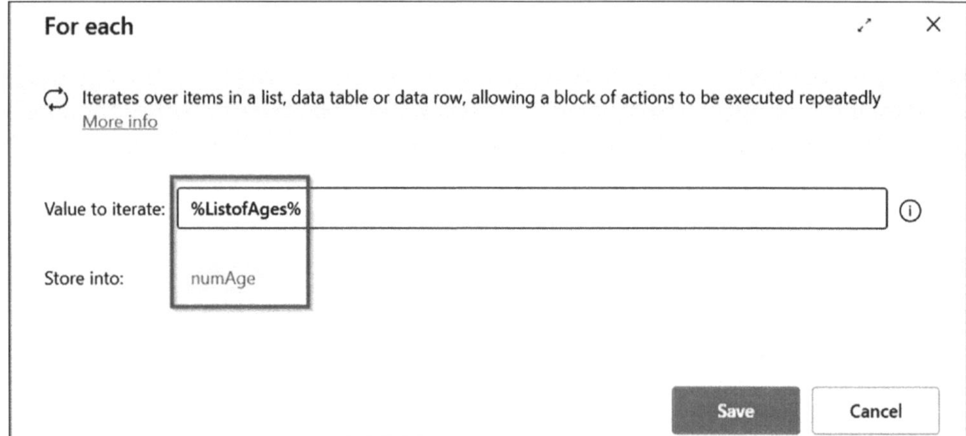

Figure 4.63: *Adding a For each loop*

The **"For each"** loop will have a corresponding **"End"** Action. Move the **"End"** Action to the very end after all the **"Switch"** structure is over. With the help of small arrows available around certain Actions (circle marked in *Figure* 4.64), one could expand/collapse the Actions, which helps in showing/hiding only the necessary Actions. After collapsing the **"Case"** Action and with the **"For each"** loop added, the Flow looks as follows:

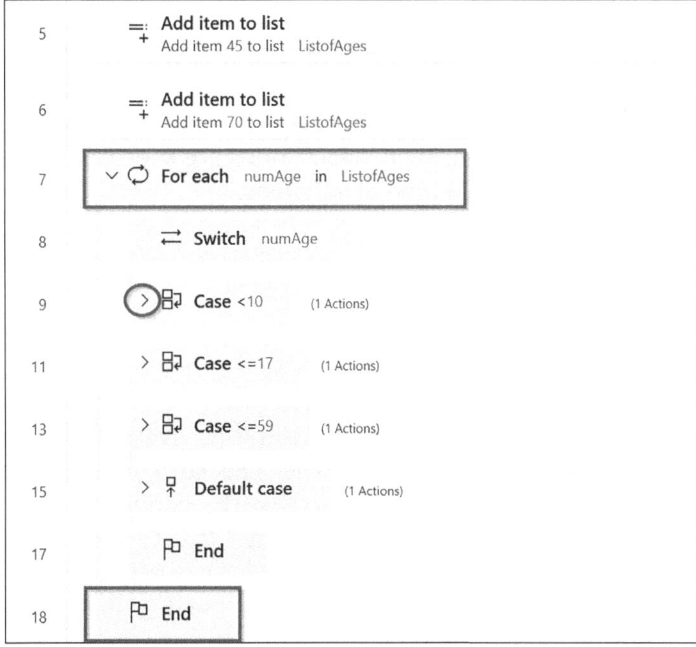

Figure 4.64: *Flow after adding For each loop*

Now, just as a quick debugging practice, disable the **"`Set variable`"** Action from line number 1 and not delete it. We do not need this Action as we are going to pass the different age inputs from the List variable. We have already set the individual ages of the list as **`numAge`.** Refer to line number 7 in the preceding figure.

By putting a breakpoint on the **"`For each`"** loop, run the Flow. This will help you to open and see the List variable values once the list is populated.

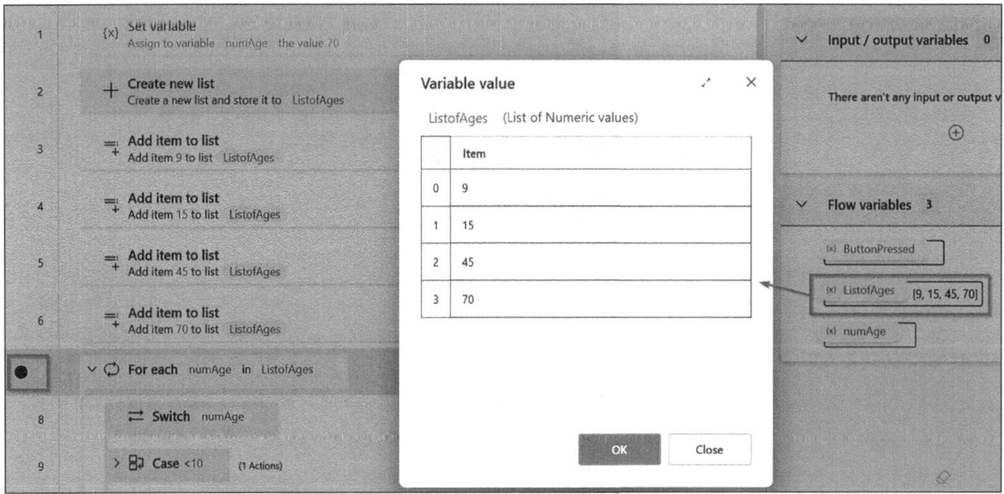

Figure 4.65: *Populated list with breakpoint*

Now you may remove the breakpoint and run the rest of the Flow. Different message boxes will show up based on each of the age groups in the above list variable, one at a time. Thus, we have looped through each of the list items and performed certain steps, that is, identifying the age group and then displaying an appropriate message box. Visualize doing this for large flows. **"For each"** loops are used for Lists as we saw, but are also majorly used for Datatable type of variables.

"Loop" Action

The **"Loop"** Action in simple terms executes for a specified number of times. From your current Flow that looks like *Figure* 4.64, delete the **"For each"** Action and replace it by dragging and dropping a **"Loop"** Action in its place. As soon as you drag, PAD will ask you to fill up the parameters. We will start iterating from 0 because, if you recall, the indexing of List variable starts from 0. For the **"End to"** parameter, use the variable picker and expand the **ListofAges** variable to find the count property. Double-click the **".Count"**, and the **"End to"** parameter will have **%ListofAges.Count%**. However, since the indexing starts from 0, if the list contains 10 items as an example, then we need to iterate the List from 0 to 9, which means we need to subtract 1 from the final list count. We do this by modifying the parameter to **%ListofAges.Count-1%**.

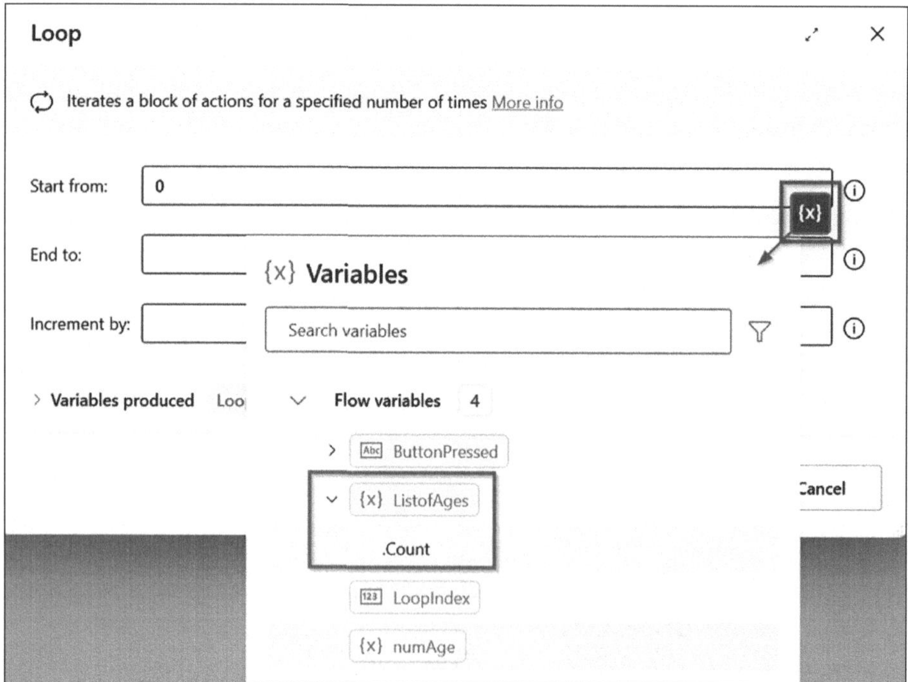

Figure 4.66: *Filling parameters of Loop action*

Increment the loop by 1. The Action with the complete parameters would look as follows:

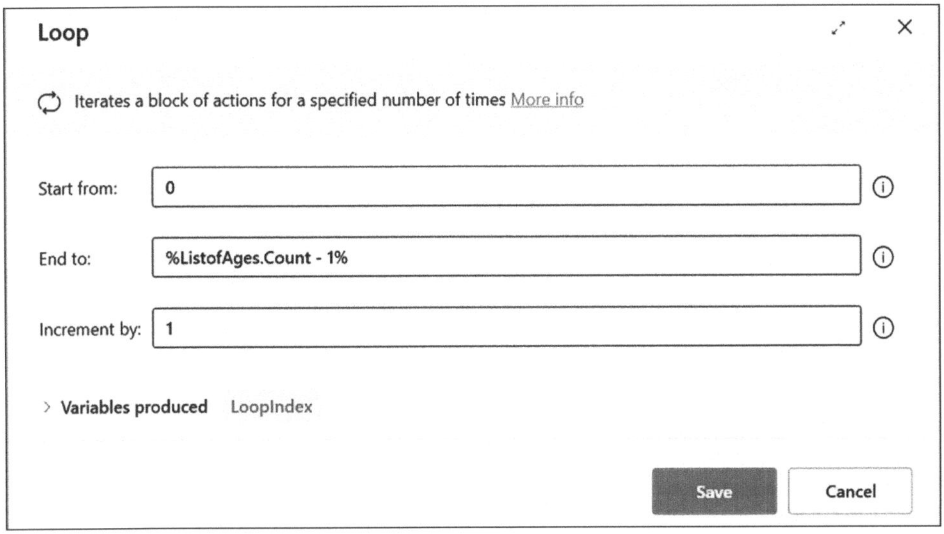

***Figure 4.67:** After filling all parameters of Loop action*

Click on **"Save"**. Remember to match the **"End"** Action for the corresponding **"Loop"** Action of line number 7 with that on line number 18. If you get a temporary error, it may be because of the mismatch of **"End"** Actions. Make sure to have the **"End"** Actions for the corresponding Actions that require them.

As shown in *Figure* 4.67, the output variable produced from the Action is **`LoopIndex`**.

Right after the **"Loop"** Action, drag and drop a **"Set variable"** Action and set its parameter as follows:

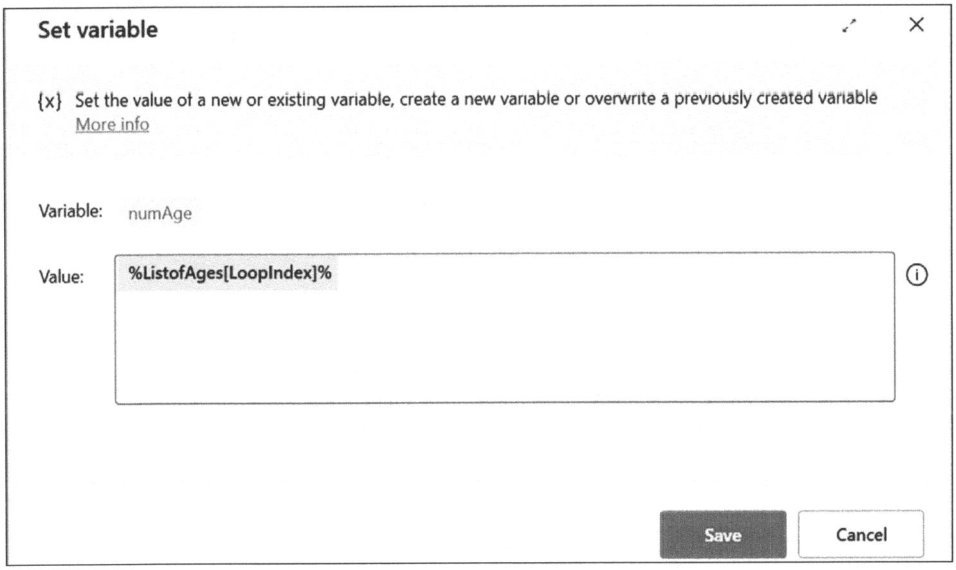

***Figure 4.68:** Accessing each value of the List*

Since this is inside a loop, the **`LoopIndex`** variable will hold values as 0, 1, 2, and so on as the loop iterates. What we are doing here is accessing each value of the **`ListofAges`** list variable by passing each of these index values to it. In other words, since this is within a loop,

`ListofAges[0]` will hold the first item of the list.

`ListofAges[1]` will hold the second item of the list and so on.

Observe in the preceding figure that each of these values is going to be stored in the **numAge** variable. Your Flow after adding the **"Loop"** Action and the **"`Set variable`"** would look as follows:

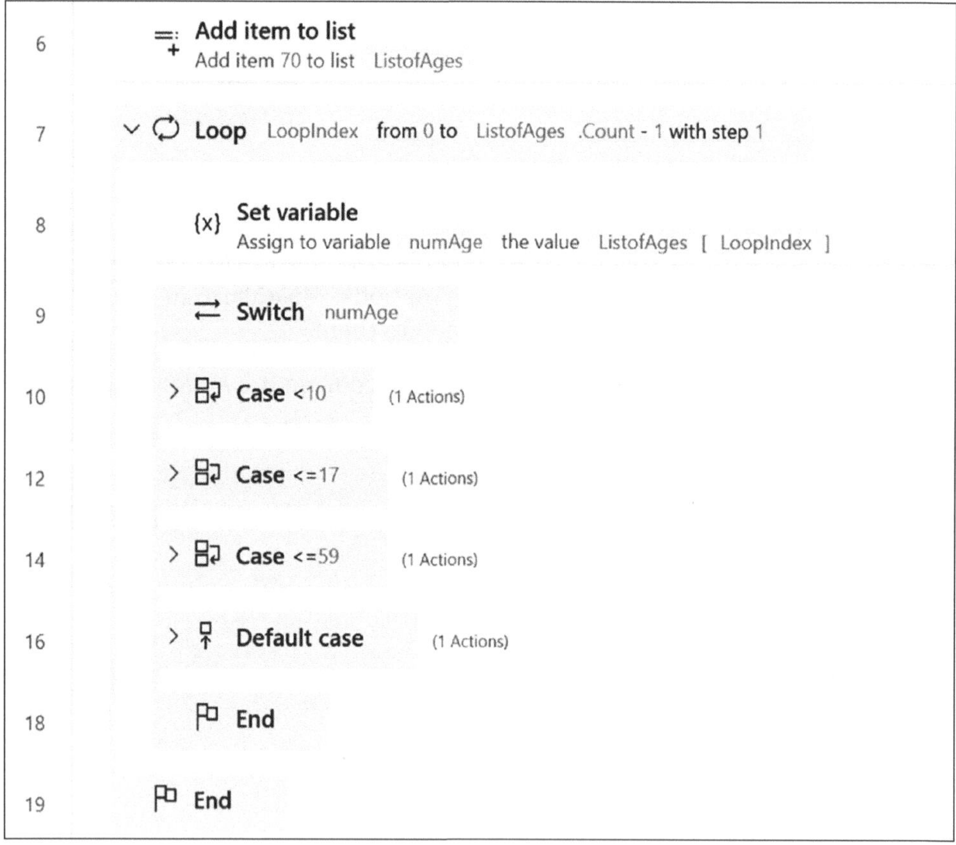

Figure 4.69: *Flow after adding Loop and Set variable actions*

We initialized the **numAge** in line number 8 to hold each of the age values coming from the list because the **"`Switch`"** in line number 9 is going to check the values of the same **numAge** variable against different age groups.

When you run the process, you will see the message boxes for different age groups from the List. Following is an example of a message box for the first item in the list, that is, for age 9. The process will continue to show message boxes for every age group in the list, that is, till the **"Loop"** finishes.

Figure 4.70: *Output for first item of the List*

Thus, with the help of **"Loop"**, we have specified the number of times it should iterate after getting the count of items in the List.

"Loop condition" Action

The **"Loop condition"** Action executes till a specified condition is true, whereas the **"Loop"** Action discussed earlier executes for a specified number of times.

With the help of this hint that the **"Loop condition"** iterates until a condition is true and by making use of the Actions in the previous section, how about doing a practical exercise using the **"Loop condition"**.

Practical Exercise

1. Use a *Counter* variable that will iterate from 0 till **%ListofAges.Count-1%**.
2. This is how the Flow will look like after creating the list, adding items to the list, and after initializing the **Counter** variable.

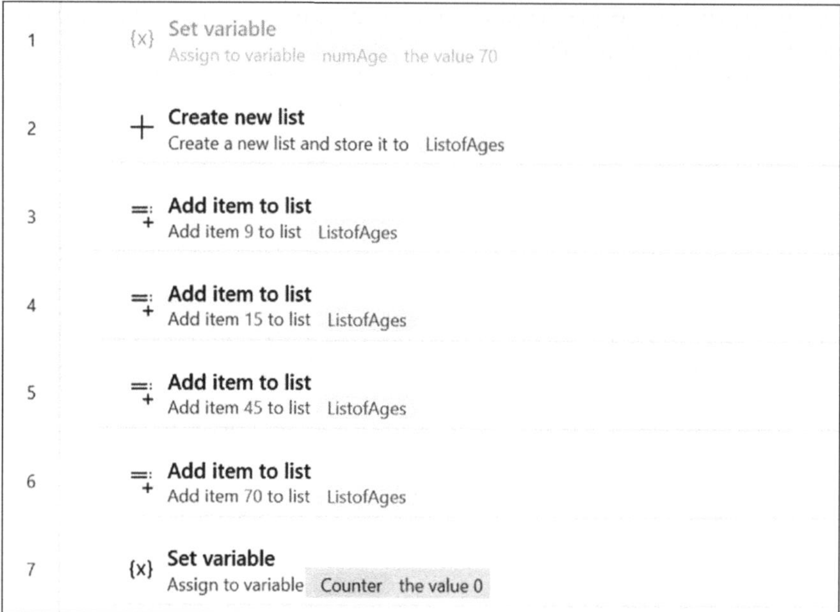

Figure 4.71: *Create and add items to List and set Counter variable*

3. The remaining part of the Flow with the **"`Loop condition`"** Action and a new Action to increment any variable.

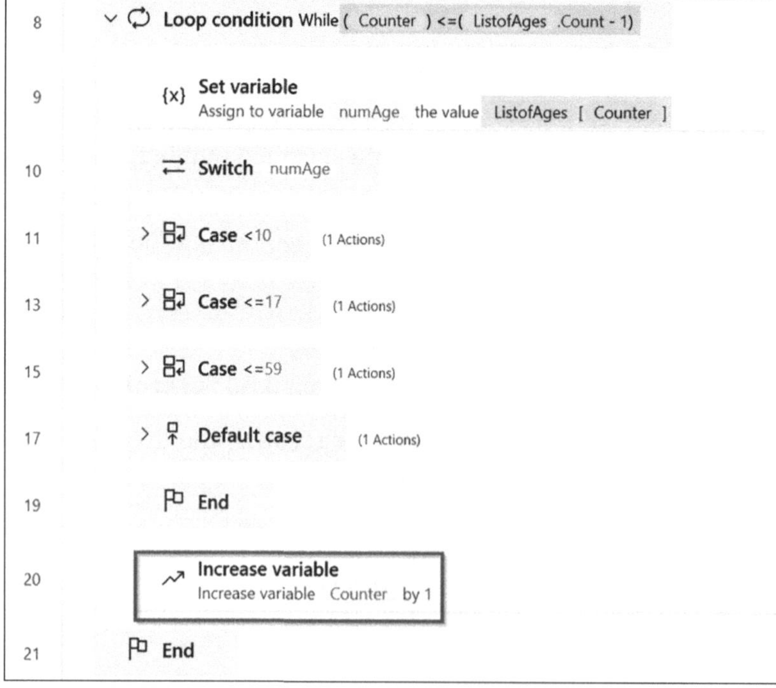

Figure 4.72: *Loop condition action with Increase variable*

The loop will run till the number of items in the List and display the message boxes for each of the input age groups in the List.

"`Next Loop`" Action

The **"`Next Loop`"** Action, as the name suggests, simply moves on to the next item in the loop. This is useful when we do not want to process a specific condition or a set of Actions. To exemplify this, let us make use of the Flow with the **"`Loop`"** Action from *Figure* 4.69.

After the **"`Case <= 17`"** from line number 12, drag and drop a **"`Next loop`"** Action. What we are doing here is, if there is any age that falls in this **"`Case`"**, the Flow will not display the message box for that age, and simply move on to pick the next age from the List.

Figure 4.73: *Use of Next loop action*

Put a breakpoint and step through to run the Flow, and you will observe that only the message boxes for ages **`9`**, **`45`**, and **`70`** from the List show up, while the case for age **`15`** is skipped.

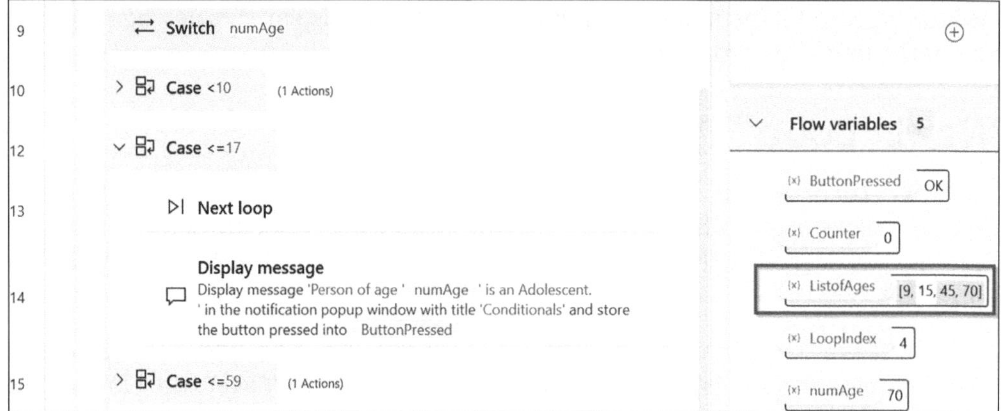

Figure 4.74: *List items that will be processed*

"Exit Loop" Action

The **"Exit loop"** works on the similar lines of the **"Next loop"** Action, with the only difference that when the Flow encounters the **"Exit loop"**, it comes out of the loop, whereas in the case of **"Next loop"**, the execution will skip the current item in the loop and move on to the next item.

Let's replace the **"Next loop"** Action and replace it with the **"Exit loop"** Action at the same place. When you run the below Flow, only the age 9 will be processed and the execution comes out of the loop without showing any messages for the rest of the ages in the List variable. In our hypothetical example, **"Exit loop"** is used here since we do not want to process any of the other ages in the List.

If there are any Actions outside of the loop, they will be processed, else the Flow will be completed.

Figure 4.75: *The Exit loop action*

Let us now look at a variable called Datarow. In the Datatables section under the **"Variables"** topic, we mentioned discussing another type of variable in the **"Loops"** topic called Datarow, and now is the time to do so (refer to *Figure* 4.27). Now that you are aware of how loops work, when you iterate through a Datatable, an individual item of the table refers to as a Datarow. A Datarow type of variable is initially not visible in the **"Variables"** pane because they get generated while looping through the Datatable. This can be observed by placing a breakpoint before running the Flow and then by opening the individual Datarow variable as follows:

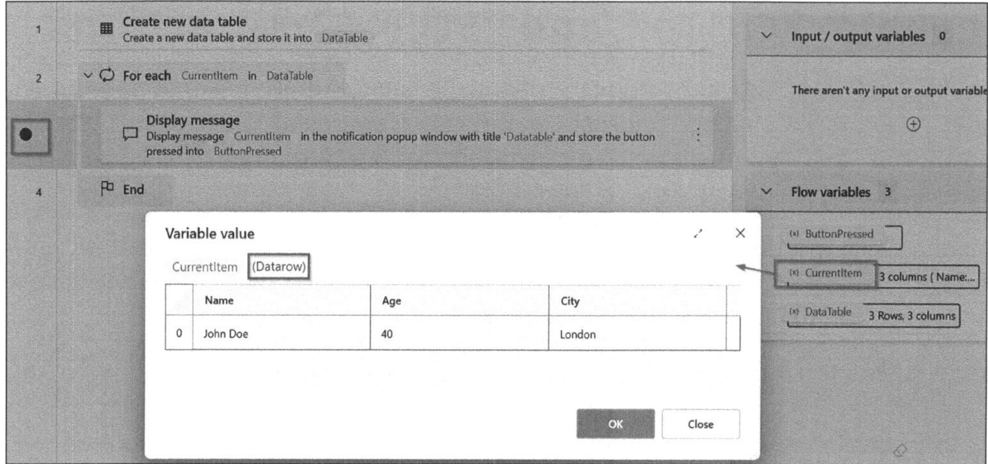

Figure 4.76: *Datarow type of variable*

Notice at the top of the preceding figure that the name of the Datarow variable is **CurrentItem**. You can also give a custom name, which is done in the **"For each"** Action. To access individual items of the Datarow within the loop, use the format as **%DatarowVariableName['ColumnName']%**.

For example, to retrieve John Doe, you would use **%CurrentItem['Name']%**.

You can also refer it with indexes, such as **%CurrentItem[0]%**, where 0 is the first column index, and this would give the same response as **John Doe**.

These are how all the Actions under the **"Loops"** category work within a Desktop Flow.

In a nutshell, the **"Exit loop"** Action stops the loop immediately, allowing the Flow to continue from the next Action after the loop. The **"For each"** Action loops through items in a List, Datatable, or Datarow, enabling a set of Actions within that loop to be executed multiple times. The **"Loop"** Action repeats a block of Actions a set number of times. The **"Loop condition"** Action repeatedly executes a set of Actions as long as the specified condition remains true. The **"Next loop"** Action triggers the next iteration of the loop, bypassing any remaining Actions in the current iteration.

Flow Control

Notice in the **"Actions"** pane that there are several Actions under the **"Flow control"** category. These Actions, as the name suggests, are used to control the navigation of the Flow. They help in performing operations like determining the order in which the execution of Flow should happen, jumping to another location of the Flow, calling a Subflow, pausing the execution of a Flow for a particular amount of time, and so on.

"Label", "Go To", and "Stop Flow" Actions

The **"Label"** and **"Go to"** Actions go hand-in-hand and are used along with each other. A label is like a named reference pointing to a particular line of code in the Flow, and the **"Go to"** Action allows the execution to jump to that particular line of code depending on a particular situation or scenario.

For simplicity purposes, let us observe the usage of these Actions with a simple example. We will set a year variable and based on the value of the year we will have the Flow execution to jump to a label for that year.

Create a skeleton as follows:

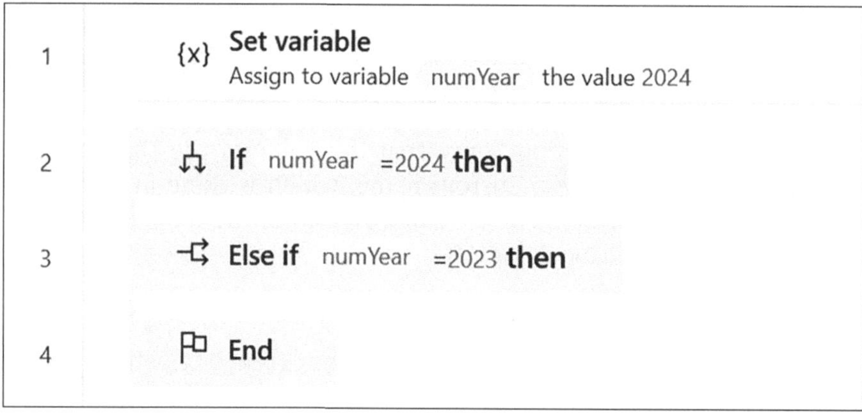

Figure 4.77: *Initialize year and add If conditions*

Create a label after the **"End"** Action by dragging and dropping the **"Label"** Action and give it a developer-friendly name, that is, **Year2024** in our case.

Label

Acts as the destination of a 'go to' statement More Info

Label name: Year2024

Save Cancel

Figure 4.78: *Label creation*

Show a display message with a message indicating that the year is 2024. After displaying the message box, we would like to stop the Flow and not process any further Actions. This is done by using the **"Stop flow"** Action. Drag and drop the **"Stop flow"** Action and set its parameter to **"Successfully"**. We are considering the automation to take a happy-path scenario here and will be looking at the error message dropdown setting in the "*Error Handling*" topic of "*Chapter 9: Leveling Up Your Automation Workflows*".

Your Flow should now have three sets of Actions, namely **"Label"**, **"Display message"**, and **"Stop flow"**.

Repeat these three Actions and modify them for the year 2023. After doing so, your Flow would look as follows:

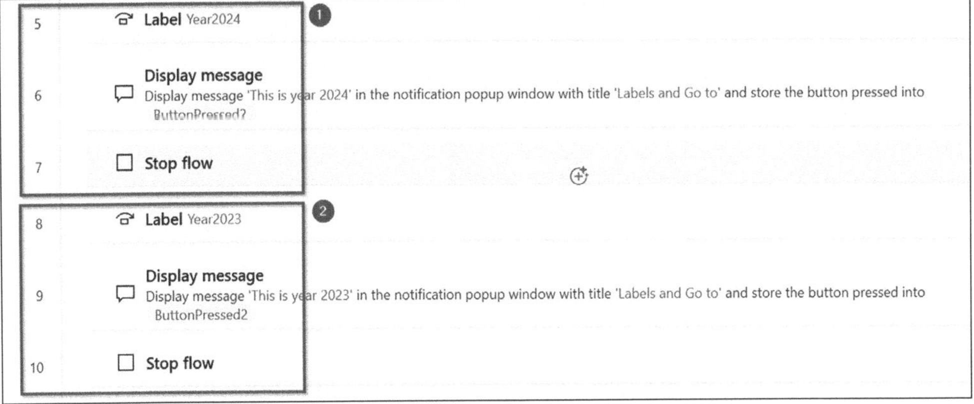

Figure 4.79: *Label and its corresponding set of actions*

We have so far only created the labels and not called them yet. This is done by using the **"Go to"** Action. We are going to call both the labels for the years 2024 and 2023 from within the **"If/Else If"** conditions for these years, respectively. As soon as you drag and drop the **"Go to"** Action between lines 2 and 3 of *Figure* 4.77, Power Automate Desktop will show a list of all available labels in that current Flow module. Note the important point that the scope of labels is *local* as opposed to that of variables which is *global*. This means that if you create a label in the **"Main"** Flow, it will be available to be called only in the **"Main"** Flow and not in any of the Subflows. Likewise, if you create a label in a Subflow, it will be available only in that Subflow and not in the **"Main"** Flow or any of the other Subflows.

Since we have created the labels for both the years within the same Flow module, the dropdown for the **"Go to"** Action will show the labels for both the years.

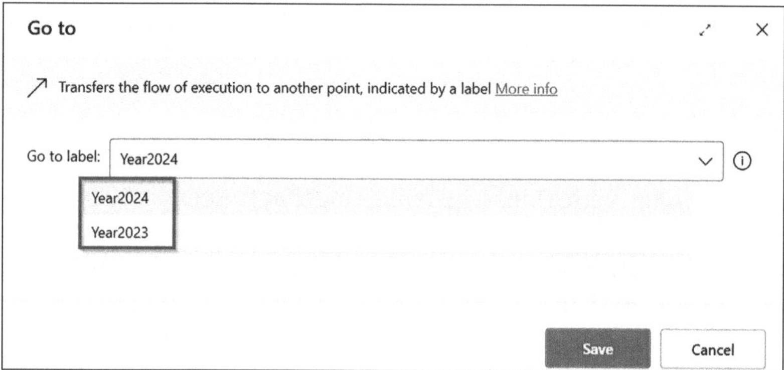

Figure 4.80: *Go to action with all available labels*

After adding the **"Go to"** statements for both years, the initial part of the Flow is as follows:

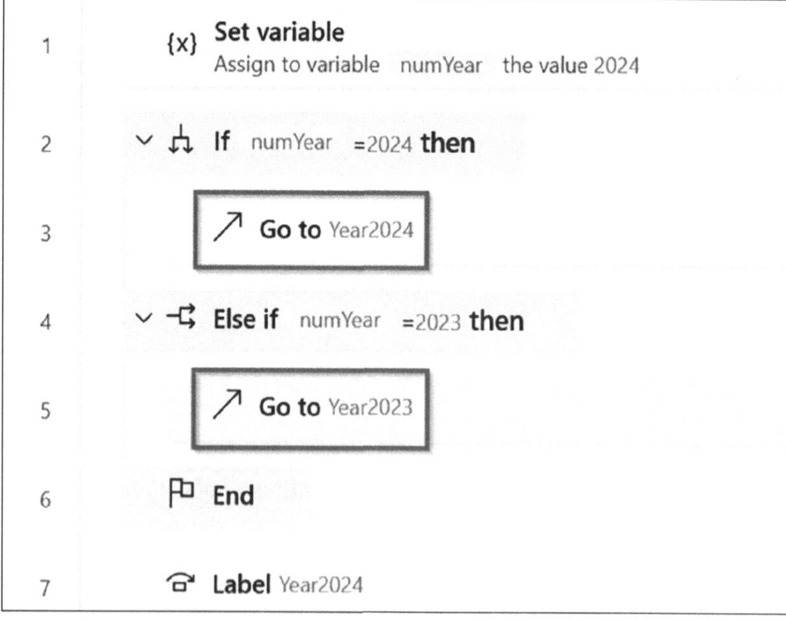

Figure 4.81: *Flow with the Go to actions*

The building of the Flow is complete and it's time to run the Flow. Insert a breakpoint on line number 2, that is, the **"If"** statement, and step through the Flow. First, run the Flow for an input value of 2024, and then for 2023, and notice how the execution jumps to the label as soon as it encounters the **"Go to"** Action and displays only its corresponding message boxes. The main idea of adding the **"Stop flow"** Actions was to stop the Flow after the message box for a year is displayed. You can try out what happens if the **"Stop flow"** Action is removed or disabled. If you figured it out, both the message boxes will be displayed one after the other even when a single year of 2024 is chosen, which is what we do not want. Assume a larger Flow with more such labels and we want to stop the execution of other Actions in the same Flow module with the help of **"Stop flow"**.

This concludes the use of **"Labels"** and **"Go to"**. However, since the programming times, excessive use of **"Go to"** statements are not considered a best practice as they make the code harder to read and debug. Instead, more use of **"Conditionals"** is recommended for better code readability and maintainability. **"Go to"** statements can still be used for simpler scenarios.

"Exit Subflow" Action

How to create Subflows and run a Subflow are already discussed in *Figure* 3.27 of "*Chapter 3: Debugging the Desktop Flows*". Let us take a quick look at using the **"Exit subflow"** Action.

Develop the **"Main"** Flow and a Subflow called **"Display Year"** as follows. The **"Main"** Flow sets a year variable and calls the **"Display Year"** Subflow:

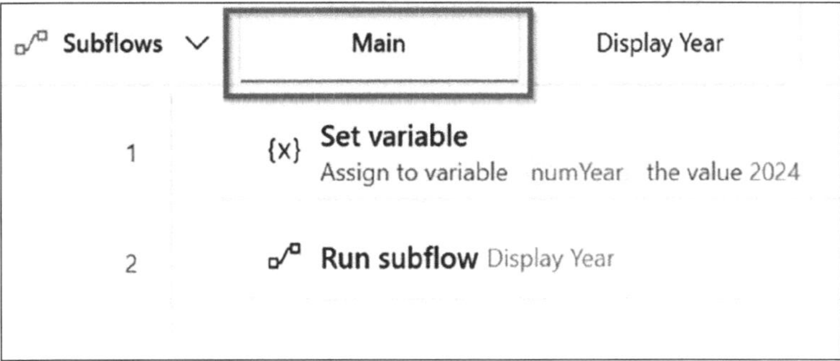

Figure 4.82: *Main flow calling the Subflow*

What we are trying to do in the Subflow is to display a message if the year is 2024, and if not, then simply come out of the Subflow without doing anything.

Figure 4.83: *Subflow with Exit subflow action*

Run from the **"Main"** Flow and observe the Flow's behavior for different year inputs, such as 2023 or 2024. For an input of 2023, the execution simply comes out of the Subflow and goes back to the calling location, that is, the **"Main"** Flow, whereas an input of 2024 will display the message box and then navigate to the calling location. This Action benefits in situations of a larger group of Actions within Subflows.

"Run Desktop Flow" Action

The **"Run desktop flow"** Action does not fall under the **"Flow control"** list of Actions, but under the **"Run flow"** category. As the name states, this Action is used to call an altogether another Desktop Flow (not a Subflow). It can also pass input variables and retrieve output variables. Let us see it in action.

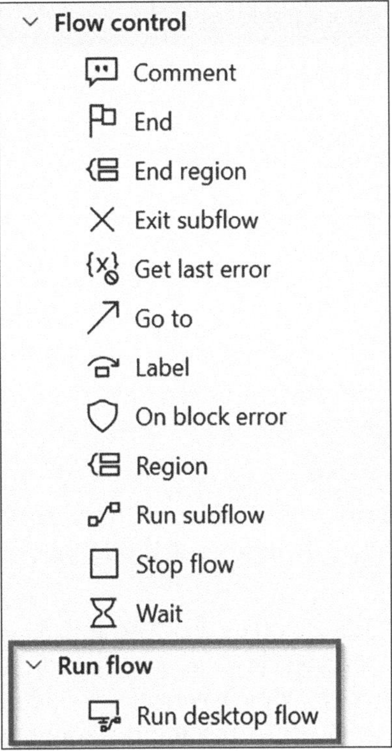

Figure 4.84: *Run desktop flow action*

Since this is about two different Desktop Flows, let us build each of them. For simplicity, let us call them as Flow 1 and Flow 2. We will be building Flow 1, which will evaluate whether any number passed to it is Odd or Even, whereas we will build Flow 2, which will pass any number to Flow 1 and display the result.

Flow 1:

1. Take an input variable from the **"`Variables`"** pane and name it as **`InputValue.`** Its external name is chosen as **`extInputValue.`**
2. Take an output variable and name it as **`Answer`**. Its external name is **`extAnswer.`**
3. The logic to check whether a number is odd or even is to divide it by 2 and then if the remainder is 0, then it is EVEN, else it is an ODD number.
4. Use an **"`If`"** statement to check if the following logic is 0:
   `%InputValue mod 2%`
5. If it is, then set the **`Answer`** output variable as **`The input value of %InputValue% is EVEN.`**

   If it is not, then set the **`Answer`** output variable as **`The input value of %InputValue% is ODD.`**

Save the Flow. Following is how the Flow 1 looks like:

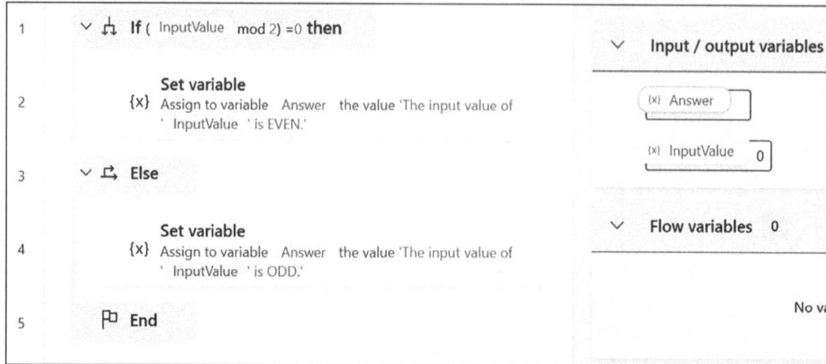

Figure 4.85: *Flow 1 to check odd or even*

Flow 2:

1. Use the **"Set variable"** which you will be using to pass a random number that needs to be checked whether it is odd or even. Let's call this variable as *Number.*
2. Drag and drop the **"Run desktop flow"** Action. As soon as you do so, it will pull up the list of all the Desktop Flows in your environment. Select **"Flow 1"** as that is our Flow, which has the logic to check for odd or even. The **extInputValue** is the external name given to the input parameter in Flow 1. Refer to point number 1 in the steps for Flow 1. The variable **%Number%** is the one you just created in Flow 2. The output from **Answer** variable of Flow 1 will be stored in the **Result** variable of Flow 2.

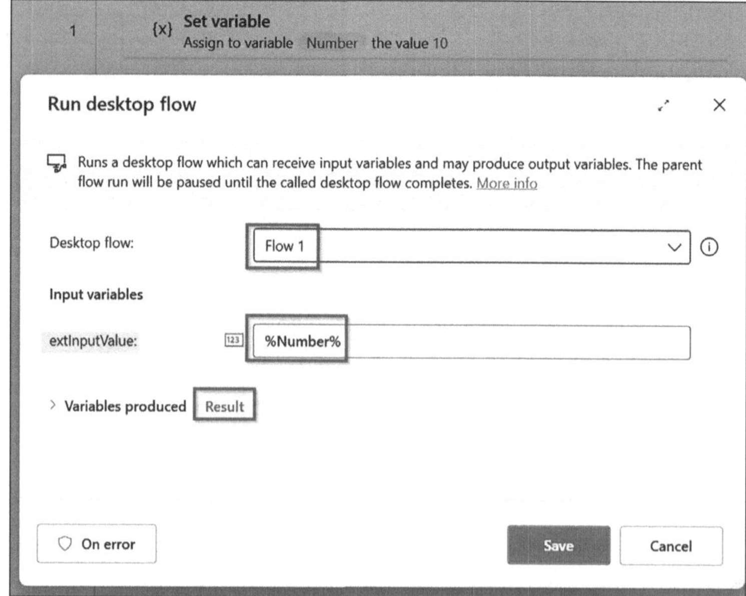

Figure 4.86: *Run desktop flow action*

We have got the result and it's time to display it. Use a **"`Display message`"** Action to display the **`Result`** variable.

Following is how the overall Flow 2 looks like:

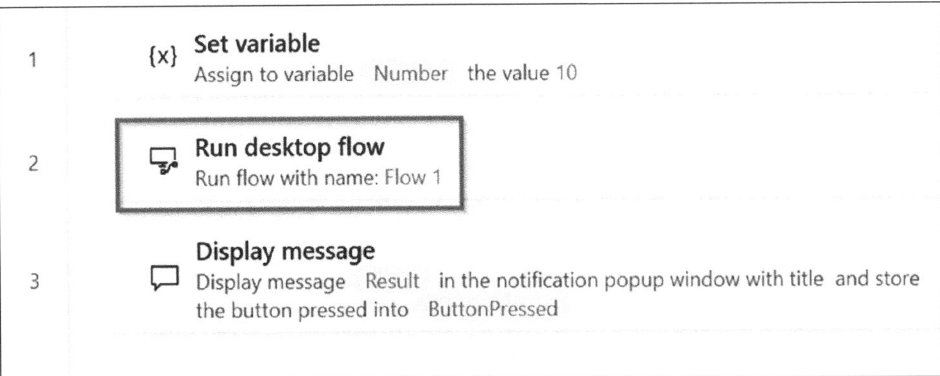

Figure 4.87: *Flow 2 to pass inputs and display the results*

Step through Flow 2 and observe how the input number (10) is passed to Flow 1 while calling it, and the response received from Flow 1 gets stored in the **`Result`** variable of Flow 2 before finally displaying it.

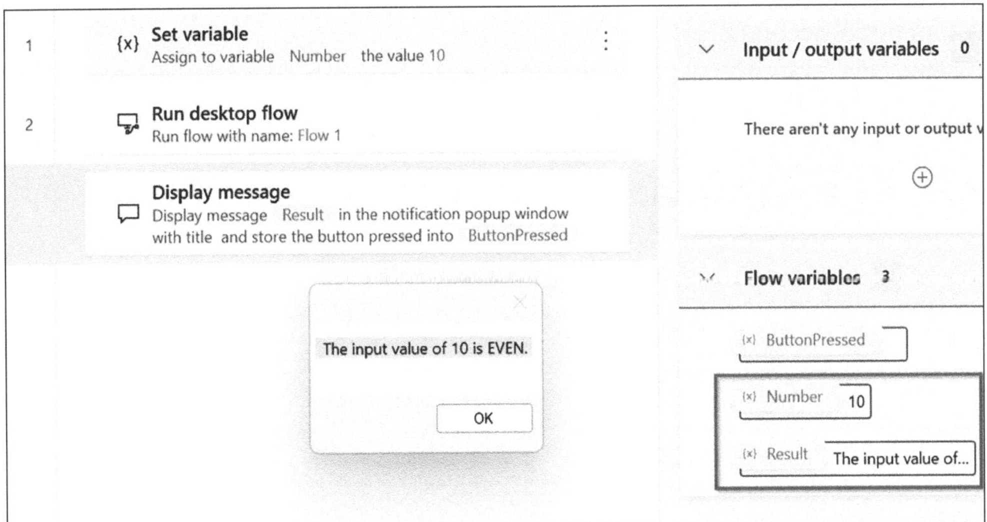

Figure 4.88: *Output after running Flow 2*

Try out the same, this time by passing an odd number like 11.

This was an example of how one Flow can call another Flow and pass inputs and outputs between them. This is used in scenarios where a Desktop Flow already automates a screen or an entire external application and can be used as a reusable Desktop Flow, which has to be called out again and again. This could be anything that will be repeatedly used in multiple Desktop Flows, such as log in to an application, run a query to get results from a database, and so on.

"`Wait`" Action

There is a last Action called as **"`Wait`"** in the **"`Flow control`"** list of Actions. This Action is used to pause the execution of the Flow for a specified number of seconds. This can be used in situations where you need to intentionally introduce a delay between two Actions. These situations could be anything like a data refresh where you are already aware that it would take approximately 10 seconds for the data to be refreshed as an example, or would like to wait for a few seconds before sending multiple emails one after the other, or you are renaming files with the date and time and want to keep a gap of a few seconds between two file names, or wherever keystrokes and mouse clicks are sent to an external application to give a lag between them such that they do not happen so fast that they fail.

Just to showcase this Action, let us add two variables that would capture the start and end time using the **"`Get current date and time`"** Action and store them in **`StartCurrentDateTime`** and **`EndCurrentDateTime`** variables, respectively. Add a **"`Wait`"** Action of 5 seconds between them before displaying the start and end times. The entire Flow with the output after running is as follows. Notice the difference in the number of seconds:

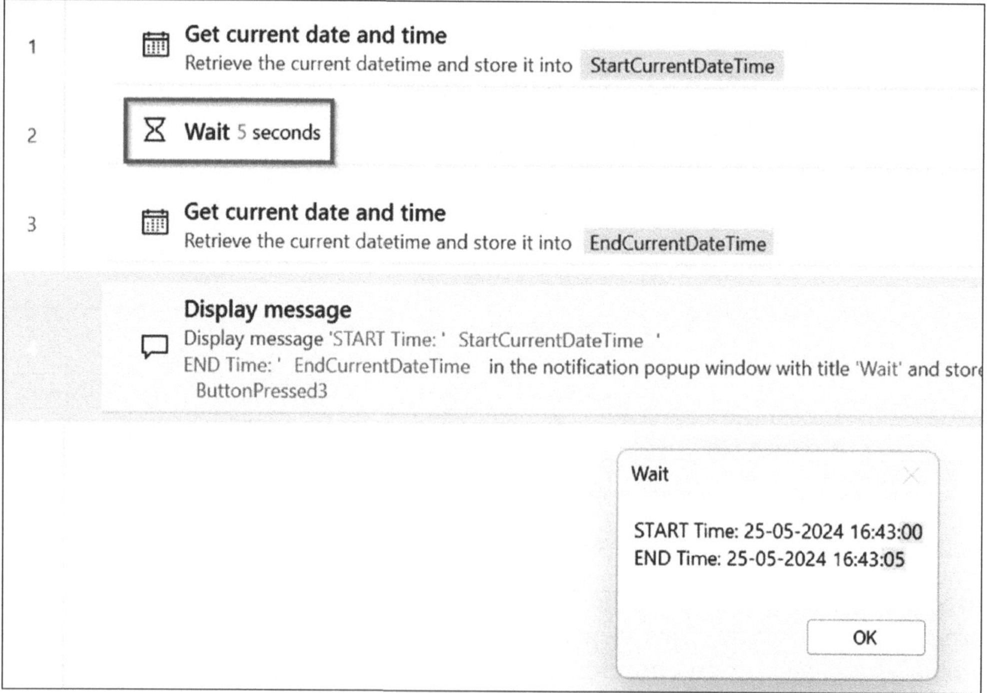

Figure 4.89: *Output after using Wait action*

Other Actions from the **"`Flow control`"** category that are not explained here will be covered in subsequent chapters and topics where they are more relevant.

Reserved Keywords

PAD has several keywords that cannot be used at multiple places, especially in a variable name among other places, as mentioned in the following link. There may be new ones added in the future or older ones supported, so here is a webpage with a list provided by Microsoft to be bookmarked for future reference:

https://learn.microsoft.com/en-us/power-automate/desktop-flows/reserved-keywords

For example, if you try to give one of the reserved words (*action*) as a variable name, it gives an error and does not allow you to do so.

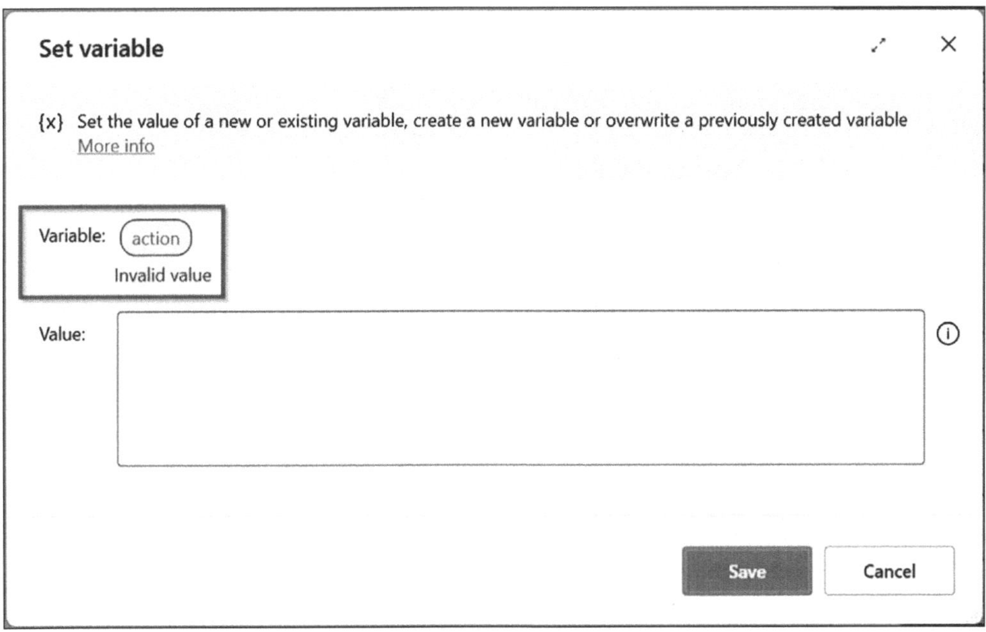

Figure 4.90: *Error for reserved keywords*

Conclusion

By mastering these essential elements, you are now well-equipped to use different variables as per their data types, use various types of conditional statements as per the logic of your requirement, different types of loops based on a scenario, how to create Subflows and call them, and how to navigate to different parts of the same Flow or an entirely different Flow using Flow Control features. As you continue to explore and experiment with these elements, you will be able to create more sophisticated and tailored automation solutions that meet your specific needs along with the topics in the upcoming chapters.

In the next chapter, we delve into the critical topics of what form the building blocks of a Desktop Flow. We will be looking at how Power Automate Desktop simplifies the process of recording automation, how UI Elements and Selectors are crucial while interacting with external applications, and about Actions, all of which form the building blocks of a Desktop Flow.

Practical Exercises

Here are some exercises for a combination of the topics we went through in this chapter.

Exercise 1:

1. Using the **"`Create new data table`"**, create a Datatable that holds the names of all the days of the week and their corresponding day numbers as follows, assuming Sunday as the first day of the week:

Variable value

DataTable (Datatable)

#	DayName	DayNumber
0	Sunday	1
1	Monday	2
2	Tuesday	3
3	Wednesday	4
4	Thursday	5
5	Friday	6
6	Saturday	7

Figure 4.91: *Datatable with day names and numbers*

2. Use a **"`Set variable`"** Action to create a variable called **`InputDayName`** and set it to a value of any day name for now, for example, Friday. This variable will be the one where you will be changing its value and testing the Flow for various day name inputs, as we did for the different input ages.

3. Use a **"`For each`"** loop to iterate through the Datatable.
4. Within the loop, add an **"`If`"** statement that will check if the value of **`InputDayName`** variable matches the one with the **`DayName`** column of the above shown Datatable. If it matches, then show a display message box along with its corresponding value from the **`DayNumber`** column of the same Datarow.

   For example, if Friday was the **`InputDayName`**, then the message should show as follows. If you see in row number 5 of the Datatable of the preceding figure, the day number for day name Friday is 6. This message should be dynamic enough to show any other input value. For example, for an input value of Wednesday, the message should read as **`The day number for Wednesday is 4`**.

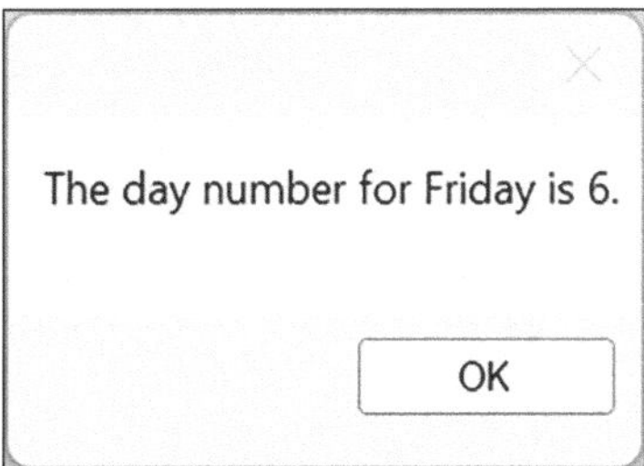

Figure 4.92: *Expected output for the given input day name*

5. After the message box, the Flow should come out of the loop and not iterate through other items of the Datatable.

Exercise 2:

1. Do the same exercise but by using Subflows.
2. Set the **`InputDayName`** variable in the **"`Main`"** Flow and evaluate the day number within a Subflow.

Exercise 3:

1. Repeat the same exercise but using two Desktop Flows, for example, Flow 1 and Flow 2.
2. Flow 1 will pass the **`InputDayName`** to Flow 2, which will identify the day number and return back the output to Flow 1.
3. Flow 1 will be responsible for displaying the message box of the final result.

Exercise 4:

1. Calculate the Area and Perimeter based on a given length and width.
2. Use two separate **"Set variable"** Actions, each for **numLength** and **numWidth** variables. Set their values as 10 and 20, respectively.
3. Perform an arithmetic operation using the following formula and display the results in a message box:

    Area is **length * width**

    Perimeter is **2 * (length + width)**
4. For the aforementioned inputs of length and width, the output would be as follows:

Figure 4.93: *Expected output for the given length and width*

Exercise 5:

This exercise is on how to use an AND and an OR operator within the same **"If"** statement.

1. Set two **Input** variables from the **"Variables"** pane as **PerformanceRating** and **YearsOfService.**
2. **PerformanceRating** is any value from 1 to 5 and **YearsOfService** is any value from 1 or more.
3. Use an **"If"** statement with an AND and an OR operator in the same **"If"** statement for the following logic:

    If the employee's performance rating is 4 or higher and years of service are 5 or more, or if the performance rating is 5 and years of service are 3 or more, then the employee is eligible for a bonus. Display a message box with the outcome of whether or not the employee is eligible for a bonus.

    Here is the logic to be used within a single **"If"** statement:
    If **(PerformanceRating >= 4 And YearsOfService >= 5)**
    Or **(PerformanceRating = 5 And YearsOfService >= 3)**
    Then, the employee is eligible for a bonus.

The sample inputs and outputs would be as follows:

If Performance Rating: 4, Years of Service: 6, Output: **`The employee is eligible for a bonus.`**

If Performance Rating: 3, Years of Service: 10, Output: **`The employee is not eligible for a bonus.`**

If Performance Rating: 5, Years of Service: 3, Output: **`The employee is eligible for a bonus.`**

If Performance Rating: 5, Years of Service: 2, Output: **`The employee is not eligible for a bonus.`**

The above logic may appear simple but not when it is practically done on PAD. The correct use of brackets and the percent variable notation should be of proper use. Testing out the Flow for various combinations of inputs and their outputs will tell whether the logic is built as expected or not.

Questions

Here are some questions that may either have answers in any of the current or previous chapters or would force the reader to practically try out the question on the PAD tool. In the case of multiple-choice questions, there is only one answer.

1. Does the index of the Datatable start from 0 or 1?
2. If a Datatable called **`'MyDatatable'`** is defined as the following figure, what would be the output of **`%MyDatatable[1][0]%`**?
    a. 1
    b. 2
    c. Error: Invalid index 0
    d. TWO

Column1	Column2
1	ONE
2	TWO
3	THREE
4	FOUR
5	FIVE

***Figure 4.94:** Input datatable*

3. For the input Datatable in *Figure* 4.94, what would be the output of **%MyDatatable[1]['Column2']%?**

   a. ONE

   b. TWO

   c. Error: Index number and column name cannot be used at the same time

   d. 1

4. If a Datatable called **'MyDatatable'** is defined as follows:

Column1	Column2
1	ONE ❶
2	TWO ❷
3	THREE ❸
4	FOUR ❹
5	FIVE ❺

***Figure* 4.95:** *Input datatable with row number markings*

What would be the output of **%MyDatatable[:3]%?**

Note: *For the sake of answering, consider the Datatable row numbers as marked in red.*

   a. This will display all Datarows from the first row of the Datatable to the third row

   b. This will display all Datarows from the first row of the Datatable to the fourth row

   c. This will display the third Datarow

   d. Error: Invalid syntax

5. What is the correct syntax to add the values of three numeric variables, namely Var1, Var2, and Var3?

   a. **%Var1% + %Var2% + %Var3%**

   b. **%Var1 + Var2 + Var3%**

   c. Both are valid

6. What is the correct syntax to multiply a value of 10 by a numeric variable called Var1?
   a. **`%Var1 * 10%`**
   b. **`%Var1% * 10`**
   c. Both are valid
7. What does the **"`Run delay`"** option at the bottom of the Flow designer do?

Figure 4.96: *Run delay option of Flow designer*

8. If you try to display the **`Result`** variable in a message box with a value as follows, what would be the output?

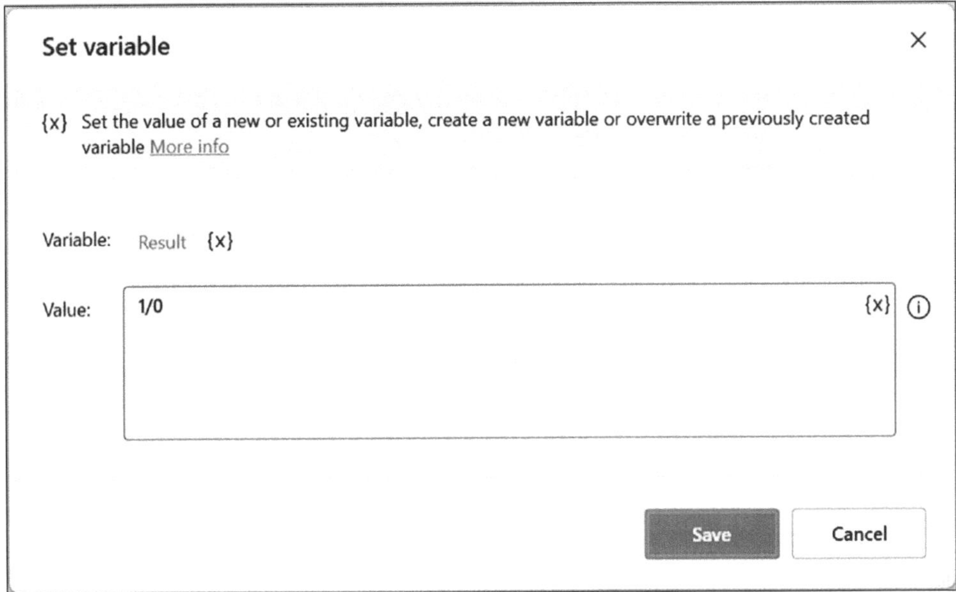

Figure 4.97: *Outcome of Set variable*

   a. The display box will show the result as 1/0
   b. PAD will give a division by 0 error
   c. The remainder of the division will be displayed
9. What is the difference between the **"`End`"** and **"`Stop flow`"** Actions?
10. Name all the different data types available for an Input variable.

11. In the **"Wait"** Action, you can provide the time in milliseconds in the **"Duration"** box.

    a. True

    b. False

12. What is the difference between **"Loop"** and **"Loop condition"** Action?

13. Scope of Labels:

    A process has 1 **"Main"** Flow and 1 Subflow.
    You set a new Label in the **"Main"** Flow (Using **"Label"** Action).
    Will you be able to call the new Label from the Subflow (Using **"Go to"** Action)?

14. Scope of Variables:

    A process has 1 **"Main"** Flow and 1 Subflow.
    You set a new variable in the **"Main"** Flow (Using **"Set Variable"** Action).
    Will you be able to use the value of the new variable in the Subflow?

15. On the right-hand side of the Flow designer, what are the three different panes available and what are they used for?

Figure 4.98: *Different panes of the Flow designer*

16. If you would like to set a variable as follows, it throws an error.
    Why is the error and most importantly how can it be fixed? Fix the error and display the text in a message box exactly as **I scored 90% marks in the exam.**

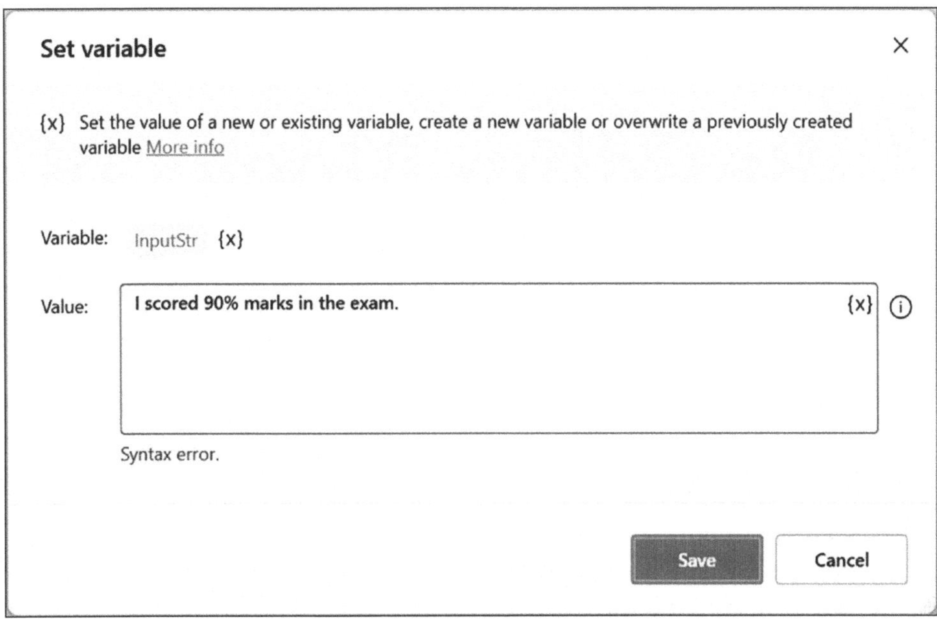

Figure 4.99: *Set variable error*

CHAPTER 5
Building Blocks of a Desktop Flow

Introduction

This chapter explores the components that form the building block of any Desktop Flow, especially for user interface-based automation. We will delve into the Unified Recorder, which simplifies the automation process by capturing user actions; UI Elements and Selectors, which are vital for interacting with application interfaces; and Actions, the individual tasks that drive the actual automation forward. Understanding these building blocks is key to leveraging the full potential of accessing external applications via Power Automate Desktop and thereby creating efficient and reliable automation solutions.

Structure

The following topics will be discussed in this chapter:

- The Unified Recorder
- UI Elements and Selectors
- Actions

The Unified Recorder

The earlier versions of the Power Automate Desktop tool had separate recorders for Web applications and Desktop applications. However, now these have been unified into a single recording button. The **"`Recorder`"** is a tool that allows you to build the Desktop Flow Actions by manually mimicking the tasks and activities that you want to perform just like a human would do. For example, you would like to perform an addition of 4 + 6 on the Windows Calculator application and get its result. To generate the Flow Actions for this automation, you need to turn on the in-built recorder and manually perform the addition on the Calculator application by pressing the appropriate buttons.

Once this is done and the recorder is closed, it will straight away generate all the Flow Actions for this automation onto the Workspace of the PAD tool. You could very well perform arithmetic calculations as explained in the topic "*Arithmetic Operations Using Variables*" of "*Chapter 4: Essential Elements of a Desktop Flow*". Hence, using the Calculator here is for demonstration purposes. Let's check it out in action.

Recording a Desktop Application Using the Unified Recorder

Create a new Flow from the main Console and give it a name, such as **"Chapter 5: Calculator"** or anything of your choice.

Once you are inside the Flow designer, there are two ways to start the recorder. One from the dedicated recorder button at the top command bar and the other from the **"Tools"** menu, both of which are shown in *Figure* 5.1:

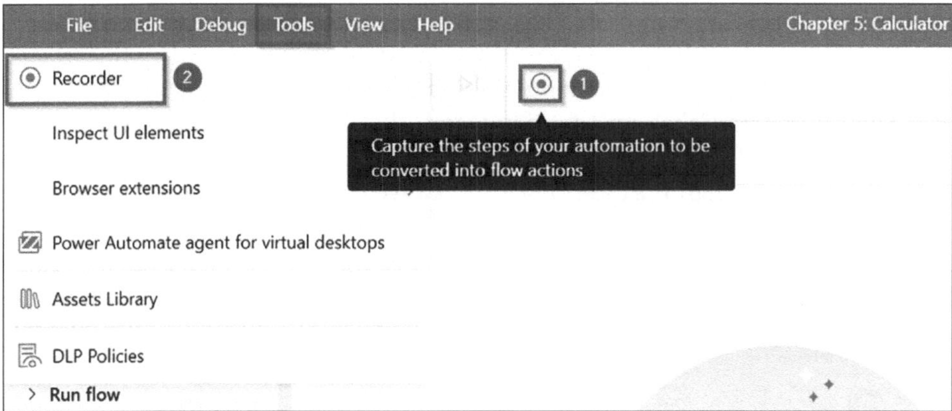

***Figure 5.1:** The Recorder buttons*

Follow the below steps to perform the desired automation on the Calculator application. First, glance through the below steps and then start with the recording process, otherwise any manual activities that you perform on the screen, such as waiting or switching between applications, will also get recorded.

1. Start the Recorder from any of the options in the preceding figure.
2. Once you do this, the Recorder window opens up. Click any one of the **"Record"** buttons shown in *Figure* 5.2 to begin the actual recording process. After clicking this button, anything that you do on the screen after this point will be recorded, unless you pause it, which is shown in the upcoming steps.

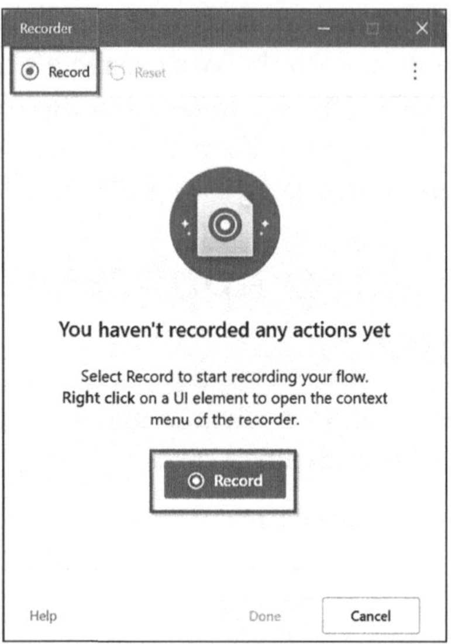

Figure 5.2: *Start recording via any one of these buttons*

3. Click the Windows Start menu, then type in the word **"calculator"** without the quotes and click on the menu item that shows the Calculator app on it. There is a different way of opening executables of applications via an in-built Action **("Run application")** in PAD, but we will be going through it in the next chapter titled "*Automating Common Applications*". The following figure might be different depending on the Windows version you are using, but the idea is to click the Start menu, type **"calculator"**, and then click the appropriate app.

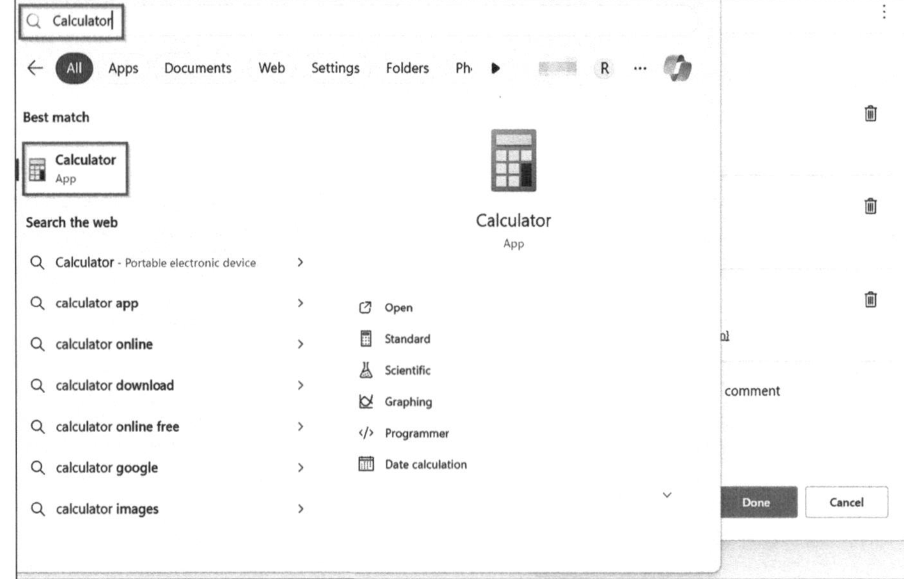

Figure 5.3: *Open calculator from the Windows Start menu*

4. The actual Calculator app opens up and now click each of the buttons gradually for **`4 + 6 =`**.
   As you do that on the Calculator app, the corresponding Actions for each of those button clicks start getting generated on the **"`Recorder`"** window. Also, as you hover the mouse over each of the elements on the screen, the recorder shows the type of element, such as the **"`Button`"**, as shown in the following figure:

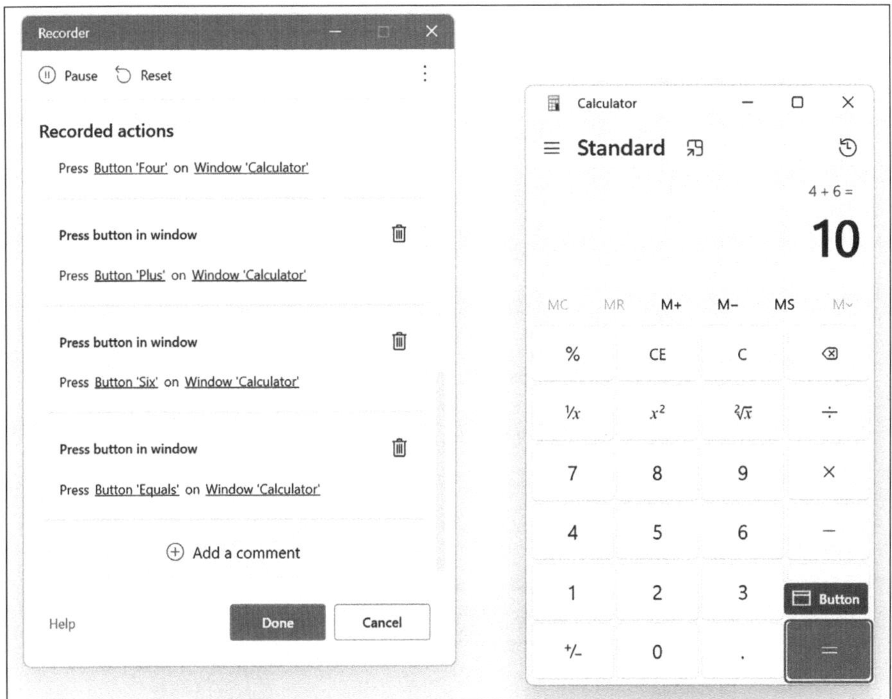

***Figure 5.4:** Actions generated for the respective button clicks*

5. We have so far clicked the buttons for **`4 + 6`** = and now we need to capture the results too. To do that, right-click on the result, which is the section that shows 10 in the above Calculator window. This further shows up a context menu, and the one we need is the last option that shows **"`Get name`"** since it shows a preview of rightly extracting the result as 10. It also has an additional text that says **"`Display is`"**, but this can be stripped off with the help of **"`Text functions`"**. However, that is not the focus of this exercise, which is more about how to perform a recording.

   Notice the **"`Pause`"** option at the top left portion of the **"`Recorder`"** in the preceding figure, which is to temporarily suspend the recording activity in case you want to perform certain operations on the screen but do not want them to be recorded. Also, if you suspect that the recording steps did not occur as expected, you can restart again using the **"`Reset`"** button seen on the same figure. You can even delete any unwanted Actions on the Recorder window. Refer to the delete button against each Action in the preceding figure.

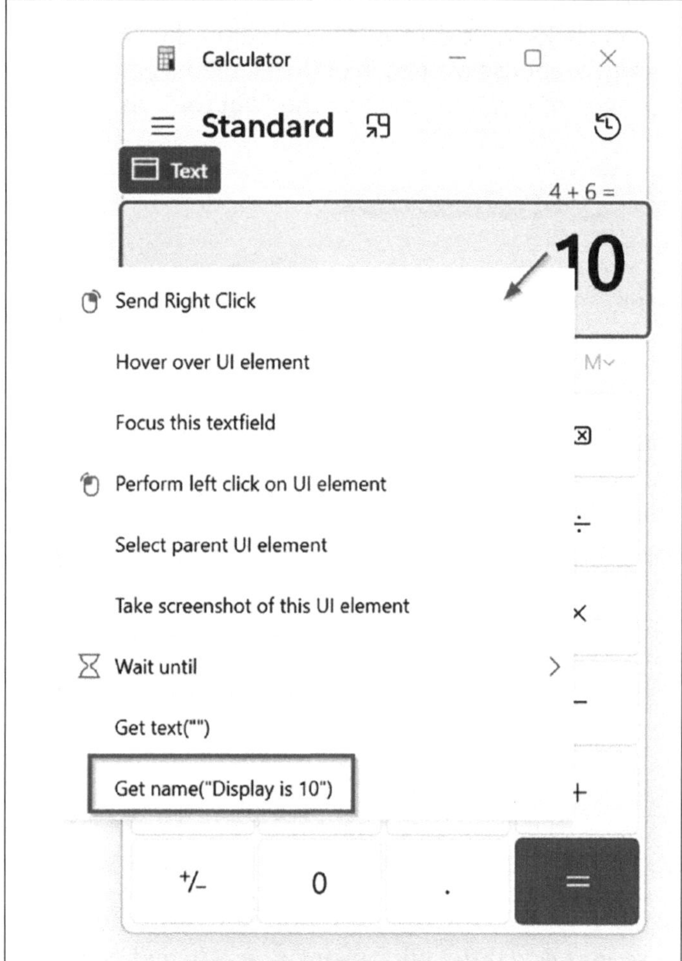

***Figure 5.5:** Right-click context menu and Get name menu item*

6. Finally, click on the **"Done"** button in the **"Recorder"** window. As soon as you do that, Power Automate Desktop generates Flow Actions for all the manual activities that were just performed. The following figure shows the initial part of the auto-generated Flow from line numbers 1 to 9 and an explanation for each one of them as follows:

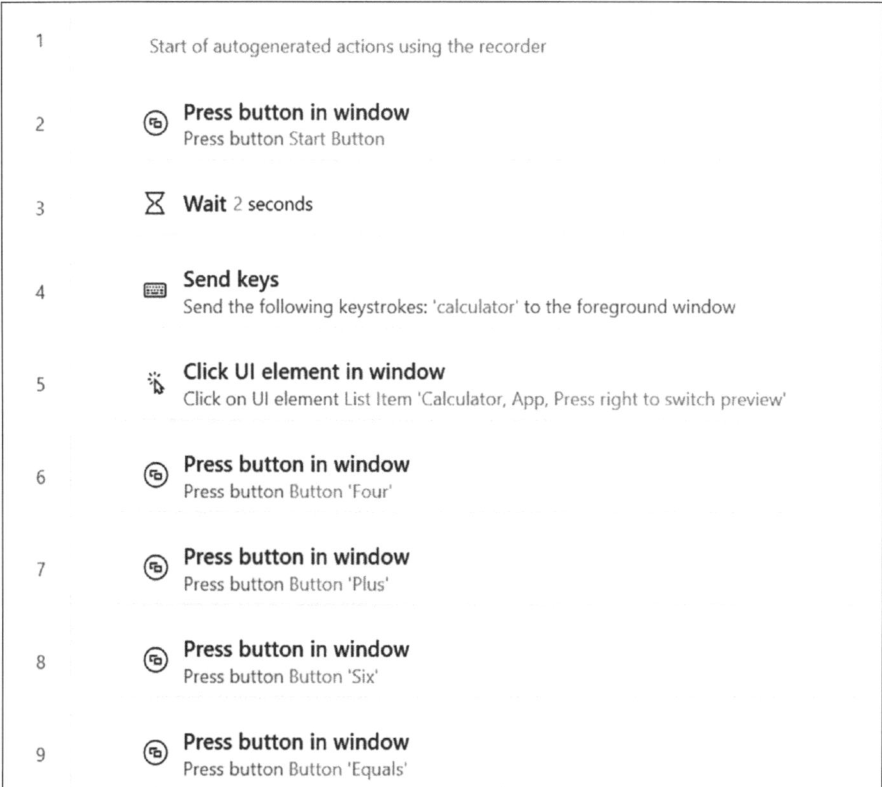

***Figure 5.6:** Auto-generated Flow from line numbers 1 to 9*

- **Line number 1**: This is a **"`Comment`"** Action available under the **"`Flow control`"** group of Actions to write any note for the developer's reference and does not produce any output variables nor obstruct the execution even if left blank. In our case, since we conducted a recording, the comment was auto-generated by the recorder. During Flow development, it is a good practice to mention comments wherever possible for better Flow readability.
- **Line number 2:** This Action denotes the clicking of the Windows Start button.
- **Line number 3**: A **"`Wait`"** Action was introduced automatically by the recorder as there was a delay in bringing up the start menu. You may or may not notice it in your case, which depends on the speed of processing.
- **Line number 4**: The **"`Send keys`"** Action was used to send keystrokes for the word **"`calculator`"** that was typed-in on the search box of the start menu.
- **Line number 5**: This click was performed on the Calculator app menu item of the search results. Hover the mouse, as shown in the following figure, on the UI elements button, which will display a snapshot image of the element that was clicked. It is a good practice to view this image so as to verify whether we clicked the right button or not.

UI stands for User Interface and UI elements indicate elements on the UI, such as text boxes, labels, buttons, and more.

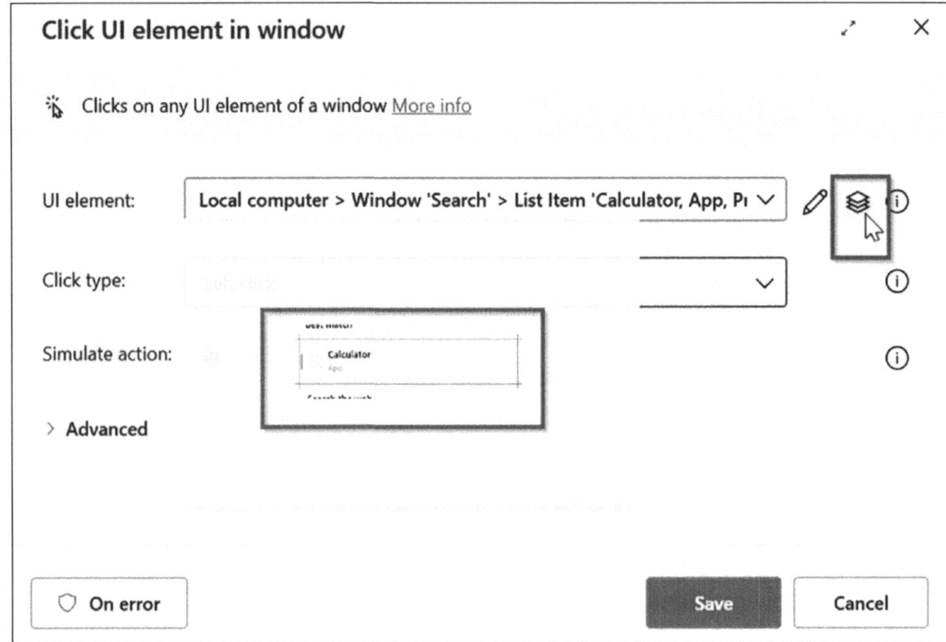

Figure 5.7: *Image preview of the element clicked*

- **Line numbers 6 to 9**: All of these lines correspond to the Actions for clicking the buttons for **`4 + 6 =`**, respectively. Open any of these Actions, hover the mouse on the UI element button, and notice the image snapshot of the button that was clicked.
- **Line number 10**: Below is the figure for line number 10, which has an Action to get the details of the calculator results box. If you recall a few steps above, we right-clicked and used the **"`Get name`"** context menu item to capture the results.

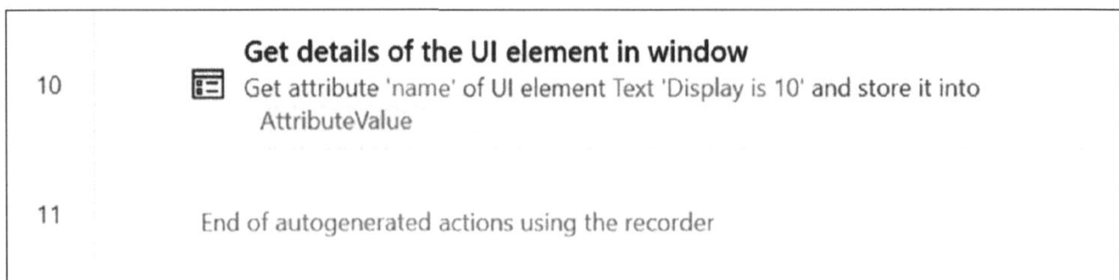

Figure 5.8: *Auto-generated Flow from lines 10 to 11*

- **Line number 11:** This denotes the ending comment by the recorder, indicating the completion of auto-generated Actions from lines 2 to 10.

The Actions from the recorder are ready; however, there is one more thing remaining and that is to display the results of the calculation. As we notice in line number 10 of the preceding figure, the results are stored as an output variable coming out of this Action and is called **`AttributeValue`**.

7. As a final step, drag and drop a **"`Display message`"** Action and display the variable called **`AttributeValue`**.

As you run the Flow, you will notice that as each of the lines of the Flow is executing, the corresponding operations are performed by the bot on the Calculator application, such as clicking on each of the buttons, and finally displaying the result in a message box, as follows. In an ideal automation scenario, we would strip off the wordings **"`Display is`"** using **"`Text functions`"** to give an exact arithmetic value and use it in any further processing. We will manipulate such data in "*Chapter 7: File Management and Data Manipulation*".

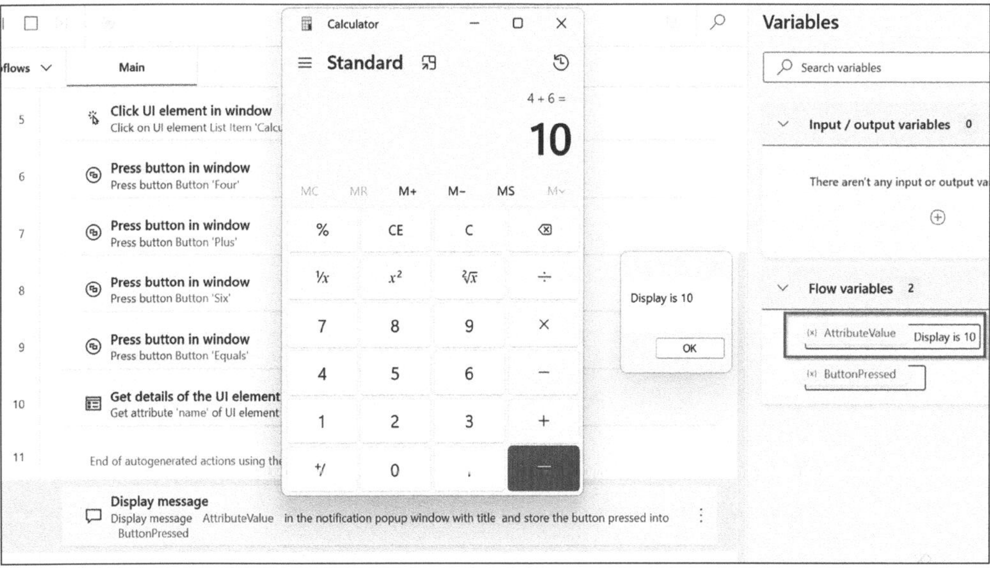

Figure 5.9: *Final output of the Flow*

Recording a Web Application Using the Unified Recorder

The process of recording a web application is similar to that we saw for a Desktop application, but let us make use of the same Unified Recorder against a web application too.

Before we begin, PAD requires browser extensions to be installed to interact with the elements on a web page. If you have not installed the extensions while installing the PAD tool in "*Chapter 2: Getting into Action with PAD*", here is another way to do it. From the Flow designer, go to the **"Tools"** menu and the **"Browser extensions"** menu item, and then click on any of your preferred browser choices.

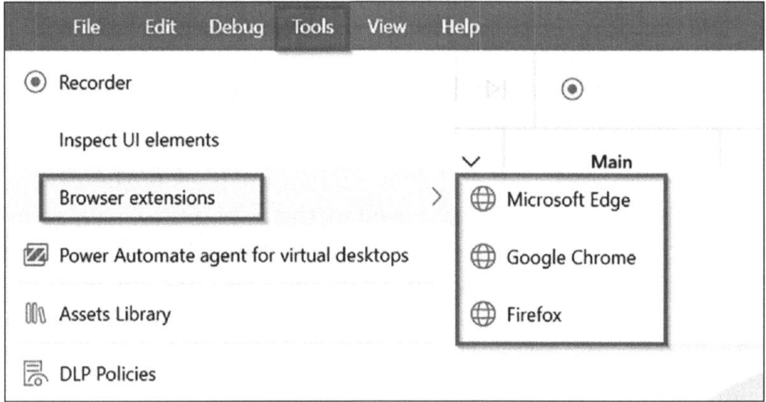

Figure 5.10: *Installing browser extensions*

For future reference or troubleshooting, you can visit the **"Extensions"** section of the browser and verify if the Power Automate extension is enabled or not. In some cases, if the browser Actions are causing issues, then re-installing the extensions can be of help.

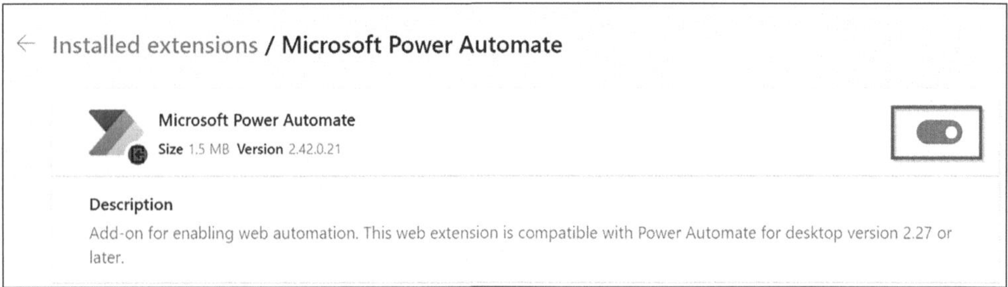

Figure 5.11: *Extensions section of browser for Power Automate*

Let us begin with the recording of activities on a web application. First, take a look at the steps and then proceed with the recording.

As a note, since websites have HyperText Markup Language (HTML) tags, it would be good to have a fair understanding of it, and you can learn more about it from the website: https://www.w3schools.com/html

1. For simplicity, first, we will manually open a browser and navigate to the following URL, and then have PAD interact with it:

   https://www.w3schools.com/tags/tryit.asp?filename=tryhtml_input_test

   In an ideal automation scenario, the browser will be launched via an in-built PAD Action, which we will use in the "*Web Automation*" topic of "*Chapter 6: Automating Common Applications*".

2. The web page contains two text boxes where we will enter values via recording, as well as a button that needs to be clicked.

***Figure 5.12:** Sample web page with text boxes and button*

3. The web page is already manually opened on the browser. Now, start the recorder from one of the options of the Flow designer, and then click on the **"Record"** button of the **"Recorder"**.

4. For the **"First name"** text box, manually type the name *John* or anything of your choice. For the **"Last name"** text box, let's see a different approach to entering values: right-click on the text box and choose the **"Populate text field"** item from the context menu.

   The following figure shows the corresponding Action in the **"Recorder"** window for the name **John** entered and also shows the context menu option for entering the last name:

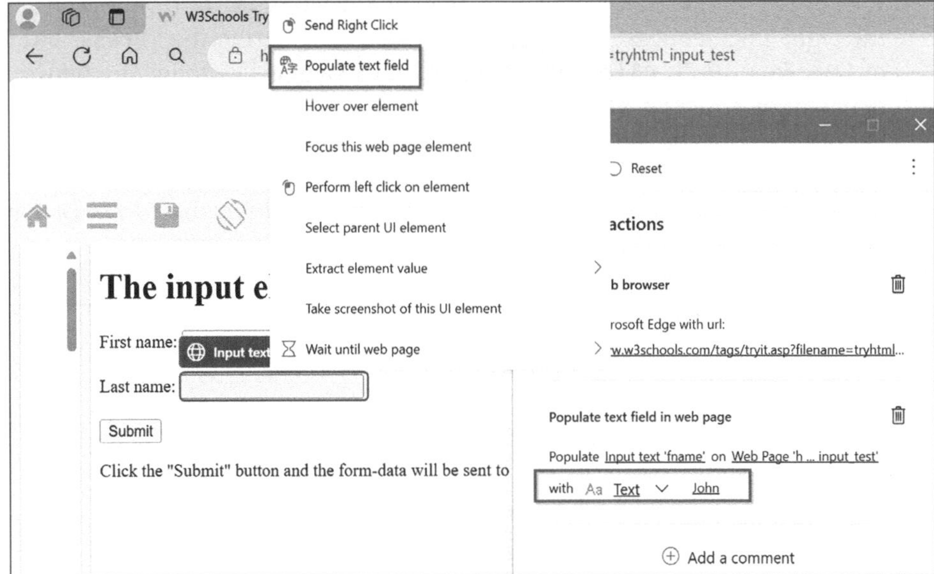

***Figure 5.13:** First name already entered and Context menu for Last name*

5. A free text box will be provided to type in the last name. Go ahead and type a last name. Finally, click on **"`Add text`"**.

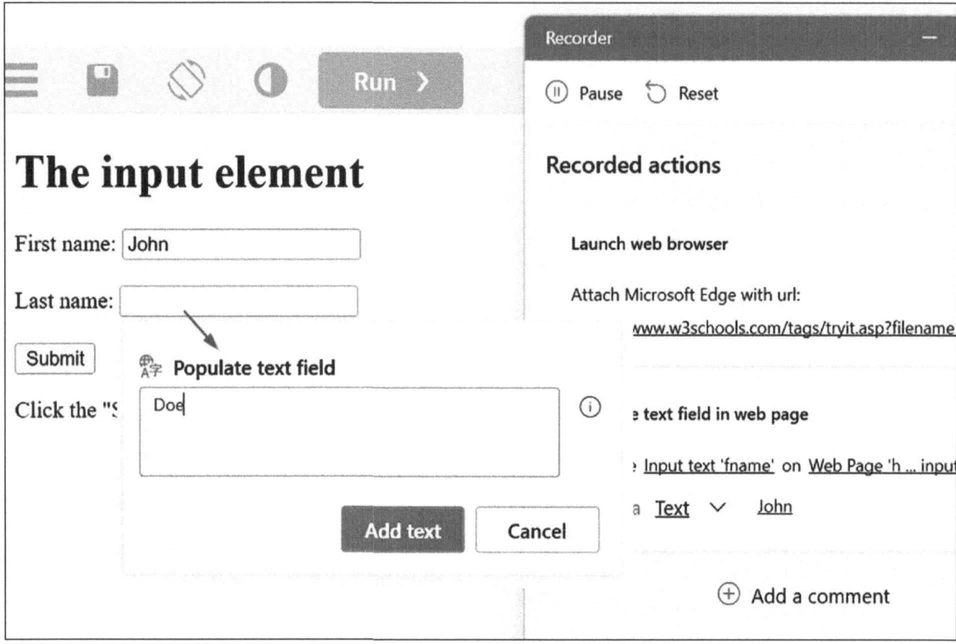

***Figure 5.14:** Populate text field option for entering value*

6. Both the text box values have been entered and it's time to click the **"`Submit`"** button. Left-click the button and finally the **"`Done`"** button of the recorder. There are two more alternate ways to click the **"`Submit`"** button, which are via the right-click context menu options of either selecting the **"`Press button`"** or **"`Perform left click on element`"**, as shown in the following figure. The behavior of different web pages is different; hence, it is a standard practice to try out each of the different options and finally select the one that gives the expected results. Also, the list of options on the context menu will be different depending on the type of element. For example, a text box will not have a **"`Press button`"** option in its context menu.

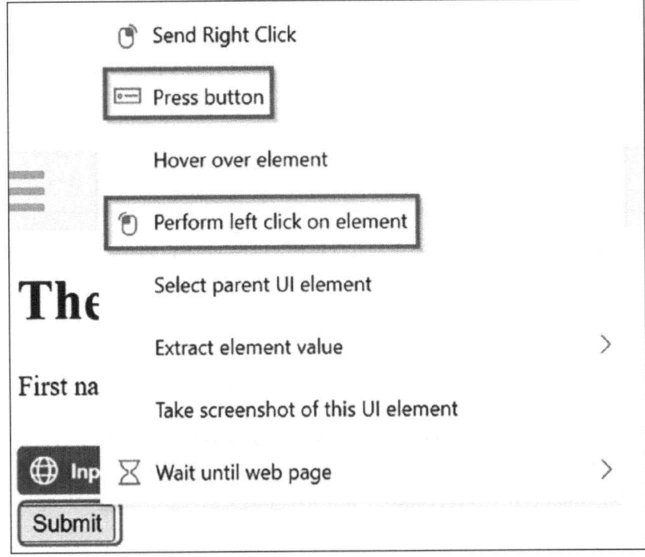

Figure 5.15: *Context menu options for clicking a button*

7. Following is the auto-generated Flow of Actions for the activities performed on the web page, such as entering values in the text fields and clicking the button. If you find that there are any unwanted Actions on the Workspace, you can delete them. To understand which Actions are required and which ones to delete, it will come along with practice.

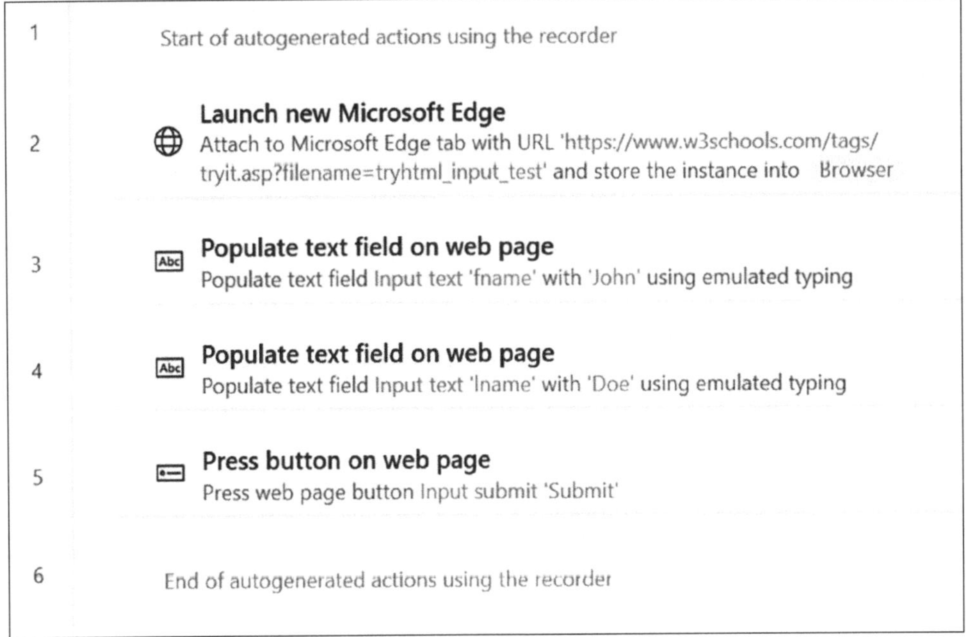

Figure 5.16: *Auto-generated Flow actions*

Let us go through the list of Actions generated:

- **Line number 1:** This is a **"Comment"** Action similar to the one we saw while recording a Desktop application.
- **Line number 2**: If you edit this line of Action, you will see that an appropriate Action for launching the correct browser was used. It has also connected (attached) to an already running instance of the browser because we had opened it manually before the recording. In the same dropdown, there is another option to launch a new instance, which is what you will use if you want the automation to launch a URL without attaching to an already opened instance.

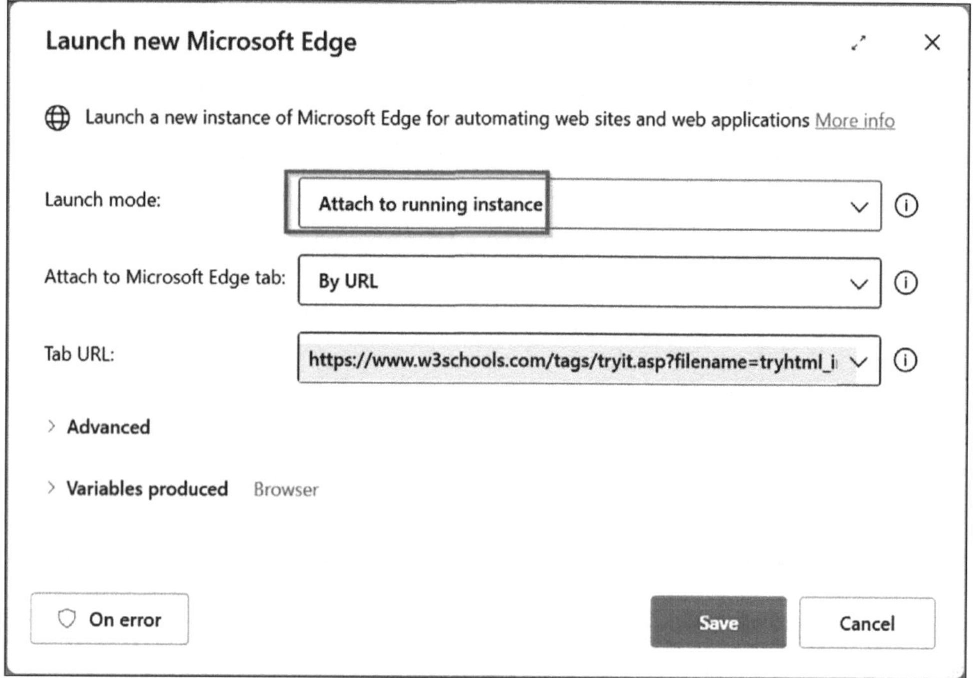

Figure 5.17: *Launch browser action and its parameters*

- **Line numbers 3 and 4**: These Actions were to enter the first name and last name values, respectively. If you recall, we used two different approaches for each of these text boxes and both of them have generated the same line of Action.
- **Line number 5**: This Action is to click the final **"Submit"** button. Again, open the Action, hover the mouse over the stack of UI elements button, and you will see the snapshot image of the element that was clicked, indicating that we are on the right track.

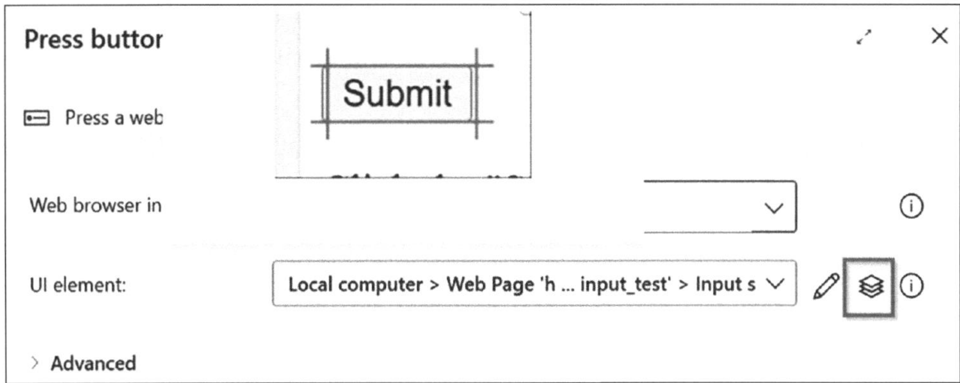

Figure 5.18: *Image of Submit button on mouse hover of UI elements button*

- **Line number 6**: Finally, the **"Comments"** Action to indicate the end of Actions generated by the recording.

It's time to run and test the outcome of the automation generated by the recorder.

Do not close the browser. Bring it back to the main page where the text boxes are empty, as shown in *Figure* 5.12. You could do this by refreshing the URL.

Run the automation and you will see the bot entering the values for the text boxes and finally clicking the **"Submit"** button. The submitted data with the text box values will show up on the next page, indicating that the automation generated by the recorder ran successfully.

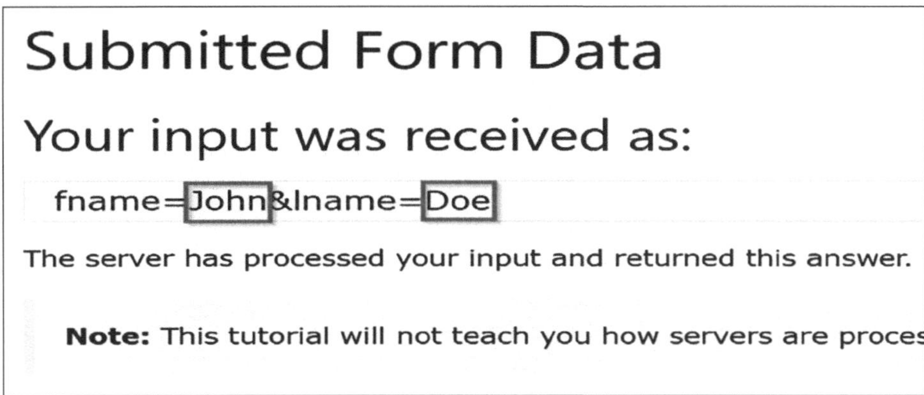

Figure 5.19: *Output after running the Flow*

Reading Values

So far, we have seen **writing** values into a text box and **clicking** a button with the help of the Unified Recorder. Let us see what it takes for **reading** values from a web page, which is similar to what we did for a Windows Desktop application on the Calculator application while reading the results box.

1. Manually open the following URL on a browser window: https://www.w3schools.com/html/tryit.asp?filename=tryhtml_form_submit

2. There are values already written in each of the first name and last name text boxes. Let us read the first name and display it in a message box.

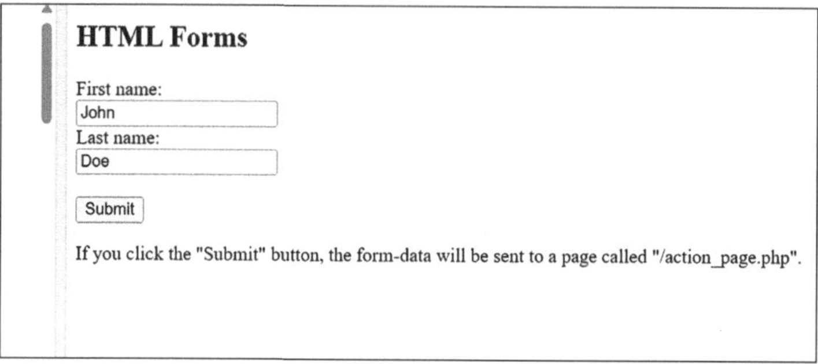

Figure 5.20: *Text boxes with filled values*

3. Start the **"Recorder"**, click the **"Record"** button, and then right-click on the first text box on the above web page. This will give a context menu and a submenu, as shown in the following figure. Click on **"Extract element value"** and the submenu that already gives a preview of what is there inside the text box, that is, **John.**

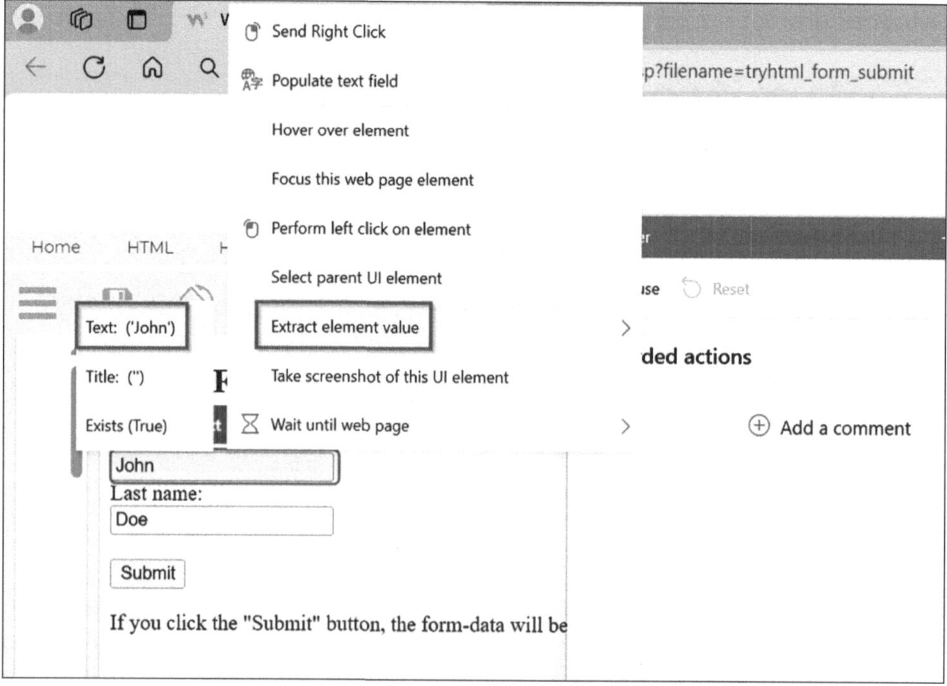

Figure 5.21: *Context menu for reading element value*

4. Corresponding Actions will be added to the **"Recorder"** window. You do not need to read the other text box or click the button as we are only trying to read a single text box value. Click **"Done"** on the **"Recorder"** window.

5. After the auto-generated Actions, add an Action for displaying the first name. In line number 3 of the following figure, the captured first name is stored in an output variable called **`innertext`**. Let us make use of that and display its value in a message box. After running the Flow, the first name would show up on the message box.

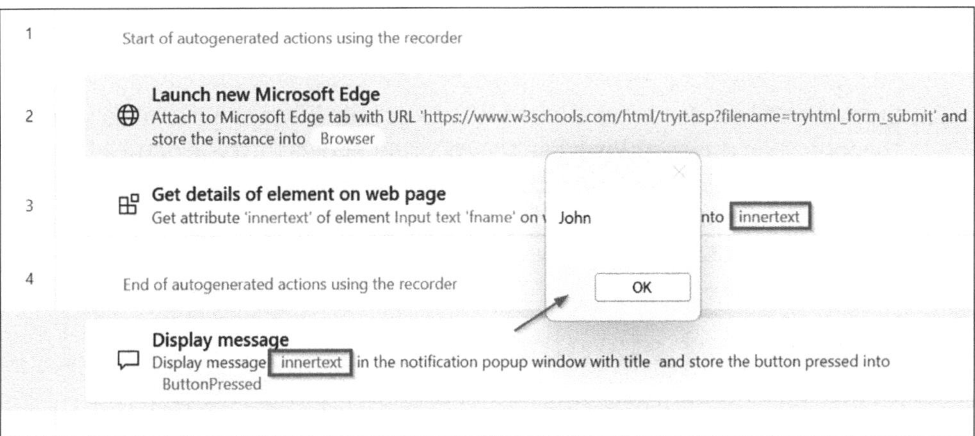

Figure 5.22: *Output after running the Flow*

Selecting Dropdown List Options

After writing, reading values, and clicking a button, let us now see what options the Unified Recorder provides for **selecting** an item from a dropdown list:

1. Manually launch the following URL in a fresh browser window. For simplicity, close all other browser tabs/windows.
   URL: https://www.w3schools.com/tags/tryit.asp?filename=tryhtml_select

   The page has a dropdown with four list items. By the bot, let us select any one of them, click the **"Submit"** button, and see if the selected value shows up on the next page.

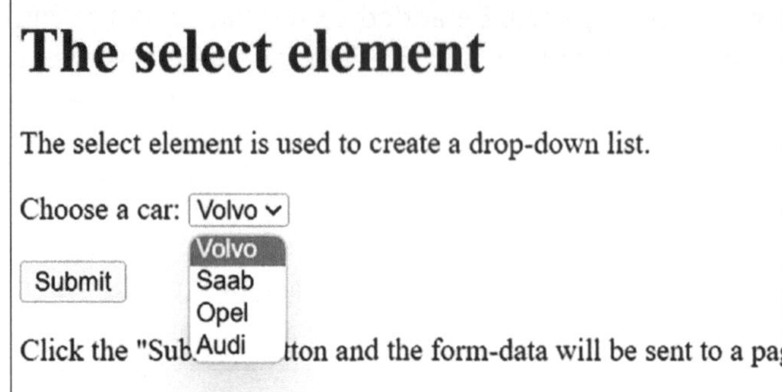

Figure 5.23: *The dropdown options on web page*

2. Start the **"Recorder"** and click on the **"Record"** button. As soon as you hover the mouse on the dropdown list, the recorder shows the type of the element, as shown in the following figure, that is, a **`Select`** element in this case. In HTML, a dropdown is represented by a **"`Select`"** tag. Right-click on the dropdown and choose the **"`Select drop down option`"** menu.

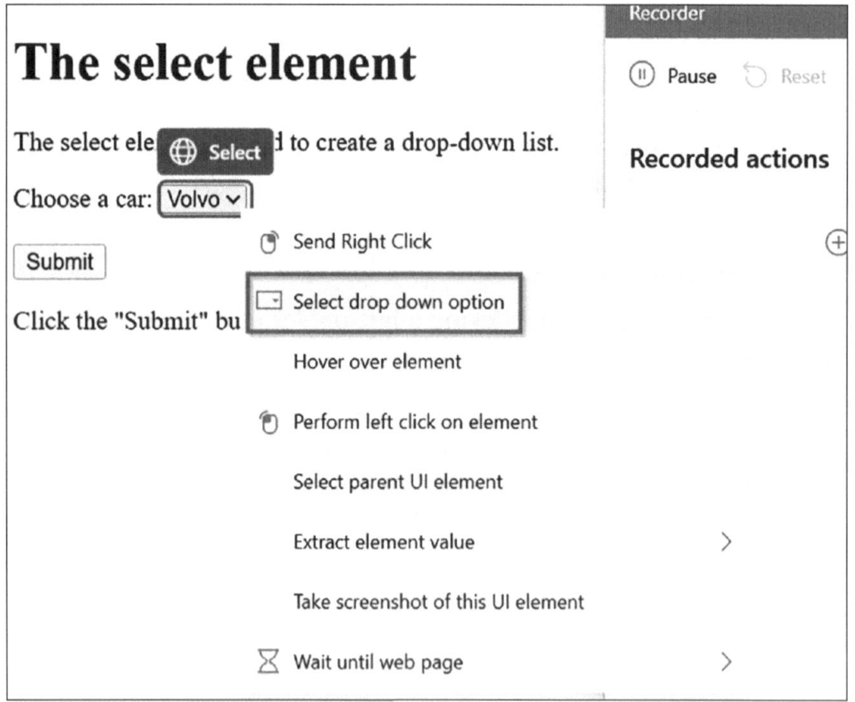

Figure 5.24: *Right-click context menu for selecting dropdown options*

3. On doing so, a list with all of the options available in the dropdown shows up. Select **"`Audi`"** from the list or any item of your choice, click **"`OK`"**, and finally click the **"`Submit`"** button. Finish the recording session by clicking the **"`Done`"** button.

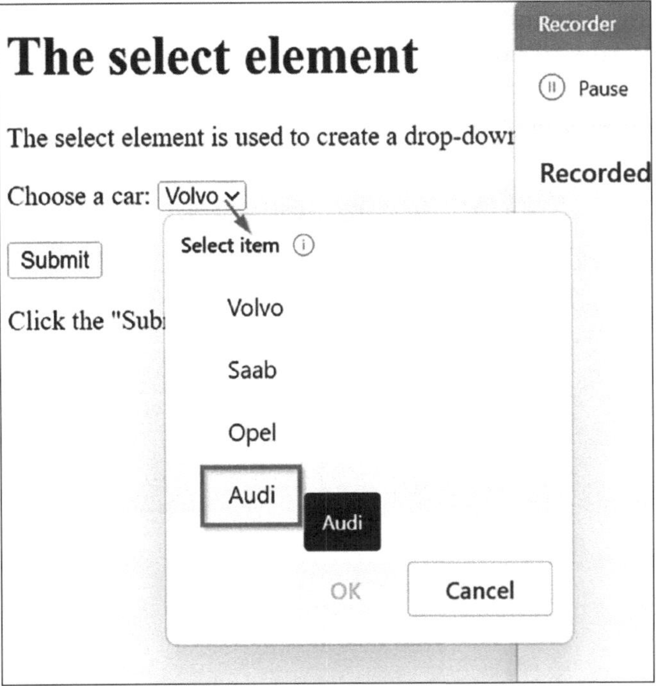

***Figure 5.25:** List of dropdown options for selection*

4. Following is the auto-generated list of Actions for the recorded automation:

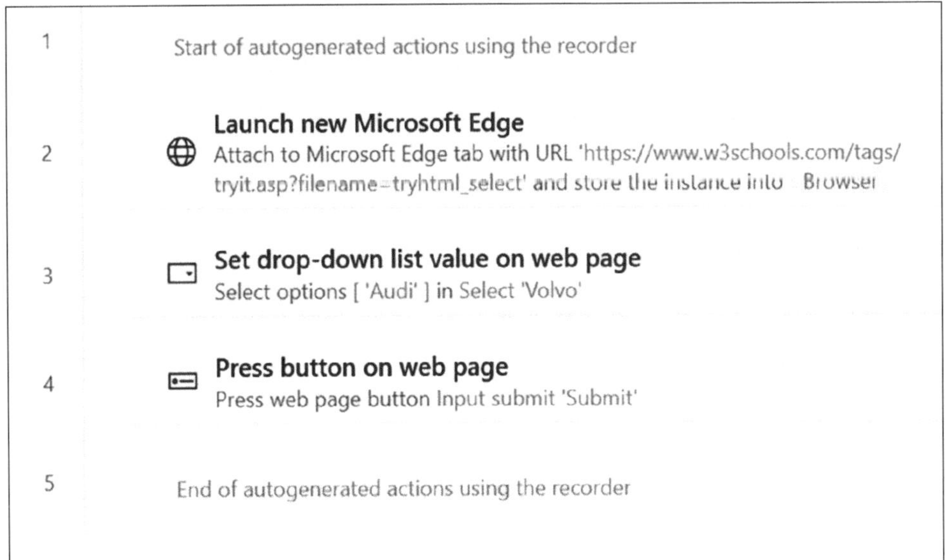

***Figure 5.26:** Final auto-generated Flow of actions*

5. Edit the Action on line number 3 and notice how the recorder automatically selected the below-highlighted parameters: one to select the dropdown

options by name, which also has the option to select by index, that is, 0, 1, and so on, and another that inserts the selected option of the dropdown, which is *Audi* in this case. Also, hover the stack of UI elements icon to verify if the right element was targeted as a good practice.

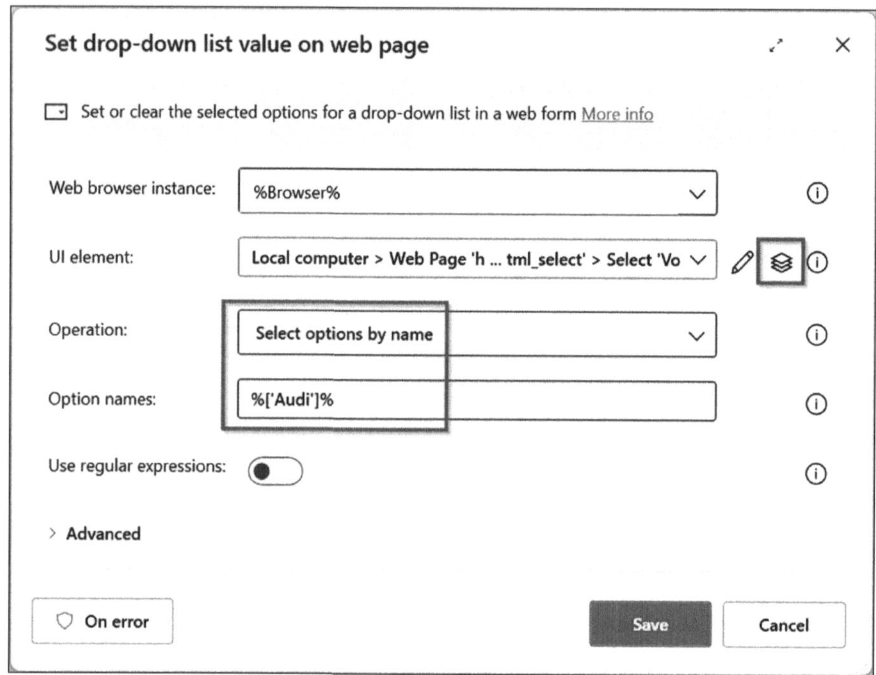

Figure 5.27: *Selection of correct dropdown option*

6. Manually take the web page to the URL from Step 1, or hit the refresh button of the web page and run the Flow.
   If the correct value shows up on the submitted page, then the automation has worked successfully. The first alphabet of the value is small as opposed to the large case in the dropdown because that is how it is configured in the HTML tag of the dropdown, and you can see that in the HTML code editor from the URL in Step 1 on the left-hand side.

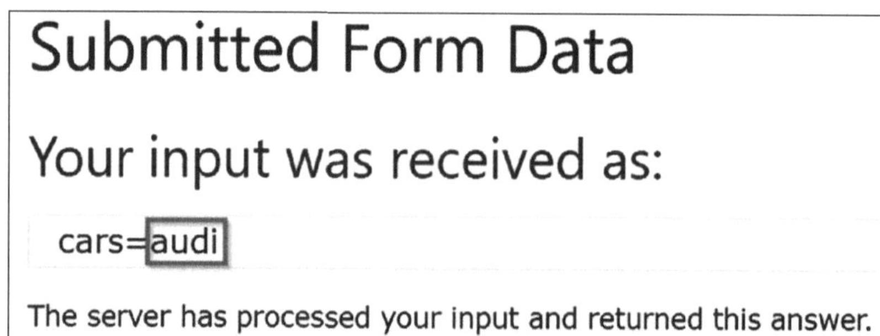

Figure 5.28: *Output after running the Flow*

Selecting and Unselecting Checkboxes

The recorder gives a provision for **checking** or **unchecking** a checkbox irrespective of its current state, that is, whether it is already checked or unchecked:

1. Manually launch the following URL in a new browser window: https://www.w3schools.com/tags/tryit.asp?filename=tryhtml5_input_type_checkbox
   There are three checkboxes, as shown in the following figure. Let us check any one of them and hit the **"`Submit`"** button:

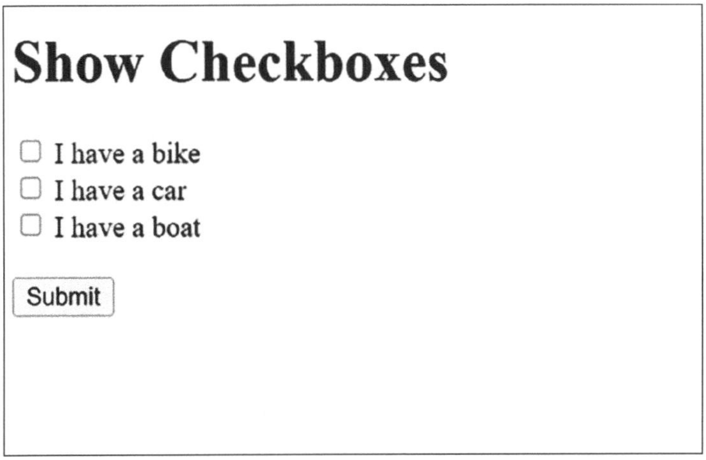

   Figure 5.29: *Checkboxes on web page*

2. Start the recording process. Make sure to verify by hovering the mouse on the actual checkbox element and not on the wording written next to each of the checkboxes as that will be a different UI element. The element we are targeting is an **"`Input checkbox`"**, as shown in the following figure. Right-click on the checkbox, and from the context menu, choose **"`Set checkbox state`"**, then choose **"`Checked`"** from the submenu. This feature also takes care of **"`checking`"** the checkbox even though it was already **"`checked`"**, so there is no need to explicitly verify in the Flow whether it was already **"`checked`"** or not.

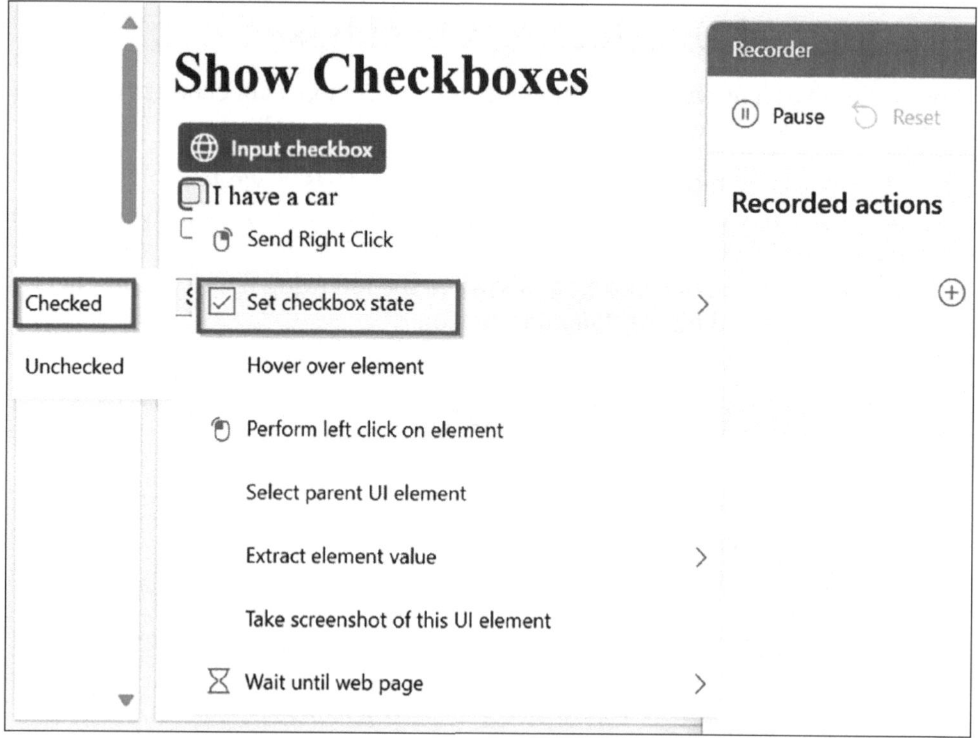

Figure 5.30: *Context menu and submenu for a checkbox*

3. Finally, record the clicking of the **"Submit"** button and press **"Done"** on the recorder window. The list of generated Actions is as follows:

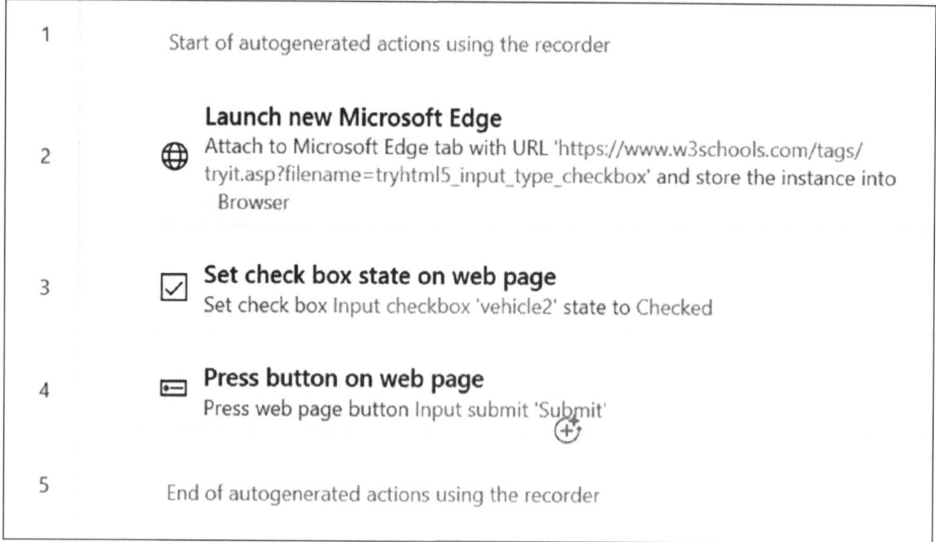

Figure 5.31: *Auto-generated actions for the recorded actions*

4. Run the Flow, and the output will show which checkbox was selected.

Submitted Form Data

Your input was received as:

vehicle2=Car

The server has processed your input and returned this answer.

Figure 5.32: *Output after running the Flow*

5. For future reference in the "*Web Automation*" topic in the next chapter, titled "*Automating Common Applications*", note that **`vehicle2`**, shown in the preceding figure, is the unique ID given to the **"`Car`"** checkbox. This is seen in the HTML code editor on the left-hand side of the same URL from Step 1. This example uses an HTML editor on the left-hand side to generate the corresponding web elements on the right-hand side. However, in an ideal website, one can see the HTML code by right-clicking on the web page and then selecting the **"`View page source`"** from the menu. The wording of this option may slightly vary depending on the browser used.

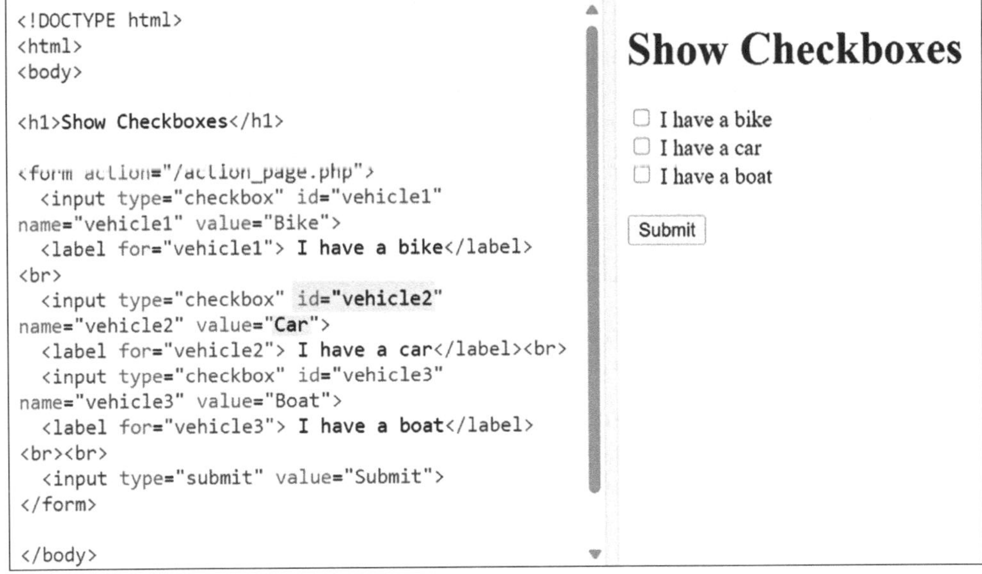

```
<!DOCTYPE html>
<html>
<body>

<h1>Show Checkboxes</h1>

<form action="/action_page.php">
  <input type="checkbox" id="vehicle1"
name="vehicle1" value="Bike">
  <label for="vehicle1"> I have a bike</label>
<br>
  <input type="checkbox" id="vehicle2"
name="vehicle2" value="Car">
  <label for="vehicle2"> I have a car</label><br>
  <input type="checkbox" id="vehicle3"
name="vehicle3" value="Boat">
  <label for="vehicle3"> I have a boat</label>
<br><br>
  <input type="submit" value="Submit">
</form>

</body>
```


Figure 5.33: *Unique ID for the Car checkbox*

The main Action that performs the actual ticking and unticking of the checkboxes is as follows:

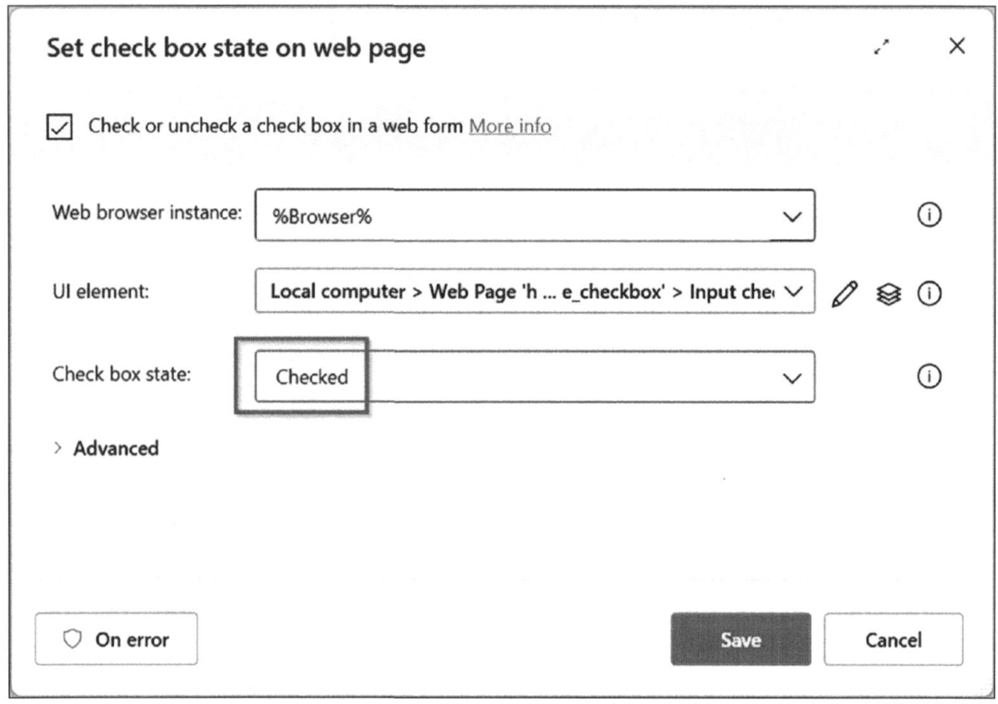

Figure 5.34: *Action to check/uncheck a checkbox*

Try out running the Flow by **"checking"** multiple checkboxes and notice the unique IDs shown on the output page. Try another run with a combination of checked and unchecked checkboxes. Observe the Flow behavior and its outputs. Make sure to manually navigate to the URL in Step 1 each time you rerun the Flow for a fresh run, or click the green **"Run"** button on the web page.

Selecting Option Buttons

In this section, we will select option buttons on a web page with the help of the **"Recorder"**:

1. Manually open the following URL in a browser window, which shows different groups of option buttons, one for **"Web language"** and the other for **"age"**, as shown in the following figure. They are also known as radio buttons:
   https://www.w3schools.com/tags/tryit.asp?filename=tryhtml5_input_type_radio
   Notice the HTML tags for the radio buttons are categorized into different groups based on the **"name"** attribute as follows:

Figure 5.35: *Groups of Radio buttons*

2. Start the recording, right-click any of the radio buttons for the preferred language category, and choose **"`Select radio button`"** from the context menu. Do the same for the age group of radio buttons. Finally, click the **"`Submit`"** button and finish the recording process by clicking **"`Done`"** on the recorder window.

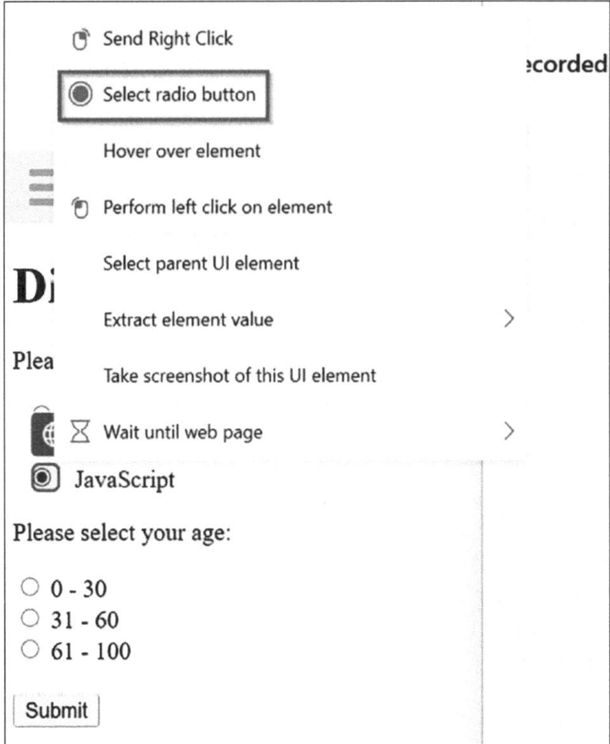

Figure 5.36: *Recorder options for selecting a radio button*

3. The generated Flow of Actions is as follows:

1	Start of autogenerated actions using the recorder
2	**Launch new Microsoft Edge** Attach to Microsoft Edge tab with URL 'https://www.w3schools.com/tags/tryit.asp?filename=tryhtml5_input_type_radio' and store the instance into Browser
3	**Select radio button on web page** Select radio button Input radio 'fav_language'
4	**Select radio button on web page** Select radio button Input radio 'age'
5	**Press button on web page** Press web page button Input submit 'Submit'
6	End of autogenerated actions using the recorder

***Figure* 5.37:** *Autogenerated Flow of actions*

4. Run the Flow and observe the outputs for the selected radio buttons, as shown in the following figure. The names **`fav_language`** and **`age`** come from the **"`name`"** attribute, as highlighted in *Figure* 5.35. The responses **`JavaScript`** and **`60`** come from the **"`value`"** attribute, from the same figure. Down the Flow, the developer will have to build logic in such a way that if the age is coming as 60 in the output, then it would imply that the automation has pressed the **"`31 - 60`"** age group radio button.

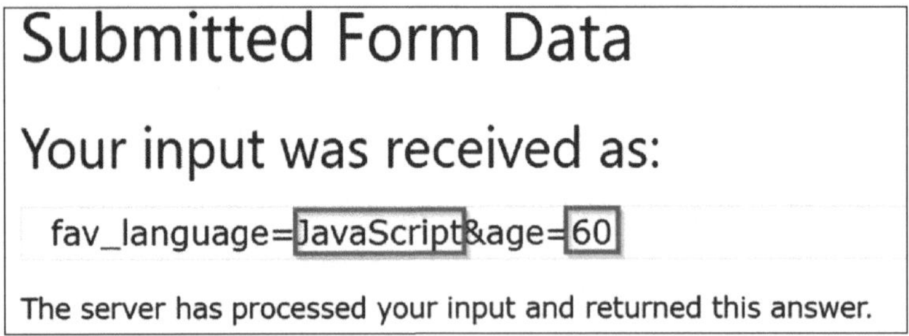

***Figure* 5.38:** *Output after running the Flow*

Try rerunning the Flow for multiple combinations of the radio buttons and observe the Flow by selecting the radio buttons and their submitted outputs. Before a rerun, remember to click the **"`Run`"** button on the web page, refresh the web page, or manually navigate to the URL in Step 1.

For the Action on line number 4 of *Figure* 5.37, hover the mouse on the UI elements button, and the snapshot image of which radio button was captured as a UI element will be shown. Check the same for the Action on line number 3 too.

The Action for selecting a Radio button does not have an option to **"select/ unselect"** similar to **"check/uncheck"** as that of a checkbox (*Figure* 5.34), which is due to the nature of radio buttons that when one is selected, another radio button gets automatically unselected.

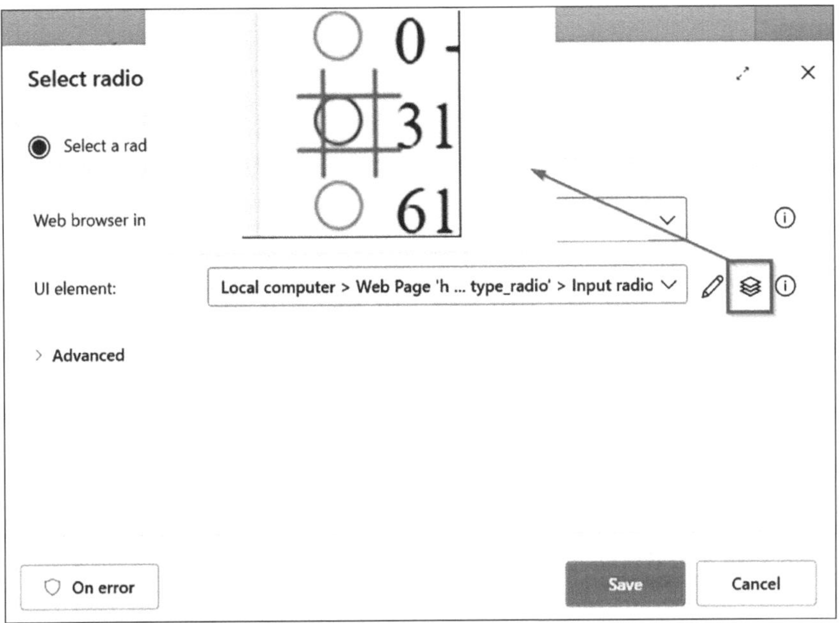

***Figure* 5.39:** *Captured radio button UI element*

Final Words About the Unified Recorder

Recorders can be useful at most times to give you a good idea about which Actions to be used within the Flow. It can also generate your entire workflow in most situations. In some cases, it greatly helps to build a skeleton of the automation and in some cases may not be of any use at all.

However, even if you use the recorder, you might have to make some tweaks and changes to the recorded steps to make your automation work correctly. Or in some cases, you may find out that the recorded steps are not of much help or certain operations do not get recorded.

It is recommended to build Flows using the in-built Actions available in PAD versus the recording because you have the flexibility to use any Action as required and write your own logic as per the automation you are trying to develop, and this comes with experience.

Having said that, since automation could be for different types of applications, experiment with and without the recorder and choose the most feasible option as per the one you are trying to build.

UI Elements and Selectors

If you practically tried out recording the Desktop and Web applications, as explained in the previous section, you already have got the UI elements and their Selectors.

UI Elements

UI elements, as stated earlier, are the elements that form the user interface (UI), such as text boxes, labels, list boxes, check boxes, frames, buttons, the window, and so on. Power Automate Desktop uses UI elements for their interaction with external applications and web pages.

UI elements captured for any application are visible in the **"`UI elements`"** pane on the right-hand side of the Flow designer, just below the button for the **"`Variables`"** pane.

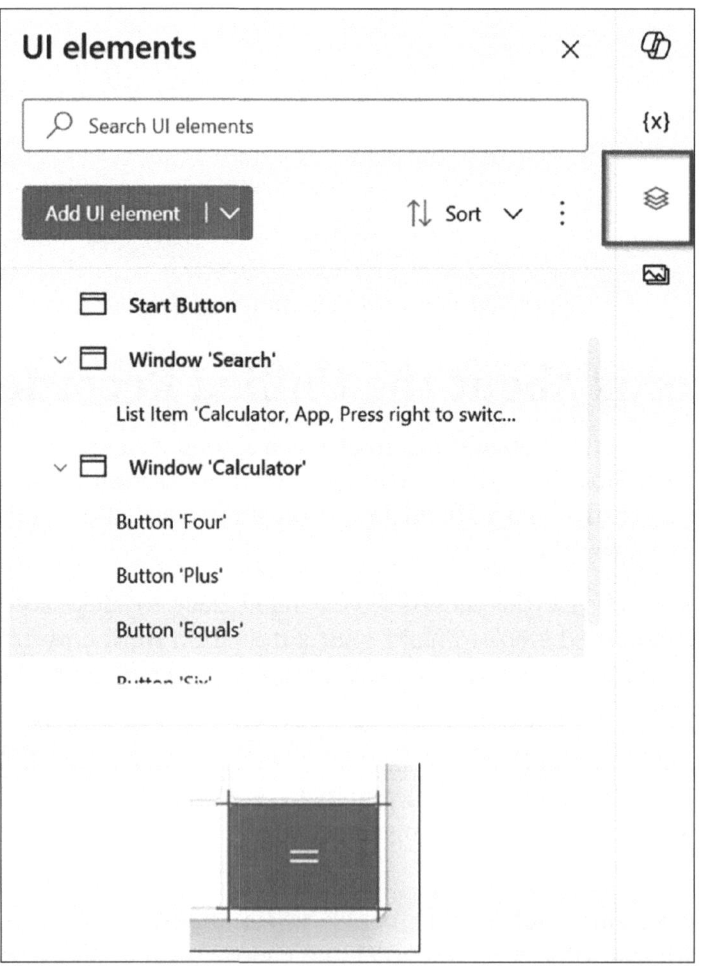

Figure 5.40: *UI elements pane with the elements for the Calculator app*

If you scroll through all the UI elements generated so far for the Calculator application, you will see a UI element created for every single element we captured using the recorder to interact with the Calculator application, for example, the buttons for number 4, number 6, the equals sign, and so on. When you click on any of these UI elements, its preview image will be shown like the equals button, as shown in the preceding figure, when the **"Button 'Equals'"** element is selected.

Likewise, when the main top-level group of each section is selected, its own preview image is seen, for example, a snapshot image of the Calculator application itself is seen when the **"Window 'Calculator'"** group is clicked. The **"Start Button"** is a section group and so is the **"Window 'Search'"**. Click on each of those to see what preview image they show up.

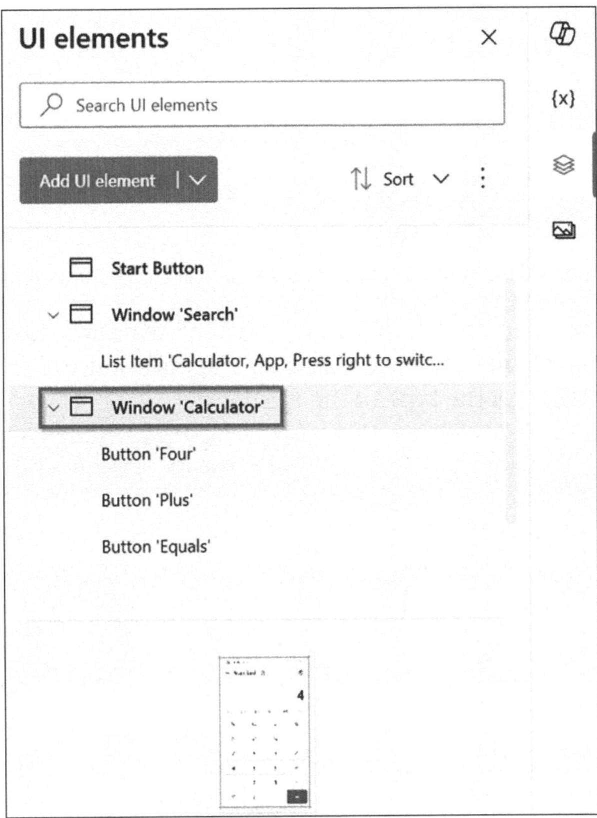

Figure 5.41: *UI elements group*

Multiple Ways of Creating UI Elements

Following are the various ways by which UI elements can be created:

- From the **"Add UI element"** button of the **"UI elements"** pane

- From the **"Add UI element"** button of respective Actions that are used for UI-based automation
- From the Recorder

Let us create UI elements through the first two options as we have already created them using the Recorder in the previous topic.

- **From the "Add UI element" button of the "UI elements" pane:**

  Perform the following steps:

  1. Manually open the Calculator application.
  2. From the **"UI elements"** pane, click the **"Add UI element"** button.

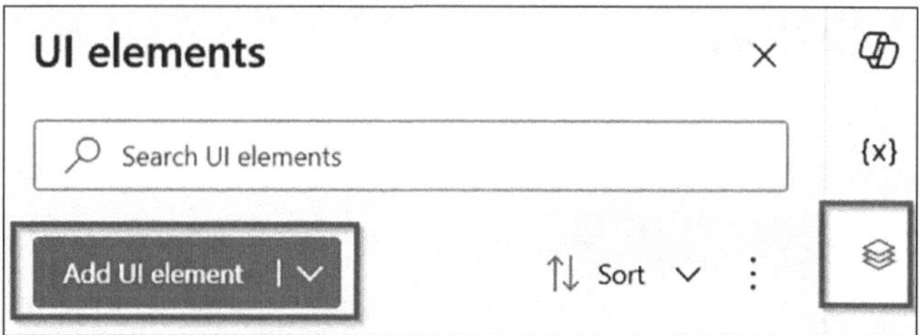

Figure 5.42: *Add UI element button of the UI elements pane*

  3. This will open an **"UI element picker"** window. Hover the mouse over different elements of the Calculator application to see how the element picker displays the type of the element.

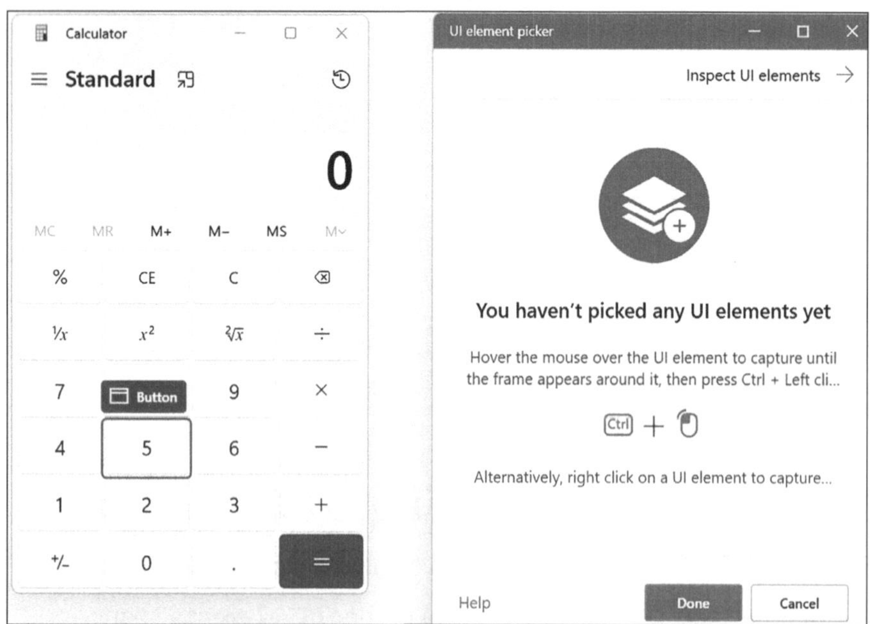

Figure 5.43: *Capturing the element with the UI element picker*

4. We are going to capture the element for the button for number 5. As per the instructions mentioned on the **"UI element picker"** window, hover the mouse on the button for 5, press the *Control* key on the keyboard, and simultaneously do a left-click by the mouse on that button. On doing so, this will create a group for the root application, which is the calculator in this case, and then the UI element for button 5, as shown in the following figure. Also seen is the preview image of the button, when clicked on the UI element in the element picker window, indicating we have clicked the desired button.

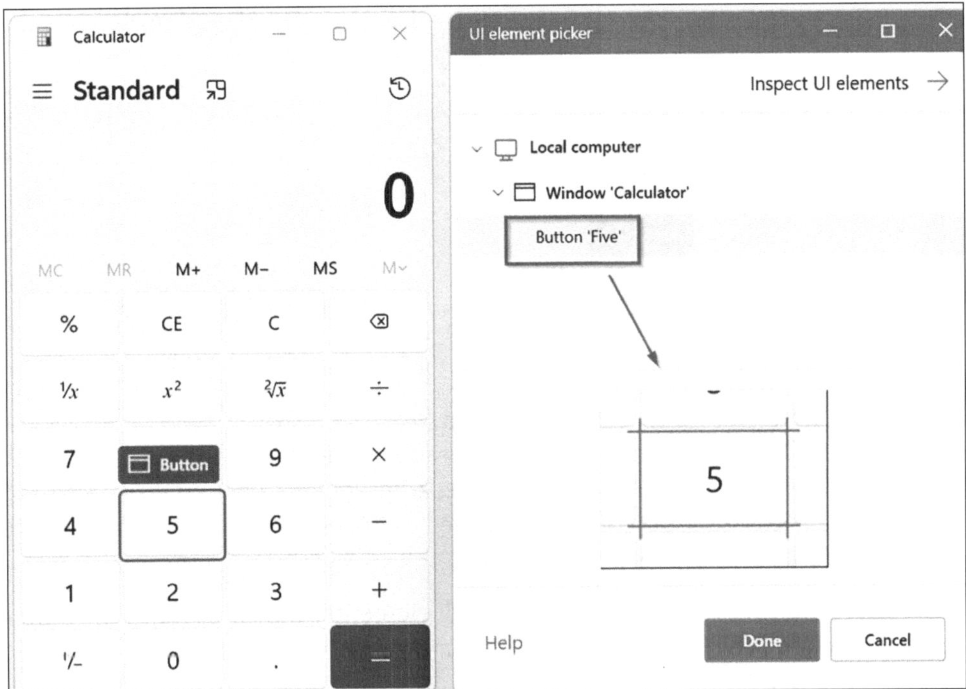

Figure 5.44: *UI element for button 5 with the root Window element*

5. Clicking on the **"Done"** button will immediately add a UI element called **"Button 'Five'"** in the **"UI elements"** pane, as shown on the right-hand side of the following figure. Also, we know from the recording session that to click a button on a Desktop application, we make use of the **"Press button in window"** Action. So, let's drag and drop that Action onto the Workspace. Clicking the **"UI element"** dropdown of this Action will bring up all the list of available **desktop UI elements**, which includes the one that we just created. Also, a preview image for the number 5 button will be displayed, which we can use to verify whether we have captured the intended element or not.

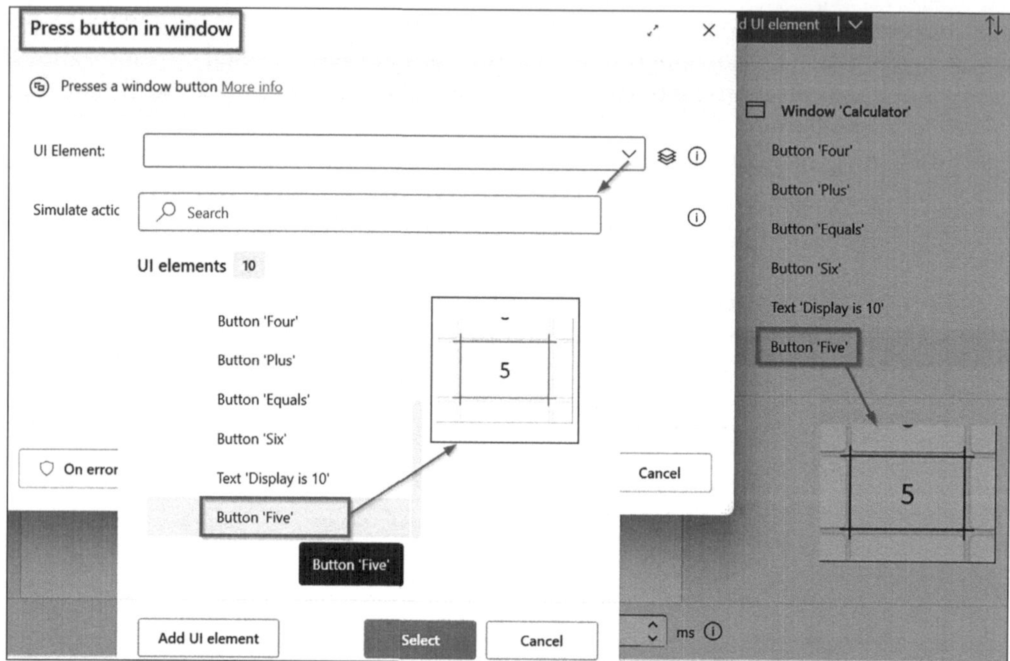

Figure 5.45: *UI element for button 5 in the list of available UI elements*

If there were any **web UI elements** captured from a web page, they will not show up in this dropdown because this Action pertains to the **"UI automation"** group of Actions (desktop application elements), and there is a separate group of Actions called as **"Browser automation"** to access web UI elements.

Therefore, there are two types of UI elements, namely desktop UI elements and web UI elements. Be noted that a web application can also have a desktop UI element, for example, the title bar, the outside window of the browser, and so on are all part of the desktop UI element and not a web UI element. Hence, the elements like the title bar, address bar, the window are to be automated using the Actions for desktop UI elements, whereas the webpage portion of the browser window is to be automated using the Actions for web UI elements. Refer to *Figure* 5.46 for these different categories of Actions for doing the same operation, that is, pressing a button.

Take the Actions under each of these categories (UI automation and Browser automation), use the **"Add UI element"** button, hover around the UI elements on the screen, and you will start getting a knack of knowing them once you see which elements of the screen are detectable by which category of Actions.

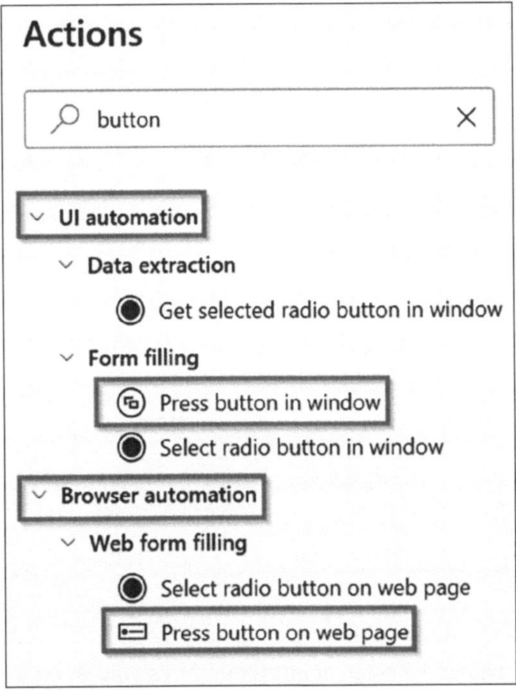

***Figure* 5.46:** *Press button in window under UI automation*

6. After choosing the UI element for button 5, click the **"`Select`"** button from *Figure* 5.45, save the Action, and run the Flow.
   The button number 5 will be pressed by the automation on the Calculator application.

- **From the "`Add UI element`" button of respective Actions that are used for UI-based automation**

This time we will press button 8 but via the second option of creating UI elements.

Perform the following steps:

1. Manually open the Calculator application.
2. Refer to *Figure* 5.6 of the recording exercise and see that the Action to click a button on a desktop application is **"`Press button in window`"**. Knowing which Action is used for what purpose comes with exploring the **"`Actions`"** pane, with trial and error and with a little learning and practice.
3. Drag and drop the **"`Press button in window`"** Action onto the Workspace. You will notice an **"`Add UI element`"** button on this Action when you pull down the **"`UI Element`"** dropdown. This button is available for relevant Actions that require a UI element to interact with. This is another way to create a UI element directly from the Action itself.

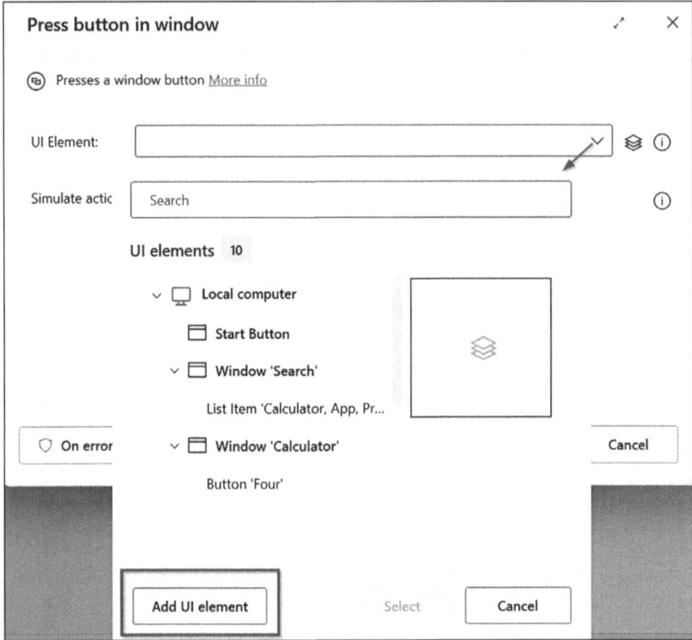

Figure 5.47: *Add UI element button within a corresponding action*

4. Click the **"Add UI element"** button. Hover the mouse on the desired UI element, which is the button for 8 in our case. Press the *Control* key on the keyboard and simultaneously do a left-click with the mouse in the same way as in the previous section.

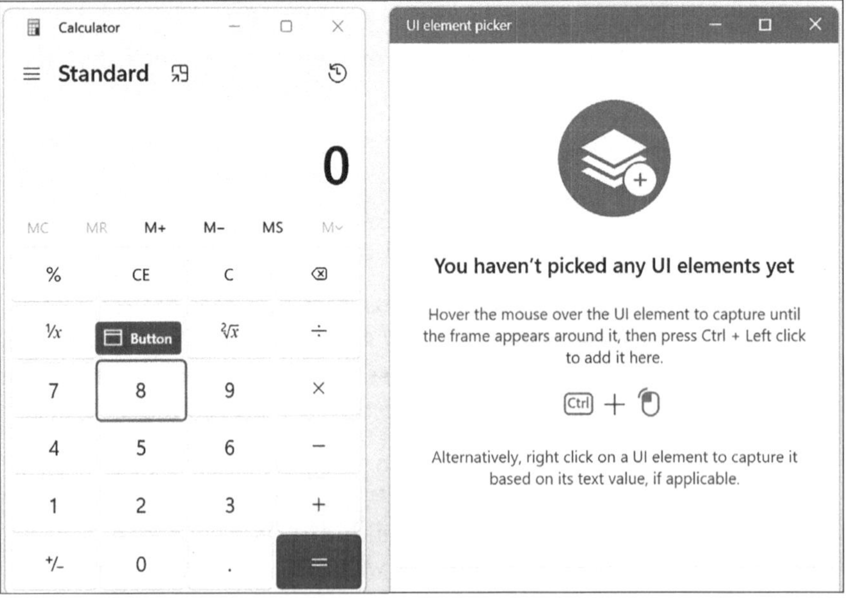

Figure 5.48: *Capturing the element with the UI element picker*

5. As soon as you do that, the UI element for button 8 gets captured and you can verify that by hovering the mouse on the stack of UI elements button to see the preview image.

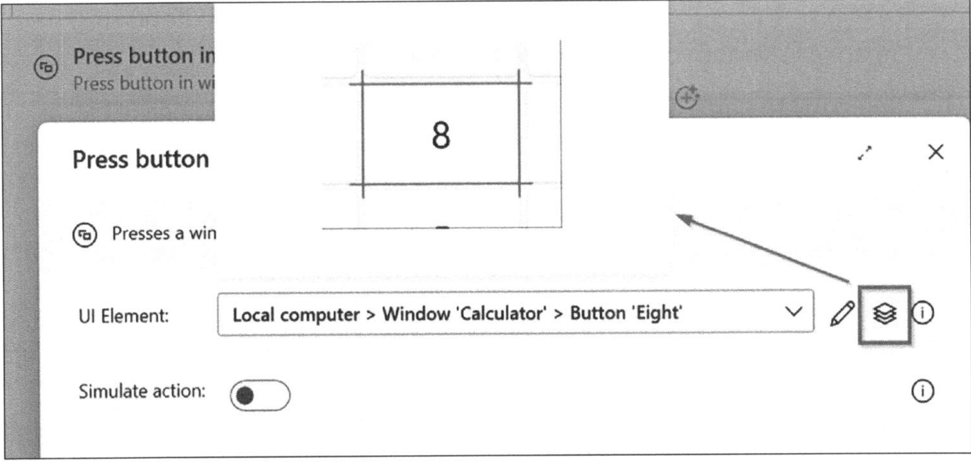

Figure 5.49: *UI element extracted for button 8*

6. Just run this single line of Action and you will see that the button 8 gets pressed on the Calculator application.

   Go to the **"UI elements"** pane and you will find the UI elements created for button 5 and button 8, captured via the two different above approaches.

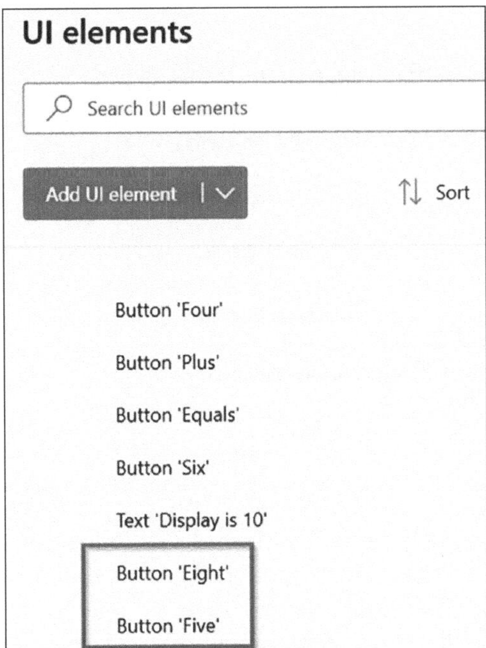

Figure 5.50: *UI elements for button 5 and button 8*

- **From the Recorder:**

  Refer to the topic of using the Unified Recorder at the beginning of this chapter to see how the UI elements were automatically created by it. Referring to *Figure* 5.50, the UI elements seen for the buttons **`4 + 6 =`** and the result of **`10`** are all the ones created by the Recorder.

  Referring to point number 5 of the section titled **`From the "Add UI element" button of the "UI elements" pane`**, here we talked about two types of UI elements, namely desktop UI elements and web UI elements. Now that we have both in our **`"UI elements"`** pane after the Calculator and the web application exercises, we can differentiate them both via separate icons in the list of captured UI elements. The first marked icon in the following figure indicates a web UI element that we used to interact with a web application, whereas the second marked is the desktop UI element that we created while interacting with the Calculator application.

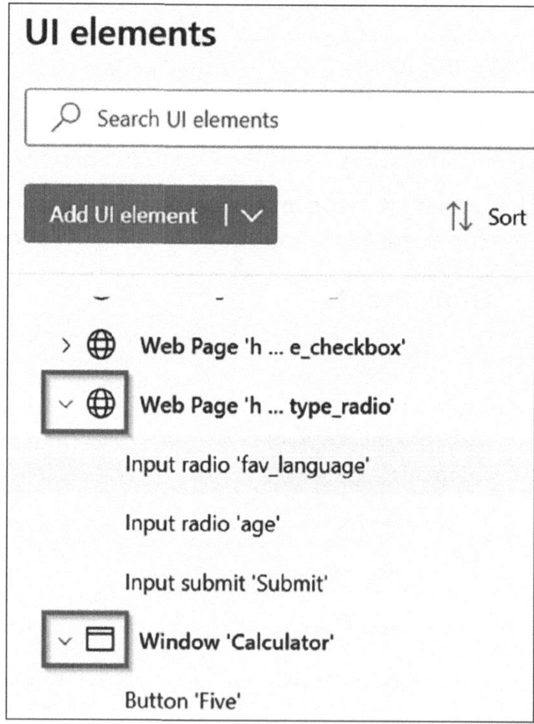

***Figure* 5.51:** *Desktop UI elements and web UI elements*

A UI element in the **`"UI elements"`** pane has the following options: to edit the UI element to open up its Selector (explained in the next topic), to rename it by giving a developer-friendly name, to find its usages so as to quickly jump to the Action where it is used, and to delete it. These options can be seen by either right-clicking a UI element or using the ellipsis button next to that element.

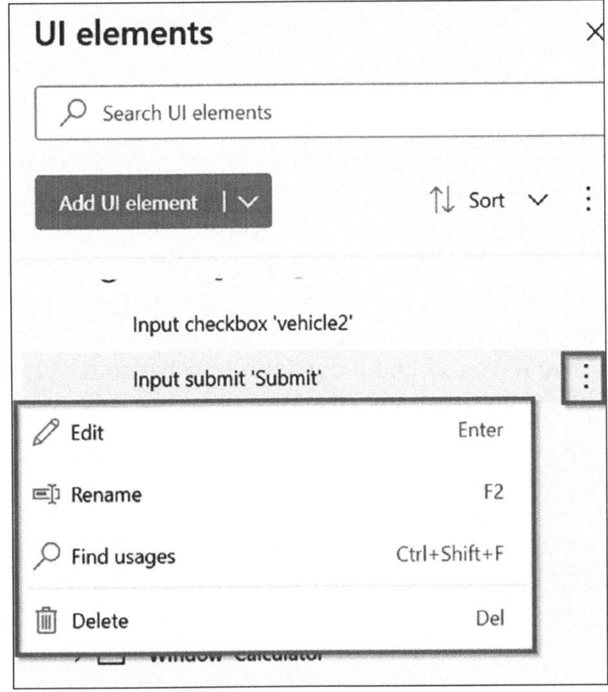

Figure 5.52: *Options for UI elements*

Another handy feature is to use the **"Remove unused UI elements"** context menu item from the top ellipsis button to remove all UI elements that were added for trial-and-error purposes but are not used in any of the Actions. You will also have an option to sort the UI elements in ascending or descending order and to expand/collapse the list of all UI elements available in the pane.

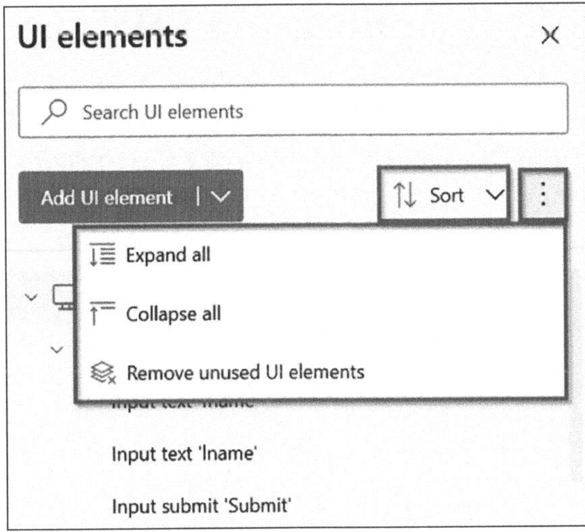

Figure 5.53: *Additional options for UI elements*

Selectors

In simple terms, Selectors are used to uniquely identify the UI elements. They contain a combination of attributes that help to point to the right UI element. These attributes could be anything, such as the UI element's Id, name, class, text, and position among several other properties. We do not have to worry about how to retrieve these attributes for a UI element. This is made available by the Power Automate Desktop tool. However, since UI elements have different attributes across different applications, our job is to accurately target the desired UI element by tweaking the available Selectors in such a way that it correctly points to the element under various conditions. In certain situations, we may also have to build a dynamic selector to cover multiple scenarios, which we will also be discussing in this topic.

In short, Selectors are a way to uniquely identify and interact with the specific elements of an application's User Interface (UI).

Just imagine if a Selector points to 5 text boxes (UI elements) at the same time and the automation has to write to only a specific text box, then that will not give us the desired outcome. In most cases, the default Selector options provided by the PAD tool serve our purpose. However, in some cases, they have to be newly built or modified. Also, the Selectors for web and desktop applications share the same structure and capabilities, but the point of difference lies in what attributes are available for each of them. While web selectors show the HTML attributes by which the page was designed, the desktop selectors have attributes based on their own design of the application (for example, an application built in Java may show different attributes as compared to an application built using .Net). Let us take a look at how Selectors look like, their features, and their functionalities.

A Sample Desktop Application Selector

Recall the calculator exercise that was done for recording the `4 + 6 =` operation. As seen earlier (see *Figure* 5.50), the UI elements for these buttons are already created. To view a Selector for these UI elements, double-click any UI element or use the ellipsis button of that UI element to open up the Selector window.

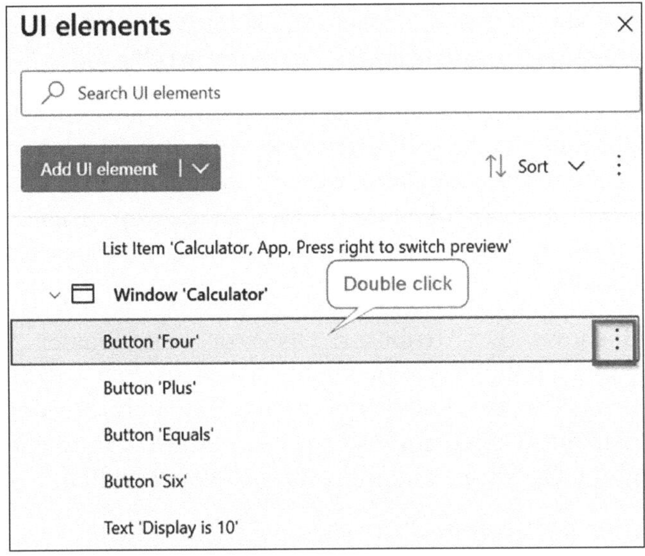

Figure 5.54: *Opening the Selector window*

Following is the Selector window for button 4 of the calculator:

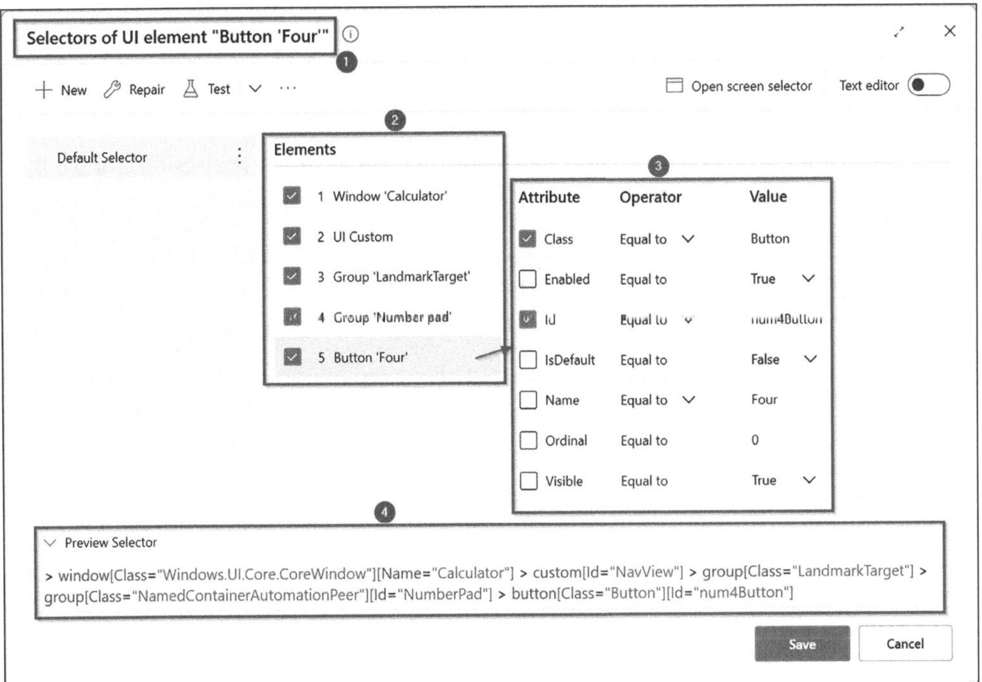

Figure 5.55: *The Selector window*

Refer to the numbering in the preceding figure and follow along as below:

1. This section shows that the Selector(s) is for which UI element. The name of the UI element is the one from the **"UI elements"** pane.

2. Section 2 shows the elements that are behind the scenes of the Calculator application, and not to confuse these with the UI elements. This means that just assume the Calculator was built using a certain technology. These elements are the layers of all the elements that were used while building the application using that technology. They can be selected or unselected using the checkboxes.

3. Section 3 shows the Attributes, Operators, and Values for the selected element. For example, in the preceding figure, clicking the Button 'Four' from the **"Elements"** section shows the Attributes, Operators, and Values for that selected element. The Attributes can be selected and unselected using the tick boxes, and the Operators and the Values can be modified.

   The selection of **"Elements"** (of section 2) and the selection of Attributes and the modifications of the Operators and the Values (from section 3) determine the uniqueness of pointing to the right UI element. This means that if these combinations are configured accurately, the Selector will point to the desired UI element and automation can be performed smoothly. As mentioned earlier, most of the times these default combinations provided by PAD can point to the right UI element, but there arise situations where these have to be modified on an experimenting and trial-and-error basis.

4. This is the **"Preview Selector"** pane. All the options and combinations that were selected in sections 2 and 3 will be shown up in this pane.

Notice in the pane that they are represented in the format: **Element[Attribute1="Value"][Attribute2="Value"]** and so on, based on the selections made in sections 2 and 3. Two elements are separated by the **">"** symbol.

For example, referring to the second row of the preview pane, the **"group"** element with **"Class"** and **"Id"** attributes comes from the 4th element of section 2. The **"button"** element with **"Class"** and **"Id"** attributes comes from the 5th element of section 2. Both of these are separated by the **">"** symbol after **[Id="NumberPad"]** as follows:

```
 > window[Class=»Windows.UI.Core.CoreWindow"][Name="Calculator"]
> custom[Id="NavView"] > group[Class="LandmarkTarget"] > group
[Class="NamedContainerAutomationPeer"][Id="NumberPad"] > button
[Class="Button"][Id="num4Button"]
```

As soon as any of the Attribute, for example, the **"Id"** of the button in this case, is removed by unticking it, the same Attribute disappears from the preview pane, as shown in the following figure. The same will happen if an Element (from section 2 of the preceding figure) is unticked.

Even if an Attribute for an element is ticked, but if the element itself is not ticked, the element and its Attribute won't show up in the preview pane. Try that out.

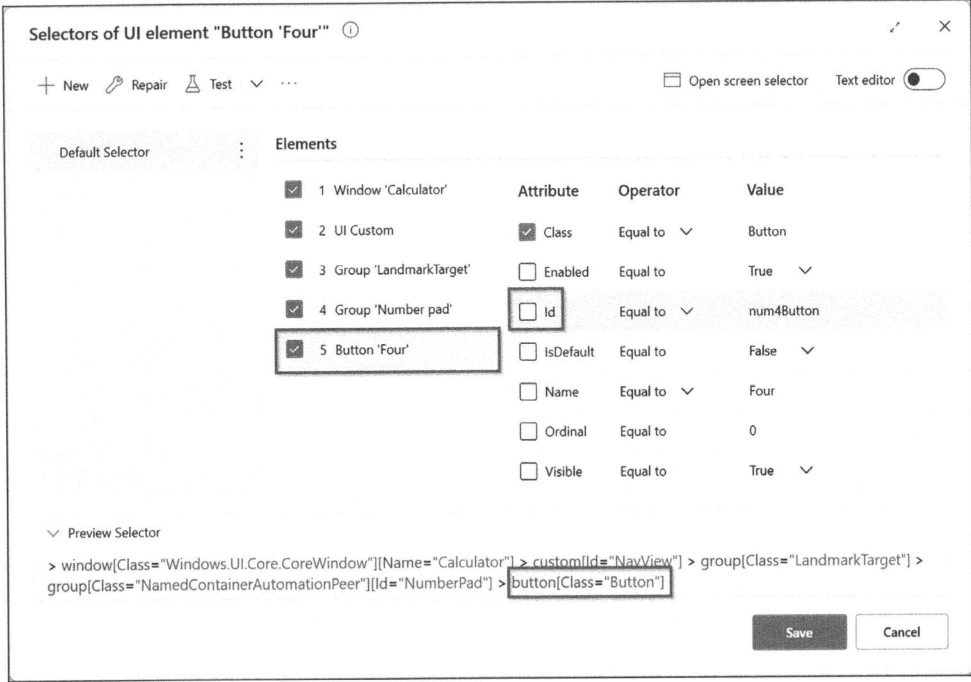

Figure 5.56: *Unchecking an attribute in the Selector window*

Testing the Selector

PAD provides a very good feature of testing whether the Selectors point to the expected UI element.

Add back the **"`Id`"** Attribute checkbox and hit the **"`Test`"** button at the top left of the Selector window.

On doing so, PAD highlights the UI element on the external application. In this case, you can see it marked as **"`Default Selector`"** on button 4 of the Calculator application. On the left-hand side, there is the name of this Selector, that is, **"`Default Selector`"**, which has a green tick next to it indicating that there were no failures while testing the Selector. One can right-click on the Selector name and change its name. Since the current name of the Selector is **"`Default Selector`"**, the one marked on the Calculator application shows up as **"`Default Selector`"**. Renaming the Selector name will be displayed as that new name on the Calculator application. Also, notice that all of the Elements (of section 2) have a green tick next to them.

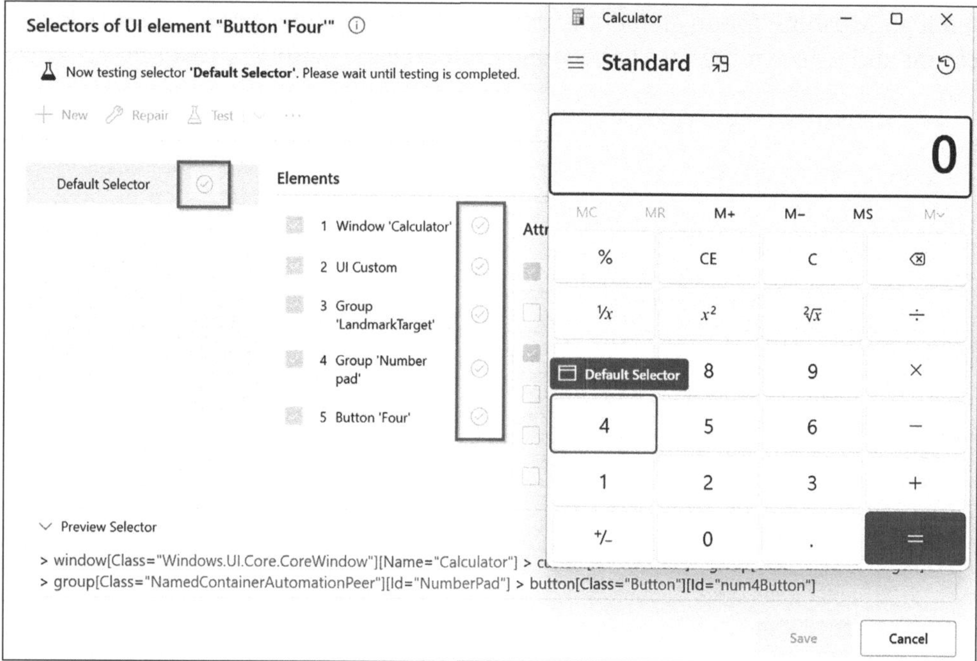

Figure 5.57: *Testing the Selector*

Now, let us see a different scenario. Untick the **"Id"** attribute of the button. As seen in the **"Preview Selector"** section of the following figure, there is no **"Id"** attribute for the button. Also, the arrow indicates that the **"Id"** checkbox is not checked. Test the Selector again, and this time although it does not give any failure, it incorrectly points to a button, that is, button for 7, whereas our Selector was for button 4. The **"Id"** Attribute of the button, with a value of **"num4Button"**, was uniquely identifying the button for 4, which we have now removed.

Click the yellow icon next to the **"Default Selector"** and refer to the message it shows. It does not show a failure, but it says multiple UI elements have matched for the Selector. In such cases, PAD points to the first UI element from the top left corner of the Calculator window that matches with the specified Selector. This is the reason it highlights the button for 7, because, in the **"Number pad"** group, the button for 7 is the first one starting from the top left corner of the Calculator window matching the Selector.

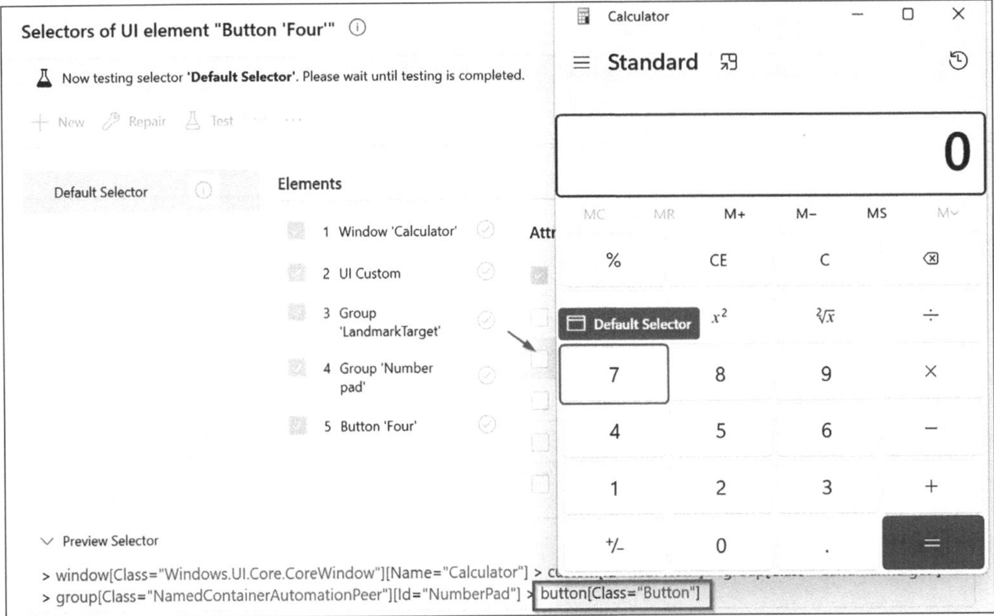

***Figure 5.58:** Incorrect Selector output during testing*

Furthermore, this time remove the button element altogether from the Selector by unchecking it from the **"Elements"** section. As marked by an arrow in the following figure, the button element is unchecked in the **"Elements"** section and therefore got removed from the **"Preview Selector"** section too. Test the selector and you will see, as shown in the following figure, that the **"Default Selector"** highlights all the numeric buttons on the Calculator application, which is totally not what we intended. Although there is a green tick because PAD was able to find a matching Selector without any issues based on the combinations given, it is pointing to a different set of UI elements because we have not uniquely drilled it down to the element for button 4.

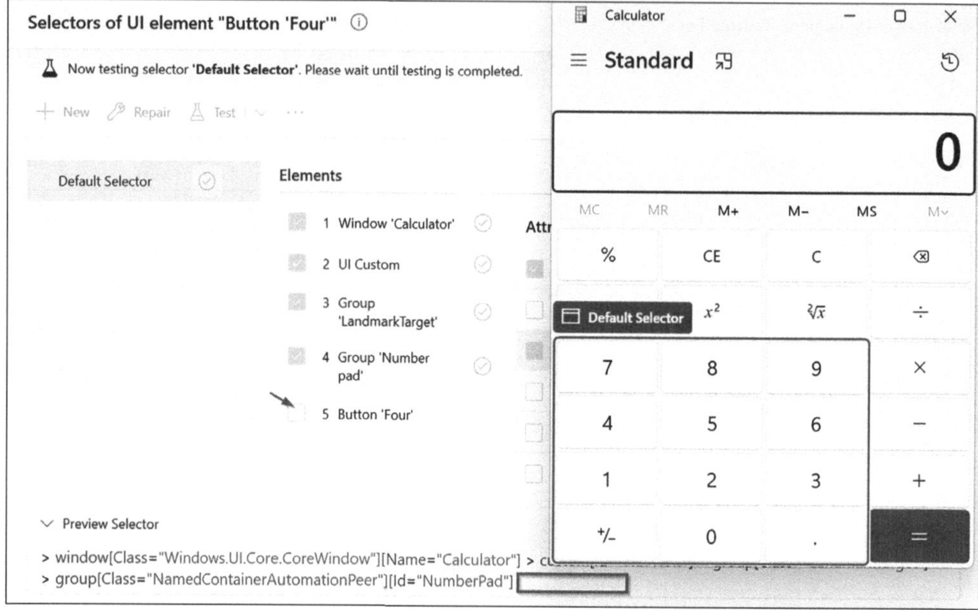

Figure 5.59: *Another incorrect Selector output during testing*

We have been seeing the green ticks for successful scenarios. Let us see a failure scenario.

1. Add back the button element from the **"Elements"** section and tick the **"Id"** Attribute.

2. As stated earlier, the Operator and the Values of the Attributes can be modified. Change the Value for the **"Id"** Attribute to something other than what it already is, for example, from **num4Button** to **num4Button1**, as yellow highlighted in the following figure. As expected, the **"Preview Selector"** section also shows the same value of **num4Button1** in the Selector.

3. Test the Selector and now we have a red marked failure icon indicated by an arrow and has a message.

   There are situations where we are going to make a Selector dynamic, and if the Values or Operators or the selected combinations are incorrect, then they will fail as shown in the following figure. We will see how to make a Selector dynamic in a short while.

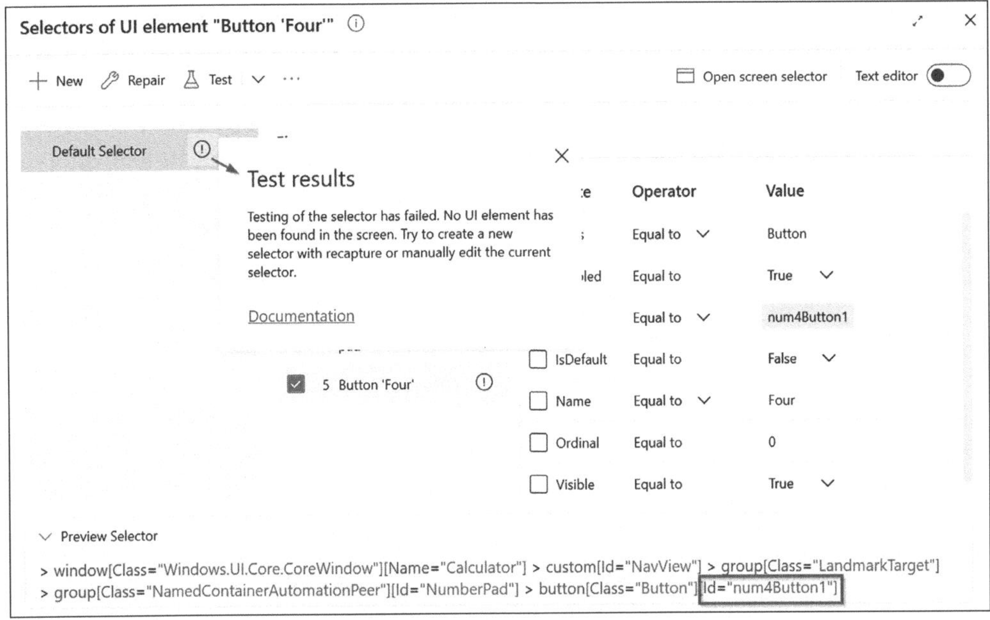

Figure 5.60: *Failed Selector testing*

So far, we have been seeing a single Selector, that is, for button 4. Let us see how Selectors for two UI elements are different. Copy the Selectors from the **"Preview Selector"** section for button 4, button 6, and the button for equals symbol, and paste them one below the other in a text editor like Notepad, and notice any differences. Here they are as follows:

Button 4

```
> window[Class="Windows.UI.Core.CoreWindow"][Name="Calculator"] >
custom[Id="NavView"] > group[Class="LandmarkTarget"] > group
[Class="NamedContainerAutomationPeer"][Id="NumberPad"] > button
[Class="Button"][Id="num4Button"]
```

Button 6

```
> window[Class="Windows.UI.Core.CoreWindow"][Name="Calculator"] >
custom[Id="NavView"] > group[Class="LandmarkTarget"] > group
[Class="NamedContainerAutomationPeer"][Id="NumberPad"] > button
[Class="Button"][Id="num6Button"]
```

Button =

```
> window[Class="Windows.UI.Core.CoreWindow"][Name="Calculator"] >
custom[Id="NavView"] > group[Class="LandmarkTarget"] > group
[Class="NamedContainerAutomationPeer"][Id="StandardOperators"] > button
[Class="Button"][Id="equalButton"]
```

As seen, the group Ids for the numeric buttons (**"NumberPad"**) are different than the ones for the operator button (**"StandardOperators"**). The **"Id"** Attribute under the **"button"** element is different for every single button, which makes them unique (**num4Button, num6Button and equalButton**). These Ids are given during the development of the Calculator application in the technology it was built in. PAD is just presenting them to us in the Selector window. Now, it will be our task as a developer of the Desktop Flow to mix and match and uniquely identify a UI element with the help of Selectors in case they are not rightly pointed by the **"Default Selector"**.

The **"Test"** Selector feature is certainly a useful and handy one. Also, be noted that at times even if the testing points to the right UI element, the Selector may fail during the execution of the Flow in certain situations. In such cases, keep making tweaks to the various combinations of the Elements, Attributes, Operators, and their Values to make it work correctly. Therefore, identifying the right Selector involves research and analysis and a trial-and-error type of work in particular scenarios.

A Sample Web Application Selector

If you refer to our recording session for the web application in *Figure* 5.12, we already have the UI elements and the Selectors for the **"First name"**, **"Last name"** text boxes, and for the **"Submit"** button, and they are as follows:

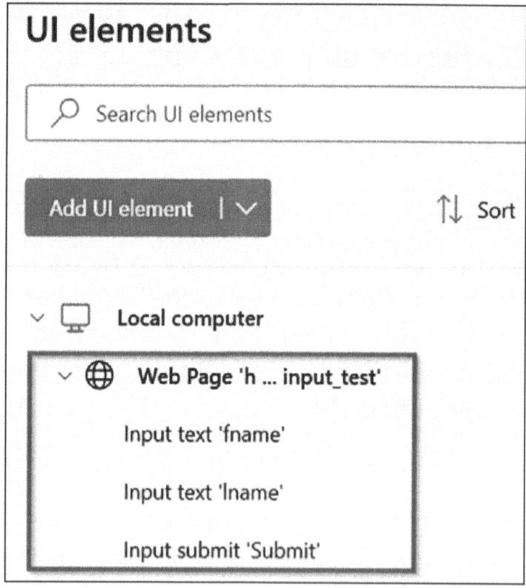

Figure 5.61: *UI elements for text boxes and button*

Open the Selector for each of them and notice that the Selector window looks the same as the one for a Desktop application seen in the previous section. The Elements, Attributes, and their Values are at the top section, and their corresponding **"Preview Selector"** is at the bottom based on whichever combinations are ticked. The format is also the same, that is, two Elements separated by the **">"** symbol and in the format as **Element[Attribute="Value"]**. The difference is that the HTML tags are displayed depending on the type of the element.

First name text box

```
iframe[Id="iframeResult"] input[Id="fname"]
```

Last name text box

```
iframe[Id="iframeResult"] input[Id="lname"]
```

Submit button

```
iframe[Id="iframeResult"] > html > body > form > input[Text="Submit"]
```

The URL of the web page is the same as earlier and is as follows:

https://www.w3schools.com/tags/tryit.asp?filename=tryhtml_input_test

Let us observe how the Selectors are retrieved in the Selector window. On the web page, right-click on the text box for the **"First name"** and click on **"Inspect"** on the context menu. The wording of this menu option may slightly differ based on the browser being used. The one used in this chapter is the Microsoft Edge browser. This will open up another pane as shown in the following figure. What we are seeing is a feature of the browser and not of the PAD tool. Here you can see the HTML of the web page and pinpoint the direct HTML tag of a particular UI element by right-clicking it and then choosing **"Inspect"**.

You will see in the following figure the entire hierarchy of HTML tags for the **"First name"** text box. If you are seeing the pane for the HTML tags as left-right instead of top-bottom as shown below, you can change the view setting using the available buttons on that pane if that is how you want to analyze the tags and their corresponding elements.

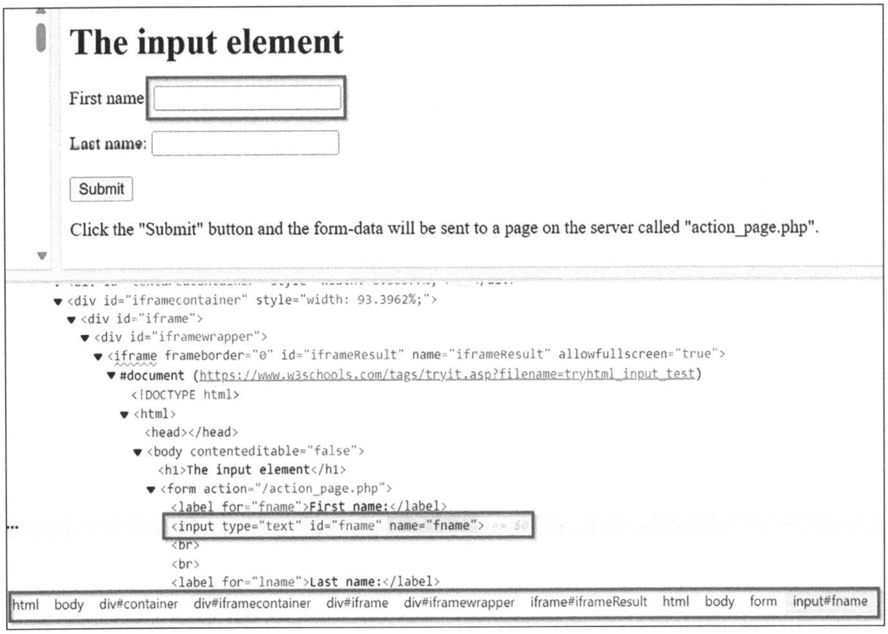

Figure 5.62: *Hierarchy of HTML tags for the First name text box*

The same structure is seen in the **"Elements"** section for the **"First name"** text box. In this case, only the **"Iframe"** and the **"Input"** HTML tag of the text box are ticked to uniquely identify the **"First name"** text box. These default combinations are presented to us by the PAD tool.

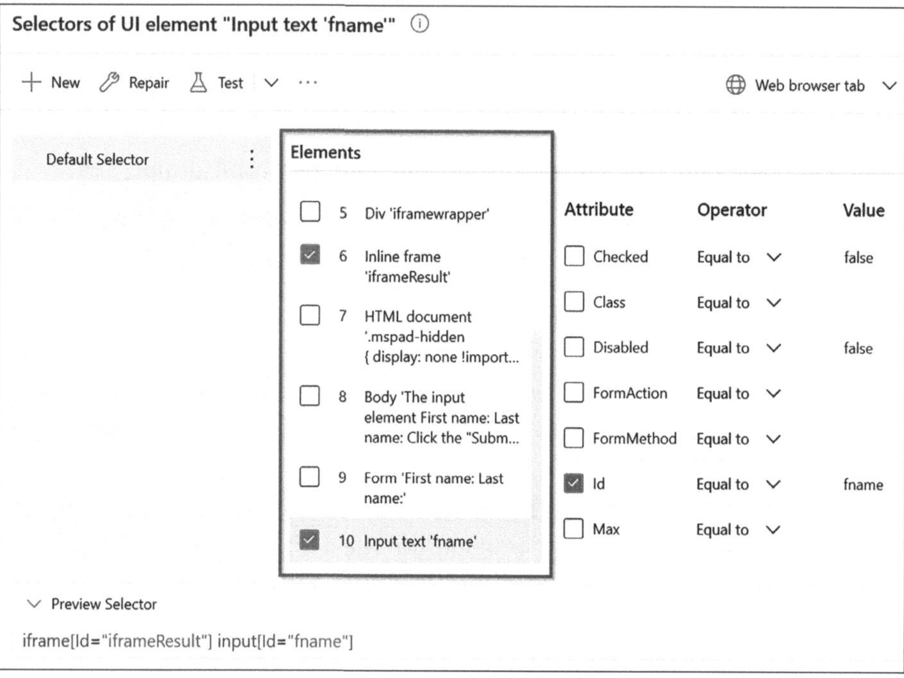

Figure 5.63: *Elements and Selector for the First name text box*

Let's go ahead and test out whether these default combinations assist us in uniquely identifying the **"First name"** text box. Click the **"Test"** button on the top left, just like the way we did for testing the Selectors of the Calculator application. As you do that, a pop-up window shows up asking you to choose the browser tab for the Selector being tested. This can also be selected beforehand by using the **"Web browser tab"** dropdown, as shown in the top right-hand corner of the preceding figure.

Select web browser tab

Select the web browser tab that contains the UI element to test.

Web browser tab

OK Cancel

Figure 5.64: *Test Selector after choosing the right browser tab*

Once you select the correct browser tab, the text box for the **"`First name`"** gets highlighted along with the name of the Selector on top of it as follows:

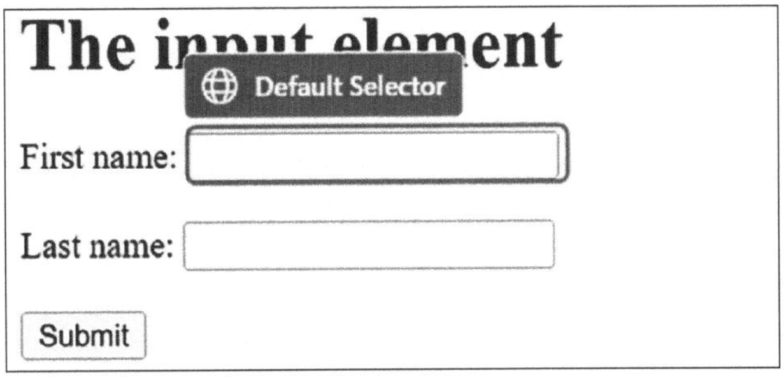

Figure 5.65: *Highlighting of First name text box during Selector testing*

Also, all of the ticked individual **"`Elements`"** and therefore the name of the Selector gets a green tick next to them, indicating that there were no failures while testing the Selector. Remember from the testing of the Selectors for the Calculator application, even though there is a green tick, it could be possible that some other unwanted UI element gets highlighted during the testing than the one we are expecting. So, it needs to be verified thoroughly before finalizing a Selector for a UI element.

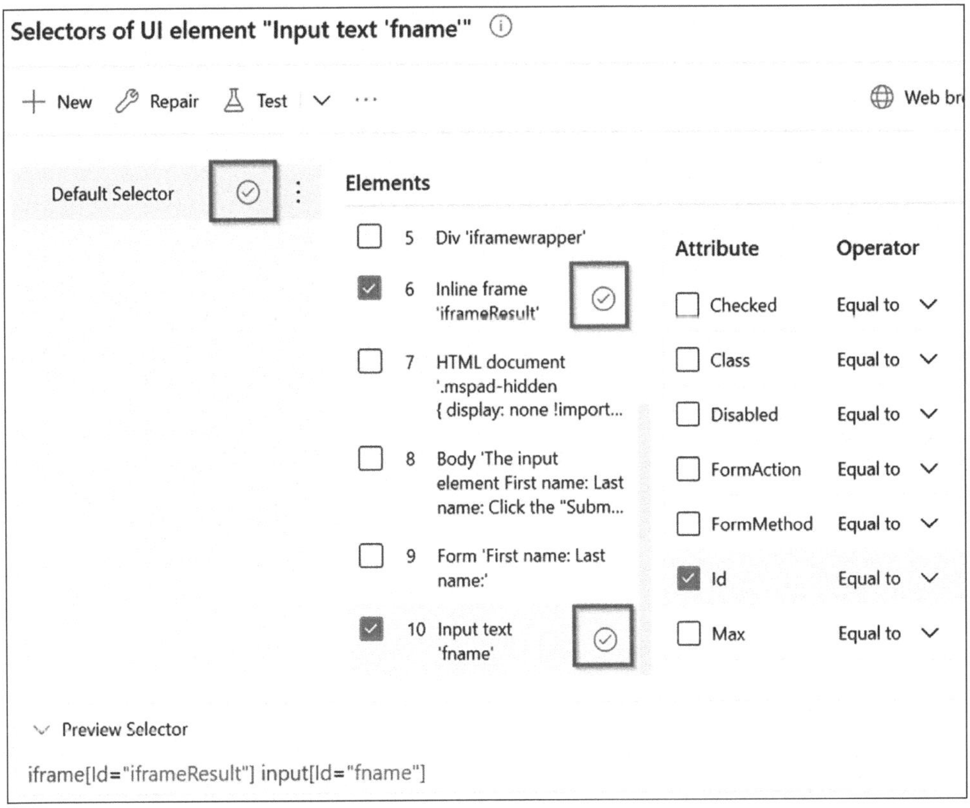

Figure 5.66: *Result of testing the Selector for First name text box*

You can experiment by ticking/unticking various combinations of Elements and their Attributes and observe the Selector testing outputs just like the way we did for the Calculator application. This part of playing around with the Elements, their Attributes, and Values plays a crucial role in identifying the right Selector if the default one does not work as expected and it comes only through practice.

The other way around is also a possible option while finding a Selector, that is, pointing to a UI element from its HTML tag. While inspecting a UI element from the browser, hovering the mouse over the HTML tag of a particular UI element in the pane will highlight that element on the browser page. This is also a feature that comes in handy while choosing the right Selector. In the following figure, hovering the mouse on the HTML tag for the **`"Last name"`** text box highlights the corresponding text box on the browser page.

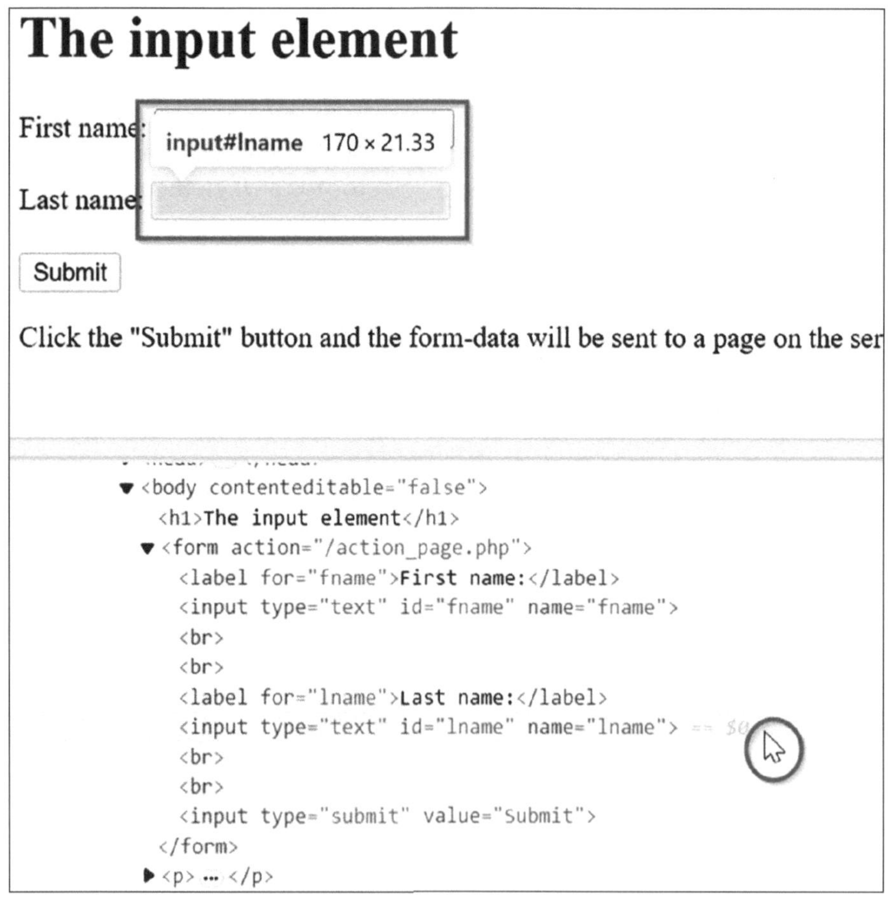

***Figure 5.67:** Highlighting an UI element by hovering its HTML tag*

In the bottom pane of the following figure, the HTML tags of all three UI elements are seen. Hover over all of them and see how their corresponding UI elements get highlighted on the browser page. This is just to see which HTML tag pertains to which

UI element and the same can then be helpful while ticking/unticking the elements in the Selector window.

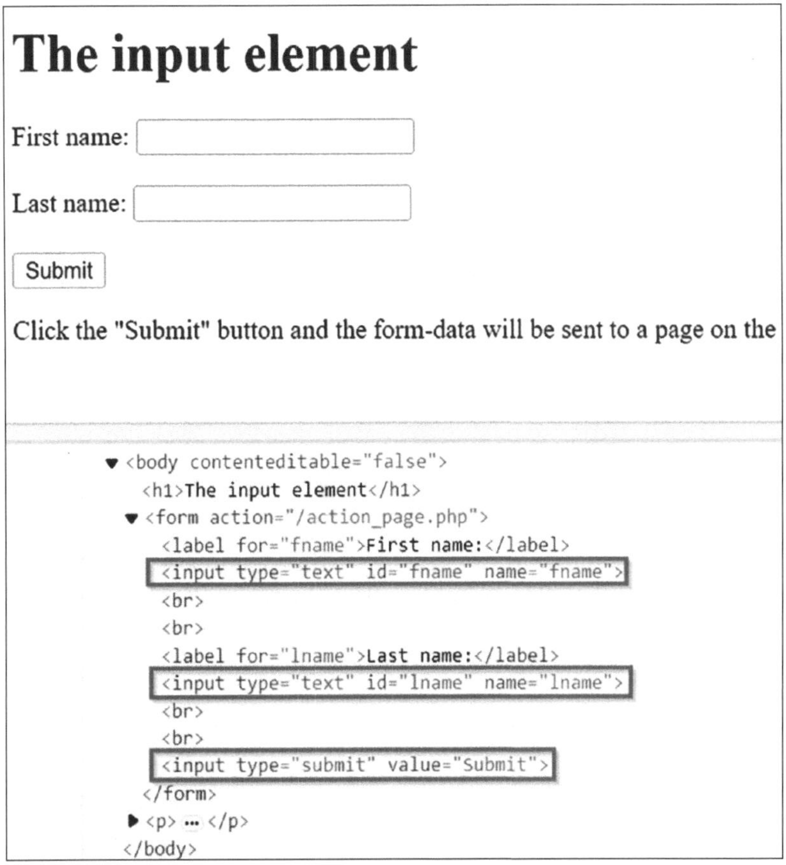

The input element

First name:

Last name:

Submit

Click the "Submit" button and the form-data will be sent to a page on the

```
▼<body contenteditable="false">
  <h1>The input element</h1>
 ▼<form action="/action_page.php">
    <label for="fname">First name:</label>
    <input type="text" id="fname" name="fname">
    <br>
    <br>
    <label for="lname">Last name:</label>
    <input type="text" id="lname" name="lname">
    <br>
    <br>
    <input type="submit" value="Submit">
  </form>
 ▶<p> … </p>
</body>
```

Figure 5.68: *Hover on HTML tags of all three UI elements*

Modifying a Selector Using the Text Editor Toggle

To understand the use of this feature, we are going to make use of a webpage for RPA Challenge, which is well-known among all RPA enthusiasts. It is like a challenge assignment that every RPA person tries to complete after learning an RPA tool. This is because the webpage uses changing positions of elements and Ids, making it difficult to identify a unique Selector, and therefore gives a good learning of the tool. The URL of the webpage is https://rpachallenge.com. What is required to be done is mentioned in the instructions on the left-hand side of the web page. For now, our focus is to uniquely identify the Selectors for the changing text boxes on the page.

Visit the preceding URL manually on a browser window. Add the UI element for the text box of the **"First Name"** using any of the options to capture a UI element ("*Multiple Ways of Creating* UI *Elements*" section of this chapter).

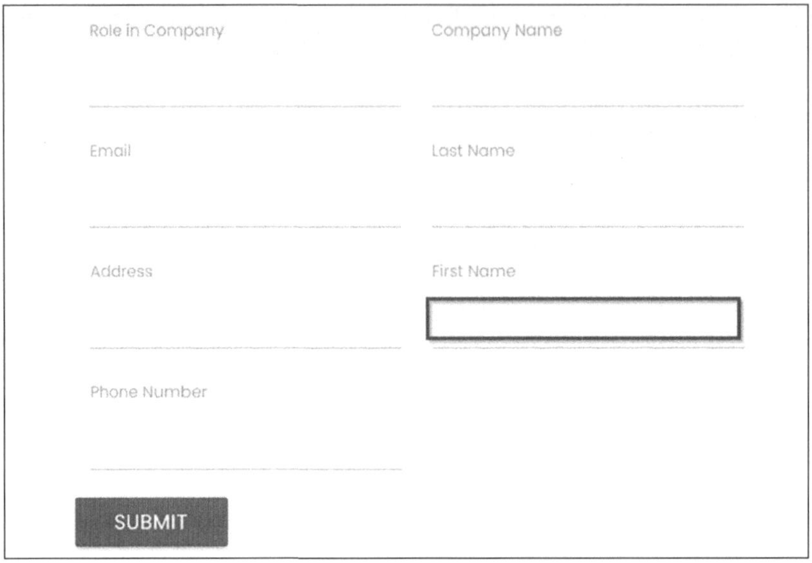

Figure 5.69: *Preview of the web page*

Open the Selector window for the UI element that gets captured. You will see that the text box for the **"`First Name`"** gets captured with an **"`input`"** HTML tag having an Attribute as its **"`Id`"** and with a Value (**`7Vavf`**). The Value that you are seeing in the following figure may be different from the one that you see on your Selector. Shortly you will know why.

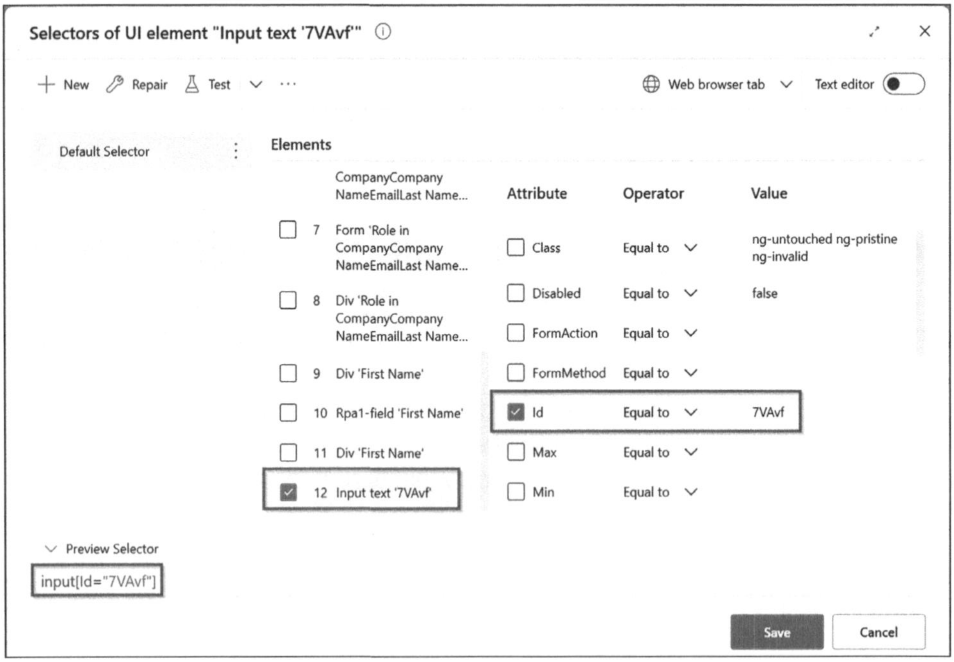

Figure 5.70: *Selector for the First Name text box*

Either Refresh the page using the browser button or click the **"`Submit`"** button (without filling any values is fine). Once again capture the UI element for the **"`First Name`"** text box. You may very well find out that the position of the text box has changed. Compare *Figure* 5.69 with the following figure:

Figure 5.71: *Changing position of the First Name text box*

You will also see one major change when you open the Selector for this recently captured UI element for the **"`First Name`"** text box. The Id of the text box (**`xVnFh`**) is different from the one captured earlier in *Figure* 5.70 (**`7Vavf`**).

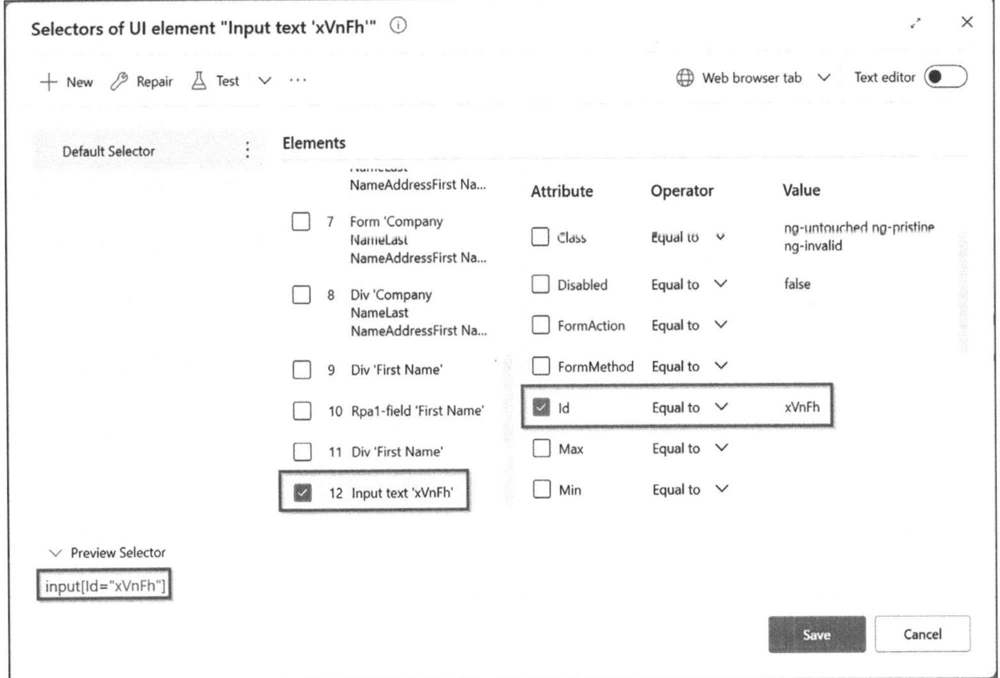

Figure 5.72: *New Id for the First Name text box*

This Id is randomly generated by the web application on every refresh or submit and that is the real challenge since it requires taking 10 different records from a spreadsheet and submitting them one by one on the page. After submission of each record, the Id of not only the **"First Name"** text box but that of all other text boxes gets changed too. If a UI element has a randomly changing Value of an Attribute on every submit, then what can be done to uniquely point to that specific element with the help of Selectors? Let's check it out in action.

What we have learned in the earlier sections is going to come in handy here. Right-click on the text box for the **"First Name"** and **"Inspect"** element. Click on the HTML tag for this text box (shown in the following figure) and copy it by pressing *Ctrl C*. You can also right-click and choose **"Copy"** and then **"Copy element"** from the menu items. Paste it into Notepad.

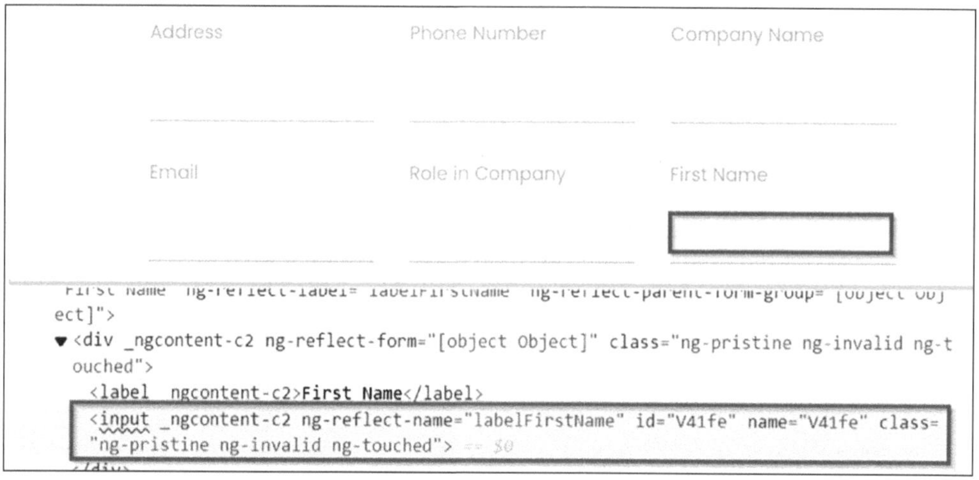

Figure 5.73: *HTML tag for the First Name text box*

Refresh the page or hit the **"Submit"** button, repeat the above procedure, and note down the HTML tag for the **"First Name"** once again. Following are HTML tags for two different instances of the text box. By doing this, we come to know which Elements, Attributes, and Values are constant and which ones are changing. It is clear that the **"id"** and **"name"** Attribute Values are different for different **"First Name"** text boxes. However, the **"ng-reflect-name"** Attribute and its Value are the same for both. For the text boxes in *Figures* 5.69 and 5.71, the HTML tags are as follows:

```
<input _ngcontent-c2=”’’’ ng-reflect-name=”labelFirstName” id=”7Vavf”
name=”7Vavf” class=”ng-pristine ng-invalid ng-touched”>


<input _ngcontent-c2=”’’’ ng-reflect-name=”labelFirstName” id=”xVnFh”
name=”xVnFh” class=”ng-pristine ng-invalid ng-touched”>
```

This would mean that we cannot use the **"id"** and **"name"** Attributes and we need to use **ng-reflect-name="labelFirstName"**. You can use the **"Test"** Selector feature using the above Selectors on various pages and will find out that they fail to identify the UI element. It will work only on the page that has a text box with the above **"id"** and **"name"**, but this is not going to be the case on every single submitted page.

In the Selector window, you won't find a check box to select the Attribute and its Value as **ng-reflect-name="labelFirstName"**. Hence, there is a need to manually add these to the Selector. This is done with the help of the **"Text editor"** toggle at the top-right corner. Click the toggle to enter into a text editor.

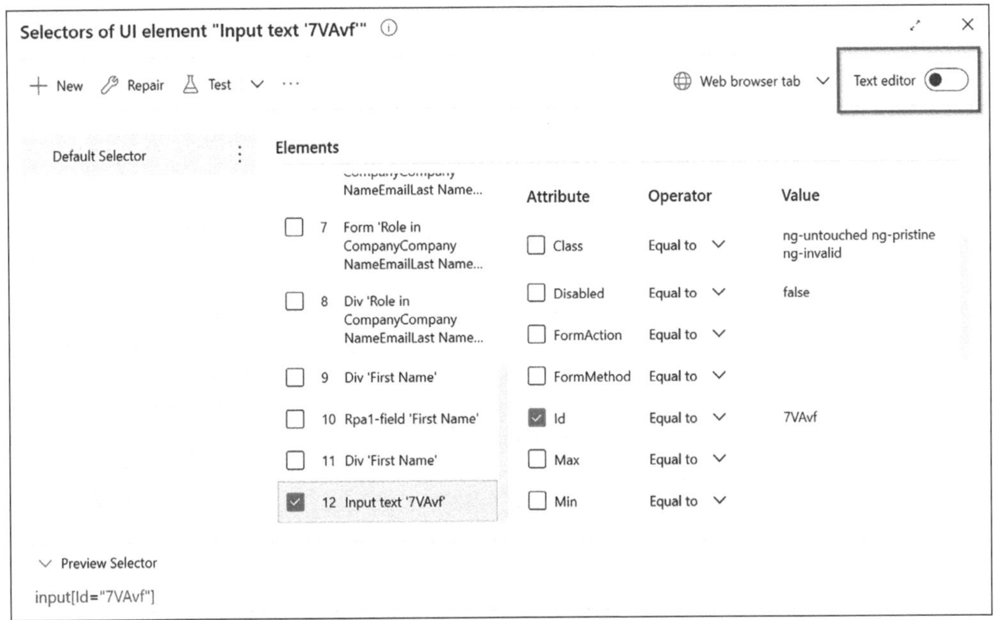

Figure 5.74: Text editor toggle option

Modify the Selector value as **input[ng-reflect-name="labelFirstName"].**

We have removed all other Attributes and their Values and used only the **"input"** element along with the Attribute and Value as **ng-reflect-name** and **labelFirstName**, respectively. Following is the window with the **"Text editor"** toggle enabled after modifying the Selector manually. Also, notice that there is a **{x}** variable picker button, which gives the ability to insert variables into a Selector.

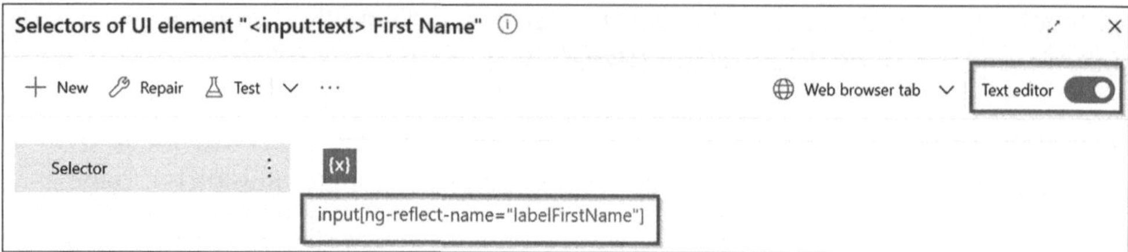

Figure 5.75: *Modified Selector using the Text editor*

This implies that if you had a variable called **`LabelForFirstName`**, which holds a value as **`labelFirstName`**, and if you used the variable picker button, then the Selector would look as follows:

```
Input[ng-reflect-name=%LabelForFirstName%]
```

Coming back to the Selector in *Figure* 5.75, hit the **"`Test`"** button and select the correct browser tab. You will see that the Selector has rightly pointed to the text box for the **"`First Name`"**.

Figure 5.76: *Testing the modified Selector for First Name*

You will also see that the green tick has appeared for the modified Selector:

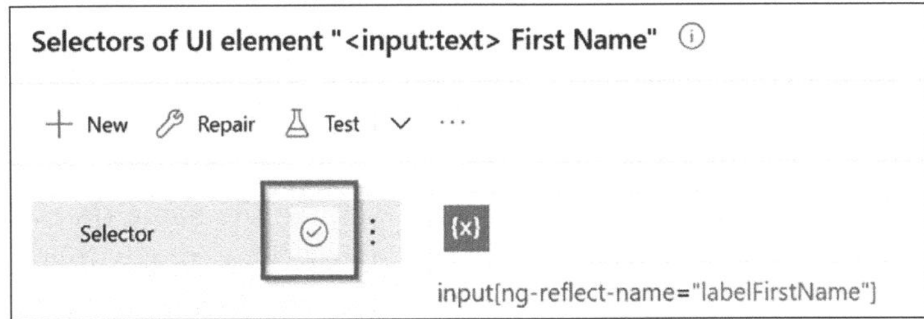

Figure 5.77: *Result of the testing for the modified Selector*

Test the Selector for different pages of the challenge website and it should point to the same text box. By using this option, the Selector provided in the **"`Text editor`"** takes precedence, and the one in the Selector window (see *Figure* 5.74) is not considered by the tool. We have successfully identified this for one UI element, that is, for the **"`First Name`"** text box, but we need to check the same for other text boxes too before finalizing this as our Selector. To identify this pattern, use the same approach of **"`Inspecting`"** the element by right-clicking on each of the text boxes, copying them, and writing them down one below the other.

```
First Name:
<input _ngcontent-c2=””” ng-reflect-name=”labelFirstName” id=”kuLcc”
name=”kuLcc” class=”ng-pristine ng-invalid ng-touched”>


Last Name:
<input _ngcontent-c2=””” ng-reflect-name=”labelLastName” id=”aPm0I”
name=”aPm0I” class=”ng-pristine ng-invalid ng-touched”>


Company:
<input _ngcontent-c2=””” ng-reflect-name=”labelCompanyName” id=”B1I1P”
name=”B1I1P” class=”ng-pristine ng-invalid ng-touched”>


Role:
<input _ngcontent-c2=””” ng-reflect-name=”labelRole” id=”2L6nJ” name=”2L-
6nJ” class=”ng-pristine ng-invalid ng-touched”>


Address:
<input _ngcontent-c2=””” ng-reflect-name=”labelAddress” id=”bcStQ”
name=”bcStQ” class=”ng-pristine ng-invalid ng-touched”>


Email:
<input _ngcontent-c2=””” ng-reflect-name=”labelEmail” id=”w6mnA”
name=”w6mnA” class=”ng-pristine ng-invalid ng-touched”>
```

Phone Number:

```
<input _ngcontent-c2="" ng-reflect-name="labelPhone" id="LytSq"
name="LytSq" class="ng-pristine ng-invalid ng-touched">
```

Do this for a couple more pages and note them down. You will find that the "**ng-reflect-name**" Values for the respective text boxes are the same on every page even though the **"id"** and **"name"** Attributes are changing. This means that we are on the right track of identifying the Selectors. It's time to add a UI element for each of the other text boxes and give their Selector values similar to that of the **"First Name"** text box.

Add a UI element for the **"Last Name"** text box, open the Selector window, enable the toggle for the **"Text editor"**, and provide the Selector as follows. Test the Selector for different pages of the challenge, and it should highlight only the **"Last Name"** text box:

```
Input[ng-reflect-name="labelLastName"]
```

Repeat the above by adding another UI element for every other text box, keeping in mind to use the Values of **ng-reflect-name**, as mentioned earlier. After doing the same for all seven fields, you should have UI elements for each of them, with their Selector correctly modified in the **"Text editor"**.

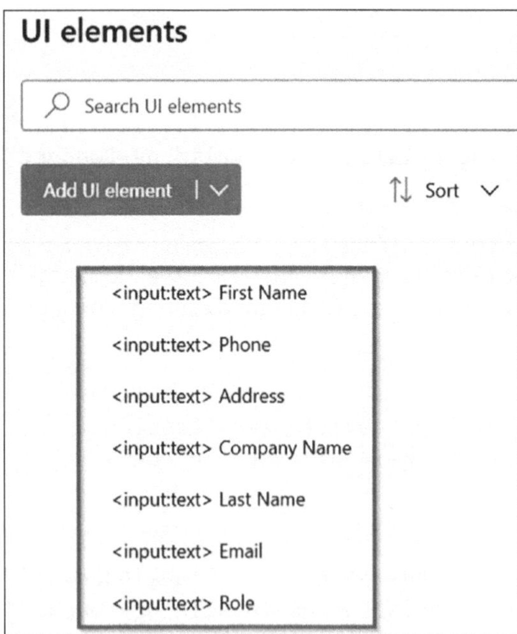

Figure 5.78: *UI elements for all the fields with their modified Selector*

As there are multiple ways, we will look at another way of finding a different Selector for this same exercise. It is an approach that is used while automating most web applications.

Right-click the text box for the **"First Name"** and **"Inspect"** the element. There is a pattern of HTML tags for each of the seven fields. There is a **<div>** tag followed by the label text followed by the **<input>** tag of the text box.

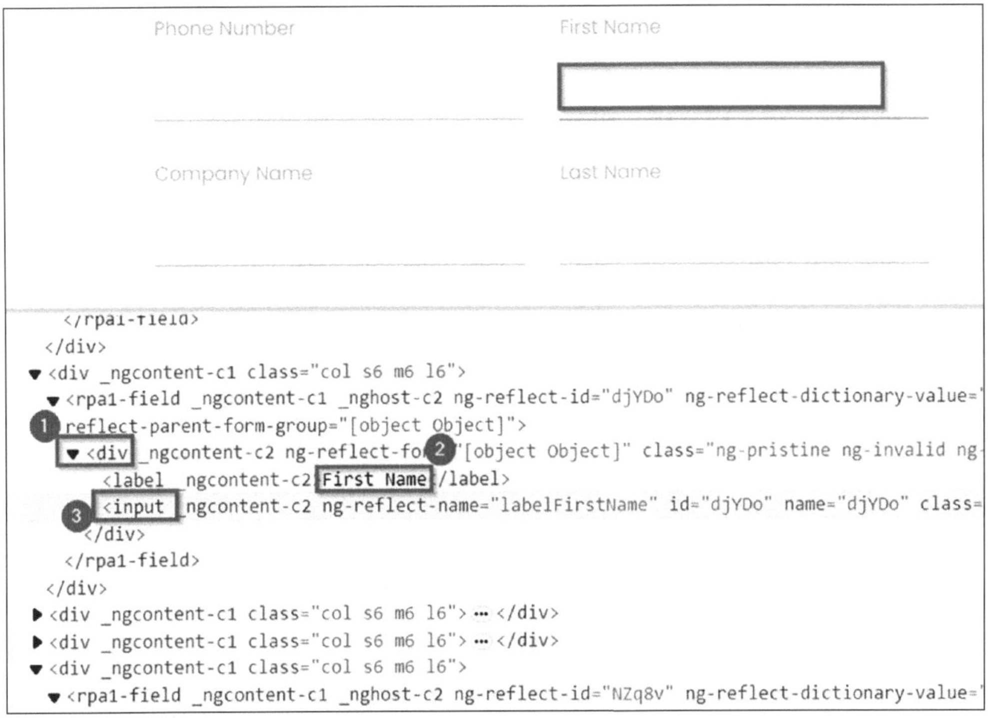

Figure 5.79: *Identifying another approach for a different Selector*

The text box for the **"First Name"** can be pointed by the following Selector syntax. Either create a new UI element for each of the seven fields (giving a different name to the UI element such as **FirstName_AnotherApproach**) or modify the Selectors of the same UI element we created using the toggle option in the previous section. Test this Selector and see that the tool highlights the **"First Name"** text box:

```
Div:contains("First Name") > input
```

Likewise, the Selectors for all the other fields based on their label text are as follows:

```
Last Name:
div:contains("Last Name") > input

Company:
div:contains("Company Name") > input

Role:
div:contains("Role in Company") > input
```

Address:
```
div:contains("Address") > input
```

Email:
```
div:contains("Email") > input
```

Phone Number:
```
div:contains("Phone Number") > input
```

You can learn about the content required for such web-related topics on the same website we have been using. Navigate through the different sections on the left-hand side of the following links:

HTML:

https://www.w3schools.com/html/

CSS Selector Reference:

https://www.w3schools.com/cssref/css_selectors.php

CSS Attribute Selectors:

https://www.w3schools.com/css/css_attribute_selectors.asp

jQuery Selectors:

https://www.w3schools.com/jquery/jquery_ref_selectors.asp

We have found two working approaches for identifying the right Selectors. Completing this exercise further requires knowledge of Excel automation. Save this Desktop Flow by a suitable name such as **"RPA Challenge"**, and we will continue on this Flow in the "*Web Automation*" topic of the next chapter after learning how to perform Excel automation.

Creating a Custom Selector with Variables and Operators

Creating a custom Selector by using variables and Operators allows to create dynamic Selectors, which helps to automate scenarios having dynamic or changing content. One way of creating a custom Selector is by passing a variable to the Selector as in the example for **input[ng-reflect-name=%LabelForFirstName%]**, where the name enclosed within the percent sign is a variable. PAD will dynamically fill in the variable's value into the Selector and point to a corresponding UI element if it matches. A hypothetical example is, let's say there are multiple links to download a file that has a caption based on a date. For example, assuming today's date is 11-06-24 and if the captions for different links are **"Download file for 11-06-24"**, **"Download file for**

10-06-24", and so on for the past five days, then the tool will get today's date into a variable and pass that variable to the Selector text after the wordings **"Download file for "** and point to today's link. Along with the **"Text editor"** option we saw earlier, variables can also be passed from the Selector window. *Figure* 5.80 shows the **{x}** variable picker button with a variable inserted after getting the current date and how the **"Preview Selector"** section looks like after doing so.

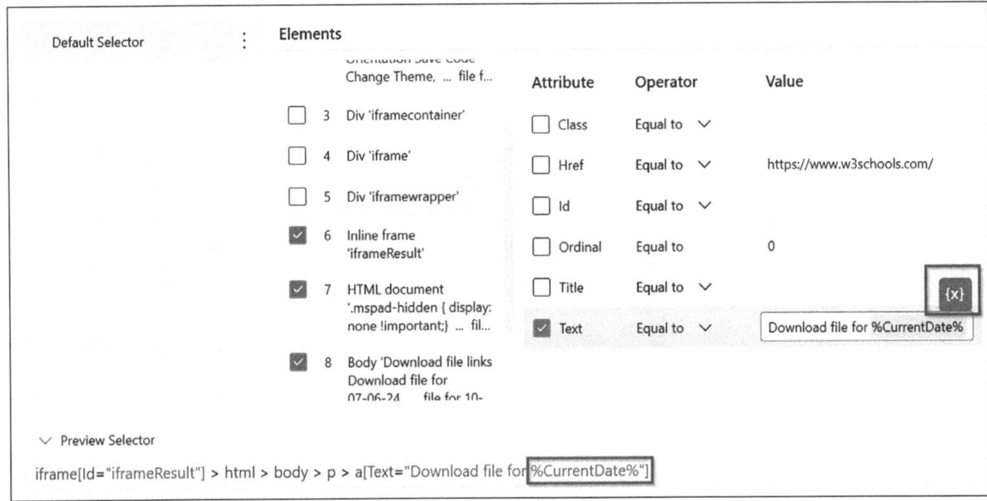

***Figure* 5.80:** *Variables in Selector*

As another way to create a custom Selector, the Selector window in Power Automate Desktop provides multiple operators. These operators are seen in the dropdown of relevant Attributes.

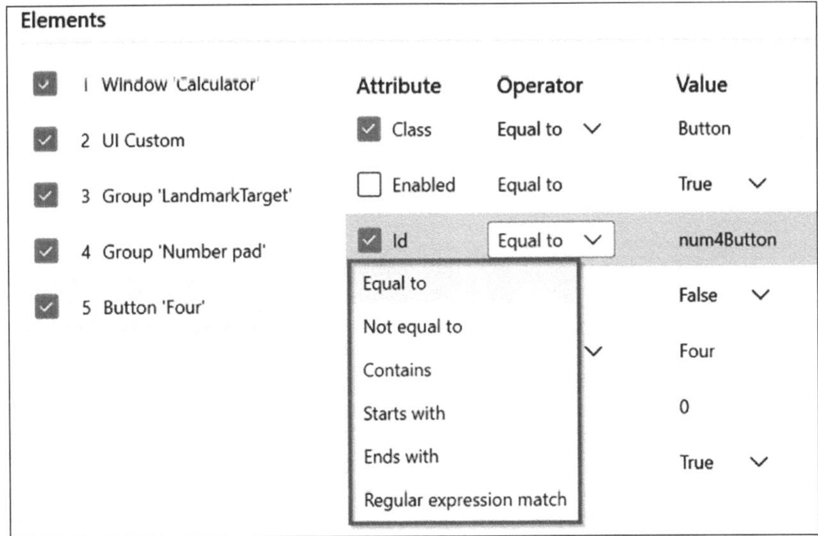

***Figure* 5.81:** *Operators context menu for Selectors*

We already have a Selector for button 4 of the Calculator application. As in the preceding figure, it is currently identifying this button when the **"Id"** Attribute is **"Equal to"** a Value of **"num4Button"**. This Value contains 4 in its text so we will use the **"Contains"** operator and give its Value to compare as 4 as shown in the following figure:

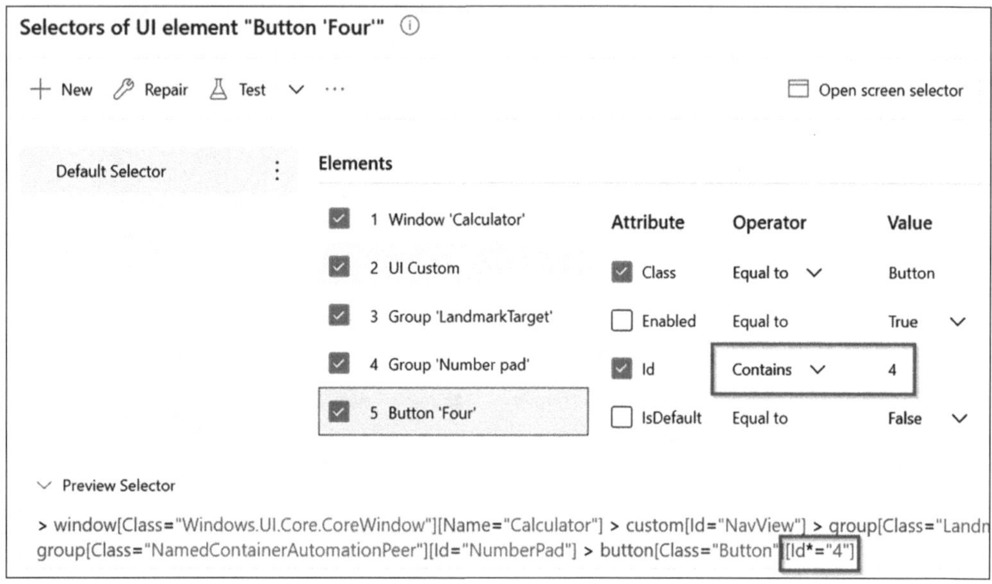

Figure 5.82: *Example of Contains operator in Selector*

When you use this Selector and run the Flow that was generated by the Recorder for **4 + 6 =**, then the Flow rightly clicks the button 4 on the Calculator app.

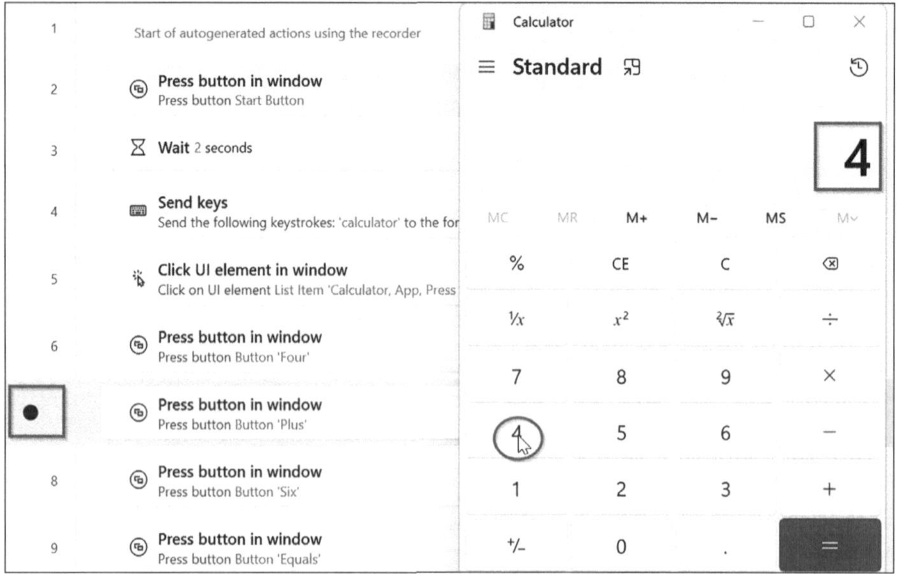

Figure 5.83: *Output of Flow with Contains operator in Selector*

You need to use these Operators when you are sure that there are not going to be multiple elements with the same Value. For example, if there was another button that contained 4 in its Value for the **"Id"** Attribute, then the Selector would have pointed to multiple UI elements and would give an undesired outcome.

Like the **"Contains"** and the **"Equal to"** operators, there are a few more Operators that can be made use of depending on the scenario we are trying to automate. Also notice in the **"Preview Selector"** section of *Figure* 5.82, that a **"*"** symbol is added to represent a **"Contains"** operator. Likewise, let's see what other Operators we have and what are their symbolic representations for the same Attribute Value of button 4 as an example.

Equal to - **[Id="4"]** - The Selector searches for Attribute with a specific value.

Contains - **[Id*="4"]** - The Selector searches for Attribute that will always have a specific text anywhere in its value (like the Calculator example we just saw using Contains).

Not equal to - **[Id!="4"]** - The Selector searches for Attributes that have anything other than the specified value.

Starts with - **[Id^="4"]** - The Selector searches for Attribute that begins with the specified value.

Ends with - **[Id$="4"]** - The Selector searches for Attribute that ends with the specified value.

Regular expression match - **[Id@="4"]** - The Selector searches for Attribute that match with the specified regular expression.

(A regular expression is a sequence of characters that specifies a matching pattern within a given text.)

Text-Based Selectors

PAD gives a provision to create Selectors based on a text on a UI element. These are used in scenarios where UI elements always have a specific text in Web or Desktop applications. Text-based Selectors can be created from the **"Add UI element"** button from the right-hand side pane of the Flow designer or from the Actions, which allow to create UI elements, for example, the **"Press button in window"** has an **"Add UI element"** option. They cannot be created by the Recorder.

Let's say there is a text on the screen that will hold the names of different Students in the following format. The text **"Name:"** will always be fixed and the actual first name and last namc will changc:

```
Name: John Doe
```

Our idea will be to create a text-based Selector that starts with **"Name:"** so that we get the entire text along with the full name of the person, and then later we can extract only the first name and last name of the person with the help of Text functions (used in "*Chapter 7: File Management and Data Manipulation*"). Following is a sample screen:

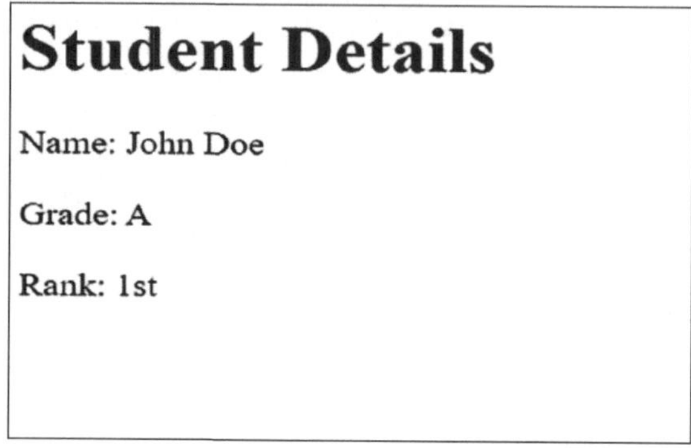

Figure 5.84: *Sample screen with specific text*

To create a text-based Selector, click the **"Add UI element"** button from the **"UI elements"** pane. Right-click on the desired element and choose **"Capture based on text"** from the context menu.

Figure 5.85: *Context menu for creating text-based Selectors*

A small window shows up with the list of operators seen earlier along with the text value that the Selector should be generated for. We will choose the **"Starts with"** operator and the value as **"Name:"** since we want to capture anything that begins with **"Name:"** on the screen. Notice that there is also a provision to use a variable picker in case the **"Text value"** parameter should come dynamically from a variable.

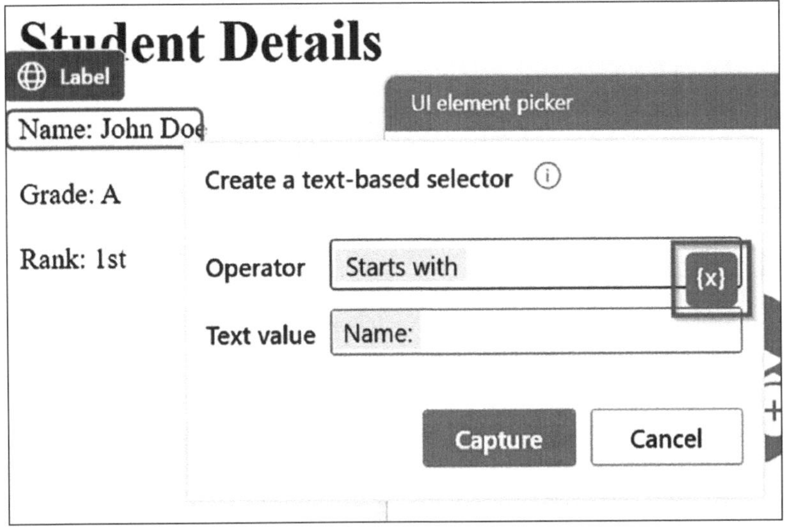

***Figure 5.86:** Setting the operator and value for the text-based Selector*

Notice how the Selector gets created. An Element with a **Text** Attribute with Operator as **"`Starts with`"** and a Value as **"`Name:`"** exactly as the way we chose on the small window above while creating the text-based Selector. When the Flow runs, the Selector will try to find an element that matches the given conditions. It will return us the full value of the Label as **"`Name: John Doe`"**, and then we will extract only the first and last name, which can be any name. We can do the same with the Grade and Rank from *Figure* 5.84 as they all have specific texts.

Elements

5 Div 'iframewrapper'
6 Inline frame 'iframeResult'
7 HTML document '.mspad-hidden { display: none !important;} ... }...
8 Body 'Student Details Name: John Doe Grade: A Rank: 1st'
9 Form 'Name: John Doe Grade: A Rank: 1st'
10 Label 'Name: John Doe'

Attribute	Operator	Value
Class	Equal to	
For	Equal to	
Id	Equal to	
Ordinal	Equal to	0
Title	Equal to	
Text	Starts with	Name:

***Figure 5.87:** Text-based Selector in the Selector window*

As you see in the above example, the **Text** Attribute is automatically used. This is for web-based applications. For a Desktop application, the process of capturing a text-based Selector is the same but instead of the Text Attribute, the **Name** Attribute of the captured element is used. In short, this type of Selector can be used for UI elements with a Name or Text Attribute that hold a value for Desktop and Web applications, respectively.

Multiple Selectors

Power Automate Desktop has a feature to create multiple Selectors for the same UI element. This is handy when the UI elements on the screen are tricky and you found out that a particular Selector works in one situation but another Selector works in a different situation for the same UI element. This is done either via the **"`New`"** button on the Selector window or through the **"`Create a copy`"** menu item from the ellipsis button.

Once created, PAD has a unique feature such that when the Flow runs and if a Selector fails, automatically the next Selector is checked against the UI element, and the next if that too fails. This happens in sequential order as per the multiple Selectors listed. You can very well change the order of the Selectors listed.

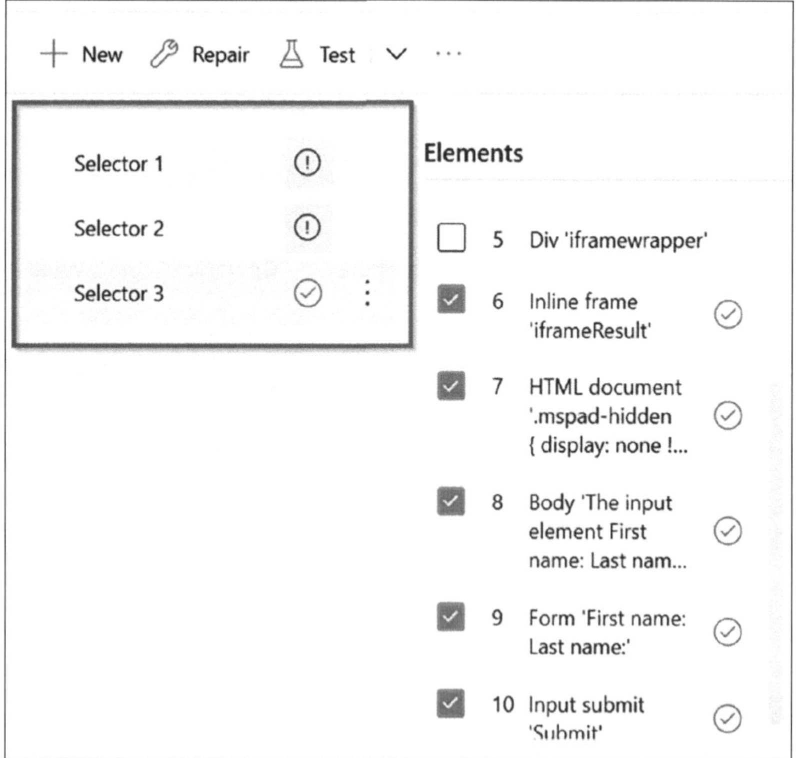

Figure 5.88: *Sequential verification of multiple Selectors*

There are certain operations that can be performed on a Selector such as follows. This context menu can be pulled out from the ellipsis button. The menu options to disable, move up and down, and delete get enabled when there is at least one more additional Selector.

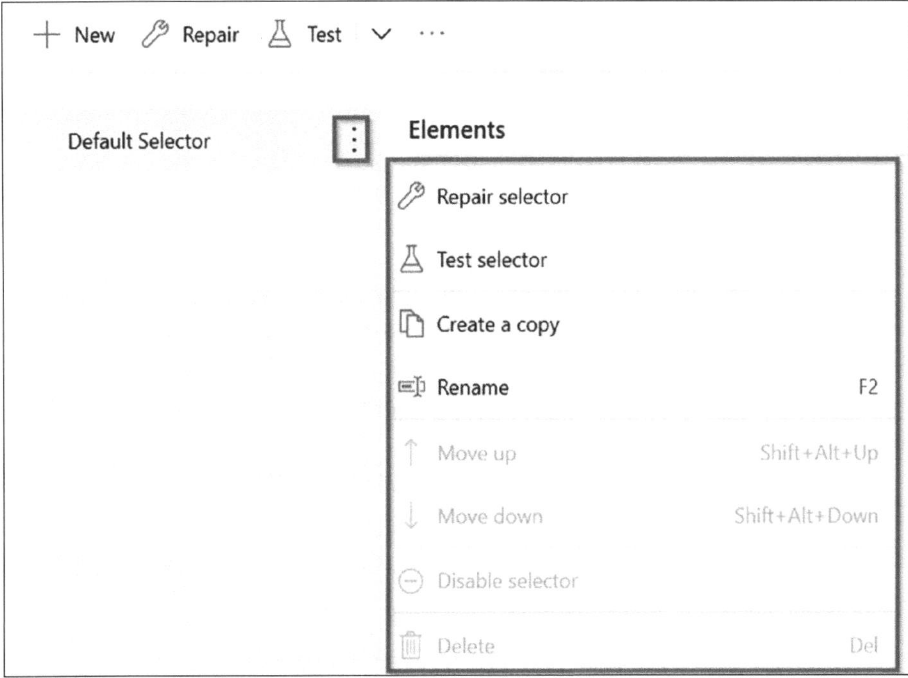

Figure 5.89: *Selector context menu options*

UI elements and Selectors are the keys to interact with external applications where data is scraped from the screens by accessing the graphical user interface (GUI) of that application. The technique is also called as Screen Scraping. To reiterate, while it is straightforward in some cases, but at times for certain applications, finding the right Selector for a UI element needs research and analysis, trial and error, and experimenting. Hence good hands-on on these topics and techniques is necessary.

You will also need to have a continued exploration and understand any currently known issues, limitations, and their workarounds, which will keep on changing as and how new updates of the PAD tool are released. Following are some links to go through:

- Inspect a UI element (different from the Inspect element feature of the browser explained in this chapter):
  https://learn.microsoft.com/en-us/power-automate/desktop-flows/inspect-ui-elements
- Automate using UI elements:
  https://learn.microsoft.com/en-us/power-automate/desktop-flows/ui-elements

- Repair a Selector:
  https://learn.microsoft.com/en-us/power-automate/desktop-flows/repair-selector
- Handle date and color pickers on web pages:
  https://learn.microsoft.com/en-us/power-automate/desktop-flows/recording-flow#handle-date-and-color-pickers-on-web-pages

Actions

We have been using plenty of Actions all along our way from the previous chapters. As mentioned earlier in this chapter, understanding which Action is used for what purpose comes with exploring the details of each Action in the **"Actions"** pane, with a little learning and practice, and with trial and error on certain occasions based on how the Action behaves for the given inputs. They are so important that a Desktop Flow cannot work without an Action.

In general, Actions have a common set of features. Follow along the numbering in the below figure:

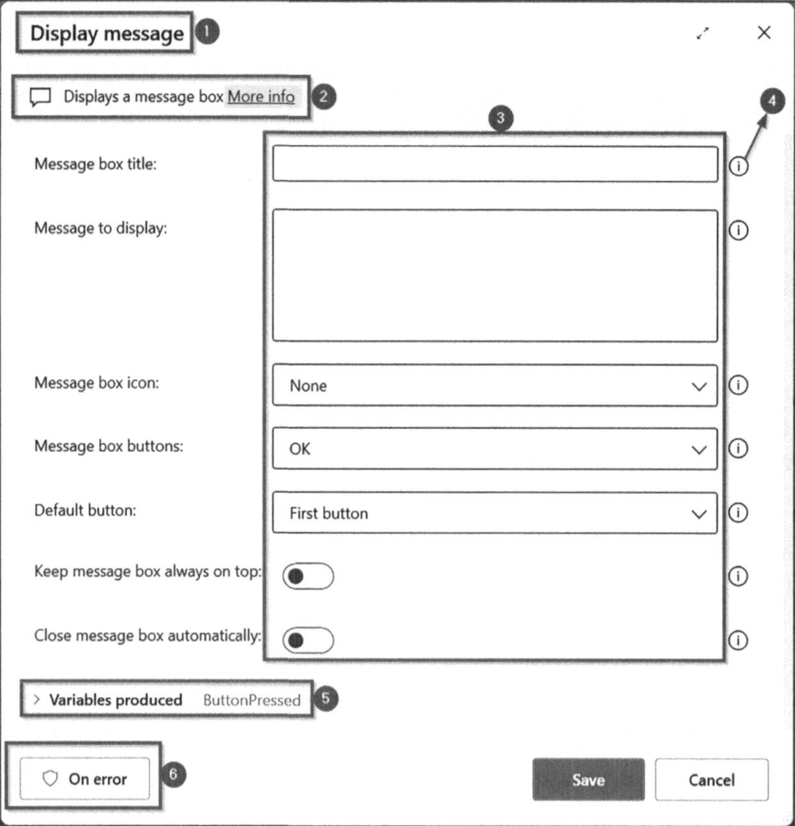

Figure 5.90: *Different parts of an Action*

1. This section shows the name of the Action.
2. Hovering the mouse on each of the Actions in the **"Actions"** pane gives a little tooltip text showing what that Action is used for. A similar short description is displayed after opening the properties of that Action, as shown in section 2 of the figure. The **"More info"** link points to the Microsoft documentation for this Action.
3. These sections indicate what input parameters need to be passed to the Action for it to function appropriately. The inputs could be a text box, a toggle button, a dropdown, or anything suitable to provide that input. Some Actions also have an **"Advanced"** section to choose the input parameters.
4. Hovering the mouse over the **'i'** information icon next to a parameter gives a tip text about what that parameter does or is used for.
5. The **"Variables produced"** section shows a list of variables and their short description. They are produced as an output of the Action.
6. Most of the Actions have the **"On error"** button, and we will be looking at it in detail in the "*Error Handling*" topic of "*Chapter 9: Leveling Up Your Automation Workflows*".

Conclusion

In this chapter, we have explored the building blocks that make up a Desktop Flow in Microsoft Power Automate Desktop. The Unified Recorder, UI Elements and Selectors, and Actions collectively form the backbone of any automation workflow, particularly in UI-based automations. Mastery of these features is essential for creating effective and efficient automation processes. Hence to reiterate again, hands-on knowledge of these features is a must.

In the next chapter, "*Automating Common Applications*", we will delve into practical applications of these concepts. You will learn how to automate tasks in Excel and Outlook, interact with databases, control Windows applications, and perform web automation. These skills will enable you to tackle a wide range of automation scenarios, further enhancing your ability to create robust and streamlined workflows.

Practical Exercise

All that has been demonstrated in this chapter must be practically tried out on the PAD tool.

Along with that, here is an exercise that asks to create one single Selector to perform arithmetic operations on the Calculator application. This means that one custom dynamic Selector to click the buttons on the Calculator, instead of separate UI elements and Selectors for each button.

You will be using a combination of features such as creating and adding items to a List, using variables, iterating Loops, Switch Actions, creating a dynamic custom Selector, adding UI elements, using the Recorder, reading data from the screen, and so on.

Before we begin with the stepwise instructions, the idea is to have an arithmetic operation as separate items in a List (for example, **4 + 6 =**). Then, read these List items one by one. There will be a Switch case for each of the numbers 0 to 9 and for the operators like **+**, **-**, **x**, **/**, **=**. A custom dynamic Selector will be created such that according to the number or operator in the List, the Flow will click that button. Finally, the Flow should display the result of the calculation.

1. Open the Calculator application via the bot from the Start menu similar to how it was done at the beginning of this chapter.
2. Create a List using the in-built Action.
3. Add separate items to the list via the in-built Action such as follows:
    1. **4**
    2. **+**
    3. **6**
    4. **=**

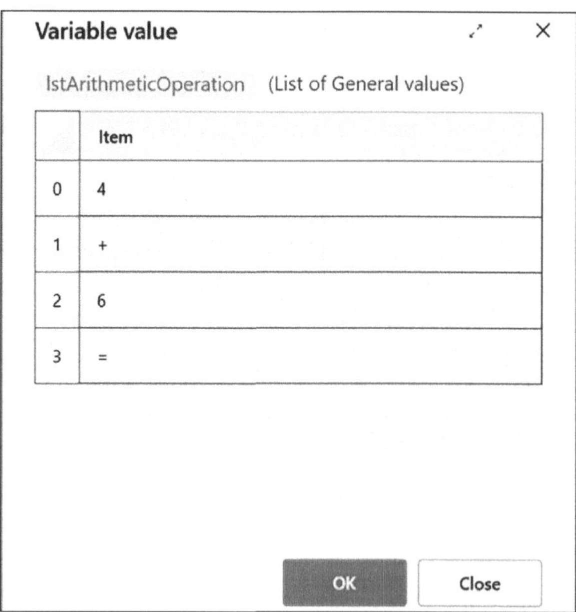

Figure 5.91: *Different items in List*

4. Add a UI element for any one of the Calculator buttons. Modify the Selector of this UI element and make it so dynamic that it will work for each of the numbers 0 to 9 and for the operators like +, -, x, /, =. There should be only one UI element and its Selector that will work for all of the above buttons. Play around with the Elements and Attributes, tick/untick them, write down the Selectors in a text editor one below the other and observe their commonality and differences, add variables where needed. Use the features explained in this chapter. Since the division sign of ÷ as shown on the Calculator application may not be easily typed in the PAD list, you can use a forward slash symbol as /. When this symbol is encountered by the Flow, it should perform a division.
5. Loop through the List created in Step 2.
6. Inside the Loop, include Switch cases for each of the numbers 0 to 9, as well as for the operators +, -, x, /, =.
7. Whenever the Flow reads an item from the List (for example, 4), it should enter into the Switch case for 4 and click the number 4 button on the Calculator. Likewise, it should do the same for the operators too using the same UI element and its dynamic Selector.
8. After the Loop is complete, the Calculator will show the result of the arithmetic operation because the last item in the List is the **"="** symbol. Show the result of the output in a message box (as shown in *Figure* 5.9), such as **"Display is 10"** for this example.
9. Once this works fine, test it for other inputs. Manually remove the old items from the List while you added items to it in Step 3 and add a new arithmetic operation to the List such as **2 x 9 =**. The output message box should show as **"Display is 18"**.

Remember, that the goal of the exercise is to have only one UI element and one single custom dynamic Selector that will click all the buttons for the given inputs and produce the desired output.

CHAPTER 6
Automating Common Applications

Introduction

This chapter will take you through a journey of interacting with the most commonly used external applications in an RPA automation process. To interact with these applications, we will be using all that we have learnt so far like Loops, Variables, UI elements, Selectors, and so on. By the end of this chapter, you will have gained a good understanding on how to read, write and interact with these common applications and use them in your automation scenario.

Structure

The topics covered in this chapter are as follows:

- Excel Automation
- Outlook Automation
- Database Interaction
- Windows Automation
- Web Automation

Excel Automation

It goes without saying that one of the most widely used applications in an RPA process is an Excel spreadsheet application. They are used either to read as input data, to process some data, to write as output or to produce a report at the end of the process. Let us take a look at the key Actions that are required for interacting with Excel applications.

Reading from Excel

All Actions for interacting with an Excel file are seen in the **"Excel"** group of Actions in the **"Actions"** pane. To read an Excel file, drag and drop the **"Launch Excel"** Action onto the Workspace. The dropdown parameter of this Action has an option to start with a blank document or to read an already existing Excel file.

Have an Excel file with some dummy data, including all types of data like columns with Date, Text and Number, a column with formula, and so on. You can also make use of the **SampleData.xlsx** file included in the GitHub folder of this chapter (https://github.com/ava-orange-education/Ultimate-Microsoft-Power-Automate-Desktop).

Use the second dropdown option and provide the full path to the existing Excel Workbook. Leave all other options as they are. Whenever an Excel file is launched, it produces an output variable of an Excel Instance type. This can be seen in the **"Variables produced"** section of the following figure. This variable can be renamed and can be used in situations where there are multiple Excel files involved, for example, to copy from one Excel file and paste data into another. In that case, there will be two Excel Instance variables which can be referred to by their own instance variable.

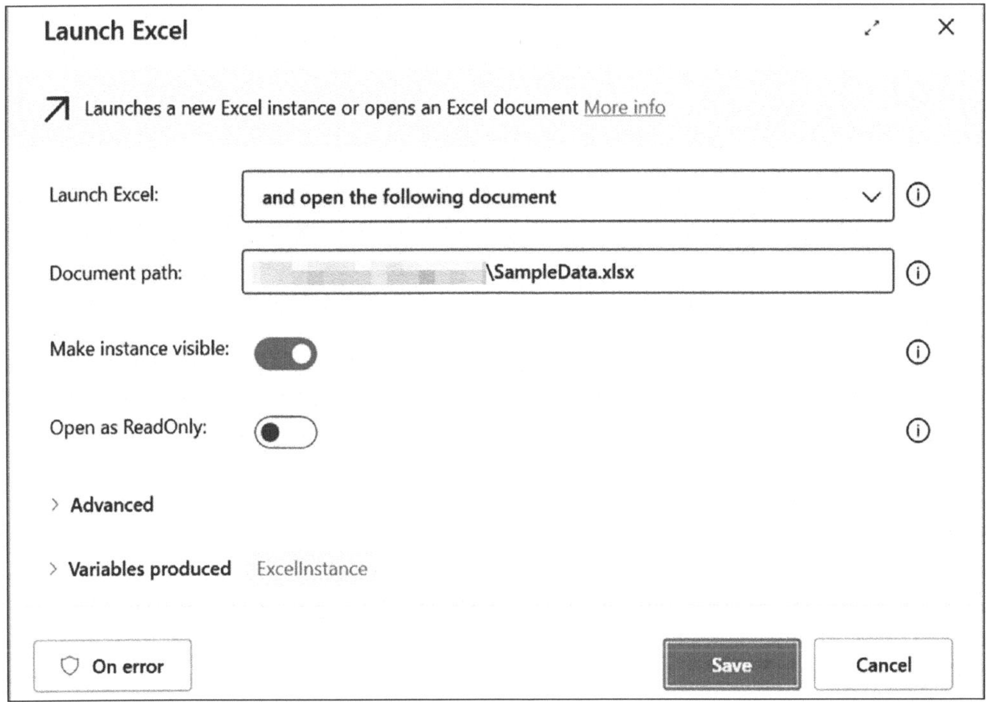

Figure 6.1: *The Launch Excel action*

We would like to read data from this Excel, but there could be several sheets already existing in this file. So, it is a good practice to tell Power Automate Desktop to point to the right sheet before starting to read, else data would be read from an incorrect sheet. To do this, use the **"Set active Excel worksheet"** Action. Provide the **ExcelInstance** that was used for this file, configure the Action to read the sheet by its name by providing the name of the sheet. The Action also has an option to read from the index number of the sheet in case the name is not known but the sequence number of the sheet is known. For example, to read data from the first sheet, use the index as 1 and so on.

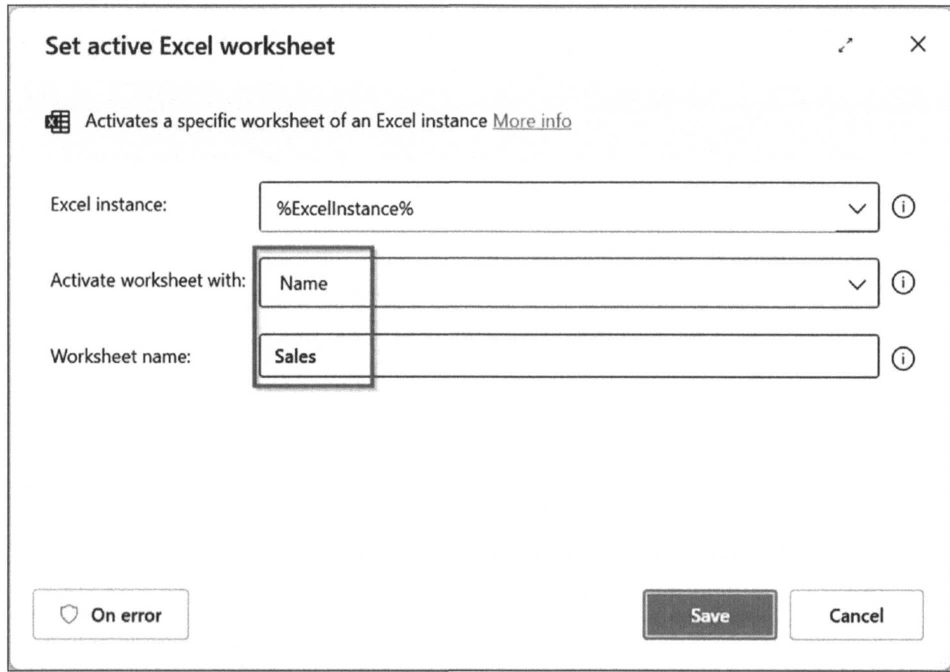

Figure 6.2: *The Set active Excel worksheet action*

To read data from this sheet, drag and drop the **"Read from Excel worksheet"** Action. This Action as the earlier one, takes the first parameter as an Instance that was opened for this file, so we will be using the **ExcelInstance** variable generated in the first figure. We would also like to read all the data from a sheet so we will make use of the **"All available values from worksheet"** option. There are multiple other options in the second dropdown and can be made use of depending on the automation scenario. For example, to read the data of only one cell we would use the option as **"The value of a single cell"** and then provide the row and column details of the cell to read the data from. Notice the **"Variables produced"** section that the output of this Action will be stored in a variable called **ExcelData**, which can be renamed though.

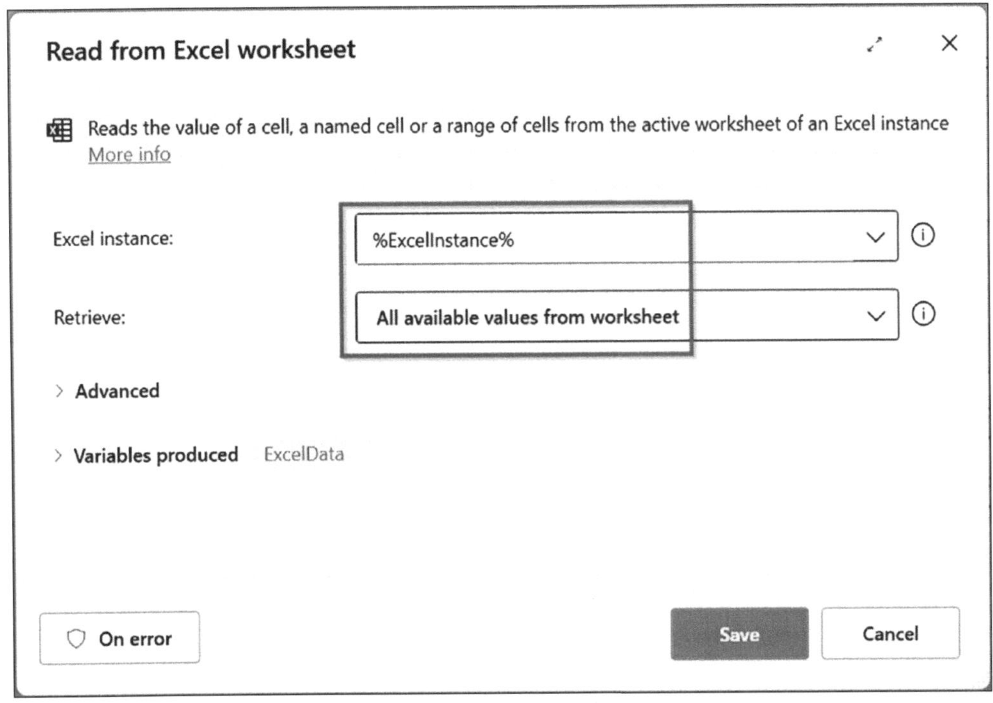

Figure 6.3: *The Read from Excel worksheet action*

Since an Excel Instance gets created in the memory, they are necessary to be closed soon after any work is done on the Excel file. This is done with the help of the **"`Close Excel`"** Action. Drag and drop this Action. The file that we want to close is the one that was opened using **`ExcelInstance`**. Provide this as the instance name in the first dropdown. This dropdown will show the list of all Excel Instances already available in our Desktop Flow. Since we did not make any changes to the file, select the second parameter to not save the document, and finally save the Action.

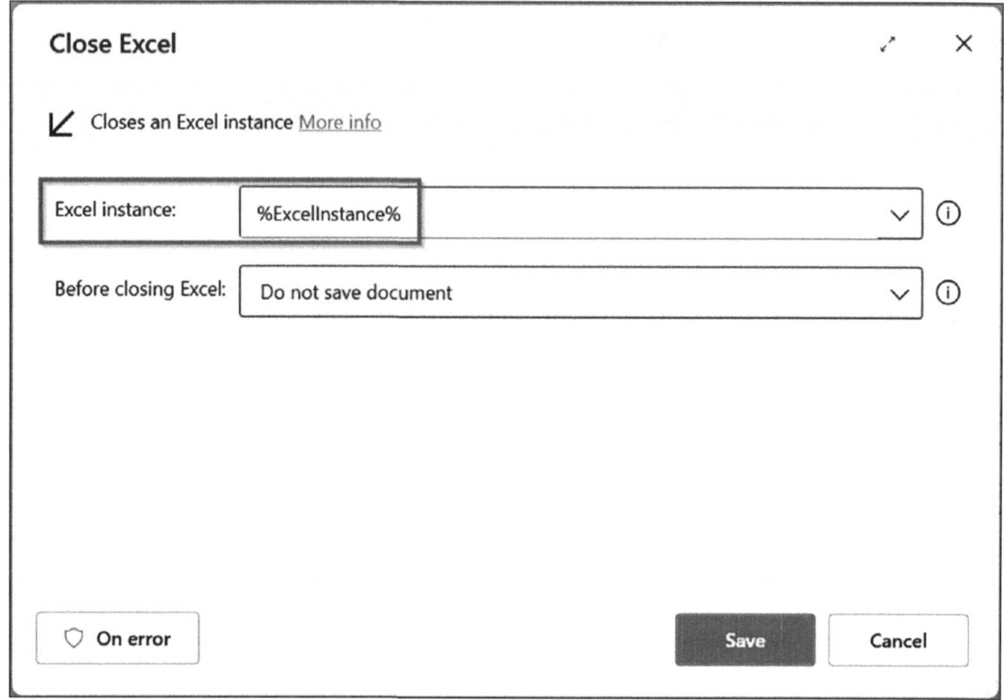

Figure 6.4: *The Close Excel action*

The Flow should now have four Actions as above ones and it's time to run it. Run the Flow and notice the `ExcelData` output variable. Following is a sample of how the input Excel looked like that was read by the tool. It has a combination of Date, Text, Number with and without decimals and a Formula column (Total Price).

	A	B	C	D	E	F	G
1	Date	City	Category	Product	Quantity	Unit Price	Total Price
2	1-Jan	Boston	Bars	Carrot	33	1.77	58.41
3	4-Jan	Boston	Crackers	Whole Wheat	87	3.49	303.63
4	7-Jan	Los Angeles	Cookies	Chocolate Chip	58	1.87	108.46
5	10-Jan	New York	Cookies	Chocolate Chip	82	1.87	153.34
6	13-Jan	Boston	Cookies	Arrowroot	38	2.18	82.84
7	16-Jan	Boston	Bars	Carrot	54	1.77	95.58
8	19-Jan	Boston	Crackers	Whole Wheat	149	3.49	520.01
9	22-Jan	Los Angeles	Bars	Carrot	51	1.77	90.27
10	25-Jan	New York	Bars	Carrot	100	1.77	177

Figure 6.5: *Sample Input Excel*

And the corresponding `ExcelData` variable after reading the file is as follows:

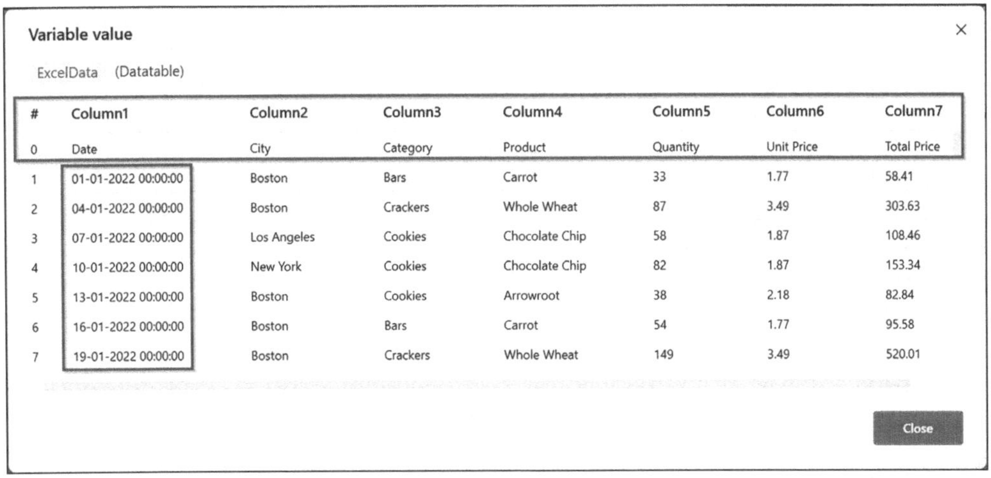

Variable value

ExcelData (Datatable)

#	Column1	Column2	Column3	Column4	Column5	Column6	Column7
0	Date	City	Category	Product	Quantity	Unit Price	Total Price
1	01-01-2022 00:00:00	Boston	Bars	Carrot	33	1.77	58.41
2	04-01-2022 00:00:00	Boston	Crackers	Whole Wheat	87	3.49	303.63
3	07-01-2022 00:00:00	Los Angeles	Cookies	Chocolate Chip	58	1.87	108.46
4	10-01-2022 00:00:00	New York	Cookies	Chocolate Chip	82	1.87	153.34
5	13-01-2022 00:00:00	Boston	Cookies	Arrowroot	38	2.18	82.84
6	16-01-2022 00:00:00	Boston	Bars	Carrot	54	1.77	95.58
7	19-01-2022 00:00:00	Boston	Crackers	Whole Wheat	149	3.49	520.01

Close

Figure 6.6: *Output variable after reading the Excel*

The **"Read from Excel worksheet"** Action was able to read all values from the provided sheet. However, there are two issues and they are marked in *Figure* 6.6. The actual column names in the Excel file are represented as the first row of the **ExcelData** Datatable variable. Also, the cell value of the **"Date"** column in Excel is extracted as date and time values in the **ExcelData** variable instead of dates given in the Excel.

These two issues can be circumvented by enabling both the toggle buttons as shown in the following figure, which are available in the **"Advanced"** section of the Action.

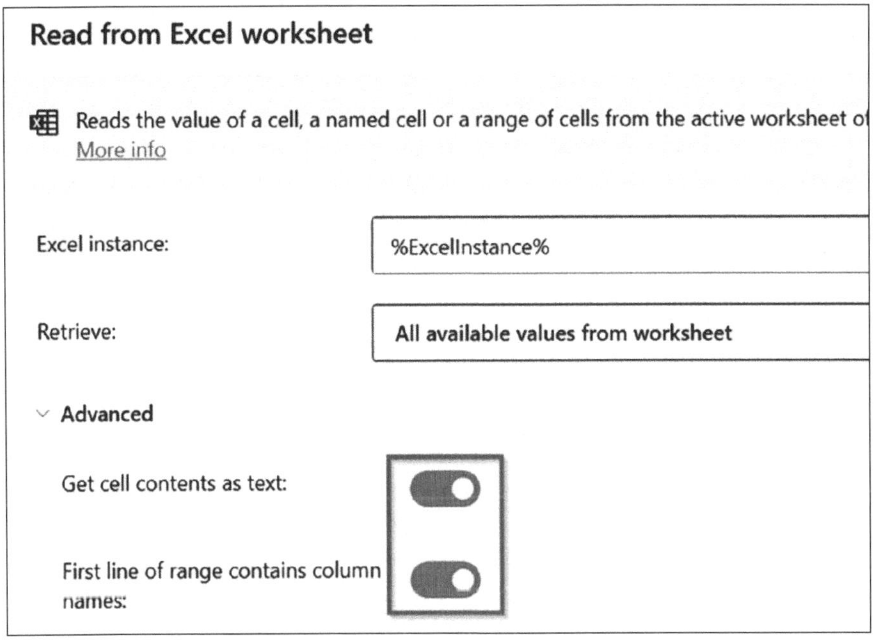

Read from Excel worksheet

Reads the value of a cell, a named cell or a range of cells from the active worksheet o
More info

Excel instance: %ExcelInstance%

Retrieve: All available values from worksheet

Advanced

Get cell contents as text:

First line of range contains column names:

Figure 6.7: *Toggle options to fix the issues*

The **"Get cell contents as text"** will extract the value of an Excel cell as they are in the form of a text. This is useful when you want to process the data in your Flow as per what is given on the Excel cell and not as per the date and time returned in the Datatable.

The option of **"First line of range contains column names"** tells the Action that the first row on the Excel sheet has column headers and therefore shows them as headers on the **ExcelData** output variable. This is particularly useful to interact with the Datatable by using the actual column names and not as the one seen above in the form of **Column1**, **Column2**, and so on. Recall the topic of variables for interacting with a Datarow of a Datatable as **%VariableName['ColumnName']%** and to access a specific row of a Datatable that has a column header use the convention as **%VariableName[RowNumber]['ColumnName']%**.

After enabling the two toggle buttons, rerun the Flow and once again observe the **ExcelData** output variable. We now have both the issues fixed and the output as expected.

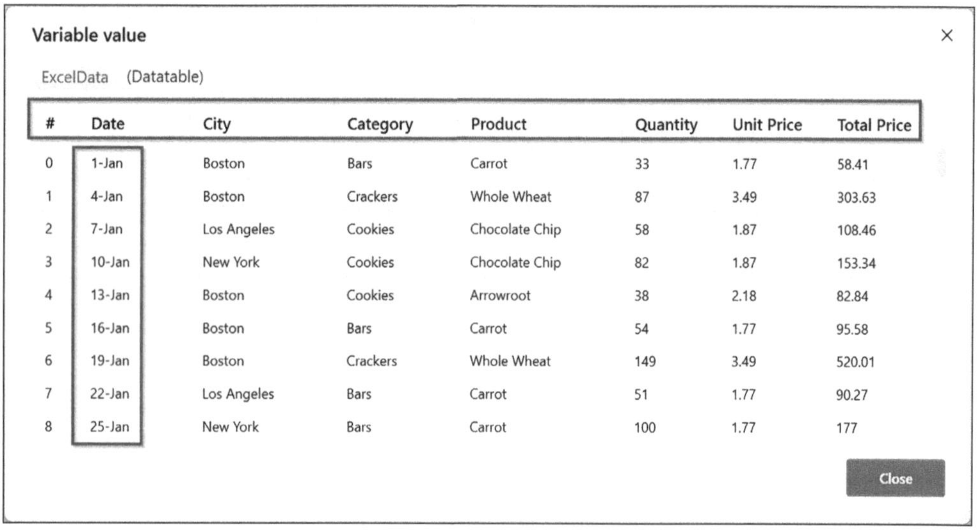

Variable value

ExcelData (Datatable)

#	Date	City	Category	Product	Quantity	Unit Price	Total Price
0	1-Jan	Boston	Bars	Carrot	33	1.77	58.41
1	4-Jan	Boston	Crackers	Whole Wheat	87	3.49	303.63
2	7-Jan	Los Angeles	Cookies	Chocolate Chip	58	1.87	108.46
3	10-Jan	New York	Cookies	Chocolate Chip	82	1.87	153.34
4	13-Jan	Boston	Cookies	Arrowroot	38	2.18	82.84
5	16-Jan	Boston	Bars	Carrot	54	1.77	95.58
6	19-Jan	Boston	Crackers	Whole Wheat	149	3.49	520.01
7	22-Jan	Los Angeles	Bars	Carrot	51	1.77	90.27
8	25-Jan	New York	Bars	Carrot	100	1.77	177

Close

Figure 6.8: *Expected output after rerunning the Flow*

These are key issues encountered while accessing Excel files and hence are showcased here.

There are two other options in the **"Launch Excel"** Action of *Figure* 6.1 that can be handy depending on the automation scenario. The first is the **"Make instance visible"** toggle which is used to tell PAD whether or not to show the Excel file during its reading or writing. Some automation scenarios require to perform Excel operations invisibly without the need to show the Excel file on the machine where the Flow is running.

The second option is the toggle for **"Open as ReadOnly"**. If enabled, a read only copy of the Excel file will be launched and interacted with. This is used in situations where no writing is required into the Excel file and only has to be used for reading data from it.

Iterating Through Data Read from Excel

To navigate through the records of a Datatable after reading from an Excel file, a **"For each"** loop is used. Drag and drop this loop onto the Workspace after the **"Read from Excel worksheet"** and before the **"Close Excel"**. It asks for only one parameter which is either a Datatable or a List or a Datarow. In our case we have the **ExcelData** Datatable, so let's pass this variable as the parameter. Notice that the output variable produced from this Action is **CurrentItem**, which is a Datarow type of variable pointing to a single row of the Datatable. The name of this variable can be changed as required.

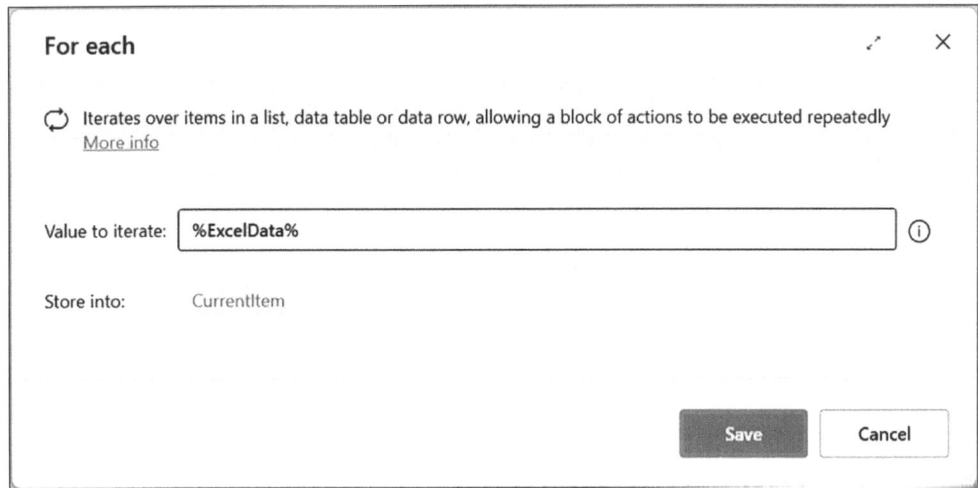

Figure 6.9: *For each loop to iterate through the Datatable rows*

Between the start of **"For each"** loop and its corresponding **"End"**, add a message box that will display the value as **%CurrentItem['City']%**. While the loop is iterating, this will display the City value of each row. Once read, these can then be stored into variables and used for further processing in the Desktop Flow as per our requirements. Another way of accessing the City value is using the indexes as seen in the topic of Datatables, that is, by using **%CurrentItem[1]%**. Both the options will give the same result. Here is the output of the first row as the loop iterates and also how the entire Flow built so far looks:

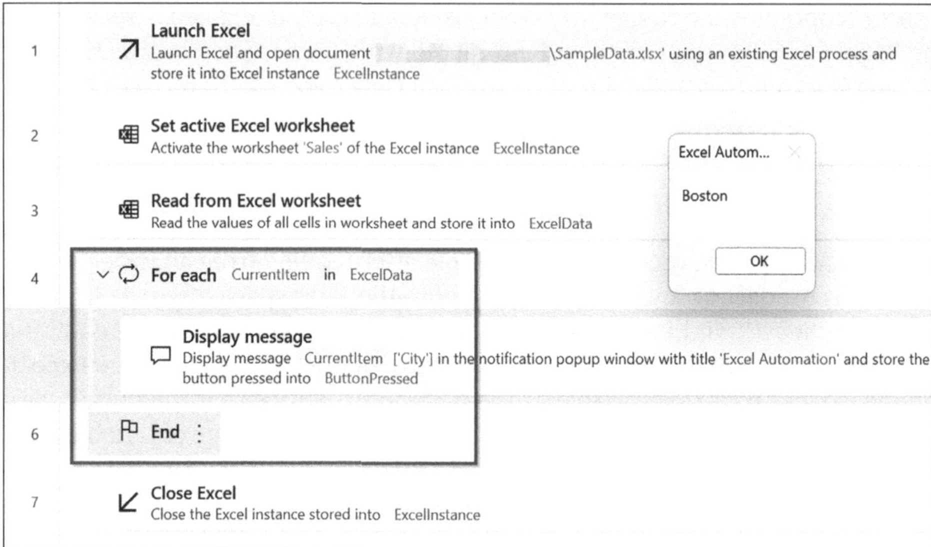

Figure 6.10: *Entire Flow with the output of the City for first row*

If you already know which row and column indexes of the Datatable you would like to read, then this can also be possible without looping and directly referring it in the format **`%VariableName[RowIndex][ColumnIndex]%`** such as **`%ExcelData[2][3]%`** or using a column name as **`%ExcelData[2]['Product']%`**.

Getting the First Empty Row and Column

During automation there arises several situations where an Excel file is already filled with rows and columns and there is a need to start writing new data from where the previous data ended in the file. In such cases getting to know the first row or column that does not have any data becomes mandatory. For this situation, Power Automate Desktop gives us an Action to identify this and the name of the Action is **"`Get first free column/row from Excel worksheet`"**. Let us make use of this Action. Disable the **"`For each`"** loop and everything inside it. Referring to the preceding figure, add this new Action after line number 3. It takes only one parameter and that is the **`ExcelInstance`** we have been using all this while. But for this Action to work as expected, we need to correctly set an active sheet which we have already done. As shown in the following figure, the output variables produced are going to tell us the first row and column that do not have any data.

Get first free column/row from Excel worksheet

Retrieves the first free column and/or row of the active worksheet. This is useful for adding new data into a worksheet that already has data in it More info

Excel instance: %ExcelInstance%

> Variables produced FirstFreeColumn FirstFreeRow

On error Save Cancel

Figure 6.11: *Getting the first free row and column that does not have data*

To see the values of these two output variables, further add a message box and print them as follows:

```
FREE COLUMN: %FirstFreeColumn%
FREE ROW: %FirstFreeRow%
```

The Excel file used here has 7 columns and 50 rows, hence the result is the next available column and row numbers of 8 and 51, respectively (refer to *Figure* 6.12).

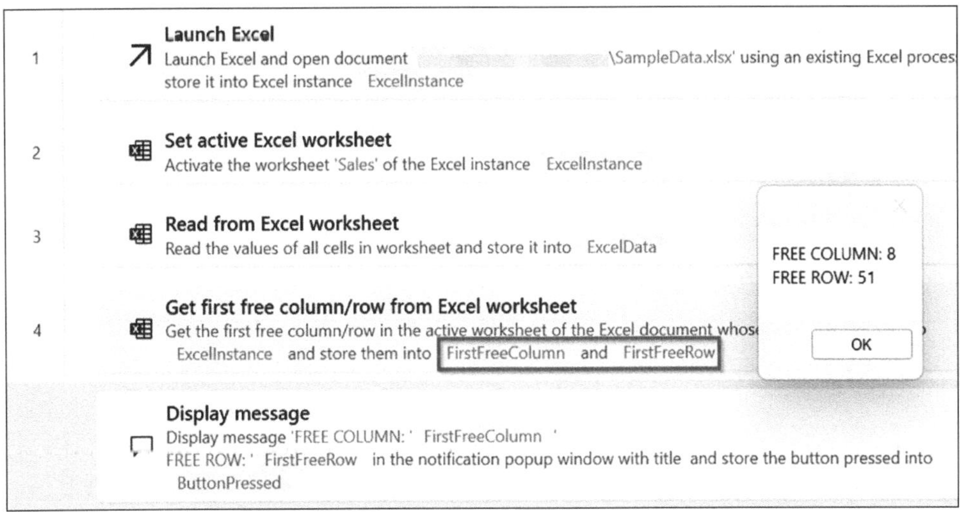

Figure 6.12: *Output of first free row and column*

There is another similar Action called **"Get first free row on column from Excel worksheet"**. In this Action, you need to specify a column number or alphabet and it will return the first empty row of that column. This is specifically used if you have a different number of rows of data for different columns. For example, have 10 rows in Column A and 15 rows in Column B and verify the difference in outputs for both the aforementioned Actions. Make sure to *not* use any Excel tables while testing the outputs. This is because if an Excel table has blank rows at the bottom of its table, the output seen will be the free row of the Excel table and not the actual free row that has no data. All of these are worth practically trying them out on the tool.

Reading Directly from the Excel File

Without retrieving the sheet data into a Datatable we can also directly read and iterate on the Excel file itself. This is particularly useful when there is a need to read certain cell values of each row, do some processing on it or even write the values on one or more cells of that row during the iteration. In this case, you do not have to read the sheet's data into a Datatable, as shown earlier, make the changes in the Datatable to write it back to the sheet.

Disable the message box Action from line number 5 of the previous section. Add a **"Loop"** Action. This loop will iterate through the rows of the Excel file. Start the loop from 2 as the Excel row number 1 has the column headers and the data starts from row number 2. As in the previous figure, the first free row is 51 which means the data resides till row number 50. Hence, subtract 1 from the first free row as **%FirstFreeRow - 1%** and increment the loop by 1 since we need to iterate through every 1 row of the Excel. **LoopIndex** is the output variable produced from this Action.

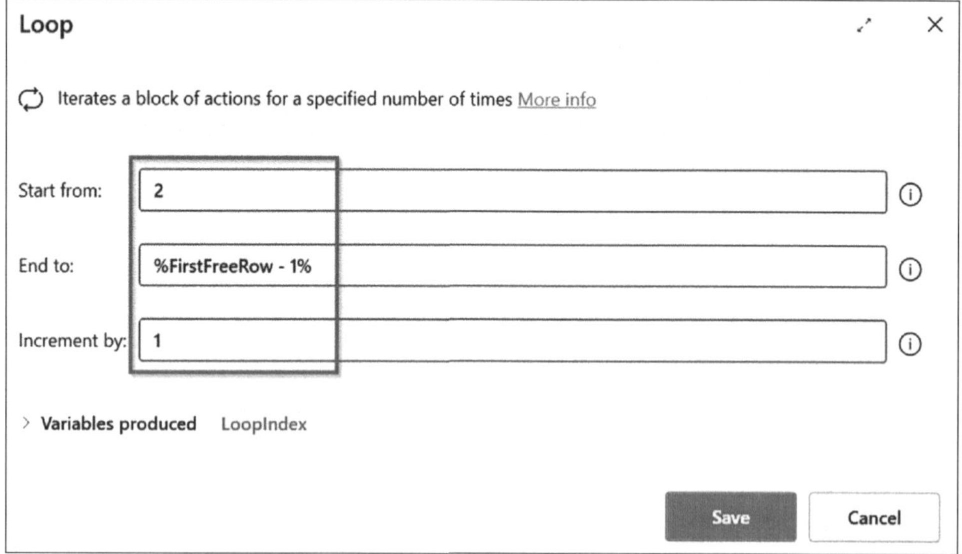

Figure 6.13: *Loop for iterating through the Excel rows*

Drag and drop the **"Read from Excel worksheet"** Action to read the value of a single cell as its parameter after providing the instance. The start column to read can be the index number or a column alphabet such as 'B' without the quotes. Provide the starting row as the **LoopIndex** variable since we are reading from row number 2. This variable will be incremented by 1 each time the loop iterates using the previous Action. In other words, as per the Excel shown in *Figure* 6.5, this Action will begin by reading the values from 2nd row of the 2nd column, then 3rd row of 2nd column and so on, or the values from cells B2, B3 and so on. Capture the output of this Action in a variable called **SingleValue** as follows:

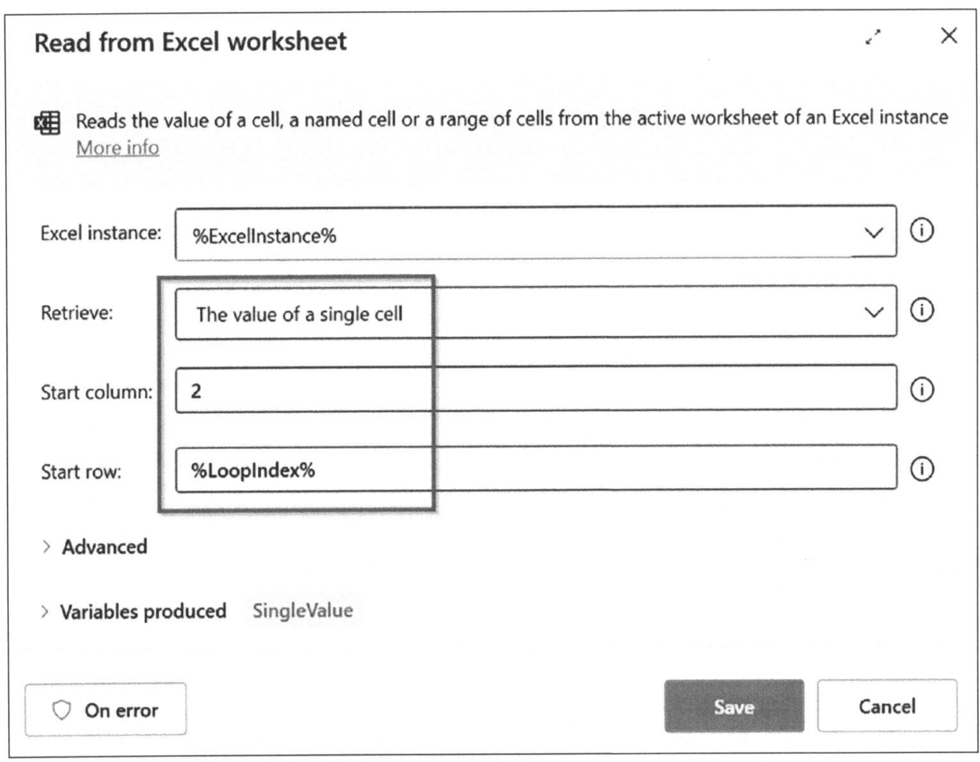

***Figure 6.14:** Reading a single cell directly from the Excel*

Display the **SingleValue** in a message box and run the Flow which will start showing the output starting from cell B2 then value of cell B3 and so on, as the loop iterates till the end. These values can be stored in variables and used for further processing in the Flow. Note that your automation is going to have several Actions within the loop and hence these variable values can be used anywhere.

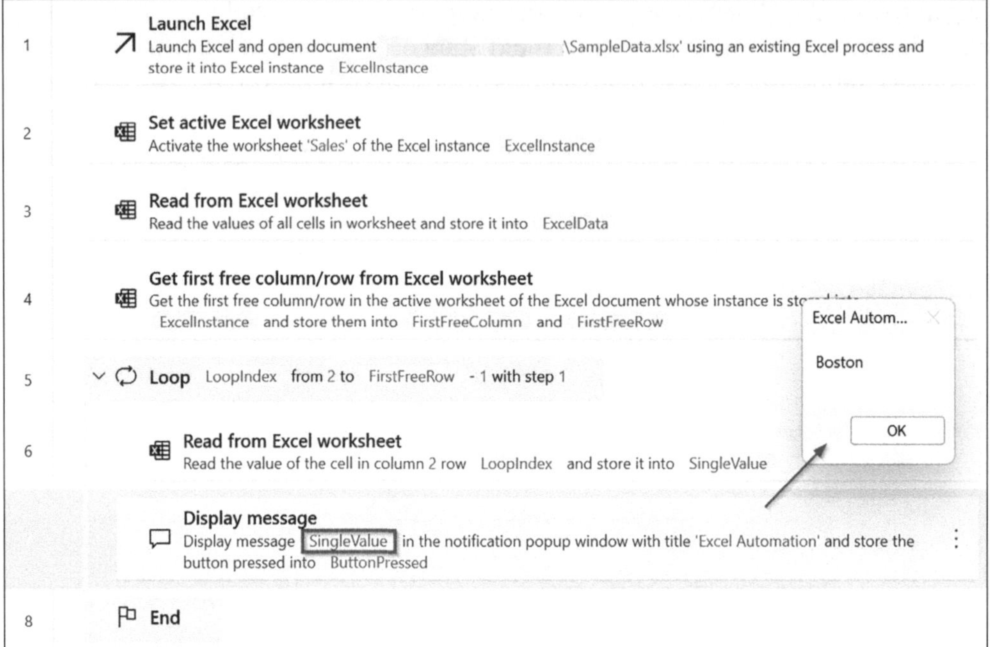

Figure 6.15: *Output of a single cell directly from the Excel*

Remember that there is also a **"Close Excel"** Action at the end of the above Flow which we haven't yet disabled and is very much needed to close the Excel after the processing is done.

Writing to Excel

A variable value holding anything like a text or a number, or a List, or even an entire Datatable can be written into an Excel file. We already have a Datatable in the form of **ExcelData** read from the **Sales** sheet in the previous section. We will write this data into another new sheet called **Sales Copy**. In our case, consider that this worksheet is already present. If a sheet is not present it can be dynamically created using the **"Add new worksheet"** Action.

We will keep the following Actions in our Flow:

1. **"Launch Excel"**,
2. **"Set active Excel worksheet"** for **Sales** sheet,
3. **"Read from Excel worksheet"** – This returns the **ExcelData** Datatable.

After these, add another Action as **"Set active Excel worksheet"** for the **Sales Copy** sheet.

The Action to write data to an Excel is **"Write to Excel worksheet"**. Provide the

ExcelInstance and the Datatable returned from Step 3 above. Since we want to start writing from the very first cell of the sheet with the column headers, choose the writing mode as **"On specified cell"**, Column as A and Row as 1. Instead of the column alphabet, a column number as 1 can also be specified.

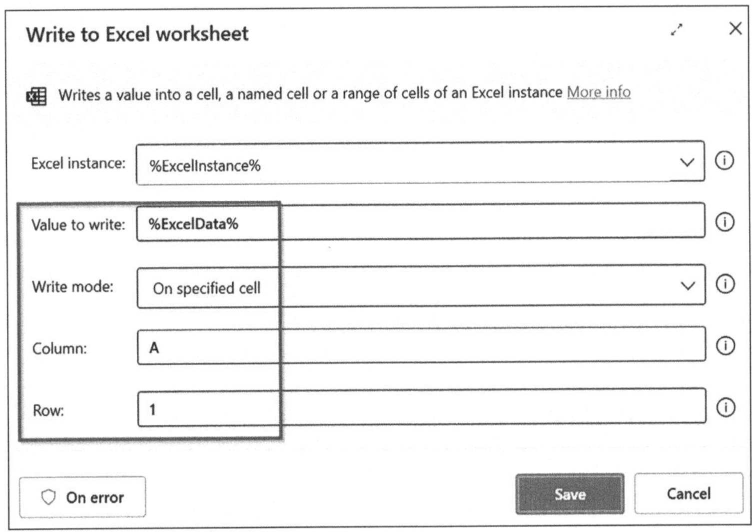

Figure 6.16: *Writing to an Excel sheet*

And then finally the **"Close Excel"** Action.

Run the Flow, and as you see in the following figure all the rows from the Datatable have been written onto the **Sales Copy** sheet. However, did you notice one issue?

	A	B	C	D	E	F	G
1	01-Jan	Boston	Bars	Carrot	33	1.77	58.41
2	04-Jan	Boston	Crackers	Whole Wheat	87	3.49	303.63
3	07-Jan	Los Angeles	Cookies	Chocolate Chip	58	1.87	108.46
4	10-Jan	New York	Cookies	Chocolate Chip	82	1.87	153.34
5	13-Jan	Boston	Cookies	Arrowroot	38	2.18	82.84
6	16-Jan	Boston	Bars	Carrot	54	1.77	95.58
7	19-Jan	Boston	Crackers	Whole Wheat	149	3.49	520.01
8	22-Jan	Los Angeles	Bars	Carrot	51	1.77	90.27
9	25-Jan	New York	Bars	Carrot	100	1.77	177
10	28-Jan	New York	Snacks	Potato Chips	28	1.35	37.8
11	31-Jan	Boston	Cookies	Arrowroot	36	2.18	78.48
12	03-Feb	Boston	Cookies	Chocolate Chip	31	1.87	57.97
13	06-Feb	Boston	Crackers	Whole Wheat	28	3.49	97.72
14	09-Feb	Los Angeles	Bars	Carrot	44	1.77	77.88
15	12-Feb	New York	[illegible]	[illegible]	23	1.77	40.71

Sales | Orders | Sales Copy

Figure 6.17: *Data written to an Excel sheet*

The column headers are not written along with the data. To fix this, edit the **"Write to Excel worksheet"** Action. In the **"Value to write"** parameter, from the variable picker button select the **`.ColumnHeadersRow`** property of the **`ExcelData`** variable by double clicking it. The parameter box will now show up as **`%ExcelData.ColumnHeadersRow%`**.

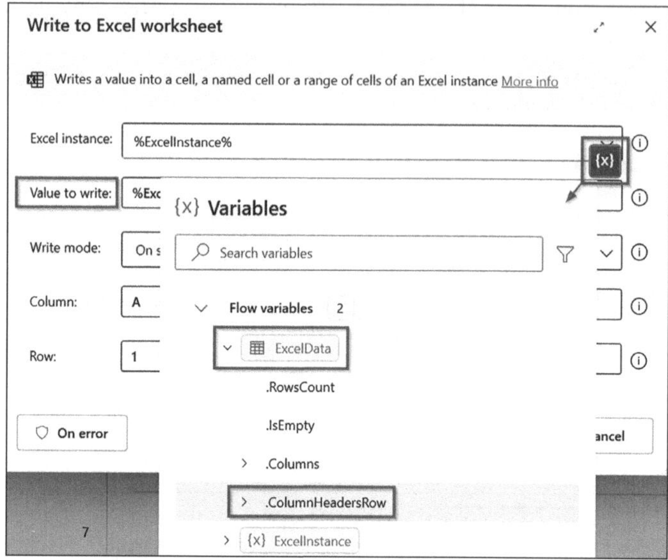

Figure 6.18: *Adding the column headers to the Excel sheet*

However, we have now only modified the Action to add the header row. To add the data, use another **"`Write to Excel worksheet`"** exactly as *Figure* 6.16, but this time the data will start from A2 because the first row now has the column headers. The entire Flow now looks as follows:

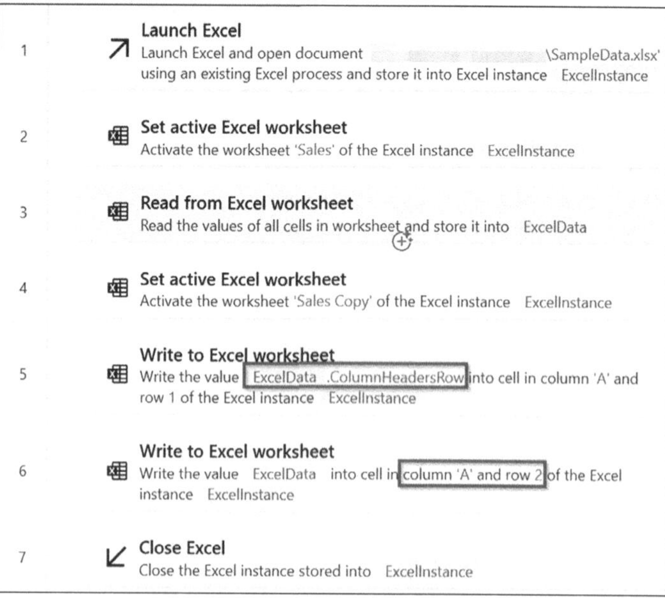

Figure 6.19: *Entire Flow after adding the column headers and data*

Rerun the Flow and the column headers show up along with the Data.

	A	B	C	D	E	F	G
1	Date	City	Category	Product	Quantity	Unit Price	Total Price
2	01-Jan	Boston	Bars	Carrot	33	1.77	58.41
3	04-Jan	Boston	Crackers	Whole Wheat	87	3.49	303.63
4	07-Jan	Los Angeles	Cookies	Chocolate Chip	58	1.87	108.46
5	10-Jan	New York	Cookies	Chocolate Chip	82	1.87	153.34
6	13-Jan	Boston	Cookies	Arrowroot	38	2.18	82.84
7	16-Jan	Boston	Bars	Carrot	54	1.77	95.58
8	19-Jan	Boston	Crackers	Whole Wheat	149	3.49	520.01
9	22-Jan	Los Angeles	Bars	Carrot	51	1.77	90.27
10	25-Jan	New York	Bars	Carrot	100	1.77	177
11	28-Jan	New York	Snacks	Potato Chips	28	1.35	37.8
12	31-Jan	Boston	Cookies	Arrowroot	36	2.18	78.48
13	03-Feb	Boston	Cookies	Chocolate Chip	31	1.87	57.97
14	06-Feb	Boston	Crackers	Whole Wheat	28	3.49	97.72
15	09-Feb	Los Angeles	Bars	Carrot	44	1.77	77.88

Sales | Orders | Sales Copy

Figure 6.20: *Output after rerunning the Flow*

You would not be seeing the same formatting and coloring as originally seen in *Figure* 6.5, since we are writing the data from the Datatable which does not hold the formatting.

To need the formatting and coloring too, use the Copy cells and Paste cells Actions. Try the following sequence of Actions:

1. **"Launch Excel"**,
2. **"Set active Excel worksheet"** for **Sales** sheet,
3. **"Copy cells from Excel worksheet"** with parameter set as **"All available values from worksheet"**,
4. **"Set active Excel worksheet"** for **Sales Copy** sheet,
5. **"Paste cells to Excel worksheet"** on the specified cell A1,
6. Close Excel

Practical Exercise

1. Have a manually created sheet with randomly added data of your choice with a few columns and few rows. You can use the *Id Column* sheet of the **SampleData.xlsx** filc in thc GitHub folder. Before building the Flow, manually remove the ID column from the sheet, as it was added to show *Figure* 6.22.

   The ID column and its data has to be added by the bot.

	A	B	C	D
1	Name	Age	City	
2	John Doe	40	London	
3	Jane Doe	35	New York	
4	Michael Smith	34	Chicago	
5	Emily Johnson	27	San Francisco	
6				
7				

Figure 6.21: *Sheet with sample rows and columns*

2. The exercise is to add a column header as ID and each row should have an ID starting from 1 till the last available row in an incremented way. If the sheet has 10 rows, then the numbering of the ID column should be from 1 to 9 after the header row.

	A	B	C	D
1	Name	Age	City	ID
2	John Doe	40	London	1
3	Jane Doe	35	New York	2
4	Michael Smith	34	Chicago	3
5	Emily Johnson	27	San Francisco	4
6				
7				

Figure 6.22: Expected output of the exercise

Saving the Excel

There are two options to save the Excel we are working with. One is saving the Excel while closing itself through the **"`Close Excel`"** Action that we have already been using. If you want to save the changes made by the bot then select the option as follows:

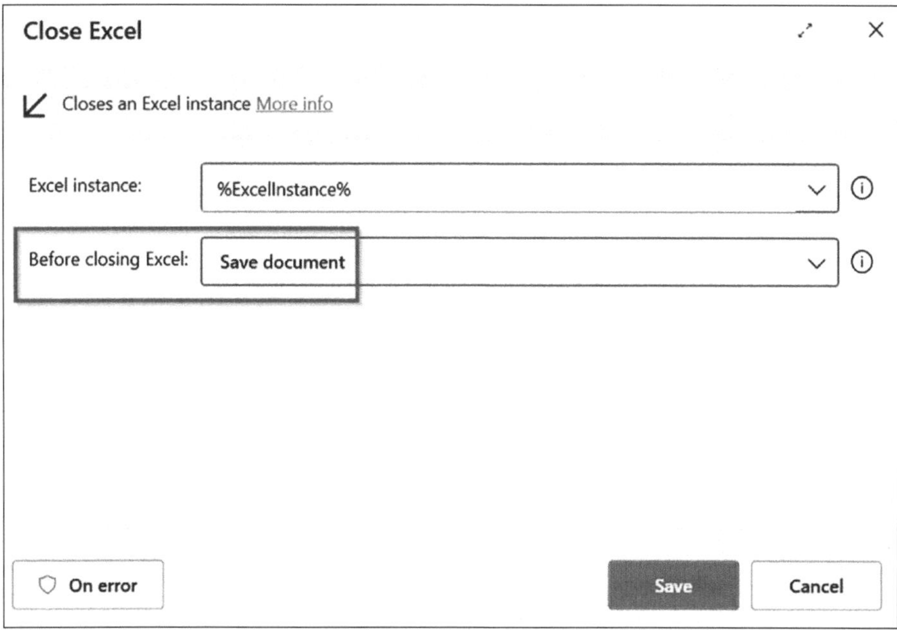

Figure 6.23: *Saving the Excel while closing*

However, if you want to save it as another copy or even in another file extension then the way to do that is as follows by selecting the extension and giving the destination folder along with a file name. In the following example, a separate copy as **`File Name.xlsx`** will be created in the mentioned folder path.

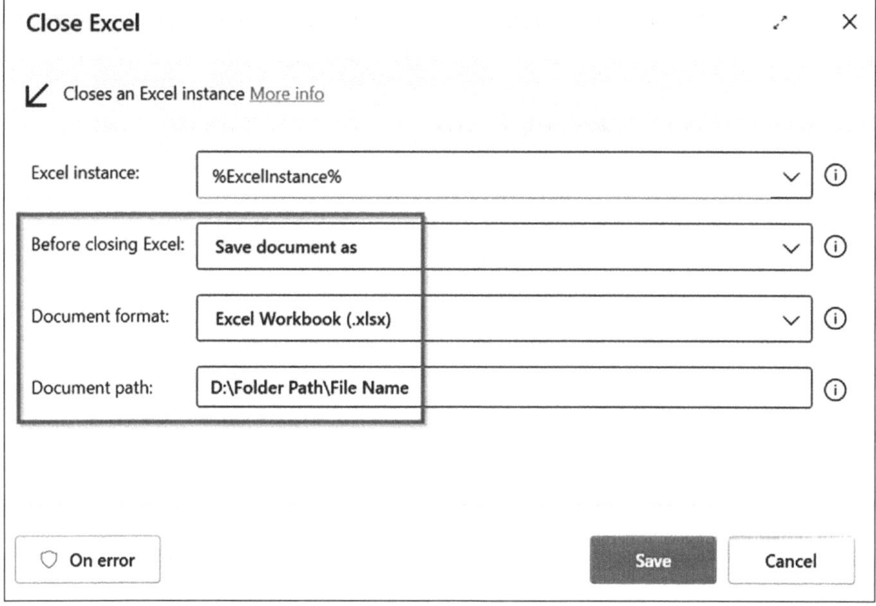

Figure 6.24: *Saving a copy while closing*

The second option is via another Action called **"`Save Excel`"**.

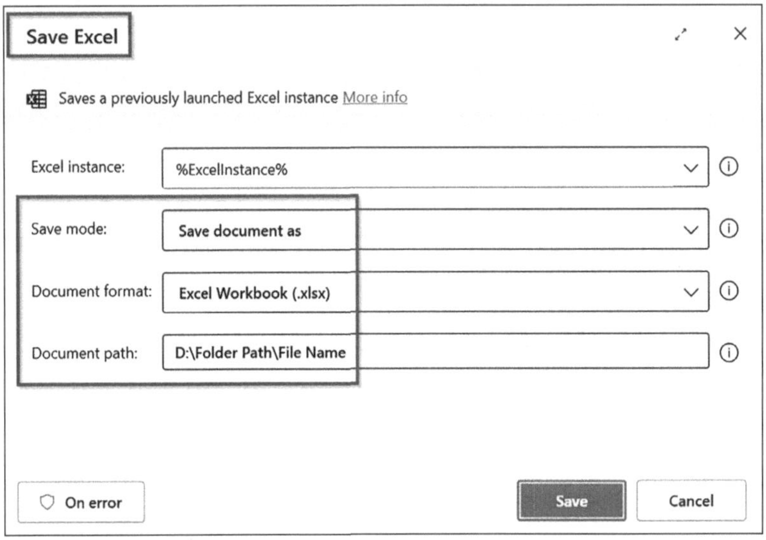

Save Excel

Saves a previously launched Excel instance More info

Excel instance:	%ExcelInstance%
Save mode:	Save document as
Document format:	Excel Workbook (.xlsx)
Document path:	D:\Folder Path\File Name

On error | Save | Cancel

Figure 6.25: *The Save Excel action*

If a Developer wants to only save the modified Excel data and continue the bot without closing it, then the **"`Save Excel`"** Action with a parameter as **"`Save document`"** can be used.

Sorting Cells

Sorting of Excel data is regularly required in automation scenarios on a need basis. In the following data sample, we will be sorting the **`Units`** column in ascending order.

	A	B	C	D	E	F
1	Region	Rep	Item	Units	Unit Cost	Total
2	East	Jones	Pencil	95	1.99	189.05
3	Central	Kivell	Binder	50	19.99	999.50
4	Central	Jardine	Pencil	36	4.99	179.64
5	Central	Gill	Pen	27	19.99	539.73
6	West	Sorvino	Pencil	56	2.99	167.44
7	East	Jones	Binder	60	4.99	299.40
8	Central	Andrews	Pencil	75	1.99	149.25
9	Central	Jardine	Pencil	90	4.99	449.10
10	West	Thompson	Pencil	32	1.99	63.68
11	East	Jones	Binder	60	8.99	539.40
12	Central	Morgan	Pencil	90	4.99	449.10
13	East	Howard	Binder	29	1.99	57.71
14	East	Parent	Binder	81	19.99	1,619.19
15	East	Jones	Pencil	35	4.99	174.65

Figure 6.26: *Input data for sorting the Units column*

Here are the steps to achieve the same:

1. **"Launch Excel"** Action
2. **"Set active Excel worksheet"** to a sheet called **Orders.**
3. Add the **"Sort cells in Excel worksheet"** Action. Click the marked **"Edit"** button. In the **"Column"** box for the **"Sort by"** you can add either the column alphabet (for example, D) or the column number (like 4). If it is an Excel table you can also add the name of the column. For multiple sort columns use the plus button at the bottom of the **"Sort by"** window. Remember to enable the **"First row is header"** toggle.

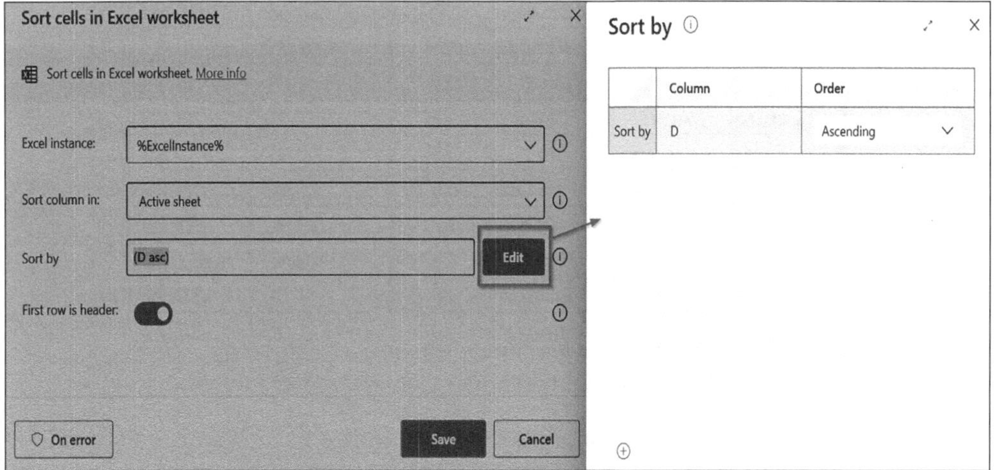

Figure 6.27: *Adding the sort column*

4. Following is the Flow built. You can then use a read related action to get the sorted data for further processing. When no further operations are needed on the Excel, you can choose to close it.

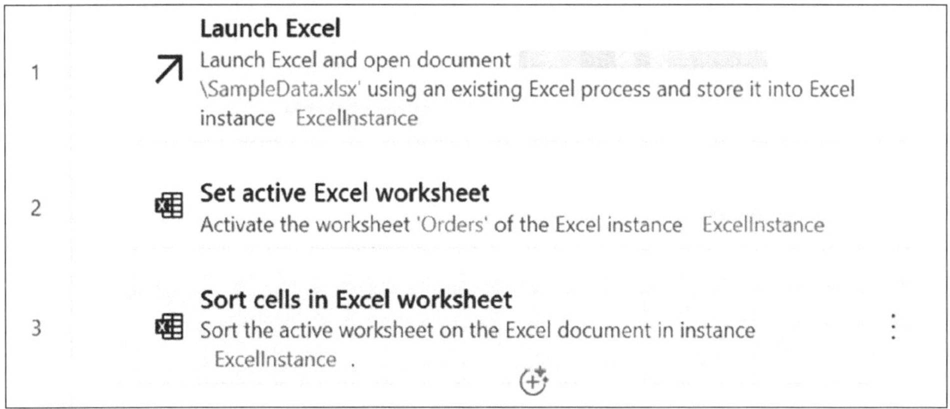

Figure 6.28: *Flow built for sorting*

5. Run the Flow and the output will be the sorted data as per Column D in ascending order.
   Only the first 15 rows are shown here but all the data in the sheet gets sorted based on the **Units** column.

	A	B	C	D	E	F
1	Region	Rep	Item	Units	Unit Cost	Total
2	Central	Smith	Desk	2	125.00	250.00
3	West	Sorvino	Desk	3	275.00	825.00
4	East	Jones	Binder	4	4.99	19.96
5	Central	Kivell	Desk	5	125.00	625.00
6	West	Sorvino	Binder	7	19.99	139.93
7	Central	Gill	Pencil	7	1.29	9.03
8	Central	Jardine	Binder	11	4.99	54.89
9	Central	Andrews	Pencil	14	1.29	18.06
10	East	Parent	Pen	15	19.99	299.85
11	East	Jones	Pen Set	16	15.99	255.84
12	Central	Gill	Pen	27	19.99	539.73
13	Central	Morgan	Binder	28	8.99	251.72
14	Central	Andrews	Binder	28	4.99	139.72
15	East	Howard	Binder	29	1.99	57.71

Figure 6.29: *Output after running the Flow*

The **"Filter cells in Excel worksheet"** is configured in the same way by passing the column alphabet or number in the **"Column to filter"** parameter. Then using the **"Edit"** button set a rule by selecting the given list of dropdown conditions using the **"Advanced"** toggle if required. As of this writing, a direct way of reading the filtered data after using this Action is not yet achievable using the given **"Read from Excel worksheet"** Action. It would have been nice to have an output variable coming out of the Action itself to give the filtered data, but this is not available as of now. To read the filtered data, after applying the filters, get the first free row and column, then copy the cells with the dropdown option of **"Values from a range of cells"**, pass the start column and row both as 1, end column as **%FirstFreeColumn - 1%**, and end row as **%FirstFreeRow - 1%**. Then use the Paste cells to paste it into a new sheet by setting the new sheet as the active one. Now read all the cells of this new sheet into a Datatable, which will have the filtered data. A different option is to read the complete sheet into a Datatable and then use the **"Filter data table"** Action (not available in the PAD version of this book) to filter within the Datatable. The first option gives the filtered data in a sheet which can then be read into a Datatable, whereas the second one gives the filtered data in the Datatable which can then be written onto the sheet. So, use the one that suits your situation. Let us wait for a few updates on the PAD tool for attaining this in a straightforward way without using any complicated reading techniques.

Finding and Replacing cells

Power Automate Desktop provides a native Action to find something on a sheet and optionally replace it with anything else. This is done with the help of the **"Find and replace cells Excel worksheet"** Action. From the sheet called **Formula** in the same sample Excel file, let's find the word **"Bars"** and replace it with **"Flavoured Bars"** all over the sheet.

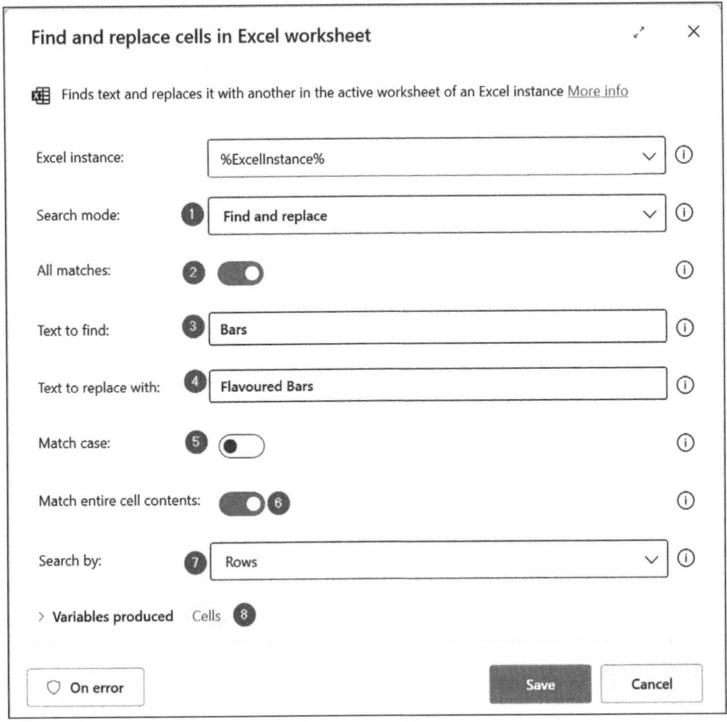

Figure 6.30: *The Find and replace Action and its parameters*

Follow along the numbering in the preceding figure.

1. After providing the Excel Instance, this Action gives an option to either do only a Find or a Find and Replace.
2. This toggle is to look for all available matches or only the first one.
3. We will be searching for the text **"Bars"** in this Excel.
4. And replace all of them with the words **"Flavoured Bars"**.
5. This toggle is to tell PAD whether to look for an exact matching case (as in small or large case letters), or without any case matching.
6. This toggle specifies whether to match for all the contents of a cell or if the text to find can be anywhere within the contents of a cell.

7. Provides the order to search for, that is, by rows or columns.
8. The output variable produced after running the Action will contain the details of the Find or Replace.

If you look at these options, they are very much similar to the options available in the Find and Replace dialog box of an Excel file as follows.

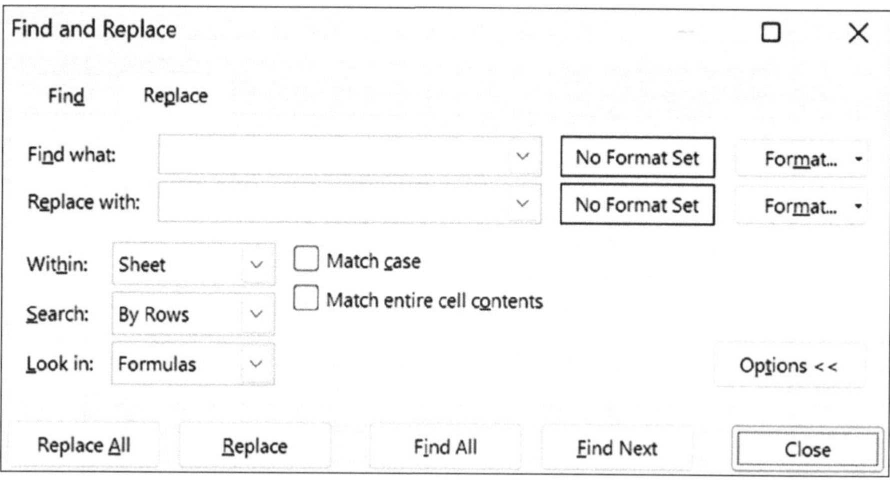

Figure 6.31: *The Find and Replace dialog box of Excel*

Run the Flow with the Actions and a bookmark to observe the output. As shown in *Figure 6.32*, all of the cells that had **"`Bars`"** written in them are replaced by the wordings **"`Flavoured Bars`"**. Visit the **"`Variables`"** pane and observe that the **`Cells`** variable will have the details of all the cell addresses (row index and column index) where this text was found.

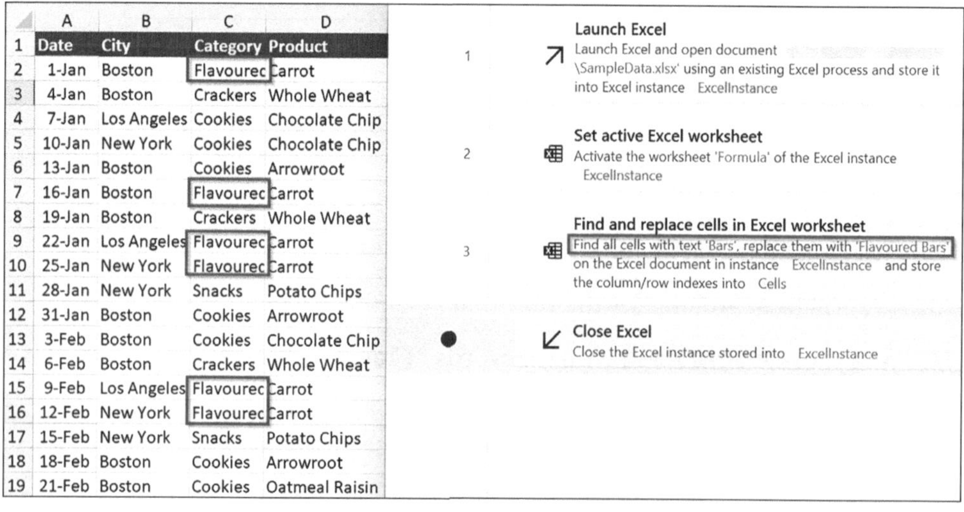

Figure 6.32: *Output after running the Flow*

Autofit Rows and Columns

If you questioned yourself after noticing the output as to how can I make the wordings **"`Flavoured Bars`"** completely visible as they are not seen fully in the column, then you can be assured that there is an in-built Action for that. You might have noticed this scenario several times while interacting with an Excel file that certain columns show **#** symbols rather than the full content. Let us go into the file and intentionally reduce the width of Column A manually such that it shows up the **#** symbols. Now we have two columns that are not showing their data fully and we will fix this using an Action called **"`Resize columns/rows in Excel worksheet`"**.

	A	B	C	D	E	F	G
1	Date	City	Category	Product	Quantity	Unit Price	Total Price
2	####	Boston	Flavourec	Carrot	33	1.77	58.41
3	####	Boston	Crackers	Whole Wheat	87	3.49	303.63
4	####	Los Angeles	Cookies	Chocolate Chip	58	1.87	108.46
5	####	New York	Cookies	Chocolate Chip	82	1.87	153.34
6	####	Boston	Cookies	Arrowroot	38	2.18	82.84
7	####	Boston	Flavourec	Carrot	54	1.77	95.58
8	####	Boston	Crackers	Whole Wheat	149	3.49	520.01
9	####	Los Angeles	Flavourec	Carrot	51	1.77	90.27
10	####	New York	Flavourec	Carrot	100	1.77	177

Figure 6.33: *Column values not showing fully*

Add this Action after the find and replace and before closing the Excel. Set the parameters of this Action as shown in the following figure to autofit all available columns. The same options are also available for rows.

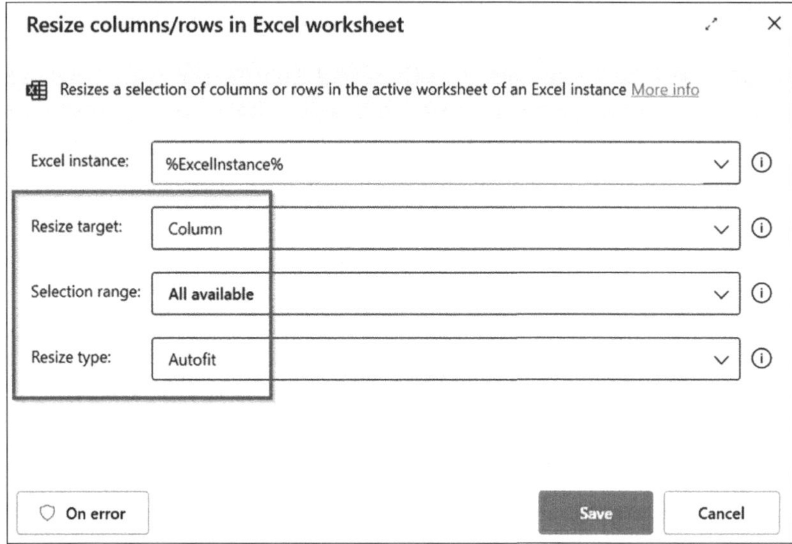

Figure 6.34: *Autofit all available columns*

The entire workflow looks as follows: If you completed the previous replacement exercise then you might want to manually replace **Flavoured Bars** back to **Bars** before running the Flow for resizing the columns, so that the replacement happens correctly when you rerun it. Insert a breakpoint before the file gets closed so that you can view the output while debugging, and then run the Flow. The two columns in question now display their full content.

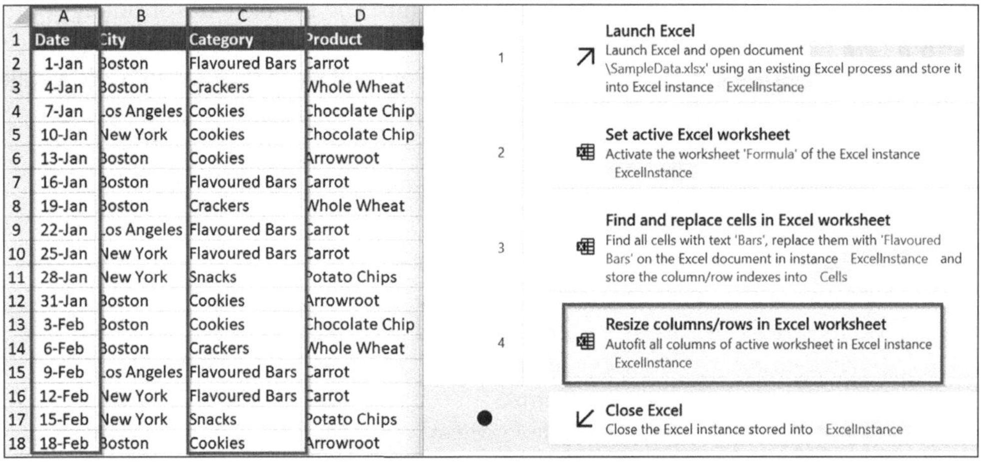

	A	B	C	D
1	Date	City	Category	Product
2	1-Jan	Boston	Flavoured Bars	Carrot
3	4-Jan	Boston	Crackers	Whole Wheat
4	7-Jan	Los Angeles	Cookies	Chocolate Chip
5	10-Jan	New York	Cookies	Chocolate Chip
6	13-Jan	Boston	Cookies	Arrowroot
7	16-Jan	Boston	Flavoured Bars	Carrot
8	19-Jan	Boston	Crackers	Whole Wheat
9	22-Jan	Los Angeles	Flavoured Bars	Carrot
10	25-Jan	New York	Flavoured Bars	Carrot
11	28-Jan	New York	Snacks	Potato Chips
12	31-Jan	Boston	Cookies	Arrowroot
13	3-Feb	Boston	Cookies	Chocolate Chip
14	6-Feb	Boston	Crackers	Whole Wheat
15	9-Feb	Los Angeles	Flavoured Bars	Carrot
16	12-Feb	New York	Flavoured Bars	Carrot
17	15-Feb	New York	Snacks	Potato Chips
18	18-Feb	Boston	Cookies	Arrowroot

Figure 6.35: *Output after running the Flow*

Running a Macro of an Excel file

During your automation development journey, there will arise scenarios where a lot of automation already happens through a macro and therefore you do not want to modify it. Then you may use RPA Power Automate Desktop to focus on automating other external applications. For example, you have to take the output coming from an Excel file after running a macro, and then use that output into other applications like a Desktop or a Web application. In such cases, it becomes mandatory to call the macro from PAD, then get its output and use that output for automating other external applications.

Consider that we have an Excel file named **"`Excel with Macro.xlsm`"** that contains two macros as follows. A macro file has an extension as **"`.xlsm`"**.

1. **`MacroWithoutParams:`**
   This is a macro that does not accept any parameters. When called, it will simply show a message box as **"`This is a message from the macro.`"**

2. **`MacroWithParams:`**
   This is a macro that accepts two numbers as parameters and the macro will display the sum of those two numbers. The macro also inserts the value of the sum in cell A1 and in a moment you will know why.

Following is the VBA macro code of both the above-mentioned macros in the **"`Excel with Macro.xlsm`"** file, and this file is also available in the GitHub folder of this chapter by the same name.

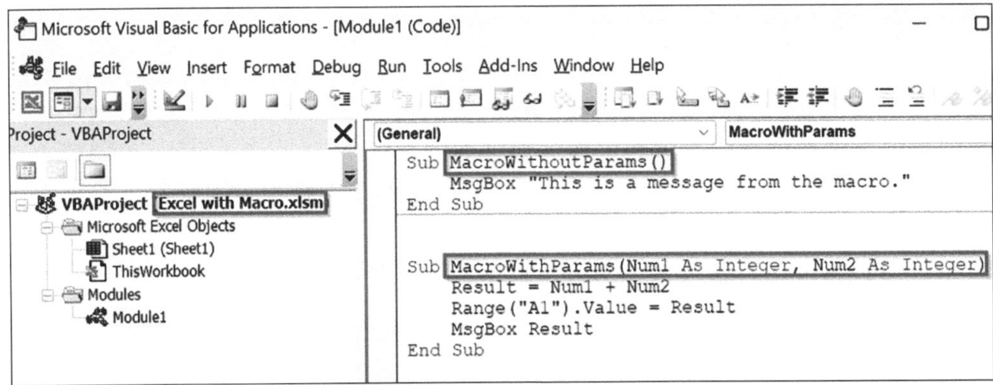

Figure 6.36: *Macro with and without parameters*

After using a **"`Launch Excel`"**, the PAD Action to call a macro is **"`Run Excel macro`"** and the procedure to call a macro "without" parameters is simply by passing its name in this Action after providing the instance.

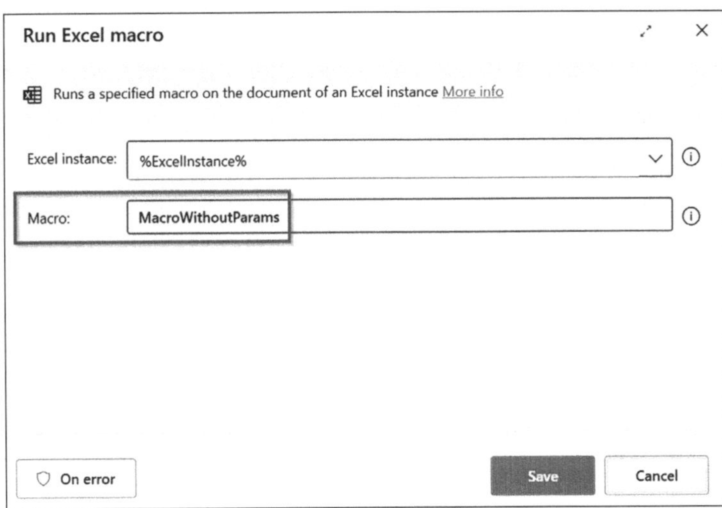

Figure 6.37: *Calling a Macro without parameters*

In the same PAD Flow, we will also call the macro "with" parameters. The Action is the same, but the way to call a macro with parameters is to pass the values separated by semicolon **"`;`"** after the macro name.

Example: **MacroName;Param1;Param2** and so on.

Let's add another **"`Run Excel macro`"** and use the preceding format to pass the two numbers as parameters.

This is what we have passed - **MacroWithParams;20;30**

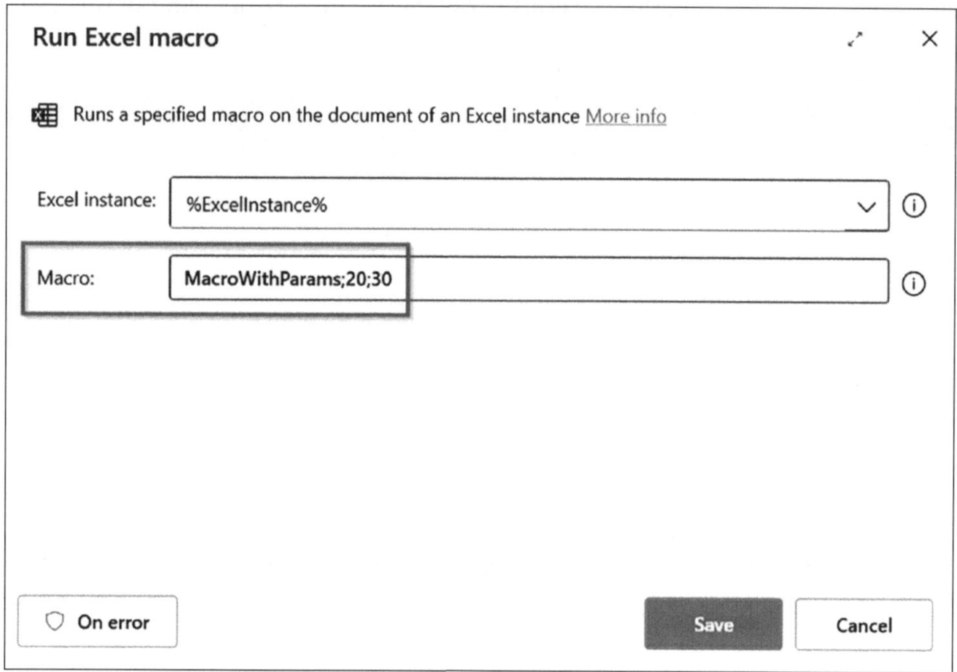

Figure 6.38: *Calling a Macro with parameters*

As a best practice add a **"`Close Excel`"** Action and run the Flow.

As you can see the first macro without the parameters has run and displayed the intended message box.

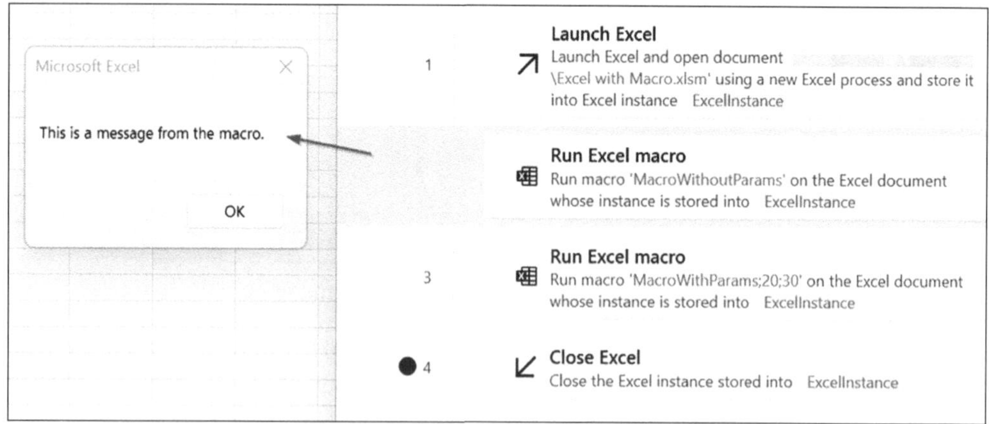

Figure 6.39: *Output of Macro without parameters*

In the next line of the Flow, the macro with the parameters has run producing the sum of the two numbers that were passed (20 and 30) via PAD. If you can also notice that we had printed the result in cell A1 so that PAD can now read the sum from this cell and use it for further processing within the Desktop Flow. This is done because the **"Run Excel macro"** Action does not have any output variables produced, so it cannot receive the value of 50 calculated by the macro.

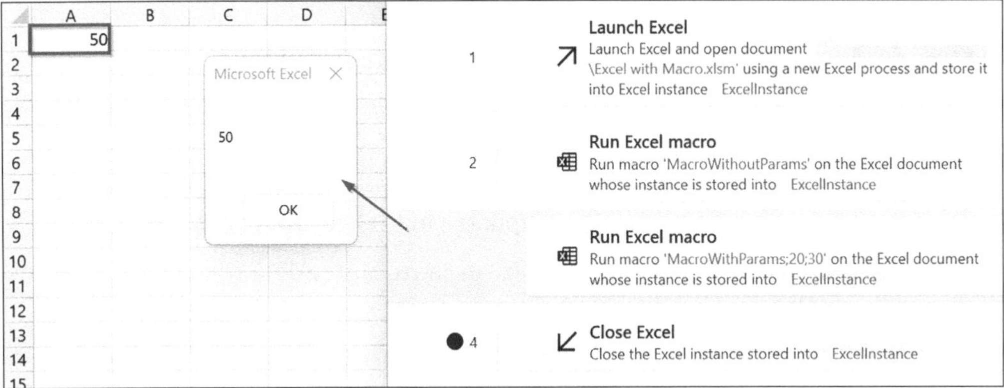

Figure 6.40: *Output of Macro with parameters*

Some important final words on interacting with an Excel is that if an Action is not available in PAD to reproduce an Excel functionality (for example, creating a Pivot table), then other options like calling a macro, or writing a VBScript via an in-built Action called **"Run VBScript"** should be made use of. Using UI based automation to perform mouse clicks on different menus of Excel is not recommended at all. This is because they are not reliable and may fail in situations where a mouse click is not registered correctly or if the right window does not have the right focus. Whereas, a macro or a VBScript is highly reliable as the code and the scripts will be using the **"Excel object model"** for generating the desired output.

Newer Actions will be added as the PAD tool progresses with its latest updates by which you will be able to perform an operation mentioned here using any other alternative approach. Feel free to use them. Keep a watch on newer Excel related Actions in the following link:

https://learn.microsoft.com/en-us/power-automate/desktop-flows/actions-reference/excel

Outlook Automation

Another widely used common application for RPA automation is Outlook for performing various email related processing, such as reading, sending, auto-replying, forwarding, or moving of emails, and so on. PAD has a group of Actions called **"Outlook"** in the **"Actions"** pane for anything related to Outlook emails. Let's take a look at the key Actions used for Outlook automation.

Reading Emails

Reading emails is needed in any automation scenario in RPA. It could be an email from a specific sender or a specific subject, or both, or even emails from a specific Outlook folder and so on.

To read emails from Outlook, the following Actions are performed.

Use the **"`Launch Outlook`"** Action, just like the way you did for launching Excel.

A key thing to note is that, at the point of this writing the Outlook automation Actions do not support the new Outlook for Windows. You need to use the Outlook desktop application. Keep a watch on its related updates in the following link:

https://learn.microsoft.com/en-us/power-automate/desktop-flows/actions-reference/outlook

Another thing to note is that, to connect to an already running Outlook, the **"`Launch Outlook`"** Action is required for creating an instance. But in case of Excel, you can use a separate Action called **"`Attach to running Excel`"** and not the **"`Launch Excel`"** Action.

Then drag and drop the **"`Retrieve email message from Outlook`"** Action.

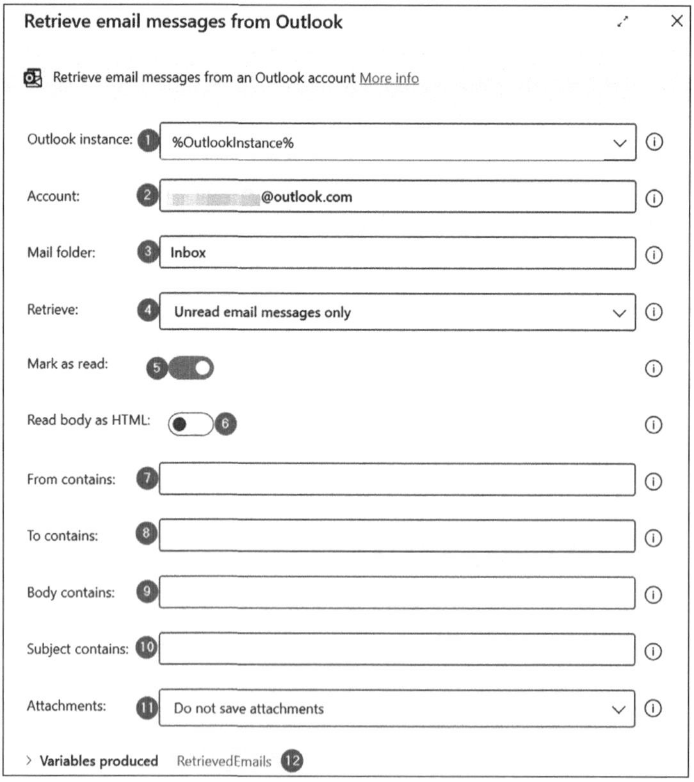

Figure 6.41: *The Retrieve email messages from Outlook action*

Follow along the numbering in the preceding figure:

1. This is the **`OutlookInstance`** variable produced after the **"`Launch Outlook`"** Action.
2. This is the Email Account that shows up on the left-hand side just above the Inbox and the list of other folders. You can also see the list of accounts in the File menu of Outlook, then under the Account Settings button in the Account Settings menu.
3. This could be either Inbox or any of the Outlook folders and subfolders that you want to read the emails from. In case of specifying a folder structure, refer to the tooltip text of the **'`i`'** information icon.

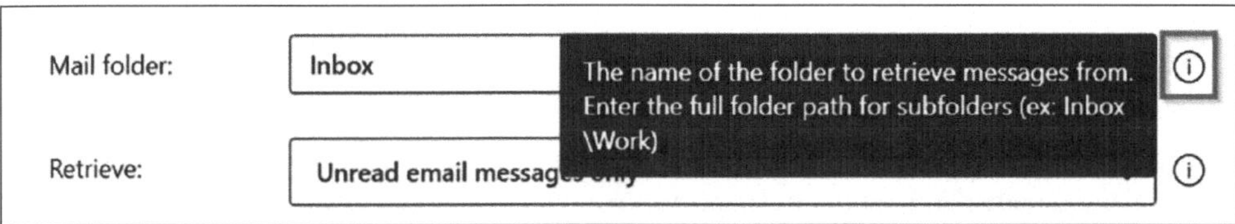

Figure 6.42: *The Mail folder parameter*

4. This parameter is to determine whether the bot should read all emails, or only unread emails or only read emails.
5. This toggle button when enabled will mark an email as read if it was originally unread, after the **"`Retrieve email messages from Outlook`"** Action is executed.
6. This toggle determines whether to read the body of the email as HTML or not. The body will contain the HTML tags and the contents of certain emails are easy to read in HTML format.
7. This box holds the email address of the sender. It can be left blank if emails from all senders are to be retrieved by this Action.
8. This box contains one or more recipient email addresses. Refer to the tooltip text for characters to be used in case of multiple addresses. The parameter can be left blank if emails to any recipients are to be retrieved by this Action.

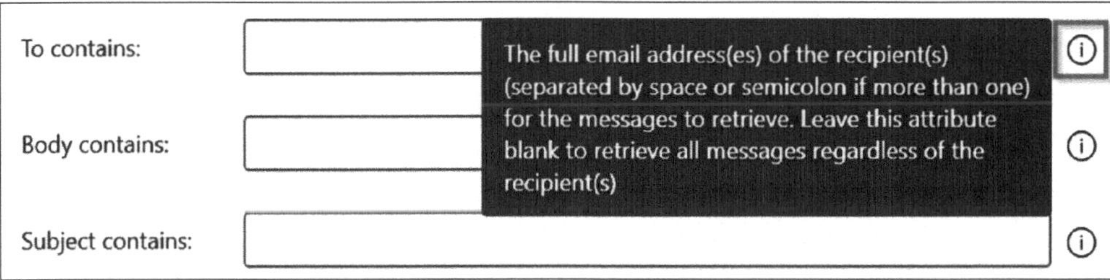

Figure 6.43: *The To contains parameter*

9. The **"`Body contains`"** parameter can hold words or phrases to be searched within the email body while retrieving the emails by this Action. Like the above two parameters, this box can be left blank to read all the emails without any specific body criteria.

10. Likewise, the **"`Subject contains`"** can hold words or phrases to be searched within the subject of the email. No parameters can be provided in this box to read all emails having any subject.

11. This dropdown will tell Power Automate Desktop whether or not to save the attachments that are contained in the email, if any. If they are chosen to be saved then it gives a box to provide the full folder path for saving the attachment files.

12. This is an output variable holding a list of all email messages that match the criteria configured in the above options.

Once the **`RetrievedEmails`** variable is populated after executing the above Action, it has to be iterated with the help of a **"`For each`"** loop similar to how we read the **`ExcelData`** variable for Excel. Drag and drop this loop and pass the **`RetrievedEmails`** variable to it. Notice that the **`CurrentItem`** is the output variable produced by the loop just like how it was for the Excel automation. The variable can be given a developer-friendly name.

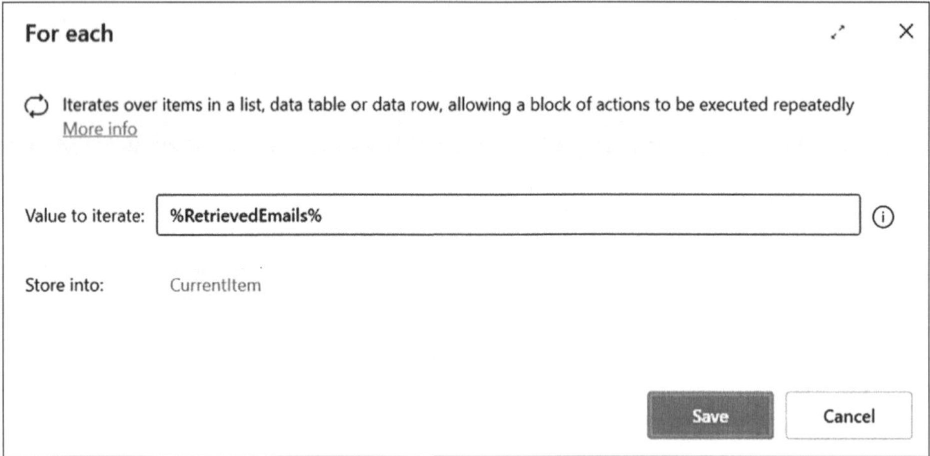

Figure 6.44: *Iterating the emails using a For each loop*

Drag and drop an Action for a message box to see what the **`CurrentItem`** variable holds.

The following figure shows the different properties available for **`CurrentItem`** for the email being currently processed within the loop. These properties give a good amount and nature of information. With their help you can store these in other variables and use them for further processing. For example, you can read the **`.Date`** property of the email and use it to process only those emails of a specific date criteria if that is what the automation asks for.

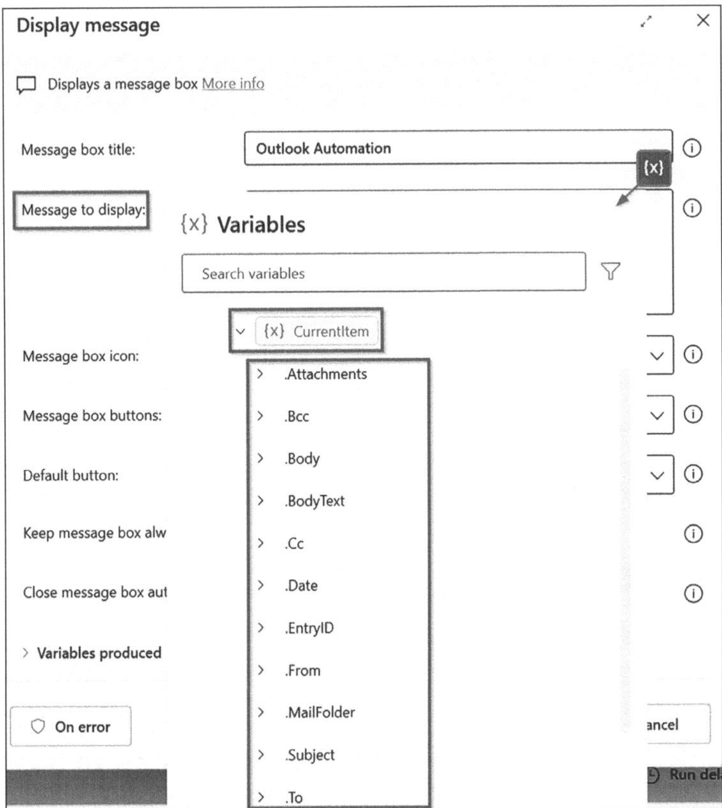

Figure 6.45: *Different properties of an email*

During your practice, observe these in the **"Variables"** pane or display them in a message box, and verify what they show for your learning. The message box is only to see what these properties show, but this area inside the loop can hold any other operations related to the email being currently processed. For example, if the requirement is to create an IT ticket from the email body, then this area will read the email body contents, extract the necessary information, go to the ticketing system, create a ticket using Web automation, make an entry into a spreadsheet with the ticket number, pick up the next email for processing, and so on.

Finally, a **"Close Outlook"** Action can be optionally used depending on whether the instance of Outlook has to be closed or kept open for any further email related processing by the bot. Following is how the entire Flow looks like after using all of the above steps for iterating through emails from Outlook.

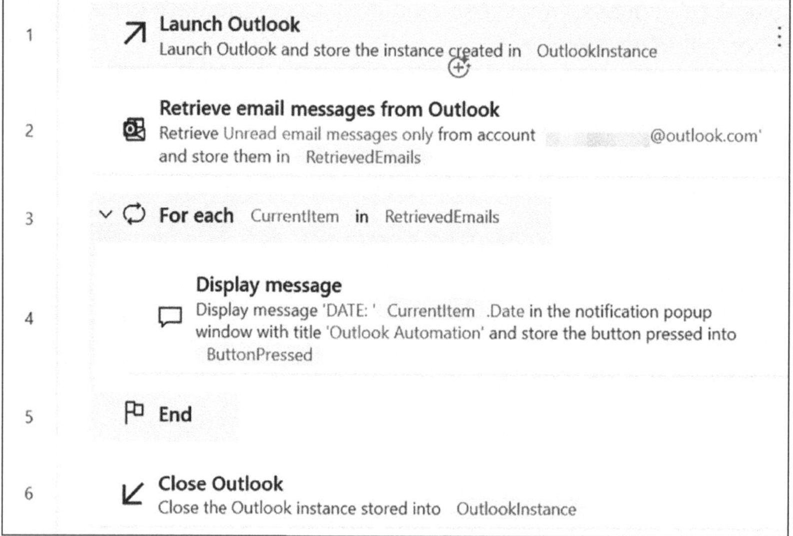

***Figure 6.46**: Final Flow for iterating through Outlook emails*

Sending Emails

Sending an email also forms a major part of an RPA automation process. Be it for sending a final report after all the processing is done, for notifying about any errors, for auto-replying to a sender stating that their email has been received, and so on.

Following are two parts of the **"`Send email message through Outlook`"** Action available in PAD.

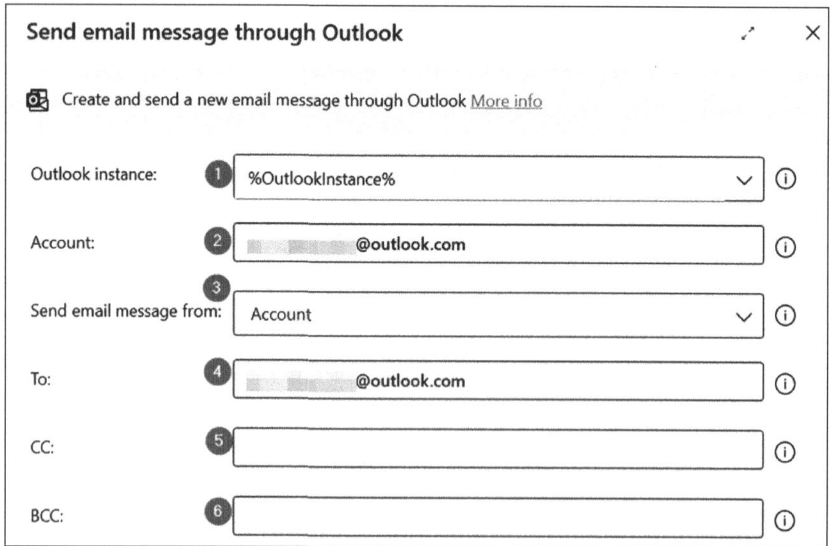

***Figure 6.47**: Part 1 of action for sending an email*

Follow along the numbers from the preceding figure:

1. The **`OutlookInstance`** generated from the **"`Launch Outlook`"** Action. This dropdown shows the list of all Outlook instances created in any other parts of the Flow.
2. The Email account for sending the email.
3. This gives an option to send the email via the account in point 2 or has an option to send via another mailbox.
4. One or more recipient's email addresses to be added here. Multiple recipients to be separated by spaces or semicolons.
5. A provision to CC (carbon copy) the email to one or more email addresses. Multiple addresses to be separated by spaces or semicolons.
6. A provision to BCC (blind carbon copy) the email to one or more email addresses. Multiple addresses to be separated by spaces or semicolons. Recipients in the BCC will also receive the email but their email addresses will not be shown to other recipients.

   Following is the remaining part of the **"`Send email message through Outlook`"** Action.

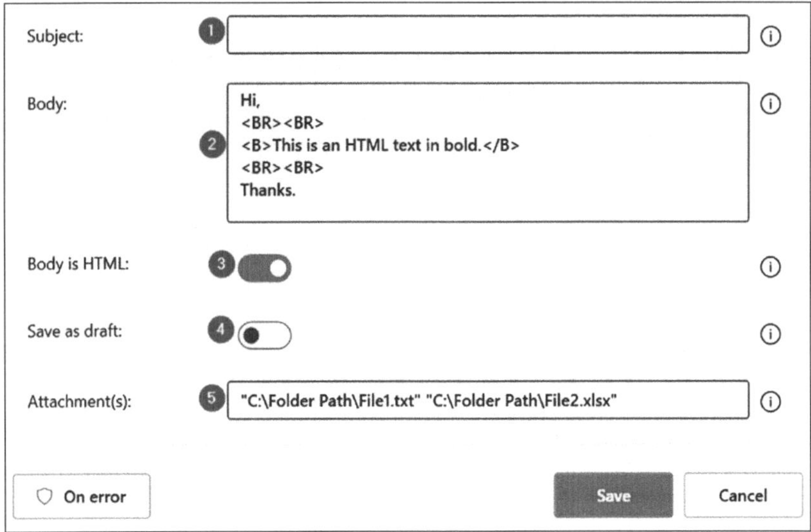

Figure 6.48: *Part 2 of action for sending an email*

Follow along for the above shown numbering.

1. A box for entering the subject of the email to be sent.
2. The content of the email body to be sent.

3. If this toggle is enabled, then the developer has the provision to add HTML markup tags in the **"Body"** parameter for formatting or for any other purpose.

For example, the HTML added in the preceding figure will produce the following text which would not have formatted the text if this option was disabled.

Hi,

This is an HTML text in bold.

Thanks.

The **
** tag is for inserting line breaks hence you see them in the output text. The starting and closing **<B>** tag is responsible for making the text bold. You could also add colors, change the font name and size, and anything else possible with the help of HTML tags when this option is enabled.

4. This toggle when enabled creates the email but saves it in the **"Drafts"** folder of Outlook and can be referred to at a later stage down the Flow.

5. Has an option to attach one or more files when specified the full path in double quotes. When multiple files are attached, they have to be separated by a space character as shown in the figure. You can also use a List variable containing a list of files with their full path.

Optionally a **"Close Outlook"** Action is used after sending the email and the overall Flow looks as below. This Action will close the Outlook application on your machine but if it needs to be kept open for some kind of processing then it can be excluded and later on used as required.

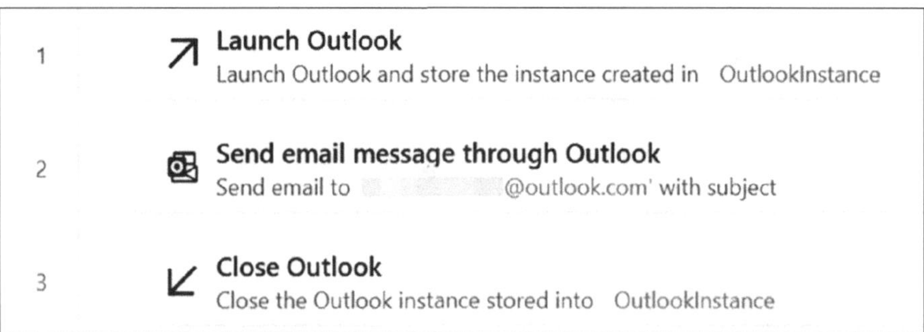

Figure 6.49: *Final Flow for sending an email*

Embed Image in Email Body

There occur several situations while sending an email to embed an image within the email body and not attach it. Power Automate Desktop gives an easy way to achieve this.

Follow these steps to achieve this functionality:

1. Launch Outlook to generate the **OutlookInstance**.
2. For this example, take a PNG image file from the disk and pass it to **the "Convert file to Base64"** Action. This Action converts the binary data of the image into string characters returned in the output variable called **Base64Text**, which will be further needed. This image file is available in the GitHub files for this chapter.

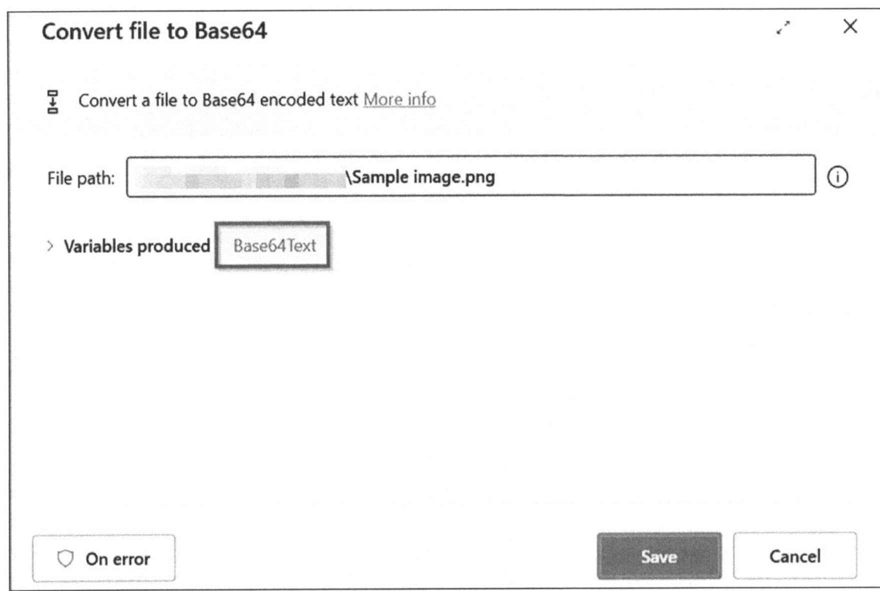

***Figure 6.50:** Convert the image file to Base64*

3. In the **"Send email message through Outlook"** Action, use the HTML **<img>** tag for images. In this tag we will specify that the data is an image of PNG type and encoded as a base64 string followed by the *Base64Text* variable generated by the previous Action. Ensure to enable the **"Body is HTML"** toggle. Following is the **<img>** tag. In this tag you could also specify the width and height of the image and give an alternate text to the image, all of which are Attributes of the **<img>** HTML tag.

```
<img src="data:image/png;base64,%Base64Text%">
```

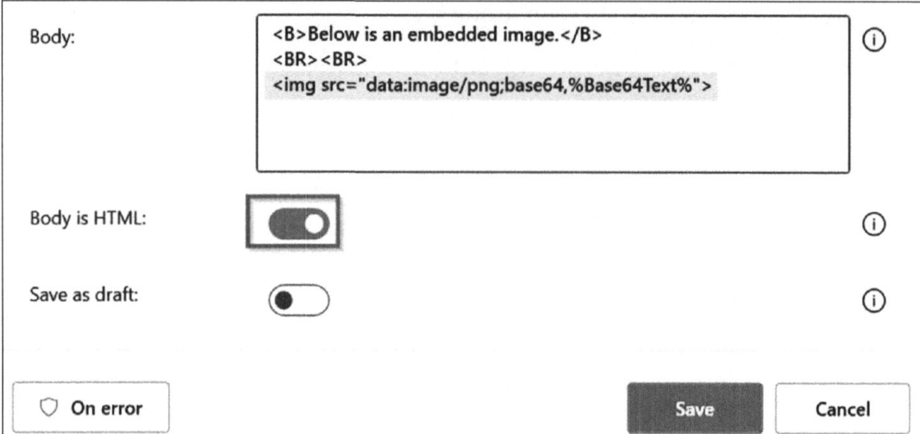

Figure 6.51: *The img tag with Base64 string*

On running the Flow, the output would appear as shown in the following figure, where the HTML bold text along with the embedded image will be shown in the email body and not as an attachment.

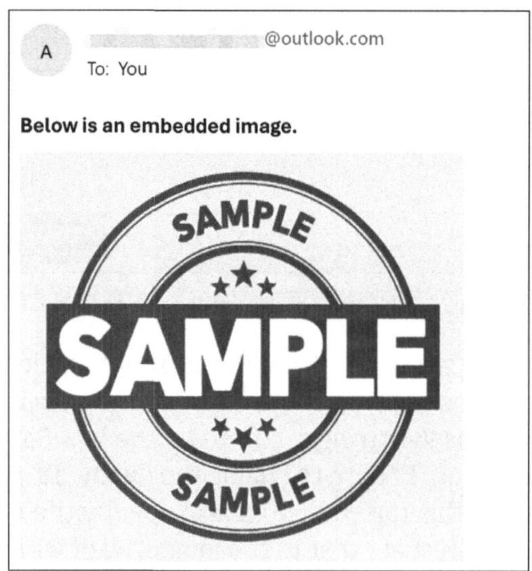

Figure 6.52: *Output after running the Flow*

In this case, the image can be other types too, for example, a JPG file, or the source of the image can be a URL as opposed to a physical file on the disk and the **`<img>`** HTML tag has to be modified accordingly.

Process Email Messages

The **"`Process email messages in Outlook`"** Action has three options to process one or more emails, namely delete email, move email to a folder, and mark email as unread.

Let us build a Flow to move emails of a specific criteria to a designated Outlook folder.

Assume that there are two folders in Outlook:

1. To be processed
2. Completed

You are building an automation scenario such that if there is an email with a subject as **"New Ticket"** then that email should be moved to the **"To be processed"** Outlook folder.

Follow the given steps to build this automation scenario:

1. Launch the Outlook to create an instance of Outlook.
2. Use the **"Retrieve email messages from Outlook"**. We could have specified the subject criteria as **"New Ticket"**, but do not give any criteria for the **"Subject"** box. For the sake of this example, we are intentionally doing this so that we can add a condition to check the subject of the email and only then move it to the desired folder. This type of checks will be needed in several automation development scenarios.

   This Action generates the **RetrievedEmails** output variable.
3. Iterate through the **RetrievedEmails** variable using a **"For each"** loop. This will generate a **CurrentItem** variable to represent every single email.
4. Use an **"If"** condition that will compare the subject of the email with the wordings **"New Ticket"**.

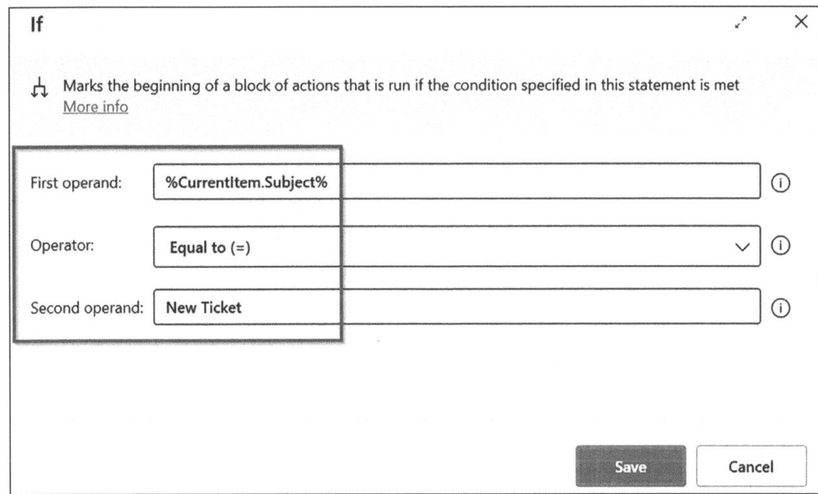

***Figure 6.53:** If condition to check the Subject*

5. If the condition matches then move the message to the **"To be processed"** Outlook folder which is under the Inbox. To do this, drag and drop the **"Process email messages in Outlook"**, which is the topic of this section.

Provide the parameters as given in the following figure to move the email pointed by the **CurrentItem** to the **"Inbox\To be processed"** Outlook folder.

The **"Operation"** dropdown has the other two options to delete or mark an email as unread.

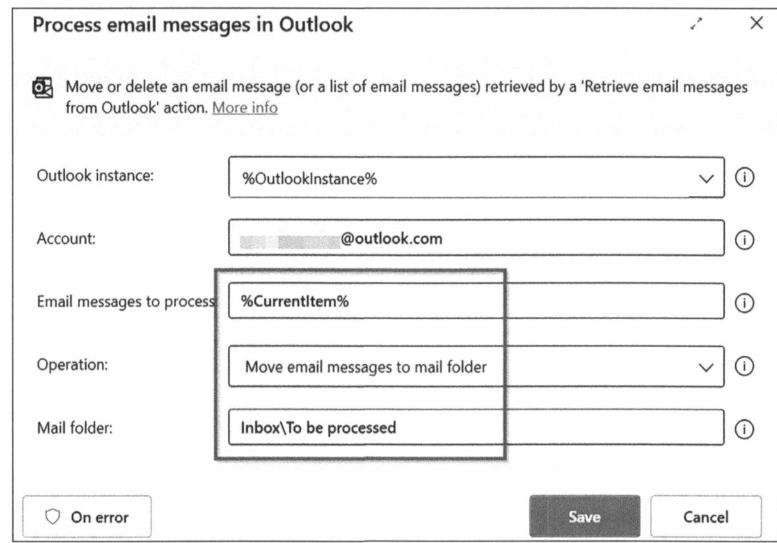

Figure 6.54: *Parameters for moving the email*

The final Flow after adding the **"Close Outlook"** Action is shown in *Figure* 6.55. When you run the Flow, only the emails that match the specified criteria will be moved to the designated folder.

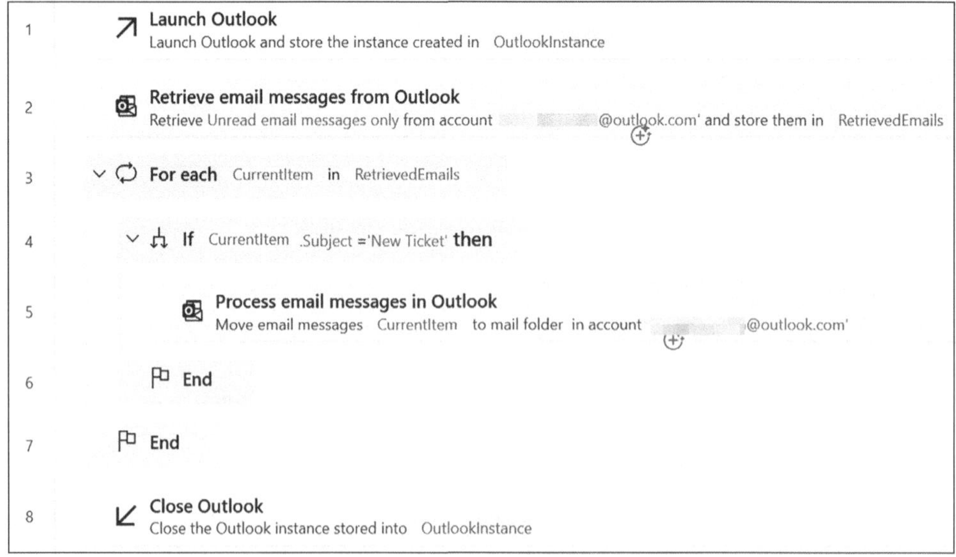

Figure 6.55: *The final Flow with all actions*

Responding to Email Messages

Responding involves replying or forwarding to an email automatically via the bot.

For the preceding steps, if the sender has to be auto-replied with a static text when the subject has **"New Ticket"** in it, then use the Action called **"Respond to Outlook message"** within the **"For each"** loop. The **"Response action"** dropdown has options for replying to all members of the original email, or replying to just the sender, or forwarding to intended recipients.

Add this Action in your Flow and verify how it works. Also review by changing the different parameter options.

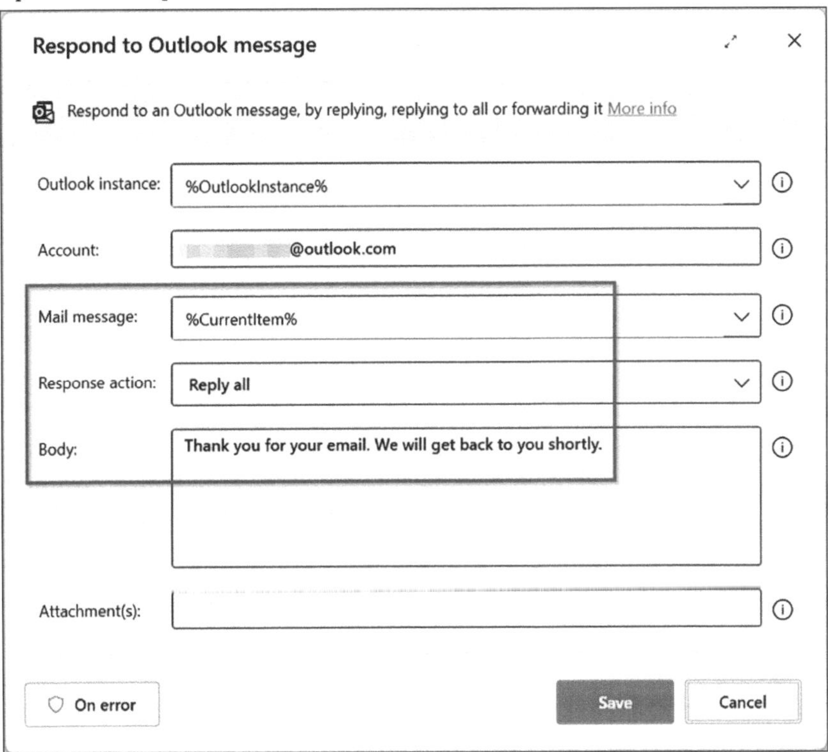

Figure 6.56: *The Respond to Outlook message action*

Saving Email Messages

One could have a requirement to save an email message for record purposes, let us say as a proof of something like resolving a ticket. PAD has an in-built Action to save an Outlook email in multiple formats, such as .txt, .msg, or even .html among others. This is done by the **"Save Outlook email messages"** Action. It is used in the same way as the above Actions where **CurrentItem** is pointing to an email after retrieving them within the **"For each"** loop.

Also, you can pass a List of email messages to this Action if you do not want to use a loop to process email messages at an individual level. It purely depends on the requirement of your automation whether you want to use a loop or pass a direct List of email messages.

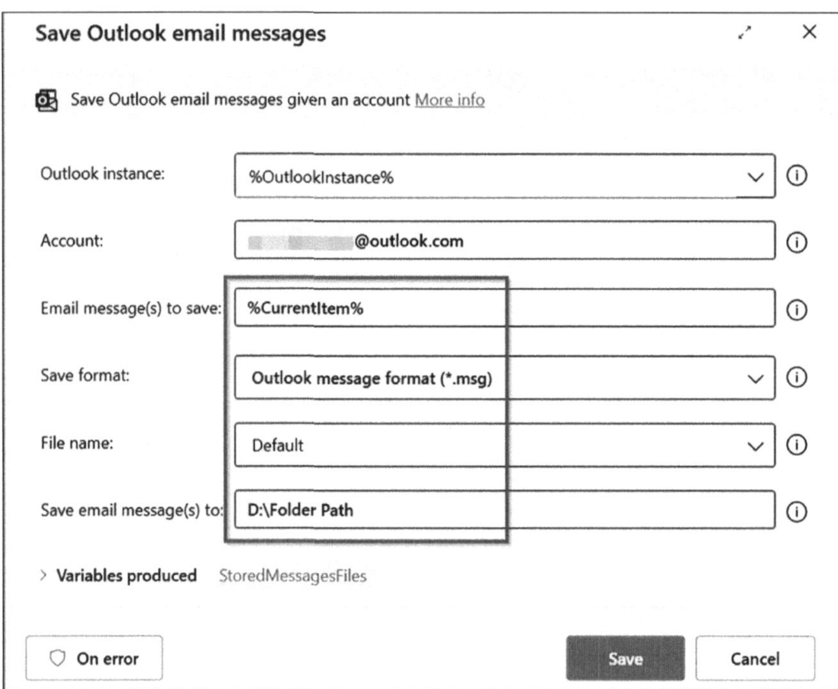

Figure 6.57: *The Save Outlook email messages action*

In this case the email pointed by the **`CurrentItem`** variable will be saved in the Outlook email message format with its default name in the specified folder path. This default name is generally the subject of the email, after stripping off the characters not allowed in a file name, followed by the extension, that is, .msg in this case. All the supported file formats can be configured in the **"`Save format`"** dropdown. The **"`File name`"** dropdown also gives an option to provide a custom name instead of the default one. Experiment with these various options. Notice the **`StoredMessagesFiles`** output variable produced which will store the paths of all the saved email files for further processing, for example to upload to a ticketing system in our case.

To perform Outlook Automation, the Outlook application has to be installed on the machine where the bot is running. In the list of Actions on the PAD Flow Designer, other than the widely used Office application of Outlook for RPA automation, there are other email related Actions like using the Exchange Server, IMAP Server and sending emails through SMTP Server. Here is a tutorial link that will assist in the continued exploration on these topics:

https://learn.microsoft.com/en-us/training/modules/pad-email/

Database Interaction

Databases have been there since a very long time and it becomes necessary to automate an application that would be having a database interaction in it, or even have a new database to store data into it by the automation.

Power Automate Desktop (PAD) provides easy in-built Actions to establish a connection with a database like Access or SQL Server, or any other, and execute SQL statements on it to Add, Update or Delete data. These Actions are available under the **"Database"** group of Actions in the **"Actions"** pane. To establish a connection with a Database, we need to first build a connection string which is done by the **"Open SQL connection"** Action.

The following figure displays a highlighted button that opens up a wizard to create a connection string. This connection string can either be manually written in the box provided or generated via the wizard. Click this button.

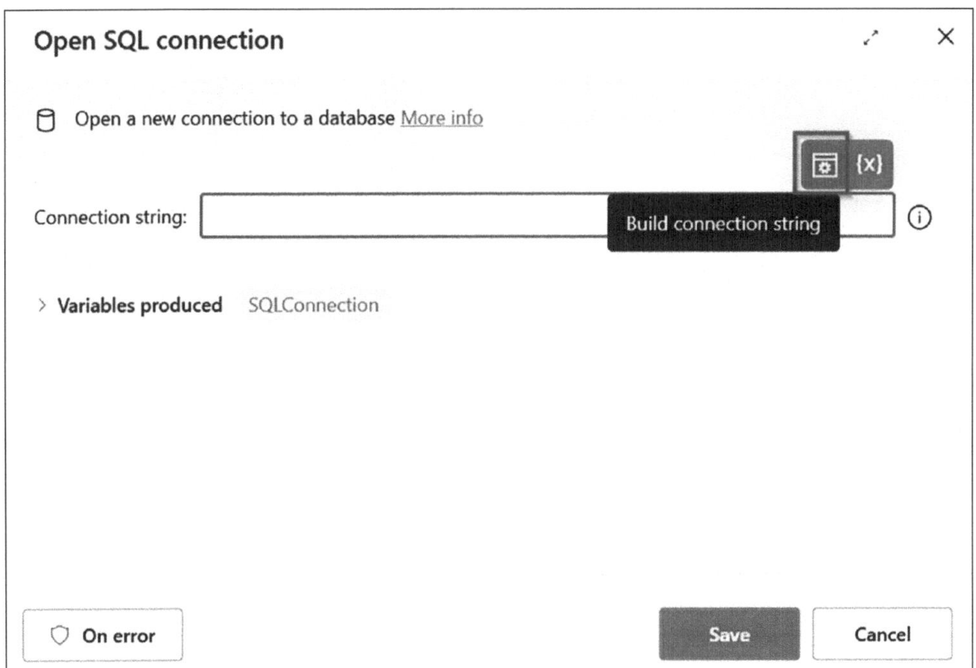

Figure 6.58: *Creating a connection string*

This will open up a dialog box showing a list of all providers available on your machine in the **"Provider"** tab. Since we are connecting to an Access database you would need the selected provider and if you can't see it in the list, or are seeing any provider-related errors when you go through the following topics, then the **"Microsoft Access Database Engine"** has to be installed from the Microsoft website. After selecting, click **"Next"** which will navigate to the **"Connection"** tab.

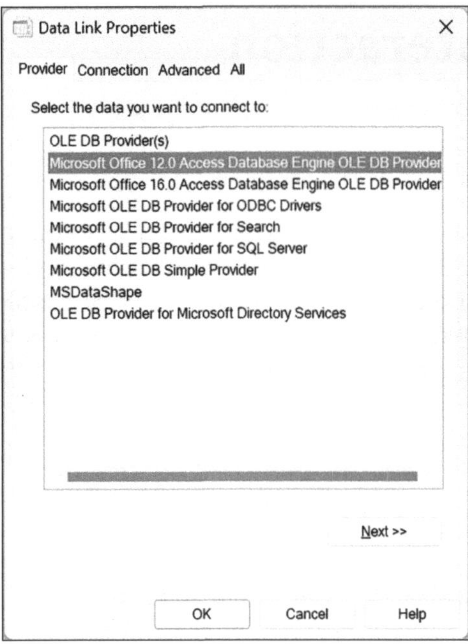

Figure 6.59: *List of available Providers*

In the **"Connection"** tab, provide the path to the Access database file in the **"Data Source"** box. A general good practice is to click the **"Test Connection"** button and verify the connection succeeded message.

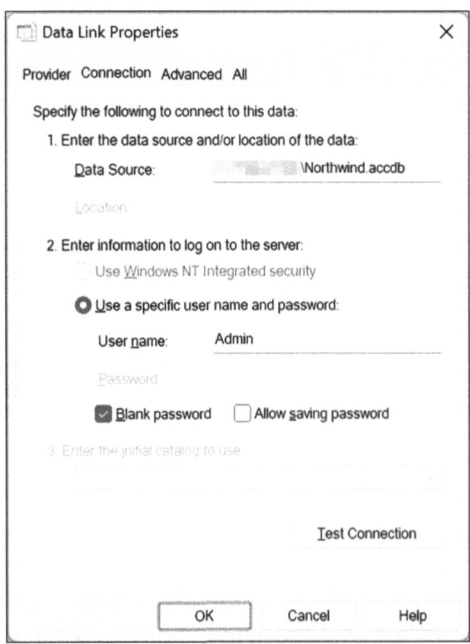

Figure 6.60: *The Connection tab*

Click the **"OK"** button and this will show the generated connection string for the selected provider and database. Also notice the **`SQLConnection`** output variable which is used to point to the connection just created.

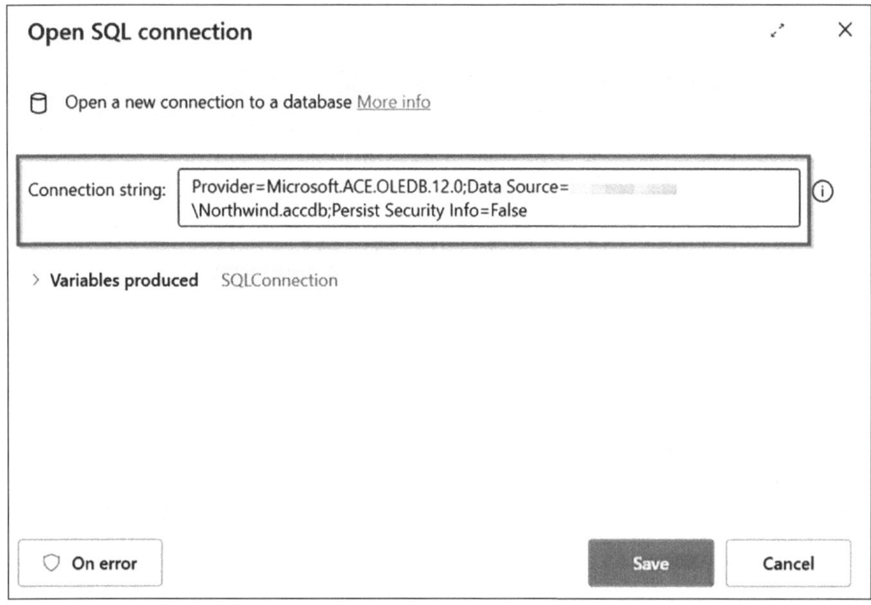

Figure 6.61: *The generated connection string*

The second way of generating a connection string is to create it manually. And this can be done with the help of a very good website called https://www.connectionstrings.com/access

The above link is for an Access database and you can see a connection string on the page is the same as the one generated by us through the wizard.

Likewise, on the homepage of the preceding website you can get a connection string to any of the listed databases.

https://www.connectionstrings.com

After a connection is established, the other Actions under the **"Database"** group of Actions are used to interact with a Database, for example, **"Execute SQL statement"** for firing SQL queries, and then **"Close SQL connection"** to close the connection generated by the **"Open SQL connection"** Action.

Let us see these in action but with the help of a unique exercise, which is not a feature of PAD but has been used since the programming times. Have you ever heard of the powerful concept of treating Excel as a Database? You can establish a connection with an Excel file and then fire SQL queries on it just like the way you would do for a Database. This is typically used in PAD where the volume of data in Excel is high or when the available Excel Actions do not serve our purpose.

Connection to the Excel is done in the same way as done via giving the connection string in **"Open SQL connection".**

Refer the connection string for **"Xlsx files"** of **"Excel 2013"** section of the following link:

https://www.connectionstrings.com/ace-oledb-12-0

Replace the full path of the Excel file with the one we need to interact with in the provided format. You can also use a variable holding the file path and pass it in the following connection string.

```
Provider=Microsoft.ACE.OLEDB.12.0;Data Source=c:\myFolder\myExcel-2007file.xlsx;Extended Properties="Excel 12.0 Xml;HDR=YES";
```

Use a **"Set variable"** Action and provide the full path of the Excel file for a variable called **%ExcelFile%.** The updated connection string with variable highlighted in bold is as shown here:

Provider=Microsoft.ACE.OLEDB.12.0;Data Source=**%ExcelFile%**;Extended Properties="Excel 12.0 Xml;HDR=YES";

Further, we will use the **"Execute SQL statement"** Action and provide an SQL query to get all the rows from a sheet named "Orders". This sheet is available in the same **SampleData.xlsx** file.

The syntax to use the table name in this query is to enclose the sheet name with square brackets and suffix a **$** symbol at the end within the brackets.

So, if **"Orders"** is the sheet name, then its corresponding Select query would be as follows:

```
Select * from [Orders$]
```

Consider several records of the **"Orders"** sheet as follows:

	A	B	C	D	E	F
1	Region	Rep	Item	Units	Unit Cost	Total
2	East	Jones	Pencil	95	1.99	189.05
3	Central	Kivell	Binder	50	19.99	999.50
4	Central	Jardine	Pencil	36	4.99	179.64
5	Central	Gill	Pen	27	19.99	539.73
6	West	Sorvino	Pencil	56	2.99	167.44
7	East	Jones	Binder	60	4.99	299.40
8	Central	Andrews	Pencil	75	1.99	149.25
9	Central	Jardine	Pencil	90	4.99	449.10
10	West	Thompson	Pencil	32	1.99	63.68
11	East	Jones	Binder	60	8.99	539.40
12	Central	Morgan	Pencil	90	4.99	449.10
13	East	Howard	Binder	29	1.99	57.71
14	East	Parent	Binder	81	19.99	1,619.19
15	East	Jones	Pencil	35	4.99	174.65

Figure 6.62: *Sample records of the Orders sheet*

After providing the **`SQLConnection`** variable, use the preceding query in the **"`SQL statement`"** box of the **"`Execute SQL statement`"** Action as shown in the following figure. The output variable **`QueryResult`** generated by this Action will hold the results of the SQL query.

Now that you are aware of how to create a connection string, you should be made aware that you can also directly use a connection string into the **"`Get connection by`"** dropdown by selecting the **"`Connection string`"** parameter. In this case you need not use the **"`Open SQL connection`"** Action and directly use the **"`Execute SQL statement`"** Action.

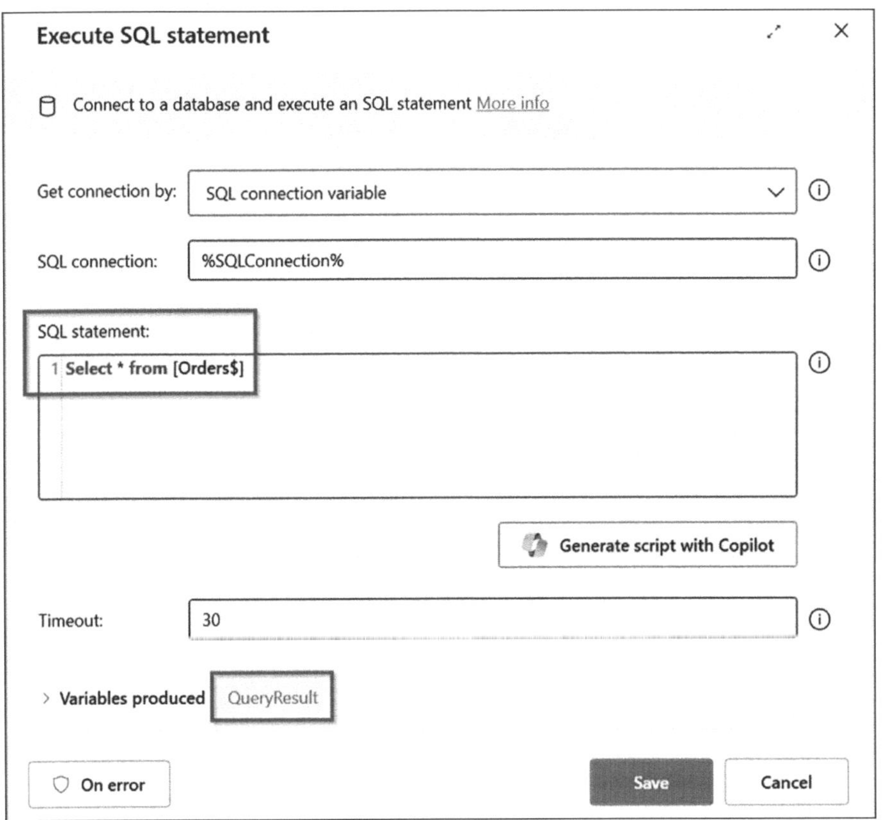

Figure 6.63: *Passing a query in Execute SQL statement action*

The **"`Close SQL connection`"** Action is used to close the connection generated by the **"`Open SQL connection`"** Action. Here is how the overall Flow looks like:

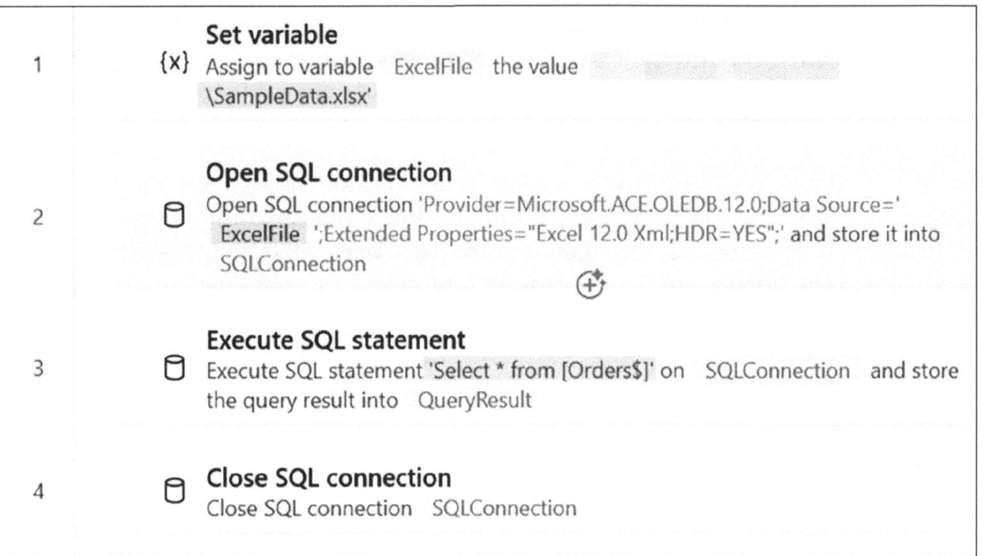

Figure 6.64: *The final Flow*

On running the Flow, the output variable gets populated with the data from the Excel sheet. Here is a sample screenshot of the top few records from the **"Orders"** sheet.

Variable value

QueryResult (Datatable)

#	Region	Rep	Item	Units	Unit Cost	Total
0	East	Jones	Pencil	95	1.99	189.05
1	Central	Kivell	Binder	50	19.99	999.5
2	Central	Jardine	Pencil	36	4.99	179.64
3	Central	Gill	Pen	27	19.99	539.73
4	West	Sorvino	Pencil	56	2.99	167.44
5	East	Jones	Binder	60	4.99	299.4
6	Central	Andrews	Pencil	75	1.99	149.25
7	Central	Jardine	Pencil	90	4.99	449.1
8	West	Thompson	Pencil	32	1.99	63.68

Figure 6.65: *Top rows of the output after running the final Flow*

Let us add a **"Where"** SQL clause to the same query for the **"Region"** column in the sheet.

We will pull all the records from the sheet where the Region is Central. The query for it will be `Select * from [Orders$] where [Region] = 'Central'`

Here the **"Region"** column is enclosed within square brackets and the text Central is enclosed within single quotes. The output after running the above query is as follows, showing only the records from the Central region:

Variable value

QueryResult (Datatable)

#	Region	Rep	Item	Units	Unit Cost	Total
0	Central	Kivell	Binder	50	19.99	999.5
1	Central	Jardine	Pencil	36	4.99	179.64
2	Central	Gill	Pen	27	19.99	539.73
3	Central	Andrews	Pencil	75	1.99	149.25
4	Central	Jardine	Pencil	90	4.99	449.1
5	Central	Morgan	Pencil	90	4.99	449.1
6	Central	Smith	Desk	2	125	250
7	Central	Morgan	Binder	28	8.99	251.72
8	Central	Kivell	Pen Set	96	4.99	479.04

Figure 6.66: *Top rows with Region as Central*

The same Action also has the capability to call Stored Procedures, and the syntax to do that is as follows, where the below names along with angular brackets are the placeholders:

```
Exec <StoredProcName> <Parameter1>,<Parameter2>…
```

Windows Automation

Another set of common applications that undergo automation are the Windows Desktop kind of applications. The Calculator application that we have been seeing is a type of Windows Desktop application. Let us look at the key Actions needed for automating these types of applications.

Before we start looking at the Actions, let us see a general guideline on how to identify the Actions from the **"Actions"** pane. The Actions needed for Windows Automation are categorized under **"UI automation"** in the **"Actions"** pane. Further down, the **"Data extraction"** sub category contains **reading** related Actions like getting or extracting something from the application. Whereas, the **"Form filling"** sub category set of Actions has anything related to **writing** like filling a text field, selecting option buttons, checkboxes, pressing a button and so on. Hovering the mouse over an Action name will give a tooltip text to give an idea as to what that Action does.

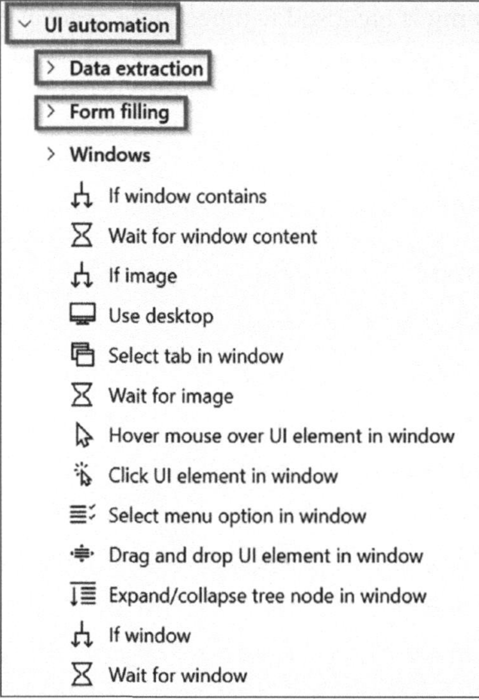

Figure 6.67: *Windows automation reading and writing actions*

Once you understand how to create UI elements and how to uniquely identify its Selectors, using the Actions to perform UI based automation becomes simpler as most of the time it involves filling in the parameter boxes with the right UI elements and values.

Launch an Application

To start an application in the Flow, the **"Run application"** Action is made use of, which is available under the **"System"** group of Actions and not under the **"UI automation"** group of Actions. The parameter accepted by this Action is the executable of the application. As examples, since Calculator and Notepad are in-built applications, they can be given as **"calc"** and **"notepad"** respectively without suffixing **".exe"** to the application name. If you type these in the Run menu of the Windows start menu and hit *Enter*, these applications would open up.

The Action also has useful options to maximize the application window or to provide an Argument to the application executable, for example, if the **"Application path"** is **"notepad"** and its command line argument is the full path of a text file then running this Action will launch the specified text file in Notepad. Another useful parameter

"After application launch" is to tell the Flow what needs to be done after the corresponding application is launched.

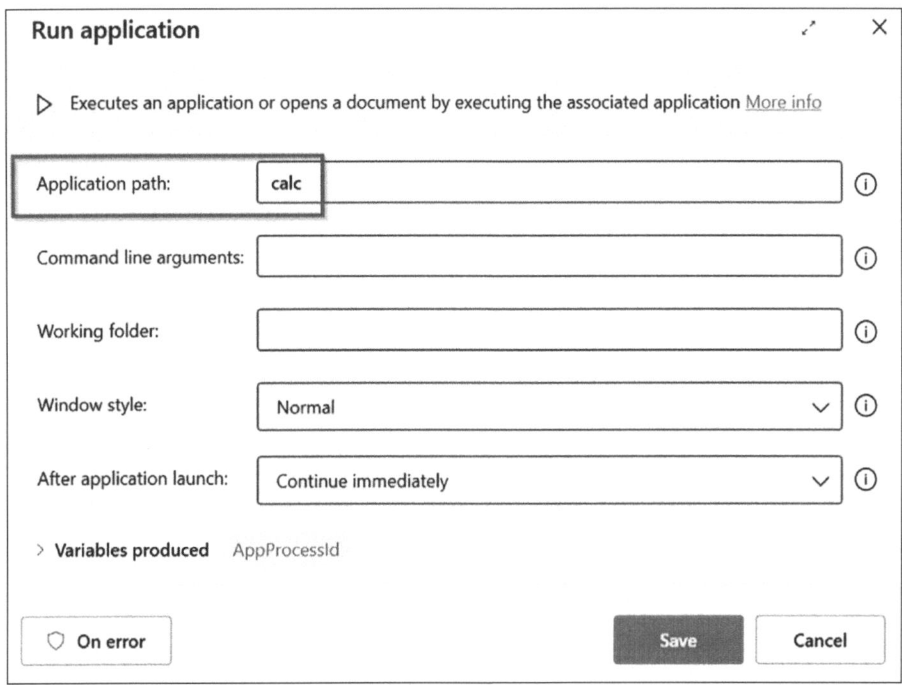

Figure 6.68: *Run application action*

The full path of the executable of the applications can be given for any other application including for in-built ones.

Reading Operations

We will be seeing the Actions for reading from an UI element or from a window. The same can be done for getting details of checkboxes, option buttons and dropdowns from an application.

For this, we will be using a sample demo application from Microsoft and is available as **ContosoInvoicingSetup.zip** file in the GitHub folder of this chapter.

The sample invoicing application in the following figure has been opened by giving its full path in the **"Application path"** box. We will read the value from the **"Account"** text box and the title of the window.

You can still use the **"Recorder"** wherever supportable but our intention here is to do the same with the help of pre-built Actions for reading content from a Windows Desktop application.

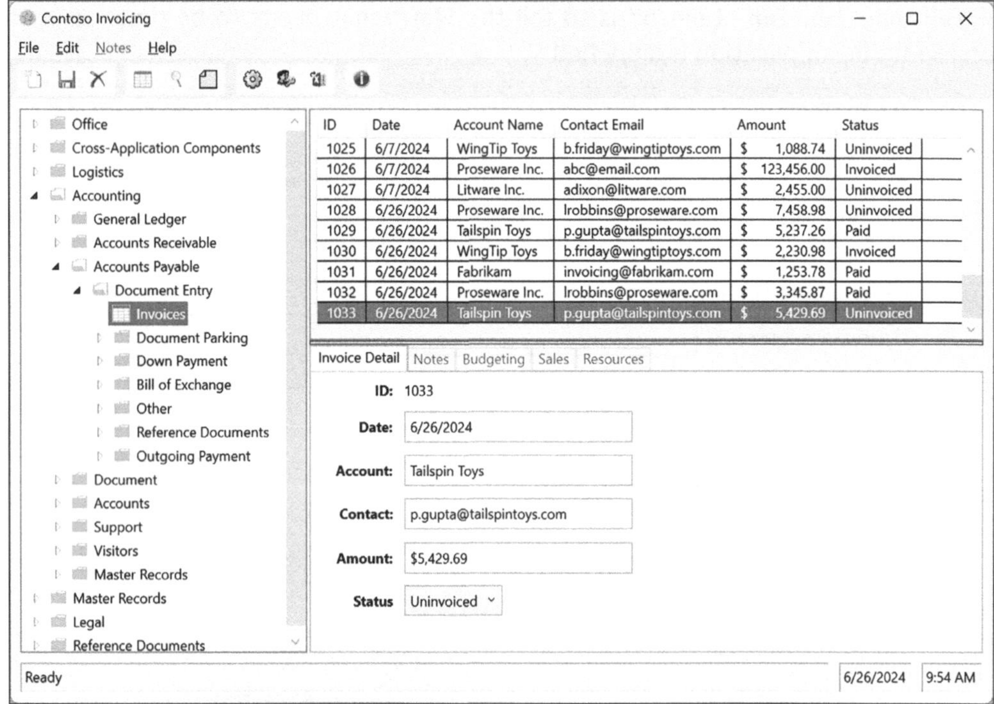

Figure 6.69: *Sample Contoso Invoicing Windows Desktop application*

The text box for **"`Account`"** is an UI element, so to read data we will use the **"`Get details of the UI element in window`"** Action. Then on adding the text box UI element from within this Action, it is populated as the following figure. Hovering the stack of UI elements button shows the text box and to extract its value we are using **"`Own Text`"** as a parameter. This dropdown is editable for giving a compatible attribute name and also has useful options to check whether the UI element exists or is enabled in which case a Boolean value of True or False will be returned by this Action. The output of the value from the **"`Accounts`"** text box is stored in the **`AttributeValue`** variable.

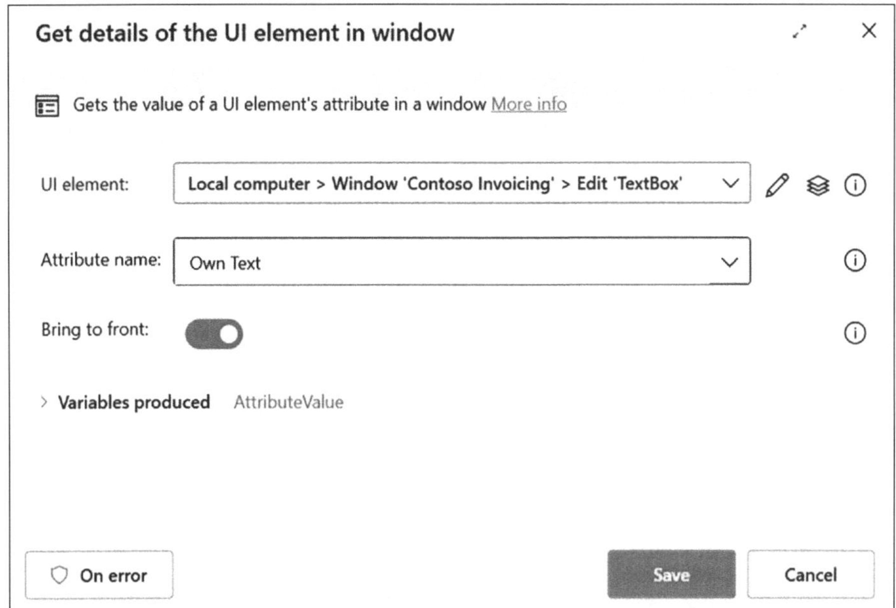

Figure 6.70: *The Get details of the UI element in window action*

Also, enabling the **`"Bring to front"`** toggle will bring the window of the invoicing application to the forefront.

To read the title of the window we make use of the **`"Get details of window"`** Action, then capture the window by pointing to the outside border of the corresponding window and set the **`"Window property"`** dropdown as **`"Get window title"`**. This dropdown can also assist in getting the process name of the application running and then used in any of the other PAD Actions that require a process name. Running the Flow with a display box for each of these extracted values will show the output as follows. These values can then be utilized for any further processing by the bot.

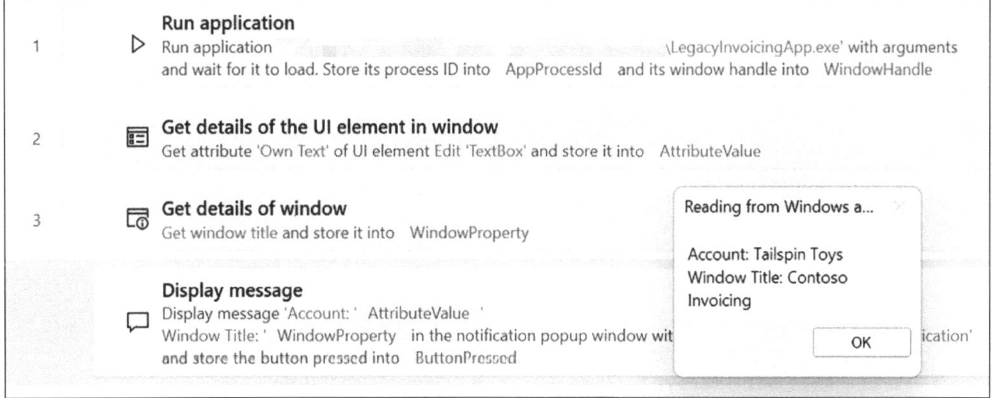

Figure 6.71: *Entire Flow and its output*

How about trying the same for checkboxes, option buttons and dropdowns from a Windows application via their designated Actions under **"Data extraction"** sub category? They simply involve adding the right UI element and filling the right parameters.

Writing Operations

Writing operations for any automation involve entering text into a text box, selecting values for dropdowns, option buttons, check boxes and so on.

As per the numbering in the next figure, following are the sequence of activities we will be performing:

1. Click the button for **"New Record"**
2. Fill a dummy value for the **"Account"** text box
3. Select the Status dropdown as **"Invoiced"**
4. Finally, click the **"Save Changes"** button

A new entry with an auto ID of 1035 should be created after running the Flow.

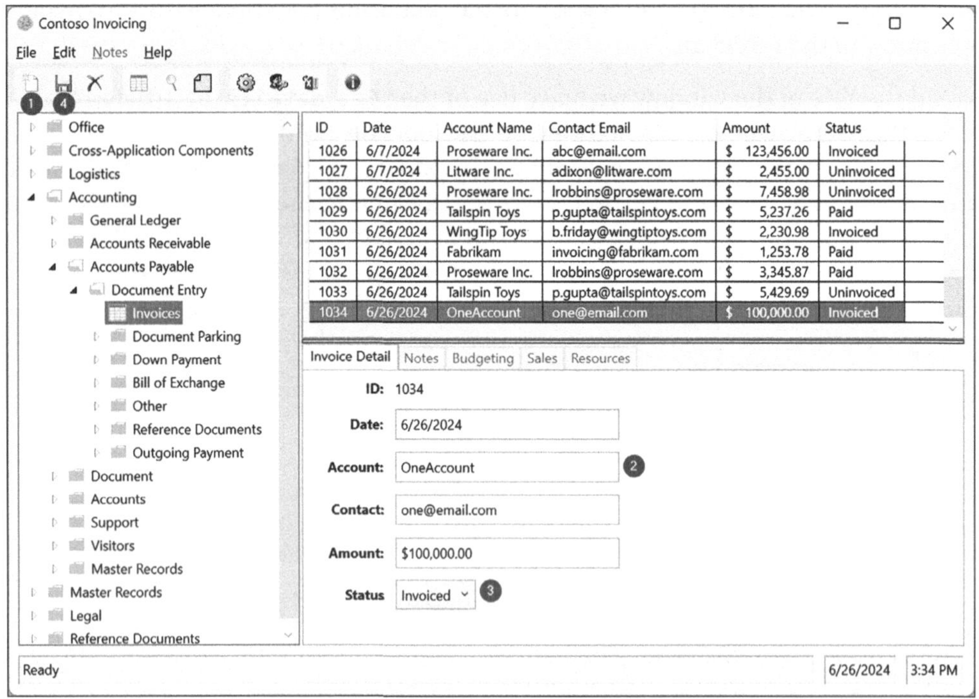

Figure 6.72: *Sequence of activities to follow*

Follow along the below steps:

1. The first Action in the Flow is to use the **"Run application"** along with the path of the executable. Use the **"Wait for application to load"** parameter so as to give it some time to load before interacting with it.

2. The **"Press button in window"** Action will assist in clicking the **"New Record"** button. Add an UI element for the button using this Action. While adding the element when you hover the mouse on the button, make sure that it shows as **"button"** and not an **"image"**.

   The **"Simulate action"** toggle button is handy in scenarios where this Action does not work when the toggle is kept disabled. On enabling, the Action will mimic the movement of the mouse to the button before clicking. In our case, we will be keeping the toggle turned off since it works fine.
   If in your case, the application on launching opens up a different tab on the tree view on the left-hand side, then through the bot click the **"Invoices"** section with the help of the **"Press button in window"** Action.

3. Next goes the **"Populate text field in window"** Action which is used to write to a text field. Via this Action, add an UI element for the **"Accounts"** text box and provide any sample account name to be written into the box. The options in the **"Advanced"** section of this Action are self-explanatory and can be used according to our requirements. When unclear, hover the mouse on the **'i'** information icon to understand the parameter.

   It is important that you capture the UI element for the text box when it is empty else the Selector might fail trying to identify a text box that already holds some value which will not be the case when entering new records.

4. Drag and drop the **"Set drop-down list value in window"** Action onto the Workspace, add an UI element for the **"Status"** dropdown, choose the **"Select options by name"** and mention the option as **"Invoiced"** without the quotes.

5. Once again use the **"Press button in window"** Action but this time add the UI element for the **"Save"** button.

The following figure depicts the entire Flow after completing the previous steps:

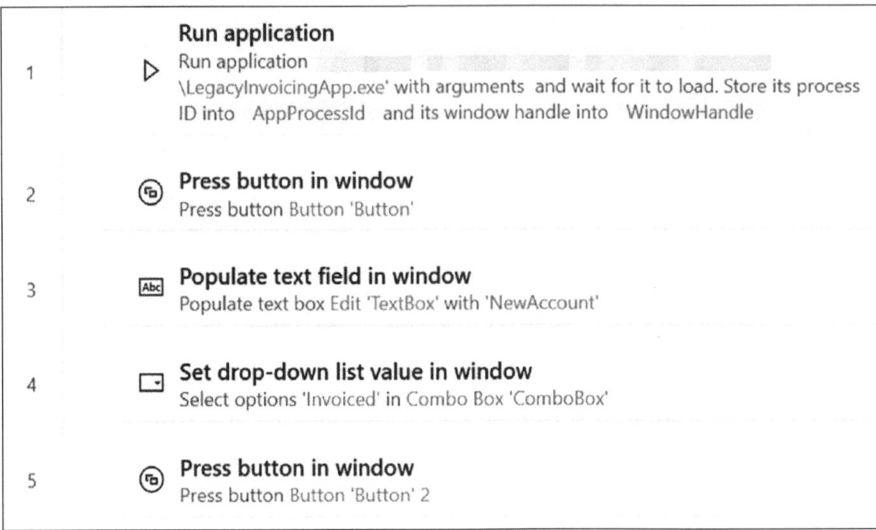

***Figure 6.73:** The final Flow with writing operations*

On running the Flow, a new entry is added to the bottom of the table with an ID of 1035 as expected, the dummy account name written to the text box and the Status dropdown selected as **"`Invoiced`"**. The date field takes the current date as default and the other boxes are shown blank as they are optional and were not interacted by the bot.

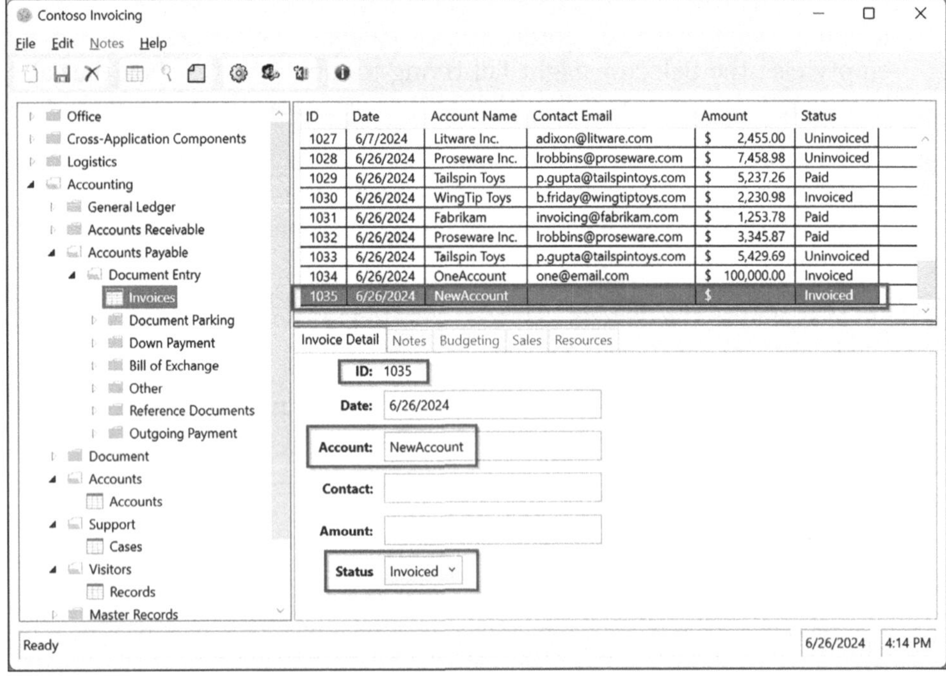

***Figure 6.74:** Output after running the Flow*

Likewise, there are writing sets of Actions under the **"Form filling"** sub group that can be used in the similar way to set a checkbox value or select a radio or option button, and are worth practicing on an application that have these UI elements.

The **"Focus text field in window"** is made use of when the focus has to be on the desired text box in which case Power Automate Desktop brings the text box in view if it is somewhere beyond visibility due to the scrolling positions.

Other Useful Windows Automation Actions

At times the **"Press button in window"** may not work as expected due to the way the underlying application is built. In such cases, the **"Click UI element in window"** Action can be made use of and tried with both, with and without the toggle for **"Simulate action".** In our case, if we try to click the **"Save Changes"** button using this Action with the toggle disabled, it works fine. Check the same for the **"New Record"** button.

This Action also works for clicking the **"Invoices"** section of the tree view on the left-hand side. So, try that out too. This means, not only buttons, but this Action can be used to click any other UI element too depending upon the requirement of the automation. Following is an example of this Action for clicking the **"Save Changes"** button.

Also, in this Action refer to the **"Click type"** parameter to see the various other possibilities like double click, right click, left down and so on.

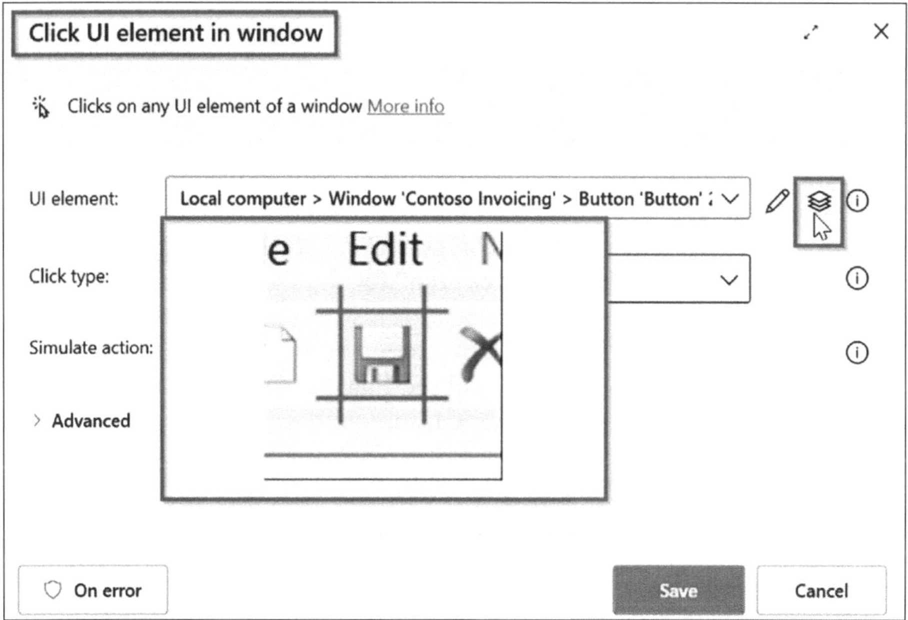

***Figure 6.75:** The Click UI element in window action for Save button*

There occur several automation scenarios where an application is already running in the background and you need to lay the focus on that application window through the bot. This could be for sending mouse clicks or keystrokes to that application or simply to put the focus on that application window to bring it to the front. To do this, PAD provides an Action called **"`Focus window`"**. The **"`Find window mode`"** has three options to find a window running in the background (refer to *Figure 6.76*). Let us see what each of them indicate.

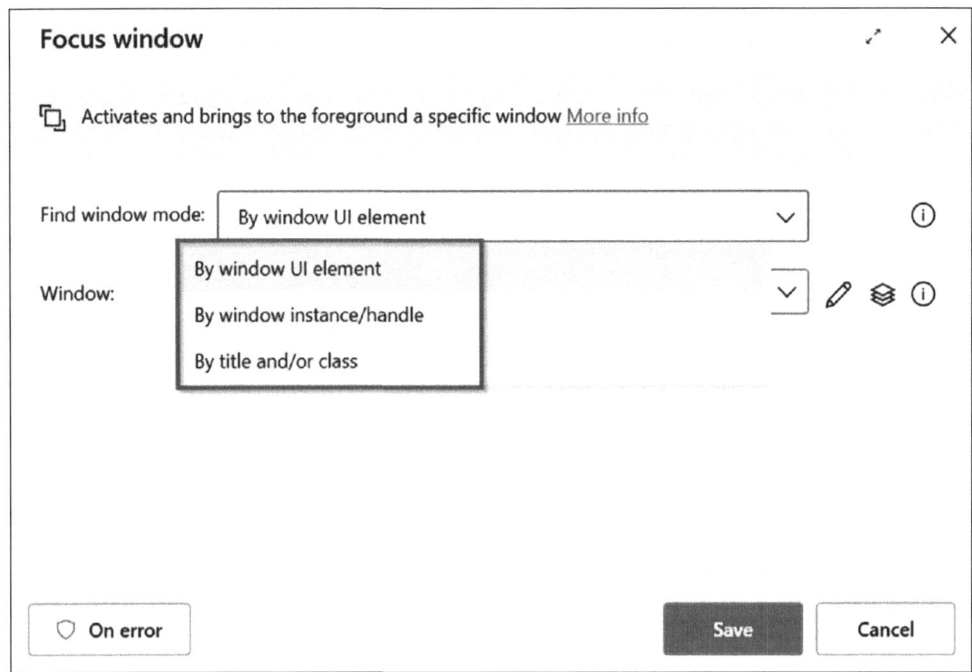

Figure 6.76: *The Focus window action and its options*

1. By window UI element:
   This option is by creating a UI element of the window for the Contoso Invoicing application through the **"`Add UI element`"** button of the **"`Window`"** dropdown. To try this, use the **"`Run application`"** for the Contoso application and then another one for opening the Calculator just to take away the focus from the Contoso application. Then use this Action to put the focus on the Contoso window. Run the Flow and you will see that the Contoso application window gets the focus and shows up on the foreground.

2. By window/instance handle:
   In this option, a window instance or a handle to a window is used in this case. This instance is returned from the **"`Get window`"** Action. So, add this Action and pass its output variable to the **"`Focus window`"** Action. Run the Flow and the Contoso application window will get the focus and the Calculator window is taken to the back.

3. By title and/or class:
   The first parameter is to pass the title of the desired window. Either you can hard-code the title, in our case as *Contoso Invoicing*, or as in *Figure* 6.71 you can get the title of a window via the **"`Get details of window`"** Action depending upon the automation scenario. Note that your automation Flows are not going to be so small that the **"`Get details of window`"** and the **"`Focus window`"** Actions will be immediately one after the another. The former could be in the Main Flow and the latter could be in some other distant Subflow, as an example. This means that you could capture the window title in the Main Flow, save it in the output variable and use it somewhere else in another part of the same Desktop Flow.
   While developing, Power Automate Desktop also gives a list of window titles of all the open windows currently open on the machine and the same can be made use of in this dropdown parameter. There is another optional parameter to provide the class of the window in case there are two windows of the same title.
   Another interesting way is via the **"`Select window`"** button which PAD provides to select the required window just like the way a UI element can be selected by pressing *Ctrl* and then left click.
   Refer to the support of the wild card characters mentioned in the tooltip text of the **"`Window title`"** parameter, which can be used in situations where the title changes dynamically.

Practically try out a mix and match of these different options and see what options are shown in the dropdown parameters and how they work against a real Windows application.

Most of the automation Flows require that the window of the application needs to be in a maximized state. This is achieved with the help of an Action called **"`Set window state`"**. This Action has dropdown parameters for minimizing, maximizing, or restoring a window to its previous state. It also has the **"`Find window mode`"** parameter which is used in the same way as in the earlier section for **"`Focus window`"**.

Run this Action for maximizing the Contoso application. Then minimize it manually and restore it via this Action and observe the different behavior of this Action.

Figure 6.77: *The Set window state action to maximize*

Be noted that the **"Run application"** itself has a parameter to open an application in a minimized or maximized state but our intention is to see the usage of these window states with the help of the **"Set window state"** Action which can be utilized later anywhere in the Flow. Practically try the same for the Calculator window.

During an automation there comes a need to check whether an UI element or a particular text on a window exists or not before taking another step. For example, while navigating from Window 1 to Window 2 of an application, there could be a delay in opening Window 2. Therefore, it is a good practice to check whether a particular UI element or a text exists or not on Window 2 and then take the necessary steps. This is achieved with the help of the **"If window contains"** Action. Let's check this out in action.

The **"Invoices"** tab on the Contoso application has an UI element for the **"Account"** text box.

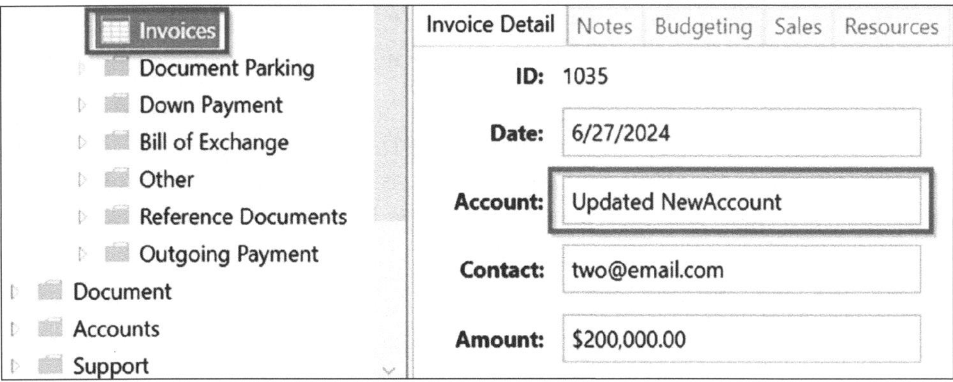

Figure 6.78: *Account text box on Invoices tab*

On adding a UI element for this text box, its Selector is as follows.

> custom[Class="ObjectEditor"][Id="ObjectEditor"] > custom[**Class="InvoiceEditorControl"**][Id="InvoiceEditor"] > tab[Class="TabControl"] > tabitem[Class="TabItem"][Name="Invoice Detail"] > edit[Class="TextBox"][**Id="txtAccount103"**]

Whereas, the **"Accounts"** tab does not have this text box. It has a different text box for **"Account Name"** with a different Selector as follows. The Class and Id Attributes are different as marked in bold.

> custom[Class="ObjectEditor"][Id="ObjectEditor"] > custom[**Class="AccountEditorControl"**][Id="AccountEditor"] > tab[Class="TabControl"] > tabitem[Class="TabItem"][Name="Account Detail"] > edit[Class="TextBox"][**Id="txtAccountName192"**]

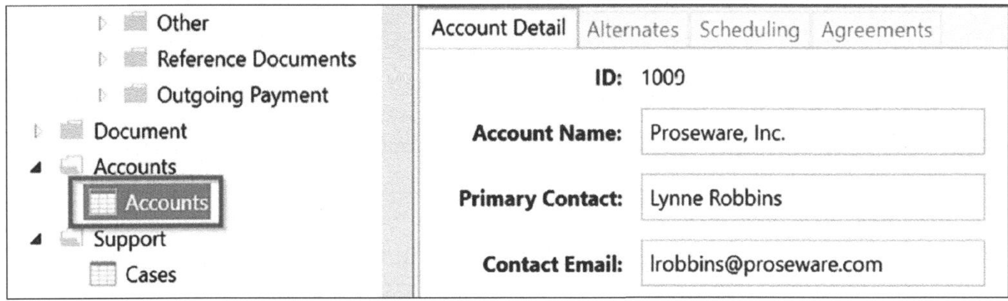

Figure 6.79: *No Account text box on Accounts tab*

With the help of the bot, we will be switching to each of these tabs and checking whether the window contains the **"Account"** text box. The bot should return True when it is on the **"Invoices"** tab whereas it should return False when on the **"Accounts"** tab.

To do this, follow the below sequence of action steps:

1. **"Run application"** with the full path of the Contoso application

2. Drag and drop the **"`If window contains`"** Action and pass the UI element for the **"`Accounts`"** text box as shown in the next figure.

You will see that on clicking the **"`Save`"** button, an **"`If`"** with an **"`End`"** Action gets inserted onto the Workspace designer. Add an **"`Else`"** Action in between the **"`If`"** and the **"`End`"** Actions. In the **"`If`"** part add a message box that says **"`Account text box exists`."** In the **"`Else`"** part add another message box that says **"`Account text box does not exist`."**

What we are doing here is, if the window contains the text box, the first message box will be displayed and if not then the second message.

For future references, the first parameter in the following Action also has options for checking whether a window contains a text or not and whether it does not contain a UI element, along with a toggle to verify whether the UI element is enabled or not.

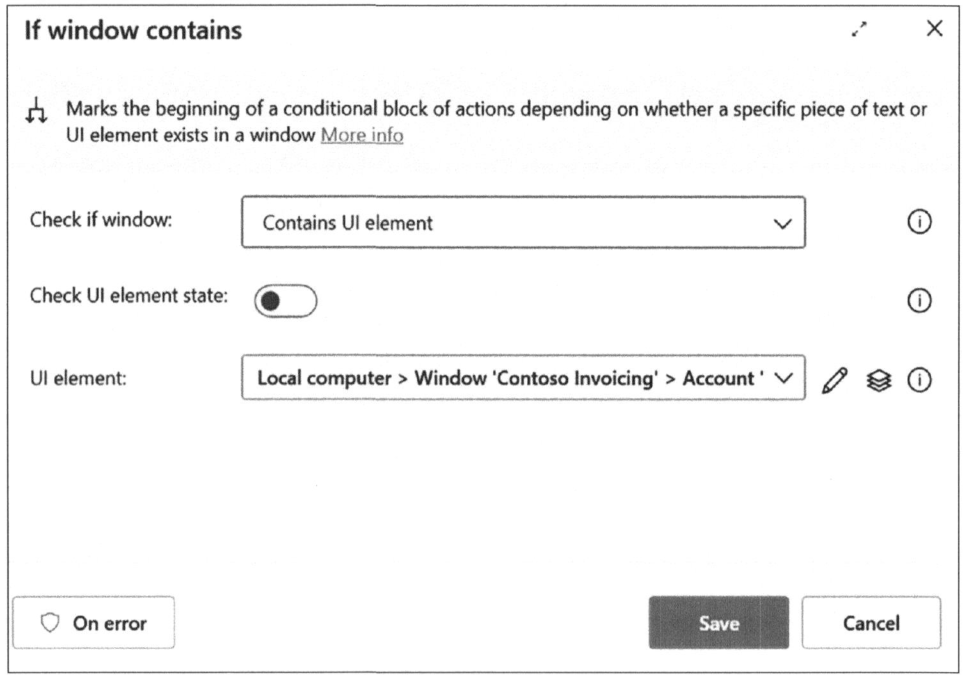

Figure 6.80: *The If window contains action*

The entire Flow after following the mentioned steps is as follows:

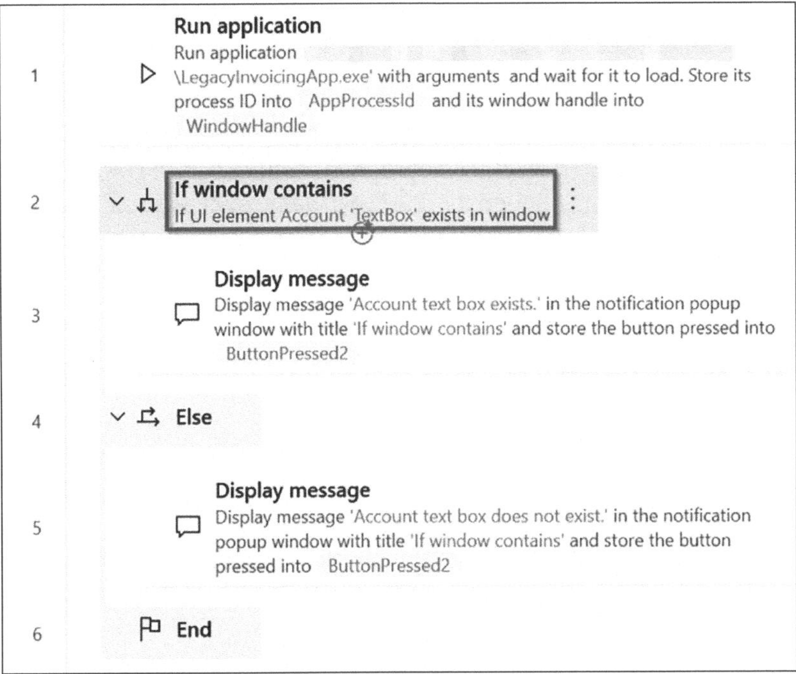

Figure 6.81: *Entire Flow after adding required actions*

Run the Flow and the **"Account text box does not exist."** message should show up if the Contoso application opens on the **"Accounts"** tab (which does not have the **"Account"** text box).

After trying this, add a **"Click UI element in window"** before the **"If"** Action to click the **"Invoices"** tab of *Figure* 6.78 by the bot. Run the Flow and the bot will navigate to the **"Invoices"** tab and hence the **"Account text box exists."** message will be shown (which has the **"Account"** text box).

The **"Wait for window content"** has the same parameters and behaves exactly the same way as the **"If window contains"** except that it has an option to wait forever or till the specified time for the given condition to be satisfied. This is typically handy when there is a delay in opening the window after the application is launched, or when switching from one window to another.

Try the following Actions as an exercise based on the aforementioned topics which would involve selecting the right UI elements and filling out the parameters.

1. Using the **"Select menu option in window"** Action, click the **"File"** menu of the Contoso application and see that it will open the menu.
2. Using the **"Close window"** Action closes the Contoso application. This Action has the exact same parameters as **"Focus window"**, which we saw in *Figure* 6.76.

Web Automation

Just like Windows automation for Desktop applications, Web automation also has a list of Actions depending on whether you are performing reading related or writing related operations on a web page. These are segregated under the **"`Browser automation`"** group of Actions. As the name suggests, the **"`Web data extraction`"** list of Actions are to read or get data from the web page and **"`Web form filling`"** Actions are to write or give inputs to the web page.

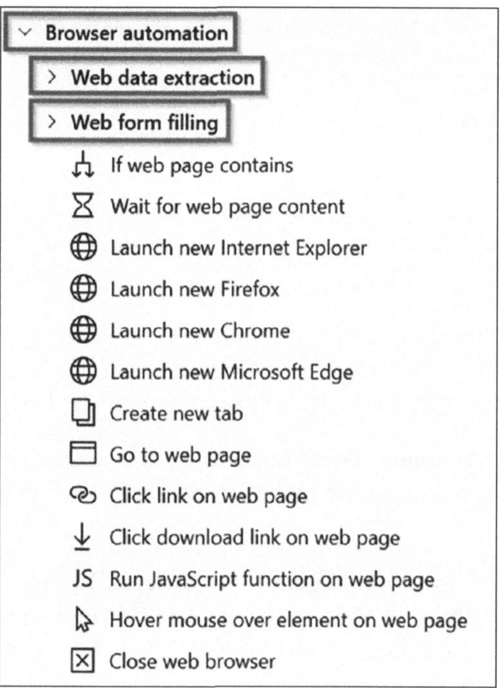

Figure 6.82: *Web automation reading and writing actions*

Once again, before you proceed you need to have browser extensions installed and enabled for performing Web automation. If not done earlier while installing PAD or during the Recording section, then they can be installed from the **"`Tools`"** menu and **"`Browser extensions`"** sub-menu of the Flow designer.

Launch a Web Application

If you recall the "*Recording a Web Application Using the Unified Recorder*" section of "*Chapter 5: Building Blocks of a Desktop Flow*", then we have been at first manually keeping a web page open and then interacting with it via PAD. That was for demonstrating the Recorder. The actual way is to have a web page open by the Flow and this is done using the **"`Launch new <browser>`"** set of Actions where a browser could be Chrome,

Edge, Firefox or Internet Explorer. In this section, we will be using the Microsoft Edge browser. You will find that the Actions and their parameters generated by the Recorder and the ones we are going to see here for launching, reading and writing will be nearly the same.

The first parameter of the **"Launch new Microsoft Edge"** Action is to tell the Flow whether to open a totally new instance or to attach to an existing instance with the specified URL. The **"Attach to running instance"** dropdown option is to be used when a browser window is already open or has to be kept mandatorily opened perhaps due to the requirements of the automation. During our recording examples, the Recorder has been automatically attaching to the running instance of the URL that was already kept open.

Select the attaching option and hover the **"i"** icon to see that it can also accept part of the URL or title name of a tab to attach to.

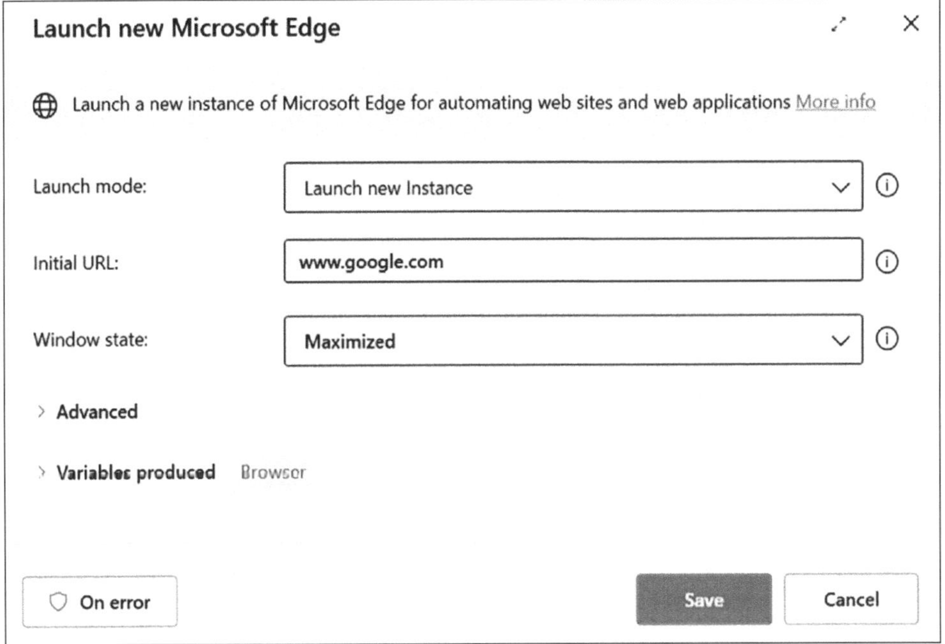

Figure 6.83: *The Launch new <Browser> action*

This Action has options to set the window state of the browser while opening. The **"Advanced"** section has some useful parameters like clearing the cache and cookies, or to wait till the web page completely loads and to specify Power Automate Desktop what to do when a pop-up appears while opening a web page. The output variable produced is of instance type and to be used in subsequent browser related Actions wherever asked.

Something that you should be aware of is that there is an Action called **"Create new**

tab" which creates a tab in a browser instance and has an option to navigate to a specified URL.

Reading Operations

Similar to getting the details of a window, we can get the details of a web page with the help of the **"Get details of web page"** Action. This Action has a varied list of options and can return the description, meta keywords, title, text, source code and URL of the web page. If the preceding figure is the launch Action, then the **WebPageProperty** output variable of the following figure would return https://www.google.com/ as the response. These various responses can then be utilized for further Actions down the Flow as per requirement. Verify getting the title and other options of any web page.

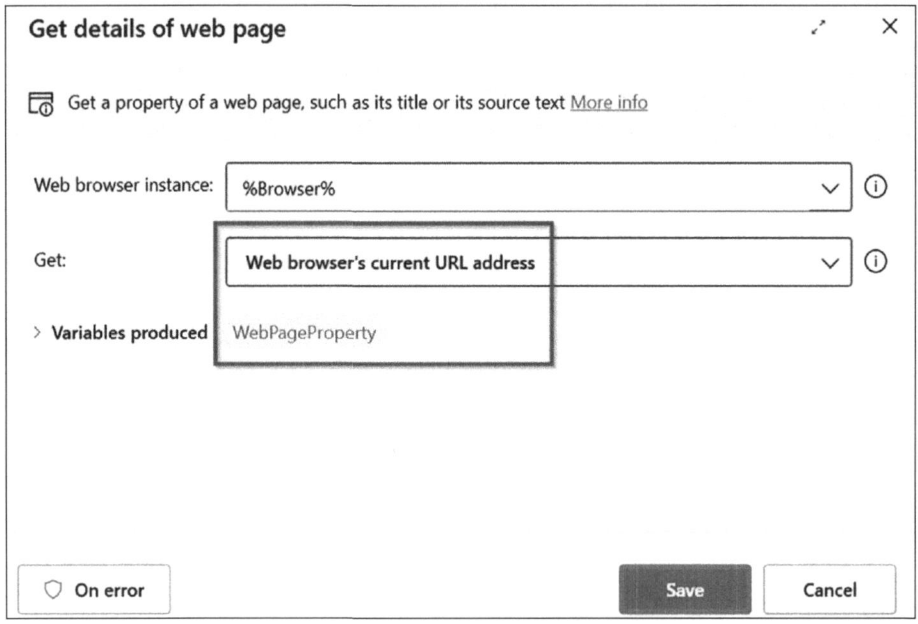

Figure 6.84: *The Get details of web page action*

When you want to get the data from a UI element on a web page, you make use of the **"Get details of element on web page"** Action. In the recording section, we read the value of a text box from a web page. Let's use the same web page and read the text box value with this Action.

1. Use the **"Launch new <browser>"** Action for the following URL: https://www.w3schools.com/html/tryit.asp?filename=tryhtml_form_submit

2. Drag and drop the **"Get details of element on web page"** Action onto the Workspace which will ask you to choose an UI element. Add an UI element for the **"First name"** text box of the preceding URL.

3. Display the output variable in a message box.

The entire Flow along with its output is as follows:

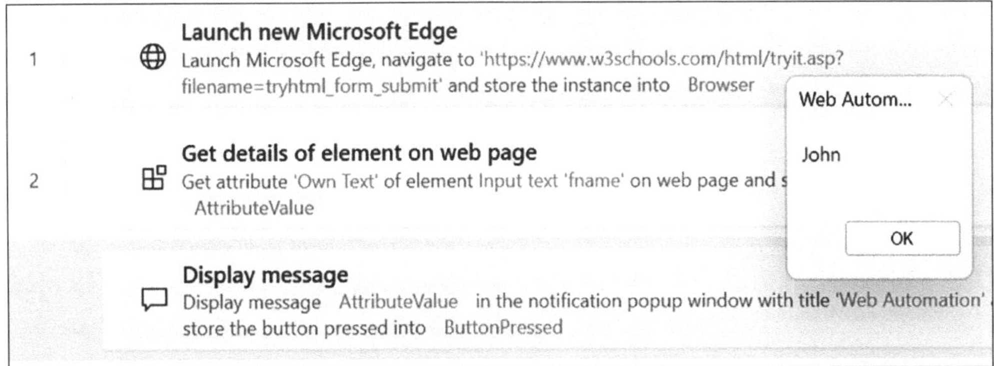

***Figure 6.85:** Reading an UI element value*

Another widely used Action especially for reading data that is in tabular or a structured format on a web page is the **"`Extract data from web page`"** Action. There is a unique way to use this Action. Follow these steps to read tabular data with this Action:

1. Manually open the web page for the following URL: https://www.w3schools.com/html/tryit.asp?filename=tryhtml_table_intro In order to extract the data from the web page, it has to be manually opened and then later closed once the extraction portion is done.

2. Use the **"`Launch new <browser>`"** Action for the above URL.

3. Drag and drop the **"`Extract data from web page`"** Action onto the Workspace. While this Action is open, manually go to the web page. As soon as you do that a **"`Live web helper`"** window opens on the page. Right-click the desired table value, use **"`Extract element value`"** and its corresponding **"`Text`"** menu item. This will add the table value on the **"`Live web helper`"** window as an **"`Extraction preview`"**.

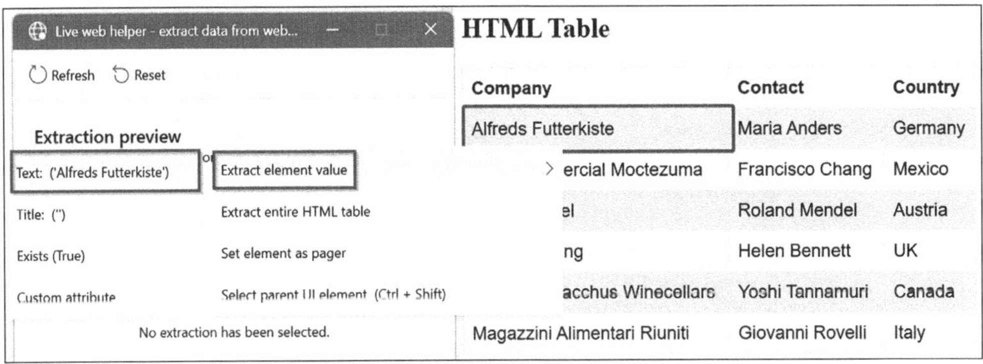

***Figure 6.86:** Extracting first table value*

Do this one more time, but for the second value in the same column, that is, for **`Centro comercial Moctezuma`**. As soon as you do that, the **"`Live web helper`"** understands the pattern of data you are trying to extract and it pulls all the values of that column and shows it in the preview, as shown in *Figure 6.87*. Also, a dotted border for the extracted data is seen indicated by the arrow in the following figure:

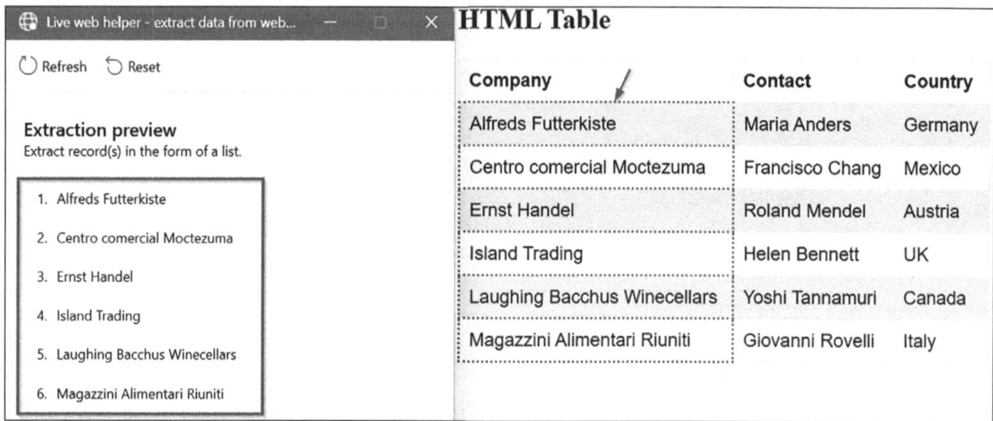

Figure 6.87: *Extraction of all values after the second value*

If you want the second column too, then do the same for the **"`Contact`"** column also. Now you can see both the column values extracted in the preview and the dotted border for both the columns. You can even edit the column name shown in the preview section from **"`Value #1`"** to something of your choice.

Extraction preview

Extract handpicked record(s) from multiple web pages in the form of a 2 -column data table.

Value #1	Value #2
Alfreds Futterkiste	Maria Anders
Centro comercial Moctezuma	Francisco Chang
Ernst Handel	Roland Mendel
Island Trading	Helen Bennett
Laughing Bacchus Winecellars	Yoshi Tannamuri
Magazzini Alimentari Riuniti	Giovanni Rovelli

HTML Table

Company	Contact	Country
Alfreds Futterkiste	Maria Anders	Germany
Centro comercial Moctezuma	Francisco Chang	Mexico
Ernst Handel	Roland Mendel	Austria
Island Trading	Helen Bennett	UK
Laughing Bacchus Winecellars	Yoshi Tannamuri	Canada
Magazzini Alimentari Riuniti	Giovanni Rovelli	Italy

Figure 6.88: *Extraction of all values after both columns*

Following is the final Flow and the web page can now be closed since the bot is going to open it. After running the Flow, open the output variable and now you can iterate through the Datatable for any further processing.

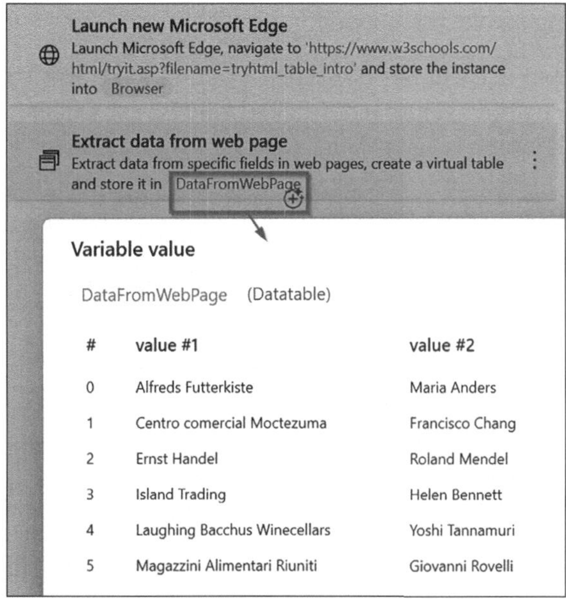

Figure 6.89: *Entire Flow and its output*

For the preceding example, when you open the **"Advanced settings"** from the bottom of the **"Live web helper"**, you will see various parameters which were automatically generated by the operations performed in the previous sections. However, you can also configure your own parameters and create CSS selectors that point to specific values or elements of the web page. References for CSS selectors are shared in the previous chapter. Navigating through different sections of the same website can be used for learning more about them.

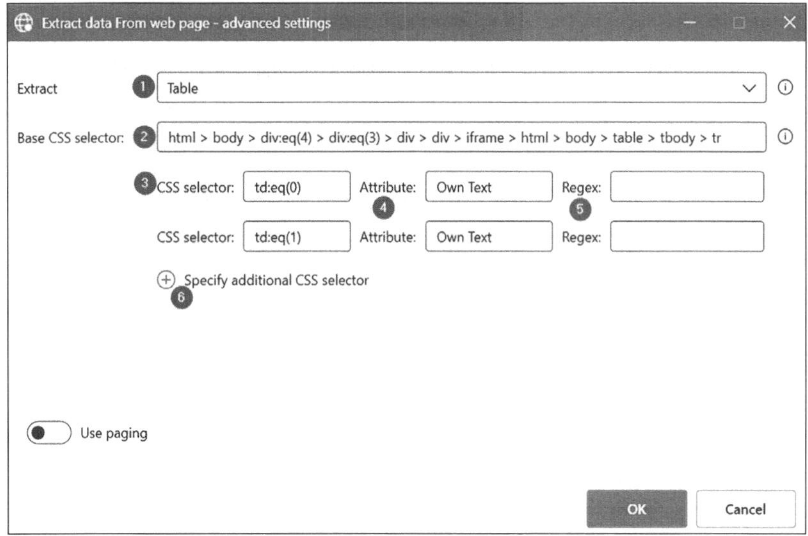

Figure 6.90: *Advanced settings from Live web helper*

Follow the numbering as per the above figure:

1. This dropdown determines the type of value to extract. These have extraction options like a single value, handpicked values, list values, table values, and an entire HTML table.
2. In this box, goes the root CSS selector that points to the element(s). In several sections of "*Chapter 5: Building Blocks of a Desktop Flow*", we have gone through HTML tags and Selectors and how to inspect elements, which also has links to learn about HTML and CSS Selectors.

   In our case, it points to the **`<tr>`** HTML tag which indicates a "table row".
3. This is the CSS selector for the first value of the table pointed by **"`td:eq(0)`"** which means "table data" shown in this case for the 0th index. Likewise, you see the same for the next index as **"`td:eq(1)`".**
4. Further, **"`Own text`"** is the Attribute we would like to extract from that "table data". PAD has by default used this Attribute and can be modified.
5. You can also configure a regular expression for pointing to an element's value, which is used in advanced or complex situations and is optional.
6. Lastly, this is a button if you would like to add more CSS selectors, which will have the same structure of options as the first two.

You can manually create a new Selector or tweak an existing one via these options from the **"`Advanced settings`"**. You can add or remove columns for your table from these settings. You can create a CSS selector in such a way that if there is a table with 5 columns then extract every alternate column like the 1st, 3rd and the 5th. You can also pick only a List of values instead of a table.

There is another use of this same **"`Extract data from web page`"** Action and that is to directly extract an entire HTML table instead of specific values. This feature works when PAD identifies the element as an HTML table.

1. Keep the web page with the following URL manually opened so that we can extract the HTML table. The URL is the same as the previous section. https://www.w3schools.com/html/tryit.asp?filename=tryhtml_table_intro
2. Add the **"`Launch new <browser>`"** Action for the above URL.
3. Add the **"`Extract data from web page`"** Action onto the Workspace. Keep this Action open and manually go to the web page and the **"`Live web helper`"** will open up. Right-click the table and choose the **"`Extract entire HTML table`"** menu item.

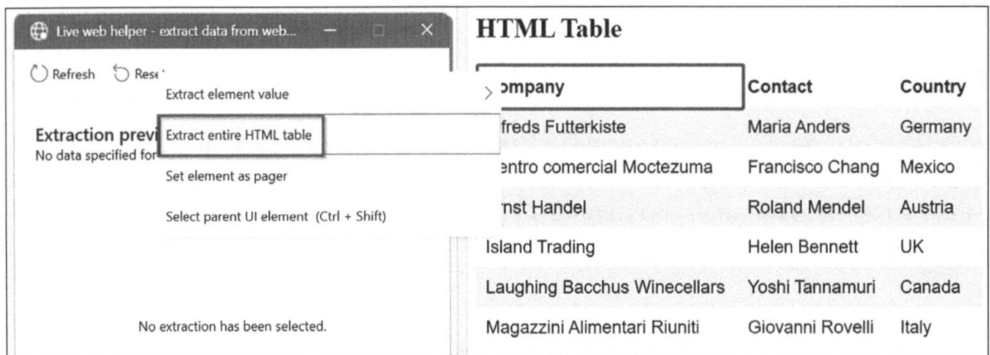

***Figure 6.91:** Extract entire HTML table*

On doing so, all the records of the HTML table will be displayed on the **"Live web helper"** with the dotted borders shown on the extracted data. If this doesn't show the preview as expected then you need to try again hovering the mouse around various positions of the table. Save all information and close the web page so that we can now run the Flow.

Company	Contact	Country
Alfreds Futterkiste	Maria Anders	Germany
Centro comercial Moctezuma	Francisco Chang	Mexico
Ernst Handel	Roland Mendel	Austria
Island Trading	Helen Bennett	UK
Laughing Bacchus Winecellars	Yoshi Tannamuri	Canada
Magazzini Alimentari Riuniti	Giovanni Rovelli	Italy

Company	Contact	Country
Alfreds Futterkiste	Maria Anders	Germany
Centro comercial Moctezuma	Francisco Chang	Mexico
Ernst Handel	Roland Mendel	Austria
Island Trading	Helen Bennett	UK
Laughing Bacchus Winecellars	Yoshi Tannamuri	Canada
Magazzini Alimentari Riuniti	Giovanni Rovelli	Italy

***Figure 6.92:** Entire HTML table extracted in the Live web helper*

When you run the Flow, the output will be populated in a variable which would be a Datatable in this case since it is a table that we are extracting. At this point, open the **"Advanced Settings"** from the **"Live web helper"** and notice the difference with the one from *Figure* 6.90.

If the HTML table extraction feature does not work as expected, either due to the design of the web page or due to PAD not being able to recognize the table, then the way of extraction discussed in the earlier section can be used.

Another scenario that is seen on web pages is the concept of paging or pagination. Pagination is when the data of a similar pattern spans across multiple pages like its first page. The following figure exemplifies the concept of paging where the table has multiple pages of data from 1 to 6 seen at the bottom of the table. In such a scenario, you need to tell PAD which paging element to look for and configure it accordingly.

When you manually want to go to the next page then you would click the button with the marked right arrow. Therefore, you can right-click that and choose the **"`Set element as pager`"** option.

As another option, just like the way you could manually configure the CSS selector for other values of a web page, you can enable the toggle for paging as seen at the bottom of *Figure* 6.90 and manually configure the CSS selector for a pager element.

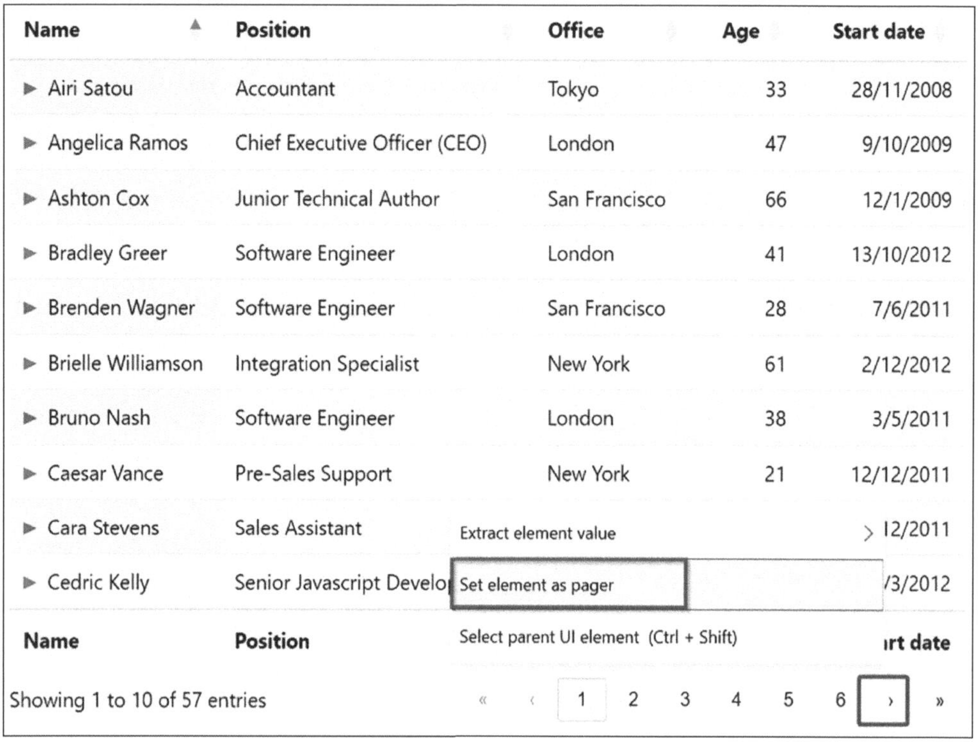

Name	Position	Office	Age	Start date
► Airi Satou	Accountant	Tokyo	33	28/11/2008
► Angelica Ramos	Chief Executive Officer (CEO)	London	47	9/10/2009
► Ashton Cox	Junior Technical Author	San Francisco	66	12/1/2009
► Bradley Greer	Software Engineer	London	41	13/10/2012
► Brenden Wagner	Software Engineer	San Francisco	28	7/6/2011
► Brielle Williamson	Integration Specialist	New York	61	2/12/2012
► Bruno Nash	Software Engineer	London	38	3/5/2011
► Caesar Vance	Pre-Sales Support	New York	21	12/12/2011
► Cara Stevens	Sales Assistant	Extract element value		12/2011
► Cedric Kelly	Senior Javascript Develo	Set element as pager		/3/2012
Name	Position	Select parent UI element (Ctrl + Shift)		rt date

Showing 1 to 10 of 57 entries « ‹ 1 2 3 4 5 6 › »

Figure 6.93: *Setting the pager element*

Even if you configure the pager element using the menu item in the preceding figure, you can go back to the toggle of the **"`Advanced settings`"** and see that a CSS selector for the pager element is automatically populated under the toggle.

If a pager element is used, closing the web helper will show the Action as follows:

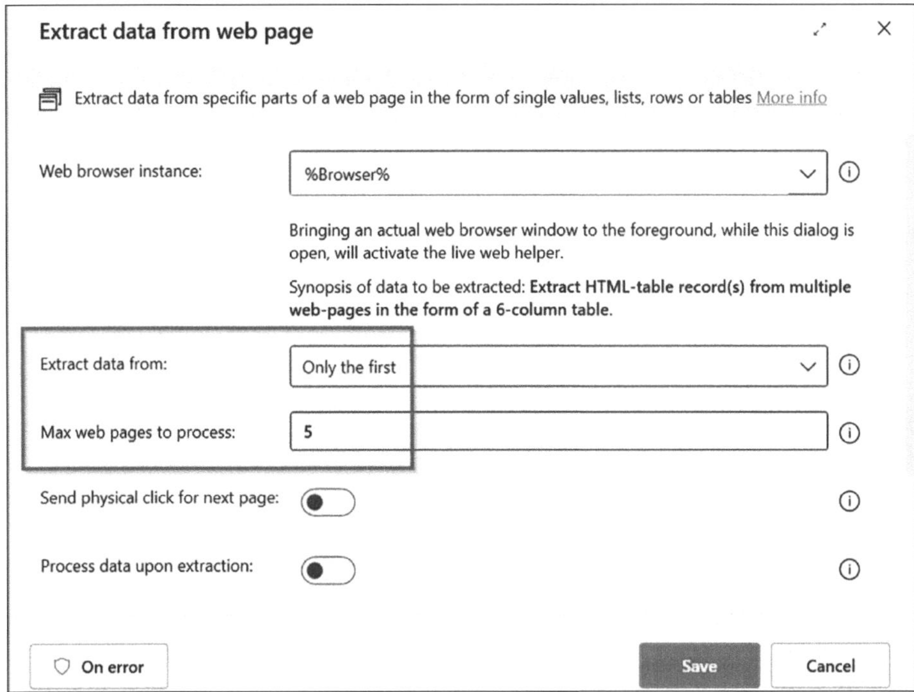

***Figure 6.94:** Configuring the number of pages to extract data from*

Whenever a pager element is configured via any of the previous ways explained, the **"`Extract data from web page`"** Action asks if all the available values need to be extracted or only the first 'n' number of pages, in which case, it gives a provision to configure the value of 'n', as shown in the preceding figure.

Hover the mouse on the information icon of each of the other parameters and identify their behavior so that they can be used in appropriate situations.

At times, each of these features for the **"`Extract data from web page`"** Action requires experimenting as they may not always work in the first go. So, a bit of trial-and-error is needed to see which feature extracts the desired data in the right way.

Writing Operations

Similar to Windows Desktop automation, writing operations for Web automation also involves the same, that is, writing some text into a text box, selecting values for option buttons, dropdowns, check boxes, pressing a button, and more.

For writing to a text box and clicking a button, follow these steps:

1. Launch the web page for the following URL which has two text boxes and a button:
   https://www.w3schools.com/tags/tryit.asp?filename=tryhtml_input_test

This is the same link used for writing values to a text box via the Recorder.

2. Drag and drop the **"Populate text field on web page"** Action which is used to write some value to a text box. Add the UI elements for the first and last name text boxes. In the **"Text"** parameter, provide a first and last name of your choice in their respective Actions.

3. Add the **"Press button on web page"** Action for the **"Submit"** button.

Following is the entire Flow with the above steps. Run the Flow and the output web page should show the values that were entered in the two text boxes.

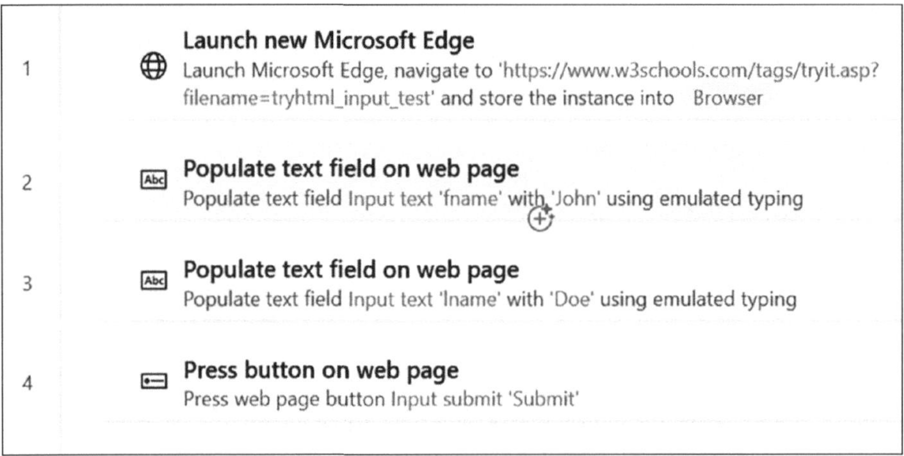

Figure 6.95: *Actions for writing text and pressing button*

Just to reiterate, once you get an idea of adding UI elements and uniquely identifying their Selectors when default ones do not work, then the basic concept of using the reading and writing Actions is just to fill and configure the appropriate parameters.

How about trying the Actions for selecting a dropdown List, selecting and unselecting checkboxes and selecting option buttons? Here are the URLs for trying these out and they are the ones that were seen in the "*Recording a Web Application Using the Unified Recorder*" section of the previous chapter. The output should be similar to the ones observed when the same operations were performed by the "Recorder".

- **Operation**: Selecting Dropdown List Options
  Action: Set drop-down list value on web page
  https://www.w3schools.com/tags/tryit.asp?filename=tryhtml_select
- **Operation**: Selecting and Unselecting Checkboxes
  Action: Set check box state on web page
  https://www.w3schools.com/tags/tryit.asp?filename=tryhtml5_input_type_checkbox

- **Operation**: Selecting Option Buttons
  Action: Select radio button on web page
  https://www.w3schools.com/tags/tryit.asp?filename=tryhtml5_input_type_radio

Other Useful Web Automation Actions

We will be looking at other key Actions used for Web automation where we will be going through multiple Actions in a single Flow. At first, we will check whether the web page contains the UI element for a desired hyperlink, if yes then the bot will click it, if not it will display a message saying that the UI element was not present. Finally, the bot will navigate to another web page. Let us see all of these in action.

Follow the steps provided here:

1. This is a web page that has a hyperlink. Manually open it so that you can capture the UI element of the hyperlink:

   https://www.w3schools.com/html/tryit.asp?filename=tryhtml_links_w3schools

2. Drag and drop the Action to launch the browser for the above URL.
3. Add a **"`If web page contains`"** Action and add a UI element for the **"`Visit W3Schools.com!`"** hyperlink seen on the right-hand side of the above URL. In HTML terminology, a hyperlink is denoted by a **`<a>`** tag also known as anchor tag.

   The **"`Wait for web page content`"** Action has the exact same parameters but with an option to wait indefinitely or till a specified time before it gets timed out. It is needless to say that waiting indefinitely is not a best practice, so providing a time out number is the way to use this parameter.

   Similar to the corresponding Windows automation Action, these two Actions have options to check for the presence or absence of a UI element or a text on the web page.

4. Use the **"`Click link on web page`"** Action that will click the hyperlink UI element captured in the previous step. This Action also has a parameter to move the mouse to the respective element while performing the click which is used in cases where it does not work without moving the mouse.
5. Inside the **"`If web page contains`"** add an **"`Else`"** which will show a display message box as **`Web page does not contain the required hyperlink`**.
6. Outside the **"`If-End`"** Actions, add a **"`Go to web page`"** Action and give some random website of your choice. This Action has some useful operations like going back or forward on a web page, reloading a web page or navigating to a URL like in our case. These operations come handy in web automation scenarios.

The entire Flow after performing these steps is as follows. Run the Flow and observe the bot clicking the hyperlink as well as the web page navigating to a different URL. Change the URL in line number 1 and you will get the message box of line 5 before the bot navigates to the URL of line 7.

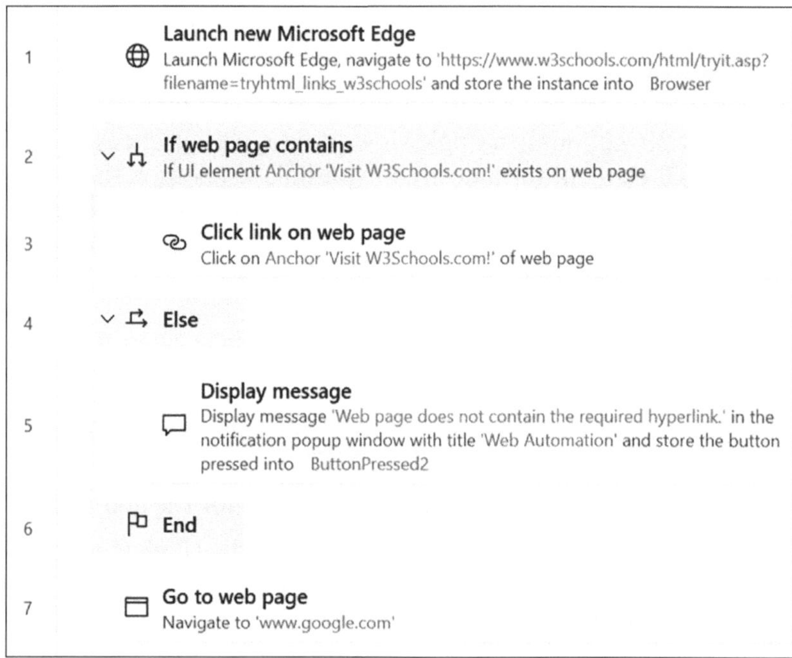

Figure 6.96: *Entire Flow after adding the web automation actions*

We are now going to see an advanced and distinct way of interacting with HTML elements. This approach is used when none of the conventional techniques work because of the way some websites are designed. It is about using JavaScript to read from or write into UI elements, to click a button on a web page, enter dates for date pickers, read all items from a dropdown, select a radio button or a checkbox and so on.

Follow along the given steps to achieve this functionality. At first, we will be manually verifying what needs to be done, then once confirmed to be working fine, we will be mimicking the same using PAD.

1. For this section, we are using www.amazon.in URL. Open the **"`Inspect element`"** feature of the browser for the search box of the above URL.

Figure 6.97: *The Search box on the web page*

In the "A *Sample Web Application Selector*" section of "*Chapter 5: Building*

Blocks of a Desktop Flow", we saw how the pane to inspect an element looks like. The following screen is the result of performing this step. Look for and click the **"`Console`"** tab shown in the figure. Here, in the HTML code, we are also able to see that the Id of the search text box is **`twotabsearchtextbox`**.

Figure 6.98: *Console tab of inspect element*

2. In the Console, type a JavaScript as follows and hit *Enter* to write a search term as **"`mobile phones`"** on an element having an Id as **`twotabsearchtextbox`**:

```
document.getElementById("twotabsearchtextbox").value = "mobile phones"
```

As soon as you do that, the search term gets written into the text box as expected.

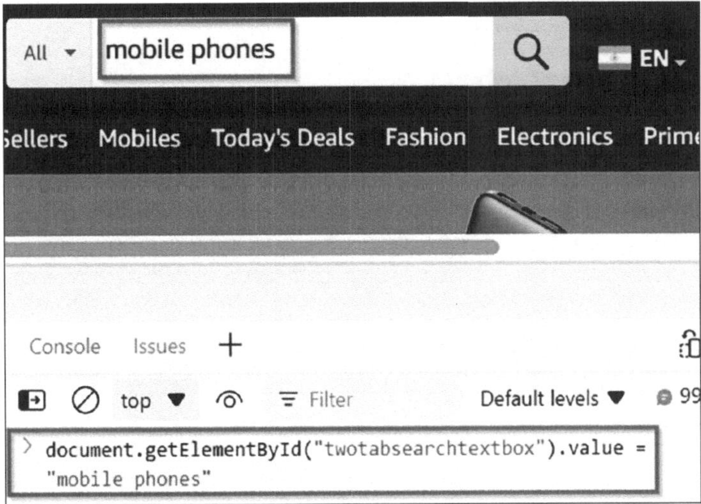

Figure 6.99: *Writing a value via JavaScript*

You can even read the value of a text box with the JavaScript statement, and the Console will show you the corresponding value.

```
document.getElementById("twotabsearchtextbox").value
```

The Id of the search button from the **"Inspect element"** panel is **nav-search-submit-button.** You can click the button with the following line. You can try it out by writing the word *books* and then hit the button from the Console.

```
document.getElementById("nav-search-submit-button").click()
```

3. We have now verified that we are able to successfully write values to this text box and even click a button with the help of JavaScript.

   You can learn JavaScript for web page elements in the same website we have been using and the URL for this function is: https://www.w3schools.com/jsref/met_document_getelementbyid.asp

   Navigate through other sections on the above link to learn other functions that can be used here like `document.querySelectorAll`, `document.querySelector`, `document.getElementsByName`, `document.getElementsByClassName` and so on.

4. We are going to do the same, that is, inject the JavaScript on the web page with the help of Power Automate Desktop. This is possible with the use of the **"Run JavaScript function on web page"** Action (not **"Run JavaScript"** Action).

Use the Action for launching the web page for www.amazon.in. Then drag and drop the intended **"Run JavaScript function on web page"** Action which already has a skeleton to write a body for the function. Add the following code with the two lines that we used in the Console to write the search term and to click the button. As per JavaScript syntax, they have to end with a semicolon.

```
function ExecuteScript()
{
document.getElementById("twotabsearchtextbox").value = "mobile
phones";
document.getElementById("nav-search-submit-button").click();
}
```

Following is the Action after incorporating the JavaScript code:

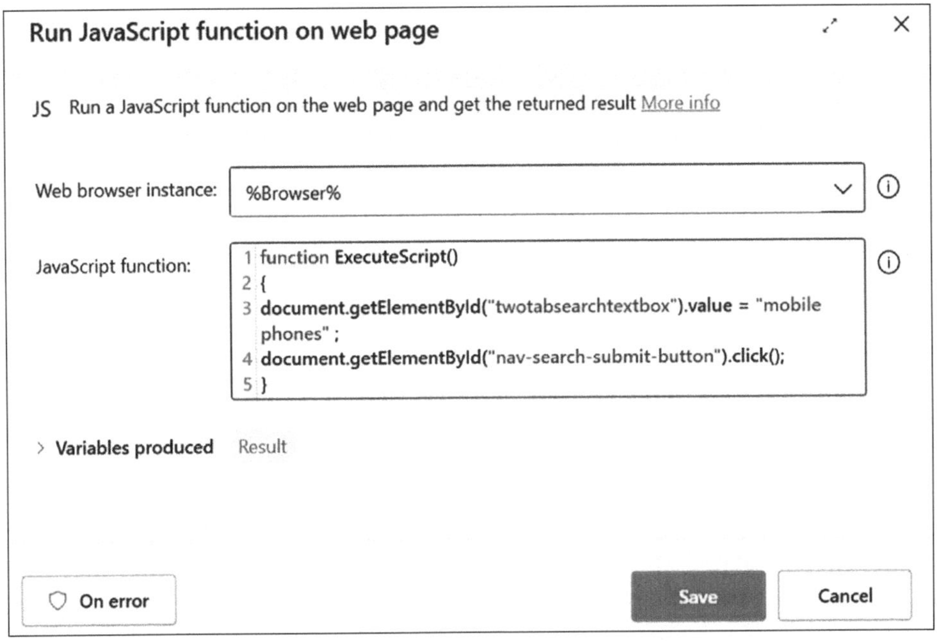

Run JavaScript function on web page

JS Run a JavaScript function on the web page and get the returned result More info

Web browser instance: %Browser%

JavaScript function:

```
function ExecuteScript()
{
document.getElementById("twotabsearchtextbox").value = "mobile phones" ;
document.getElementById("nav-search-submit-button").click();
}
```

> Variables produced Result

On error Save Cancel

***Figure 6.100:** Writing text value and clicking button via JavaScript*

Run the Flow and you will find that the browser opens for the specified URL, types-in *mobile phones* and clicks the search button showing the results for mobile phones.

A quick assignment for you is to read all the values from the dropdown that is at the beginning of the search box and display those values separated by an asterisk sign **'*'**. The dropdown to the left of the text box is shown in *Figure 6.97*.

```
function ExecuteScript()
{
  var x = document.getElementById("searchDropdownBox");
  var txt = "";
  var i;
  for (i = 0; i < x.length; i++)
  {
    txt = txt  + x.options[i].text + "*";
  }
return(txt);
}
```

In an ideal project you would use proper naming conventions for preceding variables. When you print the output variable of this Action in a message box, the following figure shows the output. In the above JavaScript code if you replace **"*"** with **"\n"** which is a newline, you will see each item on a separate line.

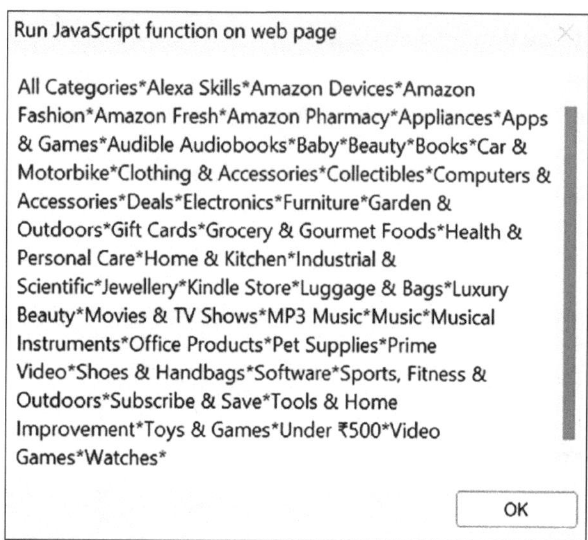

Figure 6.101: *Read all items of dropdown via JavaScript*

There are going to be several situations where this approach is going to prove beneficial especially when regular ways of interacting with web page elements are not straightforward.

To top it all off with the vital Actions used in any Web automation, just like **"`Close window`"** for Desktop automation, you close the browser with the help of **"`Close web browser`"** Action where you will provide the instance created by the **"`Launch new <browser>`"** Action.

Conclusion

In this chapter, we explored interacting with some of the most widely used applications, such as Excel, Outlook, database interaction, Windows applications, and web interfaces. Each section highlighted key Actions for automating these applications. As you move forward, continue to experiment with and expand upon the Actions and its properties under each of these application types in the **"`Actions`"** pane.

In the next chapter, "*File Management and Data Manipulation*", we will explore techniques for working with files and folders, interacting with various file types, utilizing text functions, performing datetime operations, and automating tasks with scripting to enhance your efficiency and precision in handling data.

Practical Exercises

Following are some exercises for a combination of the topics we went through in this and the previous chapters.

Exercise 1:

Here is an exercise for Excel, Windows Automation, Web Automation and Outlook.

1. Place an Excel in a folder with about 10 records and its columns as shown in the following figure. You can add dummy records of your choice matching the shown columns. The file is available in the GitHub folder of this chapter as **`"Chapter 6 Exercise 1.xlsx"`**.
2. Read each row from Excel and save them via the five fields on the **`"Invoices"`** tab of Contoso application (*Figure* 6.69).
3. An ID for the saved record is generated above the **`"Date"`** text box on the **`"Invoices"`** tab. Update that ID in the **`"ID"`** column of the Excel against that row.
4. Take the USD amount and convert it to any other currency of your choice on https://wise.com/in/currency-converter/. You can use any currency converter website. Capture the converted currency and update it into **`"Converted Amount"`** column of the Excel.
5. After the processing of all rows are complete, save this Excel, add it as an Outlook attachment and email it to any valid email address.

	A	B	C	D	E	F	G
1	Date	Account	Contact	USD Amount	Status	Converted Amount	ID
2	7/5/2024	Account70	user441@mail.com	208.46	Paid		
3	7/3/2024	Account11	user378@email.com	229.2	Uninvoiced		
4	7/1/2024	Account25	user510@email.com	797.2	Uninvoiced		
5	7/7/2024	Account43	user418@mail.com	589.17	Invoiced		
6	7/2/2024	Account8	user6@email.com	816.72	Invoiced		
7	7/5/2024	Account60	user443@email.com	431.41	Paid		
8	7/1/2024	Account16	user261@example.com	958.9	Paid		
9	7/4/2024	Account9	user786@email.com	648.09	Paid		
10	7/6/2024	Account96	user641@example.com	891.64	Uninvoiced		
11	7/1/2024	Account54	user442@mail.com	276.05	Uninvoiced		

Figure 6.102: *Sample input Excel file*

Exercise 2:

By the end of the "*Modifying a Selector Using the Text Editor Toggle*" section of "*Chapter 5: Building Blocks of a Desktop Flow*", we were able to identify two different Selectors for the text boxes with changing Ids on the www.rpachallenge.com website. We saved the Flow by the name **`"RPA Challenge"`** so that we could get back to it after understanding Excel Automation. Now that we have gone through the Actions for Excel Automation and writing operations for Web Automation, it is time to complete this challenge with the help of either one or both of the different Selector approaches explained. It is possible that you may come up with a new Selector approach but the goal of the challenge should be to fill all the fields with 100% accuracy and in quicker execution time.

Exercise 3:

This is another challenge for the RPA community and is more complex than Exercise 2. The URL is https://www.theautomationchallenge.com/. What needs to be done is explained on the left-hand side of the link.

It may get complex for two areas:

1. Finding the right Selector for the text boxes. For this, refer to the "*UI Elements and Selectors*" topic and most importantly the learning resource links mentioned in "*Chapter 5: Building Blocks of a Desktop Flow*".

2. A random reCAPTCHA pop-up will appear any time while entering the 50 records. The required topic to handle it is given in this chapter, or you may come up with your own way of handling it.

The ultimate goal of the challenge is the same as Exercise 2, that is, to fill all the fields with 100% accuracy and in quicker execution time.

Questions

Following are some questions that may either have answers in any of the current or previous chapters, or enforce you to practically try out the question on the PAD tool. In case of multiple-choice questions, there is only one answer.

Excel Automation

1. How to open an Excel file through the bot without making the file visible on the machine where the bot runs?

2. How to read data from and write data into an Excel file? Explore the step-by-step Actions and various parameters to do this.

3. What are the different range of values that can be read from an Excel sheet?

   Hint: *Refer to the* **`"Retrieve"`** *dropdown of* **`"Read from Excel worksheet"`** *Action.*

4. While reading Excel data into a Datatable, the Excel column headings do not show up on the column headers of the Datatable by default. How to make the Datatable column headings same as the Excel column headings?

5. While reading Excel data into a Datatable, if an Excel column value is 01-01-2024, but the output Datatable shows as 01-01-2024 00:00:00, then what change has to be done to correct this?

6. If a worksheet already has data in it, then without using a loop how to write a Datatable to this worksheet starting from where the previous data ended?

Example: If Excel sheet has 100 rows, then how to write a Datatable starting from the 101st row, without using a loop?

7. What are the different file formats available to save an Excel file as?
8. How to get filtered data from an Excel sheet without looping?

   Example: How to get all the rows where Qty is greater than 60 in the following figure?

Until Microsoft releases a proper way to read the filtered data after using the **"`Filter cells in Excel worksheet`"** Action, you can do it by treating Excel as a database where you can write an SQL statement to retrieve rows with Qty greater than 60. If that happens by the time of your reading this topic, feel free to use any new Actions and parameters available in the upcoming PAD versions.

	A	B	C	D	E	F	G
1	ID	Date	City	Category	Product	Qty	UnitPrice
2	ID07351	01-Jan	Boston	Bars	Carrot	33	1.77
3	ID07352	04-Jan	Boston	Crackers	Whole Wheat	87	3.49
4	ID07353	07-Jan	Los Angeles	Cookies	Chocolate Chip	58	1.87
5	ID07354	10-Jan	New York	Cookies	Chocolate Chip	82	1.87
6	ID07355	13-Jan	Boston	Cookies	Arrowroot	38	2.18
7	ID07356	16-Jan	Boston	Bars	Carrot	54	1.77
8	ID07357	19-Jan	Boston	Crackers	Whole Wheat	149	3.49
9	ID07358	22-Jan	Los Angeles	Bars	Carrot	51	1.77
10	ID07359	25-Jan	New York	Bars	Carrot	100	1.77

***Figure 6.103**: Sample input Excel for filtering data*

9. How to get sorted data from an Excel sheet?
   Example: How to sort the City column of the above Excel data.
10. While inserting a new row using a row index via the **"`Insert row to Excel worksheet`"** Action, does the row index start from 0 or 1?
11. While inserting a new row, if you pass the row index as 2, will a new row be added above the 2nd row or below it?
12. While inserting a new column via the **"`Insert column to Excel worksheet`"** Action, can you pass the column index or column alphabet or both?
13. While inserting a new column, if you pass the column index as 2, will a new column be added to the left or right of the 2nd column?
14. How to set the width of only the specific columns, for example, from columns B to D as 20?
15. What is the syntax to run an Excel macro that has arguments to that macro?

Example: Macro name is **`MyExcelMacro`** and there are two arguments, namely Arg1 and Arg2.

16. How to check if a particular worksheet exists within an Excel file or not?

17. How to copy rows from one Excel file to another?

    Example: Copy rows from Sheet1 of **`SourceFile.xlsx`** to Sheet1 of **`DestinationFile.xlsx`**

18. What is the difference between **"`Get first free row on column from Excel worksheet`"** and **"`Get first free column/row from Excel worksheet`"** Actions?

19. What are the output variables produced by the **"`Find and replace cells in Excel worksheet`"** Action?

Outlook Automation

1. How to read Outlook emails from an Inbox or its folders? Explore the step-by-step Actions and various parameters to do this.

2. Which three operations can be performed by the **"`Process email messages in Outlook`"** Action?

3. How to send an email from a shared mailbox?

4. What is the syntax to read email messages from a folder under the Inbox folder?

   Example: If you want to read the emails from a folder under Inbox called WorkItems, then what is the syntax to be given in the **"`Mail folder`"** parameter of the **"`Retrieve email messages from Outlook`"** Action?

5. While retrieving an unread email, the default setting is to automatically mark the email as read.

   a. True

   b. False

6. While sending an email, which two delimiter characters are acceptable between two recipient email addresses?

   Hint: *Refer to the information tooltip next to the* **"`To`"** *parameter of the* **"`Send email through Outlook`"** *Action.*

7. While retrieving email messages, the attachments will be saved by default.

   a. True

   b. False

Hint: *Refer to the default dropdown setting of the* ***"Attachments"*** *parameter of the* ***"Retrieve email messages from Outlook"*** Action.

8. What is the data type of the output variable produced by the **"Retrieve email messages from Outlook"** Action?

9. What are the different response actions available in the **"Respond to Outlook message"** Action?

10. What are the different file formats available to save an Outlook email message as?

11. In order to use the Outlook set of Actions, the Outlook application needs to be installed on the machine.

    a. True

    b. False

12. Other than Outlook, which other ways of sending emails are available in Power Automate Desktop?

Windows Automation

1. In the **"Attribute name"** parameter of the **"Get details of a UI element in window"** Action, you can specify an Attribute if it is not available in the list.

    a. True

    b. False

2. How to get the current status of a checkbox to see whether it is checked or not?

3. To add a new UI element to your Flow, add the element through an Action or from the **"UI elements"** pane, highlight the respective element, and press ____________

    a. *Left click*

    b. *Ctrl + Left click*

    c. *Right click*

    d. *Ctrl + Right click*

4. Which one of the following Actions is used to click a button in a window?

    a. Push button in window

    b. Click button in window

   c. Press button in window

   d. Select button in window

5. In order to focus on a window, you can find or identify a specific window by using three different options. What are they?

   Hint: *Refer to the* **"Find window mode"** *dropdown of* **"Focus window"** Action

6. How to start an external program or application, such as Calculator application?

Web Automation

1. What are the various ways of using the **"Extract data from web page"** Action? Explore the step-by-step procedure for all the various ways of using this Action explained in this chapter.

2. What are the different properties of a web page that we can read using the **"Get details of web page"** Action?

3. What are the different pre-built attributes of an element that we can read using the **"Get details of element on web page"** Action?

4. If a browser page is already open, which Action and which parameter would you use to interact with the open browser window?

5. We can extract the value of a custom attribute using the **"Get details of element on web page"** Action by entering the name of that attribute.

   a. True

   b. False

6. Which Action is used to navigate to any other URL?

7. You can set the dropdown list value on a web page using which one of the following methods?

   a. Select the options by name or property

   b. Select the options by property or index

   c. Select the options by name or index

   d. Select the options by index or attribute

8. While launching a browser with a URL, which setting is used to wait for the Flow to finish loading the page before moving to the next Action?

9. While launching a browser with a URL, what are the different options available if a pop-up dialog appears?

   Hint: *There are three options.*

10. Which different browsers are currently supported in Power Automate Desktop?
11. What are the three options available by which you can attach to a running instance of a browser?
12. Which Action is used to go back, forward or reload a webpage?
13. How to extract all links on a webpage into a Datatable, navigate to each one of them and extract some data from each of those links? Practice it on the tool.
14. What are the different Operators available for an Attribute in the Selector window?

Database Interaction

1. How to establish a database connection and run a SQL statement? Explore the step-by-step Actions and their parameters used to achieve this.
2. What is the data type of the output variable produced by the **"`Execute SQL statement`"** Action?

   Hint: *Refer to the* ***"`Variables produced`"*** *section of the* ***"`Execute SQL statement`"*** *Action.*
3. How to generate a connection string for various databases like Access, SQL Server or any other using the **"`Build connection string`"** wizard of the **"`Open SQL connection`"** Action? This will help to practice generating a connection string for different databases.

CHAPTER 7
File Management and Data Manipulation

Introduction

In this chapter, we will dive into reading and writing from and into various types of files such as CSV, Text, XML, navigating through folders, datetime handling, look into string or text functions to manipulate data and the various available Scripting options. Learning these will help to extend the capabilities of your automation solutions further enabling you to integrate with other systems and applications.

Structure

We will be going through the following topics in this chapter:

- Working with Files and Folders
- Interacting with XML files
- Text Functions
- Datetime Operations
- Scripting

Working with Files and Folders

In this topic, we will be going through several Actions pertaining to Files and Folders in the form of exercises.

Exercise 1:

In the first exercise, we will be building an automation Flow for the following:

1. With the help of Actions, identify the path of the Desktop folder for any machine.
2. With Actions, create four folders such as PDF, XLSX, JPG, and PNG.

3. There will already be a few files placed in a different folder called **"`Input files`"** that are going to be of random file types. The following figure has the different file types sorted by their type. Unzip and use the **"`File Type and Size Exercise.zip`"** file placed in the GitHub folder of this chapter.

Name	Type
Sample File 1 - 2 MB.pdf	Adobe Acrobat Document
Sample File 2 - 3 MB.pdf	Adobe Acrobat Document
Sample File 2 - 600 KB.jpg	JPG File
Sample File 1 - 24 KB.xlsx	Microsoft Excel Worksheet
Sample File 1 - 500 KB.png	PNG File
Sample File 2 - 37 KB.png	PNG File

Figure 7.1: *Different sample file types*

4. The bot will go through all the files of the **"`Input files`"** folder. Then based on their file type criteria, move them into each of their respective folders mentioned in Step 2.
   The file names are named with their file sizes for a purpose and you will know why in a moment. Also, for now, do not be much concerned with the numbering added to the files as 1 and 2. This is explained later as to why they are named that way.

5. Finally, Zip the files of the same type in its own folder.

Let us straight away head into action to build this Flow. Start with the following Actions for achieving this automation along with the explanation for each of those Actions.

1. To achieve the functionality of the first step mentioned previously, Power Automate Desktop provides us with a very useful Action called **"`Get special folder`"**. As shown in the figure, this Action has got tons of options to directly get us the required special folder path on any machine. There is a scroll bar in the dropdown and so there are more of these options. In our case, we will be getting the full path of the Desktop folder. When our bot runs on any machine, it will get the Desktop folder path of that machine and proceed to Step 2.

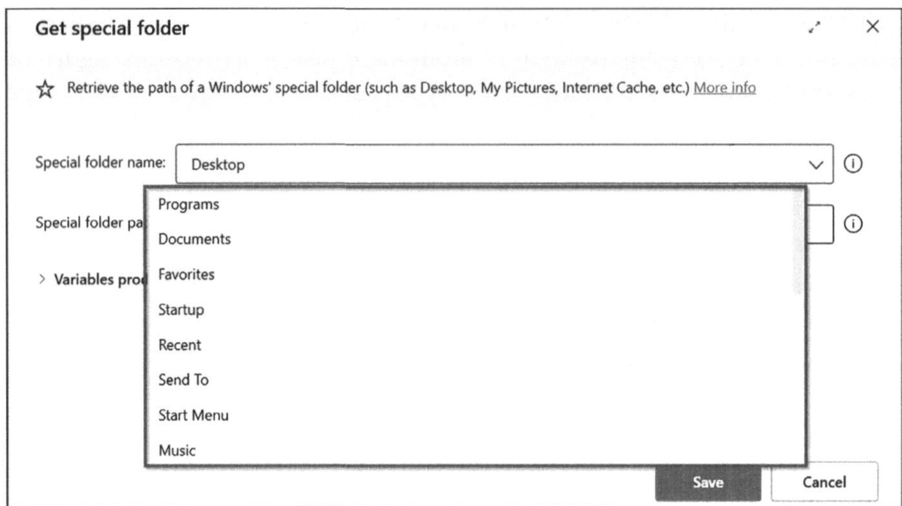

Figure 7.2: *Various options of Get special folder*

2. Next, we will create four folders for the file types shown in *Figure 7.1*. We will create the first folder as **"PDF"** under the **`%SpecialFolderPath%`** returned by the previous Action.

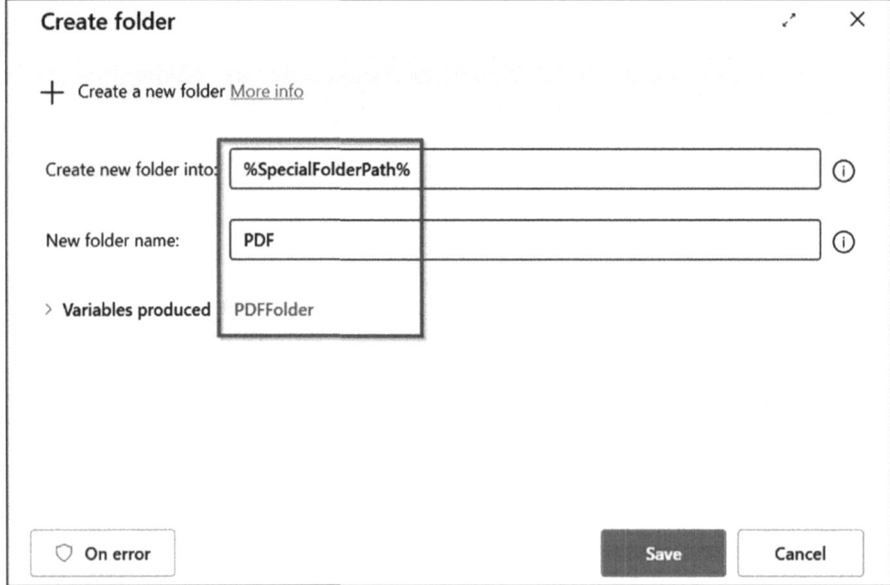

Figure 7.3: *Create folder action*

Likewise, create the folders for the other file types of XLSX, JPG, and PNG.

3. In our list of steps, we have planned to place the sample input files in a folder called **"`Input files`"**. So, the Action to read the files of a folder is **"`Get files in folder`"**.

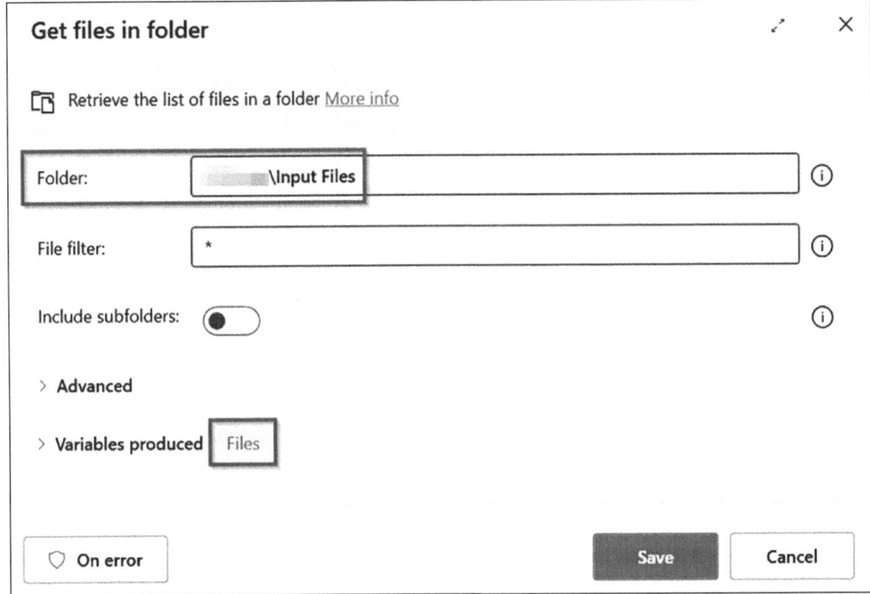

Figure 7.4: *Get files in folder action*

In this Action, since we would like to read the files of all types, we leave it with an asterisk **'*'** parameter as the filter. Hover the mouse on the **'i'** icon to see how wild cards and multiple file formats are configured. As seen, the Action has the capability to include subfolders too with the help of the toggle. The **"Advanced"** section gives a provision to sort via multiple parameters. The *Files* output variable as highlighted will provide us a list of file objects.

Our Flow built so far looks as follows:

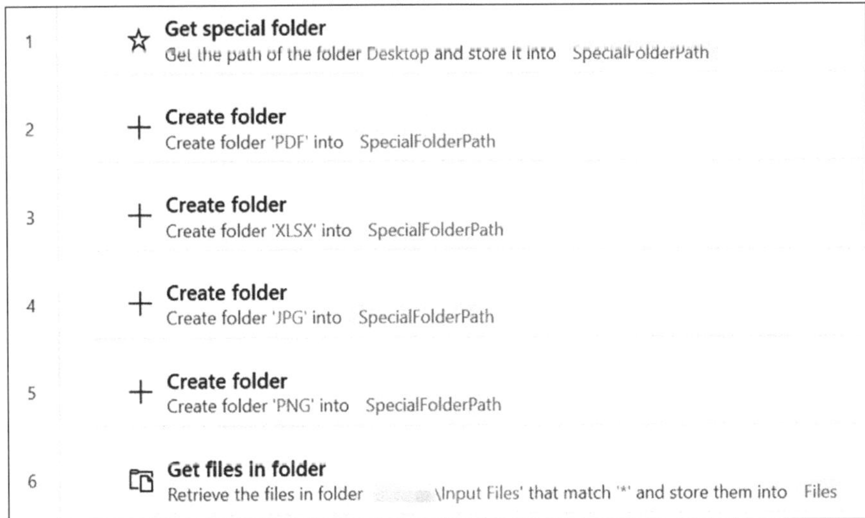

Figure 7.5: *First part of the Flow*

Just the way we iterate after retrieving all emails (Outlook) or after reading all data from a worksheet (Excel), we would read the **Files** variable with the help of a **"For each"** loop and the details of each file will be contained in the **CurrentItem** variable. Inside the loop, add a Switch Action. Since we would like to check the extension of the file and subsequently move it to its respective folder, we will get the extension from the **CurrentItem** variable that holds all the file-related information.

Refer to the following figure on the varied list of options that are available within **CurrentItem** when expanded via the variable picker. And the one we need is the **".Extension"** as highlighted. On selecting it, the switch parameter is now **%CurrentItem.Extension%**. You can verify what it shows by displaying this variable in a message box.

A **"Switch"** Action should be associated with a "**Case**" Action, so drag and drop a **"Case"** Action onto the Workspace.

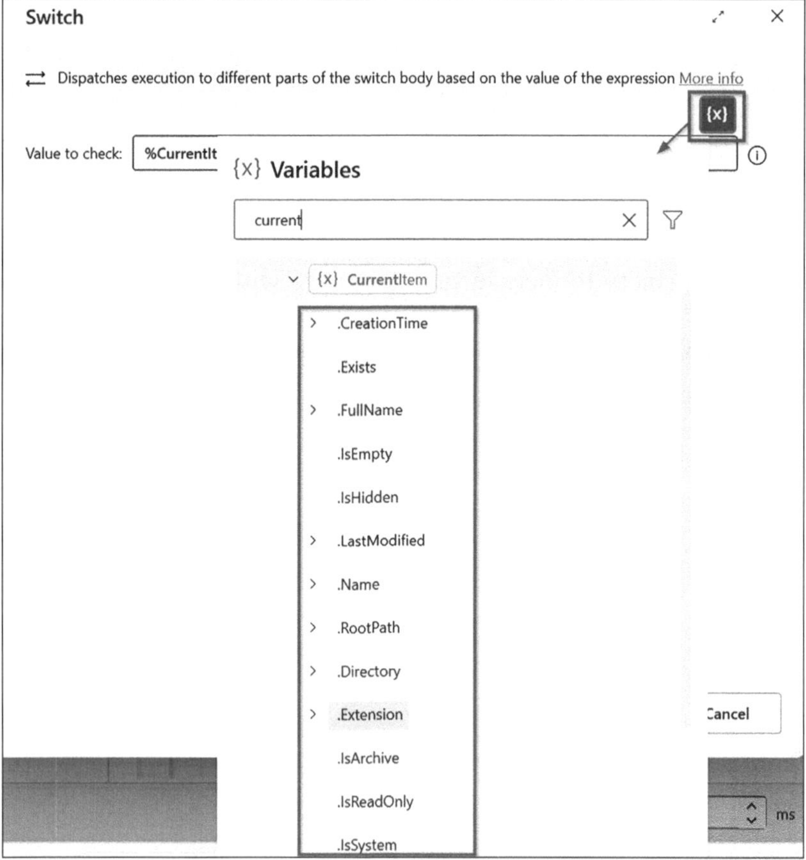

Figure 7.6: *List of file information options*

This is our first case and we will start with PDF files. Here we are comparing the file extension coming from **%CurrentItem.Extension%** with the value as **".pdf"**.

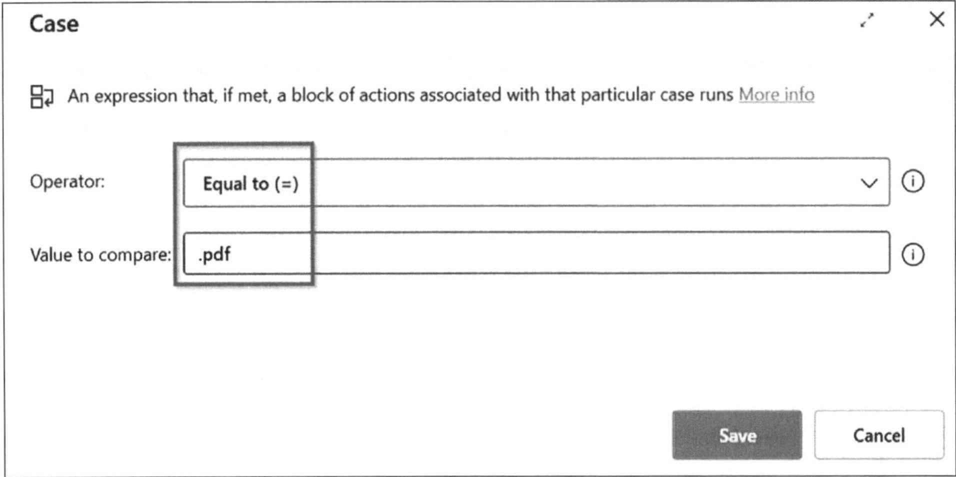

Figure 7.7: *Case action for PDF*

If the comparison turns out to be true, that is, if it's a PDF file, then we would want it to be moved to the folder that holds only PDFs and this is pointed out by the **`%PDFFolder%`** variable as returned in *Figure* 7.3. For our example, we will **"`Overwrite`"** if a file already exists. Similar to this Action, PAD also provides an Action as **"`Copy file(s)`"** which can be used in copying scenarios.

The **`MovedFiles`** output variable will be a list of files which will also have the full path of the file that was just moved by this Action.

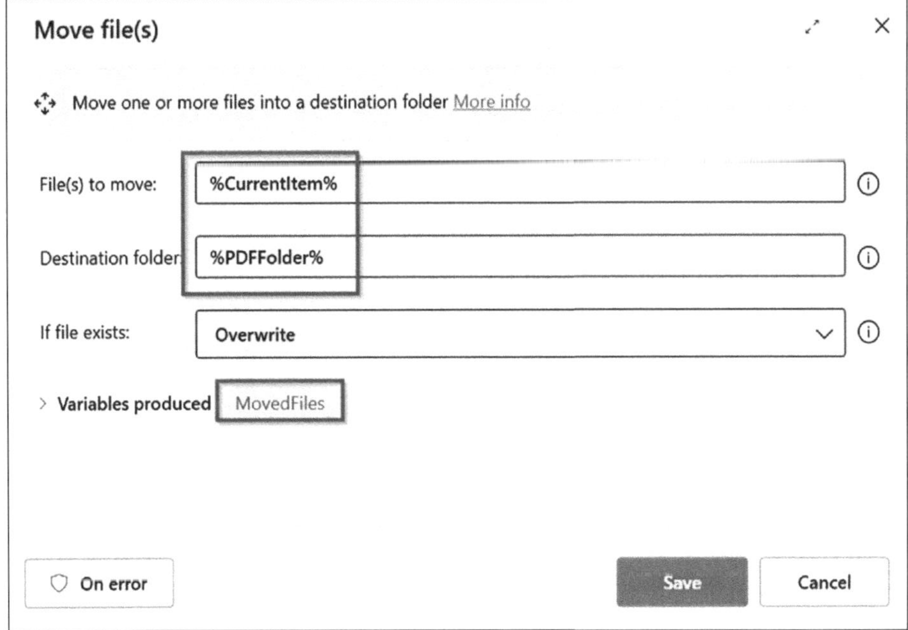

Figure 7.8: *Move files action*

Now that the file will be moved, it's time to Zip it. Note that although we are moving one file at a time, since our Actions are inside a loop, each file matching its file type criteria will be added to its own Zip file every time the loop iterates.

In the first parameter of the following figure, **`%PDFFolder%`** is the path that will hold only the PDF files followed by a backslash **'\'** for the folder structure and **`Zipped PDF Files.zip`** is a name we are giving for the new zip file that is going to hold only PDF files. The second parameter is **`%MovedFiles%`**, that will tell PAD as to which file(s) to be zipped. In our case, the PDF file is already moved and pointed by **`%MovedFiles%`**, as in the output variable of *Figure* 7.8. Similar to zipping/compressing of files, PAD also has an Action to uncompress them called **"`Unzip files`"**.

Repeat the previous three Actions of Case, Move files and Zip files for all the other file types of XLSX, JPG, and PNG. Make sure to accurately modify the names of the input and output variables as per their file types.

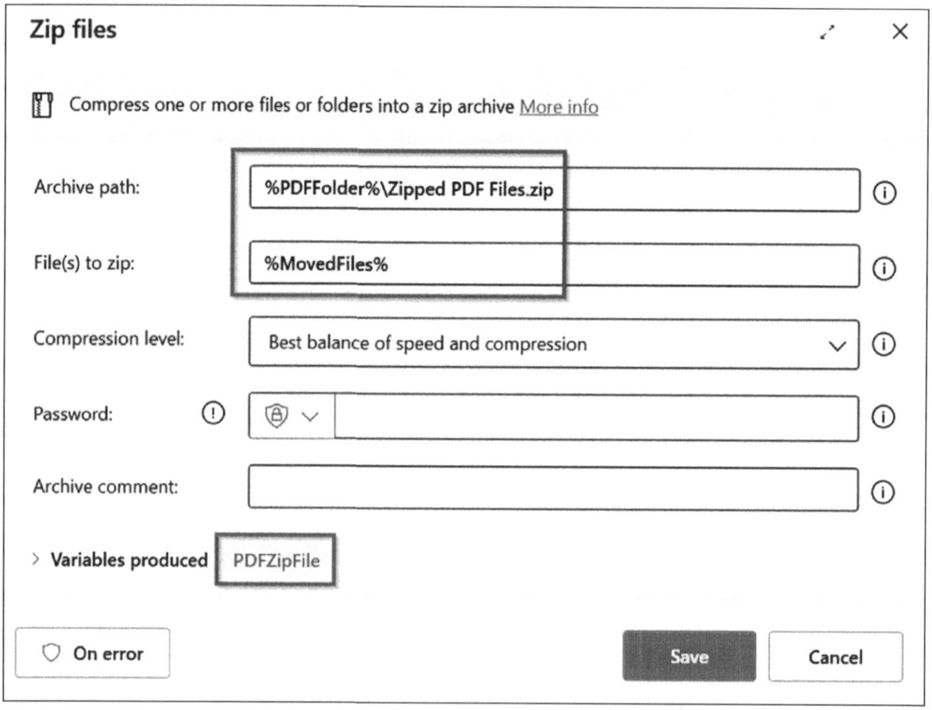

Zip files

Compress one or more files or folders into a zip archive More info

Archive path: %PDFFolder%\Zipped PDF Files.zip

File(s) to zip: %MovedFiles%

Compression level: Best balance of speed and compression

Password:

Archive comment:

> Variables produced PDFZipFile

On error Save Cancel

Figure 7.9: *Zip files action*

For the first three cases after the **"`For each`"** and the **"`Switch`"**, following is how the Flow looks like. The same has to be added for PNG too. The highlighted portions are what needs to be correctly modified for each of the cases.

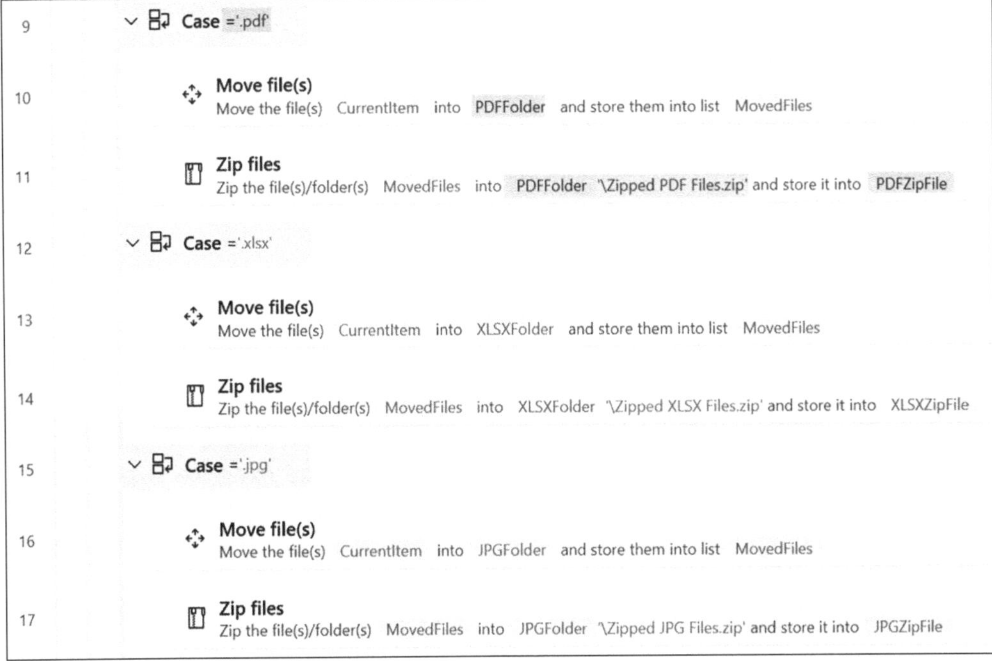

***Figure 7.10**: Flow for first three cases*

On running and completion of the Flow, the **"`Input files`"** folder should be empty. Files of each type should be moved to their respective extension wise folders and a Zip file should be created inside each of those folders. Open the Zip file and verify that it holds only the files of that same extension. Here is a sample output for only the PDF files:

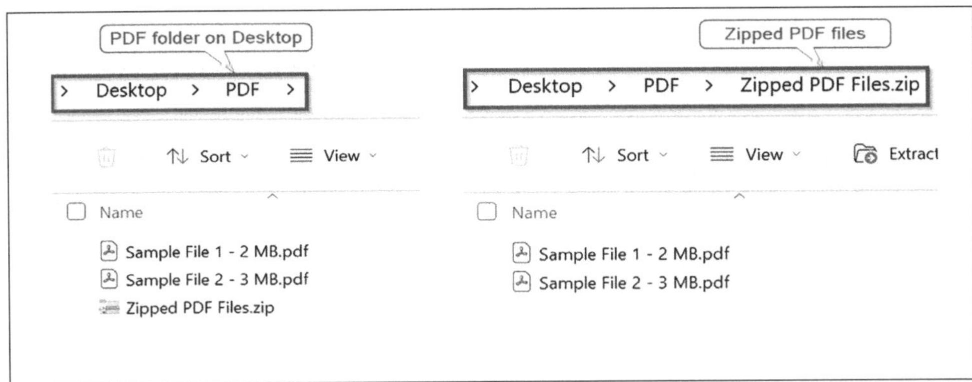

***Figure 7.11**: Output of PDF folder and Zipped file*

Now is the time to let you know why the file names have their file sizes too and that is for you to perform a practical exercise similar to what we did above.

Practical Exercise:

The file names are named with their file sizes for simplicity of this exercise, so that when the files are moved, they can be clearly understood as to files of what size are moved to which folder just by the look of it. The exercise is to move the files according to their sizes into respective folders of Small, Medium and Large.

For our exercise, we will classify the file sizes as the following:

0 KB to 100 KB : Small

101 KB to 700 KB : Medium

701 KB and above : Large

There are two files for each of these categories, as shown in *Figure 7.1*, and therefore they also hold the numbers as 1 and 2 in their names. The exercise is that the bot should go through all the files of the **"Input files"** folder. Then based on their size criteria, move them into each of their respective size wise folders. Zip all files in each of those folders.

A hint here is that there is a way to get the size of a file in PAD, just like we got the file extension. This size will be in bytes which then need to be converted to kilobytes and then compared with these categories before moving and zipping them. You can adjust these categories and create your own ones for the sake of the exercise if you find that the file size does not match closely with the above categories. Also, feel free to use your own files other than the ones in the **"File Type and Size Exercise.zip"** of GitHub.

After the movement of the files, you should see the files in their respective folders as follows:

0 KB to 100 KB (Small):
Sample File 1 - 24 KB.xlsx
Sample File 2 - 37 KB.png

101 KB to 700 KB (Medium):
Sample File 1 - 500 KB.png
Sample File 2 - 600 KB.jpg

701 KB and above (Large):
Sample File 1 - 2 MB.pdf
Sample File 2 - 3 MB.pdf

In a real-world bot, you will build the automation dynamically, that is, after getting the Desktop folder path, check if the file type (or size) folder is already present with the help of an Action in PAD called **"If folder exists"**, if not, only then create the folder and so on. You can use this Action while performing the exercise for the movement of files based on file size. **"`Empty folder`"** is another Action that can be used to empty only the contents of the folder (including subfolders) and not delete the folder itself. If the folder exists, that means there is a possibility of files present in that folder from the previous run. So, you could use the **"`Empty folder`"** in that case. On the contrary, **"`Delete folder`"** is the Action to delete all files and subfolders along with the folder itself. So, a good practice exercise would be to try both these approaches (using **"`Empty Folder`"** and **"`Delete folder`"**) for the file size exercise.

Let us do something else by making use of Files and Folders and its related Actions and operations via another useful exercise that is needed for Web automation. It is to get the most recently downloaded file after a download occurs via the bot.

The downloading of the file can happen through any relevant Actions available in PAD and is not the point of our exercise. Most of the times, when files are downloaded by the bot, it is not clear as to which is the file that is downloaded by the bot especially when the exact name of the file is not known. Also, there could be scenarios when a file with the same name gets downloaded during multiple bot reruns, in which case the browser suffixes an auto number to it like **`SampleFile.xlsx, SampleFile (1).xlsx, SampleFile (2).xlsx`**, and so on. Also imagine that you have been told by the user for whom the automation is being built to not modify the original file name by suffixing it with the date time or anything like that. In such cases, it becomes necessary to identify the most recently downloaded file.

To fulfill this scenario, the following sequence of Actions can be used:

1. Assuming that the file is already downloaded in the Desktop folder, use the **"`Get special folder`"** path for the Desktop as in the previous exercise. The path will be stored in the output variable called **`SpecialFolderPath`**. We are using the Desktop folder but the file could be downloaded in any other folder too, in which case store that folder path in a variable and use it in the following Actions.
2. Drag and drop the **"`Get files in folder`"** Action for the **`SpecialFolderPath`** and most importantly ask this Action to return the list of files sorted in descending order based on the Last modified date time criteria. The output variable from this Action is **`Files`**.

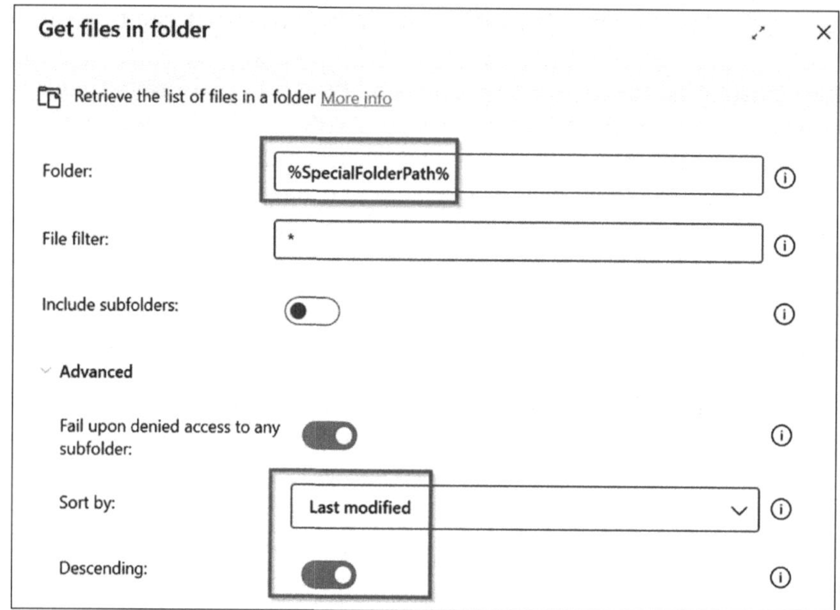

Figure 7.12: *Get files in folder action*

3. There will be several files stored in the **`Files`** variable, but we need to get only the latest. For verification purposes, display the topmost file of the **`Files`** variable in a message box which is done as **`%Files[0]%`** since it is in descending order.

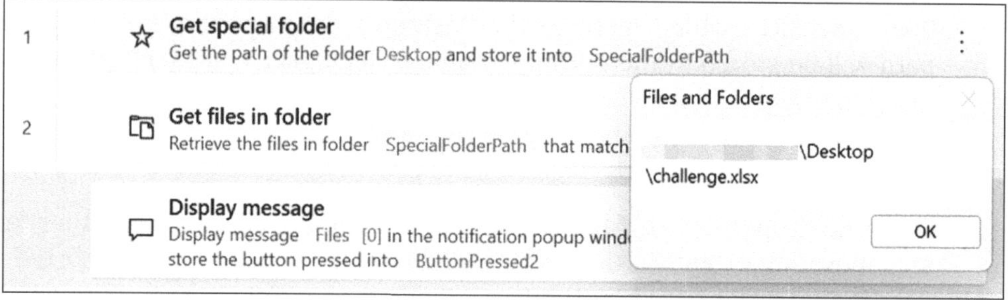

Figure 7.13: *Output of the most recent file*

If you download the same file one more time and if the browser downloads the new file suffixed by the auto number, then running this Flow will display **`challenge (1).xlsx`** as the most recently downloaded file.

Other Key Actions for Files and Folders

The **"`Get file path part`"** is an interesting Action that becomes useful in several automation scenarios. This is used when you need to get the various parts of a file path and they are the ones shown as the output variables in the following figure. When you expand the **"Variables produced"** section, you will see what each of these variables mean as well as have the option to disable any of them in case you do not need them to be returned by this Action.

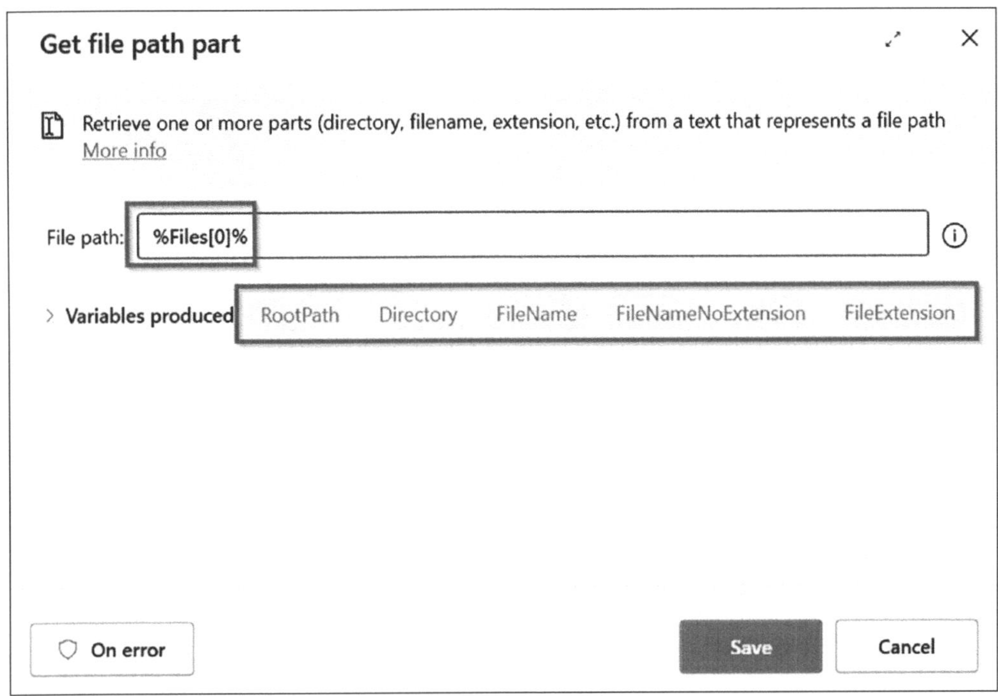

Figure 7.14: *Get file path part action*

Taking the same Flow from the previous section, pass **%Files[0]%** as the **"File path"** parameter and run the Flow. The following figure shows the unique output variables generated by this Action.

You will get the Directory of the file which is the Desktop folder path in our case, then the extension of the file, then the file name with and without the extension and the root path of the file, all of them using one single Action. Except the **Files** variable, all others have been generated by this Action and these can then be used further down the Flow.

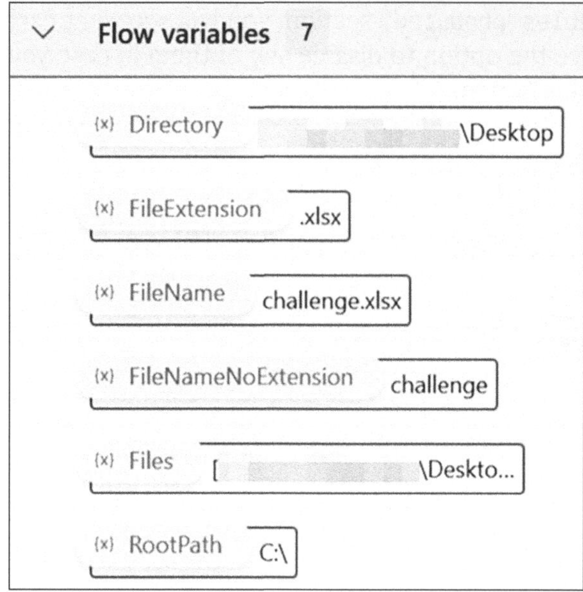

Figure 7.15: *Output of Get file path part action*

Renaming of folder is done with the help of **"`Rename folder`"** Action which takes two parameters, namely one for the folder to be renamed and the other for the new name. But the more interesting Action is for renaming a file. This is done by the **"`Rename file(s)`"** Action and is interesting because it gives a lot of options to rename the files.

Follow along the numbering in the following figure for this Action:

1. Here we give the same **`%Files[0]%`** variable as in the previous section.
2. The **"`Rename scheme`"** dropdown determines how to rename the files. Whether you would like to add a datetime to the file name, or give a totally new name, or add some predefined text to the name, remove a text from the name, replace a text with some other text of your choice, change the file extension, or even give a sequential numbering to the file name. The other parameters in the Action change according to the various options when set as any of the above ones. In our example, we will suffix the current date to the file name and exclude the time.
3. A toggle to provide a customized datetime.

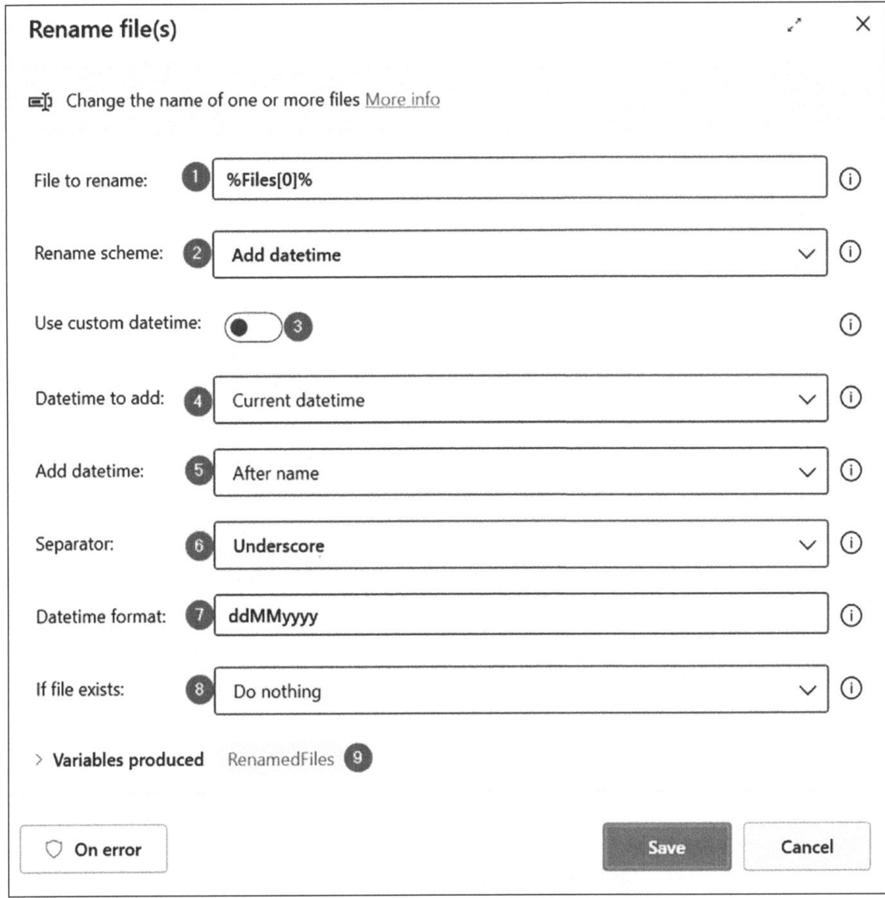

Figure 7.16: *The Rename files action*

4. Here you will see options to add the current datetime or the file's datetime like its creation, last modified or last accessed.
5. Indicates whether the datetime has to be added after or before the file name.
6. Determines what kind of separator character to be used like a space, an underscore, or even nothing to be added.
7. Here we can provide our own datetime format and since we are going to skip the time, we will give the date format as ddMMyyyy, where dd is double digit representation of the date, MM is the month (small case m stands for minute), and yyyy is the year.
8. This dropdown tells the Action what to do if the file with the new name already exists.
9. The Action returns a List type of variable of all the renamed file(s).

After running the Flow with this Action for the file name stored in **`%Files[0]%`** variable of the previous section, the file gets renamed to **`challenge_04072024.xlsx`** exactly as per the parameters configured in the preceding figure.

Similar to **"`If folder exists`"**, the **"`If file exists`"** Action generates a conditional block and comes handy in situations where some action needs to be taken based on whether a file already exists or not.

Reading/Writing CSV Files

Comma Separated Value (CSV) file is a widely supported format that is read by many programs. Interacting with CSV files becomes necessary in multiple scenarios like exporting data from a database, or data coming from any upstream system for reading in any downstream application or system. CSV files can also be used for data sharing as they can be opened in a text editor when the recipient does not have access to specialized CSV reading software like a spreadsheet application.

For our example, let's say, while you are building a Flow, you are reading some data from any source like a website and storing it into a Datatable, as shown in the following figure. And now the requirement is to write this Datatable as a CSV and send it as an email or even use it by the same bot for processing on a system that only accepts a file in CSV format.

Variable value

InputTable (Datatable)

#	ID	FirstName	LastName	Email	Department	Salary
0	1	John	Smith	john.smith@example.com	Engineering	70000
1	2	Jane	Doe	jane.doe@example.com	Marketing	65000
2	3	Michael	Brown	michael.brown@example.com	Sales	72000
3	4	Emily	Davis	emily.davis@example.com	Human Resources	60000
4	5	David	Wilson	david.wilson@example.com	Engineering	75000

Figure 7.17: *Sample input Datatable*

The Action in Power Automate Desktop to write a CSV file is **"`Write to CSV file`"**. As shown in the following figure, use the variable that needs to be written followed by the full path of the new CSV file to be created. Generally, as the name suggests, the columns in a CSV file are separated by comma as a delimiter. However, we do have options in this Action to configure delimiters like semicolon, tab or even give our own separator character. We will give a new custom character as the pipe symbol **'`|`'** and the fields of the columns in the preceding Datatable will be separated by this symbol. Also, as marked, there is a toggle to include the column names too in the CSV file in case the recipient or the downstream system needs it for processing.

Let us provide these parameters and run the Flow after seeing how the Action looks like in the following figure:

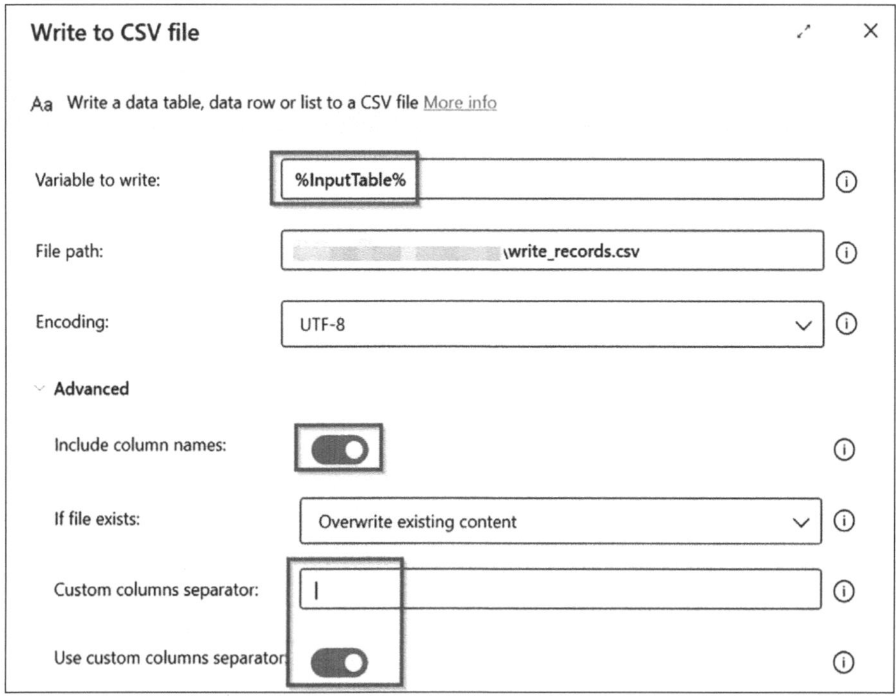

Figure 7.18: *Write to CSV file action*

For the given Datatable, **`write_records.csv`** is the CSV file generated and when opened in a text editor like Notepad appears as *Figure* 7.19. As we can see the column names are written as well as the fields are separated by the pipe delimiter.

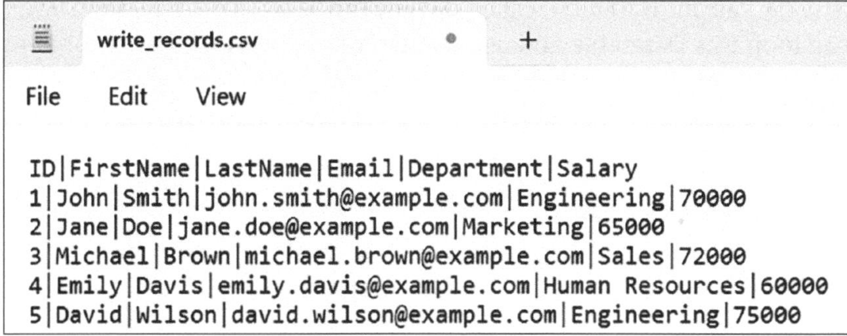

write_records.csv

File Edit View

```
ID|FirstName|LastName|Email|Department|Salary
1|John|Smith|john.smith@example.com|Engineering|70000
2|Jane|Doe|jane.doe@example.com|Marketing|65000
3|Michael|Brown|michael.brown@example.com|Sales|72000
4|Emily|Davis|emily.davis@example.com|Human Resources|60000
5|David|Wilson|david.wilson@example.com|Engineering|75000
```

Figure 7.19: *Output CSV file*

On the other hand, you may also come across certain automation scenarios where you need to do the opposite, that is, a CSV file has to be read and gathered into the Flow for further processing. Let us read the same CSV file and collect the records in a Datatable. You will find this CSV file in the GitHub files for this chapter.

The Action to do this is **"`Read from CSV file`"**. The first parameter is the CSV file that we just wrote to, followed by the parameter to include the first line as column names and the custom column separator as the pipe symbol. We should get the output in the **`OutputTable`** variable.

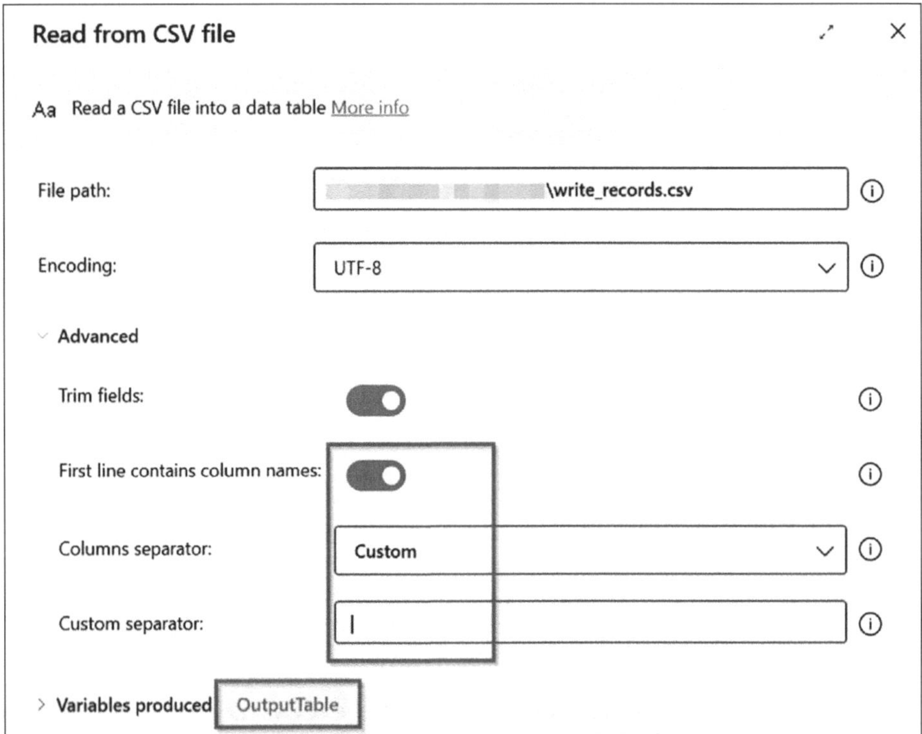

Figure 7.20: *Read from CSV file action*

Following is the output Datatable called **`OutputTable`** after running the Flow. And now the bot can loop this Datatable and use these records into any system or application.

Variable value

OutputTable (Datatable)

#	ID	FirstName	LastName	Email	Department	Salary
0	1	John	Smith	john.smith@example.com	Engineering	70000
1	2	Jane	Doe	jane.doe@example.com	Marketing	65000
2	3	Michael	Brown	michael.brown@example.com	Sales	72000
3	4	Emily	Davis	emily.davis@example.com	Human Resources	60000
4	5	David	Wilson	david.wilson@example.com	Engineering	75000

Figure 7.21: *OutputTable variable after running the Flow*

Reading/Writing Text Files

Just like the CSV files, Text files are also commonly used across RPA automation scenarios as they serve a simple and straightforward data input and output medium. RPA bots can read from and write into text files to interact with various systems and processes, they can act as a config file to store configuration settings of the bots like URLs, file paths, and more. They can be used especially to create log files of a specific format. They can even be used for temporary data storage where an RPA bot processes a batch of transactions and stores the results in a text file before uploading them to legacy systems that accept only text files.

The Action in PAD to do so is the **"`Write text to file`"** where you at first provide the full path of the file to be created followed by the text to write to it. The **"`Append new line`"** toggle allows us to add a new line at the end of the text to be written. This ensures that subsequent uses of the same Action in future Flow steps will start writing on a new line after the previous text. In other words, there would be a gap of a new line between the previous text and the new text that will be written to the file. If you do not want to overwrite the previous content of the same file which is generally the case for logging and other output reports, then this configuration can be done in the **"`If file exists`"** parameter to append the content instead of overwriting.

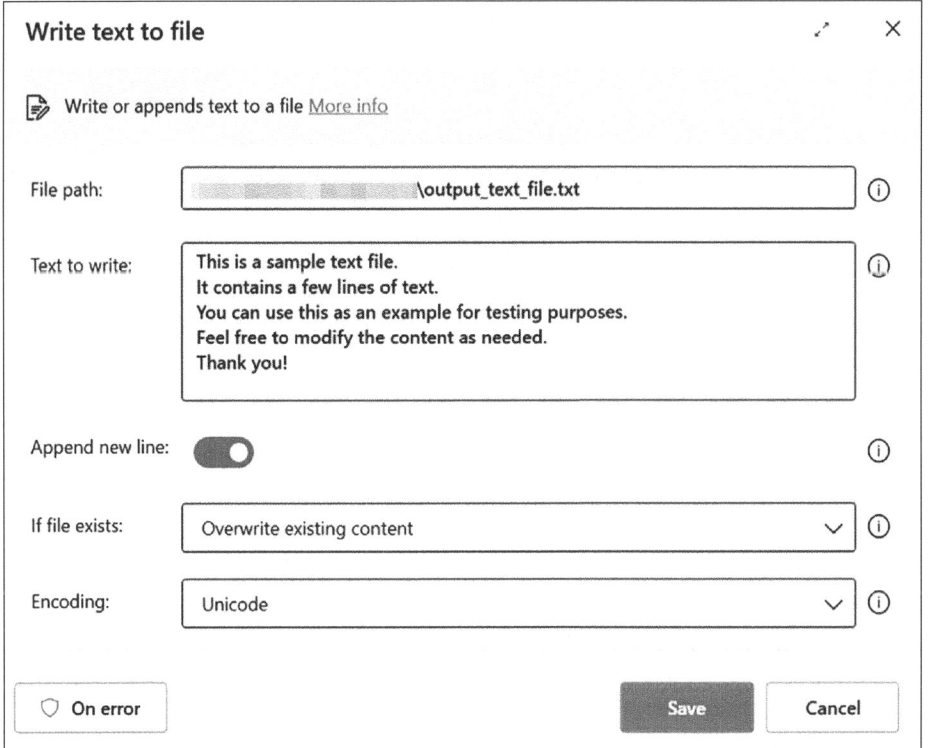

Figure 7.22: *Write text to file*

Try out the **"Read text from file"** to read the contents of the file that is written by the Action in the preceding figure or from any other already existing text file. Watch for the **"Store content as"** parameter which has the ability to read the text as a single value or in separate items of a List variable wherever it encounters a new line.

The following figure shows the output in a List variable, where each line of the input text in *Figure 7.22* is written as a separate item which can be handy when certain text needs to be extracted from the entire input data.

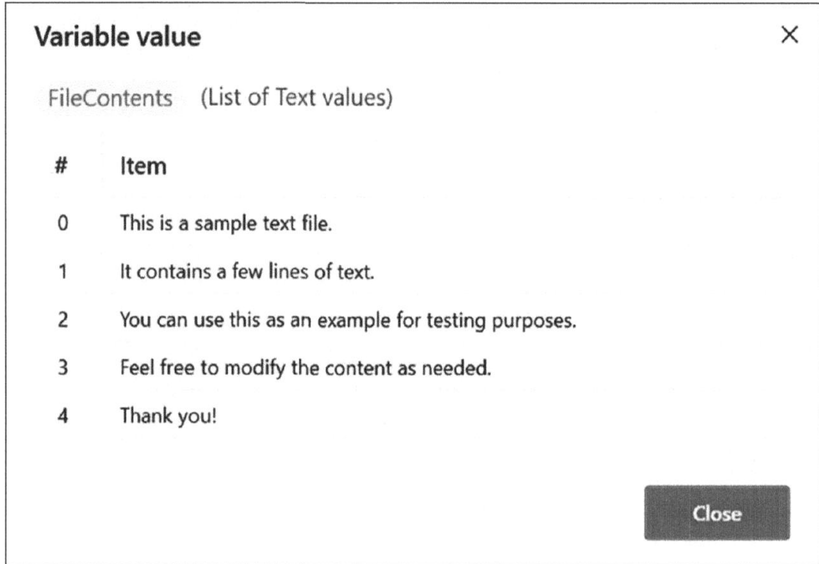

Figure 7.23: *List item output of Read text from file action*

Interacting with XML Files

Reading and writing XML (eXtensible Markup Language) files in an RPA process is vital in several scenarios due to the structured and hierarchical nature of XMLs, making it ideal for data representation and exchange. An error from an external system could be generated in the form of an XML with error description, type, reason, and more, that has to be read by the bot, or bot configuration and settings can be done via XMLs. Bot configuration XML files is one of the common ways of using this file type along with using them for logging purposes. And in some cases, they are also used to store structured data in a way that preserves the hierarchy and relationships between data elements for any kind of data exchanges.

We will see several Actions for interacting with an XML file with the help of a unique exercise.

Following is how an input XML file called **"books.xml"** looks like. As seen, this XML document represents a bookstore containing a collection of books. Each book has a category attribute and includes elements for the title, author(s), and year of publication.

This XML with the same name is available in the GitHub folder of this book for practicing the exercise.

What if you would like to add the **<price>** element for every book? In Power Automate Desktop, a new element is added with the help of the **"Insert XML element"** Action. But using this Action inserts the element only to the book that is pointed by the XPath query which is one of the parameters in the **"Insert XML element"** Action. Meaning, if the XPath query of this Action points to the third book, it will add the new **<price>** element only to the third book. However, we would like to add it for all the books of the entire XML. That is what we are going to do starting by reading the XML at first, get the count of all the **<book>** elements so that we can iterate through all of them, then insert the **<price>** element within the iteration, and then finally write the modified XML to the same input file. Let's check all of these in action.

```
▼<bookstore>
  ▼<book category="cooking">
     <title lang="en">Everyday Italian</title>
     <author>Giada De Laurentiis</author>
     <year>2005</year>
   </book>
  ▼<book category="children">
     <title lang="en">Harry Potter</title>
     <author>J K. Rowling</author>
     <year>2005</year>
   </book>
  ▼<book category="web">
     <title lang="en">XQuery Kick Start</title>
     <author>James McGovern</author>
     <author>Per Bothner</author>
     <author>Kurt Cagle</author>
     <author>James Linn</author>
     <author>Vaidyanathan Nagarajan</author>
     <year>2003</year>
   </book>
  ▼<book category="web">
     <title lang="en">Learning XML</title>
     <author>Erik T. Ray</author>
     <year>2003</year>
   </book>
 </bookstore>
```

Figure 7.24: *Sample input XML*

1. We first read the XML file and this is done in PAD via the **"Read XML from file"** Action. The first parameter is the full path of the file and the output variable to be noted in our case is **XmlDocument**, which we are going to use in the Flow.

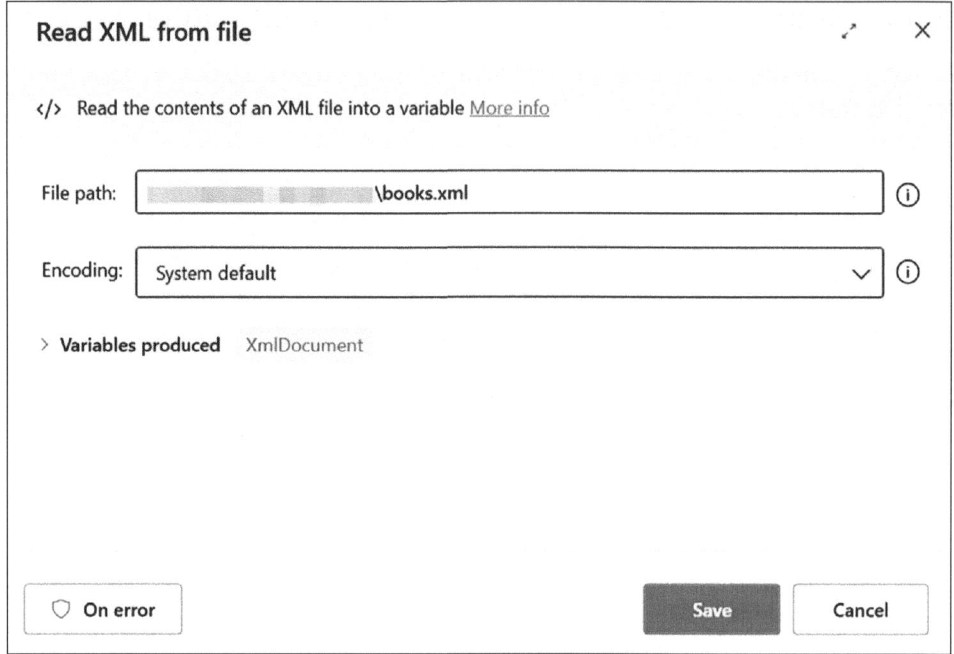

Figure 7.25: *The Read XML from file action*

2. Then we set a variable called **`Counter`** to 1. This counter is to iterate through the **`<book>`** elements.

3. Then we make use of the **"`Execute XPath expression`"** Action. XPath (not a feature of PAD) is a powerful way of navigating through the elements, filter nodes, access their attributes, and extract values of an XML document. It allows us to query and manipulate the XML data easily. In our case, we are selecting all **`<book>`** elements in the document with the help of **"`//book`"** as the XPath query. The output variable returned is **`XPathResults`** which will contain all the **`<book>`** elements and will help us to get their count.

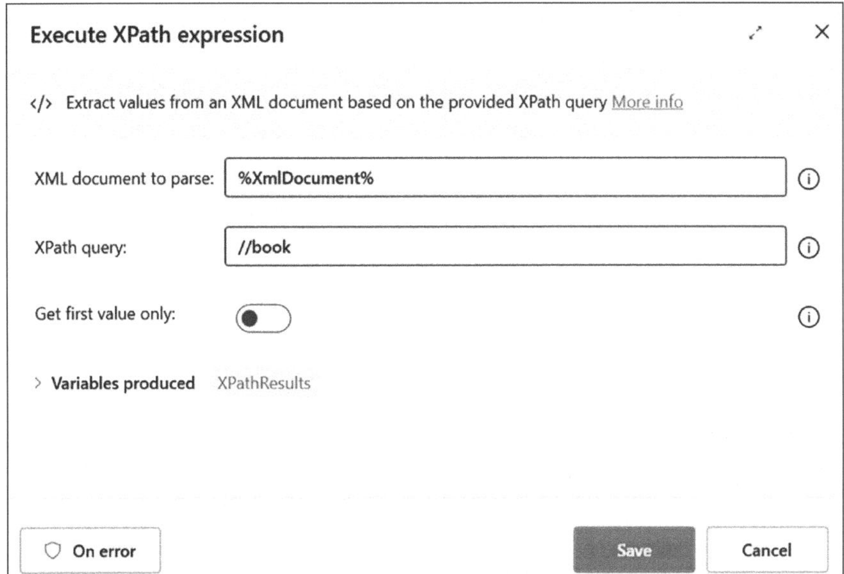

***Figure* 7.26:** *Executing an XPath expression*

You can learn XPath here or on any of the other learning resources you are already aware of: https://www.w3schools.com/xml/xpath_intro.asp.

4. We begin our iteration on the **`<book>`** elements with the help of the **"`Loop condition`"** Action. The first parameter is the **`Counter`** variable that we have already initialized to 1. (Note that you can also use a **"`Loop`"** Action which gives the **`LoopIndex`** output variable and is not needed to increment it separately. The **"`Loop condition`"** Action is used here so that you can also know how to take a separate counter variable and increment it within a loop which might be useful in any of your other automation scenarios.)

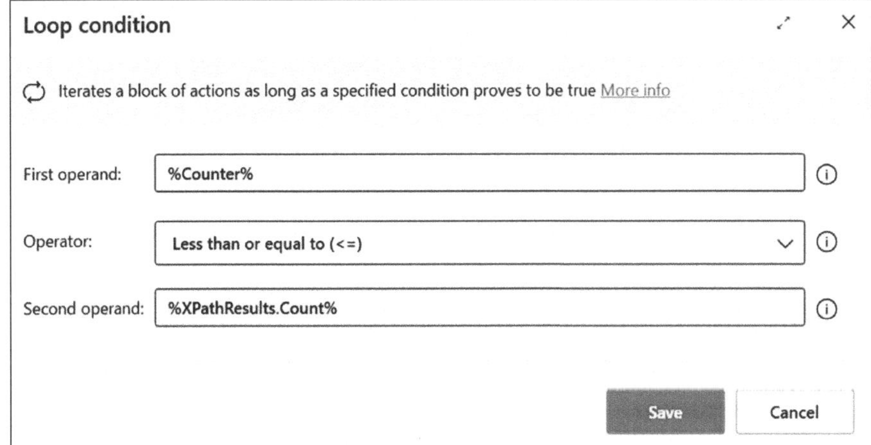

***Figure* 7.27:** *Looping through the elements*

We will loop from 1 till the number of **<book>** elements (which is 4 in our case) and that is made possible by the **.Count** property of **XPathResults**. Use the variable picker in the **"Second operand"** box to get **%XPathResults.Count%**.

5. Now is the time to insert the new **<price>** element, as specified earlier, which is possible via the **"Insert XML element"** Action. Since this Action is inside a Loop, the XPath query will be **bookstore/book[%Counter%]** meaning that it will point to **bookstore/book[1]**, **bookstore/book[2]**, and so on, as the loop iterates. **/bookstore/book[1]** selects the first book element that is the child of the bookstore element, then the second and so on.

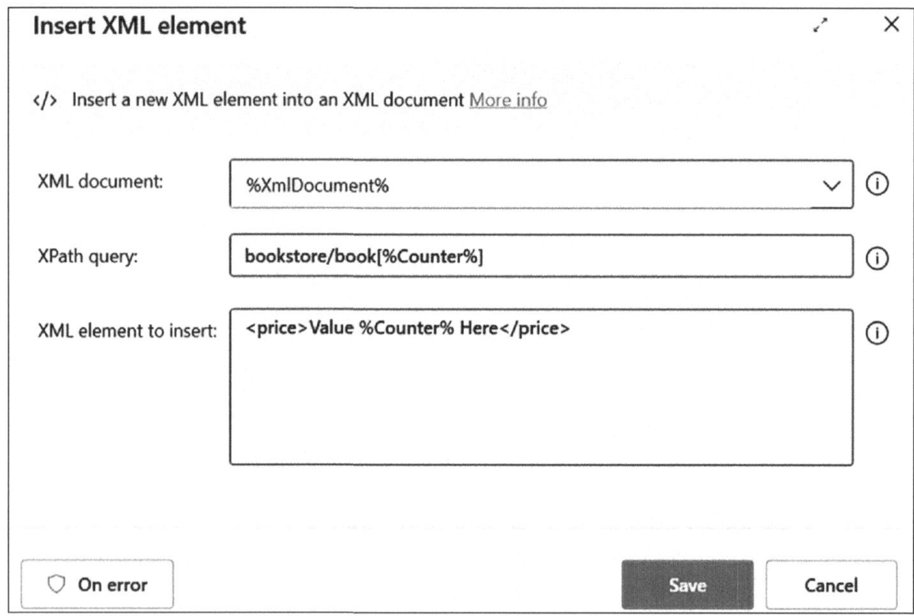

***Figure 7.28:** Inserting the new element*

The new element will have a value prefixed and suffixed by its opening and closing XML tags as **<price>Value %Counter% Here</price>**. In our example, the value will be inserted as **Value 1 Here**, **Value 2 Here**, and so on, but ideally in an automation scenario these could come from anywhere like List variables, Datatables, numeric, text variables, or from anywhere else.

6. Next, we increment the **Counter** variable by 1 using the **"Increase variable"** Action.

7. The new **<price>** elements are written to the **XmlDocument** variable in the preceding figure. It is still not saved into the original XML file and that is done with the help of the **"Write XML to file"** Action outside the loop. Here you provide **XMLDocument** as the value to write to the same file that was read originally. Leave all other default parameters as it is. Use the **'i'** icon to understand more about them.

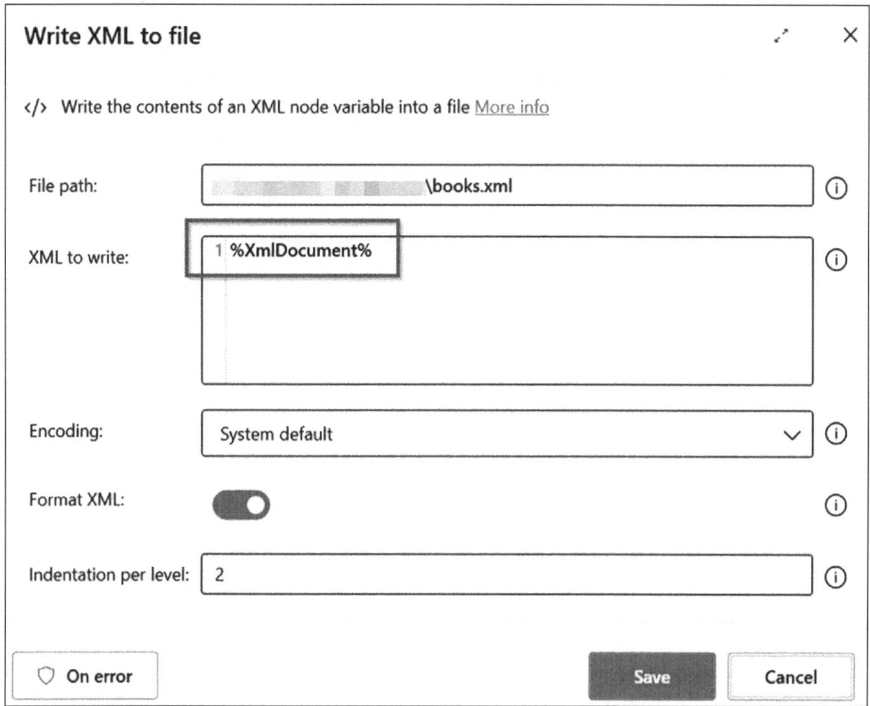

Figure 7.29: *Writing XML back to the file*

The entire list of Flow Actions for the aforementioned steps is as follows:

	Action
1	**Read XML from file** Read XML from file \books.xml' and store it into XmlDocument
2	**Set variable** Assign to variable Counter the value 1
3	**Execute XPath expression** Execute XPath query '//book' against XmlDocument and store the retrieved values into XPathResults
4	**Loop condition** While (Counter) <=(XPathResults .Count)
5	**Insert XML element** Insert XML element '<price>Value ' Counter ' Here</price>' into document XmlDocument
6	**Increase variable** Increase variable Counter by 1
7	**End**
8	**Write XML to file** Write XML XmlDocument into file \books.xml'

Figure 7.30: *Entire list of actions*

Let us run this Flow and notice the change in the XML. As highlighted, every single **<book>** element now has the **<price>** child element inserted dynamically with running values throughout the document.

```
▼<bookstore>
  ▼<book category="cooking">
     <title lang="en">Everyday Italian</title>
     <author>Giada De Laurentiis</author>
     <year>2005</year>
     <price>Value 1 Here</price>
   </book>
  ▼<book category="children">
     <title lang="en">Harry Potter</title>
     <author>J K. Rowling</author>
     <year>2005</year>
     <price>Value 2 Here</price>
   </book>
  ▼<book category="web">
     <title lang="en">XQuery Kick Start</title>
     <author>James McGovern</author>
     <author>Per Bothner</author>
     <author>Kurt Cagle</author>
     <author>James Linn</author>
     <author>Vaidyanathan Nagarajan</author>
     <year>2003</year>
     <price>Value 3 Here</price>
   </book>
  ▼<book category="web">
     <title lang="en">Learning XML</title>
     <author>Erik T. Ray</author>
     <year>2003</year>
     <price>Value 4 Here</price>
   </book>
 </bookstore>
```

Figure 7.31: *Output with price element added*

Moving on to other key Actions, in our sample XML, **category** is an Attribute and **title** is an element. If we were to read their values for the first book, then they would be **"cooking"** and **"Everyday Italian"** without the quotes, respectively.

```
<book category="cooking">
       <title lang="en">Everyday Italian</title>
       <author>Giada De Laurentiis</author>
       <year>2005</year>
       <price>Value 1 Here</price>
</book>
```

The **"Get XML element attribute"** Action is used to read an Attribute which has to be pointed by an XPath. Similarly, **"Get XML element value"** Action is used to retrieve an element's value.

With the help of the respective Action, if we point to the **category** Attribute for the first book with the help of the XPath as **/bookstore/book[1]** then the **XmlAttributeValue** output variable will return as **"cooking"** without the quotes.

Following is the usage of this Action for the aforementioned parameters.

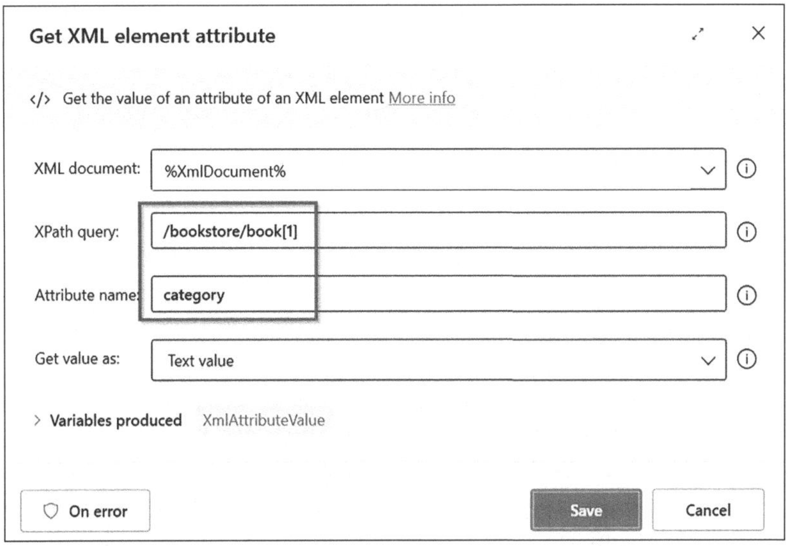

Figure 7.32: *Reading the attributes of an element*

Similarly, if we point to the **title** element for the first book with the help of the XPath as **/bookstore/book[1]/title** then the **XmlElementValue** output variable will return as **"Everyday Italian"** without the quotes.

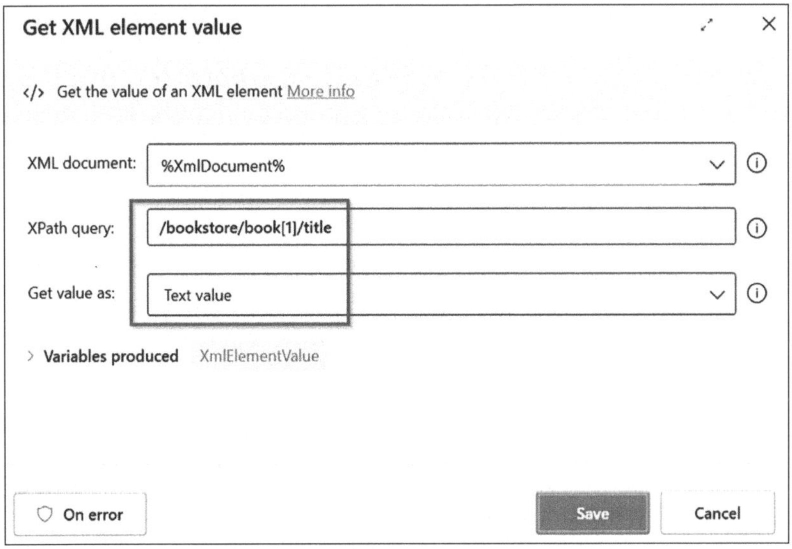

Figure 7.33: *Reading an element's value*

Add these Actions and display their output variables in a message box and verify their outputs.

Just like **reading** an XML element's attribute and an element's value, their corresponding **writing** Actions are **"`Set XML element attribute`"** and **"`Set XML element value`"**, and **"`Remove XML element attribute`"** and **"`Remove XML element`"** are their **deletion** Actions for attributes and elements respectively. How about practically trying these Actions for the **`books.xml`** file included in the GitHub folder? They take the similar kind of parameters like the Actions explained in the previous sections.

Following is one of the learning resources for understanding various aspects of an XML:

https://www.w3schools.com/xml/default.asp.

Text Functions

String Functions or Text Functions have been used since the programming times where they allow developers to analyze and manipulate text data as per the needs of the development. They provide a wide range of operations such as formatting, searching, replacing, extracting, modifying, and validating text. These are available in PAD to achieve RPA automation too. There is a varied list of text operations allowed in PAD and they are visible under the **"`Text`"** category of Actions in the **"`Actions`"** pane.

Let us go through the widely used Actions needed while building any automation.

Crop Text

Crop Text, as the name suggests is used to cut the text based on one or more specified characters called as flag. In other words, this Action extracts text that is before, after or in between any other specified text flag. To understand more, let us see it in action.

Add a **"`Set variable`"** Action for a variable called **`InputText`** and pass the value as

`Name: John Doe`

In the text **`Name: John Doe`**, we would like to extract only the first name and last name of the input text where the text **"`Name:`"** would be fixed, as an example. This input text could be anywhere from an incoming email, or a Notepad file, or on a web page. In such cases, the **"`Crop text`"** Action can come into picture.

Drag and drop the Action and pass the parameters as shown in the following figure.

The first parameter is the sample input string that we initialized. The **"`Mode`"** parameter determines whether to extract the text before, after or in between the specified flag. We would like to get the text "after" the flag. Since **`Name:`** would be static in our example, provide it as our flag. The **"`Ignore case`"** toggle tells the Action whether to match the flag in the input text using case-sensitivity or not. In our case, we have given the exact case of **`Name:`** as it would appear in the input text, but this can be changed as per our automation requirements.

Notice the output variables of **`CroppedText`** which would return us the response of the Action and we will print it in a message box, whereas **`IsFlagFound`** will tell if the flag was found or not. In an ideal scenario, you would at first check if the flag was found and then proceed further.

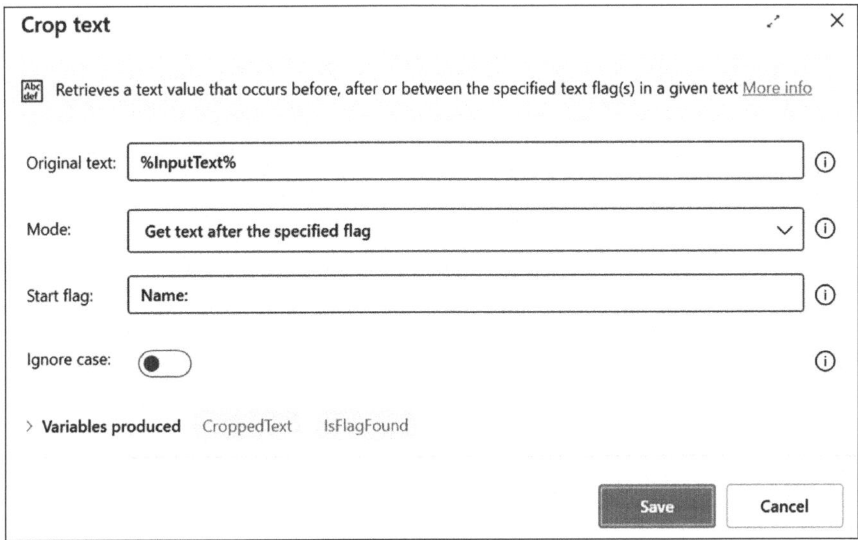

Figure 7.34: *The Crop text Action*

The entire Flow with the aforementioned Actions along with its output is as follows and we were able to successfully extract the desired output.

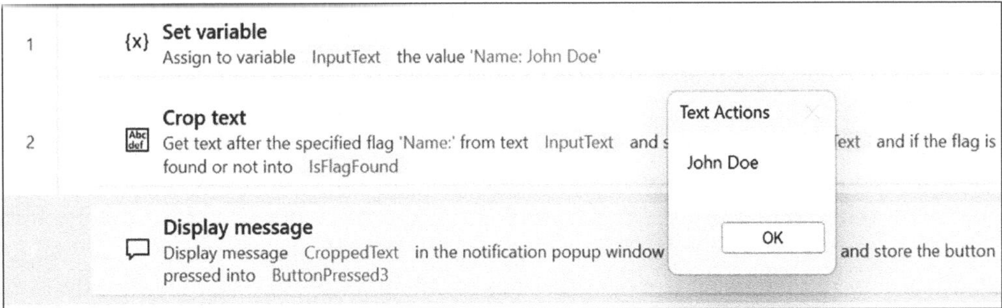

Figure 7.35: *Entire Flow and its output*

Parse Text and Get Subtext

Parse Text is a widely used Action implemented across automation scenarios. It checks for the first or multiple occurrences of a specified subtext within another text or string. It also has the ability to match a regular expression pattern. Let us see the same previous example but with the help of this Action.

Set an initial variable called **`InputText`** with the same input as **`Name: John Doe`**.

Drag and drop the **"`Parse Text`"** Action and after passing the input text as the first parameter configure the other parameters as follows:

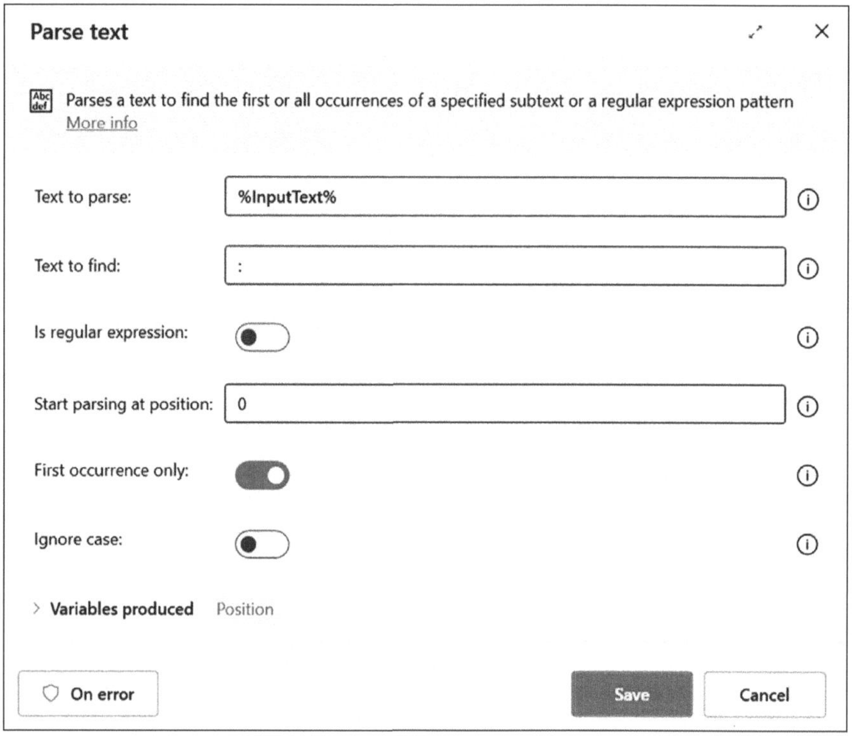

Figure 7.36: *The Parse text action*

The **"`Text to find`"** can contain one or more characters of a text that needs to be searched within the input text. In our case, this time, let us search on the basis of the colon character **'`:`'** without the quotes. The **"`Is regular expression`"** toggle is where we would tell this Action whether the text given in **"`Text to find`"** is a regular expression pattern or not. The position of the text from where to start looking for is from the beginning of the input text, that is, 0. The **"`First occurrence only`"** toggle has the ability to give us all the occurrences of the matches and not just the first one. And finally, the **"`Ignore case`"** helps to determine whether to do a case matching or not. The **`Position`** output variable will be either 0 or greater than 0 if a match is successfully found and hence can be used to add an **"`If`"** condition to read the parsed text. A value of -1 is returned if not found.

The **"`Get subtext`"** as the name suggests returns the subtext of an input string specified from a starting position till the specified length of characters.

We are at first finding the position of a character (using **"`Parse Text`"**) and then extracting a piece of text based on that position (using **"`Get subtext`"**). We are using both these Actions in conjunction with each other, but you need to know they can be used separately too depending on the situation.

Moving further with the exercise, as in the following figure, pass the same input text as the first parameter. The **"`Start index`"** can be either from the beginning of the text or from a specified position. Since we have extracted the position of the colon in the preceding Action, mention **"`Character position`"** as the dropdown option. In the input string **`Name: John Doe`**, the colon character is in the 4th position starting from 0, hence we need to add 1 to it as **`%Position + 1%`** and retrieve the rest of the text till the end.

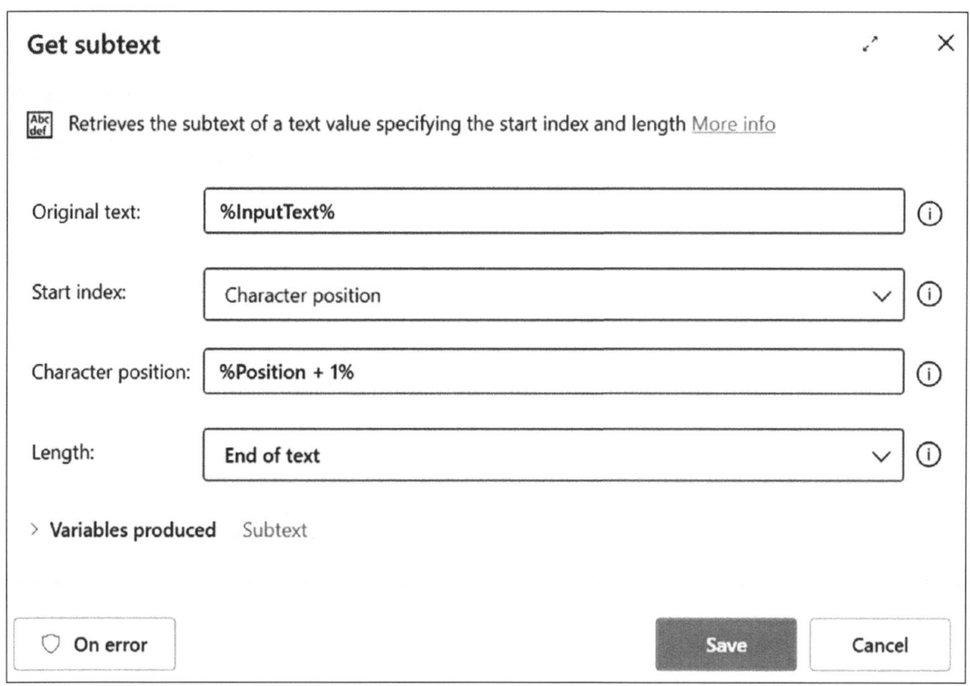

Figure 7.37: *The Get subtext action*

Display the **`Subtext`** output variable. There will be a space at the beginning (the one after colon from the input text) which is not visible in the following message box. To remove it, either you can start from **`%Position + 2%`** or use the **"`Trim text`"** Action shown shortly from here. The entire Flow along with its output on running is as follows:

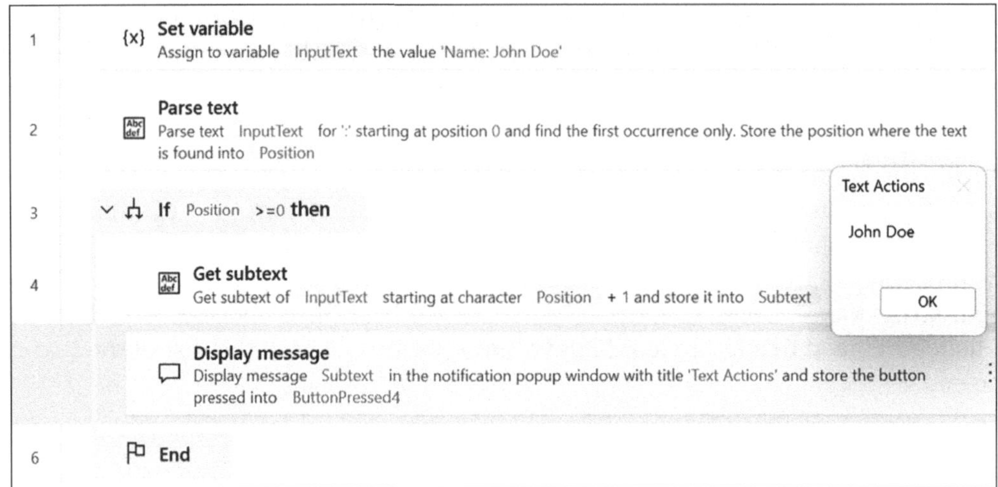

Figure 7.38: *Entire Flow and its output*

To give you an example of an isolated use of the **"Parse Text"** Action, it is widely used along with regular expressions.

For example, add **1234AB56EF** in the **"Text to parse"** parameter of the **"Parse Text"** Action and **[0-9]+** in the **"Text to find"** box. Enable the **"Is regular expression"** toggle and you will get a list output as **1234** and **56** since the regular expression was used to get all the numbers from the input.

Replace Text

The **"Replace Text"** Action is also used across various automation situations. It is used to replace a text within another text value and just like the **"Parse Text"** Action it also has the ability to match a regular expression pattern while searching for a text within another text.

Following is the usage of this Action along with its parameters.

For the same input text as in the previous sections, search for the **"Name:"** text without the quotes. We will replace this text with a blank or an empty string. In Power Automate Desktop, an empty string is denoted by two double quotes (as in some programming languages) which is then prefixed and suffixed by the PAD variable notation of percent sign. Add **%""%** in the **"Replace with"** parameter. This Action has a toggle for using a Regular Expression while performing the Find and Replace of the text values and the another one for using case-sensitivity or not, both of which are as in the **"Parse Text"** Action. It also has a third toggle called **"Activate escape sequences"** which when enabled will replace \n with a new line or \t with a tab, as examples. Use \n or \t in the **"Replace with"** box and try them out against a sample input text.

Coming back to our exercise, on clicking the **"Save"** button and re-opening the Action, you will notice that the empty string given by two **double** quotes enclosed within percent sign has turned to two **single** quotes enclosed within percent sign as **%''%** which means this can also be used to denote an empty string. A word of mention is that if you are using this as an ebook, do not copy paste the empty string from here, instead type it manually in the PAD parameter box to avoid mismatch in the font of the quotes.

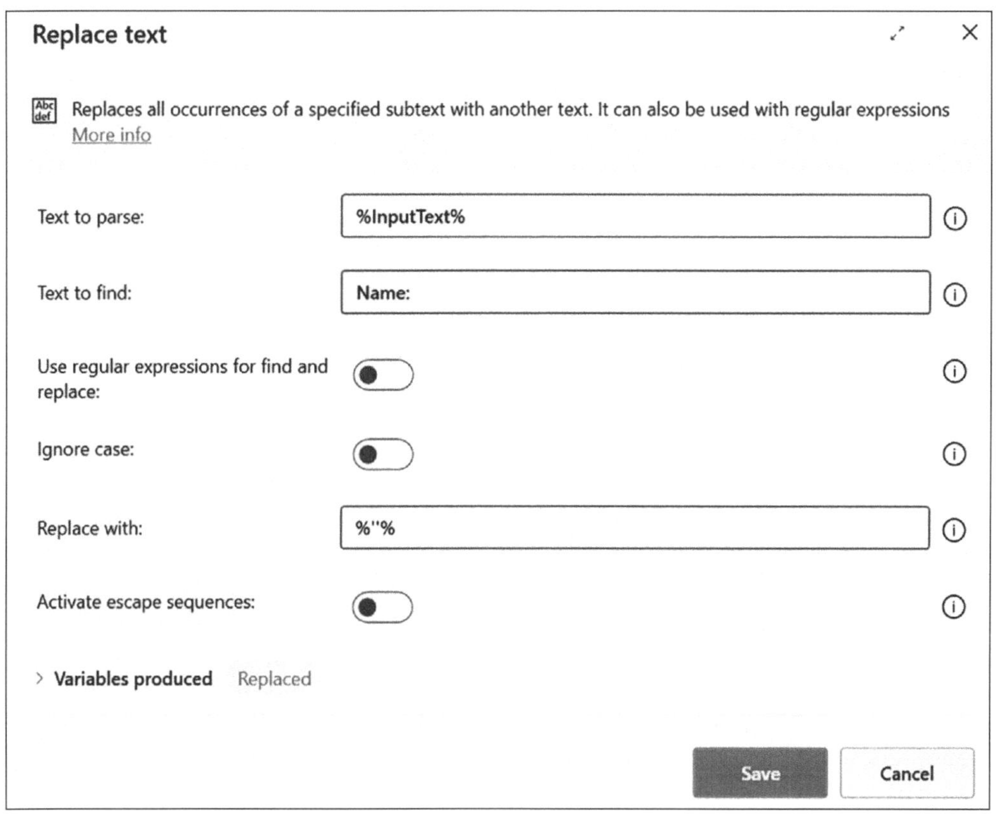

Figure 7.39: *The Replace text action*

Displaying the **Replaced** output variable in a message box will replace *Name*: with an empty string and produce the output as **John Doe**. Again, to get rid of the initial space you can include it at the end of the **"Text to find"** as **"Name: "** without quotes with a space at the end or use **"Trim text"** Action after the output retrieval.

The examples here are intentionally simple to help understand, but these Text Actions are very much used in complex scenarios.

Thus, we have stripped off the text **"Name:"** using three approaches in the previous sections. Now with these Actions, it is time that you do the same for the output of the Calculator application in "*Chapter 5: Building Blocks of a Desktop Flow*". To help recall, in *Figure* 5.9, the output of performing an arithmetic operation for 4 + 6 = shows the text in a message box as **"`Display is 10`"**. Strip off the unwanted text and store the final answer of 10 in a variable which can then be used for future reference in the automation.

This brings us to another handy Action. When you perform the above-mentioned Calculator exercise, you will notice that the value of 10 will be stored in a **"`Text`"** data type variable. This is because these Text functions return a variable of type **"`Text`"**, but 10 is a number. So, if we need the value of 10 to be stored as a number for any future purposes in the Flow then we should make use of the **"`Convert text to number`"** Action. Use this Action while performing the Calculator exercise and notice the data type of the variable before and after the conversion by opening the variable from the **"`Flow variables`"** section.

You must be made aware that, since 10 is a number, only for that reason you will be able to use the **"`Convert text to number`"** Action. If you try to convert a value that is not a number into a number then PAD throws an error. For example, if the input text is **`Name: John Doe`**, and you strip off **`Name:`** and try to convert the remaining text of **`John Doe`** into a number then you will encounter an error. So, you need to ensure before using this Action that the result would actually be a number after the conversion.

Like the conversion Action, the other way round is also possible with the help of the **"`Convert number to text`"** Action and can be used in its own automation scenario. This Action has a provision to specify the number of decimal places as well as to use a thousand separator. For example, if the input is 123456 and if the Action is configured for 2 decimal places with the thousand separator toggle turned on, then the output will be 1,23,456.00. Here, comma is the thousand separator and the output has two decimal places added to it. Practically, try this Action for various inputs and outputs. If you are getting a different output or if you want to have a different output than what is shown, then you might want to modify the number formats in the regional settings in Windows where you can change the decimal symbol as well as the digit grouping.

Split Text

The **"`Split Text`"** Action is another one that is commonly required in automation. PAD provides this Action to split a text based on a delimiter like a space, tab or a new line, or based on the number of characters to split, or even allows us to specify our own delimiter character.

Imagine an email having the following text and you would like to get the values of the name, city, and email of the person.

Name: John Doe
City: London
Email: john.doe@example.com

Add the preceding sample to the **InputText** in a **"Set variable"** Action.

Since we see that the text we would like to extract is in separate lines, we will split it with the new line as the delimiter character. To do this, drag and drop the **"Split text"** Action and provide the parameters as follows.

At first, pass the **InputText** variable, then the delimiter of **"Standard"** type because we have the **"New line"** option in the dropdown.

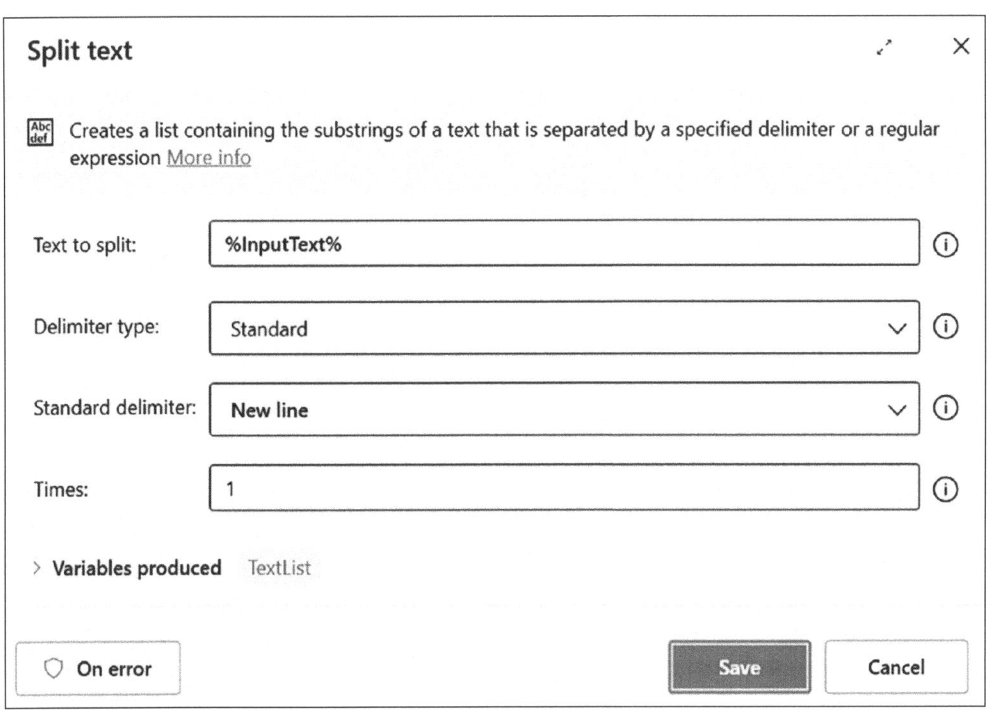

Figure 7.40: *The Split text action*

The **"Times"** value is used to indicate how many times the delimiter character will be present in the input text at a single location, which is going to be once on each line. Run the Flow and you will get a List type of variable called **TextList** which holds each line of the input text as a separate item of the List. You can then access the individual items of the List with the help of **TextList[index].**

For example, you can get the email in the third item by doing **%TextList[2]%** and then use any of the Text Actions in the above sections to strip off the wording **"Email:"** to get the actual email address.

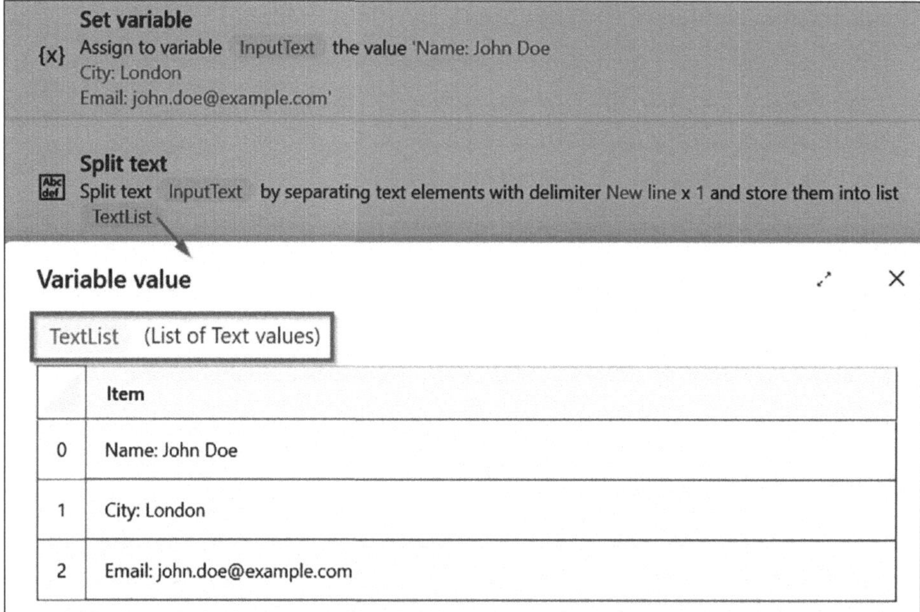

Figure 7.41: *The Entire Flow and its output*

You can do the exact opposite, that is, convert an input List into a delimiter separated text. And this is done via the **"Join text"** Action. Take the **TextList** variable coming from the previous exercise and pass it to the **"Join text"** Action. Set the delimiter as a new line and notice that the output will be exactly the same as the **InputText** variable of the previous section.

Pad Text

Several systems have a pre-defined format of storing any data. For example, a system has to mandatorily store an ID with a length of 10 characters. The system requires that if the input ID does not match this length, then it can be padded with zeros to its left.

Example, if the input text is 274A6, then the system wants to add leading zeros to its left as 00000274A6 to make it 10 characters.

This can be done with the help of the **"Pad text"** Action. Initialize 274A6 to **InputText** using a **"Set variable"**. Then drag and drop the **"Pad text"** Action. The **"Pad"** dropdown has options to perform the padding either to the left or to the right of the input string. The **"Text for padding"** in our case is **0** and we would like to make it a total length of **10** characters.

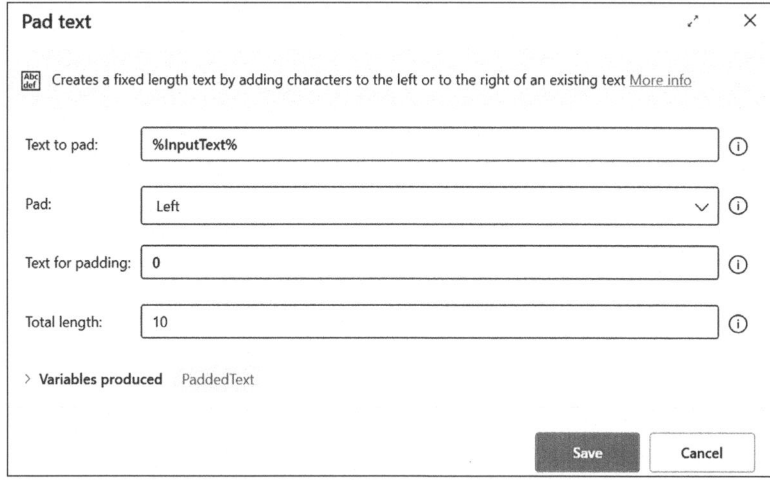

Figure 7.42: *The Pad text action*

Run the Flow and if you display the **`PaddedText`** output variable in a message box, the result you will get is 00000274A6, correctly padded by the leading zeros and making it a length of 10 characters. Likewise, you can add a trailing text to the right depending on the automation scenario you are building.

Trim Text

As seen earlier and also many times while building Flows, you would feel the need to clean up the input text by removing any unwanted characters like spaces, or new lines or tabs. This is done with the **"`Trim text`"** Action. Here is a sample input text that has a few spaces at the beginning and at the end of the text, highlighted in yellow. The cursor shown at the end of the input text is to show that there are a few spaces at the end. The Action has options to trim the start of string, end of string, or both. When you select both as the option and run the Flow, the **`TrimmedText`** output variable will have the leading and trailing spaces removed.

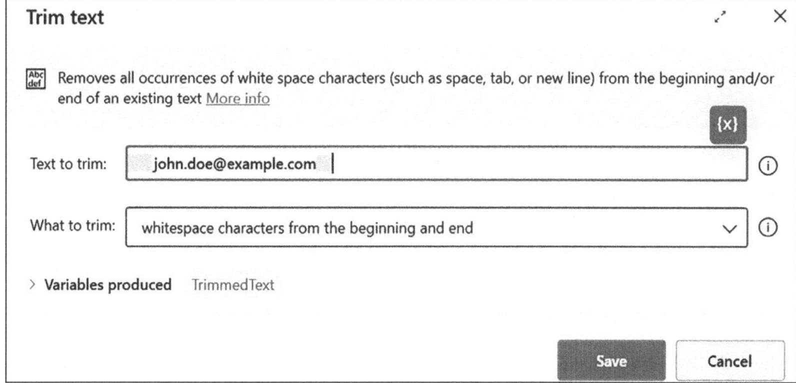

Figure 7.43: *The Trim text action*

Getting the Length of a Text

Finding the length of a string is a common real-world automation scenario. For example, you have to validate a User Id such that it should be of 8 characters in length. In this case, you would have to determine its length and this is done using the property of the variable that holds the User Id. Finding a length is not a separate Action but a property, but getting the length is generally associated when you work with Text Actions. Therefore, it has been included here in this topic alongside the Text Actions.

We have been using **`InputText`** as our variable holding the input text as **`Name: John Doe`**. To display its length, take a message box and you will see the **`.Length`** property of this variable via the variable picker button, as shown in the following figure. Select it and run the Flow to get a value of 14 for our sample text.

The display message box is just an example to print its length, but this property will be available in any other Action where variable picker can be used. In other words, you would use **`%InputText.Length%`** to get its length.

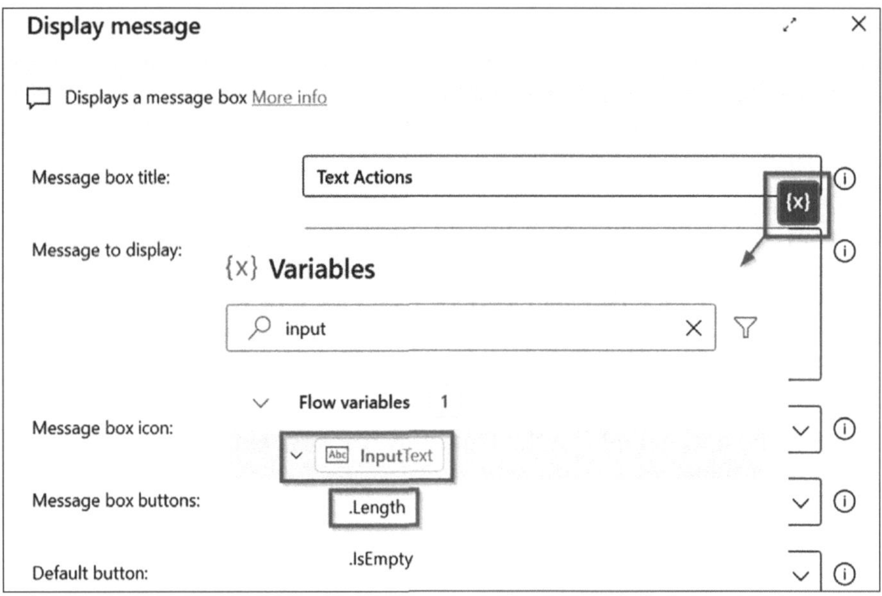

Figure 7.44: *Getting the length from the variable picker*

Create Random Text

Speaking of User Ids, if you are automating a user creation process and generating random passwords for an application and have to email it back to the user, then you would need to write a logic to create these passwords. Not only that, they have to adhere to all policies like a specific length, should or should not have certain characters and so forth. This is done by the in-built Action in PAD called **`"Create random text"`**.

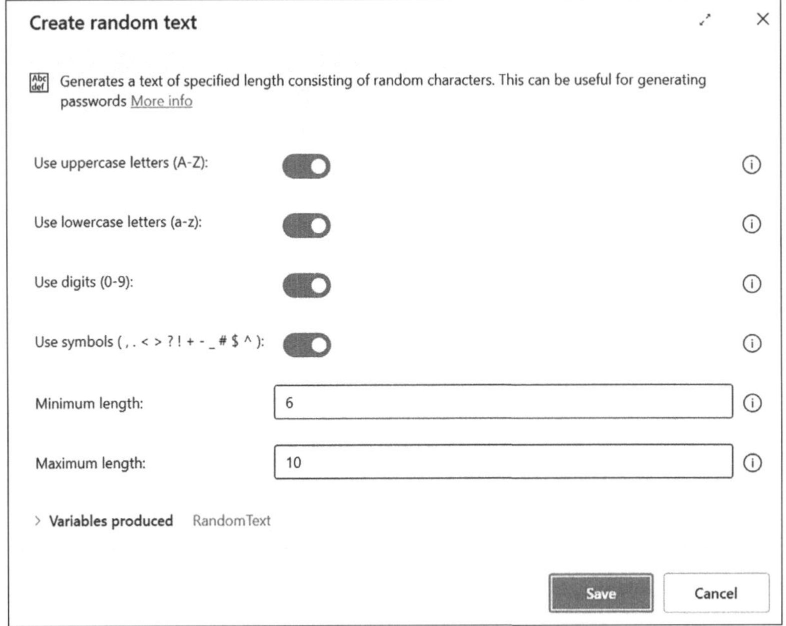

Figure 7.45: *The Create random text action*

Try generating random text by passing different combinations of the various parameters available in this Action.

Case Conversion and Comparison

During Flow development, there will arise scenarios where conversion of text to different cases like uppercase or lowercase will become necessary. For example, if there is an incoming text that has the word **"`Error`"** at some fixed location in it, but it could arrive in any case like Error, ERROR, or error. And you would like to check whether this word is present at that position and then take the next course of action. Since you do not know the case of the incoming text you cannot do a direct comparison. You will have to convert the incoming text to a specific case, that is, either to a lower case or upper case and then compare it with **"`error`"** or **"ERROR"** respectively. This is the approach that has been used since the programming times. In PAD, to change the case there is an Action called **"`Change text case`"** along with changing the input text to a Title case or a Sentence case, but we will make use of an approach that will not just change the case but also compare with a text of our choice.

Consider our sample input variable of **`InputText`** holding a text as **`Error.`** We will convert this to an upper case and compare it with a static upper case text of **ERROR**, so that both the input text and the text to compare with are the same. This conversion and comparison can be done within the same **"`If`"** Action as follows. Using the variable picker, select the **`.ToUpper`** property as the first operand and **ERROR** (all in upper case) as the text to be compared with.

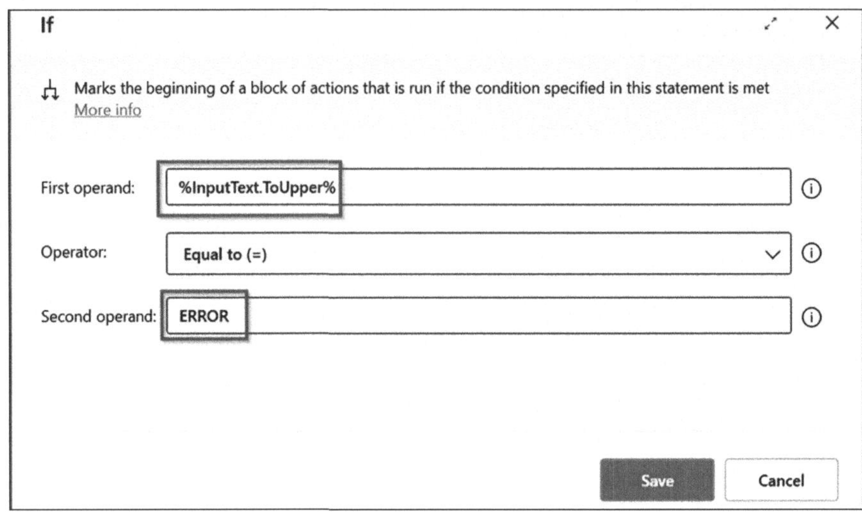

Figure 7.46: *Case conversion and comparison*

If we do this, no matter what the input text is like Error, ERROR, error, ErRor, all of these will be converted to an upper case and compared with a static upper case text of ERROR and will return True if they match. You can verify this with the help of a Flow by displaying a message box, as shown in the following figure.

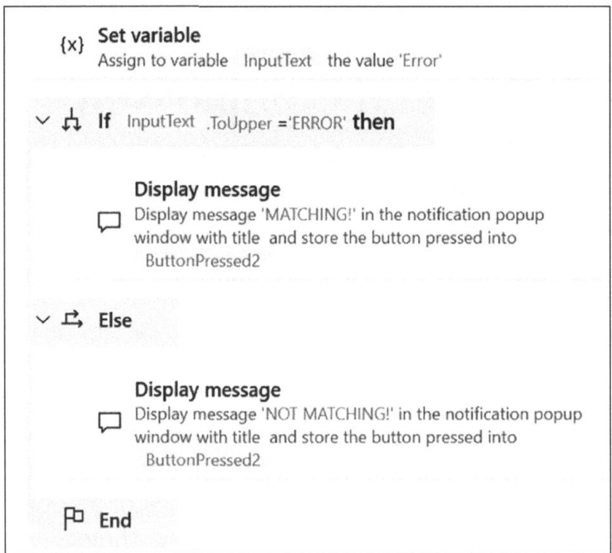

Figure 7.47: *Sample Flow to verify case conversion and comparison*

Create HTML Content

Another useful Action that has been off-lately launched is the **"Create HTML Content"**. Recall *Figure* 6.48 of "*Chapter 6: Automating Common Applications*", in the "*Outlook*

Automation" topic where we wrote an HTML text in the email body while sending an email from Outlook. We had to add the text with the help of HTML tags. For this, one would need to know the Hyper Text Markup Language. But by using the **"Create HTML Content"** Action, you will simply get an editor to create your own content and the corresponding HTML text will be generated out of it. This resulting text will be stored in a variable and can then be used anywhere in the Flow Actions where HTML is supported. Let us see this example.

The following figure shows the Action in question. We have created a text with multiple formatting features such as a text that is bold, underlined and italicized, has bullets, has font color in blue, has a hyperlink and has line breaks.

You can see the several available formatting options at the top of the editor box. It also has a variable picker **{x}** button to insert variable values anywhere in the written text. The **"Text editor"** toggle when enabled shows the same text in HTML and can be modified as required.

On running this Action, the **HTMLContent** output variable will be populated with an HTML text corresponding to the following written content. When you take the value of the **HTMLContent** variable and paste it in any HTML editor and run it to generate an HTML output from there, you will see the same content as written in this Action. Now you are ready to pass this variable in the **"Body"** parameter box while sending an Outlook email.

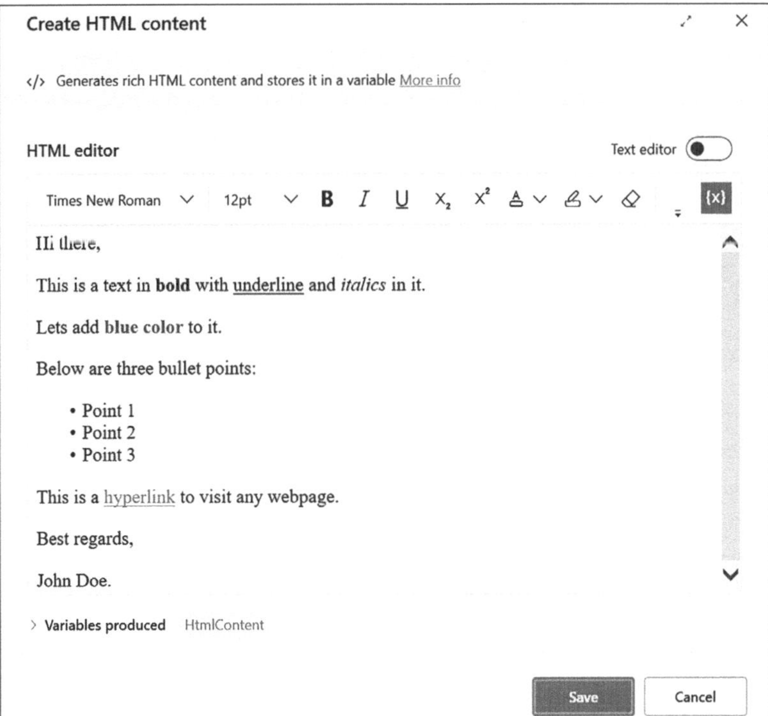

Figure 7.48: *The Create HTML content action*

Recognize Entities in Text

Did you know there is a readymade Action in-built in Power Automate Desktop to extract key known entities from a text without using Regex or any other Text functions? **"Recognize Entities in Text"** is a very powerful and useful Action in PAD and it is used to identify various key entities from any given text. These entities could be an email address, a website, a currency or a datetime value, website URLs, hashtags and mentions, and so on.

Add a **"Set variable"** Action for a variable called **InputVar** and assign it the following value:

```
Hi @John,

I will be unavailable till 15/10/2024. Could you check with @Jane about
the report that needs to be sent soon. Her email is Jane.Doe@email.com.
Alternatively, you can also contact her on +1 (555) 1234567.

If by any chance you do not get a reply then email to Rob@domain.com.

Thank you,
John
```

Drag and drop the **"Recognize entities in text"** Action, pass **InputVar** as the **"Text to recognize from"**. The **"Entity type"** dropdown has a varied list of options to extract from this text. Select the **"Email"** option as we will try to get all the email addresses from the input text. For better clarity of what the output variable is going to represent, provide its name as **RecognizedEntitiesEmail.**

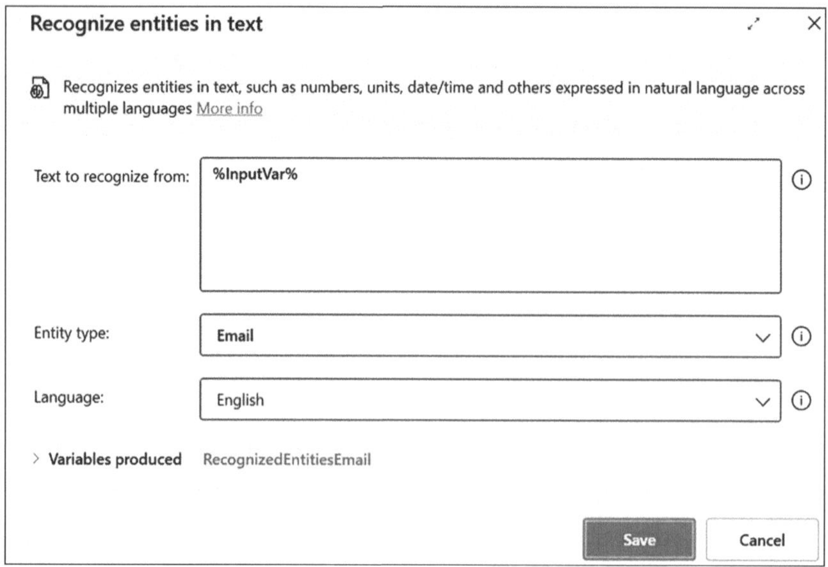

Figure 7.49: *The Recognize entities in text action*

When you run the Flow with the aforementioned Actions, the output Datatable variable will be populated with all the email addresses used in the input text, which are two in our case; **`Jane.Doe@email.com`** and **`Rob@domain.com`**. The **"`Original text`"** is what was in the input text and the **"`Value`"** is what it was interpreted as.

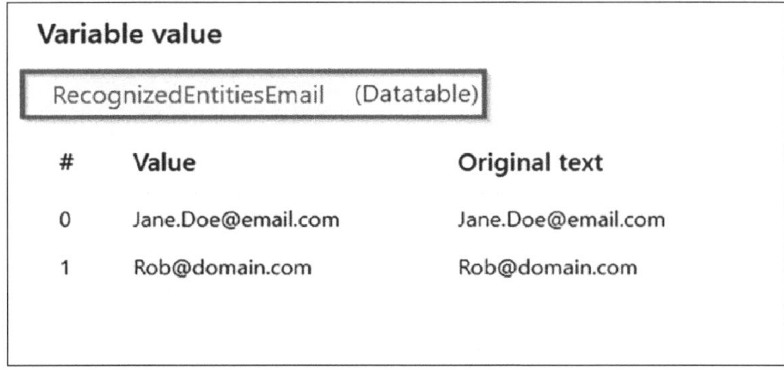

***Figure* 7.50:** *Output after extracting the Email Ids*

Similarly, if you extract the details from the output Datatable for the entities of date and time, phone number, and the mentions including the email already retrieved and write the output to a text file then it is as follows:

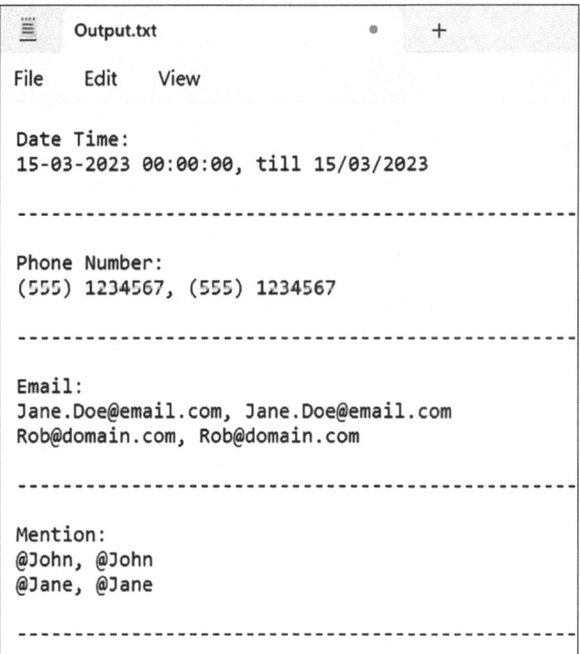


```
Date Time:
15-03-2023 00:00:00, till 15/03/2023

-----------------------------------------------

Phone Number:
(555) 1234567, (555) 1234567

-----------------------------------------------

Email:
Jane.Doe@email.com, Jane.Doe@email.com
Rob@domain.com, Rob@domain.com

-----------------------------------------------

Mention:
@John, @John
@Jane, @Jane

-----------------------------------------------
```

***Figure* 7.51:** *Output in text file after extracting required entities*

For certain portions, after using this Action, you might have to use Text Actions or Date Time formatting Actions (shown in the next topic) to extract the desired portion of the text. For instance, refer to what the Date format was in the original text and what was retrieved in the output.

Practical Exercise

Here is a practical exercise on the similar lines for this topic. There is a text file in the GitHub folder for this chapter named as **"`Exercise for Recognize Entities in Text.txt`"**. Read the text file and produce the output as shown here:

Input:

```
The real estate agent's phone number is +1 (555) 1234567 and their email
address is john.doe@realestate.com. Also, you can contact by visiting
the property website at http://203.0.113.1/mainstreetlisting.


On social media, the house is mentioned by @dreamhomes with the hashtag
#dreamhome.
```

Expected Output:

The output for various entities should be appended one after the other in a separate text file and formatted as displayed in the following figure with a separator:

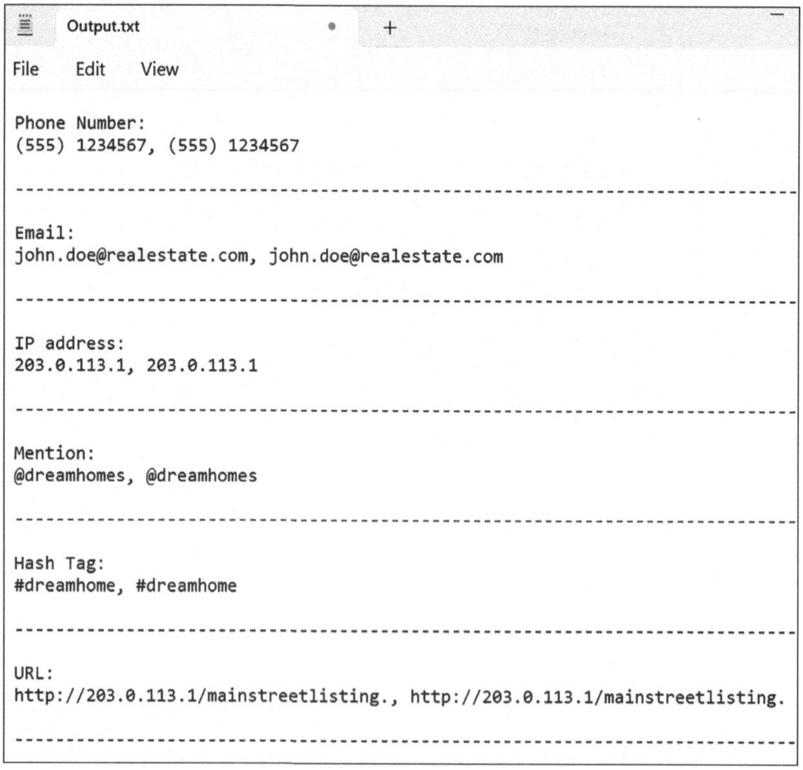

```
Output.txt
File   Edit   View

Phone Number:
(555) 1234567, (555) 1234567

-----------------------------------------------------------------------------

Email:
john.doe@realestate.com, john.doe@realestate.com

-----------------------------------------------------------------------------

IP address:
203.0.113.1, 203.0.113.1

-----------------------------------------------------------------------------

Mention:
@dreamhomes, @dreamhomes

-----------------------------------------------------------------------------

Hash Tag:
#dreamhome, #dreamhome

-----------------------------------------------------------------------------

URL:
http://203.0.113.1/mainstreetlisting., http://203.0.113.1/mainstreetlisting.

-----------------------------------------------------------------------------
```

Figure 7.52: *Expected output in text file with separator*

Identifying a New Line Character in a Text

There are going to be scenarios that you will come across while reading and writing text files, while string processing, while interacting with Web and Desktop applications, parsing of data, text display, formatting and several others. Here, it becomes necessary to identify a new line character within a text and take some action based on it. There are multiple approaches to identify a new line depending on what we are doing in the automation. You could come up with your own, but you need to know the following approaches of how we can denote a new line in PAD.

Take a **"`Set variable`"** Action and add the first name and last name of a person on separate lines in the same Action. Make sure that you hit *Enter* after the first name. Let's continue calling this variable as **`InputText`**.

```
John
Doe
```

New line characters similar to other whitespace characters such as tabs, spaces, and more, are invisible to the eye. These can be viewed with the help of text editors like Notepad++. In this editor, if you go to the **"`View`"** menu, then **"`Show Symbol`"** and click **"`Show All Characters`"**, you will see the notation for these invisible characters. When pasted in Notepad++, the new line is represented by a carriage return (CR) line feed (LF) in the editor, as illustrated in the following figure. Being able to view them can be quite handy when interacting with invisible characters and especially while troubleshooting them when you do not know the reason for a failure.

In our exercise, we will replace the invisible new line with an asterisk mark **'`*`'**. In this case, our output will be **`John*Doe`** all on a single line after replacement.

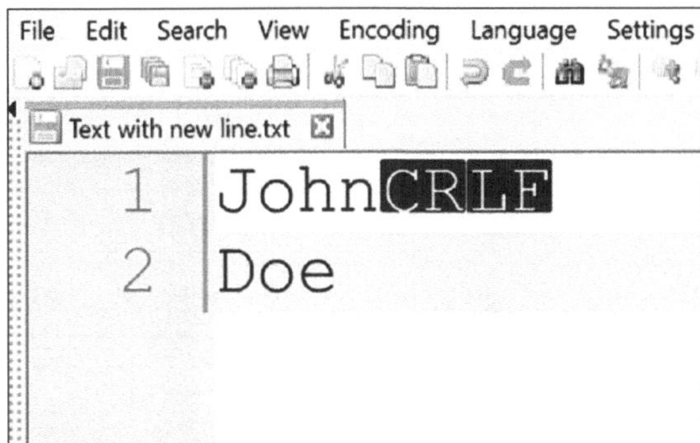

Figure 7.53: *Viewing invisible characters in Notepad++*

This can be done by adding an empty string as we saw earlier but followed by a new line character. That is, after adding an empty string as `%""%` or `%''%`, hit *Enter* so that the cursor goes to the next line as indicated in the figure. Only when you click inside this **"`Value`"** text box, you will be able to see the cursor, else the new line won't be visible. Call this variable as **`NewLine`**.

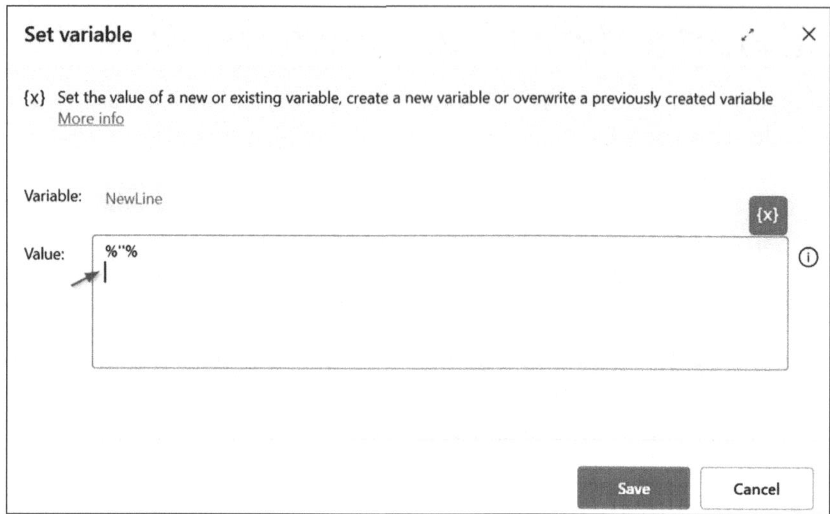

***Figure 7.54:** Initializing a variable with a new line*

Use the **"`Replace text`"** Action by passing the input variable and the new line variable, as shown in the following figure. The character to replace the new line is **'*'** without the quotes.

Run the Flow and the **`Replaced`** output variable will be populated as **`John*Doe`**, thus identifying and replacing the new line.

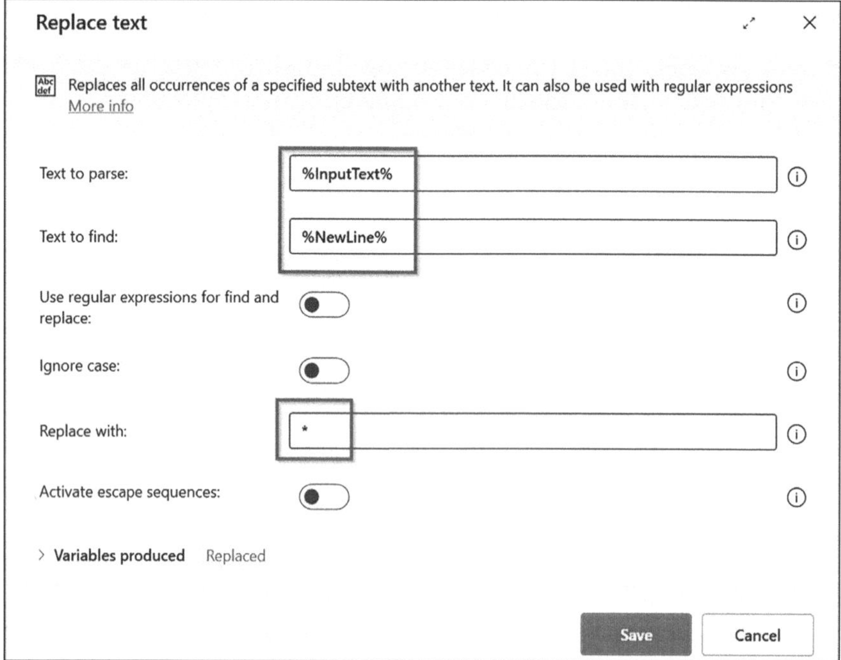

***Figure 7.55:** Identifying and replacing the new line using a variable*

Another approach is via regular expressions which are powerful. We have seen that the **"Replace text"** Action also has the ability to add regular expressions for finding and replacing text. In the preceding figure, add \r\n as the **"Text to find"**, then enable the toggle for regular expressions and keep the text to replace as it is. Run the Flow and you will find the identification of new line and its replacement successfully done. Regular expressions have been there since a long time and you can learn them at any of the available resources by simply doing a web search.

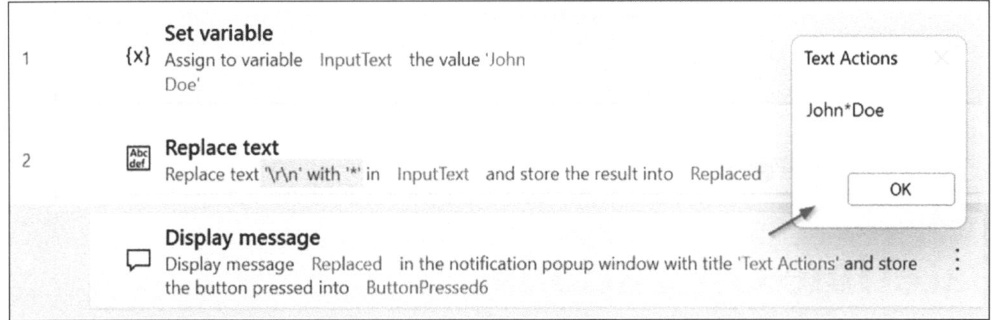

Figure 7.56: *Identifying and replacing the new line using regular expressions*

Accessing the Clipboard

The Clipboard set of Actions are not seen in the **"Text"** group of Actions in the **"Actions"** pane. However, a text can be inserted into or retrieved from the Clipboard using these Actions which are available in the **"Clipboard"** group. At times during RPA automation, you will feel the need that accessing the Clipboard is a better approach than storing information in variables. These could be ranging from data transfer between different applications or within the same application, during form filling, while text extraction and manipulation, while interacting with legacy systems, or tasks that involve more of copy-paste operations.

There are three Actions related to Clipboard in PAD and let's see all of them together. We will insert a text into the Clipboard using **"Set clipboard text"**, then retrieve the same text from the Clipboard using **"Get clipboard text"** into a variable called **ClipboardText**, clear the contents of the Clipboard via "**Clear clipboard contents**" since we have already stored it into a variable, and finally display the text that was stored in the Clipboard.

The following Flow outlines the sequence of Actions and their corresponding output:

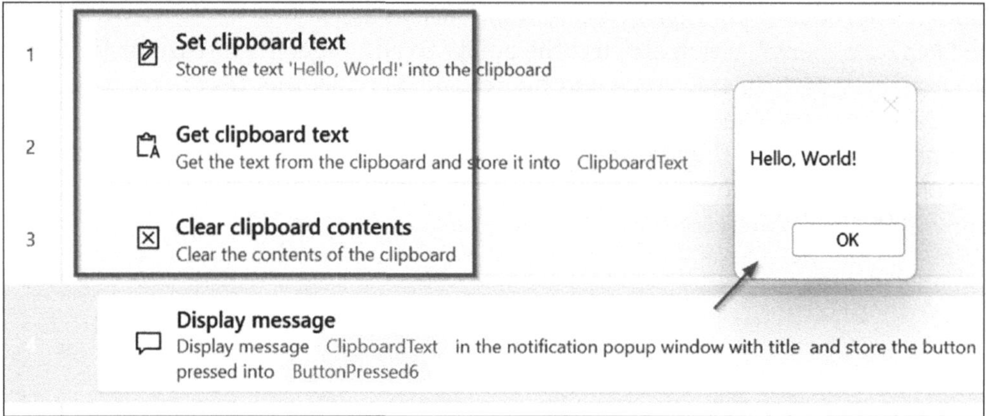

Figure 7.57: *Accessing the Clipboard*

Datetime Operations

Handling date and time operations are needed in automation activities like logging, date format conversion, date calculations like adding a time period, or subtracting dates, for report generation, email handling, for any time bound operations, for naming of files as per date-timestamp, for archiving based on datetime criteria, for querying the database based on a timeframe and for several other tasks as per automation requirements.

Power Automate Desktop has a separate group of Actions in the **"Actions"** pane called **"Date time"**.

The most widely used automation activity is to get the present date and/or time. This is achievable with the help of the **"Get current date and time"** Action. Referring to the following figure, the **"Retrieve"** dropdown has options to get only the date or both the date and time which can then be formatted to get only the time too. There are also multiple dropdown options for the time zone, but the **"Windows time zone"** is widely used because we can configure a required time zone from the listed options.

The output variable in our case is **CurrentDateTime**, which we will use in the subsequent Actions.

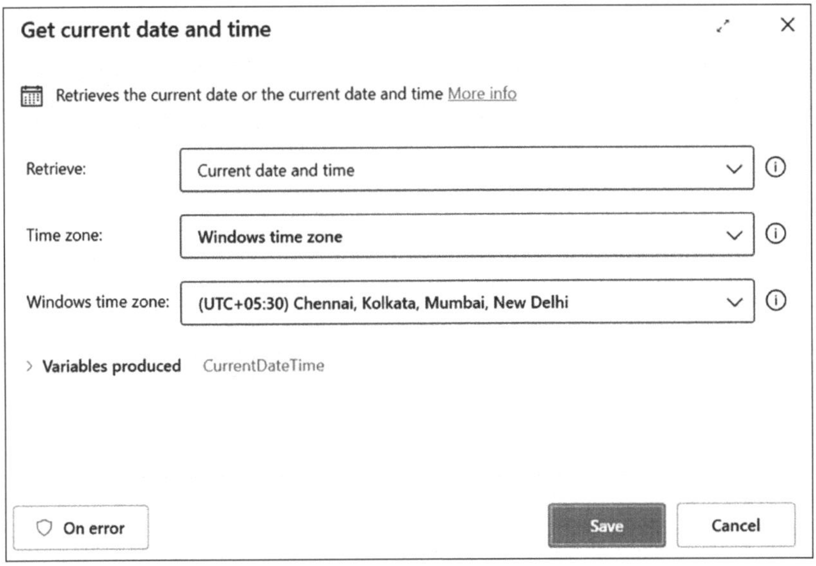

Figure 7.58: *The Get current date and time action*

Running the Flow will give the date and time in the **`CurrentDateTime`** output variable, but as a Datetime type of variable and also in a pre-defined format. If this is the need of your automation, then go ahead with it. However, generally, we have the need to get the date and time in our own format. This format can be changed with the help of the **"`Convert datetime to text`"** Action which will be available in the **"`Text`"** group of Actions. After passing the output variable coming from the previous Action, select the format as **"`Custom`"** and then give the details of the custom format we would like to have.

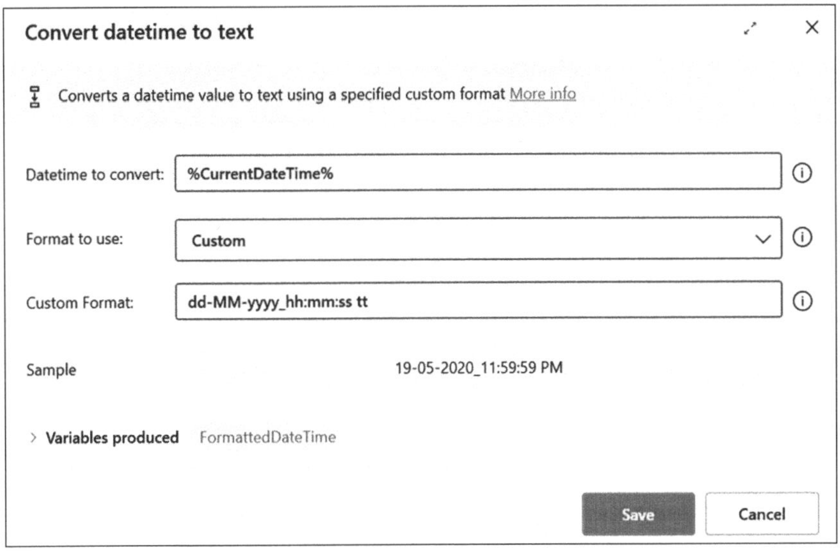

Figure 7.59: *The Convert datetime to text action*

Here are some details of what can be used in the formats:

- **dd** : To get the date part. Example: 9th of July will be represented as 09
- **MM:** To get the month. Example: 9th of July will be represented as 07
- **yyyy** : For the year
- **HH**: For the hour as 23 and small case hh for the hour as 11, if the time is 11 pm
- **mm:** Represents minutes
- **ss** : Represents seconds
- **ff** : Represents milliseconds
- **tt** : Shows AM or PM
- **zzz** : For UTC offset. Example: +5:30 for the time zone in *Figure* 7.58

Please note that you can also use the single alphabets in some cases.

Example: For 9th of July, **d** will give 9, whereas **dd** will show 09.

Check what it shows for MMM while retrieving the month.

The **FormattedDateTime** output variable from the previous figure will give an output as: 09-07-2024_02:39:57 PM.

This output, as the name of the Action says, will be returned as a text. If this suffices your requirement, then you can straight away use it anywhere in the Flow, but if you would like to convert it back to a datetime format, you would use the reverse Action of **"Convert text to datetime"** as follows. Since our datetime is in a customized format in the previous Action, we use the toggle and add the same in the following Action.

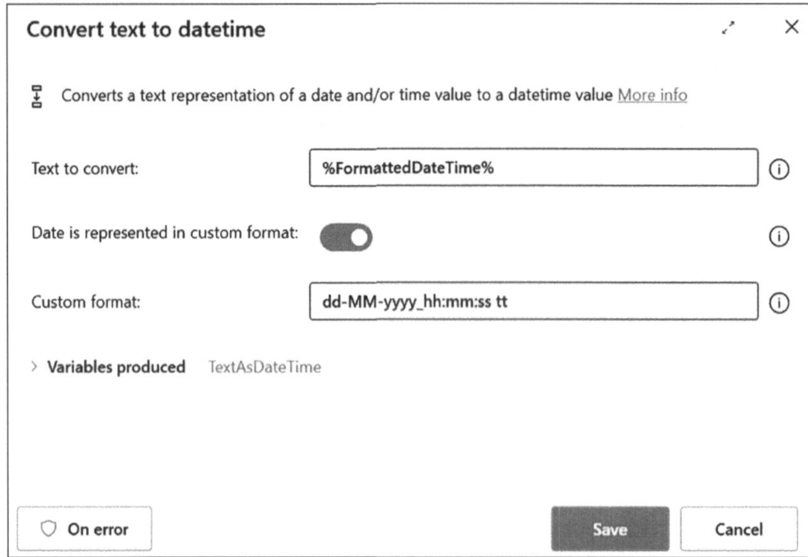

Figure 7.60: *The Convert text to datetime action*

We shall run the Flow with all the previous Actions and the variables populated will be as follows. Open each of the variables and notice their data types for a better understanding.

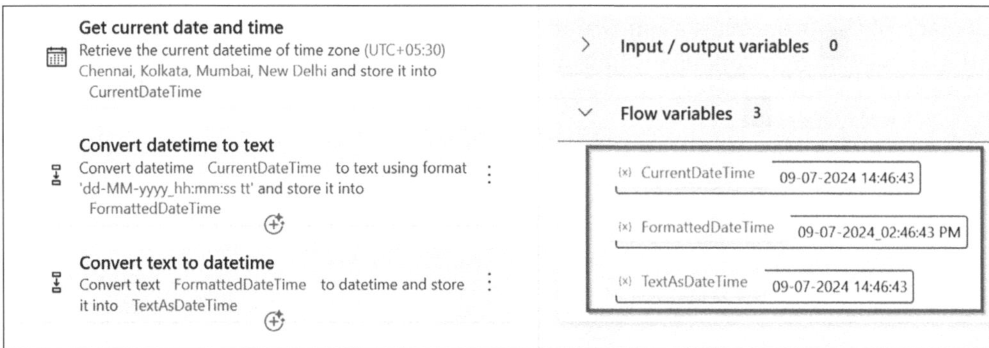

Figure 7.61: *Entire Flow and its output*

Another vital date and time related Action is the **"`Add to datetime`"** Action. This Action has a good number of options to add days, months, years, hours, minutes and seconds to any datetime input.

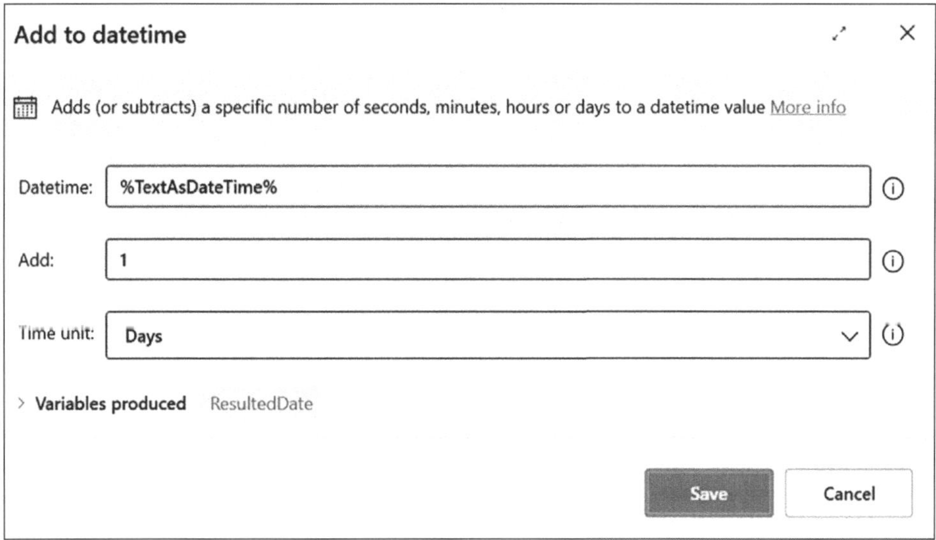

Figure 7.62: *The Add to datetime action*

In the **"`Add`"** parameter box, negative values are also supported, for example, -1 to go one day backwards for the specified **"`Time unit`"** of days.

And to sum up the date and time related Actions, PAD gives a provision to find the difference between two dates in days, hours, minutes and seconds via the **"`Subtract dates`"** Action. Try it out by passing two dates.

Something to be aware of are the list of properties available for datetime variables from the variable picker button of an Action and can be used as needed in our Desktop Flows.

Use each of the properties as shown in the following figure, add a display message box and observe the differences in their outputs.

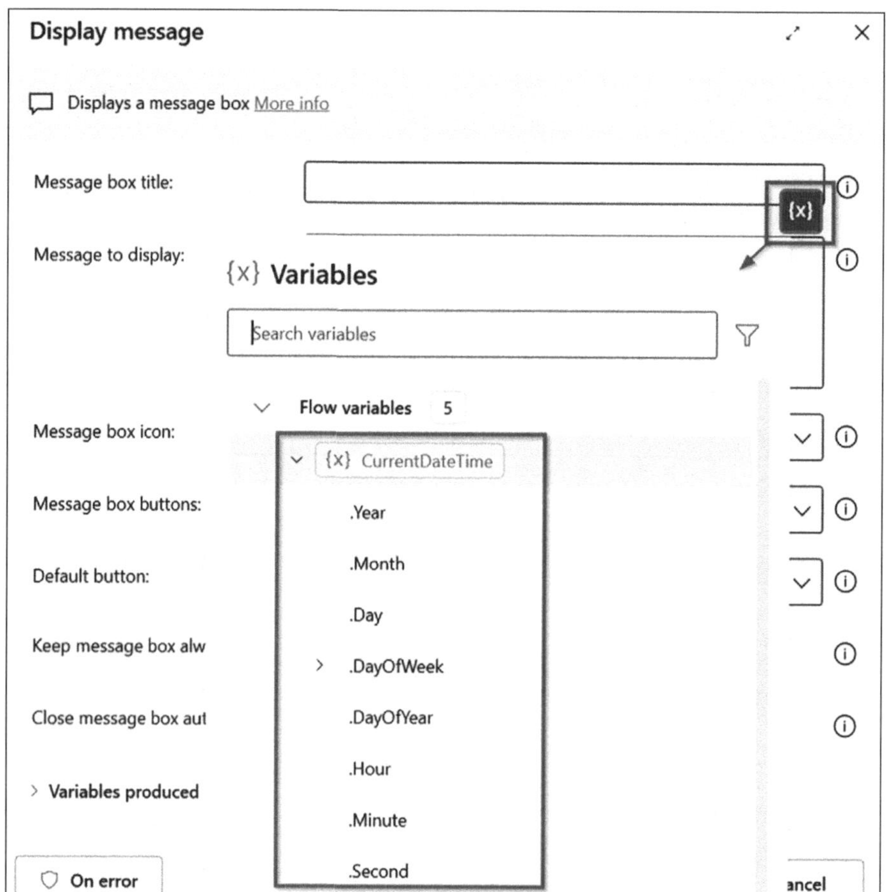

Figure 7.63: *Available datetime properties*

Scripting

Add the power of programming to your RPA automation workflows with the help of Scripting Actions. PAD provides scripting Actions for writing VBScript, PowerShell, Python, JavaScript, DOS commands and even to write a .NET script.

You can use these to perform operations that are not possible via the already available Actions in PAD. For example, write a VBScript to generate a Pivot table or set the Category or Flag of an email in Outlook, use the DOS command to get the machine related details (use the DOS command Action for **`whoami`** and see what it shows), get the list of processes running on your machine with the help of PowerShell scripts, write a .NET code in C# or VB.NET using the **"`Run .NET script`"** Action and so forth.

Here is an example usage of the **"`Run VBScript`"** Action for performing addition of two numbers where you can even make use of the PAD variables in these Actions.

The PAD variables of **`%Number1%`** and **`%Number2%`** can be assigned inside the Flow. The **`WScript.Echo`** statement at the end is a method that is commonly used in VBScript. In this case, it will return the addition of the two numbers back to this Action's output variable. Inside the Flow, display the output variable and see the result of the addition.

The code for the script is as follows:

```
Dim num1, num2, sum

num1 = %Number1%

num2 = %Number2%

sum = num1 + num2

WScript.Echo sum
```

For certain Actions. you would need to do additional activities like install modules for running a Python script or add references for the .NET Action.

You can take a look at some of these Actions in the **"`Examples`"** section of the PAD tool (refer to *Figure* 7.64).

All of the mentioned coding technologies have been there since quite some time. Once you have an awareness about writing them, there are greater possibilities with the help of these programming and scripting options. Except for **"`Run .NET script`"**, all other scripting Actions have the Copilot feature where you can take help from the AI companion to generate these scripts. The use of Copilot for scripting Actions are referenced in "*Chapter 10: Intelligent Automation via PAD*".

Also refer to the documentation link which will give details like the versions supported (example: Python, C#), using variables with Scripting Actions, and so on:

https://learn.microsoft.com/en-us/power-automate/desktop-flows/actions-reference/scripting.

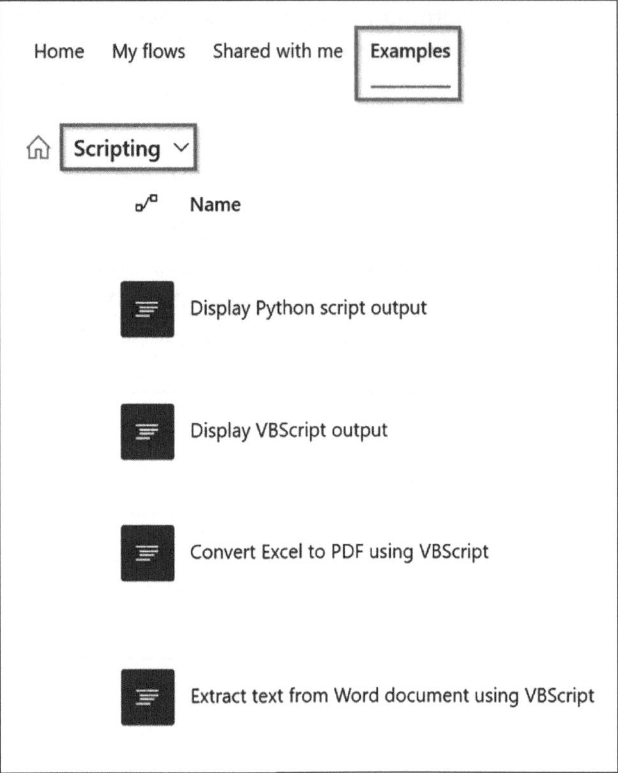

Figure 7.64: *Some examples for Scripting*

Conclusion

In this chapter, we saw the essential aspects of handling and manipulating data using the various Actions in PAD. We understood how to automate the organization, manipulation, and management of files and directories, read and write Text and CSV files, interact with XML files to parse and update structured data, and master various Text functions to find, replace, extract and format textual information. Additionally, we covered datetime operations, enabling you to automate date and time calculations and conversions with exercises on these, and finally the options to write scripts in PAD.

In the upcoming chapter, "*Beyond Conventional Automation Techniques and Strategies*", we will explore advanced methods to elevate your automation capabilities with PAD. You will learn to work with PDFs and OCR technology, automate mouse and keyboard Actions, ways of capturing screenshots, interact with APIs, and downloading options from the web. Additionally, you will discover how to use image recording to interact with applications, and what is required to automate Citrix-based environments, and terminal emulators and SAP applications.

Practical Exercises

Following exercises are based on the topics from current or previous chapters.

Exercise 1:

Develop a Flow to read the emails of Outlook from the past 1 week and store their details in Excel. In other words, get emails from the last 7 days from today and store the email details in the following Excel format. Notice the pipe separated format between two email Ids in Column C and the attachment file names are in separate lines in Column F. The date and time should be in the format as in Column E.

Refer to the **"`Outlook Email Details Format.xlsx`"** file from the GitHub folder of this chapter.

	A	B	C	D	E	F
1	Email From	Email To	Email CC	Subject	Email Date	List of Attachments
2	abc@email.com	xyz@email.com	one@email.com | two@email.com	<Subject of the email>	09-07-2024 16:53	Attachment 1 Attachment 2
3						
4						
5						

Figure 7.65: *Outlook email details Format*

Exercise 2:

Read emails from Outlook and save only specific types of attachments from those emails. Example: If an email has .xlsx and .pdf attachments, then Save only the .pdf attachments.

Exercise 3:

Download and Save the XML given here.

https://www.w3schools.com/xml/simple.xml

Make sure to remove the top text that says **'`This XML file does not…`'** while saving as XML file.

Write a Flow to find the names of all foods that have calories greater than 700.

The XML file is also available in the GitHub folder of this chapter as **"`Sample.xml`"**.

Exercise 4:

Get the following details based on today's date and write it to a text file in the shown format. This may require using a combination of in-built Datetime Actions and Scripting Actions wherever necessary. Use Scripting only where in-built Actions are not available. Different geographies have different first days of the week. You can consider your own first day of the week for the exercise.

- Last date and day name of current month
- First date and day name of current month
- Last date and day name of next month
- First date and day name of next month
- Get the date that is x weeks prior from the given date. For example, 3 weeks.
- Get the day number of the year from a given date
- First date and day name of the year from a given date
- Last date and day name of the year from a given date
- Get day number of week from given date
- Find the week number of the year from given date

Input: If today's date is 09th July 2024, then expected output are the dates shown in the following figure.

Expected output: File saved in GitHub folder as **"`Different Date Outputs.txt`"**

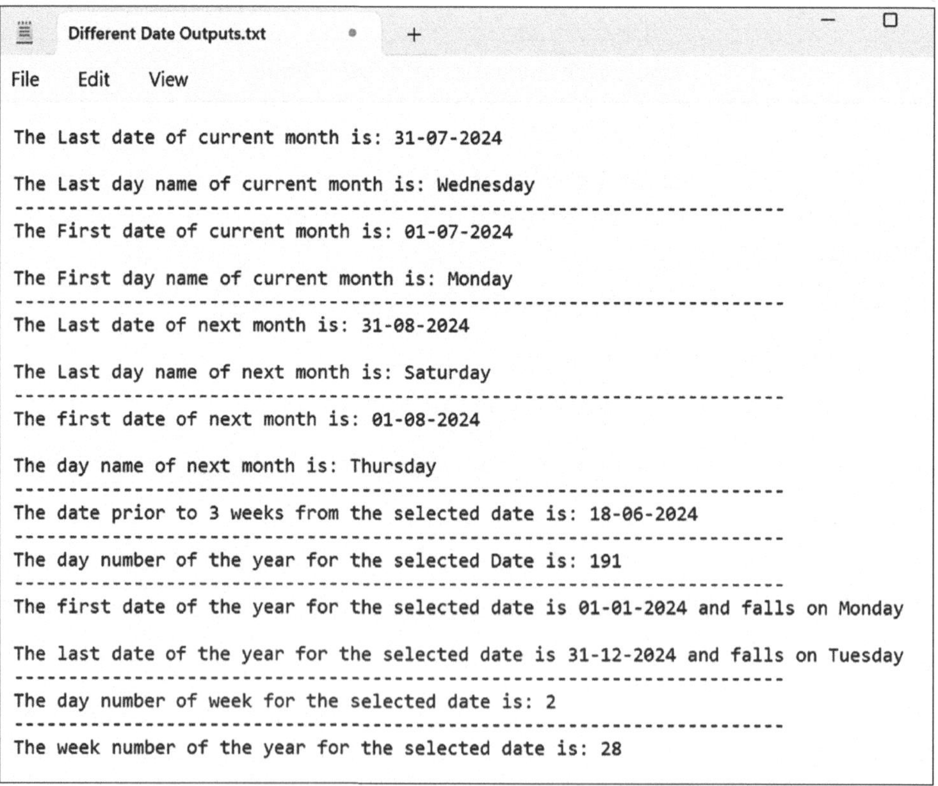

Different Date Outputs.txt

File Edit View

```
The Last date of current month is: 31-07-2024

The Last day name of current month is: Wednesday
--------------------------------------------------------------------------
The First date of current month is: 01-07-2024

The First day name of current month is: Monday
--------------------------------------------------------------------------
The Last date of next month is: 31-08-2024

The Last day name of next month is: Saturday
--------------------------------------------------------------------------
The first date of next month is: 01-08-2024

The day name of next month is: Thursday
--------------------------------------------------------------------------
The date prior to 3 weeks from the selected date is: 18-06-2024
--------------------------------------------------------------------------
The day number of the year for the selected Date is: 191
--------------------------------------------------------------------------
The first date of the year for the selected date is 01-01-2024 and falls on Monday

The last date of the year for the selected date is 31-12-2024 and falls on Tuesday
--------------------------------------------------------------------------
The day number of week for the selected date is: 2
--------------------------------------------------------------------------
The week number of the year for the selected date is: 28
```

Figure 7.66: *Format of various date outputs*

Exercise 5:

Remove the letters such as nd, rd, st, th from the dates and convert them to the format shown.

Pass any random input date as one of the following examples and generate the expected output. This should work for any input date.

Input:

Example 1: August 1st, 2024
Example 2: April 4th, 2025
Example 3: November 22nd, 2026
Example 4: October 3rd, 2026

Expected output:

Output 1: 01-Aug-2024
Output 2: 04-Apr-2025
Output 3: 22-Nov-2026
Output 4: 03-Oct-2026

Exercise 6:

1. Take all the files from **"`File Type and Size Exercise.zip`"** of *Figure* 7.1.
2. Add the last modified date as suffix to each of these file names in the format

   `<FileName - LastModifiedDate>`

   Be noted to suffix only the date and not the time. Example: File 1 – 22-10-2024

Questions

Here are some questions that might be answered by information in the current or previous chapters, or that may require hands-on experimentation with the PAD tool.

1. How to find the position of one or more characters within a given text?

   Example: If input text is **`abcdefgh`**, then how to find the position of **`'d'`**? The same approach can be used to find the position of multiple characters like **`'def'`**.

2. What is the data type of the output variable if more than one matches are found within the input text using the Action in Question 1?

   Example: If input text is **`abcdefdgh`** and the character to be searched is **`'d'`**, then what type of output variable is returned when **`'d'`** is found at two positions?

3. How to get the length of an input text in Power Automate Desktop?
4. How to clear or reset the value of a Text variable to a blank string?

   Example: Set a variable with the value as John Doe. How to clear or reset the value of this variable?

5. In the following example, find the name of the person without using "Replace text" Action or regular expressions.

   Example: If input text is
   Name: Scarlett Miller

   Output is
   Scarlett Miller

6. How to insert a new line after an input text via the Flow?

   Example: Set a variable called **`InputStr`** as **`'This is line 1.'`** without the quotes.

   Via the Flow, add a new line to **`InputStr`** and store the output in a variable called **`Result.`**

   After running the Flow, open the **`Result`** variable and it should have output as follows with a new line at the end of the first line.

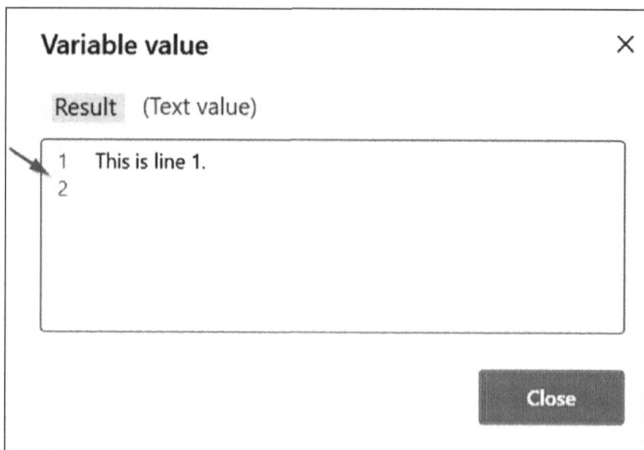

Figure 7.67: *Expected output after adding a new line*

CHAPTER 8
Beyond Conventional Automation Techniques and Strategies

Introduction

When it comes to RPA automation, the first thing that comes to mind is automating the applications with the help of UI automation, that is, by capturing the UI elements and their Selectors and then reading/writing to them. But if you want to see beyond the conventional methods of automation, then this chapter will help you understand those concepts. Also, we will see other approaches and strategies that will help to achieve greater efficiency and effectiveness while building our Desktop Flows.

Structure

The topics covered in this chapter are as follows:

- PDF and OCR
- Mouse and Keyboard
- Automating Your Workstation
- Capturing Screenshots
- HTTP Communications with Web Applications and Services
- Interacting Applications with Image Recording

- Automating Virtual Desktop-based Applications
- Terminal Emulation and SAP Automation
- Active Directory

PDF and OCR

It is needless to say PDFs are a standard format of documents in several business processes. In such processes, automating the extraction and processing of information from PDFs becomes absolutely necessary. RPA robots can be built to extract relevant data from PDFs and input it into other applications, systems, or databases. Thereby, PDF automation reduces manual data entry, minimizes errors, and accelerates workflows. PAD provides dedicated PDF-related Actions and they are available in the **"PDF"** group of Actions in the **"Actions"** pane.

Before we look into these Actions, let us see the types of PDFs available. In general, the types of PDFs are Text-based PDFs and Image-based PDFs.

Text-based PDFs have text written in them as textual data, making it easy for selecting, searching, copying, and editing of the text itself. They are generally smaller in size as they have data written in the form of text. They are also called "True PDFs" or digitally created PDFs.

Whereas, in Image-based PDFs, the text written within these files is part of an image and hence the text cannot be selected, searched, or copied directly. They are generally scanned documents or photographs, and since they are images, they are larger in size than Text-based ones.

Speaking of RPA automation, handling text-based PDFs is generally more straight-forward since the text can be directly extracted and processed. Image-based PDFs require OCR (Optical Character Recognition) technology to convert the image content into readable text, adding an extra layer of complexity to the automation process. Let us see the reading of both these types of PDFs and what options Power Automate Desktop provide to us.

Interacting with Text-based PDFs

The Action in PAD to read a Text-based PDF is **"Extract text from PDF"** where you provide the full path of the PDF to be read and the number of pages to extract the text from. The **"Advanced"** section has an option to provide a password for the PDF, if any.

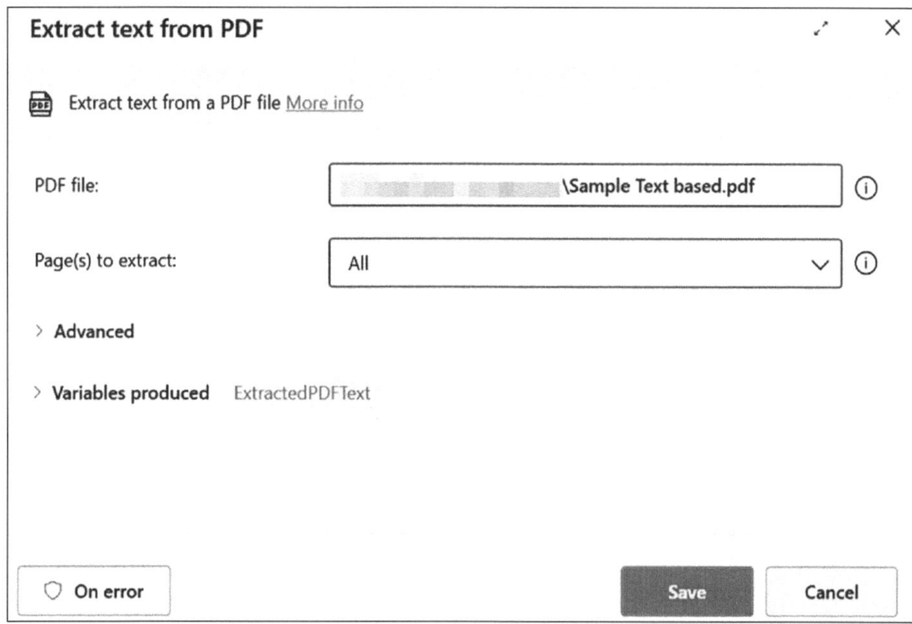

Figure 8.1: *The Extract text from PDF action*

Following is the sample extract of the PDF we are trying to read and is also available in the GitHub folder as **"`Sample Text based.pdf`"**. The output variable for this Action **`ExtractedPDFText`** will have the extracted text.

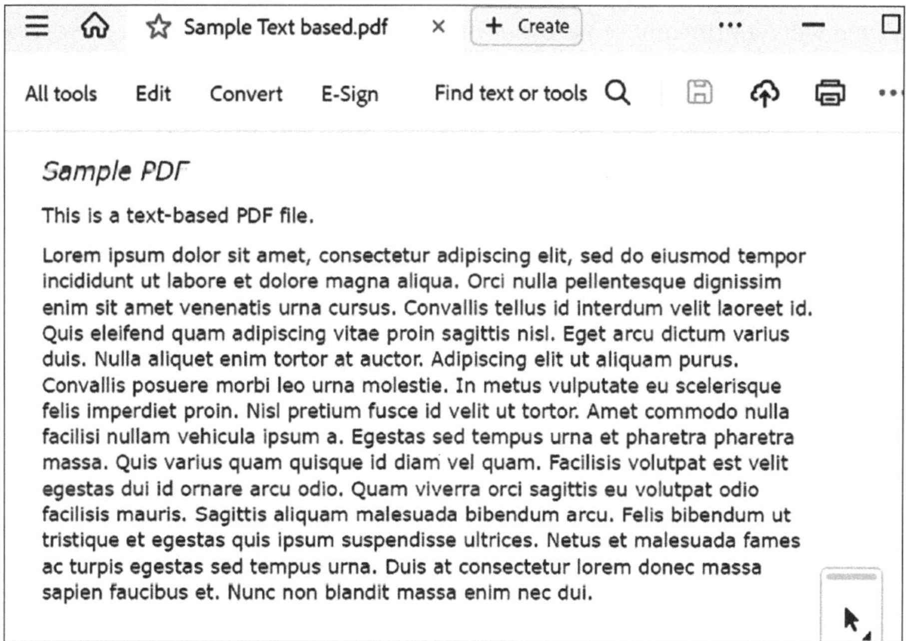

Sample PDF

This is a text-based PDF file.

Lorem ipsum dolor sit amet, consectetur adipiscing elit, sed do eiusmod tempor incididunt ut labore et dolore magna aliqua. Orci nulla pellentesque dignissim enim sit amet venenatis urna cursus. Convallis tellus id interdum velit laoreet id. Quis eleifend quam adipiscing vitae proin sagittis nisl. Eget arcu dictum varius duis. Nulla aliquet enim tortor at auctor. Adipiscing elit ut aliquam purus. Convallis posuere morbi leo urna molestie. In metus vulputate eu scelerisque felis imperdiet proin. Nisl pretium fusce id velit ut tortor. Amet commodo nulla facilisi nullam vehicula ipsum a. Egestas sed tempus urna et pharetra pharetra massa. Quis varius quam quisque id diam vel quam. Facilisis volutpat est velit egestas dui id ornare arcu odio. Quam viverra orci sagittis eu volutpat odio facilisis mauris. Sagittis aliquam malesuada bibendum arcu. Felis bibendum ut tristique et egestas quis ipsum suspendisse ultrices. Netus et malesuada fames ac turpis egestas sed tempus urna. Duis at consectetur lorem donec massa sapien faucibus et. Nunc non blandit massa enim nec dui.

Figure 8.2: *Sample Text-based PDF*

That's it. Only one Action is needed for doing this. Running the Flow populates the **ExtractedPDFText** as follows. Once done, this variable can then be used for further usage in the Flow like utilizing it in any of the **"Text"** Actions.

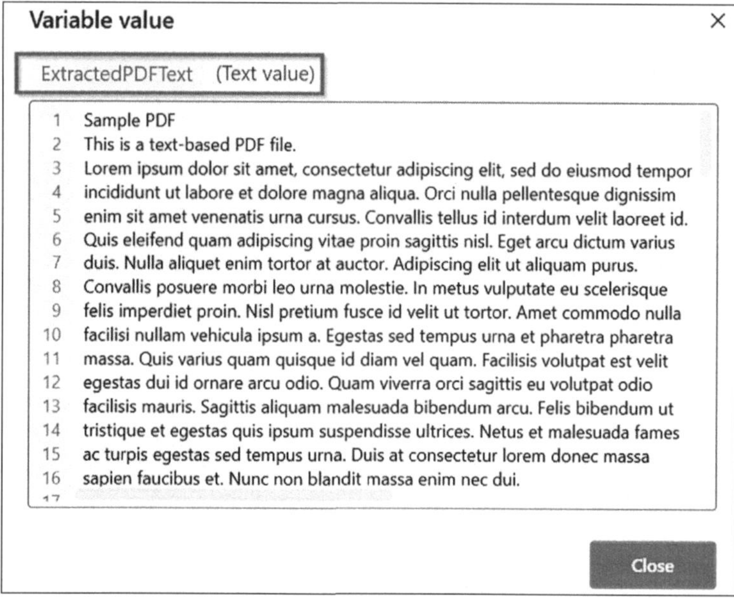

Figure 8.3: *Output on running the Flow*

The advanced setting to watch for is the **"Optimize for structured data"**. Enabling this toggle will identify any structured format in the PDF and perform the extraction accordingly. The following figure shows the output for both options, that is, when the toggle is enabled and disabled for a PDF with data in a particular structure. Use the option and see if it suits your data extraction and accordingly use it in workflows.

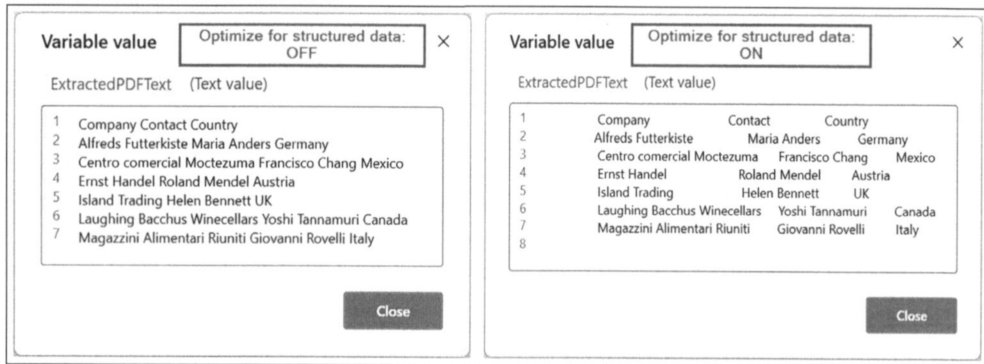

Figure 8.4: *With and without optimized structured data*

The preceding output is for a PDF that had only a table as seen in the following PDF file, and now you can review the difference in the extraction with and without the optimization setting in the preceding figure. This file with a table is available in the GitHub folder for this chapter and can also be used to extract the table for the upcoming section.

Speaking of tables, PAD has an Action specifically designated for extraction of tables, which is the **"`Extract tables from PDF`"** Action.

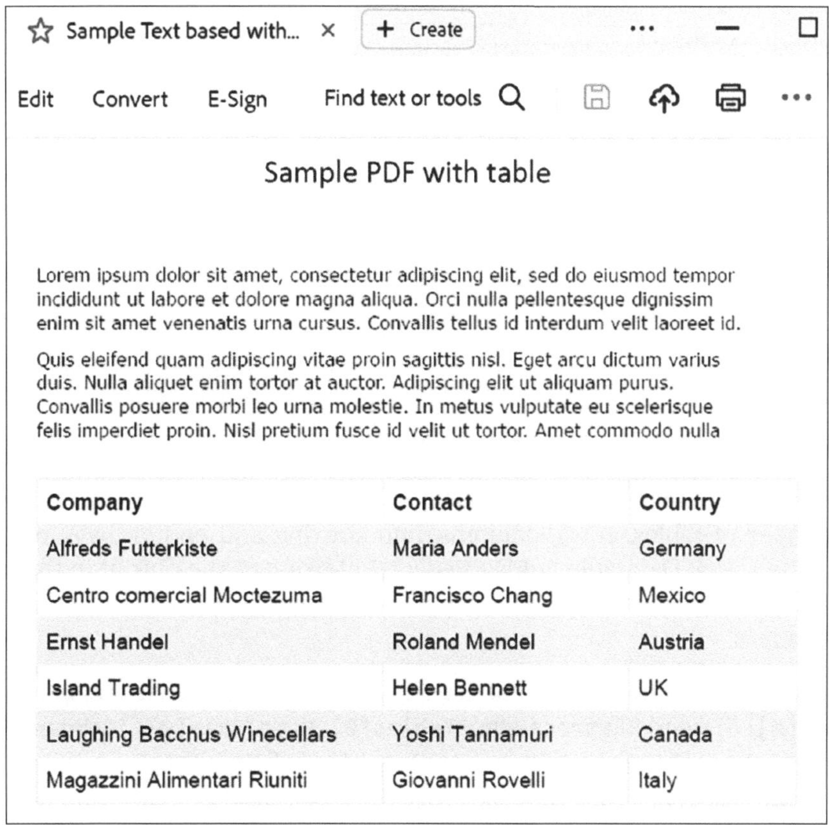

Company	Contact	Country
Alfreds Futterkiste	Maria Anders	Germany
Centro comercial Moctezuma	Francisco Chang	Mexico
Ernst Handel	Roland Mendel	Austria
Island Trading	Helen Bennett	UK
Laughing Bacchus Winecellars	Yoshi Tannamuri	Canada
Magazzini Alimentari Riuniti	Giovanni Rovelli	Italy

Figure 8.5: *Sample PDF with table*

If this is how our Text-based PDF with a table looks like, then the Action to read the table along with its parameters is as follows.

The Action has a dropdown to tell PAD whether to extract the tables from all pages, from a single page or from a range of pages. The **"`Merge tables that cross page margins`"** will merge the tables that overlap the page margins of the PDF. The **"`First line contains column names`"** setting is similar to reading from Excel and considers the first line as the column headers.

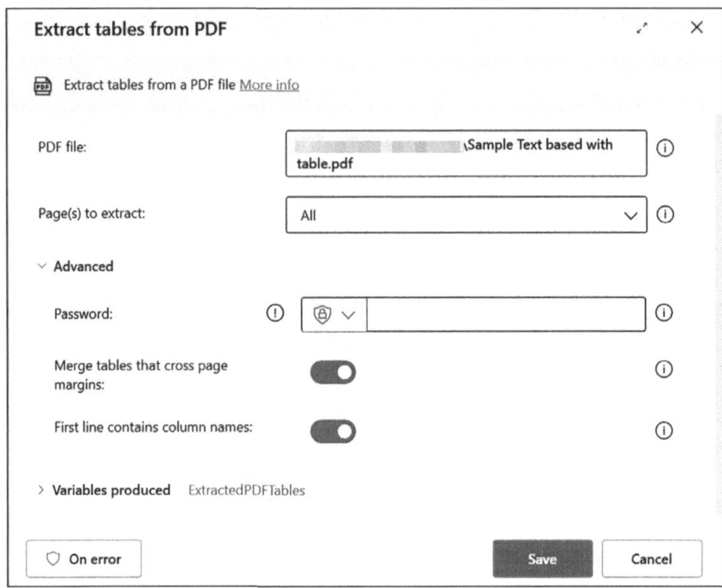

***Figure 8.6:** The Extract tables from PDF action*

The **`ExtractedPDFTables`** output variable holds a list of PDF table information, such as the number of tables, rows, columns, and starting and ending page of the table and then, the actual Datatable holds the data. Referring to the output in the following figure, this now makes it easy to read the data from the Datatable variable using its column headers.

Marked in the figure is how this Datatable can be accessed. **`%ExtractedPDFTables[0].DataTable[0][0]%`** and **`%ExtractedPDFTables[0].DataTable[0]['Company']%`**, both would return the value of the first cell, that is, Alfreds Futterkiste.

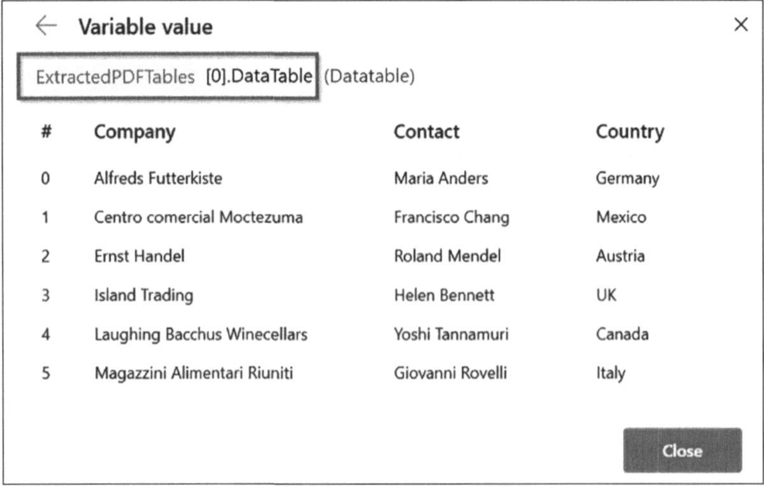

#	Company	Contact	Country
0	Alfreds Futterkiste	Maria Anders	Germany
1	Centro comercial Moctezuma	Francisco Chang	Mexico
2	Ernst Handel	Roland Mendel	Austria
3	Island Trading	Helen Bennett	UK
4	Laughing Bacchus Winecellars	Yoshi Tannamuri	Canada
5	Magazzini Alimentari Riuniti	Giovanni Rovelli	Italy

***Figure 8.7:** Output Datatable*

Interacting with Image-Based PDFs

As stated earlier, Image-based PDFs require OCR technology to allow RPA bots to read and interpret text within scanned documents or images, converting them into editable and searchable data. By integrating OCR with RPA, the automation workflow can conduct the extraction of data from PDFs, such as invoices, forms, and so on, and input them into other systems and applications.

There is a separate group of Actions in PAD called **"OCR"** and we are going to combine it with the **"PDF"** list of Actions and go through a different approach of reading Image-based PDFs. This is because PAD does not have a direct Action to read the text from an Image-based PDF, similar to the one we saw for the Text-based PDF.

Follow along the following steps to achieve the same.

Our intention in the following Flow steps will be to extract all the image-based pages of the PDF into a folder as separate image files, then retrieve all these files from that folder, loop through those files, then extract the text from those image files using OCR and keep writing the extracted text to a variable within the loop.

1. Drag and drop the **"`Extract images from PDF`"** Action.
   Refer to the Action in *Figure* 8.8. Provide the full path of the Image-based PDF which is also available in the GitHub folder. The Action has an option to read all the pages, a single page, or a range of pages. Since these pages are going to be extracted as image files, provide a prefix to those files such as the one we have given as **"`img`"**. The extracted image files will be named as img_0, img_1, and so on. Finally, provide the destination folder as to where these image files should be saved.

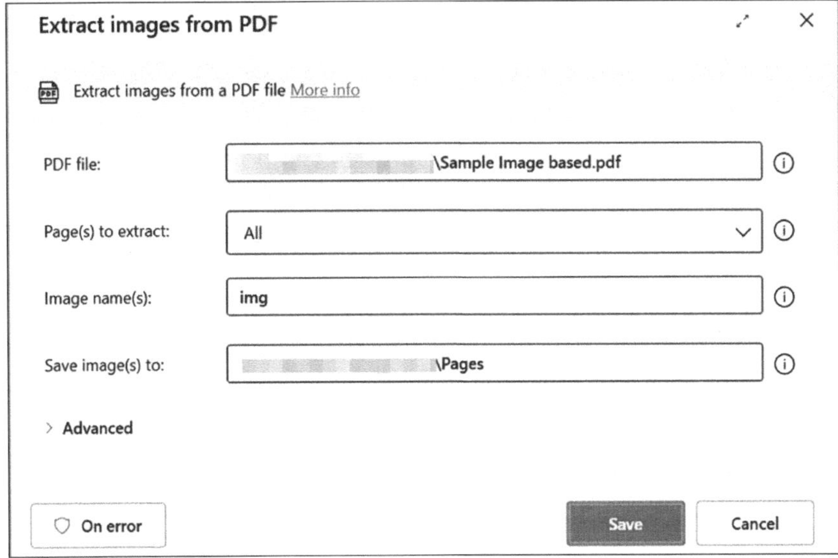

Figure 8.8: *The Extract images from PDF action*

2. The following figure shows an Image-based PDF that we are going to use and has two pages. Notice the mouse pointer when trying to select the text of the PDF which is different as compared to what you will see for Text-based PDFs. This PDF is placed in the GitHub folder as **"`Sample Image based.pdf`"**.

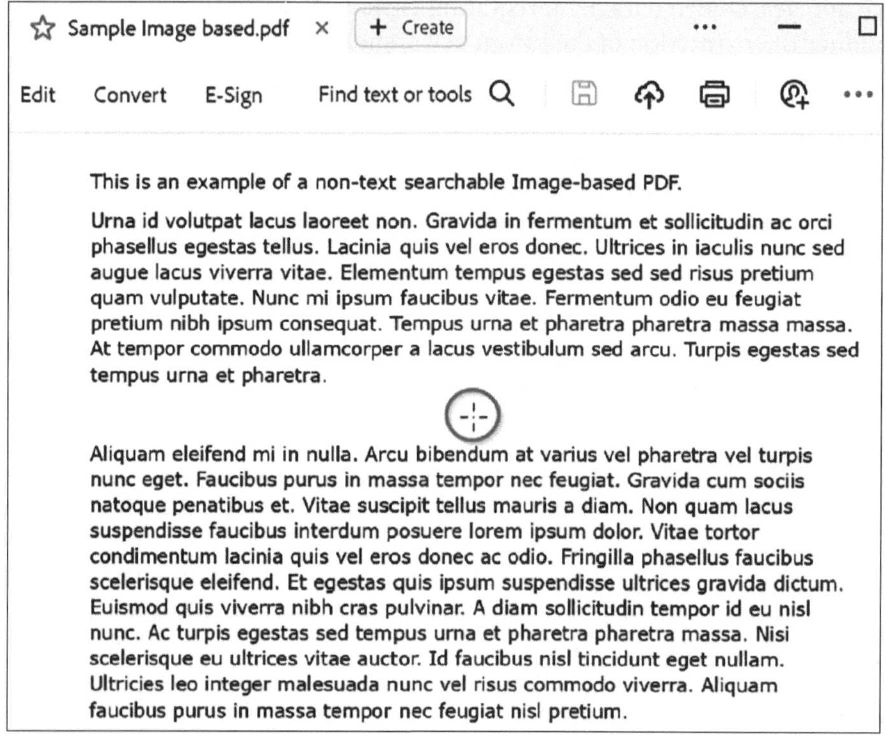

Figure 8.9: *Sample Image-based PDF*

Add the **"`Get files in folder`"** Action and supply the **"`Pages`"** folder path or the one that you used in *Figure* 8.8 to save the image files.

3. Add a **"`For each`"** loop to iterate through the **`Files`** variable returned from the previous step. This further returns a **`CurrentItem`** variable.

4. Inside the loop, drag and drop the **"`Extract text with OCR`"** Action which is responsible for extracting the text from the image files downloaded in Step 1 using OCR technology.

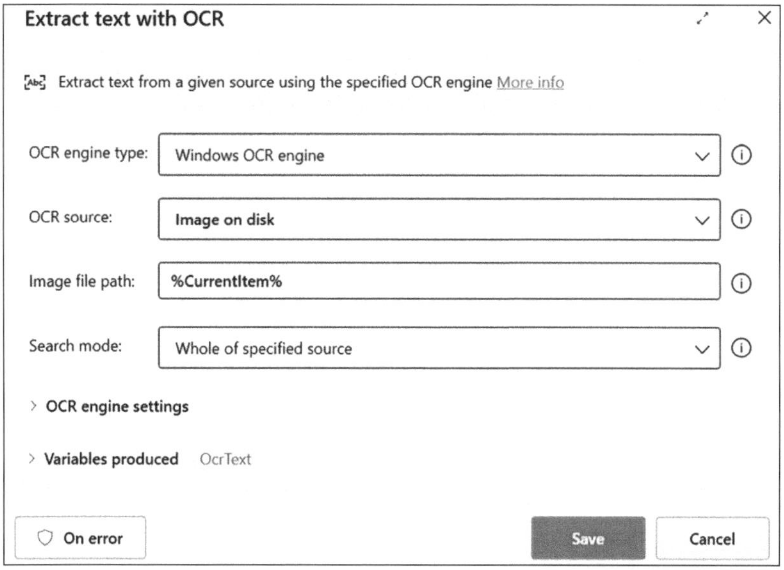

Extract text with OCR

Extract text from a given source using the specified OCR engine More info

OCR engine type: Windows OCR engine

OCR source: Image on disk

Image file path: %CurrentItem%

Search mode: Whole of specified source

> OCR engine settings

> Variables produced OcrText

On error Save Cancel

Figure 8.10: *The Extract text with OCR action*

This Action has the first option to choose the OCR engine for the extraction. Try all the options and see which one gives the nearest output as OCR extraction varies in accuracy. Since we have image files and they are stored in **`CurrentItem`,** provide the other parameters as in the figure.

5. Append the output variable of **`OcrText`** to a new variable, say **`FinalOutput`**, which holds the text of the entire PDF document one after the other.

   A word of mention is that, as per the following figure, when **`FinalOutput`** is executed for the first time, it will hold a blank value and hence a new line will be inserted followed by the contents from **`OcrText`** variable. So, if you do not need that extra new line, you may use the "**`Trim text`**" Action at the very end of the Flow to strip off any leading and trailing newline or blank characters.

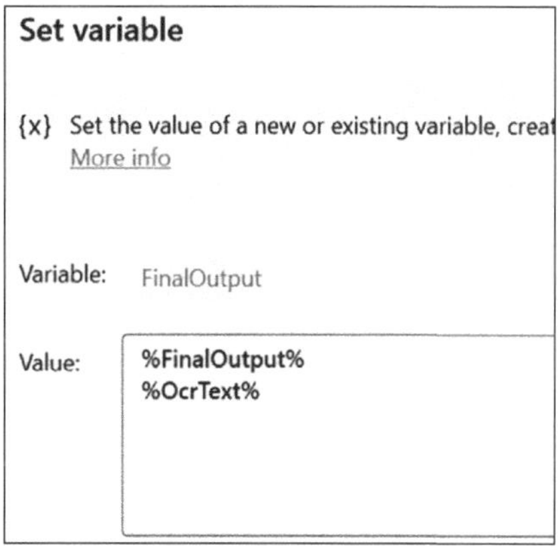

Set variable

{x} Set the value of a new or existing variable, creat
More info

Variable: FinalOutput

Value: %FinalOutput%
%OcrText%

Figure 8.11: *Appending the output to a variable*

With the end of the loop, the entire Flow looks as follows.

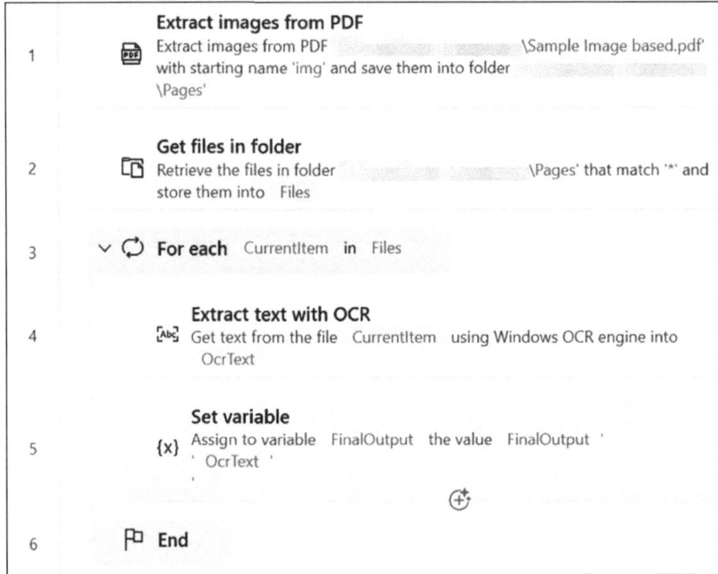

Figure 8.12: *Entire Flow with all actions*

On running the Flow, the **`FinalOutput`** variable should have the text output of all the pages of the document. Most importantly, the **"`Pages`"** folder should now have the number of image files equal to the number of pages in the PDF document indicating that the Flow was able to extract all the pages.

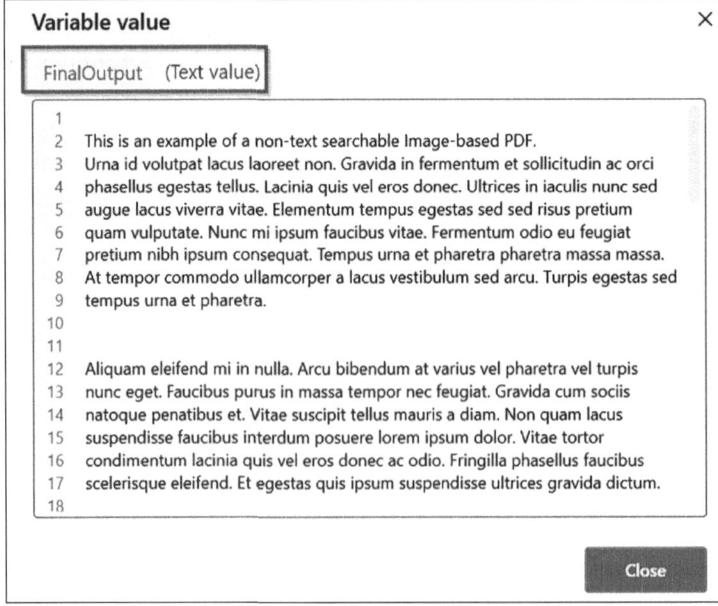

Figure 8.13: *Final output appended in a variable*

This variable can then be used to extract information just as you would do on a Text file. Instead of a variable you can even append the output in a Text file one after the other and is something to try out while performing the above exercise.

There are two other Actions under the **"PDF"** category called **"Extract PDF file pages to new PDF file"** and **"Merge PDF files"**, both of which are showcased in the **"Examples"** section of the PAD tool. There are also useful Flow examples on how to find the page count of a PDF and split a PDF.

Not all PDFs can be extracted in a desired manner. For certain PDFs, due to its structure and complexities, you may need to use enhanced features of the Power Platform like the AI Hub available via the Cloud Flows which has AI models for Document Processing, Invoice Processing, Receipt Processing, Extract text from images and PDF documents, and so on. You will understand how to have Cloud Flows and Desktop Flows interact with each other in the "*Making Use of the Cloud Portal and the Power Platform*" topic in "*Chapter 9: Leveling Up Your Automation Workflows*".

Mouse and Keyboard

As we are already aware, when it comes to RPA automation, the conventional way is to capture the elements on the screen and interact with them via the pre-built Actions in any tool. However, when this approach does not work, which it will not in many cases, then there is a need to take control of the mouse and the keyboard of the machine where the bot is running and interact with those elements on the screen. This could be moving the mouse to a particular image or a UI element, sending a mouse click after moving, sending the keys to a particular text box which otherwise couldn't have been possible to write to it, and so on. These operations are required for data entry and retrieval, application navigation, and other tasks that require direct interaction with the computer interface but are not achievable through conventional automation techniques.

To achieve this, the most widely used Action is the **"Send keys"**. Let us see an example with various keystrokes to send. These Actions are available in the **"Mouse and keyboard"** category.

1. Use the **"Run application"** Action to open *Notepad*.
2. Then use the **"Focus window"** Action for a window title of *Notepad*. Only one wild card character of the asterisk symbol '*' is sufficient at the start of the text, but we are making sure that the word *Notepad* is anywhere in that line of text, just in case. While using mouse and keyboard Actions, it is very much necessary to have the right window opened and the focus on the right window too, else the keys and the clicks will be performed on an incorrect window or application.
3. Drag and drop the Action in question. We will launch the Notepad and write some text to it, then select all the text and press *Alt* + F4 which are combination keys to close a window.

Since we have laid focus on the Notepad window, you could use the **"Foreground window"** as the first parameter. The other options in the dropdown are similar to the Window-related Actions. Then, write some text that you would like to send to the Notepad application and send the *Enter* key using **{Return}**. You will be able to select the desired keys via the two available dropdowns. Selecting all text is done via **{Control}({A})**, which you can refer to from the tooltip text of the **"Text to send"** parameter on how to use a key as a modifier. The modifier keys are the ones shown in the **"Insert modifier"** dropdown. Likewise, we have a wide range of keys to be sent via the **"Insert special keys"** dropdown. Have a look by pulling the dropdowns.

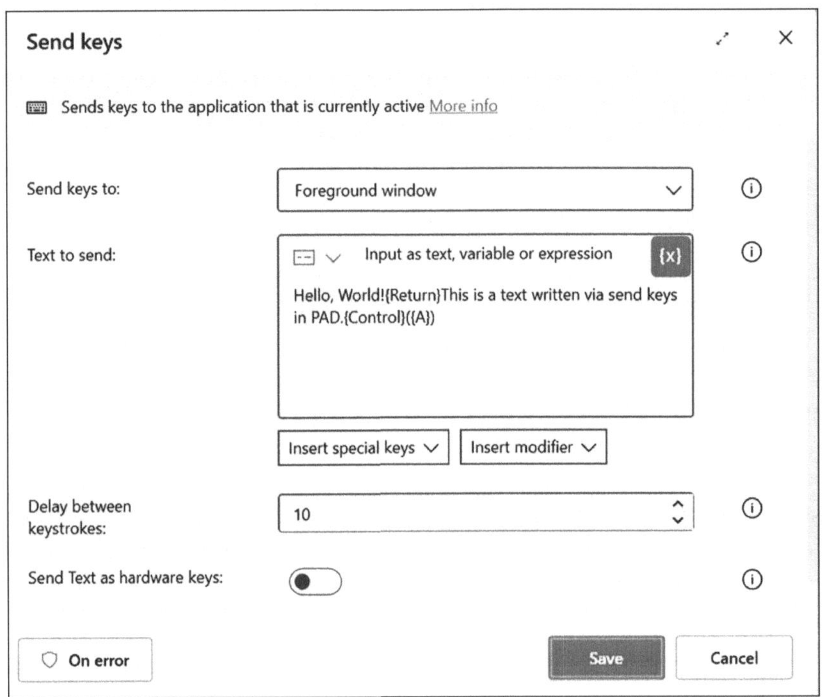

Figure 8.14: *The Send keys action*

The **"Delay between keystrokes"** as it says is to provide a time gap between two keys and be noted that it is in milliseconds. This can be used if you see that the keystrokes are incorrectly sent or way too fast. Another option to try and see is the **"Send Text as hardware keys"** to mimic the hardware keys when the keystrokes are not working with the toggle kept off.

4. Finally, add one more **"Send keys"** Action and use **{Alt}({F4})** to close the Notepad window. This could have been added in the same Action that we used in the above step, but it is better to not overwhelm a single Action with too many keystrokes. Also, while building Flows you are going to have several mouse and keyboard Actions in your Flow. So, if you see that the operations

are happening very fast, you could add a **"Wait"** Action for a few seconds between two Actions to give it some breathing time before performing the next Action. **"Wait"** Actions are very much needed while using keystrokes and mouse clicks. Type **"Wait"** in the **"Actions"** pane and use the suitable one(s) according to the situation or only the **"Wait"** in some cases.

On running the Flow, the output is as follows. The text is written as expected with the new line due to the *Enter*, with all the text selected due to the *Ctrl* + A and the close confirmation dialog box due to the *Alt* + F4.

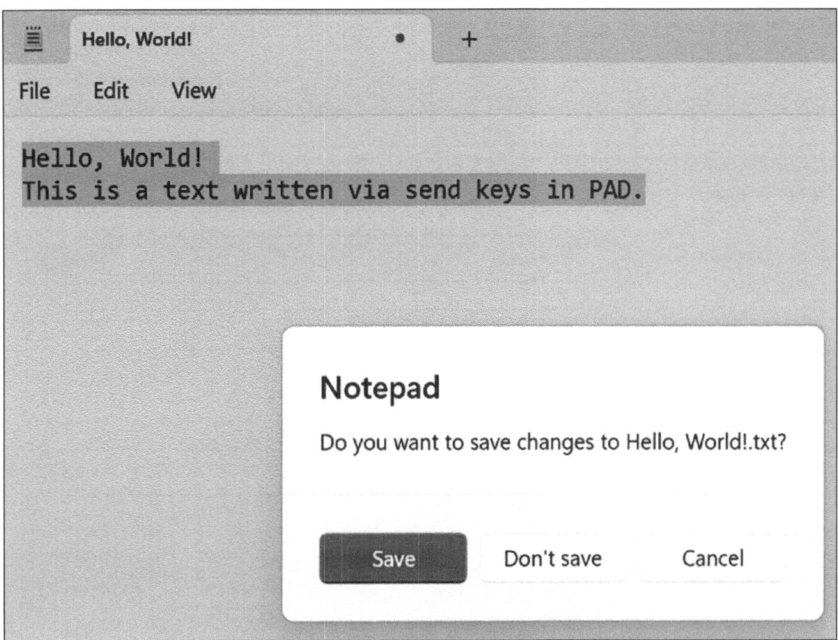

Figure 8.15: *Output after running the Flow*

Before running the Flow, the title of the notepad window was **"Untitled - Notepad"** which now got automatically changed to the first line of the text in the file after we wrote to it and is a feature of the Notepad application and not done by PAD.

We will now look to close the confirmation box without saving the file for this exercise. You could send the keys to perform a TAB operation for jumping from the **"Save"** button to the next and then hit *Enter* on the **"Don't save"** button. But we will do this by going through other vital Actions in PAD.

By the way, to send the same key multiple times the syntax is **{Down:5}**, where the down arrow key will be sent 5 times in this case. This is especially handy when navigating up and down through menus or left and right through different characters of a text or hitting TAB multiple times to jump onto the right element on the screen.

The following figure uses another crucial Action called **"Move mouse to image"**. As the name specifies, it is used to move the mouse to a captured image of an element and then optionally send a mouse click. Drag and drop this Action onto the Workspace.

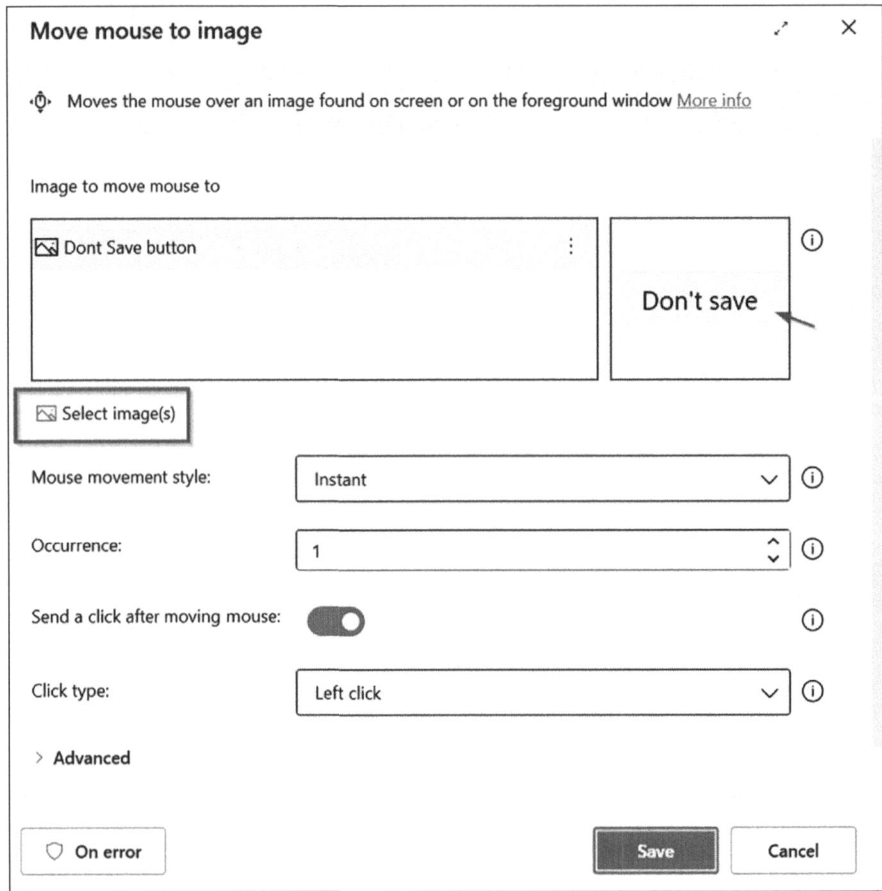

Figure 8.16: *The Move mouse to image action*

The image of the **"Don't save"** button indicated by an arrow in the preceding figure is the result of capturing the button's image via the **"Select image(s)"** option. Turn on the **"Send a click after moving mouse"** toggle so that the bot will click the **"Don't save"** button as soon as it sees it. To reduce the time to identify the image on the screen, to limit the search area, and for better reliability, you can change the **"Search for image on"** dropdown option in the **"Advanced"** section to **"Foreground window only"**. You can keep the rest of the advanced options as it is but have a look at them for learning purposes. Hover over the information icon and play with the Action.

That's all you need to serve our purpose of hitting the **"Don't Save"** button. The Action works fine by closing the Notepad application and can't be shown here. If you find the tool is not identifying the button properly, then re-capture the button's image and rerun or make changes in the settings. Image detection and matching may not always give the results at the first instance. Also, image recognition is sensitive to the resolution of the screen. This is why playing around with the Action is necessary.

Disable the above Action and this time, drag and drop the **"`Move mouse to text on screen (OCR)`"** Action. As shown in the following figure, provide the **"`Text to find`"** as **`Don't save`** since that is the text on the close confirmation box (*Figure* 8.15). Search the text on the foreground window and in the **"`Advanced`"** section, turn on the toggle for **"`Send a click after moving mouse`"**.

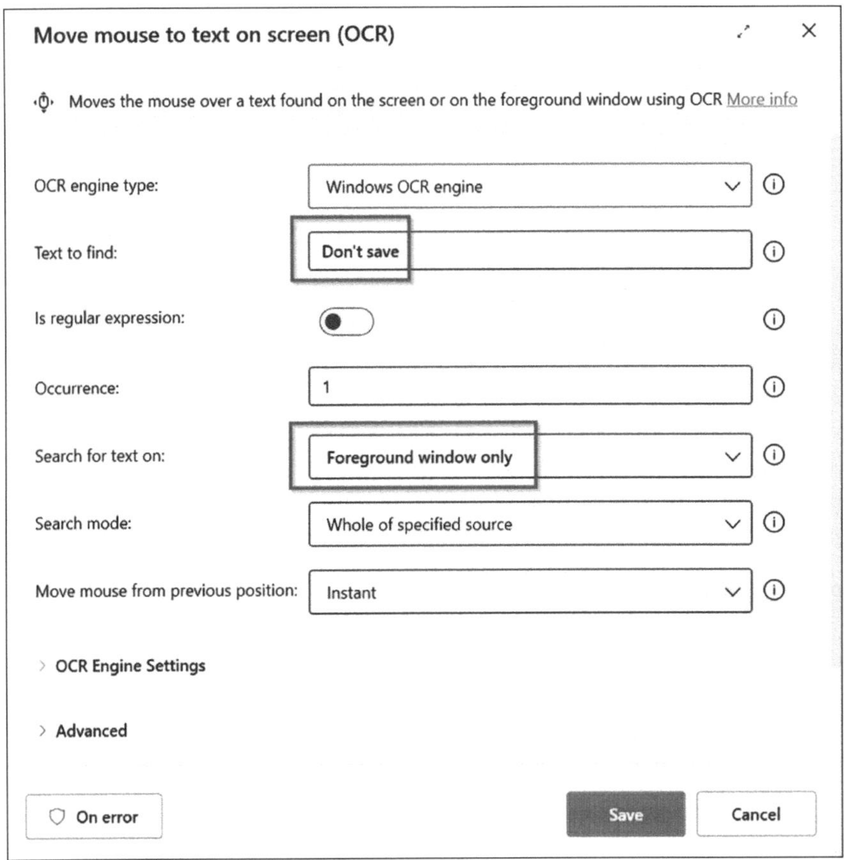

***Figure* 8.17:** *The Move mouse to text on screen (OCR) action*

This Action will search for the configured text on the foreground window and send a mouse click to it, which in our case is the **"`Don't save`"** button. This Action works perfectly fine for the aforementioned configured parameters and is something you can try out. Here is the entire Flow built so far, with the **"`Move mouse to image`"** Action disabled in our previous step. Remember to add wait Actions in between if the automation for you runs fast and is not able to perform as expected.

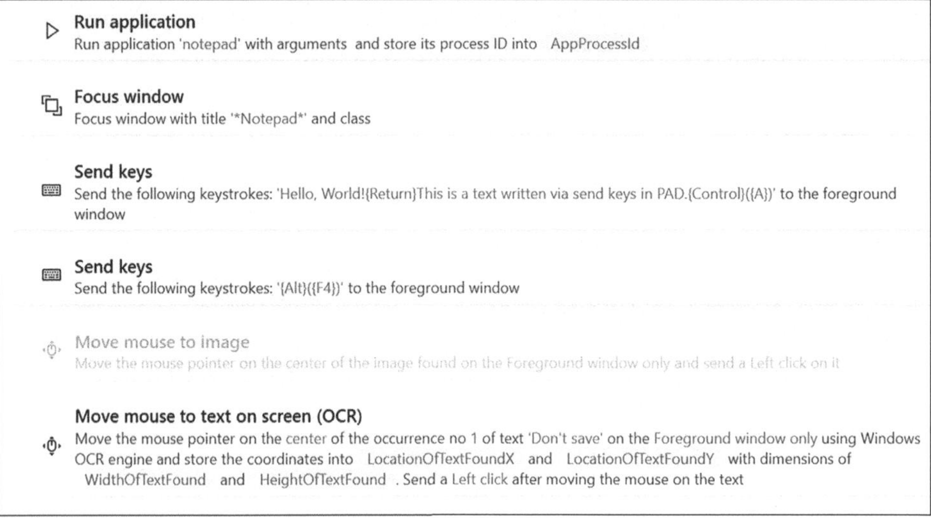

***Figure 8.18:** Entire Flow of actions*

Pressing and releasing of modifier keys has a separate Action called **"`Press/release key`"**. The Windows shortcut to open the Task Manager of the computer is *Ctrl + Shift + Escape*. Press the first two modifier keys with the Action given here and then in a separate **"`Send keys`"** Action trigger the **`{Escape}`** key. On running the Flow, you will notice that the Task Manager of the machine opens up. In certain situations, while sending the keys, you might have to run the Flow directly and not interrupt it by debugging it in the Flow designer.

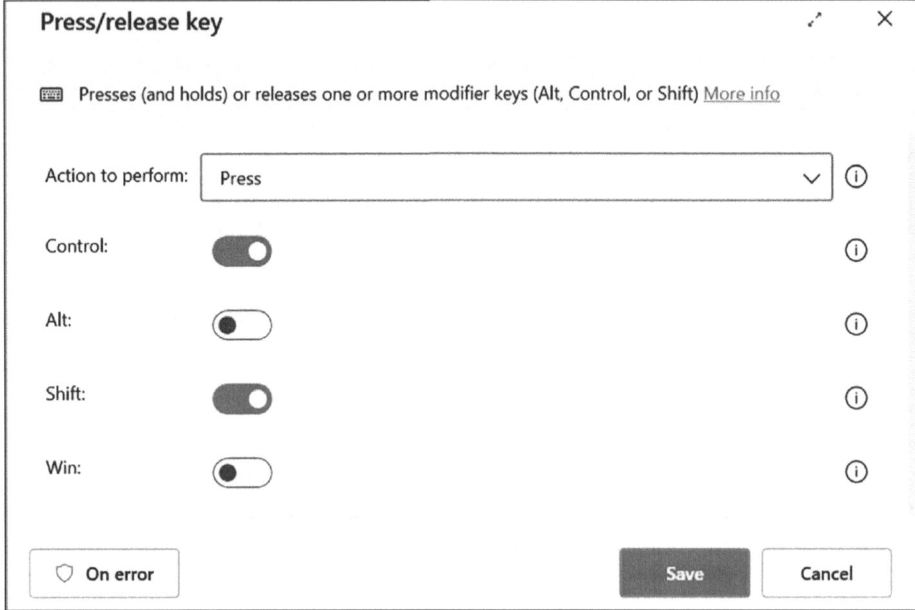

***Figure 8.19:** The Press/release key action*

It is a good practice to release the keys via this Action to bring it back to its original state.

Similarly, you could use the **"`Set key state`"** Action to enable or disable the Caps lock, Num lock, and Scroll lock.

A general issue is that when the bot is running and if it is performing any mouse or keyboard-related operations then the bot would stall or perform invalid operations if interrupted by the user of the machine. To avoid this, make use of the **"`Block Input`"** Action which blocks any user input and thus avoids any hindrance to the bot. Make sure to run Power Automate Desktop in administrative mode for this feature to work as expected. If used, the Flow should unlock it back when complete or when there is an error. An error can occur at any place in the Flow. So, having an error handler is necessary and this is the place where the unlocking should be done in case of an error. We have a separate topic on "*Error Handling*" in "*Chapter 9: Leveling Up Your Automation Workflows*".

Use the **"`Block Input`"** Action with caution as when the unblocking does not happen at the right place then you may have to manually terminate the process from the Task Manager and/or restart the machine.

Various mouse clicks, such as left, right, and middle can be done via the **"`Send mouse click`"** Action. Before using this Action, you need to move the mouse to the desired location where the click needs to happen.

A caveat for using mouse and keyboard Actions is that it may highly be possible that they may work appropriately at some times and not at the other. Hence, they should be used when all other viable options are exhausted and if used, they need to undergo a thorough testing.

Automating Your Workstation

Automating the workstation on which the bot runs can involve activities, such as shutting down the computer, logging off, printing a document, setting the screen resolution, and so on. These can be necessary in several scenarios like end-of-day processes where the bot logs off or shuts down the machine after its work is done without any manual intervention, or in print automation where documents need to be printed at specific intervals or after the generation of reports or invoices. Let's look at the key Actions to perform these types of activities which are available under the "**`Workstation`**" list of Actions.

For sending one or more documents to the printer, at first, a good practice is to configure the printer with the help of the **"`Set default printer`"** Action which will show a dropdown list to pick from or can be manually entered. Here is an example Flow of how you can loop through a list of files in a folder and then use the **"`Print document`"** Action to send each of those files to the printer.

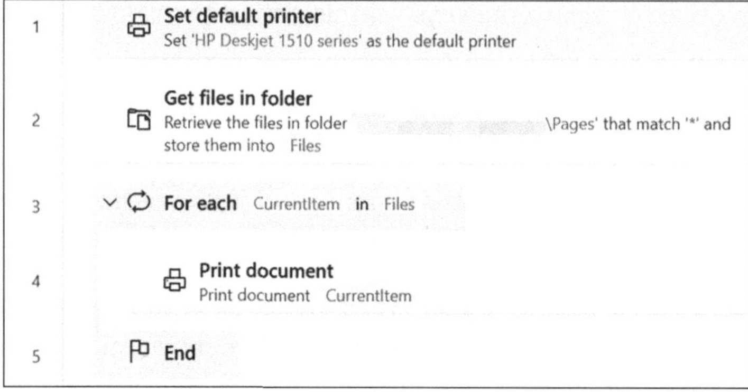

***Figure 8.20**: Setting a default printer and sending files to it*

Having the right screen resolution for RPA automation is crucial for several reasons. This is because if you develop your Flow in the DEV environment on a machine that has one resolution and move it to the TEST environment which has a different resolution, then chances of the Flow not working as expected are high. Although it is needed for any type of automation, it is especially necessary for the accuracy of UI interactions where the usage of coordinates, image recognition, mouse clicks, or keyboard activities are performed. Therefore, it is a good practice to set the expected resolution by the bot at the beginning of the Flow such that they will be the same in all the environments.

This is done with the help of the **"`Set screen resolution`"** Action. Either you can select from the list of available screen resolutions via the marked dropdown or configure your own entries in the text boxes provided. A good option is to add another Action called **"`Get screen resolution`"** prior to this, and if the resolution is not as expected, then execute the following Action using an **"`If`"** conditional statement.

Set screen resolution

Sets the width, height, bit count and frequency of a selected monitor More info

Available screen resolutions

Monitor number: 1

Monitor width: 1920

Monitor height: 1080

Monitor bit count: 32

Monitor frequency: 60

On error Save Cancel

***Figure 8.21**: Setting the screen resolution*

However, there are two other approaches for setting the screen resolution in unattended mode as mentioned in the following documentation link and that is to tweak the registry or make changes to an already available config file. Unattended automation is explained in "*Chapter 9: Leveling Up Your Automation Workflows*".

https://learn.microsoft.com/en-us/power-automate/desktop-flows/how-to/set-screen-resolution-unattended-mode

At times, you might want to minimize all the running applications and windows on the machine via the bot. The **"Show desktop"** Action will come into play. Keep several open windows and try this Action. On the contrary, the same Action can restore all the windows.

The bot can also log off, lock, or even shut down the machine with the help of the following Actions.

- **"Log off user":** This Action will stop the running Flow and log off the current user. The Action can forcibly log off the user even if something may obstruct it from logging off like an unsaved file or an application that otherwise won't close.
- **"Lock workstation":** This is similar to the locking of the machine which is generally manually done by pressing the combination keys of *Windows* + L. It is interesting to try using this Action followed by a message box and see whether the Flow executes the rest of the Actions or not after locking the machine.
- **"Shutdown computer":** Along with shutting down the machine, this Action has options to restart, sleep, or send the machine to hibernate. Similar to **"Log off user"**, this Action can also perform the operations forcibly.

Capturing Screenshots

Some automation scenarios require taking a screenshot for specific usages. For example, when there is an error, the bot will capture a screenshot and save it for further troubleshooting purposes, or as a proof of record for validation and verification purposes, for example, after a record is submitted, a transaction ID is created so the bot will take a screenshot saving it as a proof of record. Let us see the various ways of capturing a screenshot using PAD.

"Take screenshot" Action

The first way is using a direct approach of using the **"Take screenshot"** Action. The first dropdown has options to take a screenshot for any screens or for a foreground window that has the focus while the bot is running. The second dropdown determines whether the bot should store the captured image in the Clipboard or a physical file on the disk. If the **"File"** option is selected, you can provide the full path of the image file along with the format of the image, such as BMP, JPG, PNG, and so on.

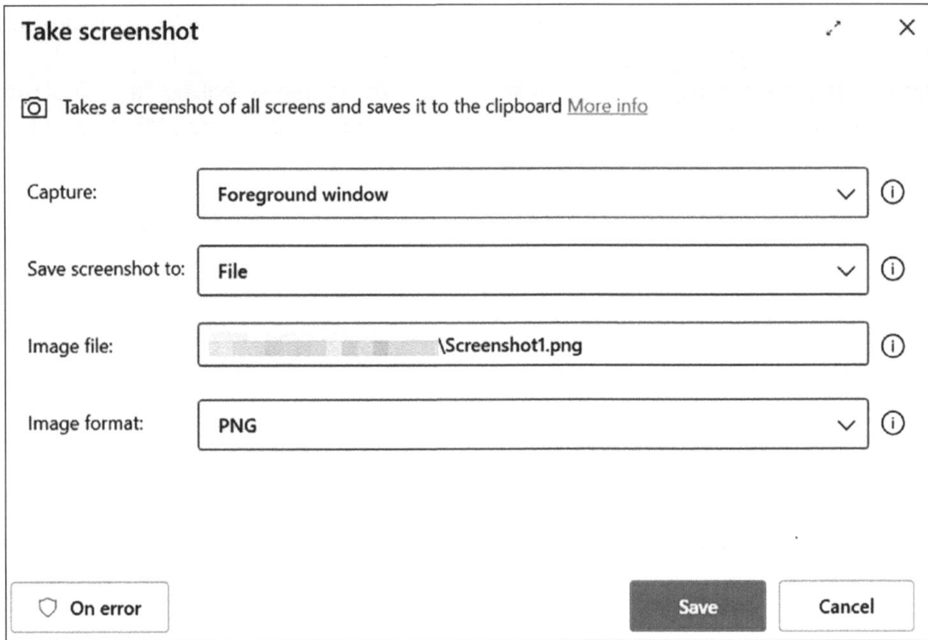

Figure 8.22: *The Take screenshot action*

Practical Exercise

1. Refer to Exercise 1 in the "*Practical Exercises*" section of "*Chapter 6: Automating Common Applications*". The exercise was for reading the records from Excel, entering them onto the Contoso Desktop application, converting the currency amount on a web application and writing it back to Excel before sending an email.

2. This exercise is to take the same exercise and add screenshot capabilities to it. After adding the fields in the Contoso application and saving the record, the bot should capture the screenshot of the Contoso screen as in the following figure with a new ID created. The following screenshot is a real example captured by the bot after ID 1037 is created. The image file is to be saved in a folder with the file name containing date and time stamp as day, month, year, hours, minutes, and seconds and the format of which is seen in `Column H` of *Figure* 8.24.

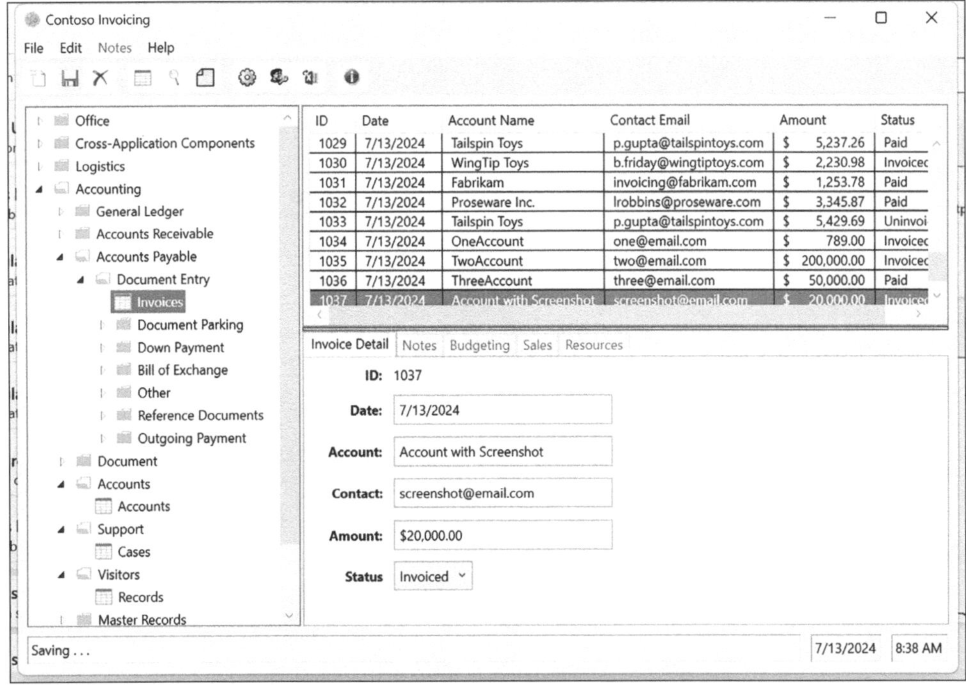

Figure 8.23: *Sample screenshot of Contoso window*

The full path of the screenshot file should be written back to Excel in a new column as highlighted in the following figure. All steps should be performed for every row in Excel.

	A	B	C	D	E	F	G	H
1	Date	Account	Contact	USD Amount	Status	Converted Amount	ID	Screenshot Path
2	7/5/2024	Account70	user441@mail.com	208.46	Paid			C:\Folder Path\13-07-2024 08_38_52.png
3	7/3/2024	Account11	user378@email.com	229.2	Uninvoiced			
4	7/1/2024	Account25	user510@email.com	707.2	Uninvoiced			
5	7/7/2024	Account43	user418@mail.com	589.17	Invoiced			
6	7/2/2024	Account8	user6@email.com	816.72	Invoiced			
7	7/5/2024	Account60	user443@email.com	431.41	Paid			
8	7/1/2024	Account16	user261@example.com	958.9	Paid			
9	7/4/2024	Account9	user786@email.com	648.09	Paid			
10	7/6/2024	Account96	user641@example.com	891.64	Uninvoiced			
11	7/1/2024	Account54	user442@mail.com	276.05	Uninvoiced			

Figure 8.24: *Screenshot path in new column*

"Take screenshot of UI element" Action

The second approach is for capturing a UI element of a Desktop application and is available under the **"UI automation"** list of Actions. Referring to this Action in the following figure, you need to pass a UI element for which the screenshot is to be captured. The other parameters are the same as in the earlier Action, that is, save as Clipboard or File, the name of the file followed by its format.

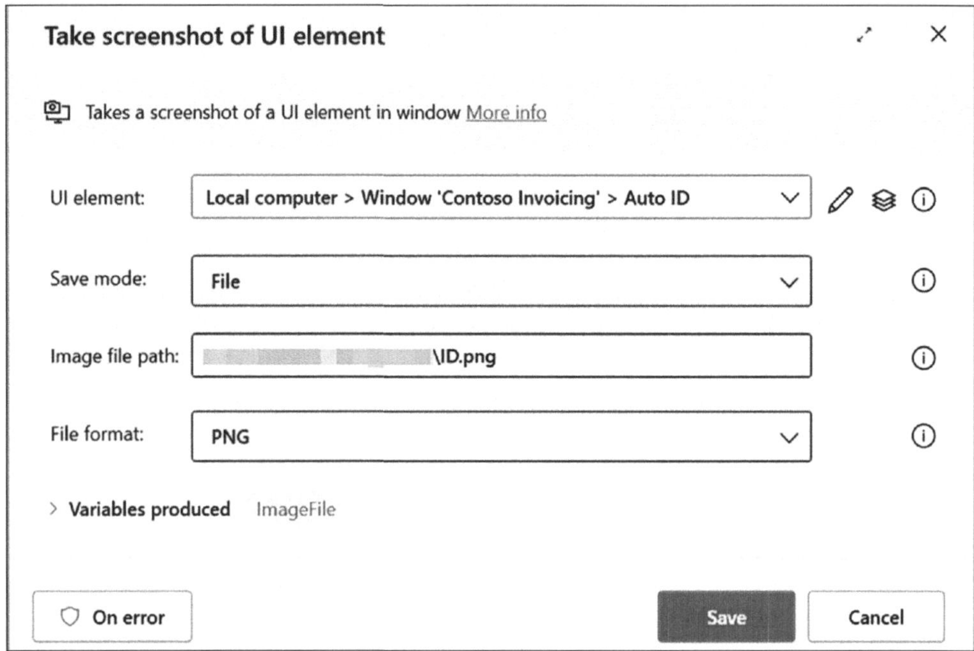

Figure 8.25: *The Take screenshot of UI element action*

Practical Exercise

1. After the record is saved in the previous exercise, capture the screenshot of the UI element where the auto-generated ID is displayed above the **"`Date`"** text box, that is, 1037 in *Figure* 8.23. An example of the ID portion is as follows. You will get a small image of about 1 KB.

Figure 8.26: *Sample screenshot of the auto generated ID*

2. The screenshot file is to be saved as the auto-generated ID in its file name and written back to the Excel file in a new column called **"`Screenshot Path of ID`".** You can create this new column by the bot itself.

   Example: C:\Folder Path**1037.png**

   This file name should change as per the generated ID and the exercise is to be completed for every record of the Excel.

"**`Take screenshot of web page`**" Action

The third Action that can capture screenshots is the **"`Take screenshot of web page`"** Action. Since you would be interacting with a web page you would already be having a *Browser* instance variable and that has to be passed to this Action. Then you are given an option to capture the entire web page or only a specific UI element of that page. All other parameters are the same as in the previous Action.

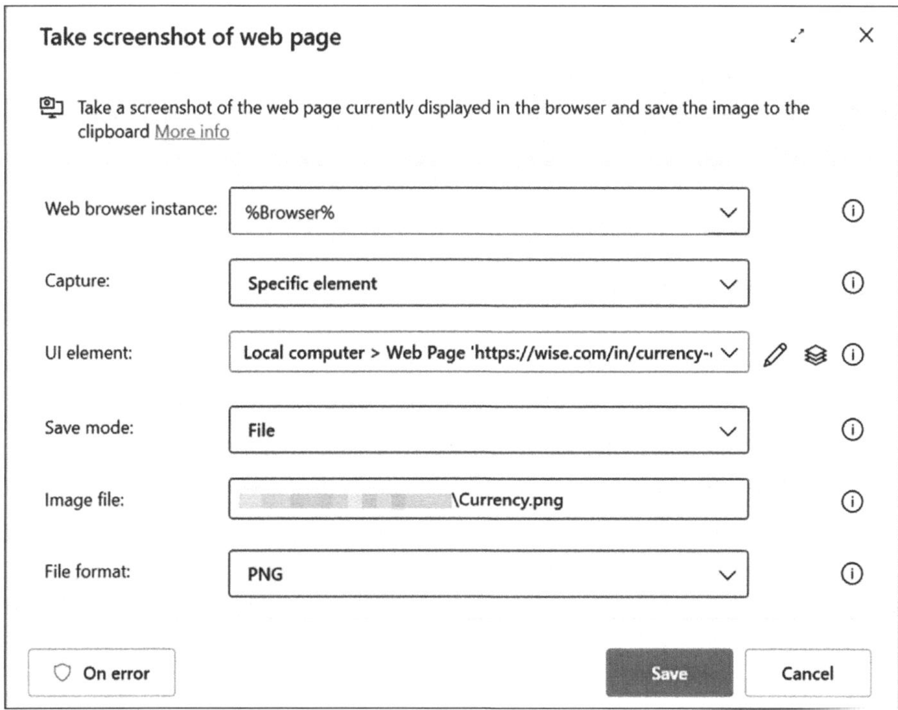

Figure 8.27: *The Take screenshot of web page action*

Practical Exercise

1. In the same exercise, you also had to take the currency amount from Excel and convert it to any currency of your choice via https://wise.com/in/currency-converter.

2. After converting the currency on the web page, you now capture the screenshot of the element where it shows the from and to conversion amounts, as shown in the following figure.

3. Save the full path of the image file to a new column in Excel called **"`Screenshot path for Currency Conversion`"** with the file name having the words **"`Currency conversion for`"** followed by a space and then the actual ID. Example: *Currency conversion for 1037.png*

Here is the actual screenshot by the bot that is expected for the exercise for all records of the Excel.

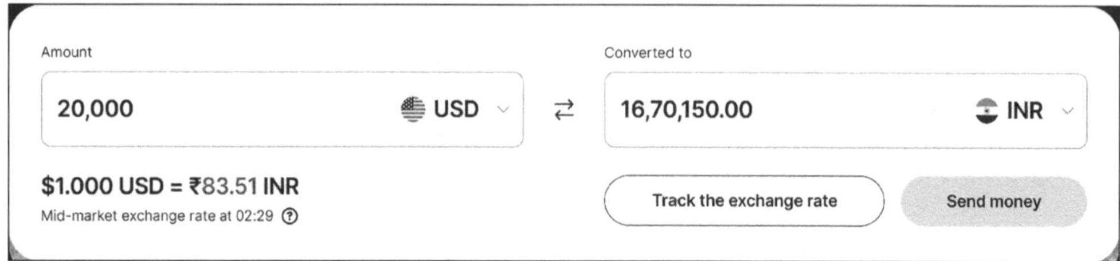

Figure 8.28: *Sample screenshot of the currency output*

HTTP Communications with Web Applications and Services

HTTP which stands for Hyper Text Transfer Protocol, in simple words, is a set of rules or protocols used by browsers and servers to communicate with each other over the internet. On typing a URL on the browser, it is HTTP that is responsible for sending the request to the server to fetch and display the webpage.

When it comes to RPA, it is generally considered to be a tool to perform screen scraping, sending mouse clicks, and keystrokes and conduct UI based automation.

Beyond this conventional and known use of RPA for UI based automation, PAD also can call an API (Application Programming Interface) or directly download files from the web without any UI interaction. In PAD the **"HTTP"** category of Actions is responsible for downloading files or for interacting with an API.

APIs

For reference, API is a set of rules that allows various software applications to comm-unicate with each other. Note that we are referring here to Web API and not Windows API. Just like you have functions in programming languages where a call is made, and it returns some data, think of Web APIs as "functions on the web" where you pass some parameters to call the API (request) and it returns data or information (response) from the server. There are two API Actions under the **"HTTP"** category in PAD and they are **"Invoke web service"** and **"Invoke SOAP web service"**.

What we are going to look ahead for calling an API are all different components of an API and they are not features of PAD. So, you need to learn about the API components from the already available resources on the web while working with them. Once you learn them, in PAD you just need to know how to pass the parameters to call the API and read its response.

"Invoke Web Service" Action

This Action is typically used to call the widely used REST (Representational State Transfer) APIs to make an API request with standard web methods like **GET** (to retrieve data), **POST** (to send data), **PUT** (to update data), **DELETE** (to remove data), and so on. A REST API is a way for different systems to communicate over the internet using HTTP requests. You can learn more from web articles on how the REST API operates behind the scenes and what its internal architecture is.

Let us take a look at using this Action in PAD.

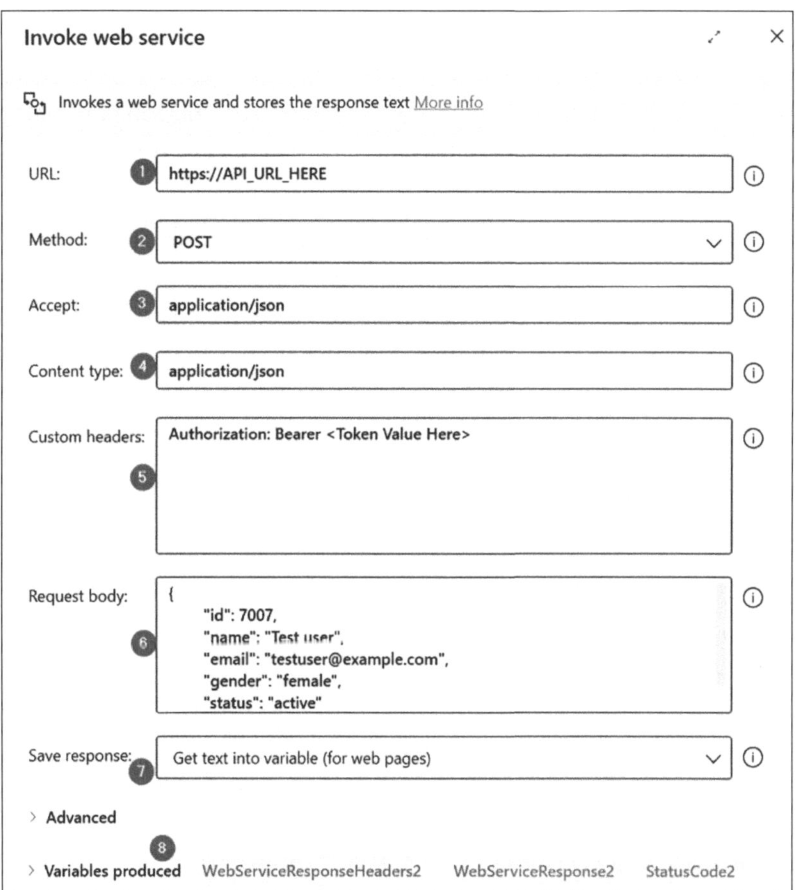

Figure 8.29: *The Invoke web service action*

Follow along as shown based on the numbering in *Figure* 8.29:

1. This is the URL or address to access the API and is called the API endpoint. Without this URL you cannot call the API, and it will be available from the API documentation and is generally available with the person or organization for whom you are building this automation.

2. This tells the server what action you want to perform using any of the standard methods mentioned earlier (For example, **GET**, **POST**). You can pick from the available list of methods from the dropdown.

3. This tells the server what type of response you want to receive and is usually a specific format like JSON or XML given in the format as *application/json* or *application/xml*.

4. On the other hand, **"Content type"** tells the server what type of data you are sending in the request, such as JSON, XML, or plain text and is given in a similar format as *application/json*. There could also be additional parameters (like character set) to be added here and you can separate them with a semicolon.

5. Only if necessary, as per the API documentation, here you can provide custom-based headers which are additional pieces of information sent along with the request. They can include things like authentication tokens or user-specific data.

   Here is an example to pass a token in this box if the API uses any.

   ```
   Authorization: Bearer <Token Value Here>
   ```

6. Here goes the actual data being sent to the server, typically used with methods (such as POST or PUT) which are responsible for sending any data. As an example, if the content is to be sent in JSON and you are adding a new user, the **"Request body"** parameter would include the user's details in key-value pairs as follows, where text values are enclosed within double quotes and numeric values without anything.

   ```
   {
    "id": 7007,
    "name": "Test user",
    "email": "testuser@example.com",
    "gender": "female",
    "status": "active"
   }
   ```

7. This dropdown has options to save the response from the API as text inside a variable or save them to the disk in case they are files.

8. The output parameter of **WebServiceResponseHeaders** (suffixed with 2 in the preceding figure and can be renamed as required) returns the pieces of information sent back by the server like the content type, length, date and time of the response, and much more. The **WebServiceResponse** output is the main information that we asked for via the API call and is generally in the form of JSON or XML, and the **StatusCode** will tell the outcome of the request in the

form of a numeric code that helps to determine whether the call was a success or a failure. Therefore, you might want to learn the different status codes and their meaning from learning tutorials related to API responses.

The setting to watch for is in the **"Advanced"** section of this Action and it is the **"Encode request body"** toggle. Enabling this will tell PAD to encode the request body (which will also contain the URL) while making the call. URL encoding replaces non-allowed characters into their equivalent allowed characters, for example, %20 with space. Learn more about this concept here: https://www.w3schools.com/tags/ref_urlencode.ASP.

The point to be noted here is, whether to enable or disable this toggle depends on the configuration of the API at the receiving end. If the API documentation has these details, then well and good. But if not, then try enabling or disabling it if you are having issues getting successful API responses.

The **"Advanced"** section also has an option to provide the username and password in case the web server requires it.

Even before calling an API from PAD, to verify whether your API is working as expected or not, a widely used API platform for developers called Postman accessible via https://www.postman.com is made use of, where you can provide these same parameters as earlier and test the API. This also helps in detecting issues in case you are calling the API incorrectly. Something to be noted is that if you are using any sensitive data or do not want to interact with your data on a third-party website, then you should refrain from using any external API testing platform.

In the "*Practical Exercises*" section at the end of the chapter, you will have sample REST API endpoints to practice using these parameters.

Reading the Response

In the case of the previous figure, if **WebServiceResponse2** is the output variable that is going to hold the actual response, then pass this variable to the **"Convert JSON to custom object"** Action to simplify the output and further read it. You can then loop through this custom object output variable. If the JSON returned by the API is similar to the format as in point number 6 above, then after conversion, the **CurrentItem** variable of the loop followed by the dot operator with one of its keys (for example, name) will give its value. For example, **%CurrentItem.name%** will return the **Test user**.

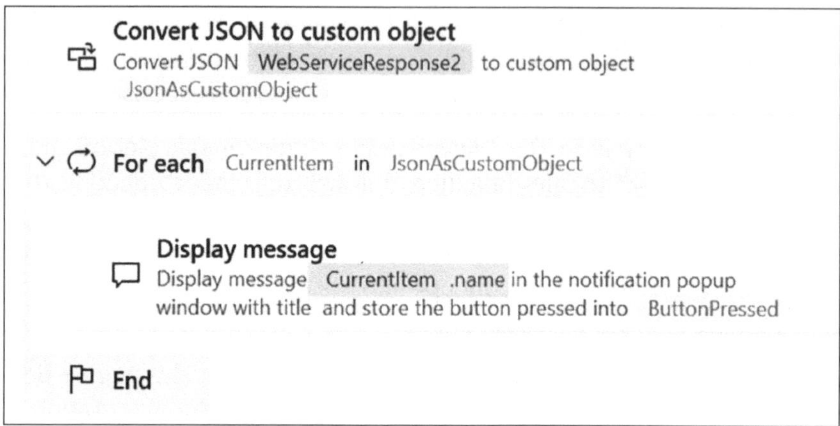

Figure 8.30: *Reading the API response*

Depending on the way the output is returned in **`JsonAsCustomObject`**, at times, you might have to go certain levels further to extract the direct desired value, for example, **`%JsonAsCustomObject['Name'][0].text%`** or you might have to pass a level further of the **`JsonAsCustomObject`** to the **"`For each`"** loop to iterate through it. You will get to know this after opening the **`JsonAsCustomObject`** variable from the **"`Variables`"** pane and by referring to its top section where it shows the variable name and levels when you keep clicking the **"`more`"** link button within the output rows.

A word of mention is that not all custom objects of PAD can be looped through. There could be several complexities and layers of hierarchy within it depending on how the input JSON is structured. Let us hope that Microsoft makes the provision to read any custom object structure coming from any JSON format.

"`Invoke SOAP Web Service`" Action

As the name suggests, this Action is used to call a SOAP API which is used less frequently compared to the latest REST API. SOAP which stands for Simple Object Access Protocol was largely used prior to the introduction of REST for communicating between applications via HTTP and it has its own set of syntax and rules. It uses XML to format the messages being sent and received. They are still used for legacy applications, and if you come across any during your automation journey, then you can make use of the **"`Invoke SOAP web service`"** Action via Power Automate Desktop.

1. Within the **"`Invoke SOAP web service`"** Action, the first thing you would see is the **"`Build request`"** button (*Figure* 8.32). Click the button and the parameter it takes (*Figure* 8.31) is either a WSDL file on the disk or a WSDL URL (that is, a URL pointing to a WSDL) which you will need to obtain from the end-user for whom the automation is being built. You can learn more about it but in simple terms, a WSDL (Web Services Description Language) is an XML-based content that describes the functionalities offered by the SOAP web service. Once you

import the file or URL, all the details will be read and automatically populated in the subsequent fields except for the **"Request envelope"**.

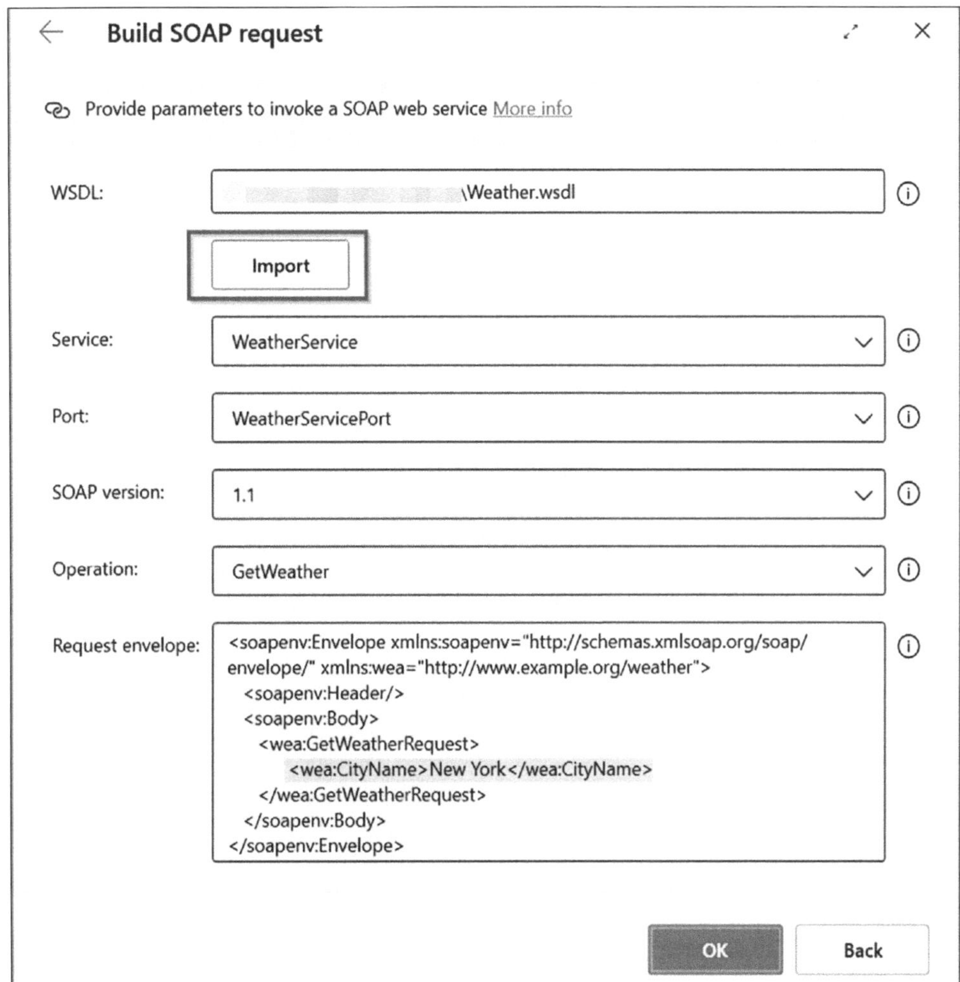

Figure 8.31: *The Build SOAP request screen*

If there are multiple services in the WSDL, then the **"Service"** dropdown would list them all. Likewise, if there is another operation in addition to **GetWeather**, for example, **GetZipCode**, then it would show up in the **"Operation"** dropdown.

For generating a request body/envelope, either you could get it if it is already available from the API's documentation or you will need to use a tool like SoapUI available at https://www.soapui.org to generate and paste it here. You can download the Open Source version of the tool which is for free and use it for testing the API as well as for generating the request body.

The above **"Request envelope"** is just an illustration to showcase how the request would look like where a city name parameter is required for getting its weather. To make it dynamic, you would need to add a variable in place of **`New York`** such as **`%CityName%`** so that the request is made for the city coming from the bot. There can be multiple parameters too, for instance, parameters for two numbers can be present to retrieve their addition.

2. Clicking **"`OK`"** will take you back to the main screen of the Action and all the rest of the parameters will be pre-filled including the endpoint and the headers along with the request body from the earlier screen.

***Figure 8.32:** The Invoke SOAP web service action*

Again, the URLs shown in the preceding figure are for illustration purposes, not for trying it as a SOAP web service. The output variables are similar to the ones for REST APIs, and the result you are looking for will be in the **`SoapServiceResponse`** variable.

Like the **"`Invoke web service`"** Action, this Action also has the provision to pass the username and password for HTTP authentication.

The output format of SOAP URLs is typically XML, so you would need to perform XML operations to retrieve the desired output from the response by making use of XML Actions as per "*Chapter 7: File Management and Data Manipulation*".

Downloading from Web

Another very useful Action that is used to do a direct download of some text or a file without performing any kind of UI interactions is the **"`Download from web`"** Action. Let's straight away head on to the practical usage of this Action.

On the https://rpachallenge.com webpage, if you hover the mouse on the **"`DOWNLOAD EXCEL`"** link button, you will notice in the status bar of the browser (marked by an arrow) that the URL directly points to a file download (**`challenge.xlsx`**). This is a perfect example of using this Action. Without even clicking the UI element by the bot, the file would be downloaded to the specified folder using this Action.

In the applications that you would automate, even if you won't see any URL in the status bar as this, then you could always use the **"`Inspect`"** browser feature of that element and see if it is pointing to a direct download URL. Another option is to capture the UI element and then go to the Selector window, and observe if any of the Attributes point to a direct download. Even if not, you can still try this Action and see if it causes the desired download wherever manually clicking an element does some kind of download. Apart from a file download, this Action is also for getting the web page HTML text configured in the **"`Save response`"** dropdown to save the text as a variable.

Figure 8.33: *URL of file download in status bar*

In our example, right-click on the link button, copy the URL, and paste it into the **"`Download from web`"** Action, as shown in the following figure. This Action has two method options, **`GET`** and **`POST`**. Since we are getting the file, so choose the GET method. Save the file to a disk and choose a destination folder. The **`DownloadedFile`** output variable will give us several details about the file along with its full path which can then be used further in our automation.

In the **"`Advanced`"** section, the **"`Connection timeout`"** parameter is available for these three HTTP Actions which are used to pass the number of seconds to wait for a successful connection. If beyond those seconds a response is not received, then the Action throws a timeout error.

Lastly, this Action also has the parameters to pass the username and password.

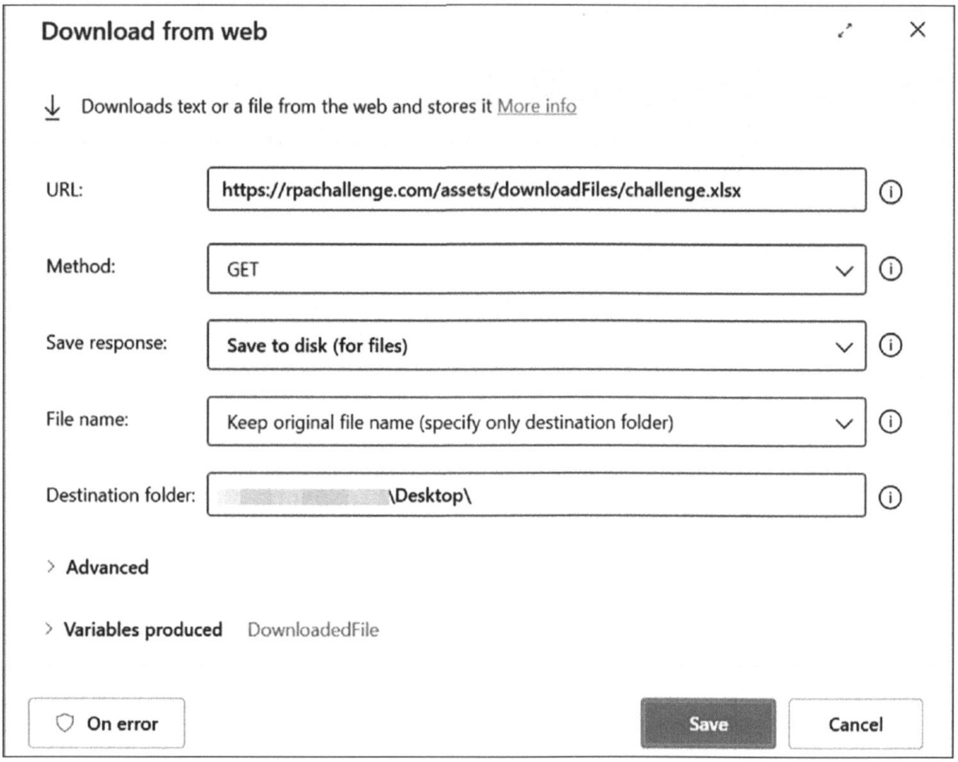

Figure 8.34: *The Download from web action*

This concludes the way of interacting with web applications and services via HTTP Actions where no UI based interactions are used.

Interacting Applications with Image Recording

You are certainly going to encounter experiences, where no matter what, you are not able to capture the UI elements and their Selectors due to the way the underlying application is built. In these cases, you would still need to read and write values to UI elements. Image recording and reading/writing using images can come to your rescue in such cases. Let us go through them in detail.

Follow the given steps:

1. We are going to use the Contoso application, assuming that we cannot capture its UI elements and its Selectors. Use the **"`Run application`"** Action for the executable of the Contoso application.

2. Add the **"Focus window"** Action, passing the window title as **"Contoso Invoicing"**.
3. Drag and drop the **"Move mouse to text on screen (OCR)"** Action. This is for clicking the **"Invoices"** tab on the left so that the tab activates and opens when the application launches. As shown in the following figure, search for the text **"Invoices"** on the foreground window, since we have already given focus to the window.

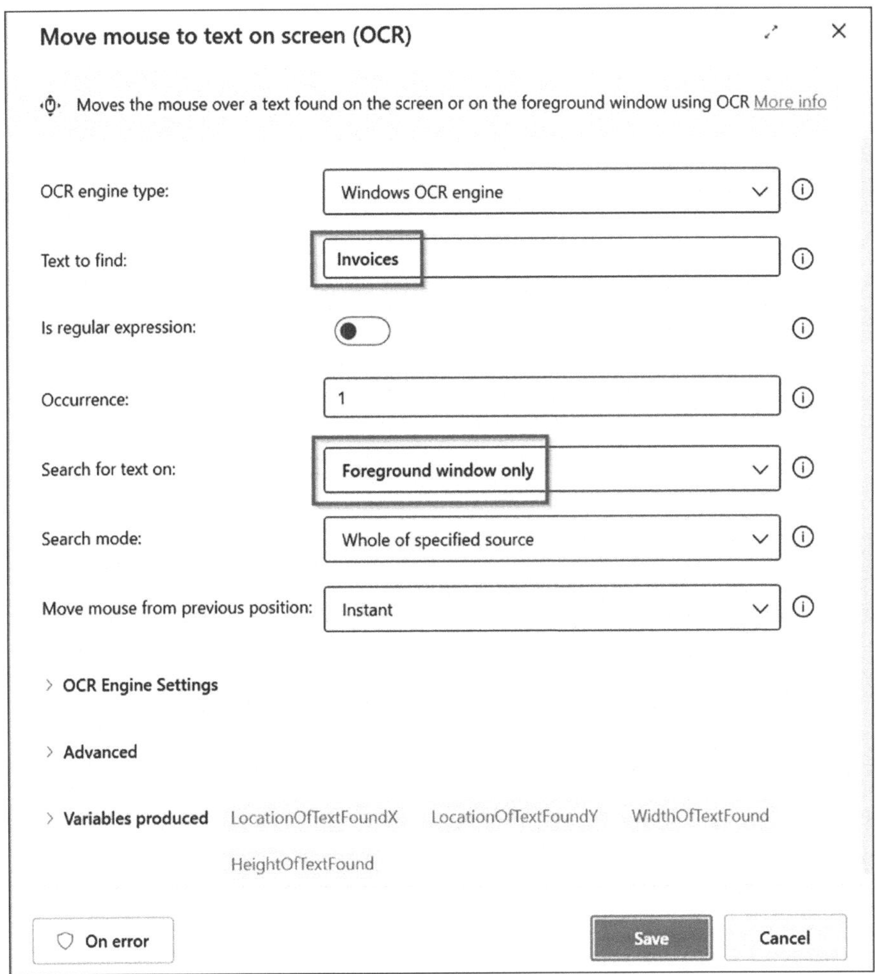

Figure 8.35: *Activate the Invoices tab*

4. It's time to create a new record. Drag and drop the **"Move mouse to image"** Action. Capture the **"New Record"** button at the top left of the Contoso application below the menu bar. Send a mouse click on the image to create a new record. Refer to the following figure. In the figure, **"NewRecord"** is the name given to the captured image.

The image for the **`"New Record"`** button after it is captured is indicated by the arrow.

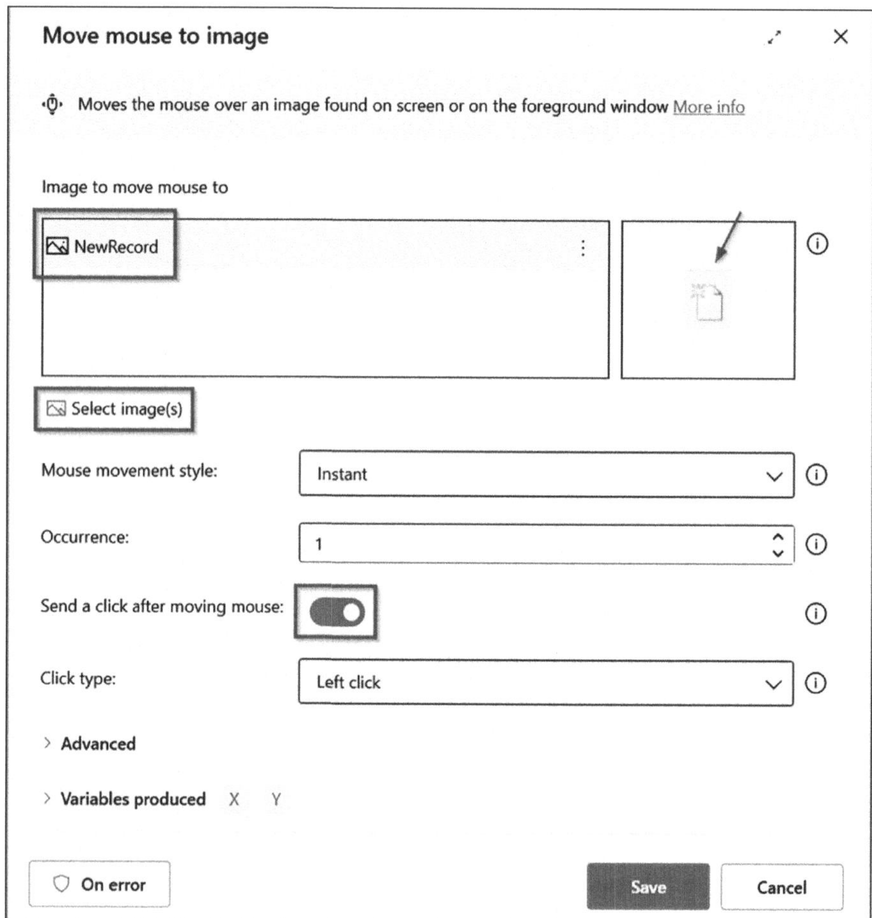

Figure 8.36: *Capture and click the new record button*

As soon as the **`"New record"`** button is clicked, an auto id is generated and indicated by an arrow in the following figure. We will be capturing this ID using Image recording.

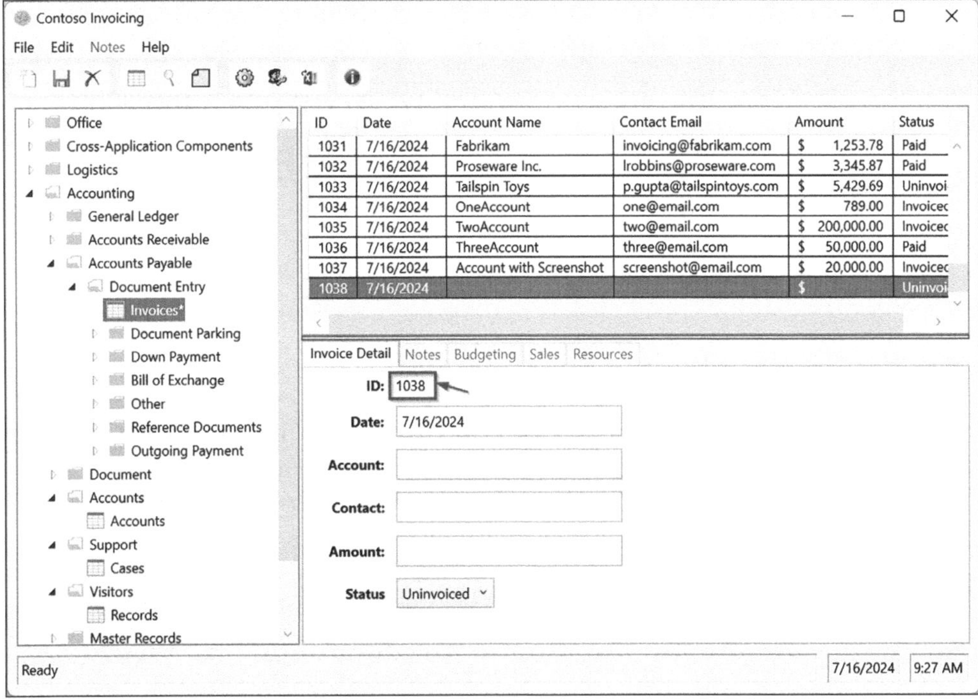

Figure 8.37: *Auto Id to be extracted using Image recording*

5. Start the recording session from the **"Recorder"** button on the Flow designer. Once the **"Recorder"** window is opened, click the ellipsis button, and you will find a toggle to turn on the Image recording. Enable the toggle. So far, we have been using the recorder without this toggle and hence were able to capture the UI elements and their Selectors. Click the **"Record"** button to start the Image recording.

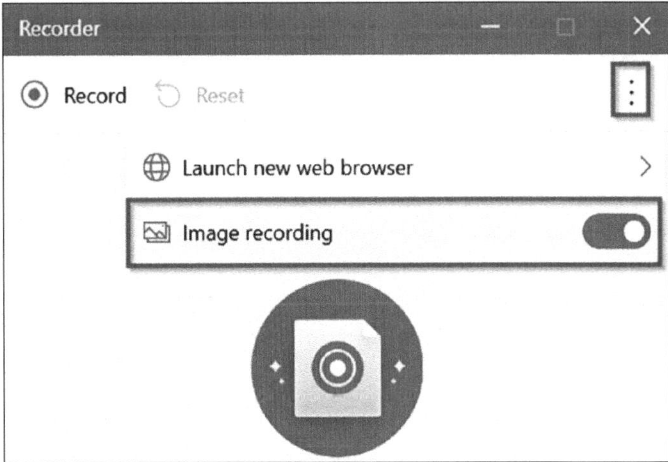

Figure 8.38: *Enabling the Image recording*

6. Right-click on the auto number which is **`1038`** in our case and click the **"`Extract text from image`"** option.

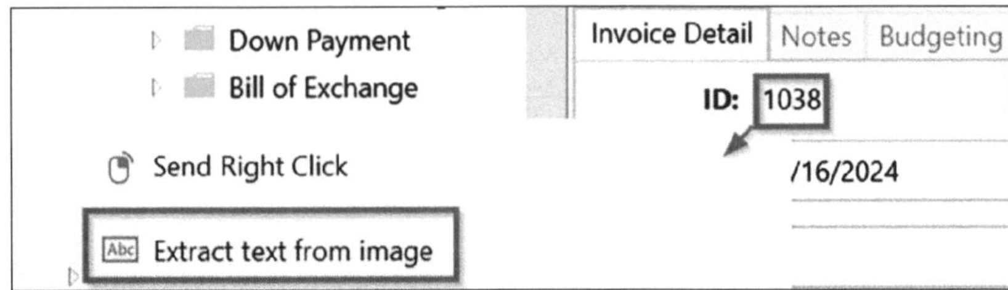

Figure 8.39: *Extract text from image*

7. Instantly as you do this, the first step of the Image recording process is shown at the top that says **"`Define text area`"**, as shown in the following figure. The big rounded circle is the mouse pointer waiting for you to define the text area that needs to be captured. Using this mouse pointer mark the text area of the auto ID that shows **`1038`**.

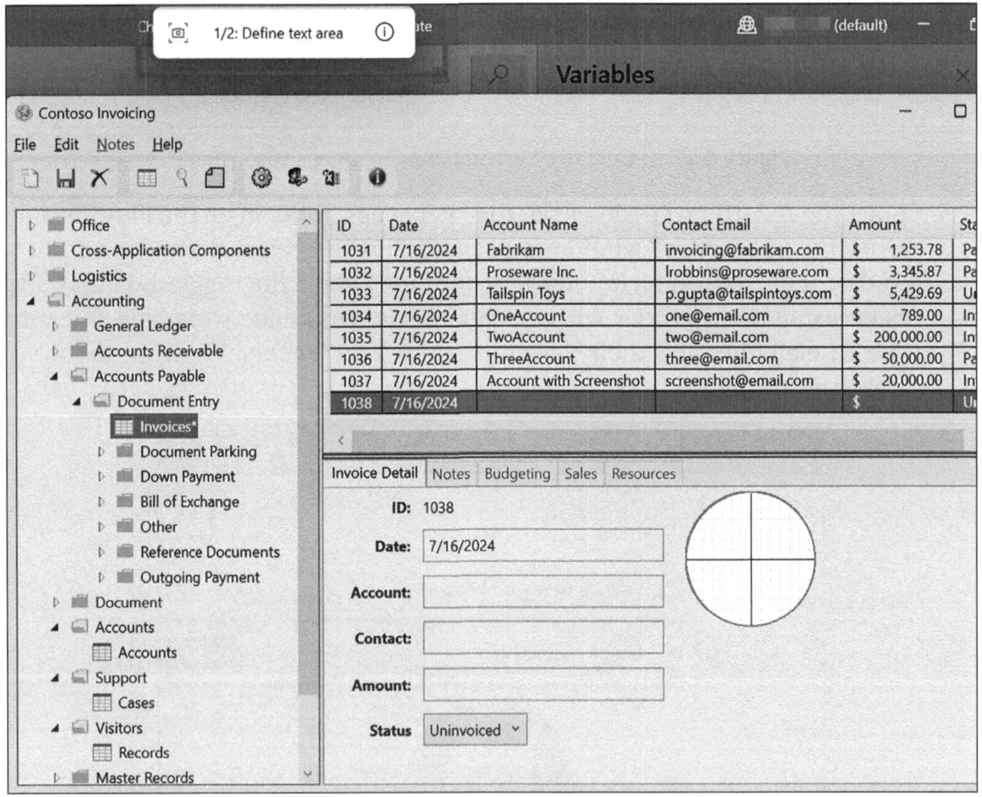

Figure 8.40: *Defining the text area*

8. As soon as you mark the area, it moves to the second step which is to define the anchor area, shown at the top of the following figure. The text **`1038`** seen in

a red box is colored by the Image recorder indicating what was marked in the first step.

For defining the anchor area, we will choose the label next to it that shows as **"ID:"**. Mark this label for the second step.

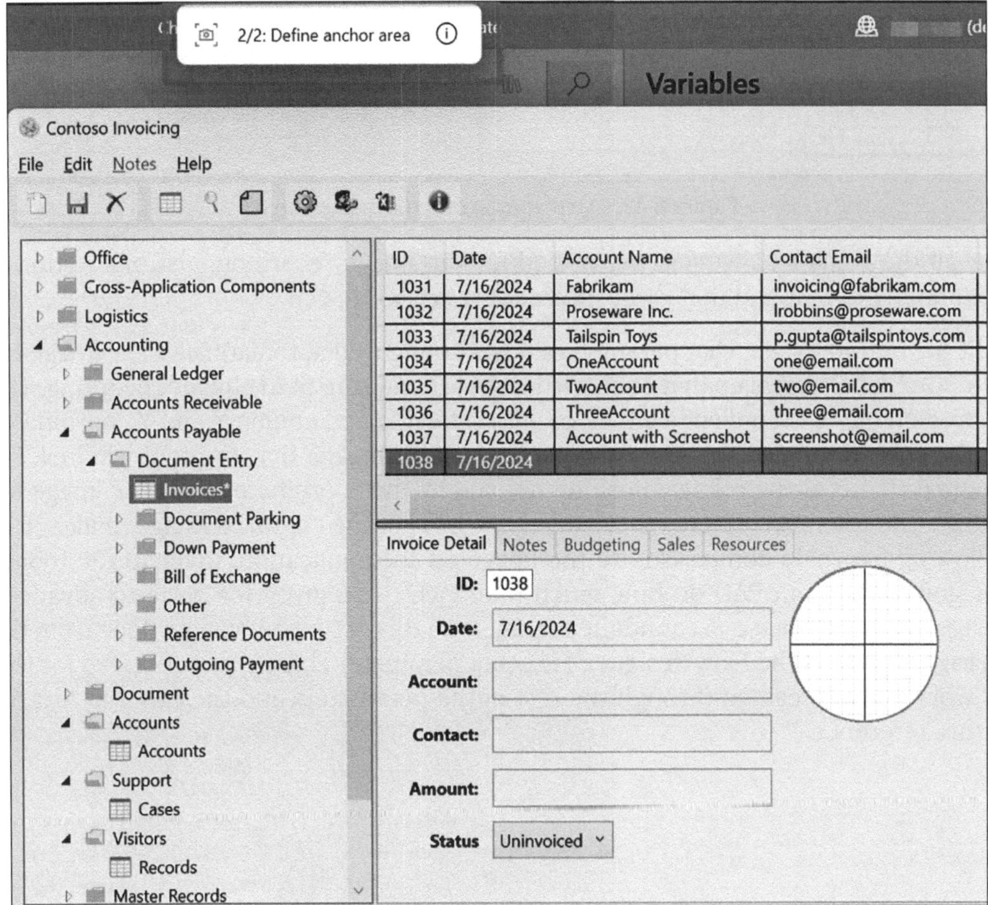

Figure 8.41: *Defining the anchor area*

9. Once the anchor area is marked, both the fields will be marked in different colors, as shown in the right-hand side of the following figure. The blue marked field **(ID:)** is the anchor area whereas the red marked **(1038)** is the text area coming from the first step of the image recording.

   The following preview can be seen when clicked on the image icon of the **"Recorder"** indicated by the arrow. The **"Sample Value"** is also visible. If all looks right, accept the changes to close the **"Recorder"**. If not, re-do the steps.

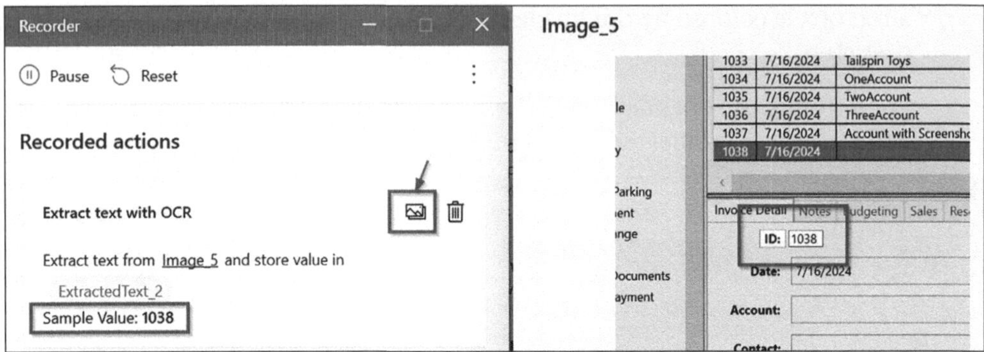

Figure 8.42: *The text area and the anchor area*

For all the steps that we just performed for the Image recording, just one Action is generated out of it and that is the **"`Extract text with OCR`"**.

Edit the Action to see what parameters it has configured automatically. The image for the **"`ID:`"** label shows up that comes from the second step of the Image recording. The subregion mode is applied in which case the starting and ending X and Y coordinates of the sub region are automatically captured. This means that the tool will look for the text that is at the relative position defined by the coordinates from the image for **"`ID:`"**. The tolerance defines the acceptance level of the captured image (*Image_5* in following figure) in comparison to the image on the application. Refer to the tooltip for guidelines from PAD on how much tolerance to be given for basic to advanced image matching. *Image_5* cannot be renamed via this Action but can be done from the **"`Images`"** pane of the Flow designer. No other parameter changes are required for this to work, but you can go through the rest of the parameters and their tooltip text for future reference.

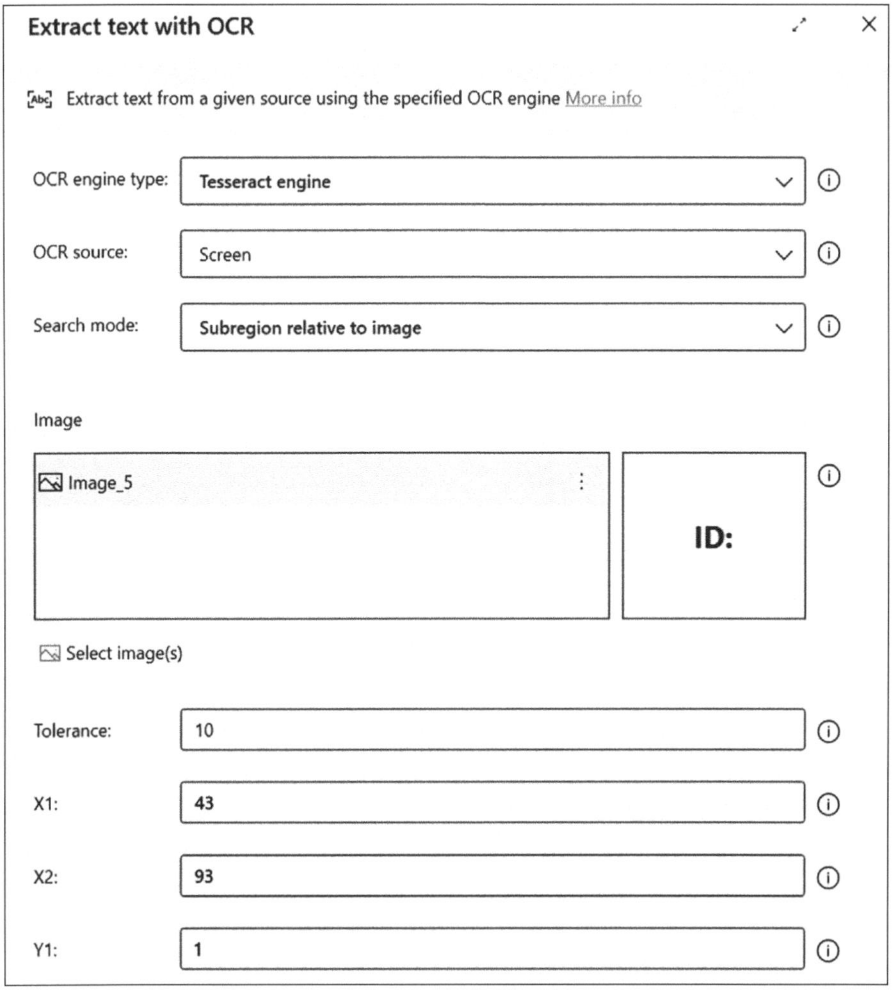

Extract text with OCR

Extract text from a given source using the specified OCR engine More info

OCR engine type: Tesseract engine

OCR source: Screen

Search mode: Subregion relative to image

Image

Image_5

ID:

Select image(s)

Tolerance: 10

X1: 43

X2: 93

Y1: 1

Figure 8.43: *The Extract text with OCR action*

10. Display the output variable coming from the above Action and run the Flow.

Here is the entire Flow of what we built so far starting from line number 2. Line 1 contains the **"`Run application`"** Action. As you can see, the bot has rightly extracted the text **"`1038`"** that was present next to the anchor **"`ID:`"**.

We have nowhere added any UI element or its Selectors during the entire process.

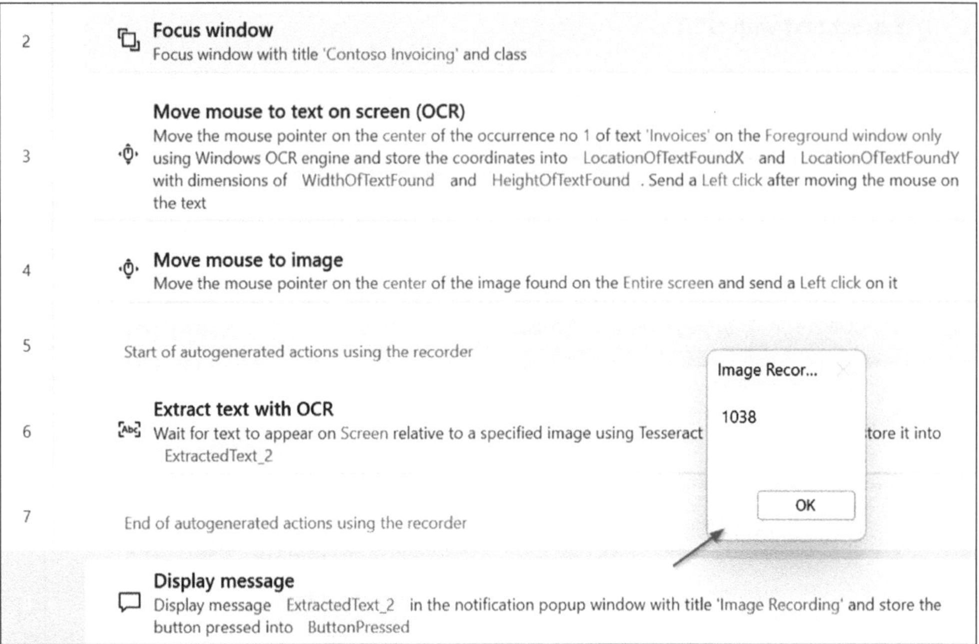

Figure 8.44: *Entire Flow and its output*

You could even perform the clicking on the **"Invoices"** tab and the **"New Record"** button via the Image recorder in place of the Actions on line numbers 3 and 4, but we wanted to see an additional approach.

In the preceding exercise, we used a text-based anchor in the form of the label **"ID:"**. Meaning, some text was written on it. Likewise, we could also use an image-based anchor. Meaning, an image would be the anchor and extract the text next to that image anchor. For example, in the following figure, we could use the red-crossed icon as the image anchor and capture any text surrounding it like **"Error message"** or **"This is the text I want to extract."**. The steps to achieve this are the same as what we did for the earlier exercise.

Figure 8.45: *Sample Image-based anchor*

Next, as a different topic, we will use a unique way to write a value to the **"Account"** text box without capturing any UI element or its Selector.

Follow the given steps:

1. Drag and drop the **"Move mouse"** Action and place it side-by-side of the Contoso application, as shown in the following figure. Place your mouse (do not click) at the beginning of the **"Account"** text box indicated by the arrow. This is to identify the place from where to start writing the text in this text box. The **"Move mouse"** Action can show the coordinates of the present position of the mouse as you move it. As per the figure, the coordinates of the mouse position are X=720 and Y=746. Do not **"Save"** the Action.

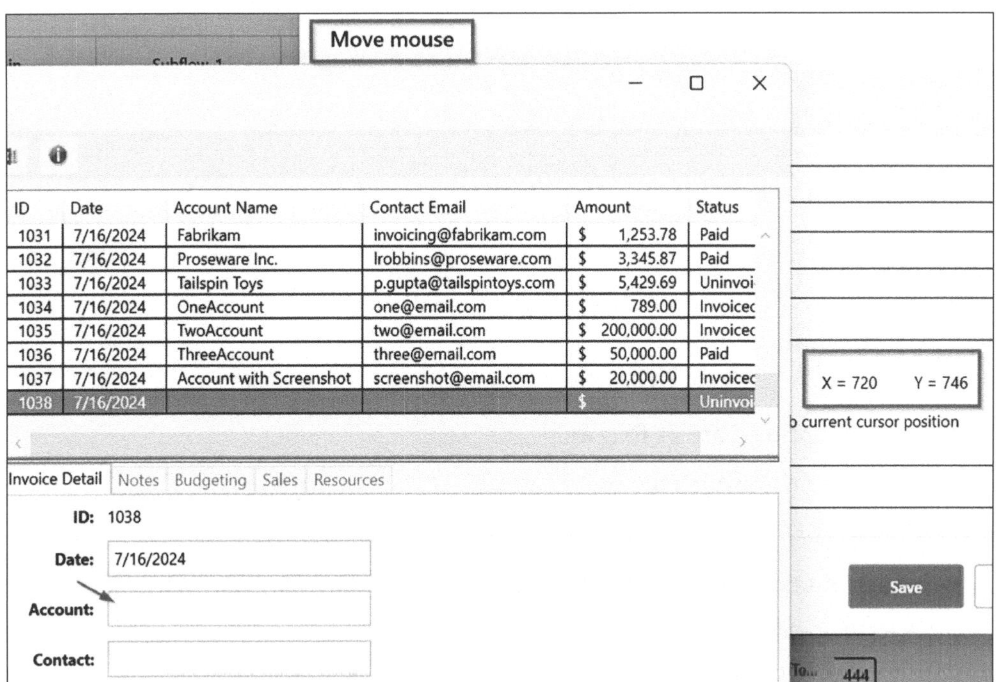

Figure 8.46: *Identifying the start position of text box for writing*

2. Do the same for the beginning of the label for **"Account:"** as shown by the mouse pointer marked by the circle in the following figure. In other words, find the coordinates for the position where the **"Account:"** label starts. Place the mouse such that the Y coordinate is the same as in Step 1 (that is, 746). This is because, the **"Account:"** label and its text box both are going to be on the same line (that is, Y axis) and only its X coordinate will change.

   As per the figure, X=620 and Y=746.

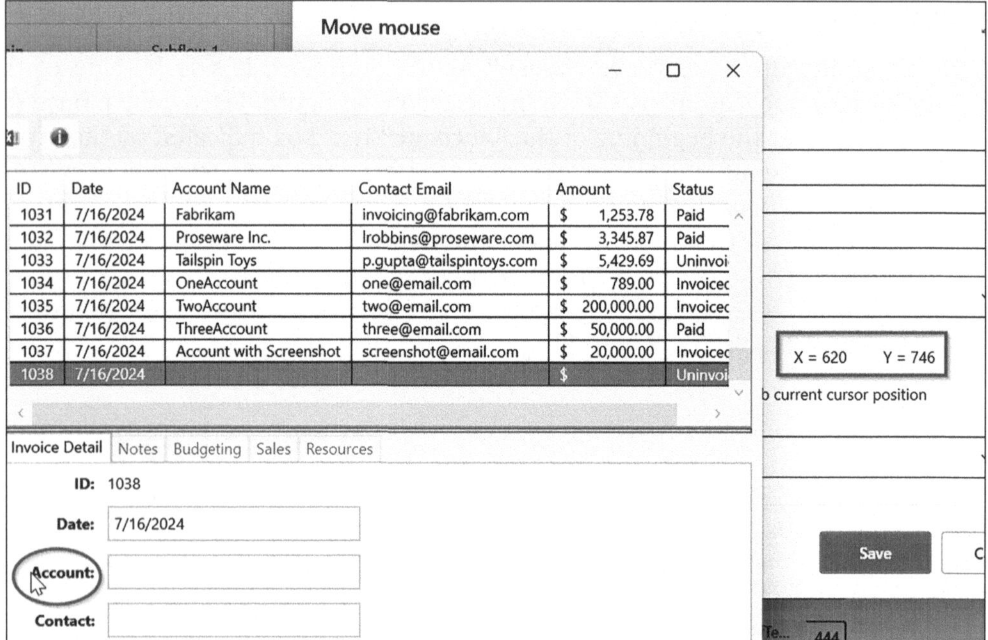

Figure 8.47: *Identifying the start position of label*

The positions captured are as follows:

- **Start of Account label:**

  X=620, Y=746

- **Start of text in Account text box:**

  X=720, Y=746

There is a difference of 100 (720 minus 620) between the X coordinates of each. This means that you need to add 100 to the X coordinate of the **"`Account:`"** label and then start writing from there. To do this, we would need to find the X and Y coordinates of the **"`Account:`"** label dynamically by the bot so that whichever position the Contoso screen opens, we will be able to capture the right coordinates of the **"`Account:`"** label.

3. This is done by the **"`Move mouse to image`"** Action where you capture the image of the **"`Account:`"** label as marked by the arrow in the following figure. See that the output variables of this Action are X and Y coordinates of the **"`Account:`"** label and that is exactly what we want.

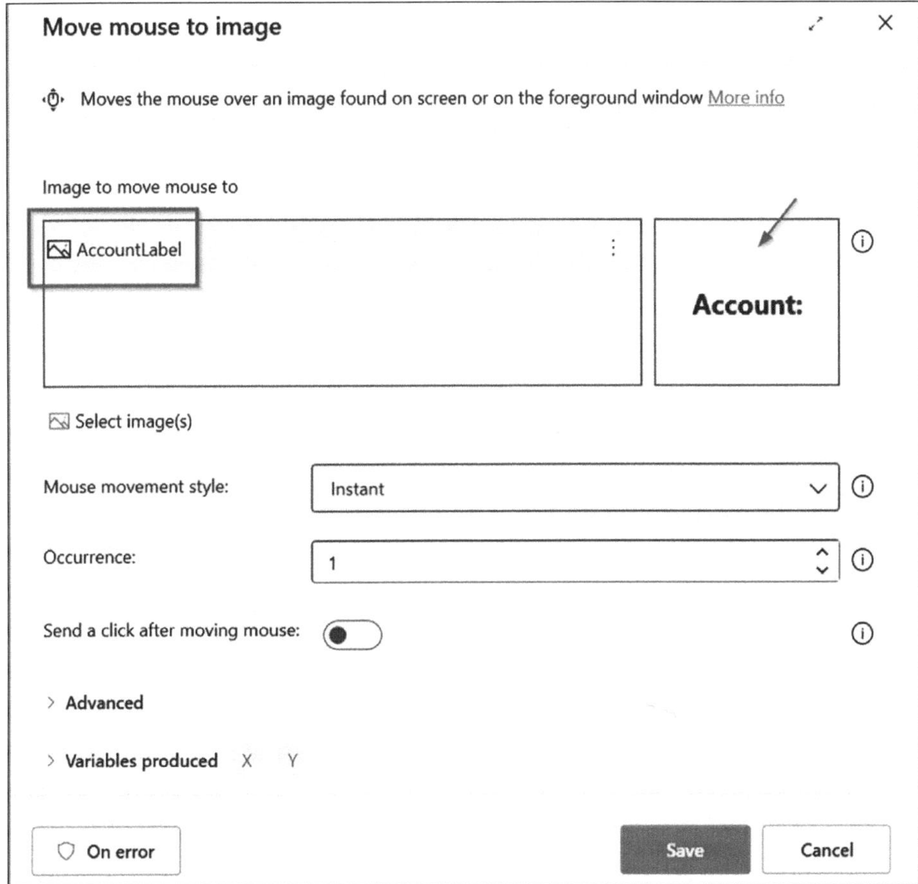

Figure 8.48: *Getting the X and Y coordinates of the label*

4. Add a **"Move mouse"** Action which can be used to move the mouse to the specified coordinates. In our case, we will add 100 to the X variable coming from the above Action and keep Y as it is. This will move the mouse to the **"Account"** text box.

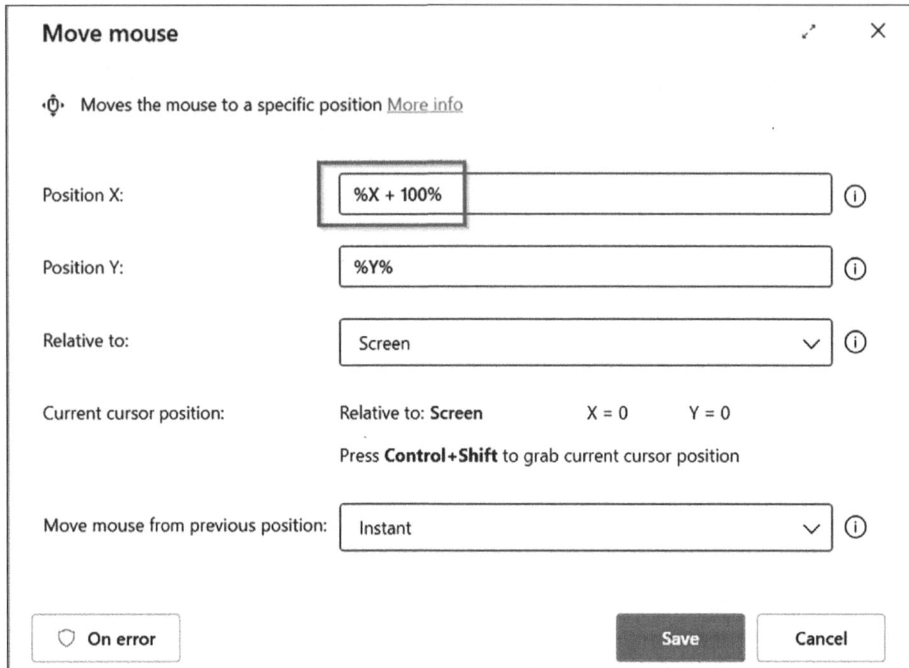

Figure 8.49: *Positioning the mouse over the Account text box*

5. The mouse pointer has only been positioned over the **"`Account`"** text box, but we need to click inside the box so that the bot can start writing. This is done by the **"`Send mouse click`"** Action. No changes in the parameters of this Action are required.
6. Lastly, drag and drop the **"`Send keys`"** Action and pass any Account Number to be written inside the text box. For this example, we are using the text **"`New Account Here`"**.

A display message of **"`Done`"** at the end is added just to add a breakpoint.

As shown in the following figure, the wordings **"`New Account Here`"** are written inside the **"`Account`"** text box with a blinking cursor at the end after the text was entered by the **"`Send keys`"**.

To summarize, we identified the static position for the start of the **"`Account:`"** label and for the start of the text inside the text box. We manually calculated the position for the start of the text box from the position of the label by finding its difference. Using Actions, we captured the image of the **"`Account:`"** label to identify its coordinates dynamically and then moved the mouse position from there by adding the difference calculated. Keeping the mouse in the same position, we clicked inside the text box via the bot so that it could start writing by sending keystrokes.

Throughout the entire exercise, we did not capture any UI elements or its Selectors.

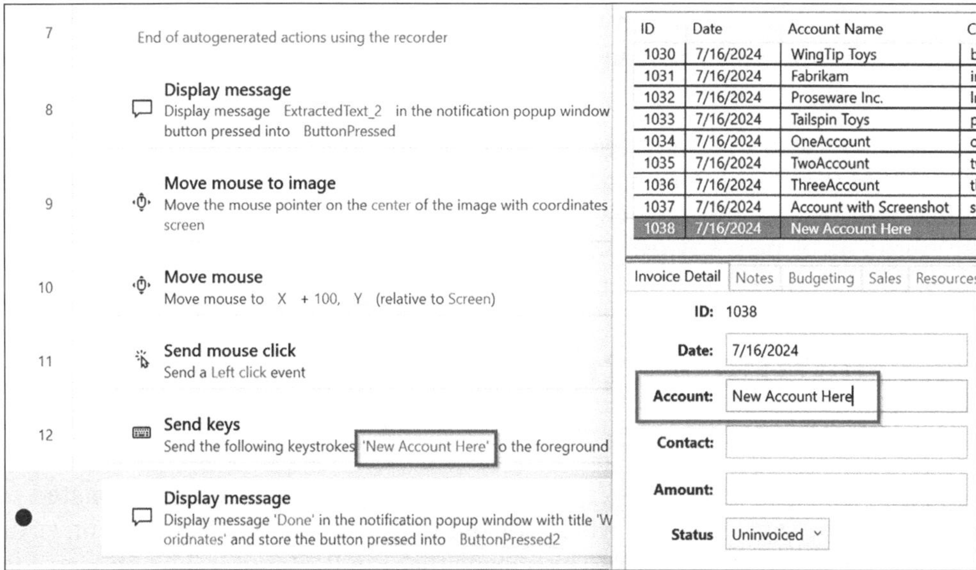

Figure 8.50: *Entire Flow and its output*

You can follow the same steps to read a value from a text box as opposed to writing a value as above. After clicking inside the text box, send keystrokes for selecting all text and copying the text using **`{Control}({A}){Control}({C})`**. The copied text will be available in the Clipboard and using the **"`Get clipboard text`"** Action will return the value that was present in the text box. Try this out.

A good practice to adhere to in such kind of automation is to use an Action like **"`If text on screen (OCR)`"** before doing a **"`Move mouse to text on screen (OCR)`"** for line number 3 of *Figure* 8.44 which will first check if the text is present and only then take the next course of action. Similar to it is the **"`Wait for text on screen (OCR)`"** which will give you an opportunity to add a time interval before failing with a timeout error.

Likewise, before **"`Move mouse to image`"** Action of line number 4 of *Figure* 8.44 and line number 9 of the figure above, make use of the **"`If image`"** Action. This will check if the image is searched and found by PAD and if yes only then proceed further.

The **"`If image`"** Action has the option to add multiple images for matching, in which case, also refer to the toggle that says **"`Find all images in the list`"** thus giving the option to match one or more images. Searching for an image on the foreground window will narrow down the image search instead of looking at the entire screen. Also, searching on a specific subregion will further narrow down the search. But use these parameters according to the scenario of the automation you are building.

The **"`Wait for image`"** has the same options but with the timeout toggle which is better to use to avoid an infinitely long time for the search.

For these kinds of automation, it is a recommended practice to keep the same screen resolution of all the machines in all environments, where the bot is built as well as where it is going to run.

Some final words on using image-based automation are that this approach heavily makes use of image searching and matching, send keys, mouse clicks, and coordinates. It is best used as a last resort when nothing else works like the conventional approaches of capturing UI elements, Selectors, use of Scripting, and so on. A thorough testing is a good way to tell the reliability of this type of automation.

Automating Virtual Desktop-Based Applications

In any conventional automation, the applications or systems to be automated are generally on the same machine where the bot runs. But they could also be on virtual desktops like Citrix, for example. This means that the PAD tool will be on your local machine while the applications to be automated are on a virtual desktop. This makes it cumbersome for the tool to capture UI elements and Selectors of an application that is on a different machine.

For this purpose, to make it easily achievable to automate virtual desktop-based applications, Power Automate Desktop needs you to install a software agent called **"`Power Automate agent for virtual desktops`"**. This is available from the **"`Tools`"** menu of the Flow designer and needs to be installed on the remote desktop.

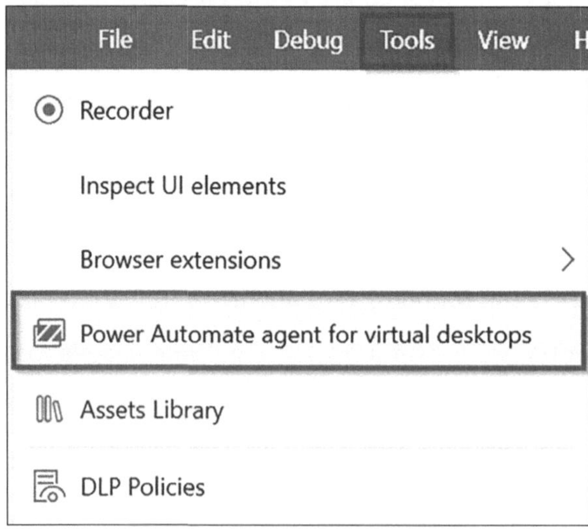

Figure 8.51: *Installing the agent*

Using this agent simplifies it to automate tasks on virtual desktops just as you would do on local machines.

Note that, at first, you should try to see if it is possible to install the PAD tool on the virtual desktop environment so that you can interact with UI elements and build Flows conventionally. By doing that, you will be able to circumvent the shortcomings of using the agent mentioned in the link at the end of this section.

Currently, Virtual desktop automation via this agent is available for Windows RDP, RemoteApp, Citrix Desktop, and Citrix Virtual Apps. There may be more additions in the future. But virtual desktop automation is available for UI automation Actions as opposed to Web automation Actions. Recall the two categories of UI automation and Browser automation from *Figure* 5.46 of "*Chapter* 5: *Building Blocks of a Desktop Flow*". However, for Browser automation you can still handle web components like desktop interface elements (meaning, try to interact with the web elements through the UI automation Actions) wherever applicable or use the features of image recognition and matching, mouse clicks, keystrokes, OCR all of which we have seen in the current chapter.

While PAD will be installed on your local machine where you will be building the Flows, the agent must be running on the remote desktop while you are developing, and designing a Flow as well as when the Flow runs.

Based on the earlier listed supported virtual desktop platforms, since the virtual desktop will be using either Citrix or Microsoft RDP (Remote Desktop Protocol), the UI elements captured in the pane will show up under a category as **"`RDP`"** or **"`Citrix`"**, whereas elements captured on your local machine will show up under the "Computer" category of elements.

The agent has a high scope for evolving further in terms of reliability and support of more types of applications. You need to be aware of its current issues and limitations, their workarounds if any, its pre-requisites, how to install and use it, and how the communication happens between PAD and the agent. All of these will keep changing in future and you will get to keep yourself abreast from the official link of this topic at https://learn.microsoft.com/en-us/power-automate/desktop-flows/virtual-desktops.

Terminal Emulation and SAP Automation

Power Automate Desktop allows interaction with terminal emulators like mainframe applications or legacy applications that have a command line interface. They are also referred to as **"`Green screen`"** applications. These types of applications still remain in use today, particularly in organizations where legacy systems are deeply integrated into their day-to-day business processes, and thereby requiring to automate them.

They mostly have a text-based interface. Automating these applications via RPA would generally involve performing operations like extract the text displayed on the terminal screen, move the cursor or place it in a particular position, simulate keyboard inputs to interact with the terminal, enter commands, press function keys, navigate menus, wait for specific output on the screen, in some places use the recorder, and so on. PAD provides us Actions to do these and they are available in the **"`Terminal emulation`"** group of Actions. Where the available pre-built Actions do not work as expected, you could certainly give a try at Image-based automation too.

These require valid software and an appropriate license of that software. Although not a comprehensive and exhaustive guide provided by Microsoft to the developer fraternity on this topic, given here is an official link that has pointers on establishing a connection with a terminal session using the Actions in PAD:

https://learn.microsoft.com/en-us/power-automate/desktop-flows/actions-reference/terminalemulation

For interacting with the SAP GUI (Graphical User Interface), a new set of SAP Actions have been released. Before the advent of these Actions, using the Recorder, or navigating through various menus of the SAP interface, sending keystrokes, and mouse clicks were used. Additionally, using SAP's recording engine and then implementing the VBScript generated by it in PAD's VBScript Action was also one of the approaches used. Even now these can still be used wherever automating SAP is not possible via the pre-built Actions, but you could start with the available ones at first. Actions dedicated to SAP are included in the **"`SAP automation`"** category in the **"`Actions`"** pane.

For all the approaches listed above, the link given here is a good resource from Microsoft that will take you through those topics including the GUI scripting configuration needed for automating SAP applications. The link for the resource is https://learn.microsoft.com/en-us/power-automate/guidance/rpa-sap-playbook/introduction and you need to go through all of the topics shown in the following figure along with the videos.

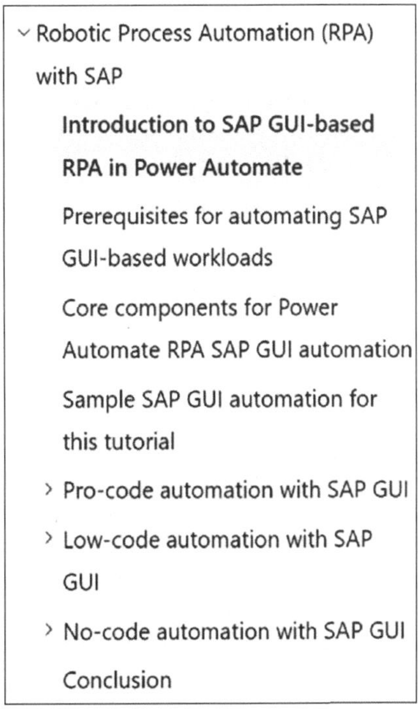

˅ Robotic Process Automation (RPA) with SAP

- **Introduction to SAP GUI-based RPA in Power Automate**
- Prerequisites for automating SAP GUI-based workloads
- Core components for Power Automate RPA SAP GUI automation
- Sample SAP GUI automation for this tutorial
- › Pro-code automation with SAP GUI
- › Low-code automation with SAP GUI
- › No-code automation with SAP GUI
- Conclusion

Figure 8.52: *Resources for extended reading*

On the other side, the following link gives a reference on the new set of Actions:

https://learn.microsoft.com/en-us/power-automate/desktop-flows/actions-reference/sap.

Here you will know which different SAP automation Actions are available, how they could assist in interacting with SAP UI elements, that these Actions allow integration with other PAD Actions for complex SAP process automation, the supported SAP GUI version and the number of connections allowed to an SAP system as of this writing and all of these will keep on evolving.

Active Directory

In short, Active Directory (AD) is a directory service developed by Microsoft for managing permissions and accesses within Windows domain networks. It handles network resources like user accounts and machines by internally storing data in a particular structure. AD provides authentication and authorization services, which are used by IT administrators for maintaining user identities and ensuring security across any organization. They are widely used in business environments to manage users, control access to data, and enforce security policies. By integrating AD with RPA automation workflows, organizations can streamline these administrative tasks and ensure secure management of their IT infrastructure.

Demonstrating Active Directory requires a specific set-up on a server operating system to function but cannot be installed on a client machine. A tutorial from Microsoft on using AD via Power Automate Desktop is provided here. It talks about automating AD tasks with PAD allowing administrators to streamline the process of adding, removing, or updating users and objects in AD. The link gives a practical example, such as creating a new user from HR email details. Make sure to click on the **"Next"** button and go through all the pages of the learning module:

https://learn.microsoft.com/en-us/training/modules/pad-active-directory/1-introduction

Conclusion

In this chapter, we explored advanced automation techniques and strategies that extend the capabilities of PAD on top of the usual ways of UI automation. We went through PDF and OCR Actions for data extraction from Text-based and Image-based PDFs, mouse and keyboard automation for simulating user interactions and automating your workstation. HTTP Actions highlighted the use of APIs and downloading from the web without a single click. We saw some unique approaches to interact with applications using Image Recording, sending keystrokes, mouse clicks on images, and coordinates-based automation. Additionally, some topics like automating virtual desktop-based applications, Terminal Emulation, and SAP automation require further deep dive and continued exploration to automate tasks in virtual and legacy environments. It also has a direction on integrating PAD with Active Directory to ease up its activities and related tasks.

In the next chapter, "*Leveling Up Your Automation Workflows*", we will explore essential topics to optimize your automation processes. We will cover Work Queues for efficient workload management, Error Handling for creating robust workflows, and Logging and Monitoring to track and diagnose automation activities. Additionally, we will discuss how to utilize the Cloud portal for Desktop Flows and see the two types of automation, namely Attended and Unattended.

Practical Exercises

The exercises based on topics from current or previous chapters are as follows:

Exercise 1:

1. Refer the following file placed in the GitHub folder of this chapter by the name **`"Chapter 8: Exercise 1.xlsx"`**.

	A	B	C	D	E	F
1	Date	Account	Contact	USD Amount	Status	ID
2	7/5/2024	Account70	user441@mail.com	208.46	Paid	
3	7/3/2024	Account11	user378@email.com	229.2	Uninvoiced	
4	7/1/2024	Account25	user510@email.com	797.2	Uninvoiced	
5	7/7/2024	Account43	user418@mail.com	589.17	Invoiced	
6	7/2/2024	Account8	user6@email.com	816.72	Invoiced	
7	7/5/2024	Account60	user443@email.com	431.41	Paid	
8	7/1/2024	Account16	user261@example.com	958.9	Paid	
9	7/4/2024	Account9	user786@email.com	648.09	Paid	
10	7/6/2024	Account96	user641@example.com	891.64	Uninvoiced	
11	7/1/2024	Account54	user442@mail.com	276.05	Uninvoiced	

Figure 8.53: *Sample input file*

2. Read the records from the Excel file using Excel operations.
3. Add these records into the Contoso application using Image automation and **without capturing UI elements and their Selectors**. Make use of image recording, send keystrokes, mouse clicks on images, capture images of labels and insert values in their textboxes using coordinates. Selecting the value of the Status dropdown will require sending the keys once there is focus on it.
4. After saving the record, capture the text of the auto ID using Image automation and save it to the Column F of the Excel above using Excel operations. Repeat the same for all rows in the Excel.

Exercise 2:

If you have any supported virtual desktop environment, then using the **"`Power Automate agent for virtual desktop`"** add a record to the Contoso application.

Exercise 3:

Practice performing the REST API operations using API testing websites like https://reqres.in and https://gorest.co.in.

Note: *If the websites are down due to heavy usage at times, then revisit them later.*

Questions

These questions could be addressed using details from the current or earlier chapters, or by exploring the PAD tool.

1. What setting is used to detect the formatted layout in a PDF document and extract text accordingly, thus retaining the structure of the data?

2. Explore how to extract text from all pages of an Image-based PDF.
3. Explore how to extract tables from a Text-based PDF.
4. Which Scripting languages are supported in Power Automate Desktop?
5. Which five parts of a file can be retrieved from the **"Get file path part"** Action?
6. What is the syntax to send the same key multiple times using **"Send keys"** Action?

   Example: How to send the TAB key 10 times?
7. How to use an AND operator and an OR operator within a single **"If"** Action?
8. How to turn on the CAPS lock via Power Automate Desktop?
9. Which OCR Engine types are available in OCR-related Actions?
10. While writing to a text file, if there is already any content in it, how to append new content in the same file without overwriting the previous text?
11. Where to find the **"Image recording"** option?
12. Take the current system date time and convert it to the following format. The month name should be in full and should add AM/PM to the time.

    Output Format: 20-February-25 09:40:35 AM
13. What needs to be installed to automate processes on a virtual desktop like Citrix?
14. How to get the name of the computer on which the Flow is running?
15. What is the difference between the **"Run JavaScript"** and **"Run JavaScript function on web page"** Action?
16. Which Action is used to call a SOAP API?
17. Which Action is used to call a REST API?

CHAPTER 9
Leveling Up Your Automation Workflows

Introduction

In this chapter, you will learn to level up your Automation workflows by leveraging the use of Work Queues for workload management, adding error handling and logging mechanisms for building robust and reliable Flows, making use of the Cloud portal and understanding how can Cloud Flows work in conjunction with Desktop Flows, monitoring the automation for higher uptimes, using Unattended and Attended automation as required.

Structure

We will cover the following topics in this chapter:

- Making Use of the Cloud Portal and the Power Platform
- Work Queues
- Error Handling
- Logging and Monitoring
- Unattended and Attended Automation

Making Use of the Cloud Portal and the Power Platform

We are going to use some features of the Power Automate Cloud portal and the Cloud Flows in the upcoming topics of this chapter in collaboration with Desktop Flows, so it is necessary for you to know them. In the "*Ways of Running a Desktop Flow*" topic of

"*Chapter 2: Getting into Action with PAD*", we had a hint of calling a Desktop Flow from a Cloud Flow as one of the ways of running Desktop Flows.

To build Cloud Flows or to open the Cloud portal, you will use the following URL:

https://make.powerautomate.com

Here, you will see the three types of Cloud Flows where you could leverage Desktop Flows via these. We will see what these three types are in a moment, but for now know that they are **Automated** Cloud Flows, **Instant** Cloud Flows, and **Scheduled** Cloud Flows.

Figure 9.1: *Types of Cloud Flows for leveraging Desktop Flows*

Note that calling a Desktop Flow from the Cloud portal is a premium feature and requires a valid license. The licensing required for Power Automate is mentioned in the "*Licensing*" topic of "*Chapter 12: Extending the Landscape of Your Desktop Flows*".

Manage Machines and Machine Groups

Before calling a Desktop Flow from a Cloud Flow, you need to add a machine so that Cloud Flows will know which machine to connect to and where to run the bot. You can also add multiple machines and create machine groups.

Recalling the "*Installation*" topic of "*Chapter 2: Getting into Action with PAD*", if you are using a Windows version other than the Home edition, then you will have the **machine-runtime app** installed on your machine which is what is used for this purpose. This app is specifically for managing the machine settings, ranging from registering your machine to creating machine groups and accessing the troubleshooting tool to export the service logs and the machine's configuration into a single file, all of these directly from the machine-runtime app. Microsoft has provided a good amount of information for everything about machine and machine groups including registering your machine needed for calling Desktop Flows in the given link: https://learn.microsoft.com/en-us/power-automate/desktop-flows/manage-machines.

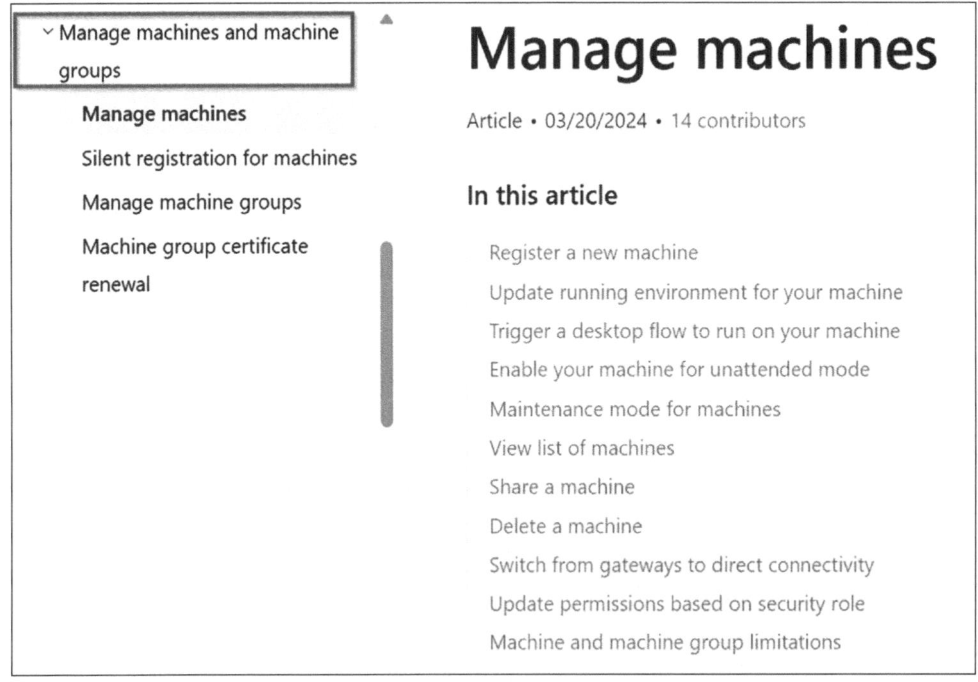

Figure 9.2: *Learning resource on Machine and Machine groups*

A vital point to be aware of is that in the case of multiple machines (groups), the platform can perform a load balancing by automatically running the Desktop Flow on another machine while one is occupied with another bot, thus distributing the load across machines.

Creating a Desktop Flow Connection

Once a machine is created, you need to establish a connection with that machine.

There are two different ways to connect Cloud Flows with the machines or machine groups, namely **Connect with username and password** and **Connect with sign-in for attended runs**. We will be focusing more on the interaction between Cloud Flows and Desktop Flows, so for the configuration, setup, pre-requisites, and limitations refer to the following link where both of the approaches are explained.

https://learn.microsoft.com/en-us/power-automate/desktop-flows/desktop-flow-connections

In this link, you may come across terms, such as attended and unattended runs. Although we will be going through them as a separate topic in this same chapter, but for now you must know that there are different modes of automation execution based on the human involvement required. In simple words, the unattended runs involve bots that operate independently without human intervention on dedicated machines and attended runs involve bots that work with human involvement, generally on the user's machine.

This was information about the setup and configuration required for calling a Desktop Flow from the Cloud and now we can see what the **three types of Cloud Flows** are, as shown in *Figure* 9.1 from where Desktop Flows are called.

While calling the Desktop Flow within a Cloud Flow, you will get to select the already populated list of connections, machines, and groups that were configured earlier. Once these parameters are configured, the tool will show the list of Desktop Flows in that environment and ask the user to set the run mode (attended/unattended) and the priority of the Desktop Flow which determines the order of its execution when multiple bots are run.

How to build Cloud Flows is not our intent and focus of this book, but we will go through the three types of Cloud Flows in a nutshell, so you know when to call Desktop Flows using which type of Cloud Flows.

You can get a direction for triggering Desktop Flows from the Cloud via the following documentation link from Microsoft.

https://learn.microsoft.com/en-us/power-automate/desktop-flows/trigger-desktop-flows.

Via an Instant Cloud Flow

An Instant Cloud Flow, as the term suggests, is a way to run the Cloud Flow at any instance as and when required at will. These must be run manually and do not kick off automatically.

A Desktop Flow is called from within any of these three types via the **"Run a flow built with Power Automate for desktop"** connector marked in *Figure* 9.3. The following figure uses a **"Manually trigger a flow"** type of trigger which implies an Instant Cloud Flow. When you need to run the Desktop Flows at will (from the Cloud), then this is the Cloud Flow to go for.

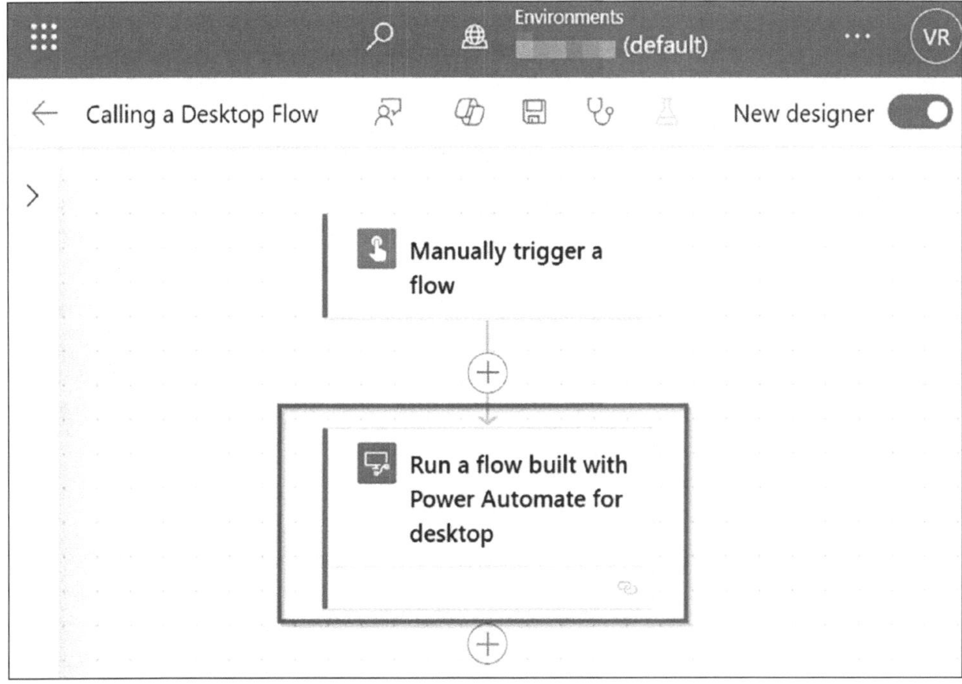

Figure 9.3: *Connector for calling Desktop Flows*

Via a Scheduled Cloud Flow

A Scheduled Cloud Flow runs on a scheduled basis. This Flow automatically starts based on a specified date and time configured in the Flow. If you would like to run your Desktop Flows on scheduled intervals, then this is the Cloud Flow to go for. The Recurrence trigger indicates a Scheduled Cloud Flow and has parameters to be configured like the ones seen on the left-hand side of the figure given here.

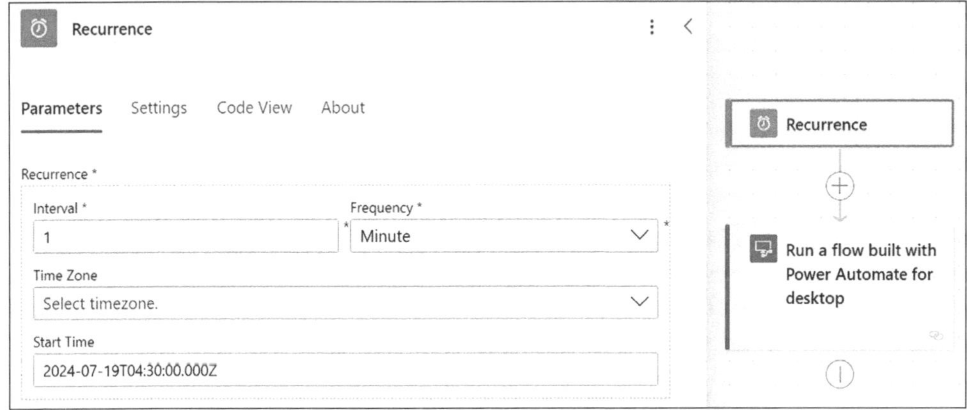

Figure 9.4: *Scheduled Cloud Flow calling a Desktop Flow*

Via an Automated Cloud Flow

An automated Cloud Flow runs by itself based on a specific event called triggers. These triggers could be anything ranging from a new email arriving in the Inbox when a SharePoint item is created, when a OneDrive file is created, when a team member is added to Teams, and so on. These triggers are available to be configured while designing the Cloud Flows. So, for example, if your Desktop Flow processes emails as soon as they arrive in the Inbox, then this is the type of Flow to go for.

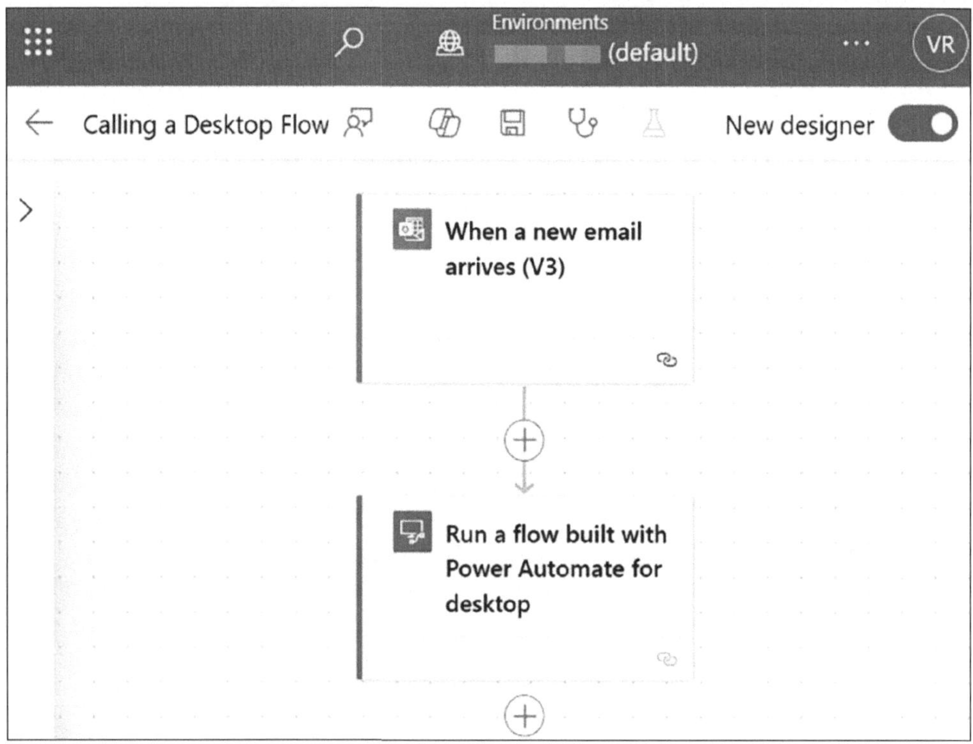

Figure 9.5: *Automated Cloud Flow calling a Desktop Flow*

Remember the topic "*Input/Output variables*" from "*Chapter 4: Essential Elements of a Desktop Flow*" where we talked about how the interaction between Desktop Flows and Cloud Flows happens via these types of variables. If you create an **`"Input variable"`** in your Desktop Flow, it will automatically show up as a parameter to be filled in the **`"Run a flow built with Power Automate for desktop"`** connector (above figure) when you select that Desktop Flow in the connector. Likewise, if you create an **`"Output variable"`** in the Desktop Flow, you will be able to retrieve that variable value in this connector in the Cloud Flow for any further processing.

Note that you will see only the list of those Desktop Flows in the connector to which you have access, and the **`"Environment"`** should be the same where the Desktop and Cloud Flows are built so that the interaction can happen. For Desktop Flows, we have already seen how and where to select the environment via the "*Environments and Tenants*" topic of "*Chapter 2: Getting into Action with* PAD". For Cloud Flows, refer to the wording **"Environments"** at the top portion of the preceding figure which is also available on the home screen when you launch the Cloud portal.

After going through the above sections and topics, if you questioned yourself when to use Cloud Flows, then,

- use it when you want to run your RPA automation (Desktop Flows) on an automated trigger as mentioned above,
- or on a schedule,
- or when you want to use a combination of Cloud Flows plus Desktop Flows (that is, when features of Cloud Flows are not available in Desktop Flows and features of Desktop Flows are not available in Cloud Flows).

No matter what, during your Desktop Flow automation journey, you are indeed going to need the Cloud portal, especially in enterprise automation because the Cloud portal is the orchestrator for the Desktop Flows (and the Cloud Flows). By that what it means is deploying, automated triggering, scheduling, managing, and monitoring of Desktop Flows are done only through the Cloud portal.

Deploying Desktop Flows

In enterprise-grade automation, there are generally three environments, such as, DEV, TEST, and PROD, while some organizations have even additional ones. Now that you have built your Desktop Flows in the DEV environment, what's next? How do you move it or deploy it to the next level environment? This is done through **"Solutions"** from the Cloud Flows portal.

"Solutions" are a packaged zip file of all the components you have used in building the automation, and they are a way of achieving Application Lifecycle Management (ALM) for Power Automate.

The following steps are taken to deploy the bots from one environment to another:

1. When you launch the Cloud portal, you will see a list of tabs on the left where the "**Solutions**" tab is available, as shown in the following figure. If you do not see the tab, then click **"More"** and pin it.

2. Via this tab, you create a Solution from the **"New solution"** button by providing a name to it. You will also be asked to select or create a new publisher. Refer to the link https://learn.microsoft.com/en-us/power-platform/alm/solution-concepts-alm#solution-publisher to understand what a publisher is and why you should create a new publisher and not use the default one. Click **"Create"** to create a Solution.

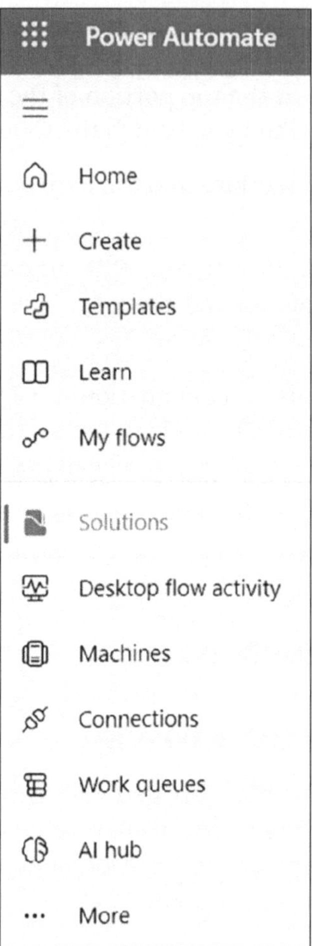

Figure 9.6: *Solutions tab on the Cloud portal*

3. This will open a screen as follows where you would use the **"Add existing"**, **"Automation"**, and **"Desktop flow"** menus to add your existing Flow to this newly created Solution. Note that even before building your Desktop Flow, you could also use the **"New"** menu to create a Desktop Flow from there so that whatever Flows you build via this option will be automatically included in this Solution.

Through this screen, you also add any other Power Platform tools and/or components to the Solution in case you are using them, for example, Cloud Flows, AI Builder, Power Apps, and so on.

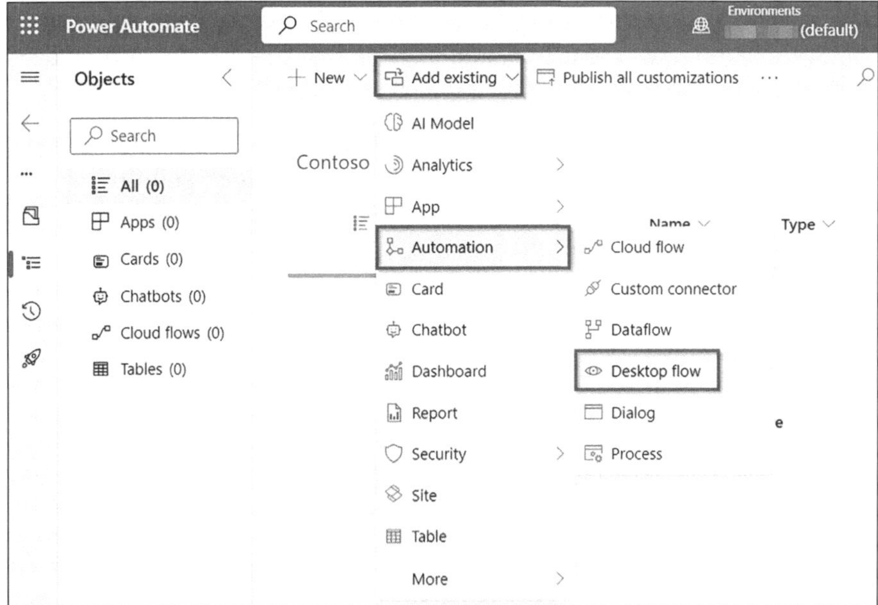

Figure 9.7: *Adding an existing Flow to the Solution*

4. Once those are added, they will be counted in the list of objects based on what you have chosen, as shown in the following figure. Click the back arrow marked in the figure.

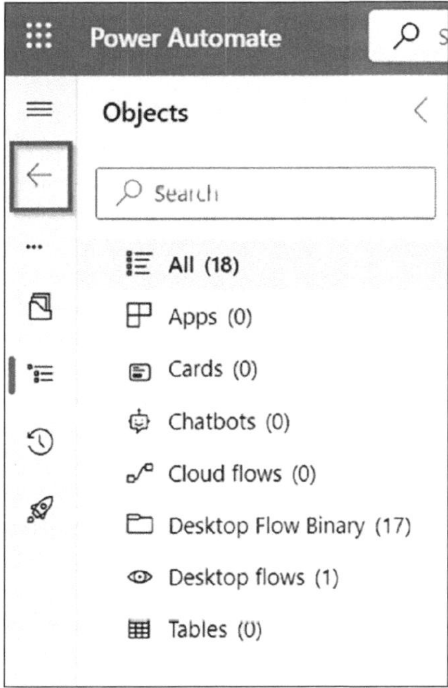

Figure 9.8: *Components added to the Solution*

5. This will take you back to the page where you created the Solution (the one in Step 2) and now, the list will include the one that you just created. Tick the appropriate Solution, click on **"Export Solution"**, and click **"Next"**.

6. At the final step, you will be asked to Export the Solution as a **Managed** or an **Unmanaged** Solution. For reference, an unmanaged solution is a Solution that is a work in progress and still under development and is not meant for distribution. When an unmanaged solution is complete and you are ready to move it from one environment to another, then export it as a managed solution. If you would like to know more, then the same link for **"Publisher"** has details on it.

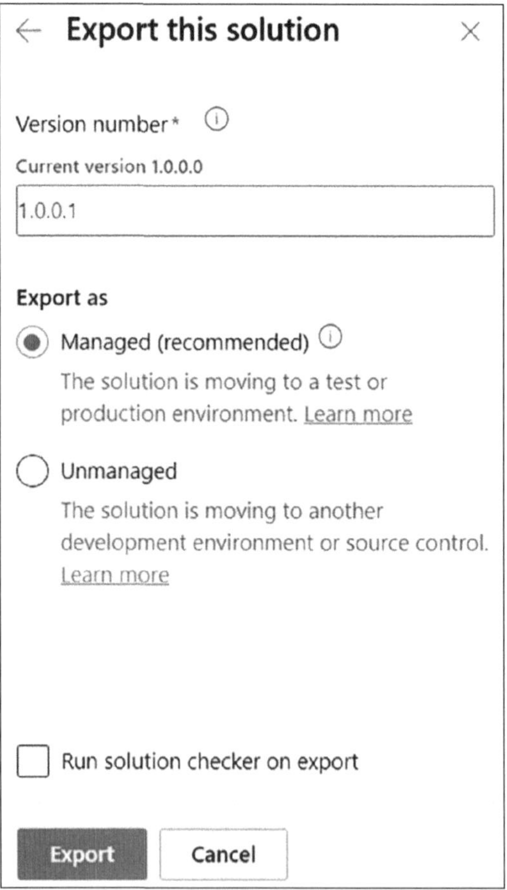

Figure 9.9: *Export as managed or unmanaged solution*

7. When the exporting process is complete, you will see a message and an option to download, which will be a packaged Zip file of all the objects of the Solution.

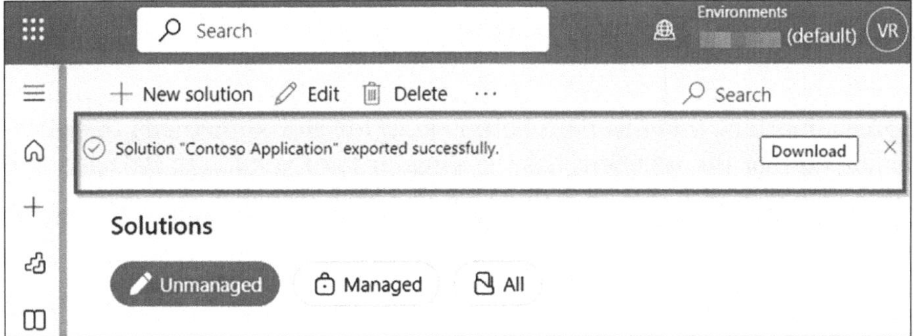

Figure 9.10: *Export message and option to download the solution*

8. Download this Zip file and save it to a location for future reference of the file.
9. Change the environment as intended via the marked arrow. In the same **"Solutions"** tab, use the **"Import solution"** option as shown and import the Zip file.

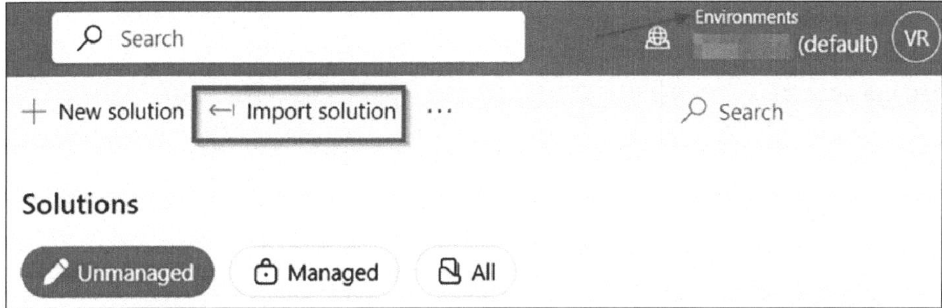

Figure 9.11: *Changing environment and Importing the solution*

After the import process is complete you should see the Solution imported in the new environment. The Desktop Flow imported via this process will now be available in the PAD tool when you choose the appropriate environment.

Manage Desktop Flows and Their Access

Managing the Desktop Flows involves activities like seeing the list of your Desktop Flows and their details like the run history and information of every run, the websites and applications used in the Flows, managing the access like editing and deleting user permissions, and so on. As a starting point, go to **"Desktop flows"** under **"My flows"** tab on the left navigation items of the Cloud portal and visit the page and other various sections to see what all information is made available.

Other various sections of the Cloud portal are explained via the following official documentation:

https://learn.microsoft.com/en-us/power-automate/desktop-flows/manage

Sharing Desktop Flows

There are three ways that Microsoft has provided to share your Desktop Flows with others. An important thing to note here is that, for all the methods of sharing, it is recommended that the recipient has the same or later version of PAD as the person sharing the Flow, or else they won't be able to edit it or may face challenges in doing so.

- **Via the Share option of Cloud Portal:**

  This option works only within the same environment. Here are the steps to use this approach:

  1. In the Cloud portal, go to **"`My flows`"** and then **"`Desktop flows`"**.
  2. Tick the Flow that you would like to share and then click **"`Share`"**.
  3. In the **"`Add people`"** box, start typing the name of the person(s) you would like to share with and select them (marked in the following figure). You can grant either of the two types of accesses to anyone, namely User or Co-owner, both of which are explained in short in the following figure:

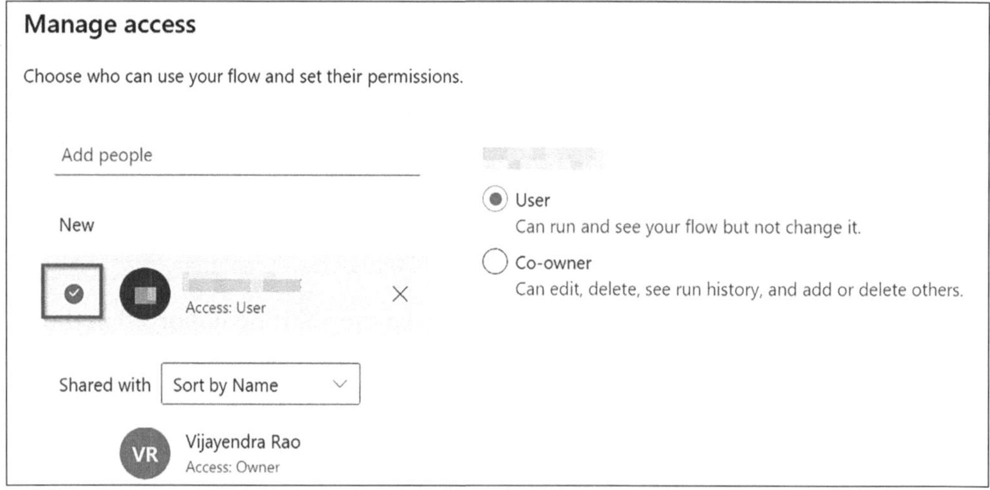

Figure 9.12: *Sharing Desktop Flows via Share option*

  4. Once done for all the required members, Click **"`Save`".**

- **Via the Export Solution of Cloud Portal:**

  In the previous section of "*Deploying Desktop Flows*", you have exported a Zip file that contains the Desktop Flow and can be sent to another person, who can then import the Zip file into their environment.

- **Via copy-pasting in the Desktop tool:**

  The preceding two options require the right account and license for the sender and the recipient to log in to the Cloud portal and use the Share option or the Solutions approach. Following is an option that can be done via the PAD tool itself.

Follow the given steps to achieve the same:

1. In the PAD tool, Select all the Actions from the Workspace and Copy them (*Ctrl* + A, *Ctrl* + C). Then Paste them in a text editor (*Ctrl* + V) like Notepad and save it as a .TXT file. You can also use the **"`Edit`"** menu of PAD for the copying.

   Only one Subflow can be copied at a time. So, you need to create separate .TXT files for each Subflow after doing it for the Main Flow. Rename the files such that they have the same name as the Subflow name for the recipient's use in Step 3. You can name the text file having the Main Flow as "Main" (or anything that would make it clear for you and the recipient).

2. Send the .TXT file(s) to the recipient.

3. The recipient should Copy the code from the text editor (*Ctrl* + C) and Paste it into the Workspace of a new Flow (*Ctrl* + V). The Flow Actions will be generated as soon as the Paste is performed.

   Rename the Subflow names as the file names, so that any calls made to the Subflows will not fail.

This option comes with certain caveats and *not* everything gets shared.
The following chart will help you to ensure what gets copied or not, and what additional tasks need to be done after copy-pasting the Flows:

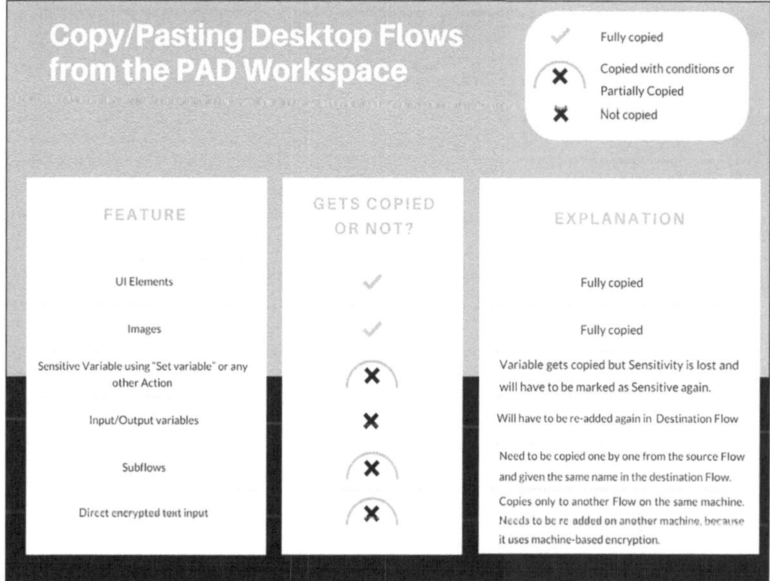

Figure 9.13: *Feature wise comparison while copy-pasting Flows*

Two items that need some understanding in the preceding figure are the Sensitive variables and Direct encrypted text input.

As you are aware that a variable is generated from either the **"Set variable"** Action or from any of the other Actions as an Output produced, or even after manually adding it as Input or Output from the **"Variables"** pane. These variables can be marked as Sensitive from the ellipsis button in the **"Variables"** pane. When Sensitive variables other than Input/Output ones are copy-pasted into the destination Flow, the variables get copied but their Sensitivity is lost and should be re-marked again. In the case of the Sensitivity of the Input/Output variables, the variable itself has to be re-created since they do not get copy-pasted and then additionally their Sensitivity has to be re-configured.

There are some Actions that have an option to add a **"Direct encrypted text input"** like the **"Send keys"**. Refer to the following figure. Text input entered as direct encrypted only works on the machine where it was initially added. This is due to the machine-specific encryption used for such inputs. After sharing the Flow, if it is opened on a different machine, the input text will not be valid and will have to be re-entered.

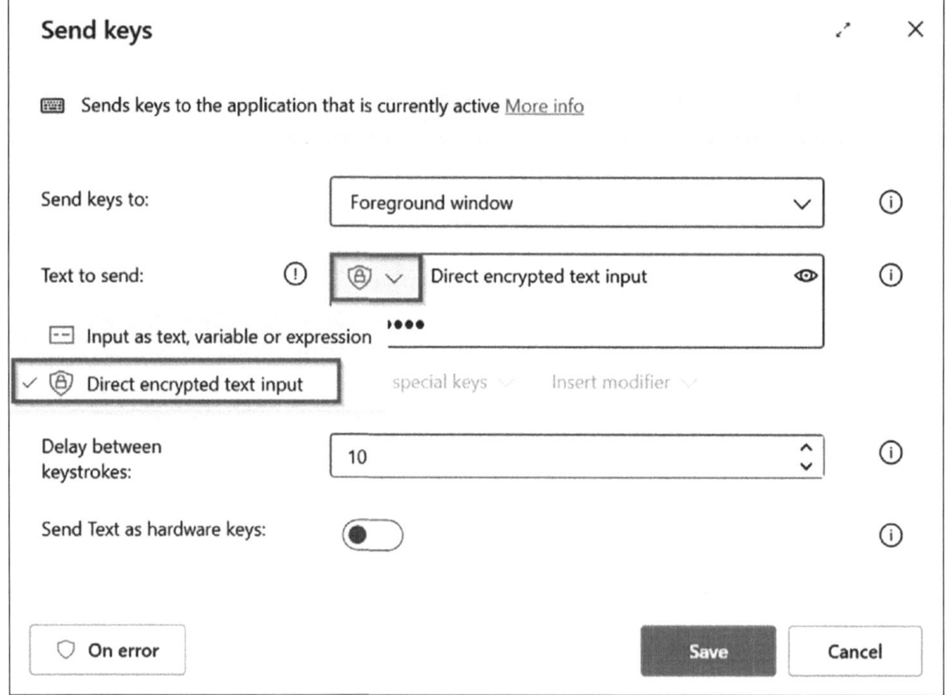

Figure 9.14: *Direct encrypted text input option*

This concludes the main topic on how to utilize the Cloud Portal and the Power Platform. For the Desktop Flows, there are other very good uses of the Power Platform like using the **"AI hub"** seen as one of the tabs on the portal (*Figure* 9.6). To give you a scenario, it can be used for document processing like the Cloud Flows can read an email as soon as it arrives with a specific subject and a specific type of attachment, download the attachment, extract values from the attachment using models from the AI hub, call and pass the values to the Desktop Flow which inserts the values into any website or application, create an Excel report, and so on.

Several Cloud Flow connectors are also now being made available as Actions in the Desktop Flows, such as SharePoint, OneDrive, Dataverse, Excel Online for Business, Word Online for Business, Teams, and so forth.

There are other usages of the Cloud portal in regard to the Desktop Flows and we will see them in the upcoming topics of this chapter.

Work Queues

In simple words, a Work Queue is a queue of **"Work"**. Here, the **"Work"** refers to a Workitem or a Case. For better clarity, consider an Excel having 100 records and each of them needs some kind of processing. If each of these records is added to the Work Queue and then used for further processing, each record of the Queue denotes a **"Workitem"** or a **"Case"**.

Work Queues are used by the bots where a considerable volume of data has to be processed and generally in RPA automation, we work with a large volume of data, which means Work Queues can be used everywhere. They not only assist in workload management but also are essential for enhancing automation efficiency and scalability. They allow prioritization of queue items, ensuring that high-priority items are addressed first, for instance, to meet a particular SLA (Service Level Agreement). A good example of SLAs can be seen in a ticketing system where they should be completed within a stipulated time or at least accepted and assigned within a given time. A bot can very well go ahead and click on an **"Accept"** button on the ticketing tool or select a team member's name from a dropdown and **"Assign"** it to them.

Items in the Queue can be also deferred to a later stage for processing and an example for this is to complete a particular financial transaction at a later stage after receiving some kind of input. Queues can be used for reporting purposes too.

Using work queues enhances bot utilization and optimizes the required number of bots to complete the items. Meaning, you can have multiple bots working on the items of the work queue thus, catering to timely completion of **"Work"**. Please do not confuse the load balancing using multiple machines mentioned in the topic of "*Manage Machines and Machine Groups*" with the workload management using Work Queues.

Imagine, in the earlier scenario of 100 queue items, if the bot stops after 10 items, the Work Queue will have the capability to tell which items were processed successfully, which ones failed and which ones are yet to be processed. Thus, they also give a centralized view to the users of the bot. They can not only track the success and failure status of items but also understand the reasons for failures, especially when errors are properly logged during bot development.

Work Queues can generally be used in two ways. Consider a bot reading the list of open tickets from a source system like ServiceNow. The bot reads the **entire** list and adds it to the Work Queue. The bot will then pick each of the tickets one by one from the Work Queue and process them as per the requirement. This is the recommended approach, but wherever this is not possible the bot could read **one** open ticket from ServiceNow, add it to the Work Queue and then process that ticket as per requirement.

If you go to the PAD tool and see the list of Actions, you will find a diamond icon next to the **"`Work queue`"** group of Actions indicating that it is a premium feature.

Let's check which Actions do we have and how Work Queues are used in Desktop Flows.

For the topic of Work Queue based Flow development in PAD, a concept of **"`Dispatcher`"** and **"`Performer`"** can be made use of for simplicity purposes. As their name says, a **"`Dispatcher`"** Flow is responsible to "dispatch" or add items to the Work Queue, whereas a **"`Performer`"** is accountable for "performing" or processing those items of the Queue. These two types could either be two separate Desktop Flows or even one Flow having each of them as Subflows. You can build your own Queue based Flow framework and choose either of these approaches based on your requirement. This will be determined by how you want to navigate the logic of the Flow, based on the automation scenario and the availability of licensing. The reason licensing is mentioned here is that, as of this writing, there is a "per-bot" licensing plan, and this means licensing will be required based on the number of bots used.

In our case, let's use the latter approach of having two Subflows within the same Flow.

Out intent will be to read the records of an Excel file, add them to the Work Queue, and see how the items can be processed from the Queue. You will find the Excel in the GitHub folder of this chapter by the name **"`Chapter 9 Work Queues.xlsx`"**.

Follow the given steps to achieve the same:

1. The way to create a Work Queue is via the Cloud portal. Launch the portal and login if required. Use the same account and environment in the Cloud that you are using in the Desktop Flows. Go to the **"`Work Queues`"** from the tabs on the left (*Figure* 9.6) and if not seen there, then click the **"`More`"** button and pin it for future ease. Click on the **"`New`"** button, give a name to the queue and create it. In our case, the name of the queue is **`WQContoso`**.

2. This will open a screen giving some details about the queue that you just created. Click on **"`See all`"** to bring up a screen as given here.

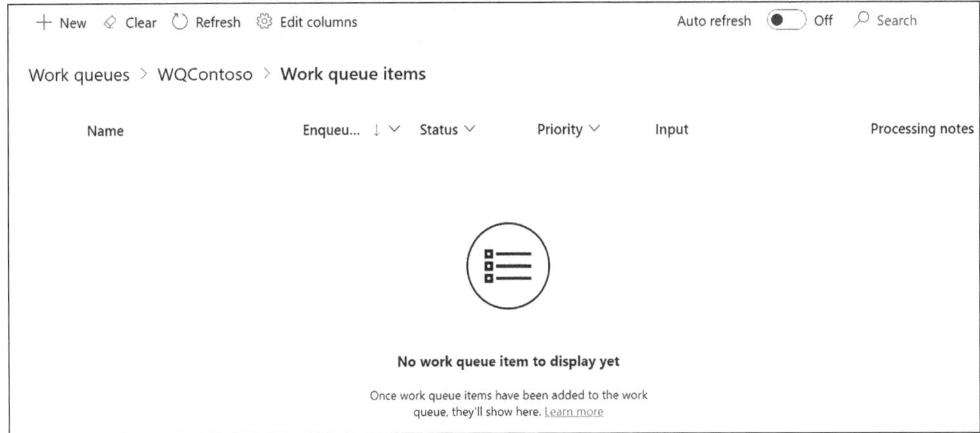

Figure 9.15: *Work queue items screen*

3. Our queue is manually created. We should now add items to this queue and that will be done via Desktop Flows. Go to the PAD tool.

4. Create a new Desktop Flow, add a Subflow, and name it as **`QueueDispatcher`**. Add Actions to launch the provided Excel (see *Figure* 9.16), read all values from it, and close it. Add a **"`For each`"** loop to iterate through the data from the sheet.

	A	B	C	D	E	F	G
1	Account	Date	Contact	USD Amount	Status	Converted Amount	ID
2	Account70	7/5/2024	user441@mail.com	208.46	Paid		
3	Account11	7/3/2024	user378@email.com		Uninvoiced		
4	Account25	7/1/2024	user510@email.com	797.2	Uninvoiced		
5	Account43	7/7/2024	user418@mail.com		Invoiced		
6	Account8	7/2/2024	user6@email.com	816.72	Invoiced		
7	Account60	7/5/2024	user443@email.com	431.41	Paid		
8	Account16	7/1/2024	user261@example.com		Paid		
9	Account9	7/4/2024	user786@email.com	648.09	Paid		
10	Account96	7/6/2024	user641@example.com		Uninvoiced		
11	Account54	7/1/2024	user442@mail.com	276.05	Uninvoiced		

Figure 9.16: *Sample input file*

The blank values in the column for the amount are intentional, where the queue will not be processing those items and marking them as failure. Remember to read the cell contents as text and the first row as column headers in the Excel Action. The Subflow built so far looks as follows:

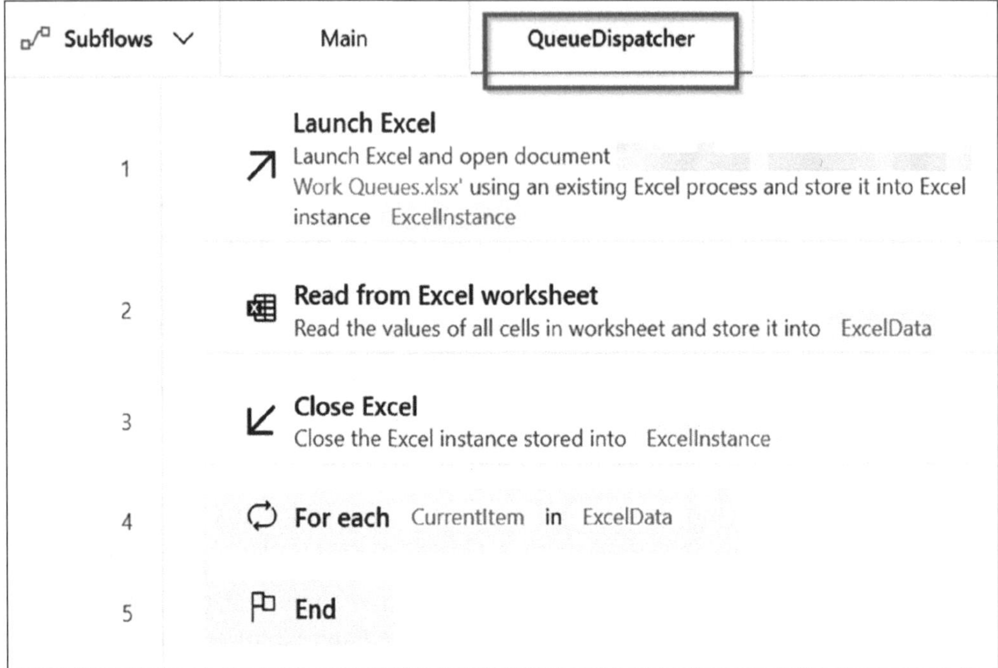

***Figure 9.17:** Dispatcher Subflow built so far*

5. Drag and drop the **"Add Work queue item"** Action inside the loop.

   Referring the following figure, add the parameters as follows:

   a. **Work queue**: This dropdown will show the list of all the accessible Work Queues created in the Cloud portal just like the way we did. Select the appropriate one (in our case **WQContoso**).

   b. **Status**: Can be **"Queued"** or **"On hold"**. Since we are queuing the items, mark it as **"Queued"**.

   c. **Priority**: A priority of "**High**", **"Normal"**, and **"Low"** can be set here to tell the Flow to process the items accordingly.

   d. **Name:** What you pass here will be used to identify a particular work queue item. We can use the Account in this case that is coming from the Excel in the form of **%CurrentItem['Account']%**. We will see shortly where this **"Name"** field will be populated and is visible.

   e. **Input**: This parameter is the data that the queue will be processing. A single value can also be passed to this parameter, but since we need all the columns of the Excel to be added and processed by the queue, we will add them all. A comma-separated format can be used here but adding it in JSON becomes more developer-friendly and you will see why in a moment.

```
{
"Account":"%CurrentItem['Account']%",
"Date":"%CurrentItem['Date']%",
"Contact":"%CurrentItem['Contact']%",
"Amount":"%CurrentItem['USD Amount']%",
"Status":"%CurrentItem['Status']%",
}
```

Since JSON contains a key-value pair, we have added a hard-coded *key* followed by its dynamic *value* coming from the Excel via the Datatable.

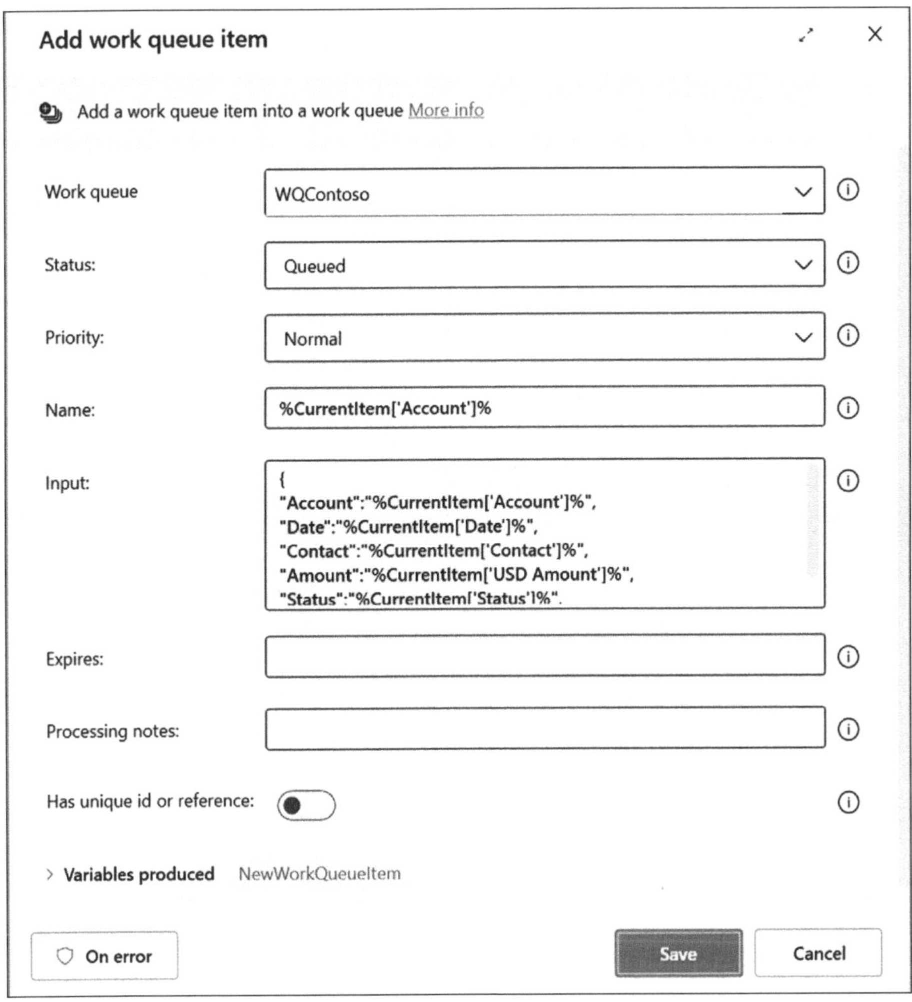

Figure 9.18: *The Add Work queue item action*

f. **Expires**: This parameter depends on the automation scenario you are trying to build. Certain items (for example, financial transactions, tickets) may no longer be valid after a certain date and time and hence may need to be added into the Queue with an expiry date and time.

g. **Processing notes**: These can be any comments or notes as the items are added to the queue or even after any processing occurs on a queue item using another Action in PAD (**"Update work queue item processing notes"**). The comments here can be, such as **New entry**, **Contact via email**, **Invoice Uploaded, Escalate to customer service**, and so on.

h. **Has unique id or reference**: This toggle when enabled will ask to provide a unique id value for the queue item. For example, if the Excel we are reading had a unique Sr. No. column, it can be used in this parameter. You could even use something like the Account we have in the Excel if you think that is always going to be unique. Since this is optional, leave it disabled for our exercise.

6. The **"Dispatcher"** is ready as follows. You don't need to save the Excel as we haven't made any modifications to it. It can even be opened as Read-only while launching it.

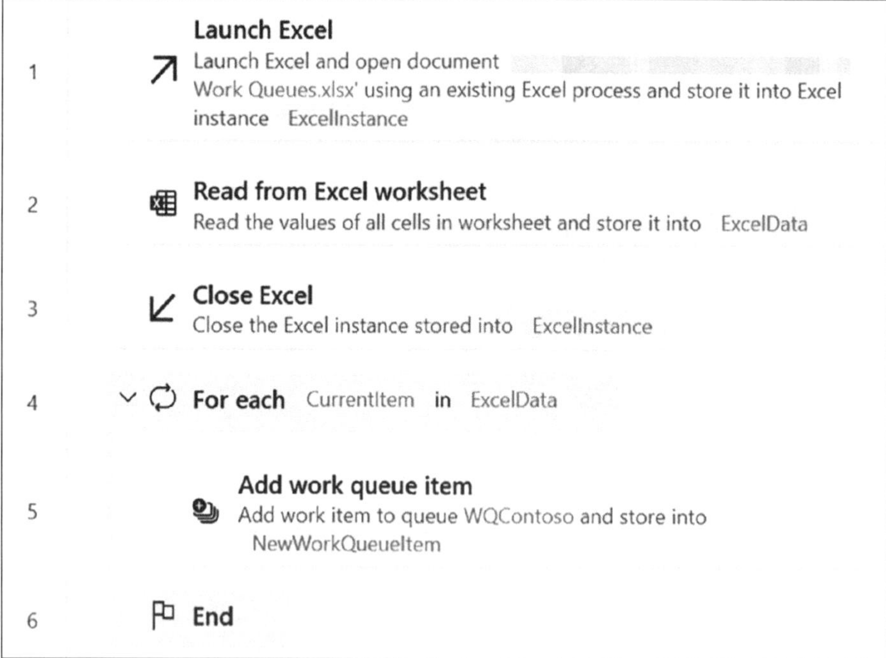

Figure 9.19: *The updated Dispatcher Subflow*

7. Add the corresponding Action to call the **QueueDispatcher** Subflow from the **"Main"** and then run the Subflow (you can use the **"Run from here"** debugging feature). On the Cloud portal, you will see that all the records of the Excel are loaded into the Work Queue, as shown in the following figure.

You will find that work items have been created as per the Action we configured in the previous step.

If you are not seeing any data yet, use the **"Refresh"** button seen at the top section. The **"Edit columns"** can be used to configure additional columns of the queue in the following view. Check it out to see which additional columns are available.

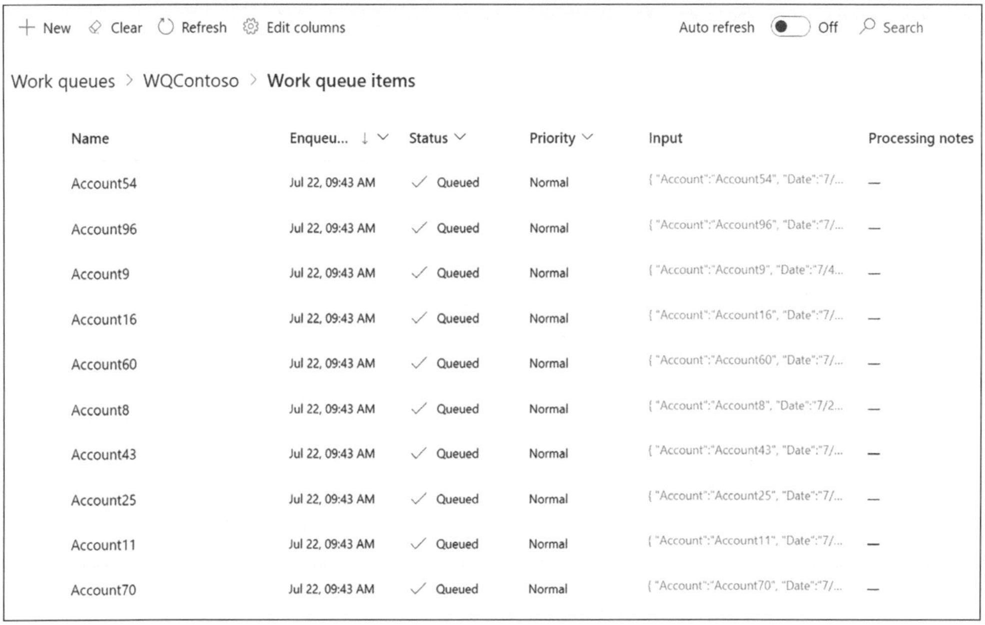

+ New Clear Refresh Edit columns Auto refresh Off Search

Work queues > WQContoso > Work queue items

Name	Enqueu... ↓	Status	Priority	Input	Processing notes
Account54	Jul 22, 09:43 AM	✓ Queued	Normal	{ "Account":"Account54", "Date":"7/...	–
Account96	Jul 22, 09:43 AM	✓ Queued	Normal	{ "Account":"Account96", "Date":"7/...	–
Account9	Jul 22, 09:43 AM	✓ Queued	Normal	{ "Account":"Account9", "Date":"7/4...	–
Account16	Jul 22, 09:43 AM	✓ Queued	Normal	{ "Account":"Account16", "Date":"7/...	–
Account60	Jul 22, 09:43 AM	✓ Queued	Normal	{ "Account":"Account60", "Date":"7/...	–
Account8	Jul 22, 09:43 AM	✓ Queued	Normal	{ "Account":"Account8", "Date":"7/2...	–
Account43	Jul 22, 09:43 AM	✓ Queued	Normal	{ "Account":"Account43", "Date":"7/...	–
Account25	Jul 22, 09:43 AM	✓ Queued	Normal	{ "Account":"Account25", "Date":"7/...	–
Account11	Jul 22, 09:43 AM	✓ Queued	Normal	{ "Account":"Account11", "Date":"7/...	–
Account70	Jul 22, 09:43 AM	✓ Queued	Normal	{ "Account":"Account70", "Date":"7/...	–

Figure 9.20: *Output of the Dispatcher*

Be noted that we are creating the **"Dispatcher"** and instantly running it only to view its output for demonstration purposes. In a real-world bot scenario, the running of the **"Dispatcher"** can be followed by the **"Performer"** one after the other so that one adds items to the queue and the other processes them. Let's go ahead and build the **"Performer"**.

8. Create a new Subflow and name it as **QueuePerformer**. The Action to process work queue items is the **"Process work queue items"**, so drag and drop the same. This Action creates a loop-like structure with an **"End"** Action (*Figure 9.23*) and the output variable of this Action needed for our further reference is **WorkQueueItem**.

9. When the Flow is running, the **WorkQueueItem** variable will hold the JSON that we had passed (via the Dispatcher) in the **.Value** property as marked below.

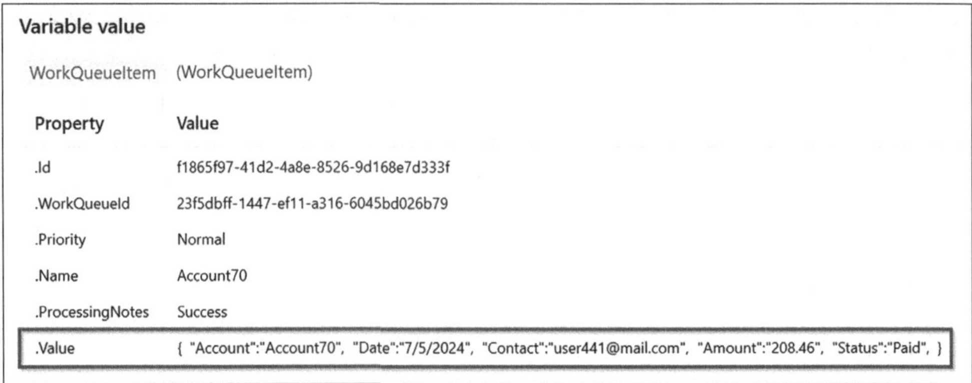

Figure 9.21: *Value property of WorkQueueItem*

10. Since this is a JSON, we need to read its values and as you already know this is done easily with the help of the **"Convert JSON to custom object"** Action. Drag and drop it inside the loop of the queue processing and pass the JSON parameter as **%WorkQueueItem.Value%** coming from the preceding figure.

11. After this Action performs the JSON conversion, the output variable **JsonAsCustomObject** resembles as follows, where each of the columns and their values can be easily extracted using **%JsonAsCustomObject['Account']%** for example. Hence we used the JSON format as opposed to comma-separated values which would have needed splitting and using other Text Actions to get the desired values.

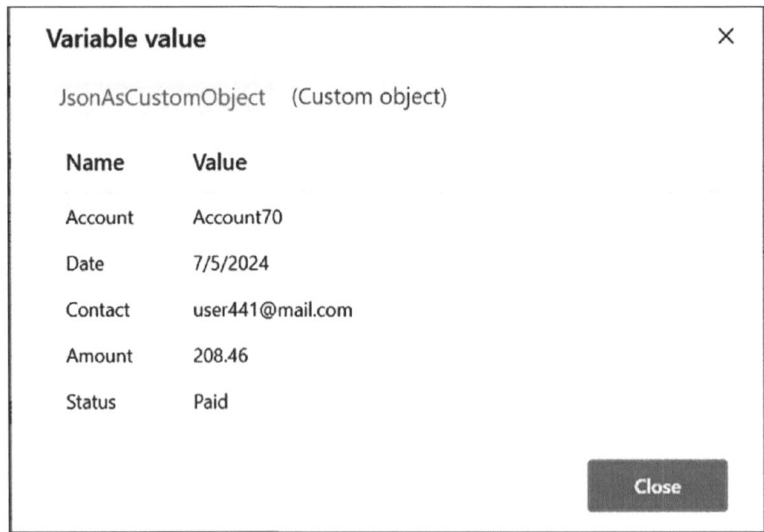

Figure 9.22: *Values after JSON conversion*

After the conversion, this is the place where you would read all the values from the JSON, such as the Account, Date and the others in separate variables, and then call the Subflows you will be building to insert data in the Contoso application. We will use a display message to see one of its outputs, that is, the Account where we use **%JsonAsCustomObject['Account']%**. Given here is the output and how the Flow looks so far. The breakpoint to the **"End"** Action is to process only one item of the queue and see its output.

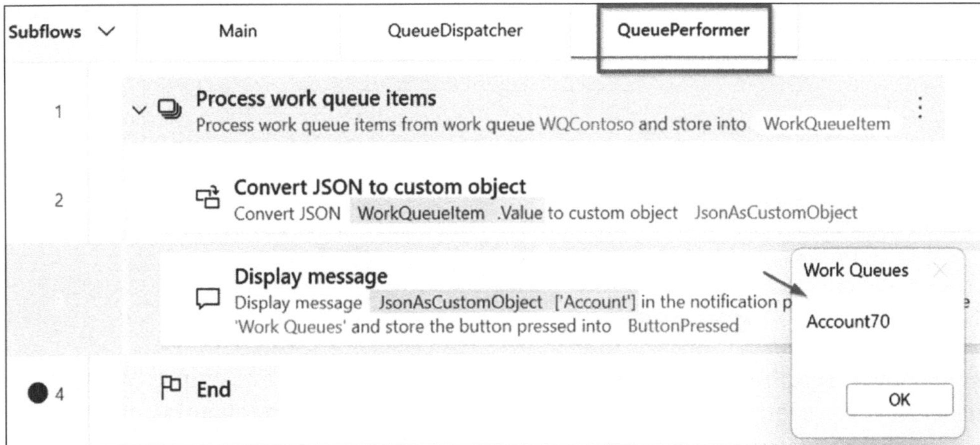

***Figure 9.23:** First Account extracted from the queue*

Once again, to emphasize, in line number 3 we are only displaying the Account of the first item of the queue. But in a real bot, this section of the Flow is where you would call other Subflows and take the necessary action, such as add the Account and other details on the Contoso application using Windows automation.

At this stage, if you visit the Work Queues on the portal for **Account70**, its Status is changed to **"Processing"** as this is the item of the queue being currently processed by the bot. The **Account70** shown in the first column is the **"Name"** parameter coming from the **"Add work queue item"** of *Figure 9.18*, which we mentioned earlier.

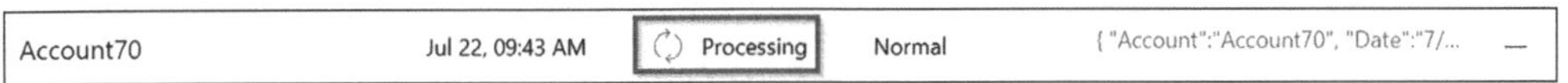

***Figure 9.24:** Status of queue item updated to Processing*

After the Account details are added to the Contoso application, the queue item needs updating with the corresponding Status depending on what happened, that is, whether it was successfully added or there was any failure. This is done by the **"Update work queue item"** Action.

12. Stop the Flow and drag and drop this Action after the display message of the preceding figure. Assuming this is a positive scenario, along with updating the Status to **"Processed"**, we will add a processing note as **"Success"**. Refer to the **Status** dropdown for the different options and this Action also has a toggle to clear any previously added notes.

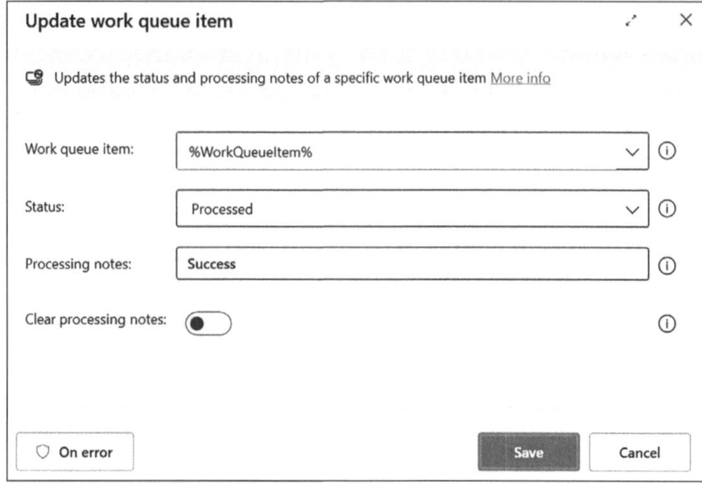

Figure 9.25: *The Update work queue item action*

As you have seen in the Amounts of *Figure* 9.11, some values are empty. We will treat this as an error scenario and the bot will not process this item (meaning, it should not be added to the Contoso application) and mark the Status and its notes accordingly.

13. This is done by a simple **"If"** statement where you check whether **%JsonAsCustomObject['Amount']%** is empty. If yes, then update the queue item as follows. The Status is marked as a Business exception whereas a customized processing note is added for our future understanding as to why the item was not processed. Business exceptions refer to those situations where a pre-defined business rule or condition is not met. In our case, we are assuming that the Amount is necessary to add the record to Contoso and it wasn't present, so we are marking it as a Business exception.

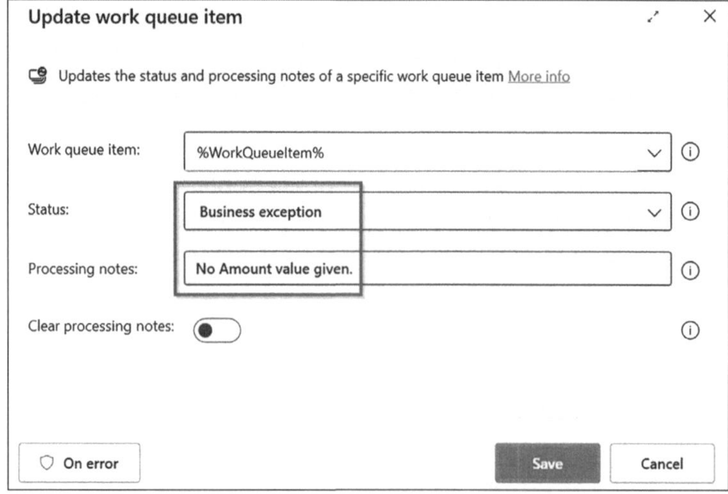

Figure 9.26: *Updating the queue item with an exception*

The **"Else"** condition will have the same success scenario as *Figure* 9.25.

The following is the complete Performer Subflow after the display message along with the **"If"** and **"Else"** conditional Actions.

Note that, now the body of the **"Else"** will have all the Actions related to calling Subflows to insert records into the Contoso application since that is the part where the Amount value is available. After the successful entry into the Contoso application, the bot should update the queue item as Success.

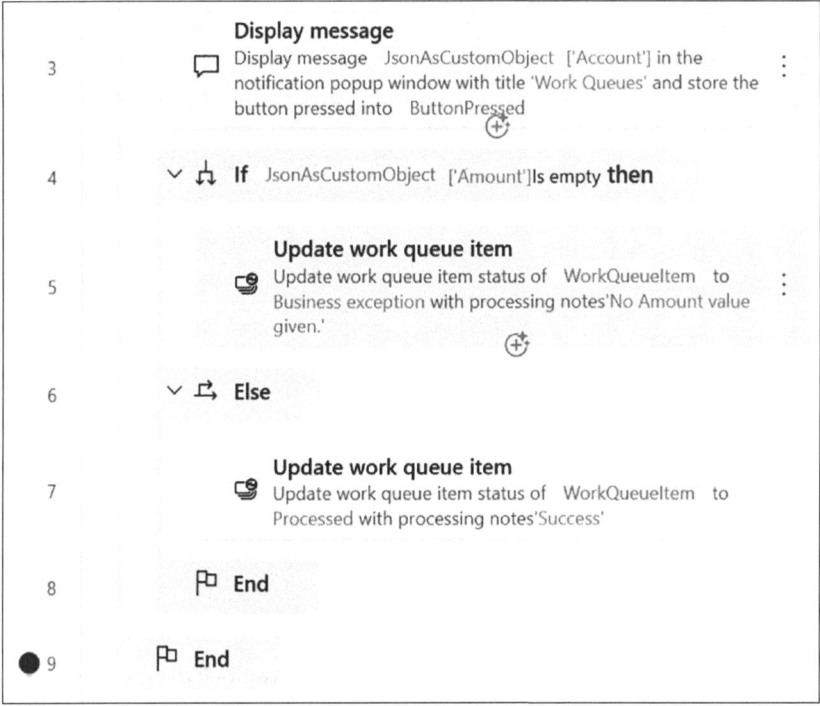

Figure 9.27: *The Performer Subflow*

When you use the **"Run from here"** option for the **"Performer"** Subflow and when complete, visit the Cloud portal. The queue items are as follows. This time **Account11** will be picked up because we had stopped the Flow while processing **Account70** (in Step 12) and the next queue item that was in **"Queued"** status was **Account11**. Since its Amount was empty, the queue is updated with Business exception and the processing notes column is shown in a way we had configured.

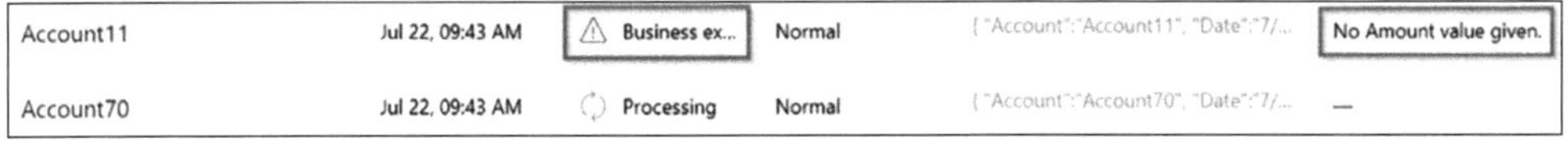

Figure 9.28: *Output with Exception scenario*

When the bot completes finishing all the items in the queue, this view would give a good picture to the users as to what happened with each of the records and take any appropriate steps, like correcting the data and processing the failed items.

"Requeue item with delay" is an Action to resubmit an item to the queue until a specified date and time that you configure in this Action. As specified earlier in the uses of Work Queue at the beginning of this topic, items can be deferred to a later date and time in those situations.

Something that you should be aware of is that a user can use the ellipsis button on the Cloud portal, and change the status of a queue item. These statuses can be changed only if they are in a certain previous state. For **Account70** in the preceding figure, you can change it to **"Processed"** and only then it can be changed to **"Queued".** Go ahead and try it out.

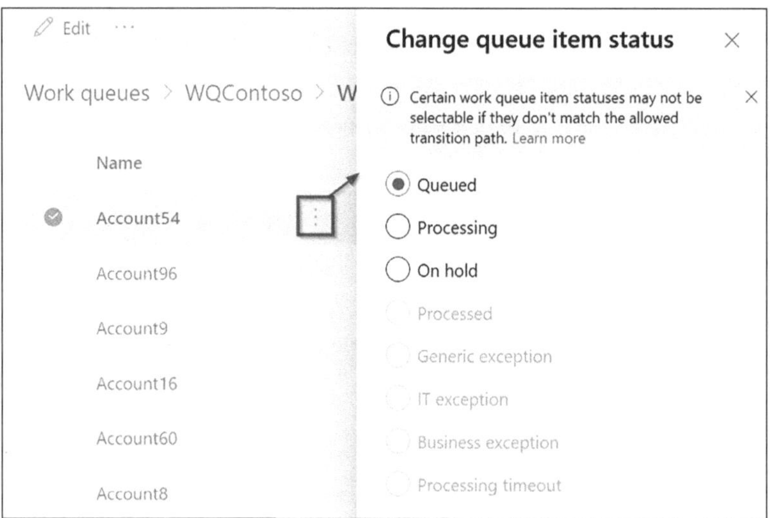

Figure 9.29: *Changing the status of queue items*

Our **"Main"** Flow with other Subflows is as follows:

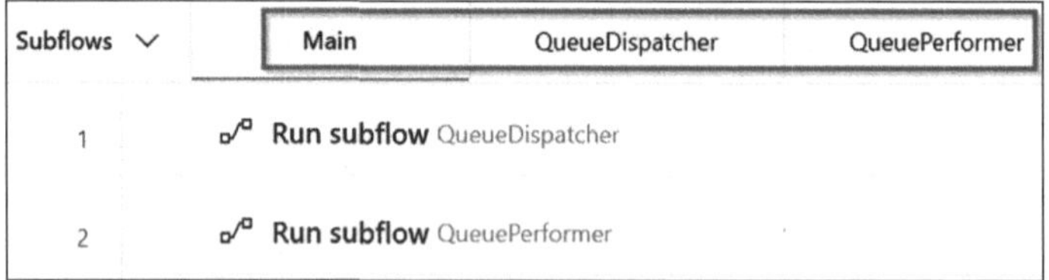

Figure 9.30: *Main flow with Subflows*

Practical exercise

Now that you are aware how to read the values, complete the remaining part of the Flow by reading the values from the Work Queue and inserting them into the Contoso application and even populating the **"Converted Amount"** and **"ID"** columns of *Figure* 9.16.

Remember that as mentioned in the topic of Subflows, you need to modularize the Flow into appropriate Subflows. Have separate Subflows for launching the Contoso application, another for adding records into the Contoso application coming from the Performer, a separate one for the currency conversion using Web automation and another one for closing the Contoso application. You can be more creative by adding the generation of Excel reports and sending emails using Outlook automation to this exercise, which of course, would be separate Subflows.

Error Handling

It goes without saying that error handling forms an integral part of not only RPA automation but also for any other tool or technology. Error handling is a "must" for every automation for proper functioning of the Flow by allowing a smooth navigation of the Flow in case of errors. The error handling should be designed in such a way that the Flow anticipates, detects, and manages the errors that may occur during the execution of the workflows. This not only increases the robustness and reliability of any automation but also minimizes downtime, improves accuracy, and maintains smoother operations in case unexpected issues occur.

There are two types of errors in PAD and generally in any other programming methodology too. They are design time errors and run time errors.

- **Design time errors**: This type of error is seen when the bot is being built or designed. These errors must be fixed before running the bot. The designer's **"Run"** button remains disabled until you fix these errors.

  Just try to set a variable with no value to get a design time error.

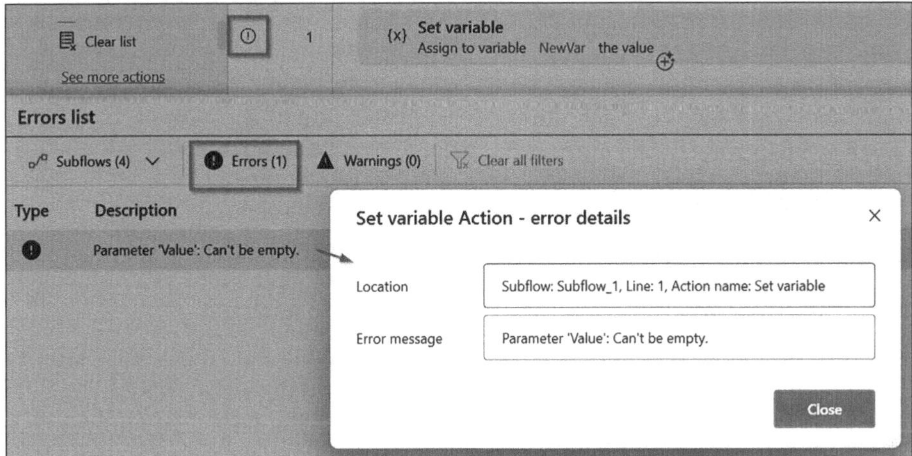

Figure 9.31: *Sample design time error*

- **Run time errors**: This type of error is seen when the bot is running. A bot might fail if it is trying to open an Excel file that does not exist, or while trying to access an UI element of a page that has not yet been loaded, and so on.

This type of error needs to be handled by the developer of the bot using error handling features for smoother functioning of the Flow. These can also be called as **Exceptions** and are further classified into two types which we will be going through.

Apart from errors, the PAD **"`Errors list`"** pane can also bring up Warnings. These are potential issues and may or may not stall the bot and are therefore shown by PAD as a warning. Meaning, they do not stop us from executing the Flow but are something to be alarmed about. In the following example, **`Subflow_1`** calls **`Subflow_2`**, and there is a call made from **`Subflow_2`** to **`Subflow_1`** and therefore shows up a warning stating that there is a recursive call and to have a look at it.

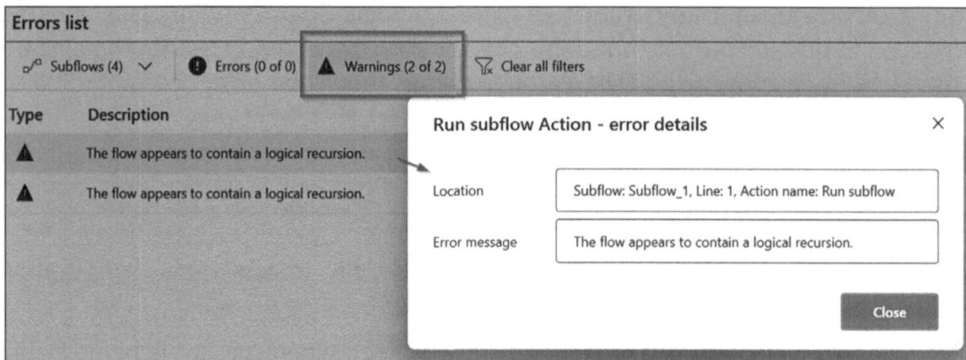

Figure 9.32: *Sample of warning*

Speaking of the two types of Exceptions, they are Business Exceptions and System Exceptions. There are other exceptions too, such as Data Exception, IOException, Memory Exception, and so on, but these can be classified as subcategories of the following two exception types. It is important to not make it overwhelming with too many exception types thus, making it difficult to identify and pin-point when it comes to troubleshooting. An exception category as either one of these mentioned here and with a valid exception reason stating the issue should suffice in that case.

- **Business Exceptions:**

  This type of exception is something that we have already seen in the Work Queues section where the Amount is not present and hence the bot does not insert data into the Contoso system. Another example is, let's say you are automating hospital records and would like to process only adult patients who are equal to or above the age of 18 years. If the data consists of patients less than the business rule of 18 years, then these records can go into business exception. Such exception records must be skipped and the Flow should move on to the next record without stopping the workflow. Also, these exceptions should not be retried or reprocessed because it makes no sense to retry the same record that does not have any Amount, as an example. A few other examples of business exceptions are Customer ID not found, Order quantity exceeds limit, missing mandatory inputs, date mismatch, and so forth.

- **System Exceptions:**

  This type of exception, as the name says, refers to errors that occur due to issues in the underlying system or application or the environment in which the automation is running. They could be hardware, software, or even network-related problems. For example, the bot has launched Outlook, but it becomes unresponsive or crashes and the bot is no longer able to read emails. It could also be that an operation takes longer than the predefined time limit to complete, such as waiting for a web page to load or a database query to execute, or even an API response. These exceptions can be retried in most cases, for example, by trying to call the API once again and see if it gives back a response this time or relaunching the web page to see if it loads again. In general, as a thumb rule, these exceptions can be retried three times, but this number can depend on the type of system issue and the automation you are trying to build. In any case, with or without a retry, the Flow should be able to record the issue, send a notification wherever possible, and smoothly exit for further manual intervention.

Power Automate Desktop has two ways of error handling, namely Action-level exception handling and Block-level exception handling. You can include either of them or both in your Flow depending on the scenario. Let us see what PAD has to offer us.

- **Action-level exception handling:**

  Error handling through this type is done at an Action level through the **"`On error`"** button, as shown in the figure. Almost all the PAD Actions have this option available.

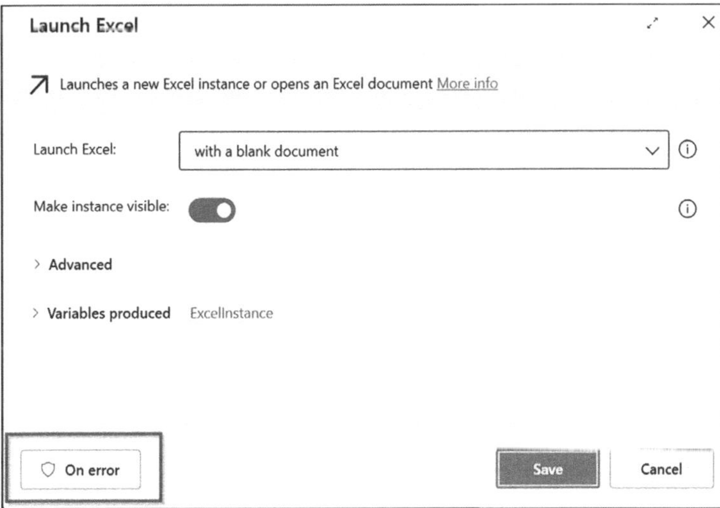

Figure 9.33: *On error button for action level error handling*

Follow the given steps to see its practical usage. We will have the bot cause an error by trying to access a sheet in Excel that does not exist:

1. Build a Flow that has Actions to Launch an Excel, activate **an invalid sheet**, read values from it, and close it.
2. Then set a variable called as **`SheetExists`** to **`True`**. You will know in a moment the reason for adding this.
3. Add a **"`Stop flow`"** Action with success.
4. Add a label and name it as **`lbl_SheetNotFound`**. Labels are explained in "*Chapter 4: Essential Elements of a Desktop Flow*".
5. Add a display message box to show the value of the **`SheetExists`** variable as **`SheetExists: %SheetExists%`**.

The entire Flow built looks as follows:

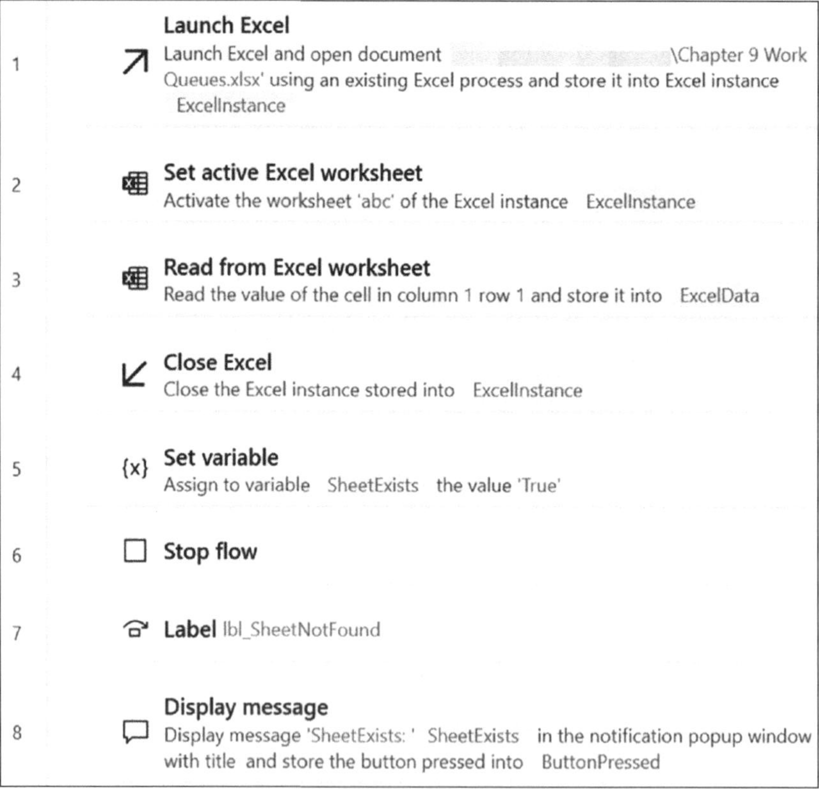

Figure 9.34: *Flow actions built so far*

The Flow will execute smoothly from line number 1 to 6, if there are no issues and finally stop the Flow (line 6). Now, we will add an action-level error handler to line number

2 and design it in such a way that if the sheet tried to be activated does not exist, then the bot will jump to the label in line 7 and display the value of the **SheetExists** variable.

6. To do this, open the **"Set active Excel worksheet"** Action and click the **"On error"** button.

   Before we configure these for our scenario, let us see what options are available for action-level exception handling (see *Figure* 9.35):

   a. The first option is where the retry goes which has parameters to set the number of times to retry this Action as well as the time interval to wait before each retry. Hover the mouse on the **'i'** information icon and refer to their explanation.

   b. The **"New rule"** button, as shown in the figure, in the **"All errors"** section has an option to set a variable value to something that we want or to call another Subflow depending on how we want to navigate the Flow of the automation in case any error comes out of this Action.

   c. The blue **"Throw error"** button when enabled will directly throw the error and stop the process.

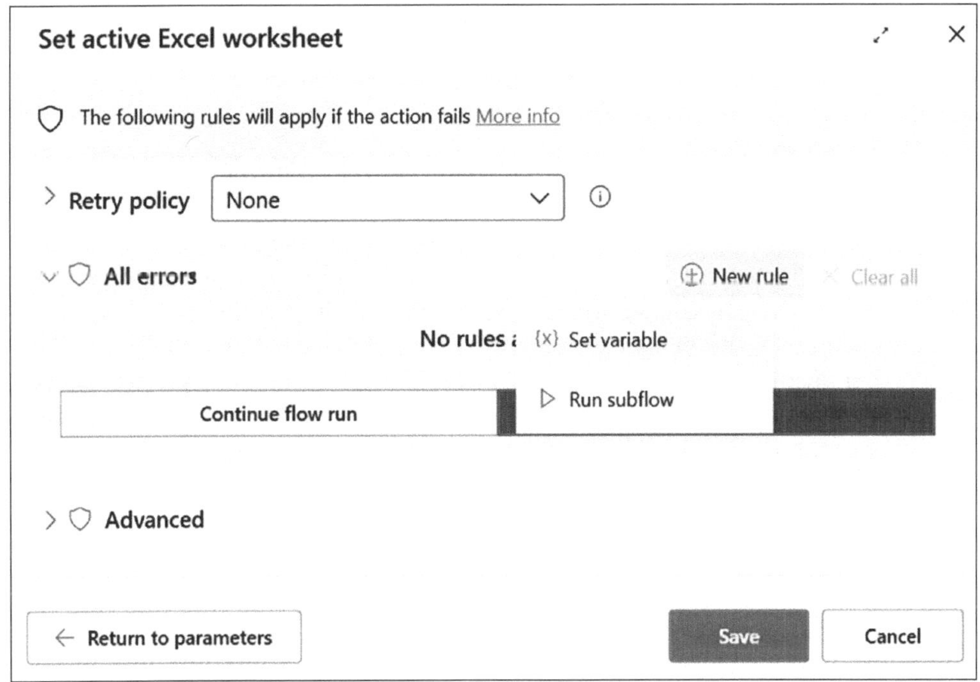

Figure 9.35: *Various options of the action-level error handling*

   d. In case the **"Continue flow run"** is enabled, the Flow will not stop and continue based on the options given in the shown dropdown of the following figure. Either it will move to the next Action (**"Read from Excel worksheet"** in our case) or repeat the same Action of setting the active worksheet or navigate to a label defined in the Flow. Repeating the same Action might cause it to go in an infinite loop as this option repeats until the Action runs successfully, this is something to be cautious about.

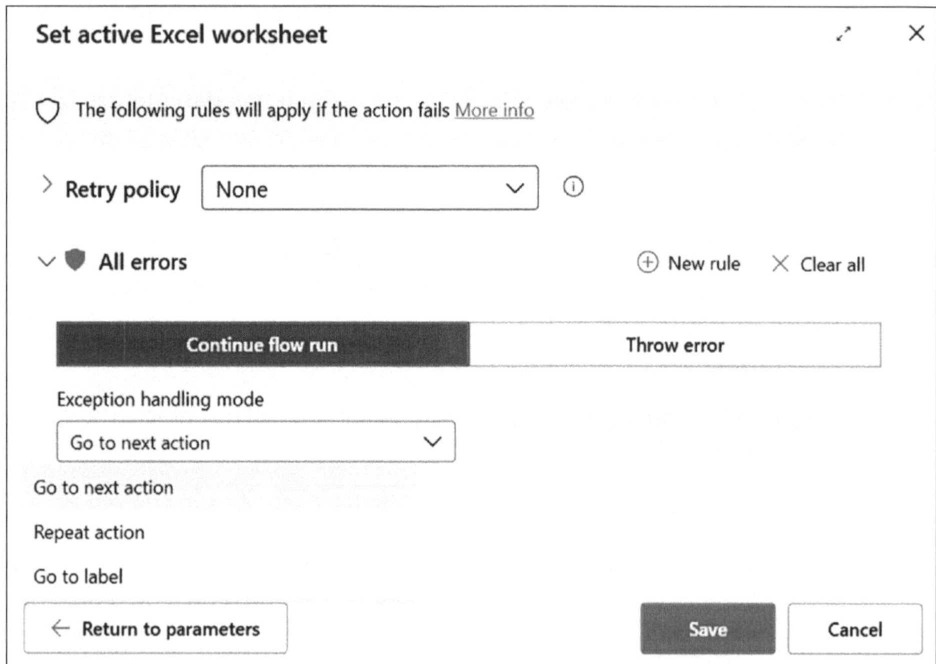

Figure 9.36: *Options for continuing the flow run*

e. The **"Advanced"** section has individual-level errors that can possibly be generated by this Action and will vary according to the Action chosen. For example, the **"Launch new Microsoft Edge"** Action will show different individual-level errors in the **"Advanced"** section. If each of the individual errors need to be handled differently, then you could use the **"Advanced"** section which has the same **"New rule"** button as described above.

Figure 9.37: *Options in advanced section*

7. For our scenario, configure the settings as follows. It is not needed to retry because no matter if the sheet doesn't exist at first instance, it will be the same at all other times. We are skipping the **"All errors"** section by keeping it as it is. You can see the difference in the blue-filled icon next to **"All errors"** and **"Advanced"** indicating which one is active. For the individual level error of **"Can't find worksheet"**, set the **SheetExists** variable to **False** helping us to understand that the sheet was not found. Then navigate the Flow to the **lbl_SheetNotFound** label which we already have in our Flow.

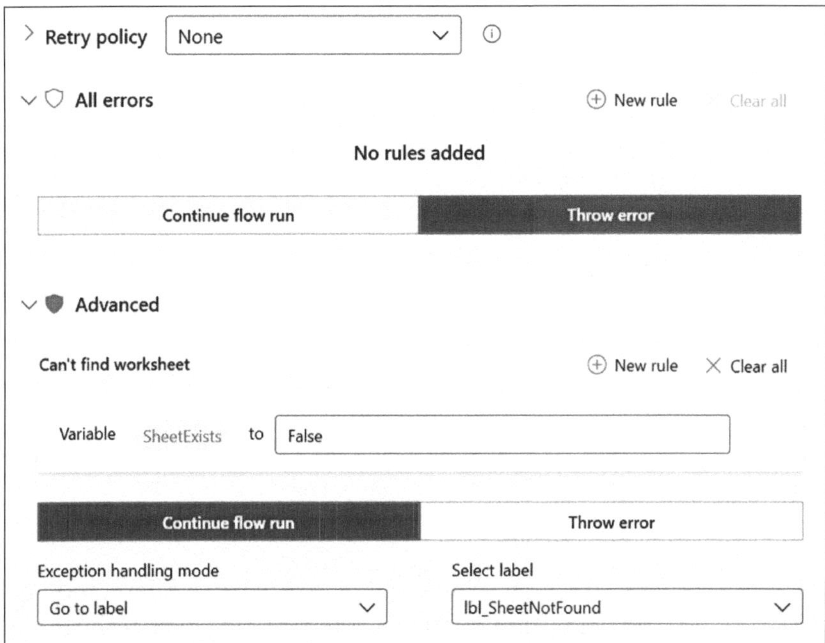

***Figure 9.38:** Configuring the parameters for our Flow*

Save the configurations to see how PAD shows us when an action-level error handler is applied to any Action (marked in the following figure). The **"On error"** button of *Figure* 9.33 also lights up similarly.

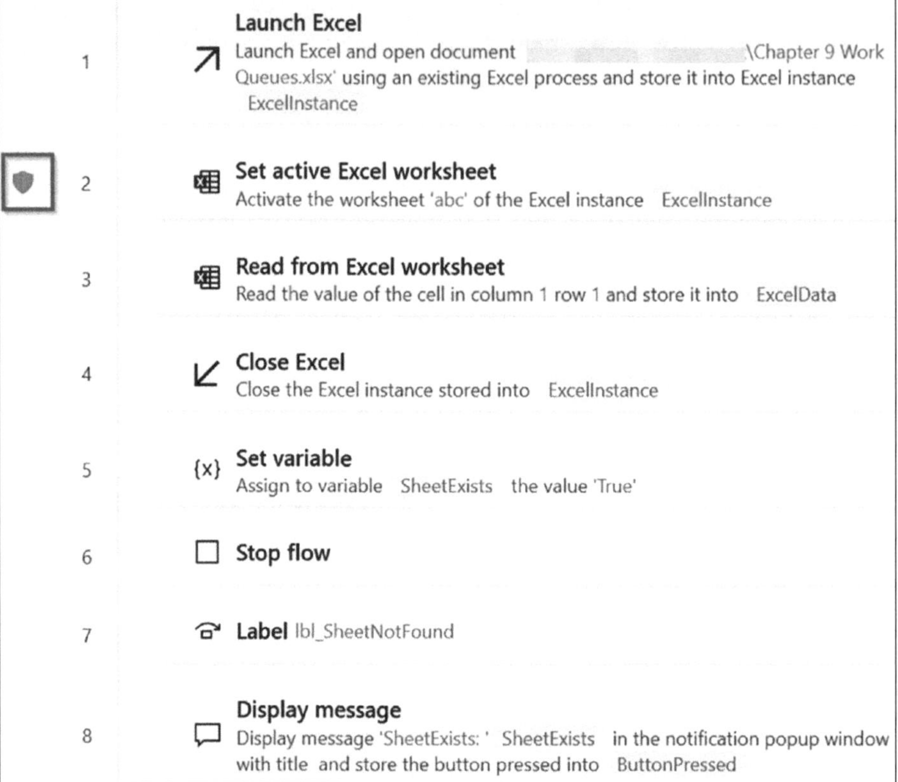

Figure 9.39: *Flow after applying action level error handling*

Run the Flow by stepping through which will give a better understanding. Refer to the following figure to see its output. If you have *incorrectly* given a sheet name in the Action on line number 2, then the Action generates an error, jumps to the label on line number 7, and displays the value of **`SheetExists`** as **`False`** which we had initialized in the error handler of **"`Set active Excel worksheet`"** Action.

The fact that the Flow jumped to the label is evident because it did not assign the value of True to **`SheetExists`** in line number 5, nor did it stop the Flow on line 6.

This is only an example of demonstrating the parameters of the action-level exception handling. What Actions are to be written under the Label is totally up to the developer of the bot to decide what needs to be done when a sheet that the bot is trying to access does not exist. As an example, the Flow can log the issue and send an email stating the error. We will see shortly how to get the details of an error. An even more creative way of building Flows is to write Actions that would first check if the required sheet exists or not, and then proceed accordingly, rather than having the error handler to identify an incorrect sheet.

In place of calling a label in the action-level error handler, the Flow could also call a

Subflow which is built only for logging the errors, sending emails, and so on, which would be the right way of error handling best practices.

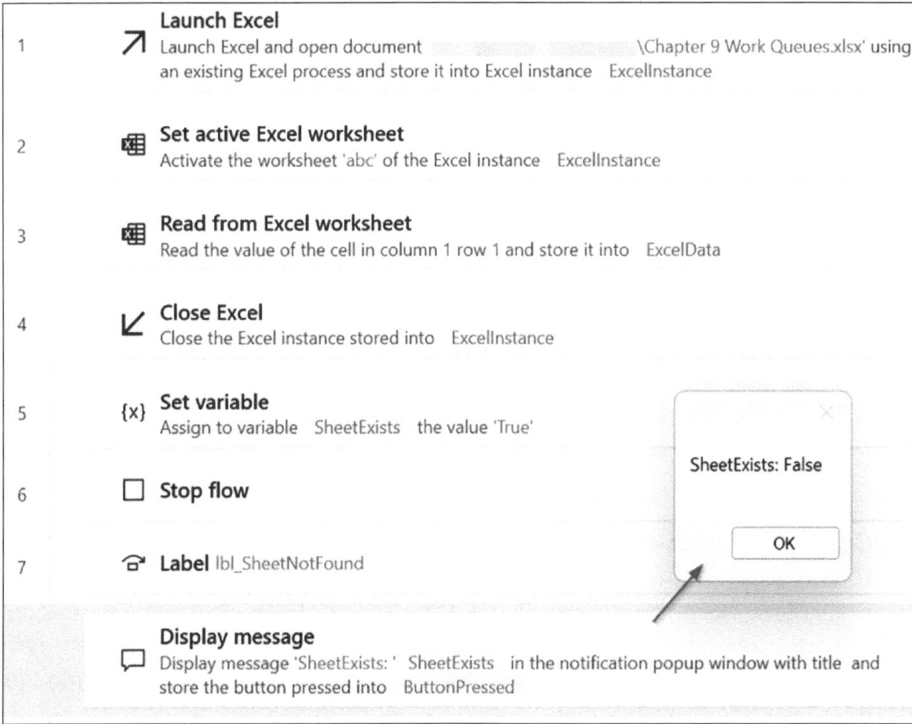

Figure 9.40: *Output after running the Flow*

- **Block-level exception handling:**

  In your Flow, there are going to be several Actions. At times, it is not practically possible to add action-level exception handling to every single Action, and also at times, it won't be clear as to which of those Actions might fail. This is where the block-level exception handling comes into play. As the name suggests, it applies to a block of several Actions.

  Follow the given steps to add block-level exception handling:

  1. Create a Flow that will Launch **an invalid** Excel file, set an active sheet, read from the sheet, and finally close the file. You can leave the earlier Flow as it is, and create a new Subflow for this exercise.

  2. Drag and drop the **"`On block error`"** at the beginning of the Flow with its corresponding **"`End`"** Action at the end of the Flow, such as the following figure.

  The file path in line number 2 is a dummy path to a non-existent file to cause an error.

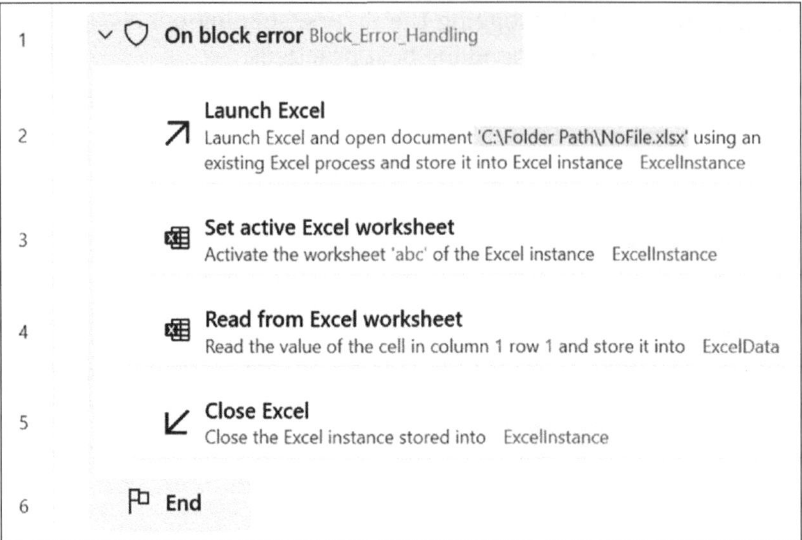

Figure 9.41: *Flow with on block error*

3. Open the properties of the **"`On block error`"** Action. Give a meaningful name to the block depending on what you are doing in that block, for example, *ErrorBlock_ReadInputExcel*. It has the same options that we saw earlier and the additional options pertaining to the block for navigating to the beginning or end of the block in the **"`Continue flow run`"** section. Select the **"`Go to end of block`"** for our exercise.

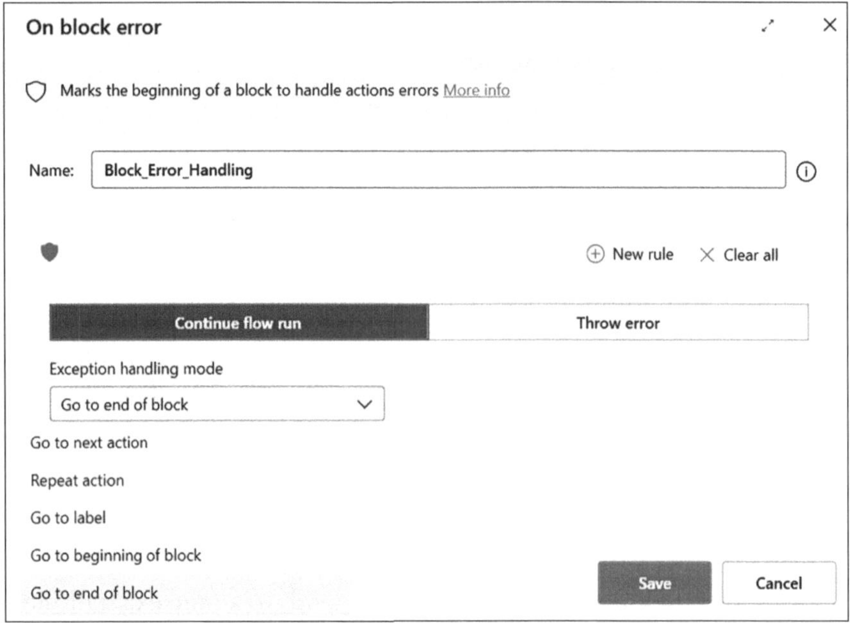

Figure 9.42: *Configuring the on block error*

4. After line 6 of *Figure* 9.41, drag and drop the **"`Get last error`"** Action followed by a display message for the **`LastError`** variable. The updated Flow is as follows:

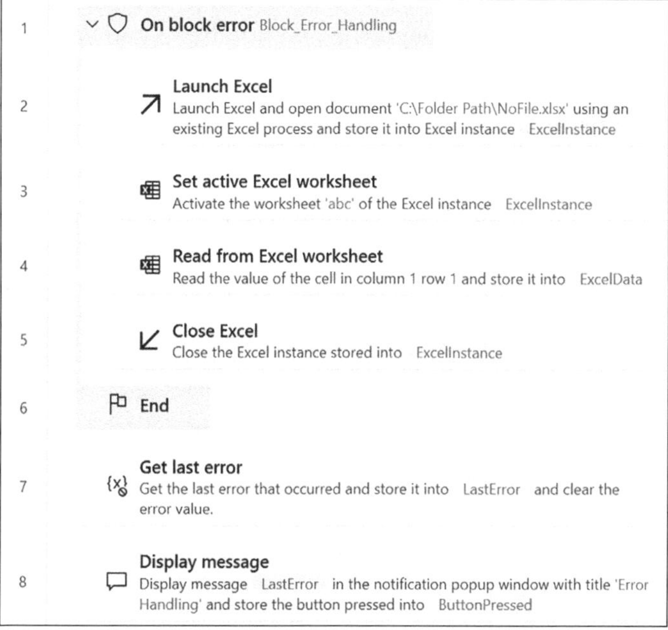

Figure 9.43: *The final flow*

The **"`Get last error`"** is the Action to give us the details of the error. Debug the Flow.

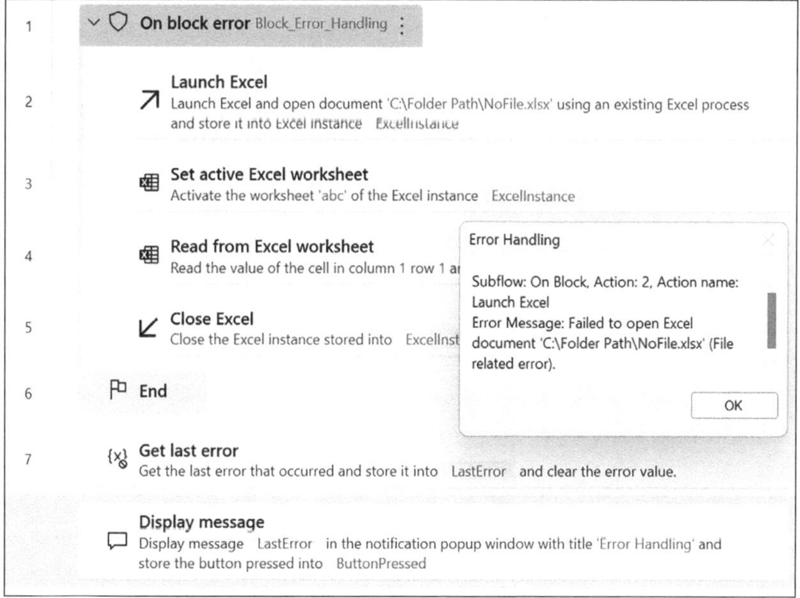

Figure 9.44: *Output after running the flow*

If you stepped through the Flow one Action at a time, you will notice that as soon as the execution encounters line number 2, it jumps to the beginning of the block where it reads what options we have configured and then goes to the end and then to line number 7 because we configured it to go to the end of the block. It did not execute any of the other Actions. Also, even though the line number 3 had an incorrect sheet, the error was at first caught in the line number 2 for an invalid file.

Moreover, have a look at the details given in the message box, such as the name of Subflow, Action line number and its name, and the error reason.

On the other hand, if you modify the Flow to add a valid file path (in line number 2) but an incorrect sheet name (in line number 3), this time it shows an error related to the incorrect sheet.

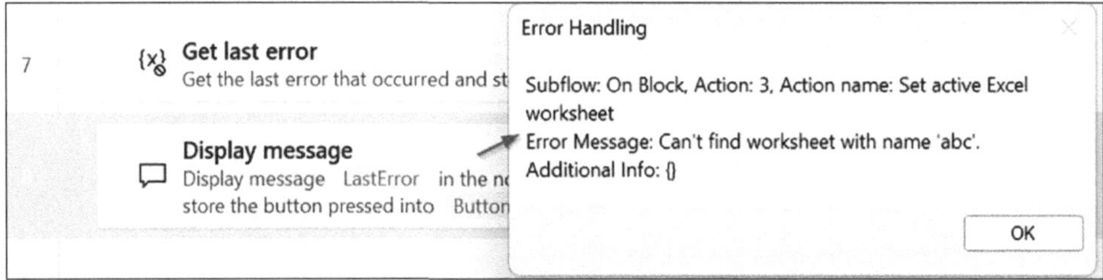

Figure 9.45: *Output for an incorrect sheet*

Thus, the block was capable of catching errors coming from any Actions within the block.

The **`LastError`** won't populate in case there is no error from the block. So, you can add an **"`If`"** statement to check if the **`LastError`** variable is empty or not, and accordingly navigate the Flow. In several situations, you can even read the various properties of the **`LastError`** variable from the variable picker (refer to the following figure) and decide the next course of action. For example, you could have the bot read the **`.Message`** property and take the appropriate steps if it contains the text **`Can't find worksheet with name`**.

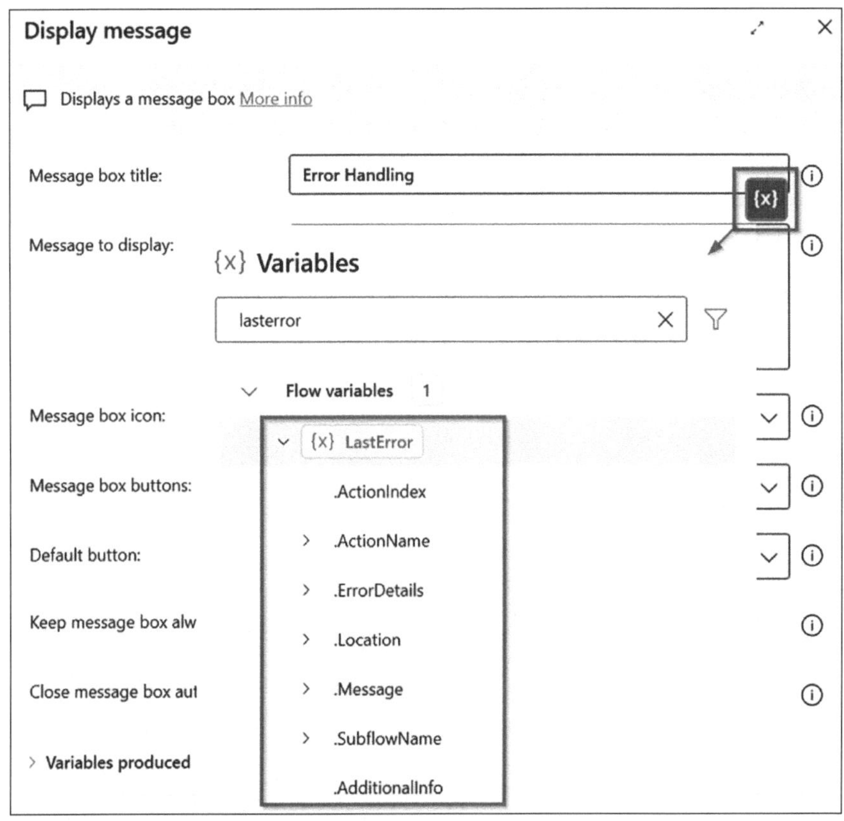

Figure 9.46: *Different properties of LastError variable*

As necessary, you can even stop the Flow with the details from the **`LastError`** variable.

Stop flow
Terminates the flow More info
End flow: With error message
Error message: %LastError%
Save
Cancel

Figure 9.47: *Stop flow with LastError variable*

The **“`On block error`”** Action also has a toggle that says **“`Capture unexpected logic`**

errors" which is used to trap errors like division by zero or index out of bounds. The error in the following figure is generated by adding only one item to a List and then accessing the second item of the list thus causing an error (List starts from 0 index). This error is caught after enabling the toggle with **"go to end of block"**. Try dividing a number by zero and see the same error coming up with a different message. Since this toggle is available only in the **"On block error"** Action, such errors can only be caught by the error block.

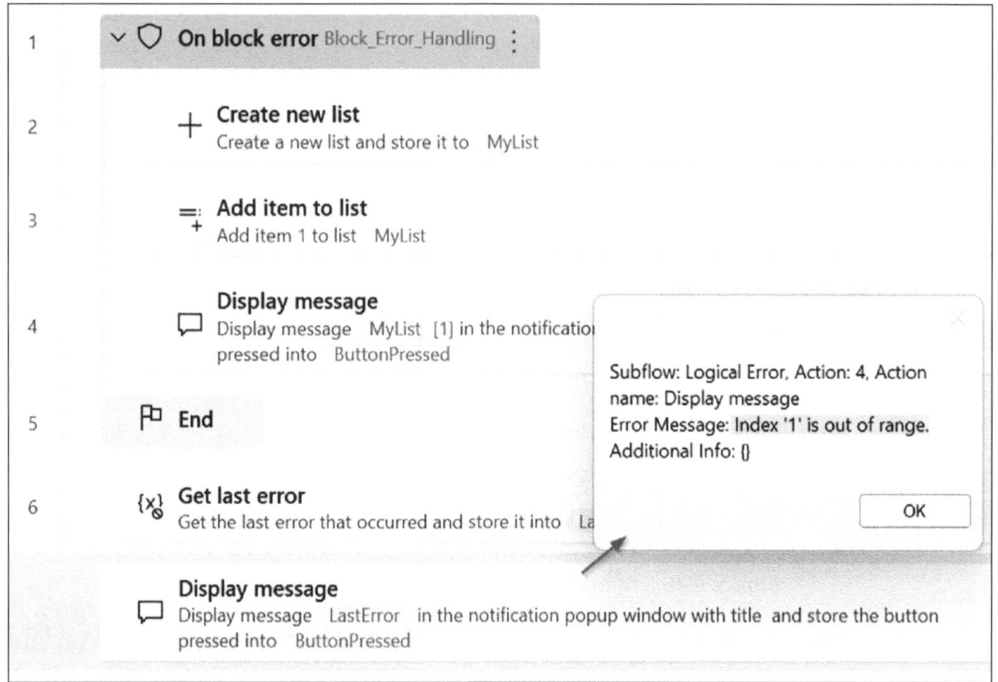

***Figure 9.48:** Capturing unexpected logic errors*

Practical Exercise 1

For all the topics and exercises you have been doing alongside in this book, practice adding action-level and block-level exception handling to those Flows wherever you suspect that they may cause Exceptions.

Practical Exercise 2

Both, action-level and block-level exception handling can co-exist with each other. Meaning, you can have an action-level exception handling for an invalid sheet as well as have a block-level to that same Flow. Your exercise will be to see which one takes priority over the other in such a situation. Add all parameters to the action-level like setting a variable, calling a Subflow, going to the next Action, and then see what happens.

Final Words on Error Handling

These explain only the features such as how the configurations and parameters are done for error handling in the PAD tool. But how to use these features and have a smooth navigation (for Business Exceptions) and a cleaner exit of the Flow (for System Exceptions), or where to use retries, is the creativity of the bot developer.

For System Exceptions, there should be fewer Actions in the next steps of the error handling part, for example, in the called Subflow or under the Label, which is to ensure that those Actions themselves do not throw any error or do not go into an endless loop.

For Business Exceptions, while processing multiple records, the Flow should have an efficient logic to skip the erroneous record, log the error details, and pick up the next record.

Note that checking certain conditions also forms a good error handling mechanism, for example, checking the status code variable after an API call to determine success or failure, checking if a file exists before accessing it, checking if a window exists before interacting with it, or checking a specific UI element that may or may not be present based on the data, and so on.

Error handling and logging (explained in the next section) go hand-in-hand and must be used in conjunction for robust and efficient error handling.

Logging and Monitoring

Logging and error handling should go in tandem with each other. Always build a Flow keeping in mind the support person or team as to what they would do, how they would troubleshoot and identify the issue in quick time with proper logging of errors. These errors could be either or both Business or System exceptions. Note that logging is not just for errors but also to list down the execution step of the process. Let us see what logging options the tool provides and how to monitor the logs and any other activity of the Desktop Flow.

Logging

PAD provides an Action called **"`Log message`"** to log a custom message with a severity logging level of Info, Warning, or Error. Note that this is a premium feature and Action logs are not uploaded to the Power Automate service when the Flow is executed through the Power Automate Desktop Flow designer. They are updated and visible on the Cloud portal when run from the PAD Console or called via a Cloud Flow. In the "*Monitoring*" section, we will see where the logs via this Action are reflected.

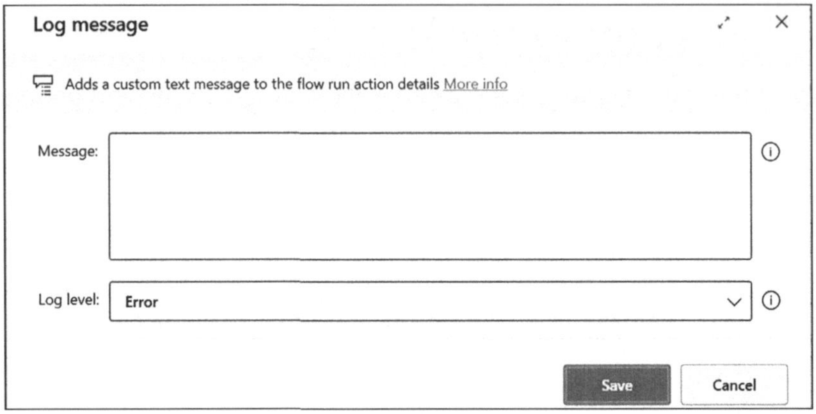

Figure 9.49: *The Log message action*

If you are not using a premium license or if you want to have additional information in the logs, you could also create your own logging mechanism.

A simple example of how to have a customized logging is:

1. Use the **"`Write text to file`"** Action with the **"`Append content`"** setting.
2. Add various logging fields such as:

   `DateTimeStamp | Subflow Name | Action Name | Error Line number | Error Description | Message | Additional Info`, and so on.

You will get these details from the properties of the **`LastError`** variable (see *Figure* 9.46).

Keep the writing of a Log file in a segregated Subflow to create a dedicated logging mechanism and call it during errors and at any key steps of the process.

You can write the execution steps of the process, such as Process Started, Starting 'Add Customer Details', Invoice Uploaded, Submitted 'Customer Details', and so on.

In the above format, a pipe delimiter is used to separate the columns. Delimiters help to give a structured look to the logs. Also, when such a Text file is imported into Excel, the logging fields can be separated into different columns based on the delimiter character which helps in readability. Choose a delimiter that is not going to be present in your data.

An Excel file can also be used as a log file with these same fields and written to it using Excel operations. Depending upon the landscape and environment of the automation, other approaches like Dataverse or Database tables can also be used for logging which enterprises have been doing.

Add your own fields in the log file as required, for example, Logging levels of High, Medium, and Low, or a column to indicate whether it is Information, Error, or Warning.

For better readability, the names of the log files can have the Desktop Flow name with a date-timestamp as follows. In situations of multiple logs and where bots run at different times, this will give a clear indication as to which process is the log for and for which run of the day. This is just a pointer and can be modified as needed.

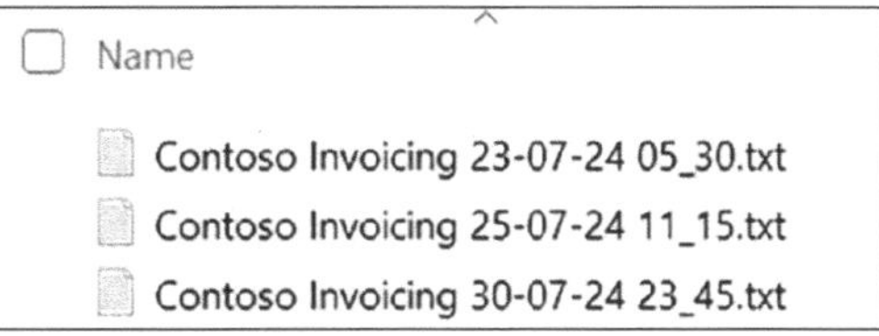

Figure 9.50: *Sample log file naming format*

Also, if there is one log file generated per run and if the Flow runs for several hours of the day, then there are chances that the sizes of these files will accumulate. So, in such scenarios, ensure building a logic inside the Flow to split the logs after a certain size so that it does not end up as a very huge file. You can add some identification suffixes like _Part1, _Part2, and so on, indicating the sequence of the log file for the same process.

Since there are going to be several logs generated by multiple processes and for multiple times of the day, also have an archival or purging mechanism after a set number of days. Meaning, that the start or end of the Flow could have a logic to check the logs folder, compare its date-timestamp with the system date and time, and if it is beyond the configurable number of retention days, then delete it or move it to a separate location. You can plan on having a separate Desktop Flow that does this and then call it at the beginning or end of the Flow, or use a Subflow if there are restrictions in licensing availability.

The log file generation logic in the Flow can also be coupled with an email functionality to send it to the support team as and when required based on a flag variable.

Monitoring

If you are adding error handling to the Flow and logging the issues and its execution steps, it is also obvious that you would need to monitor them. Monitoring is done for several reasons, such as error detection and resolution, performance tracking of the bots, ensuring that the bots are running as per the set guidelines for compliance and auditing, resource management to add bots and resources when needed, increased uptime for user satisfaction, and so on.

On the Cloud portal, go to **"`Desktop flow runs`"** either from the **"`More`"** button or if not available, then via the **"`Discover all`"** button. This section will give a view of all the Desktop Flow runs you have access to. This view gives information, such as the requested date and time of the Desktop Flow by its parent Flow, the name of the Desktop Flow, the Status of the Flow like Succeeded, Cancelled, Failed, any errors, the run mode (attended or unattended explained in the next section), and so on. Apart from these, you can also customize this view by removing existing ones or adding new columns.

Figure 9.51: *Desktop flow runs section of cloud portal*

Clicking any of the Desktop Flow will take you to another page, as shown in the following figure. It has several sections, such as Run details, Run status, Action details. The **"Run details"** section gives information, such as Parent Cloud Flow run, Parent Desktop Flow run, Start time and duration of run, Status of the run, Target machine on which the Desktop Flow is run, Target machine group if any, Run mode (attended/unattended), Version of the PAD tool used.

The **"Run status"** section gives an information like timeline from when it was requested/triggered till its final step. Additionally, it gives information such as the time taken on a step which helps in identifying if there is a longer time than expected on a particular step.

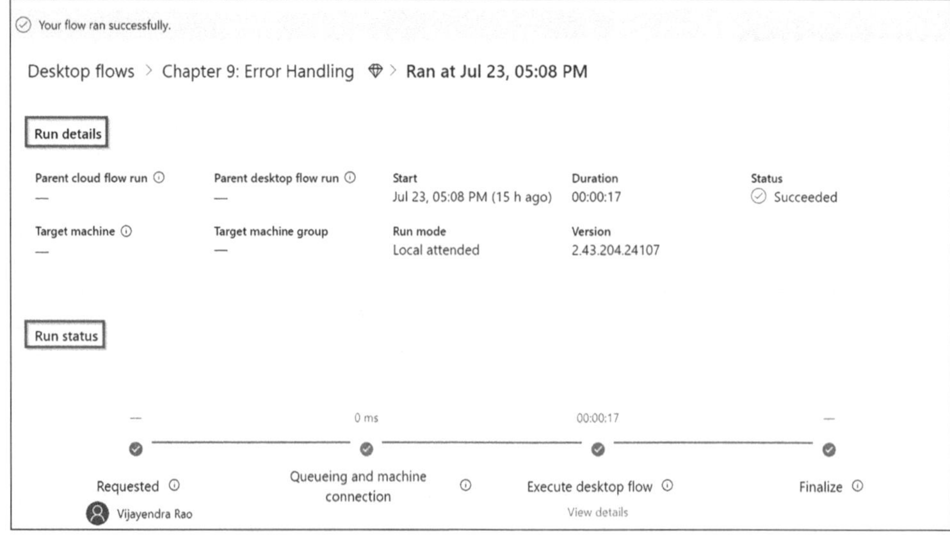

Figure 9.52: *Further details of desktop flow runs*

The **"`Action details`"** section gives the information at each Action level of the Desktop Flow. The following figure illustrates columns like Start time, Subflow name, Action index (the line number of the Action), Action name, Duration it took to run that Action, Log level and Status. The **"`Log message`"** that is showing an Error in the following figure is the Action we saw in the "*Logging*" section of this chapter (*see Figure* 9.49). The dropdown in this Action was selected to Error, hence it is showing the same, but the Action itself did not fail and went on to the next step, therefore showing as Succeeded.

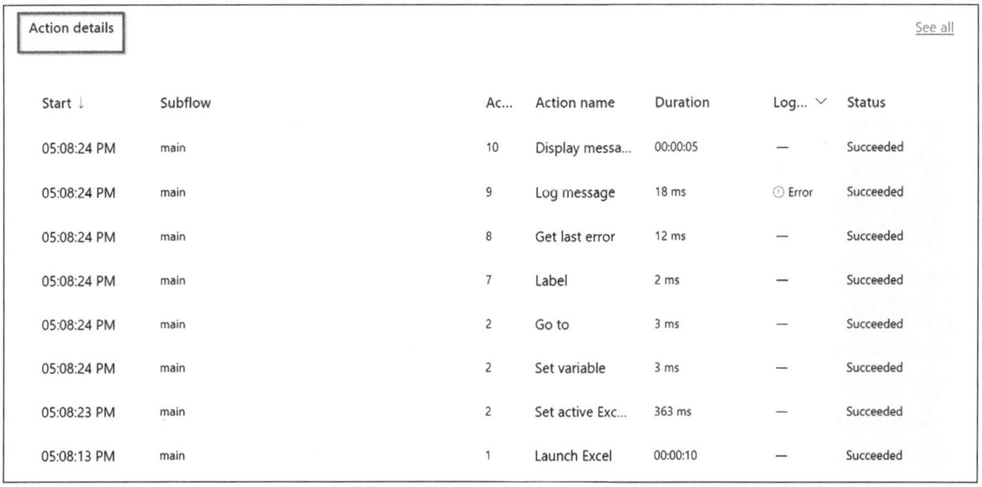

Action details

See all

Start ↓	Subflow	Ac...	Action name	Duration	Log... ∨	Status
05:08:24 PM	main	10	Display messa...	00:00:05	—	Succeeded
05:08:24 PM	main	9	Log message	18 ms	ⓘ Error	Succeeded
05:08:24 PM	main	8	Get last error	12 ms	—	Succeeded
05:08:24 PM	main	7	Label	2 ms	—	Succeeded
05:08:24 PM	main	2	Go to	3 ms	—	Succeeded
05:08:24 PM	main	2	Set variable	3 ms	—	Succeeded
05:08:23 PM	main	2	Set active Exc...	363 ms	—	Succeeded
05:08:13 PM	main	1	Launch Excel	00:00:10	—	Succeeded

Figure 9.53: *The action details section*

You can even go one level next by clicking any of the above rows. This will take you to a page shown in *Figure* 9.54. Here you can again select any of the line items and even see the input and output details of an Action. Note that variables marked as sensitive will not be shown here.

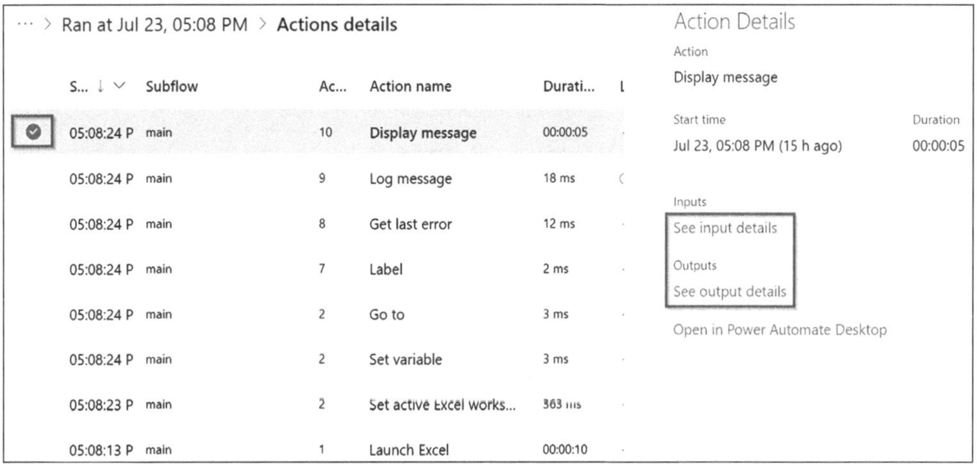

··· > Ran at Jul 23, 05:08 PM > **Actions details**

S... ↓ ∨	Subflow	Ac...	Action name	Durati...
05:08:24 P	main	10	Display message	00:00:05
05:08:24 P	main	9	Log message	18 ms
05:08:24 P	main	8	Get last error	12 ms
05:08:24 P	main	7	Label	2 ms
05:08:24 P	main	2	Go to	3 ms
05:08:24 P	main	2	Set variable	3 ms
05:08:23 P	main	2	Set active Excel works...	363 ms
05:08:13 P	main	1	Launch Excel	00:00:10

Action Details

Action

Display message

Start time: Jul 23, 05:08 PM (15 h ago)

Duration: 00:00:05

Inputs

See input details

Outputs

See output details

Open in Power Automate Desktop

Figure 9.54: *Input and output details*

The **"Desktop flow activity"** is another tab that provides a good amount of information pertaining to the Desktop Flows.

Figure 9.55: The desktop flow activity tab

Furthermore, you can view additional information, such as error trends, top machine failures, various graphs and charts, view the run queue of a machine, and so on. These are viewable via different sections of the portal and requires a continued exploration using the following link. Ensure to go through all of the sections on the left-hand side of the link, as shown in the following figure:

https://learn.microsoft.com/en-us/power-automate/desktop-flows/desktop-flow-activity

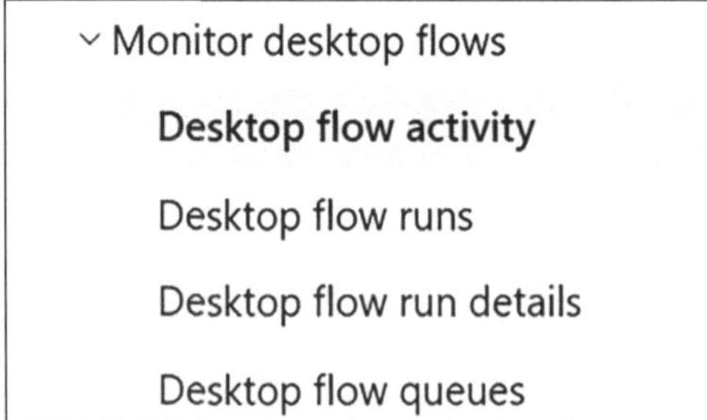

Figure 9.56: Further deep dive for monitoring desktop flows

Practical Exercise

To the error handling done in the previous section for all exercises, practice adding a logging mechanism using the Text/Excel log file approach and via the **"Log message"**

Action. View the Desktop Flow activity and details of their runs from various sections of the Cloud portal.

Unattended and Attended Automation

We have been using these two terms in this chapter as run modes. There are two types of automation or types of run modes in any RPA tool, namely Unattended and Attended automation. Let us look at what each one of them implies:

- **Unattended automation:**

  In simple terms, they refer to the execution of bots which do not have any human intervention. Meaning, no human "attends to" this kind of automation. Bots under this category are designed to work by themselves as they are fully automated. They are either automatically triggered by an event (such as when an email arrives) or run automatically on a schedule. A specified machine or group of machines are configured to execute the automation in lieu of the user's machine.

  Here is some additional information about unattended Desktop Flows, such as, for running these Flows the machine should be ON but not locked:

  https://learn.microsoft.com/en-us/power-automate/desktop-flows/run-unattended-desktop-flows

- **Attended automation:**

  On the contrary, these refer to the execution of bots where human intervention is involved and a human "attends to" these bots. Such bots are generally kicked off by a human, or even a human gets involved in the middle of the interaction or decision-making process. This intervention in between the process is also termed as "human-in-the-loop automation". For example, in an end-to-end attended bot, a human can get involved to start the bot, analyze the output given by the bot, make some decisions, feed inputs to the bot, move files, upload information, again re-run the same or another bot, and so on. These bots generally run on the user's machine.

Something to note is that Unattended and Attended Flows have different licensing plans, and these are pointed out in the "*Licensing*" topic of "*Chapter 12: Extending the Landscape of Your Desktop Flows*"

This is about the run modes. But how can users interact with bots for attended automation? Let us see the different ways of asking inputs from the user to achieve Attended automation in PAD.

The different display boxes to flash in front of the user are available under the **"Message boxes"** category in the **"Actions"** pane. There is a wide range of dialog boxes for each type of data depending on what kind of input is expected from the user. Here is a sample for the **"Display input dialog"** Action. Let us see what else do we have and their key parameters.

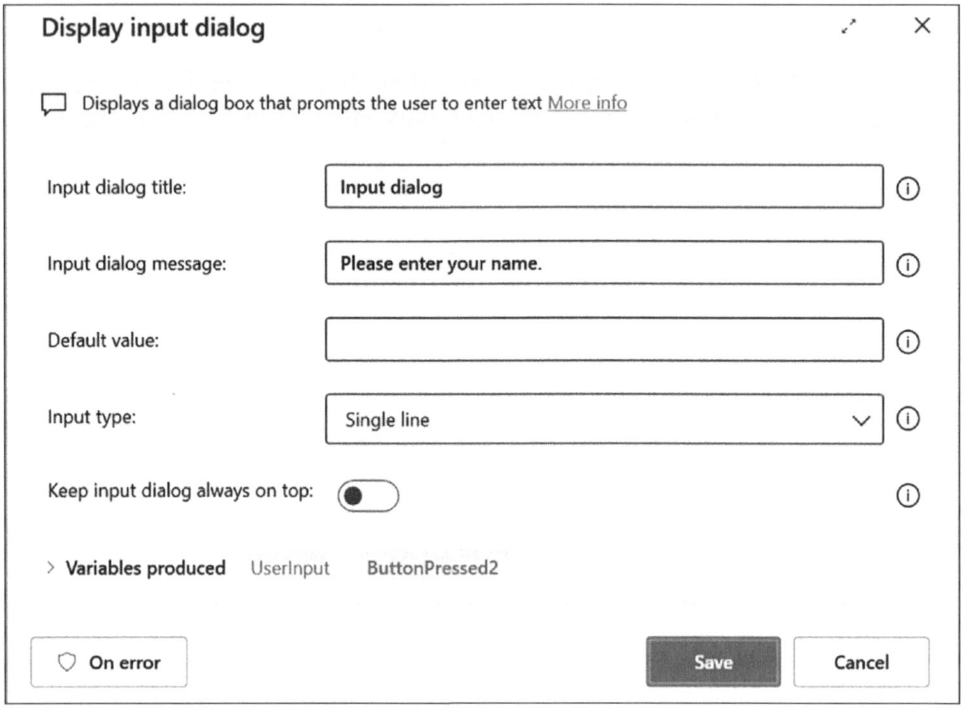

***Figure* 9.57:** *The display input dialog action*

Although the **"Display message"** Action does not directly ask for written input, even asking the user to click on any of the buttons on the message box is also a way of accepting user inputs (for example, Ok/Cancel). Apart from this Action which we have used several times from the beginning of this book, here are the other Actions in this category.

- **Display input dialog:**

  This Action displays an input dialog box to the user asking for filling an input. You can configure it to ask for a single-line value, a multi-line text box, or even a password field. A default value can also be set that will show up to the user who can then modify it if required. The toggle seen in the preceding figure is for the dialog box to overlay on top of other windows, which is available for all the dialog boxes listed below. The output variables coming out of this Action can then be used to process the input given by the user.

- **Display select date dialog:**

  This dialog box is to ask for any date input kind of information. It also has an option to ask for two dates as in a range of **"From"** and **"To"** from the user. The dialog box can be configured to ask for either date only or for a date and time, with an option to set a default value.

- **Display select from list dialog:**

  This dialog acts like a dropdown list of values to be presented to the user for their selection. The Action optionally allows the user to write their own input values to the list like a combo box. The user can choose multiple items in the list or even not select anything at all in case user input is not mandatory.

- **Display select file dialog:**

  This is a file selection dialog box with an option to show the dialog box for a specified folder and with a specified file extension filter (for example, *.xlsx). Refer to the tooltip to see the syntax for including wild card characters as well as for adding multiple file filters. It has a good feature to check if a file exists when the user makes the file selection. Meaning, if the file exists toggle is enabled, and if the user types in a file that is not present on the selected path, then the Action will not accept it by showing a message. Users can also select multiple files via this dialog.

- **Display select folder dialog:**

  Instead of a file, this Action is for the user to select a folder configured by the specified path.

The above Actions ask for individual inputs from the user. Try them out and observe how each of them appear after running the Flow. What if you need to ask multiple inputs from the user at the same time? For example, enter the name and the date of birth. It won't be user-friendly to pop up multiple dialog boxes one after the other on the user's screen. Power Automate Desktop gives us the option to add textboxes, labels, dropdowns, check boxes, file selection, and so on, all in a single window. This is done via the **"`Display custom form`"** Action. Let us see how it is created and what features it provides.

- **Building the Form**

  On the **"`Display custom form`"** Action, clicking the **"`Custom form designer`"** button will bring up a screen as shown here. Here you will see four sections, as shown in *Figure* 9.58. The **"`Form elements`"** section is where the list of control elements is available. Those can be dragged and dropped onto the **"`Form structure`"** section. The **"`Preview form`"** section will show a preview of the controls added to the **"`Form structure`"** section. The last section on the right-hand side shows the properties of the selected element.

  Drag and drop the elements as per your requirement onto the **"`Form structure`"**. In the following figure, a **"`Text input`"** element is added to the form.

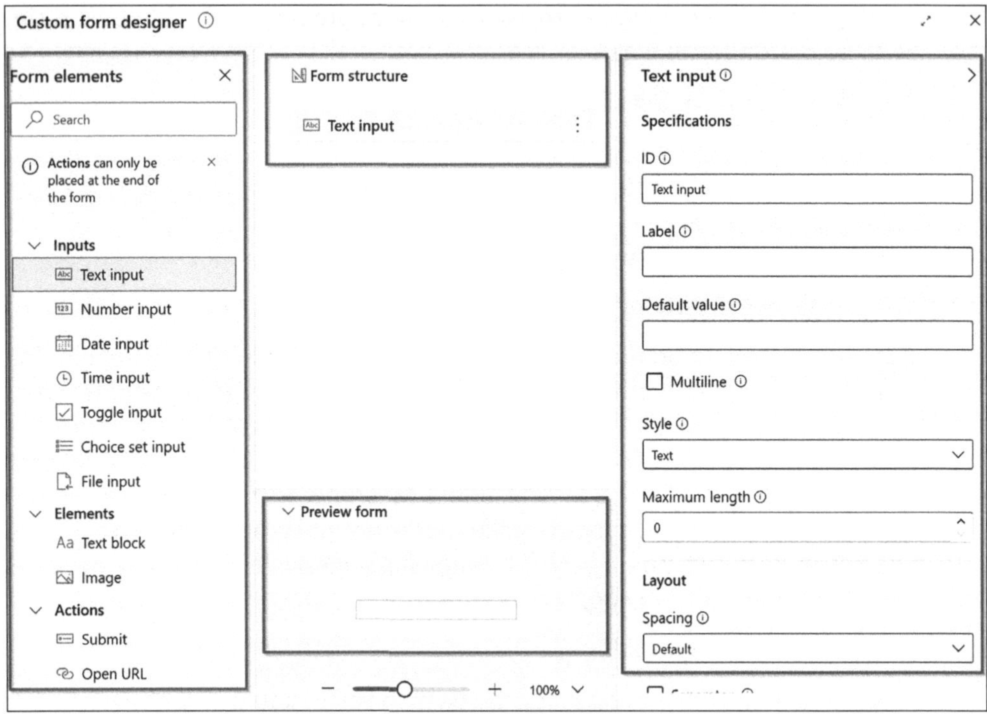

Figure 9.58: *The Custom form designer*

Here is the **"Form structure"** after adding every single available element:

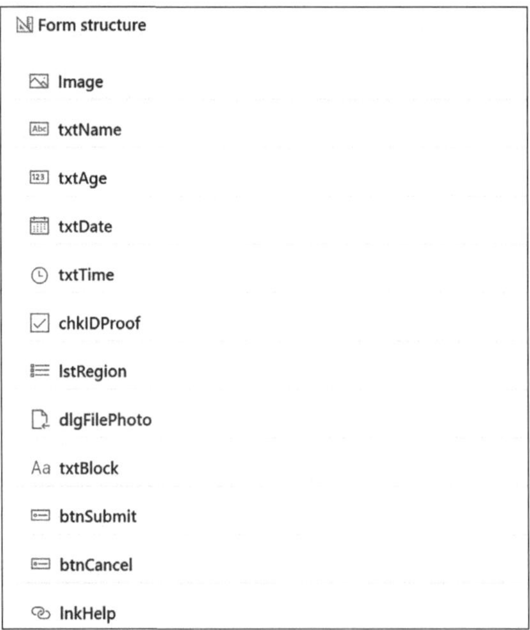

Figure 9.59: *The Form structure that includes all elements*

This is how the form looks like for the developed structure after running it and adding some user inputs. Map the small blue icons of the preceding figure with the icons in the **"Form elements"** section of *Figure* 9.58 to know the type of controls used in the form.

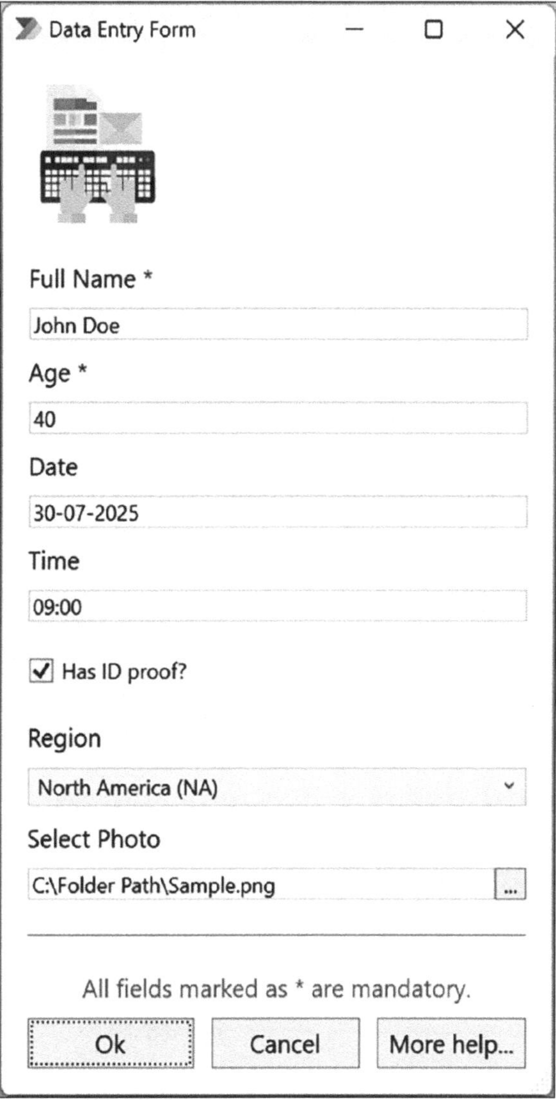

Figure 9.60: *Sample form with all elements*

Figure 9.61 shows how to add labels to the elements. The **"Label"** box in the properties that has **"Full Name"** is what shows up in the preview section for a text box.

The text given in the ID box **txtName** is the unique ID for that element and will be used to capture data from this text box by referring to its ID.

The asterisk mark next to the label comes from the **"Required"** property of the text box indicating the user that this is a required field.

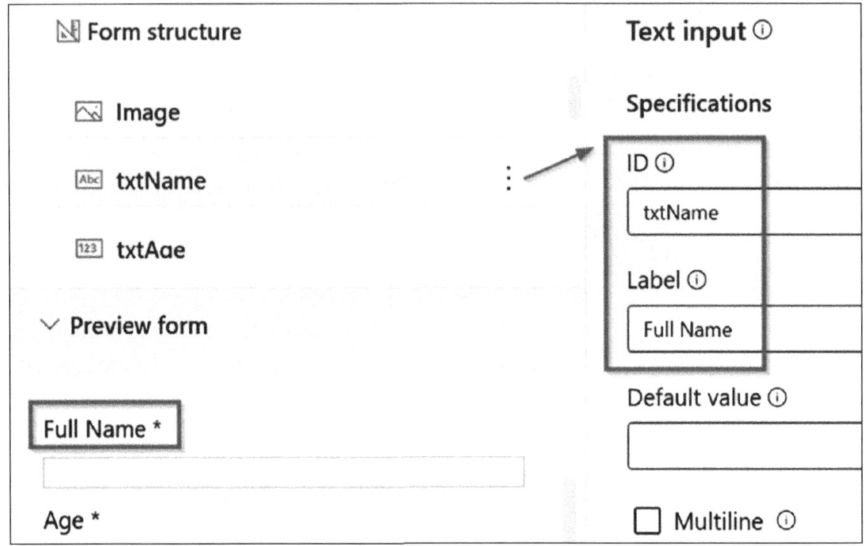

Figure 9.61: *Configuring the label and the Id*

- **Validation for mandatory fields:**

  Here is a required field example for the Age which is a **"Number input"** type of element.

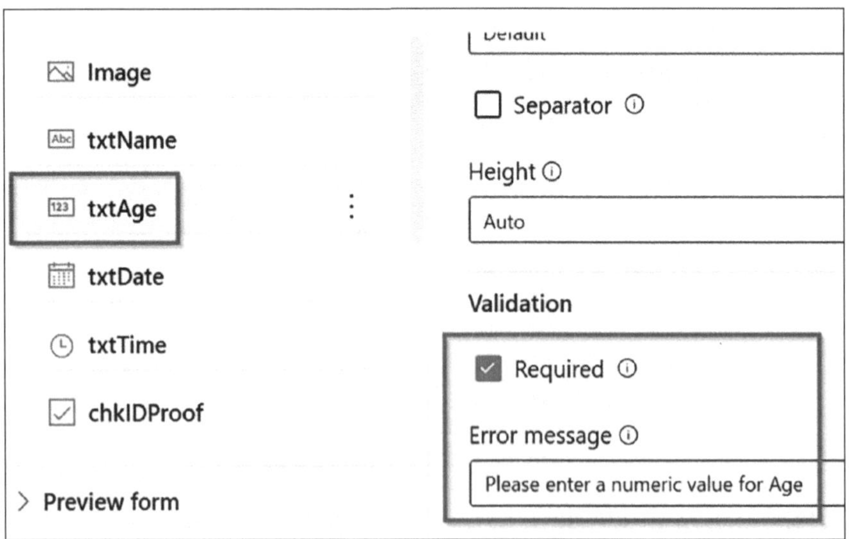

Figure 9.62: *Configuring the required property*

If you leave the box empty without entering a value and submit the form, the configured error message will be as follows. Note that since this is a **"Number Input"** field, it will also allow decimals. If you do not want to allow decimals, then use a **"`Text input`"** element and apply regex on it (shown in next point).

Full Name *

John Doe

Age *

Please enter a numeric value for Age

Figure 9.63: *Error message as per the required property*

- **Validation using regex pattern:**

  You can apply a regular expression on several data inputs, such as name, email address, phone number, and so on.

  The following is an example of a regex pattern for a first name followed by one space, an optional alphabet, another space, and a last name. Also, the first and last name would be anywhere between 2 and 30 characters long. You need to build your own regex as per the needs of the automation.

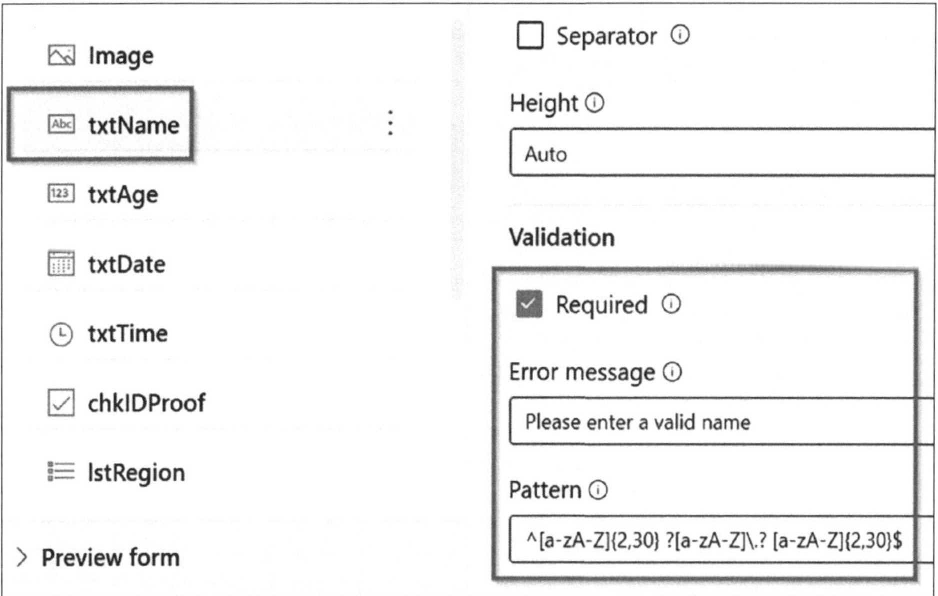

Figure 9.64: *Configuring the regular expression pattern*

The output after running it in real time and submitting the form is shown in the following figure. It won't accept if the first name is not at least 2 characters long as configured in the regular expression.

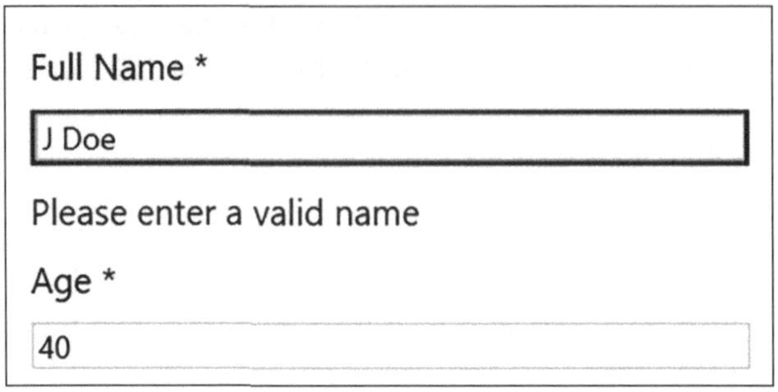

Figure 9.65: *Output error message as per the regular expression pattern*

- **Validation for date ranges:**

  You can also give a minimum and maximum value for a **"`Date input`"** field and an appropriate error message. Click the **"`i`"** information button next to the labels for the minimum and maximum values to read about regional format settings.

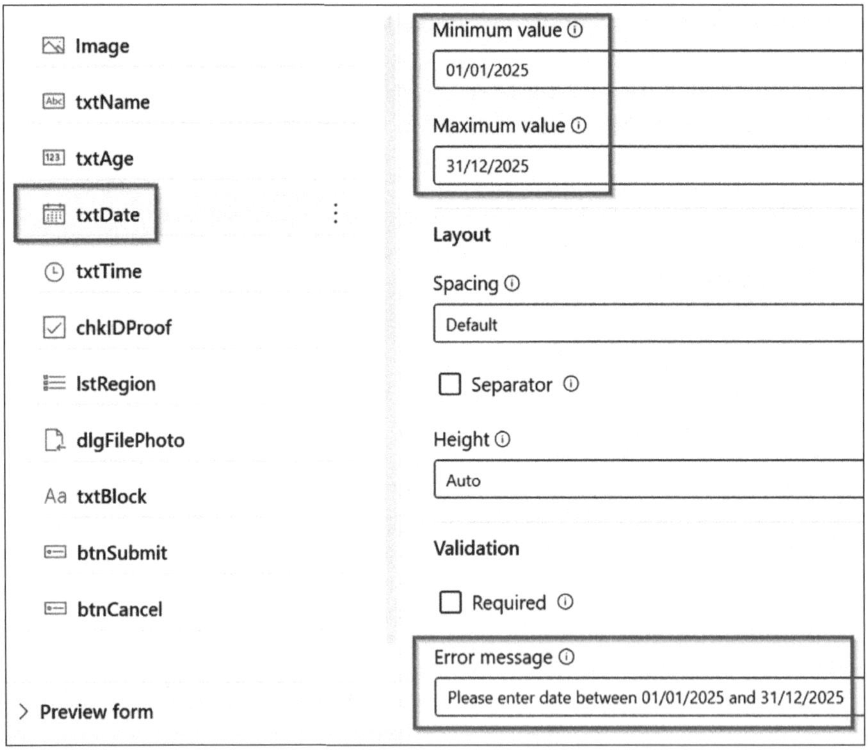

Figure 9.66: *Configuring the minimum and maximum date range with error message*

The following figure shows the error message for a date outside the configured range.

Currently, they appear as text boxes in the output. Let us expect Microsoft to change these to DatePicker and Time controls in future releases of the tool.

Full Name *

John Doe

Age *

40

Date

01/05/2026

Please enter date between 01/01/2025 and 31/12/2025

Figure 9.67: *Output for the date range validation*

- **Other design parameters:**

  The text that displays as **"`All fields marked as * are mandatory.`"** is a **"`Text Block`"** field and the color it gets is from the dropdown of the property. Change the options in the dropdown to see which different colors are available.

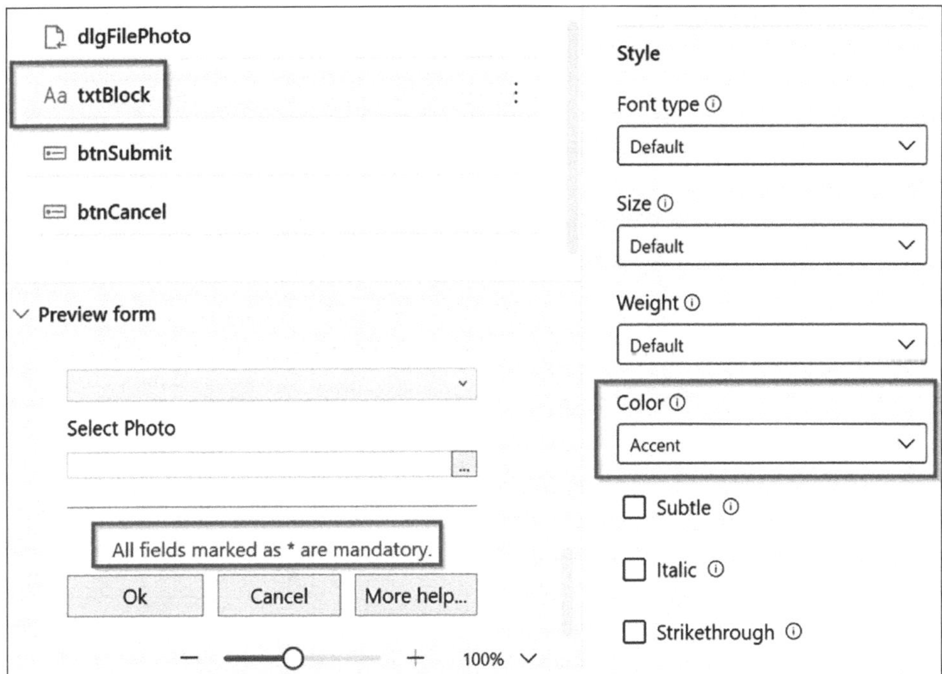

Figure 9.68: *The text block element*

The line that shows up above the Text Block is the **"`Separator`"** property. The way it works is - A separator line automatically appears to the *top* of the element which has this property ticked.

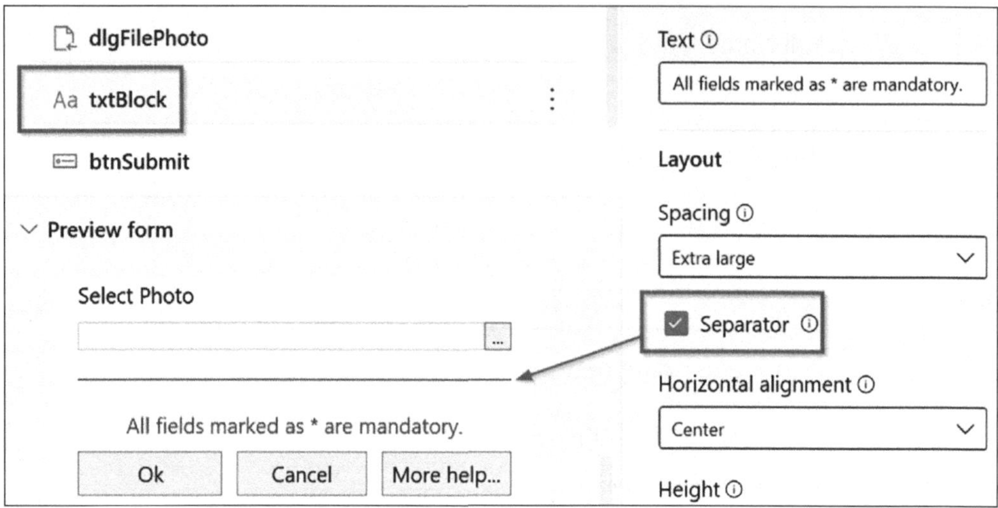

Figure 9.69: *The Separator property*

The **"Choice set input"** element (or a listbox) should be given as a combination of Title and its Value.

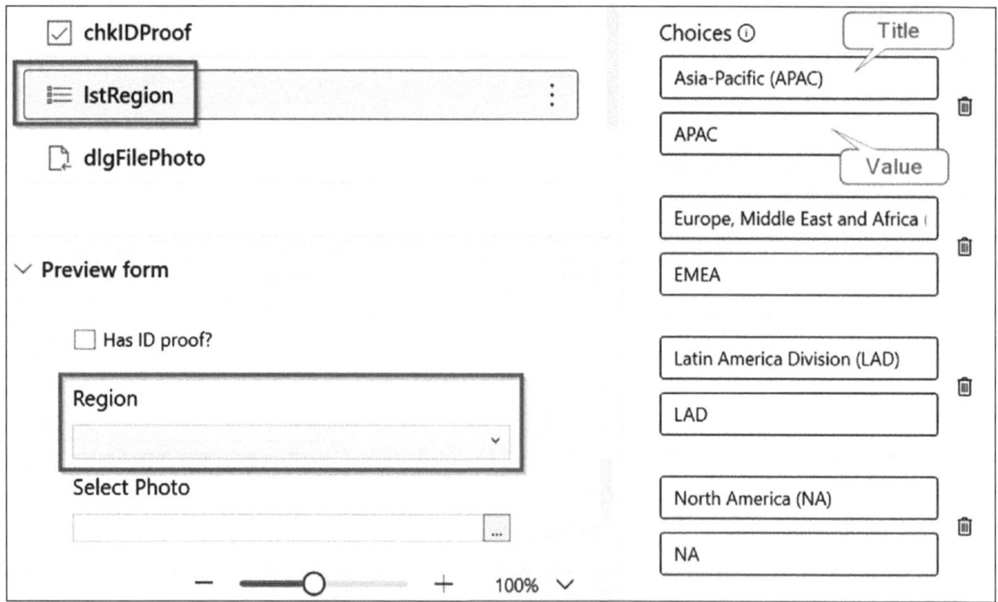

Figure 9.70: *Configuring the Choice set input element*

When the Form is run as shown in the following figure, the text added in the **"Title"** section shows up in the listbox dropdown, and the text in the **"Value"** is the one that will be saved when a user selects that particular **"Title"**.

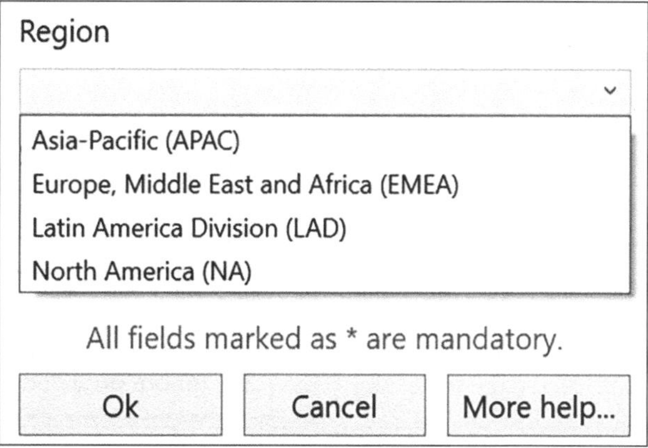

Figure 9.71: *Output of the Choice set input element*

For the **"Toggle input"** (or a checkbox), the **"Label"** can be kept as blank and the **"Title"** property can be used instead as it looks better on the output form as compared to using the **"Label"** property. Try it out and see. Also, the text box values of **"Value when on"** and **"Value when off"** determine what value is saved when the form is finally submitted depending on whether the checkbox is checked or unchecked by the user. Meaning, that if the checkbox is checked, a value of True is submitted in the response.

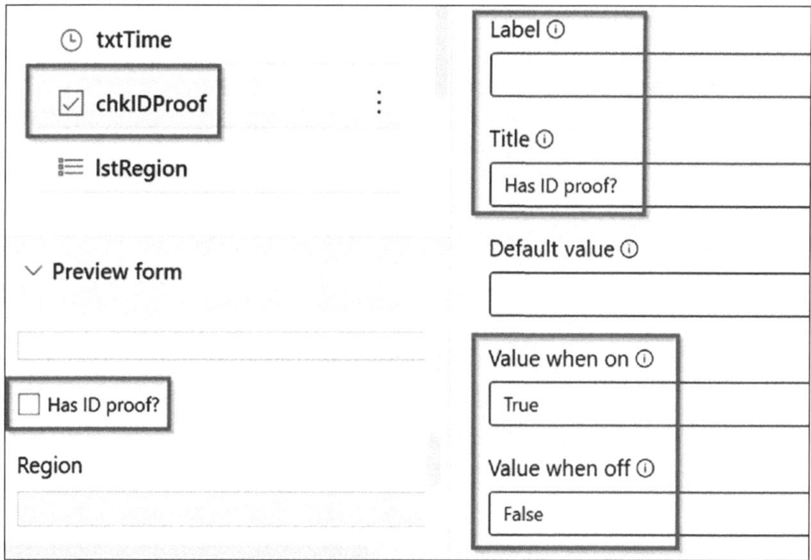

Figure 9.72: *The Toggle input element*

The **Ok** and the **Cancel** buttons at the bottom of the form (*Figure* 9.71) are one and the same, that is, they both are the **"Submit"** type of elements with the only difference being that the Cancel button has the below property ticked. The **Ok** button, which has this property unticked, will send the values back to the Flow, but the **Cancel** button won't. Refer to the **'i'** information icon shown next to the checkbox.

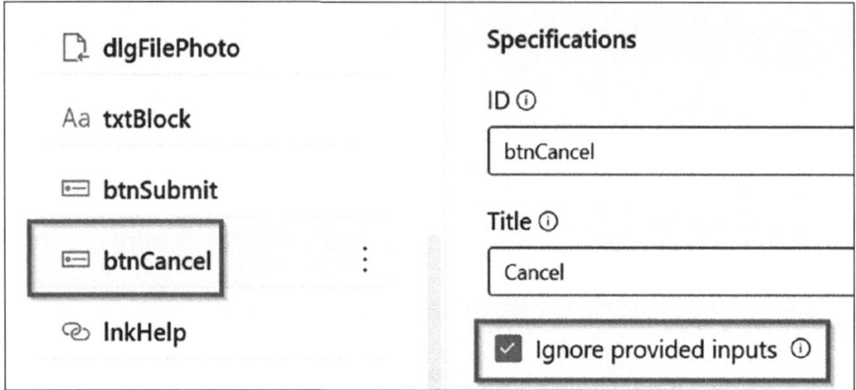

***Figure 9.73:** The Submit type of element*

The last button, the **"More Help"** button, is an **"Open URL"** type of element with the following properties. When clicked, it opens the specified URL.

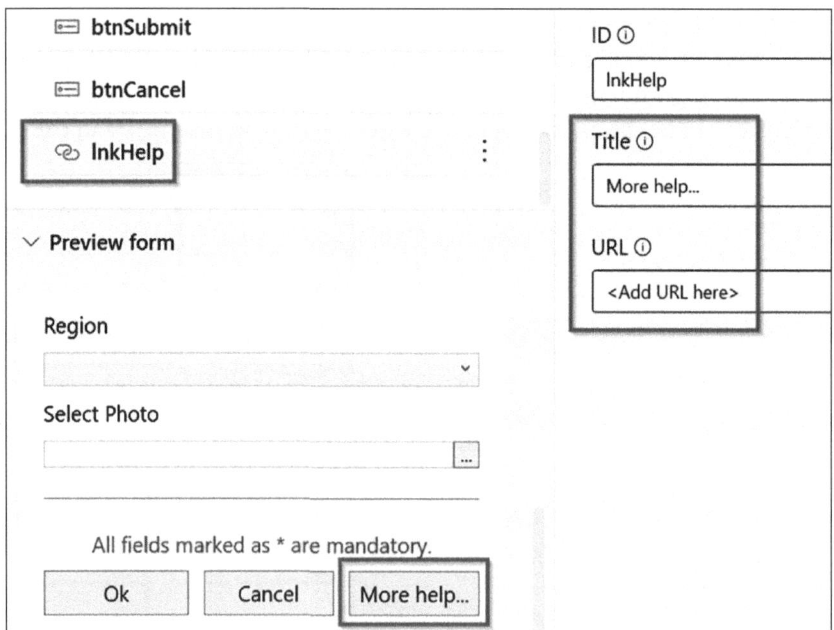

***Figure 9.74:** The Open URL type of element*

- **Reading the values from these controls:**

  This is done in a simple way. On submitting the form, the data entered by the user is stored in the **CustomFormData** output variable of the **"Display custom form"** Action. You can simply access its value via the notation as **%CustomFormData['ElementID']%** where **ElementID** is the one you supplied in the **"ID"** box while designing the form (shown in **"Name"** column in *Figure* 9.75).

For example, in *Figure* 9.61, we configured **`txtName`** as the ID of the first text box, hence **`%CustomFormData['txtName']%`** will give the value of **`John Doe`**. These can then be used anywhere down the Flow as per the automation requirements.

The following is the output variable populated after running the Flow with the Action in question:

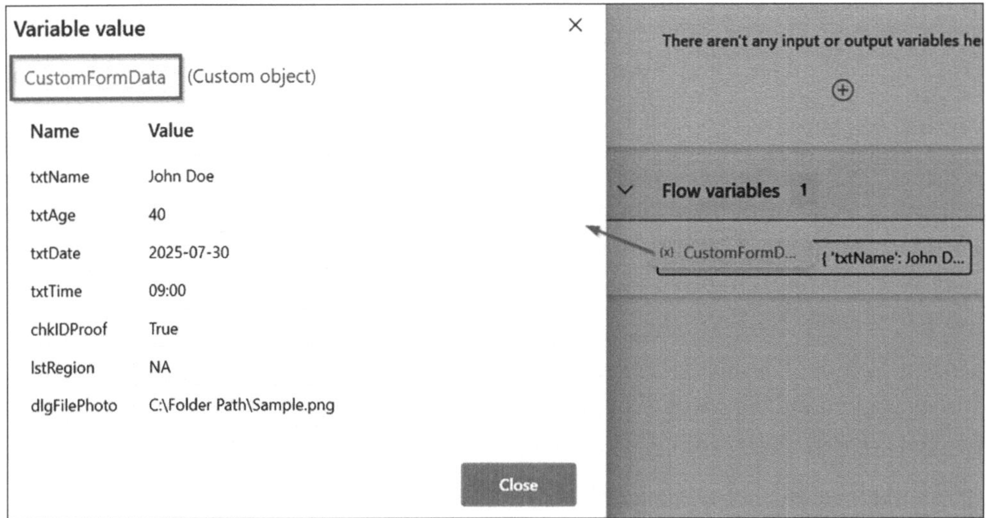

***Figure* 9.75:** *Output stored after submitting the form*

The **`ButtonPressed`** output variable will hold the ID of the button that was clicked by the user which is **`btnSubmit`** in our case. If the user has clicked the Cancel button, then this value would show as **`btnCancel`** coming from the ID, as shown in *Figure* 9.73. You can then add an **"`If`"** statement, check the value of **`ButtonPressed`**, and proceed accordingly with the next steps.

Variable value

ButtonPressed (Text value)

1 btnSubmit

Close

***Figure* 9.76:** *ID of the button that was pressed*

When a Flow runs, having Input variables in it will ask for inputs at the beginning of the Flow (*Figure* 4.5 of "*Chapter* 4: *Essential Elements of a Desktop Flow*") but they are not a user-friendly way as compared to the Display Actions or the Custom forms that we saw in this chapter, and those can be majorly used for passing values from the Cloud Flows to the Desktop Flows or for testing the Flow when run from the Console.

This concludes the topic of Unattended and Attended Automation. You should be aware that there are different licensing plans based on these run modes. The information on pricing and licensing is given in the "*Licensing*" topic of "*Chapter* 12: *Extending the Landscape of Your Desktop Flows.*"

Practical Exercise

Create a Custom form to accept manual inputs required to add details to the Contoso application. When the user submits the form, the bot should add those details to the Contoso application. The inputs to be accepted are the ones you were reading from Excel in the earlier chapters as an exercise - Date, Account, Contact, Amount, and Status.

Use appropriate elements on the form, for example, use a dropdown to show the Status with values as Paid, Uninvoiced, and Invoiced. Use validations wherever required like adding a regular expression to accept an email address.

Conclusion

In this chapter, we saw how you can make use of the Cloud portal and Cloud Flows, how you can add the concept of Work Queues in your automation for workload balancing, what are the ways available in PAD for error handling, how to include logging mechanism, how and where to continuously monitor the Desktop Flow activity for their various benefits, what are the different run modes of automation, various ways of asking inputs to the user for achieving Attended automation.

In the next chapter, "*Intelligent Automation via* PAD", we will look at the various cognitive and intelligent automation features available in PAD and how to use them via the approaches and Actions provided to us in the tool. We will also look at some automation scenarios where these can be utilized.

Questions

The following questions are either from the current or the previous chapters or require you to explore them on the PAD tool.

1. There are two types of exception-handling methods in PAD which can be interchangeably used together or separately depending on the situation. Which ones are they? Explore how they are used.

2. How can you get the Error line number and the Error description at run time when a Flow runs?
3. In the **"On block error"** Action, what are the different Flow navigation options available when **"Continue flow run"** is selected?
4. What does the toggle for **"Capture unexpected logic errors"** exactly do?
5. What are the different Actions available in PAD for asking inputs to the user to achieve Attended automation?
6. What are machines and machine groups? Which application is required to be installed to manage them?
7. Which Cloud connector is used to call a Desktop Flow from a Cloud Flow?
8. What configurations need to be made and which parameters need to be passed while calling a Desktop Flow from a Cloud Flow?
9. How to read values in a Desktop Flow that are coming from a Cloud Flow?

CHAPTER 10
Intelligent Automation via PAD

Introduction

In this era, any automation without the mention of AI is incomplete. Artificial Intelligence (AI) is the ability of computers or machines to perform tasks that usually require human intelligence. This includes things such as understanding language, recognizing patterns, solving problems, making decisions, and learning from experience, among several other things. Adding AI capabilities to RPA will enable Intelligent Automation. This chapter will guide you through leveraging various Actions in PAD to achieve this. Additionally, we'll explore the AI features available within PAD itself.

Structure

The topics we will be going through in this chapter are as follows:

- Cognitive Services in PAD
- GPT in PAD
- Copilot Features
- Suggested Actions

Cognitive Services in PAD

In the context of RPA, "*cognitive*" refers to the incorporation of AI technologies into your bots. The Cognitive services available in PAD help you to achieve Intelligent Automation and these are accessible via each of the following service providers and their Actions, namely, Google, IBM and Microsoft.

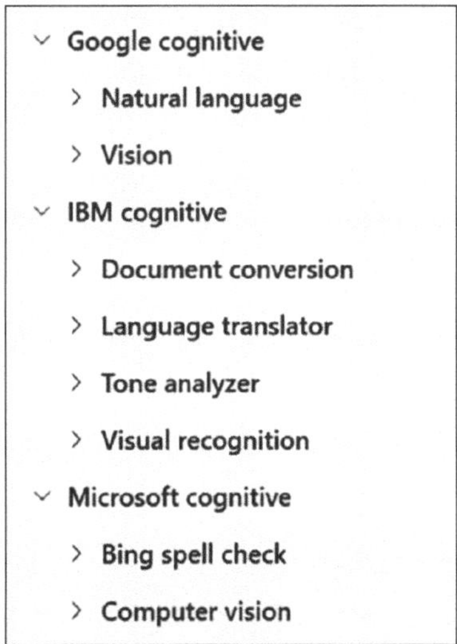

***Figure 10.1:** Cognitive services Actions in PAD*

Let us straight away jump in to use any of these services. We will perform the cognitive operations of language translation and identification using IBM services in PAD. These services may require paid licenses or would be free to use up to a certain limit.

Follow along the succeeding steps to achieve the same:

1. The language translation from IBM is done through the **"`Translate`"** Action under the **"`IBM cognitive`"** list of Actions in the **"`Actions`"** pane. But if you see the Action, it cannot be used without an API key, Instance ID, and a few other details. We are going to see how to get these details from scratch.

   To begin, create an account on https://cloud.ibm.com. If you already have ever added the Cognitive resources of language translator in your IBM account and have the details such as Instance ID, API key, and so on handy with you, then you can skip the addition of the Resource in the following steps and proceed directly on how to enter these details in the PAD Action (Step 8).

2. Once registered with an account, type **`language translator`** in the search box and choose the **service**.

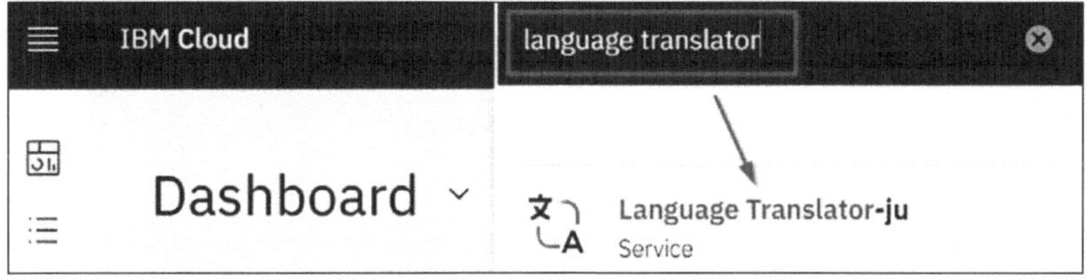

***Figure 10.2:** Picking the language translator service*

3. On the next page, you will see a **"Create"** tab similar to *Figure* 10.3. Select your location, choose the Free Lite plan, and click the **"Create"** button at the end to create a Resource.

   Read the Lite plan details to see how many characters you can use as part of this plan. Importantly, make a note of the location, which will be required in the PAD Action shortly.

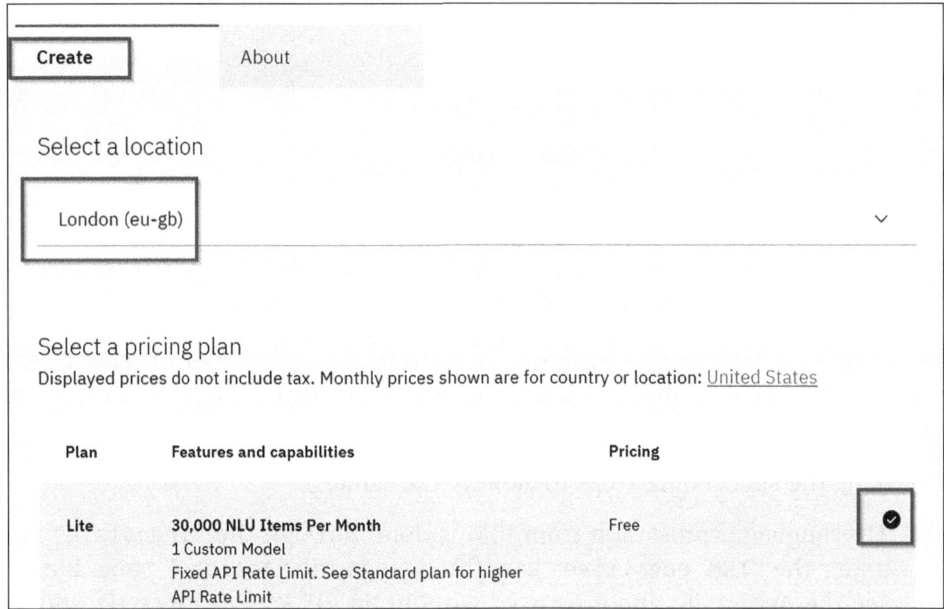

***Figure* 10.3:** *Creating a resource*

4. You will see the list of all the Resources added to your IBM account and the ones active on the Resources page via the URL https://cloud.ibm.com/resources, or navigate through the website to look for the resources section if this link changes in the future. The one that you just added for language translation will show up in the list.

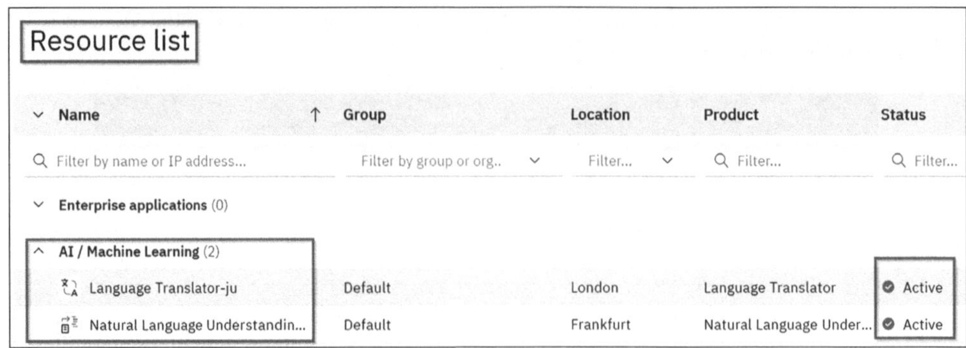

***Figure* 10.4:** *Viewing the list of added resources*

5. Click open the **`Language Translator`** resource, and we now need to create a Credential to use this Resource. Click **"`Service credentials`"** on the left-hand side, and then click the **"`New credential`"** button.

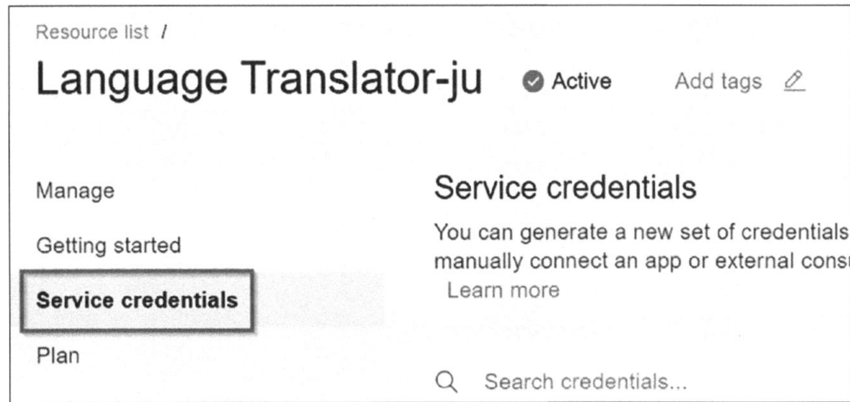

Figure 10.5: *Creating a Service credential*

6. Give a friendly name on the **"`Create credential`"** screen and click **"`Add`"**, leaving all other options as they are.

7. Once created, a credential will be added with the chosen name, and you will see a JSON when you expand the marked section of the following figure.

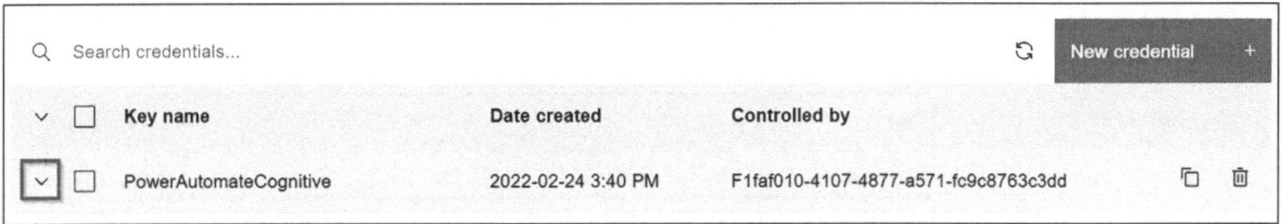

Figure 10.6: *Newly added Service credential*

8. Go to the PAD tool and drag and drop the **"`Translate`"** Action. Referring to *Figure* 10.7, add the parameter as follows:

- **Service endpoint location:**

  Select the location related to the one noted down in Step 3 (*Figure* 10.3).

- **Translate mode:**

  Either you can create your own model and give a Model ID here (which may require a paid plan) or choose **"`Source and target`"** as shown in *Figure* 10.7.

- **Source:**

  The short code for the source language of the text you would like to translate. It is selected as English for this exercise.

  Choose the Source and Target languages from the list of codes at:

https://cloud.ibm.com/docs/language-translator?topic=language-translator-translation-models

A word of mention is that IBM plans to deprecate some of their features in the upcoming future, but be noted that the way to create an API key is the same.

- **Target:**

  The short code for the target language of Hindi is selected for this exercise.

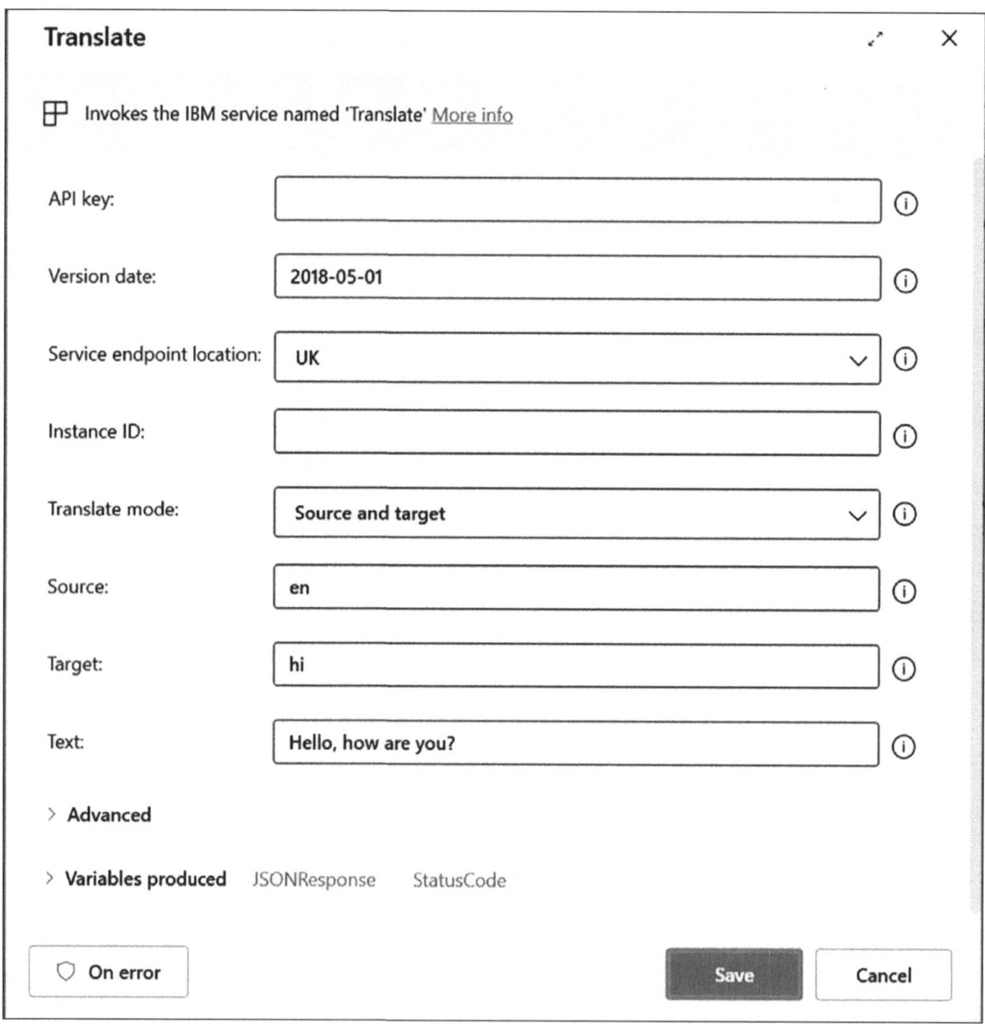

Figure 10.7: *The Translate action and its parameters*

- **Text:**

  The actual text that needs to be translated. Also supports a variable.

- **API key and Instance ID:**

  Expand the Service Credential created in *Figure* 10.6 and pick the API key and Instance ID, as shown in *Figure* 10.8. Add them without any quotes.

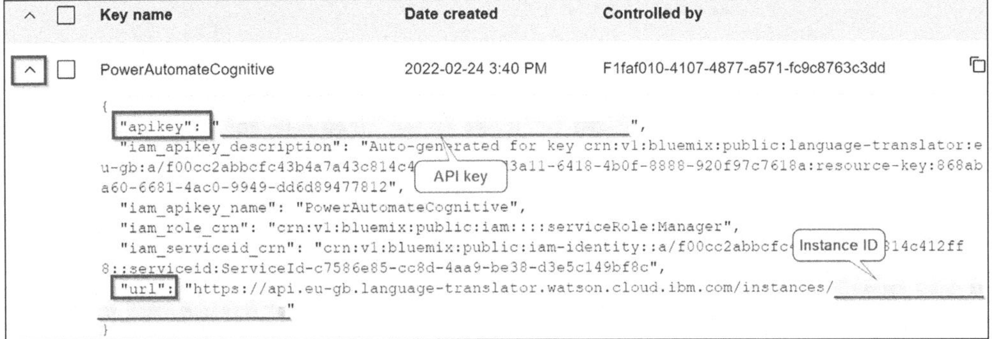

***Figure* 10.8:** *Selecting the API key and the Instance Id from the JSON*

- **Version date:**

  For the Version Date, visit the API docs of the service in question, which is the language translator: https://cloud.ibm.com/apidocs/language-translator

  For this example, the version date is 2018-05-01, as marked in the following figure.

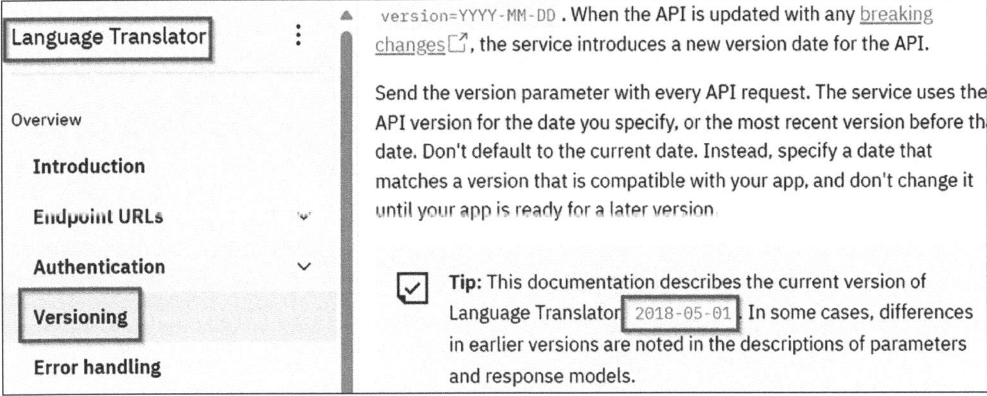

***Figure* 10.9:** *Identifying the version date*

On running the Flow, the translation in this case is stored in the **`JSONResponse`** output variable at the following variable structure.

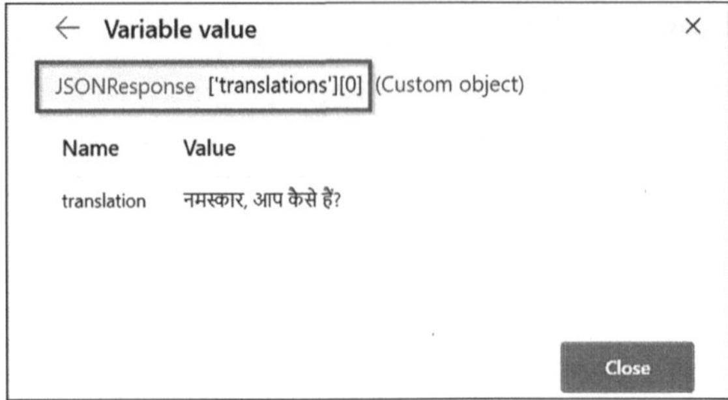

Figure 10.10: *Output variable*

So, if you print this in a message box, the output of the translation is as expected.

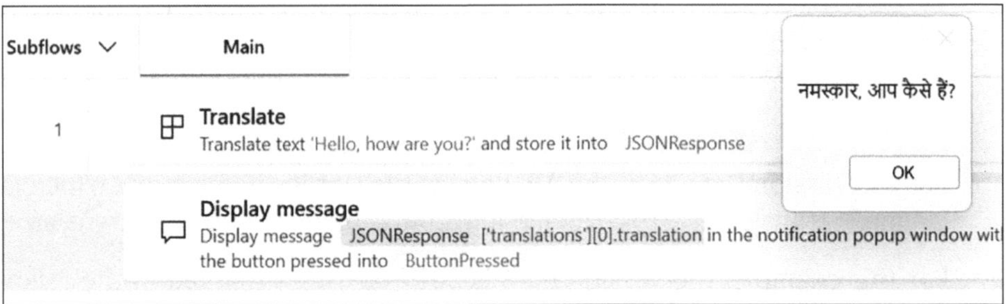

Figure 10.11: *Entire Flow and its output*

Using the same approach, here is an example of another Cognitive Action of IBM, the **"Identify language"** Action, which is used to identify the language of a given text.

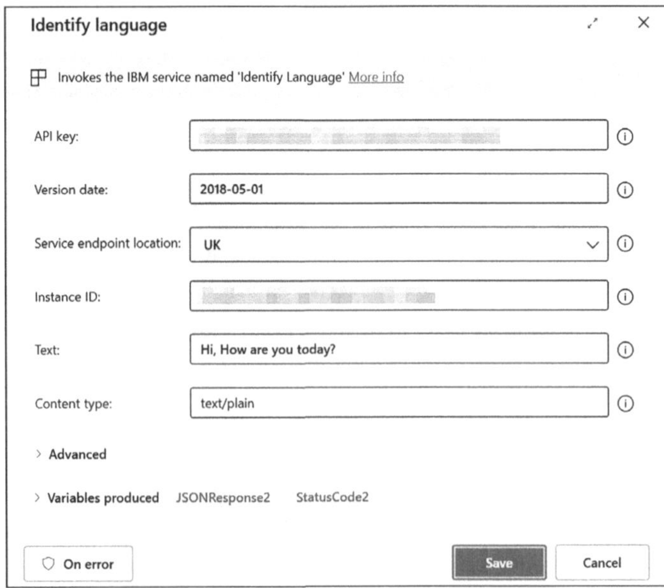

Figure 10.12: *The Identify language action*

Running this Action will give the list of potential languages along with a confidence score, as shown in the following figure. In this case, the language identification of English (en) has the highest score for the given input text.

One can even identify a language first and then use the language code (example, en) in the **"Translate"** Action.

These outputs can then be used across the Desktop Flows for any language identification and translation automation scenarios.

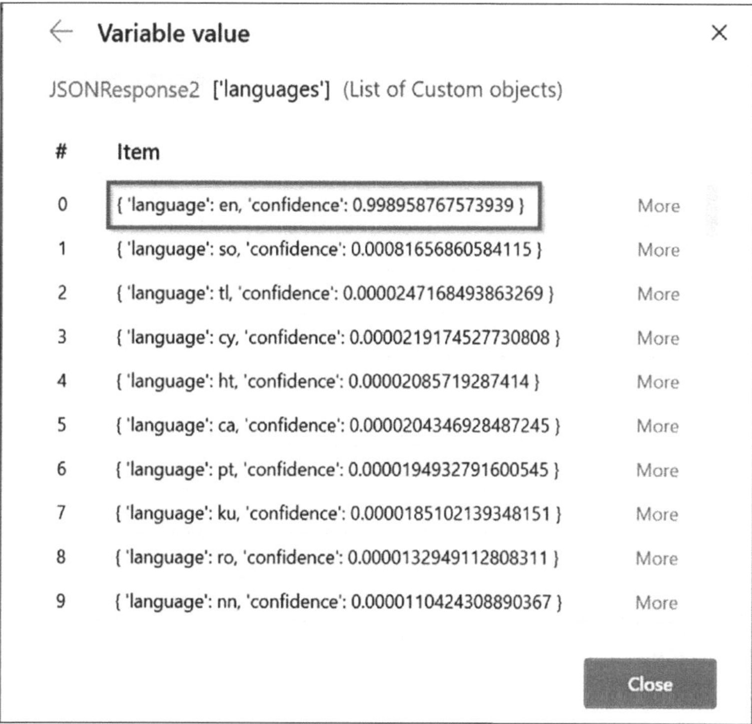

Figure 10.13: *Output of Identify language action*

You can do the same for the other IBM Cognitive Actions. Go through the list to see what each of the Actions can do. You might need to add other Resources in your IBM cloud account for using the other Cognitive services. For example, for using the **"Analyze Tone"** Action of PAD, you might need to add the *Natural Language Understanding* service in the Resources section using the aforementioned steps and use its own API key and Instance ID in the PAD Actions.

Likewise, every other service provider of Microsoft and Google has their own way of creating an API key and then using it in their respective PAD Actions. The free plan exemplified here has a certain number of free credits and units and might have a limitation after a certain point.

For paid plans used in enterprise-grade automation, you can very well fine-tune the results by creating a model of these AI services and customizing them as per the data you are using for the RPA automation.

GPT in PAD

GPT, or Generative Pre-trained Transformer, is a type of AI model. It is designed to understand and generate human-like text based on the patterns and information it has learned from large amounts of text data. PAD makes GPT available to us in the form of an Action called **"`Create text with GPT`"**. It is available under the **"`AI Builder`"** set of Actions, is a premium feature, and is under Preview as of this writing.

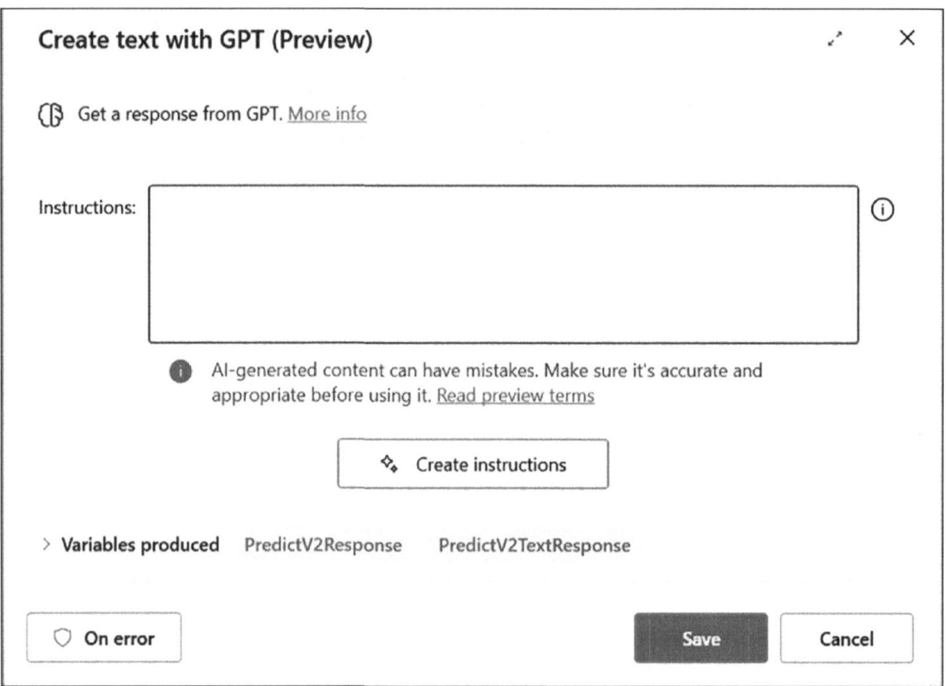

Figure 10.14: *The Create text with GPT action*

Either you give instructions to the GPT in the **"`Instructions`"** box (*Figure* 10.14) or you click the **"`Create instructions`"** button to use a pre-built template or write instructions from scratch with the help of the **"`Start from blank`"** button in the following figure.

Following is a list of those pre-built instructions template:

Open each of these templates to refer to their usage and how a text can be written to use that particular template.

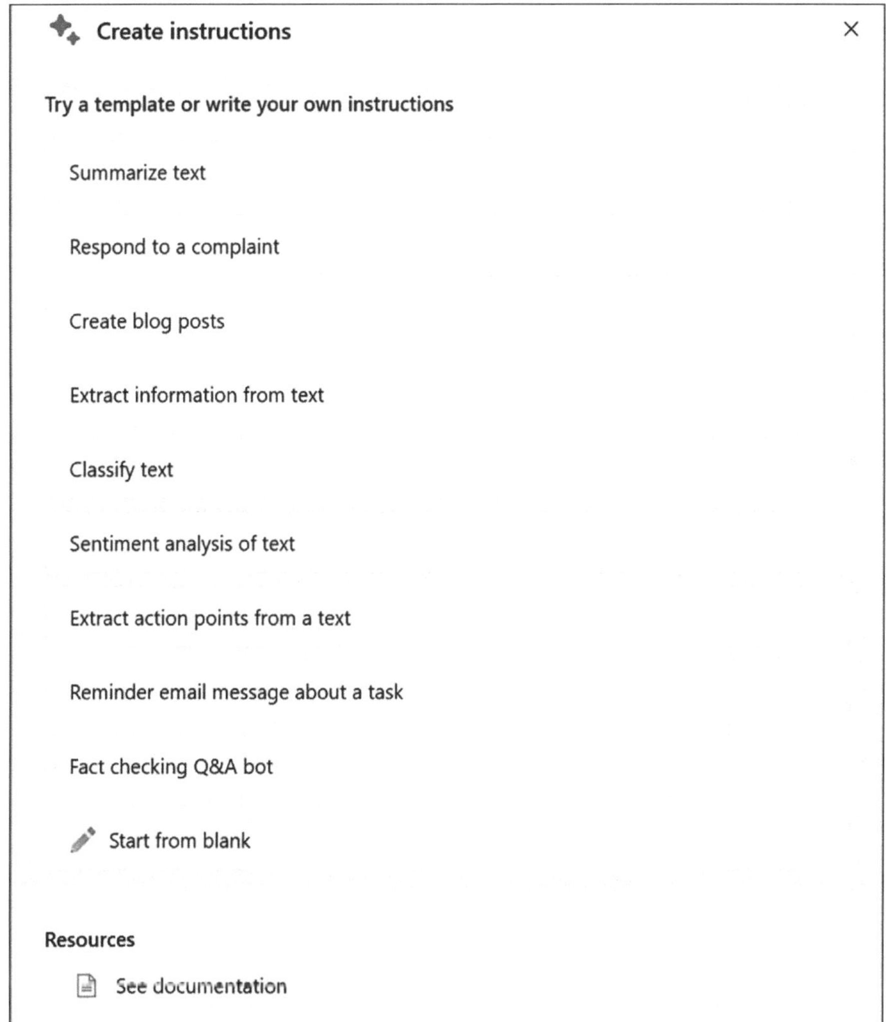

Figure 10.15: *List of pre-built instructions template*

If you start from any one of them, for example, **"`Sentiment analysis of text`"** in the following figure, you will see pre-filled instructions on how you want the sentiment analysis output to be and a way to write the input text between the wordings **"`[Start of text]`"** and **"`[End of text]`"**. On clicking the **"`Test it out`"** button, the output will be generated in the **"`Response`"** box, as shown in *Figure* 10.16. You would then click the **"`Use instructions in flow`"** button, which will paste these instructions in the previous screen, which is the one in *Figure* 10.14.

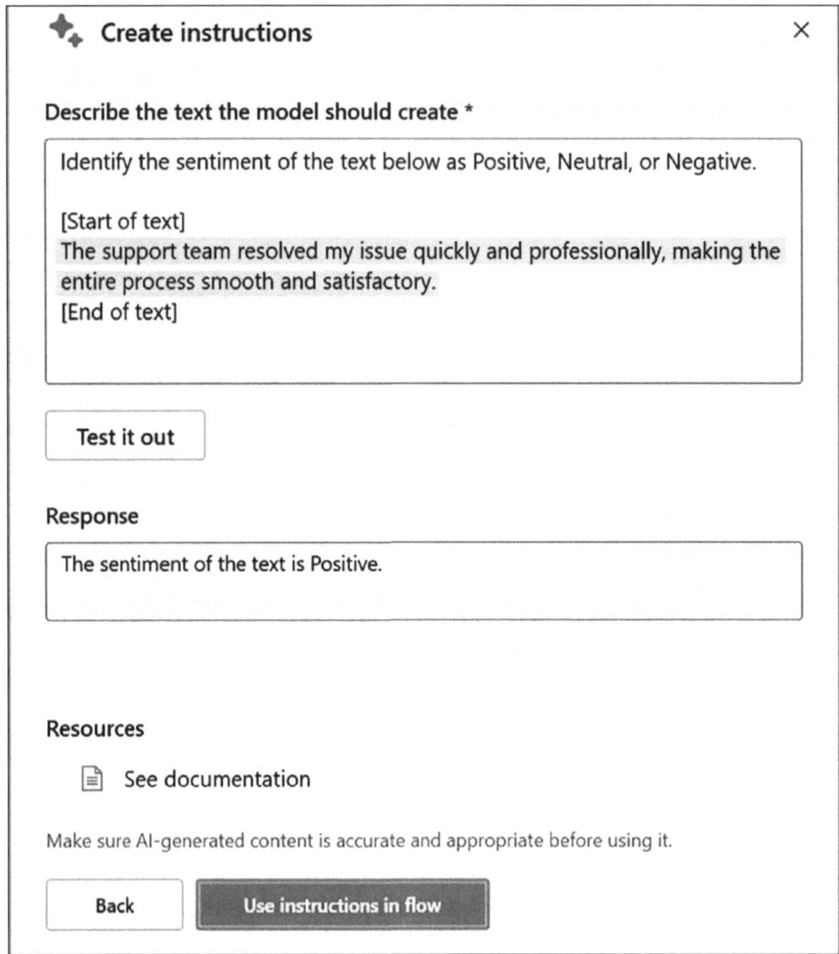

Figure 10.16: *Sample input and output of a pre-built template*

This Action generates two output variables described as follows, which can then be used in our Flows.

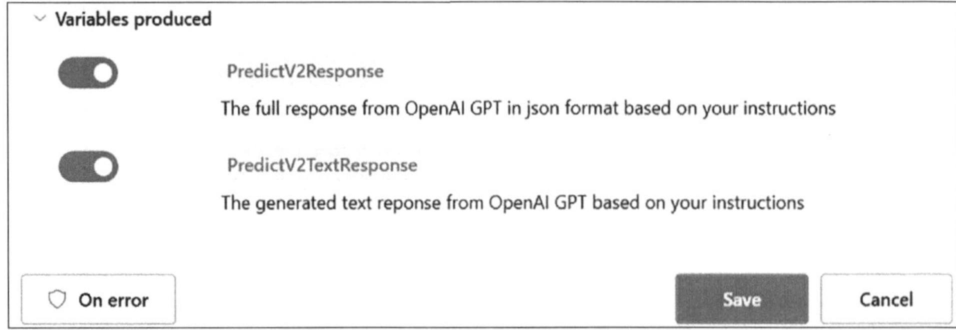

Figure 10.17: *Output variables produced*

The variables of PAD can also be used here, as shown in the following figure. For example, the RPA bot reads a ticket feedback using Web automation or APIs, stores that feedback in a variable called **`%InputText%`**, and passes it to the following Action to get its sentiment analysis. In case of an unsatisfactory feedback, the bot can escalate the priority of the ticket or even send an email to the Support team to contact the user who is dissatisfied and make things right for them, thus achieving customer satisfaction using GPT in your automation.

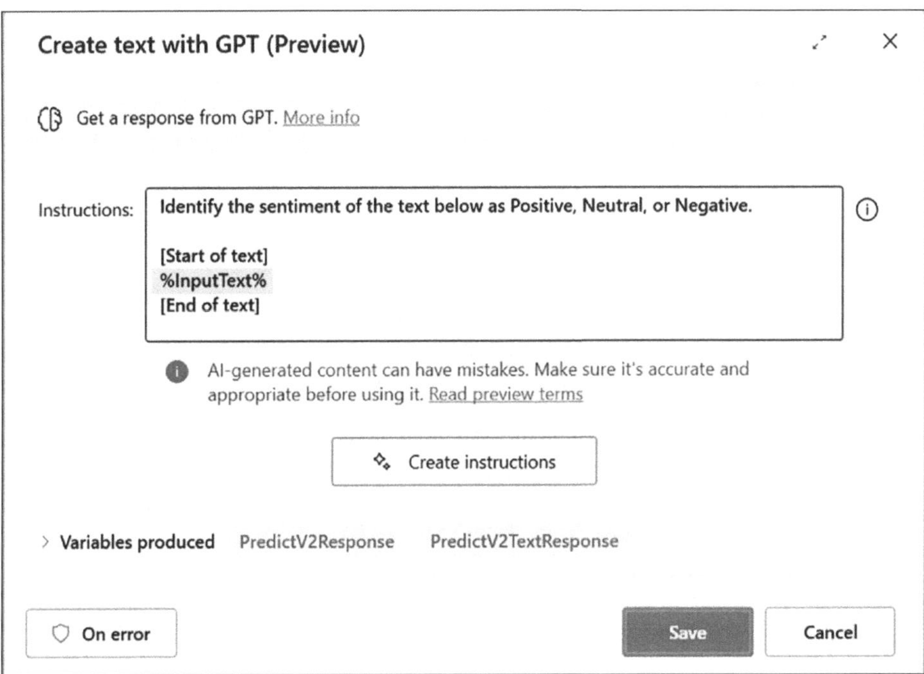

Figure 10.18: *Use of variables*

Something that you should be aware of is "prompts". Prompts are cues or inputs given to an AI model (GPT in this case) to generate a response. Refer to the newly added prompt that says **"`Write the answer in one word`"** and notice the difference in the output of *Figure* 10.16 as opposed to the one in the following figure. This would certainly make it easy for the RPA bot to pick up the response and move forward rather than using Text functions to filter out the desired response. Writing a suitable prompt is a skill and can be developed by trying various permutations and combinations of the instructions.

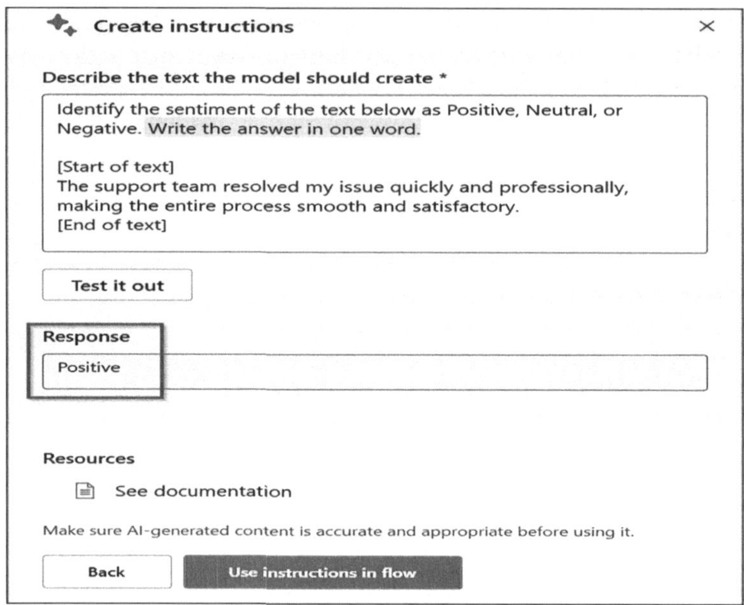

***Figure 10.19:** Using prompts*

Another important thing that you should be aware of is that when you click the **"Save"** button of the Action, you will get an error.

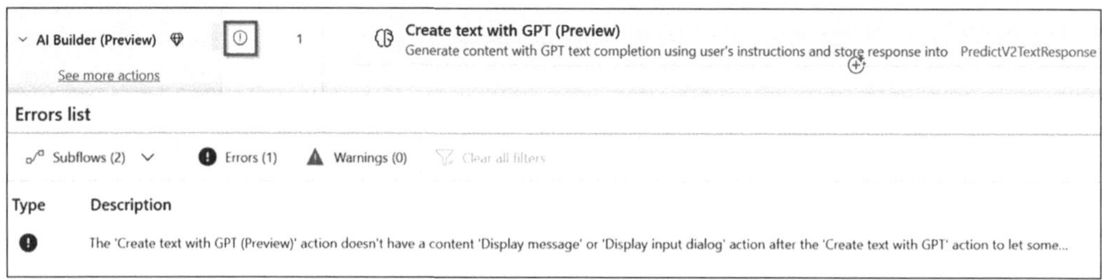

***Figure 10.20:** Responsible AI error*

The full text of the error is as follows:

```
The 'Create text with GPT (Preview)' action doesn't have a content 'Dis-
play message' or 'Display input dialog' action after the 'Create text
with GPT' action to let someone manually review the generated content.
```

The error is because, as part of the **"Responsible AI"** initiative, Microsoft wants the output coming from the GPT to be reviewed before using it. The way suggested by Microsoft is to have a **"Display input dialog"** Action or a **"Display message"** Action showing the output coming from the **"Create text with GPT"** Action.

Refer to the following link and the figure for more details. The link also has details stating that this feature is available currently as gated access, meaning you need to apply to get access to it, and is only available in specific regions yet:

https://learn.microsoft.com/en-us/power-automate/desktop-flows/actions-reference/aibuilder

> Further strengthening our commitment to responsible AI we're introducing some updates related to the utilization of **Create text with GPT (preview)** action in the Power Automate for desktop October 2023 update. Specifically:
>
> - A **Display input dialog** action or **Display message** action must accompany each use of the **Create text with GPT** action
> - The **Display input dialog** action or **Display message** action must contain the response from the **Create text with GPT** action in its body so it is clearly presented to the user

Figure 10.21: *Solution for handling the Responsible AI error*

As soon as you add **`%PredictV2TextResponse%`** (which is the text output coming from the GPT Action) in a display message, the error disappears, and when you run the Flow, following is the output in one word according to the prompt.

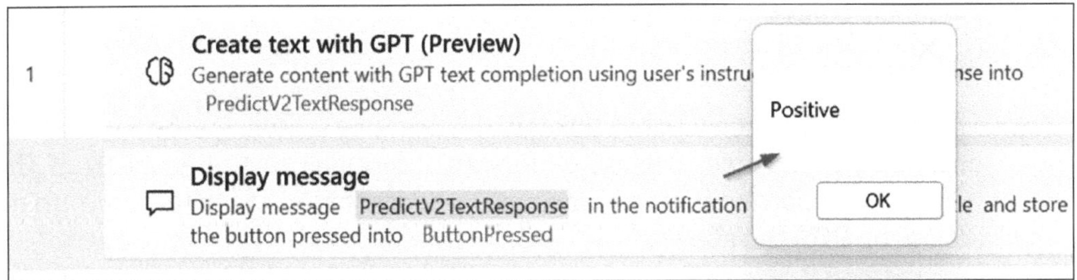

Figure 10.22: *Output after adding solution for the Responsible AI error*

GPT Scenarios Using PAD

Generally, developers, users, or anyone in RPA struggle to find out scenarios where GPT can be used in conjunction with any RPA tool. Here we will look at several automation scenarios that can be leveraged with PAD and the GPT Action we have been seeing in the previous section.

The **Source** of input text for these scenarios could be anything like an incoming email body, a ticket description, any file, or in fact any field on any application that is readable by the PAD bot.

Scenario 1: Find Out the Category/Department Name/Routing Area

In this scenario, based on the input text, GPT will identify the category, the department name, or a routing area of service and thereby help in expediting input queries.

Workflow of the bot:

1. The Power Automate Desktop bot reads the incoming data, as an example, from any of the aforementioned sources using the available Actions.

   Example 1: Billing

   Hello, I have recently received my monthly invoice and noticed that the amount charged is incorrect. I have checked my usage and it seems that I have been charged for services that I have not used. Could you please take a look at my account and resolve this issue? I would also like to receive an updated invoice reflecting the correct charges. Thank you for your assistance.

2. PAD sends the aforementioned text to the GPT along with the prompt, as shown in the following figure. Certain responses require more than one word; hence, you may modify the prompt as "in short".

   Response from the GPT Action:

   Billing Dispute

3. The PAD bot can then create a ticket in the ticketing system for the appropriate department (example, Billing), or forward the email to the email ID of the respective department, or a human can validate this and take the appropriate action, or all of the above.

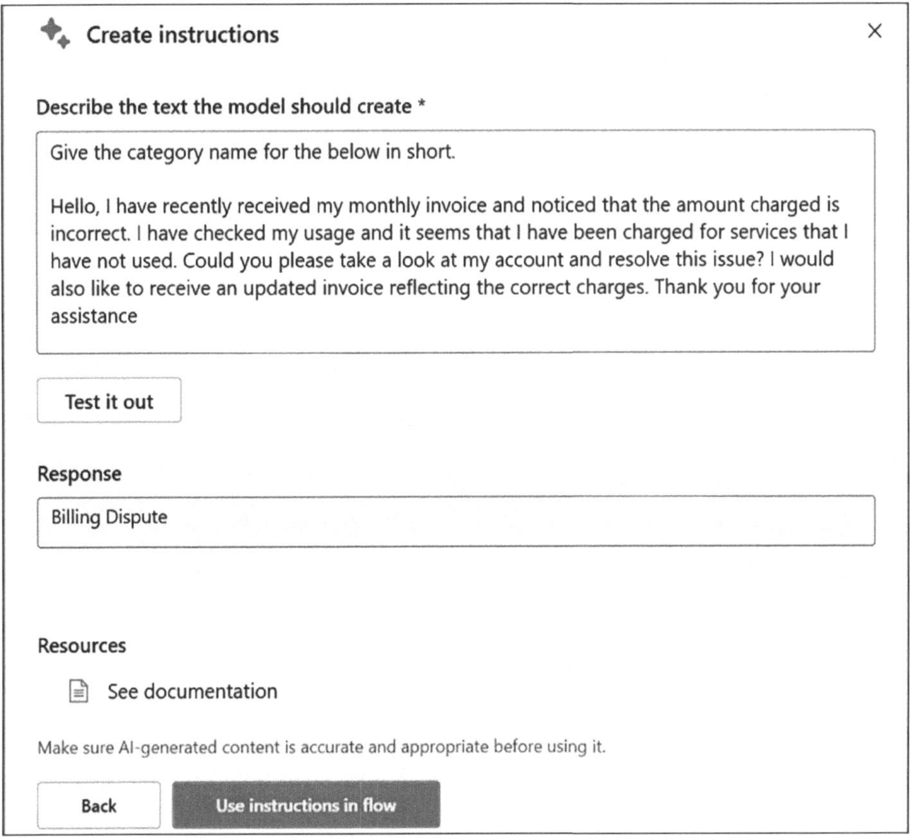

Figure 10.23: *Instructions and the Response for the scenario*

Example 2: IT Support

Instructions:

You may even add the starting and ending hash characters '#' and write the text between them.

Give the category name for the below in short.

###

Hello, I am having trouble connecting my laptop to the internet. I have tried restarting my laptop and my router but it's still not working. I am able to connect to the internet on my phone, so I think the issue is with my laptop. Can you please help me resolve this issue? Thank you in advance for your assistance.

###

Response from the GPT Action:

The category for the issue described is "Technical Support."

This may need Text Actions, or change the prompt to **"Give the category name for the below in few words"** and see what you get. Finalize the one that works best for your automation scenario.

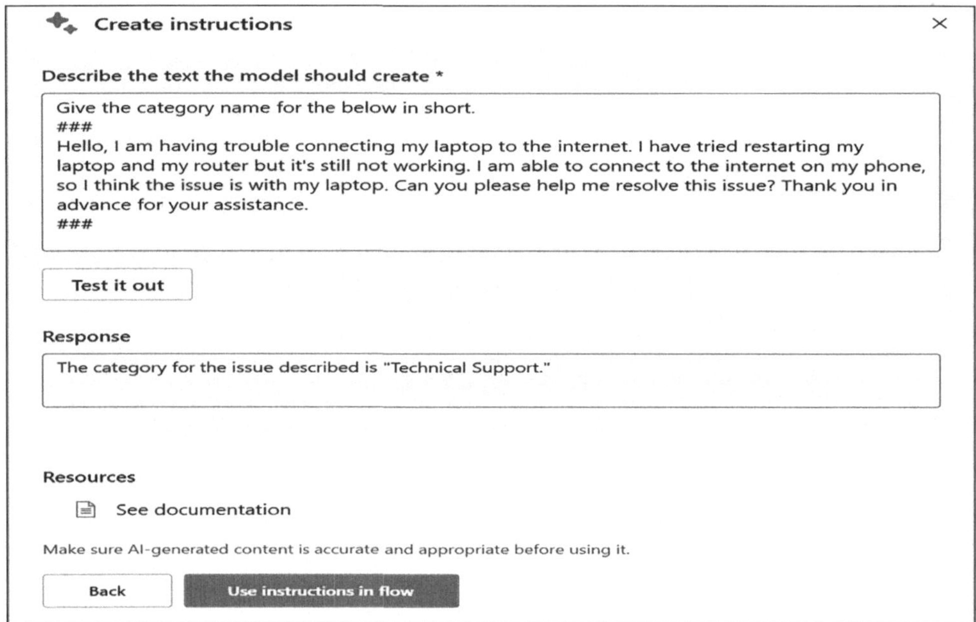

***Figure 10.24:** Instructions and the Response for the scenario*

Example 3: Sales

Instructions:

Here is an example of using **"department name"** instead of category and with the wording **"without giving multiple options"** because the GPT may give more than one option at times, such as **"Sales or Customer Service"**.

Give the department name for the below in short without giving multiple options.

I am interested in learning more about your products and services.
I would appreciate it if you could provide me with the necessary information to help me make an informed decision. Thank you for your time and assistance. Looking forward to hearing from you soon.

Response from the GPT Action:

Sales

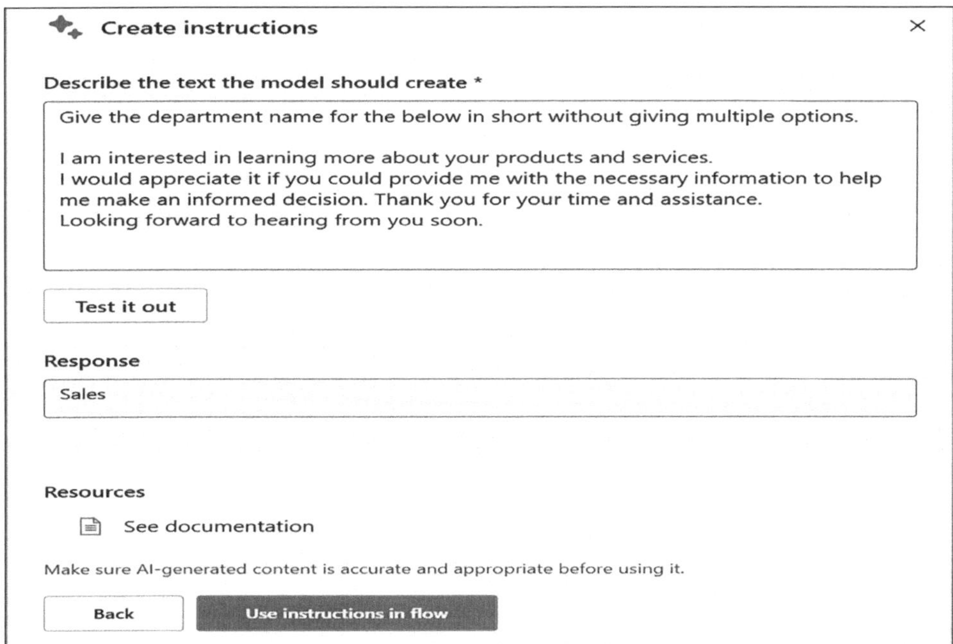

Figure 10.25: *Instructions and the Response for the scenario*

Example 4: Inquiry

Instructions:

Here is another modified version using the wording **`"just the category name"`**.

> *Provide just the category name for the below text.*
> *Hello, I am interested in using your company's product for my business and I would like to know more about its features and capabilities. Can you please provide me with a demo or brochure of the product so I can evaluate if it meets my requirements? Additionally, I would like to know if there are any customization options available. Thank you for your time and I look forward to hearing back from you soon.*

Response from the GPT Action:

Business Inquiry

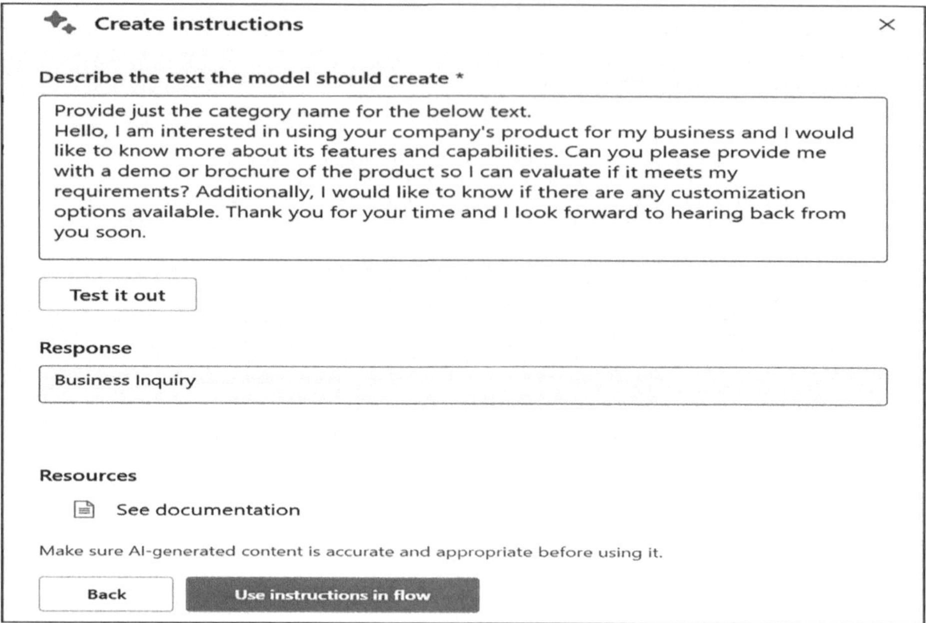

Figure 10.26: *Instructions and the Response for the scenario*

Example 5: Multiple department names

Instructions:

An example of a different variation for asking three department names for the input text.

Give 3 department names where the below feedback should be routed to in short.

Hello, I recently used your product and I was overall satisfied with my experience. However, I did have a few suggestions on how the product could be improved. I think adding a feature to export data would be very useful for me and I believe it would be appreciated by other users as well. I would also like to suggest that the user interface be simplified for better navigation. Thank you for considering my feedback.

Response from the GPT Action:

1. *Product Development*
2. *Customer Experience*
3. *User Interface Design*

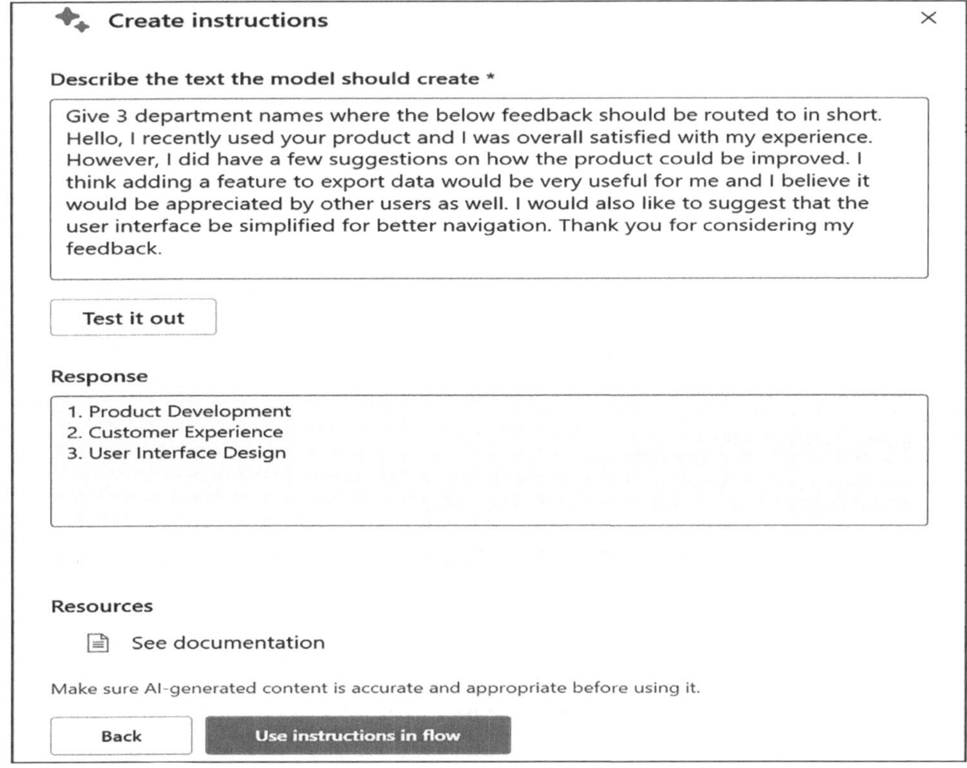

Figure 10.27: *Instructions and the Response for the scenario*

Scenario 2: Auto-Reply Based on the Type of Incoming Request

In this scenario, the GPT will read the input text and, based on the intent and the content, will suggest what should be replied back to the originator via the bot.

Workflow of the bot:

1. The PAD bot reads the incoming data from any of the mentioned sources using the available Actions.

Example 1: Complaint auto-reply

Instructions:

Write an auto-reply for the below text.
Dear Customer Service Team,

I am writing to express my disappointment with my recent purchase from your website. The product I received was not as described on the website and does not meet my expectations. I feel that I have been misled by the product description and the images provided on the website.

I would like to request a refund for this purchase, as I do not believe that it is fair for me to keep a product that does not meet my expectations.

Please let me know the next steps in this process and how I can return the product.

Thank you for your attention to this matter.

Sincerely,

John

Response from the GPT Action:

Dear John,

Thank you for reaching out to us regarding your recent purchase. We apologize for any inconvenience this may have caused you. We take customer satisfaction seriously and we are committed to resolving this issue promptly.

To assist you with your request for a refund and return of the product, please provide us with your order number and any relevant details about the item in question. Our customer service team will review your case and guide you through the next steps in the process.

We appreciate your understanding and patience as we work to resolve this matter to your satisfaction.

Thank you for bringing this to our attention.

Best regards,

Customer Service Team

2. A human can then validate the auto-reply suggested by GPT, make necessary modifications such as add URLs, attach Receipts, catalogs, ticket numbers, and so on, and reply back to the sender either manually or through the bot.

Example 2: Sales inquiry auto-reply

Instructions:

Write an auto-reply for the below text.
Dear Sales Team,

I am interested in purchasing one of your products and would like to receive more information about it. Specifically, I am interested in the specifications, pricing, and availability of the product.

Could you please provide me with more information on these aspects? Additionally, I would appreciate it if you could let me know if there are any ongoing promotions or discounts that apply to this product.

Thank you for your assistance. I look forward to hearing back from you soon.

Sincerely,

Emily

Response from the GPT Action:

GPT even returns with a placeholder text with square brackets seen at the end of the following response asking you to replace it with your company name, which even the bot can do the replacement.

Dear Emily,

Thank you for reaching out to us regarding your interest in our products. We appreciate your inquiry and are happy to provide you with more information.

To assist you better, could you please specify which product you are interested in? Once we have that information, we will promptly send you detailed specifications, pricing, availability, and any ongoing promotions or discounts that may apply.

We look forward to helping you with your purchase. Please provide us with the product name or details so we can assist you effectively.

Thank you for considering our products. We will get back to you with the information you need as soon as possible.

Best regards,

[Your Company Name] Sales Team

Example 3: IT Request auto-reply

Instructions:

Write an auto-reply for the below text.
Dear IT Team,

I am experiencing an issue with my computer and require assistance in resolving it. Specifically, I am unable to access certain files on my computer and am encountering error messages when attempting to open them.

Could you please advise on how to fix this issue? Additionally, if there are any updates or software installations that need to be performed, please let me know.

Thank you for your help.

Best regards,

Alex

Response from the GPT Action:

Here is an example where GPT also detects what the subject of the email is based on the content of the email and also provides certain recommendation steps, which can then be manually verified, modified, and replied back via the bot itself.

Subject: Re: Issue with Computer Files

Dear Alex,

Thank you for reaching out to the IT Team for assistance with the issue you are experiencing on your computer. We understand the importance of resolving this promptly.

To address the problem of being unable to access certain files and encountering error messages, we recommend the following steps:

1. *Check if the files are located in a network location that is currently unavailable.*

2. *Ensure that you have the necessary permissions to access the files.*

3. *Run a disk check to identify and repair any potential file system errors.*

4. *Update your antivirus software and perform a full system scan to rule out any malware issues.*

If the issue persists after trying these steps, please provide us with more details about the error messages you are encountering so we can offer more specific guidance.

Regarding updates and software installations, we recommend keeping your operating system and software up to date. You can check for updates in the settings of your computer or contact us for assistance with software installations.

Thank you for your cooperation, and we will do our best to help resolve this issue promptly.

Best regards,

IT Team

Scenario 3: Extract Key Value Pairs from Unstructured Data

In this scenario, the GPT will read the input text having unstructured data, make sense out of it, and extract relevant information in the form of key value pairs and/or in a format that we specify, such as JSON, and more.

Workflow of the bot:

1. The PAD bot may read this from a receipt using OCR or from any of the mentioned sources using the available Actions.

Example 1: Receipt processing

Instructions:

Can you extract the key value pairs of the below text in Json format.
ABC Supermarket
1234 Main Street
Anytown, USA 12345

Date: 01/20/2025
Time: 11:45 AM
Receipt No.: 123456789

Item Quantity Price
Product A 1 $10.00
Product B 2 $5.00 each
Product C 3 $3.00 each

Subtotal: $32.00
Tax: $2.56
Total: $34.56

Payment Method: Visa
Card Number: **** **** **** 1234
Authorization Code: 123456

Thank you for shopping at ABC Supermarket!

Visit us again soon.

Response from the GPT Action:

```
{
  "Store Information": {
```

```
    "Name": "ABC Supermarket",
    "Address": "1234 Main Street, Anytown, USA 12345"
  },
  "Transaction Details": {
    "Date": "01/20/2025",
    "Time": "11:45 AM",
    "Receipt No.": "123456789"
  },
  "Items": [
    {
      "Product": "Product A",
      "Quantity": 1,
      "Price": "$10.00"
    },
    {
      "Product": "Product B",
      "Quantity": 2,
      "Price": "$5.00 each"
    },
    {
      "Product": "Product C",
      "Quantity": 3,
      "Price": "$3.00 each"
    }
  ],
  "Payment Details": {
    "Subtotal": "$32.00",
    "Tax": "$2.56",
    "Total": "$34.56",
    "Payment Method": "Visa",
    "Card Number": "**** **** **** 1234",
    "Authorization Code": "123456"
  }
}
```


2. The bot can then process this output using the available Actions in PAD and update the data in other systems.

Example 2: Sales/Order processing

Instructions:

Here is an example of asking GPT to give the output in CSV format from an unstructured text.

Can you extract the key value pairs of the below text in CSV format.

Dear Sales team,
I would like to place an order for the following items: 10 units of Product A (SKU: A123) 5 units of Product B (SKU: B456) 20 units of Product C (SKU: C789).

Response from the GPT Action:

Product A,SKU: A123,10
Product B,SKU: B456,5
Product C,SKU: C789,20

Example 3: IT Support

Instructions:

Extract the key value pairs of the below text in JSON format.
Dear Support team,
I am having an issue with my computer. The screen keeps freezing and I can't seem to find a solution. I have tried restarting the computer several times but the problem persists. My computer model is Dell Inspiron 15 and the operating system is Windows 10. Please help me resolve this issue as soon as possible.
Thank you.
John Doe

Response from the GPT Action:

```
{
  "Issue": "Screen keeps freezing",
  "Troubleshooting Steps Taken": "Tried restarting the computer several times",
  "Computer Model": "Dell Inspiron 15",
  "Operating System": "Windows 10",
  "Name": "John Doe"
}
```

Scenario 4: Emotion and Sentiment Analysis

In this scenario, the GPT will extract the sentiment (Positive, Negative, Neutral) and emotion (Anger, Frustration, Happy, and so on) behind the input text.

Workflow of the bot:

1. The PAD bot reads the incoming data from any of the mentioned sources using the available Actions.

Example 1: Negative

Instructions:

Give the emotion and sentiment analysis of the below text each in one word.

The product I received was defective and the customer service team was unresponsive and unhelpful when I reached out for assistance. I am extremely dissatisfied with my experience and will not be purchasing from this company again.

Response from the GPT Action:

Emotion: Dissatisfaction

Sentiment: Negative

2. A human can then take the following possible follow-up actions:
   - Give a call to the sender
   - Elevate the customer service
   - Increase the priority of the ticket
   - Expedite the resolution of the sender's issue

Example 2: Positive

Instructions:

Give the emotion and sentiment analysis of the below text each in one word.

I am extremely satisfied with the service I received. The customer service representative was very helpful and resolved my issue efficiently. I will definitely be returning as a customer.

Response from the GPT Action:

Emotion: Satisfaction
Sentiment: Positive

Example 3: Neutral

Instructions:

Give the emotion and sentiment analysis of the below text each in one word.

I recently purchased a new laptop from your online store. It arrived on schedule and in good condition. The setup process was straightforward, and it seems to work as expected. There isn't anything particularly noteworthy about the experience, and the product functions as described. Overall, it's an average purchase with no significant issues to mention.

Response from the GPT Action:

> *Emotion: Satisfied*
> *Sentiment: Neutral*

Scenario 5: Language Translation Services

There are several instances where an input text from a particular language has to be converted to another language, be it for an incoming email or an IT request, or from anywhere else for that matter. In this scenario, the GPT will translate the language of the input text to the specified language. You can even ask it to give the name of the language.

Example 1: Danish to English - Billing issue

Instructions:

> *Translate the below text to English.*
> *Jeg har et problem med min faktura. Det ser ud til, at jeg er blevet opkrævet for et produkt, som jeg ikke har bestilt. Beløbet på fakturaen er også forkert. Kan I venligst hjælpe mig med at få dette løst?*

Response from the GPT Action:

> *I have a problem with my invoice. It seems that I have been charged for a product that I did not order. The amount on the invoice is also incorrect. Can you please help me resolve this?*

Example 2: English to Spanish - IT Support

Instructions:

> *Translate the below text to Spanish.*
> *Hello, I have a problem with my computer. I can't connect to the Internet, and it seems there is an issue with the network adapter. The network icon shows that there are no available connections. I have tried restarting the computer and the router, but it still doesn't work. My computer runs on Windows 10 and has an Intel 82579LM Gigabit network card. Can you help me fix this issue?*

Response from the GPT Action:

> *Hola, tengo un problema con mi computadora. No puedo conectarme a Internet y parece que hay un problema con el adaptador de red. El icono de red muestra que no hay conexiones disponibles. He intentado reiniciar la computadora y el enrutador, pero aún no funciona. Mi computadora funciona con Windows 10 y tiene una tarjeta de red Gigabit Intel 82579LM. ¿Puedes ayudarme a solucionar este problema?*

We looked at five GPT scenarios, and these are illustrations of using it with PAD, but are not limited to these. These scenarios can even be used in combination with each other. For example, identifying and translating the language of an incoming text, detecting the department from the same text, doing a sentiment analysis to identify the tone of the request, extracting key value pairs from that text, auto-replying to the same person, and so on, all of these in the same bot. The inclusion of AI gives greater possibilities, and it is up to the bot developers to explore its creativity and innovativeness.

GPT scenarios are not only limited to these but can also be implemented to format your data in PAD.

For example, you have some rows and columns in a Datatable variable. You can loop through the Datatable and create an HTML structure out of it by adding the HTML tags of header <th>, table rows as <tr>, and table data as <td>.

You can then pass the following instructions to the GPT to give you a Cascading Style Sheet (CSS) with a formatting of your choice.

Instructions:

> *Provide a CSS for the below without any description.*
> *table header as dark blue background with white font*
> *every alternate row as light gray*
> *Font as verdana*
> *text align to left*
> *border 2px with dark gray*
> *width as 80 percent*

Response from the GPT Action:

```
table {
  width: 80%;
  border: 2px solid darkgray;
  font-family: Verdana;
}

th {
  background-color: darkblue;
  color: white;
  text-align: left;
}

tr:nth-child(even) {
  background-color: lightgray;
}
```

Prefix this CSS to the HTML table that you have generated in its previous step. You can then use the final HTML containing the CSS as well as the HTML table and utilize this good-looking formatted and colored table anywhere in your PAD bots, for example, in the body of an email.

How about trying this as a practical exercise, which is a good combination to use GPT along with the data in the PAD Flow?

Here is how the input Datatable and the output HTML table will look like:

Sample Input:

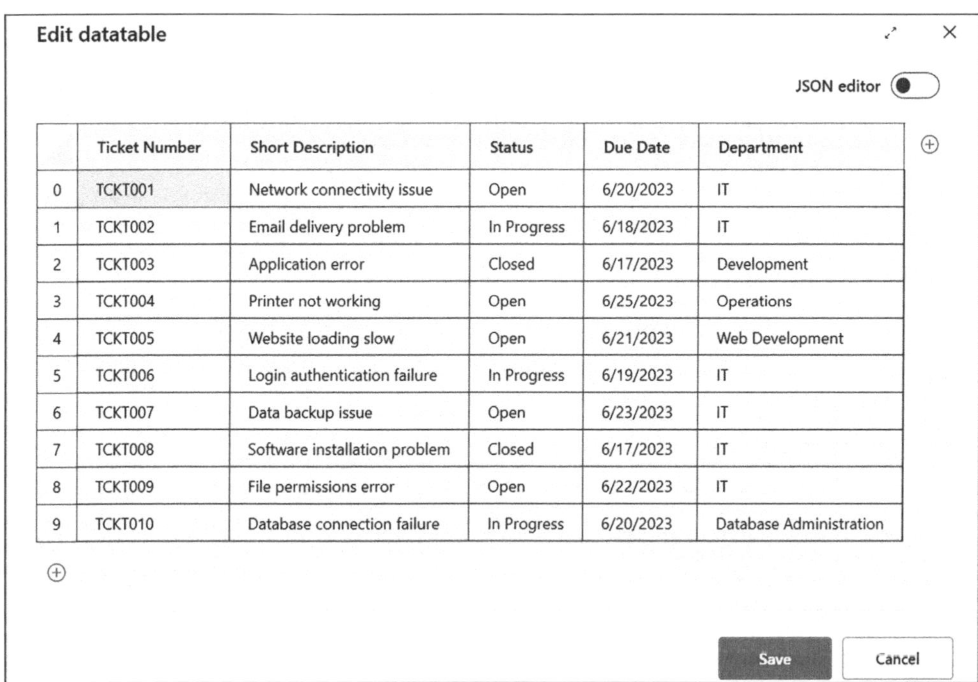

Edit datatable

JSON editor

	Ticket Number	Short Description	Status	Due Date	Department
0	TCKT001	Network connectivity issue	Open	6/20/2023	IT
1	TCKT002	Email delivery problem	In Progress	6/18/2023	IT
2	TCKT003	Application error	Closed	6/17/2023	Development
3	TCKT004	Printer not working	Open	6/25/2023	Operations
4	TCKT005	Website loading slow	Open	6/21/2023	Web Development
5	TCKT006	Login authentication failure	In Progress	6/19/2023	IT
6	TCKT007	Data backup issue	Open	6/23/2023	IT
7	TCKT008	Software installation problem	Closed	6/17/2023	IT
8	TCKT009	File permissions error	Open	6/22/2023	IT
9	TCKT010	Database connection failure	In Progress	6/20/2023	Database Administration

Save Cancel

Figure 10.28: *Sample input datatable*

Sample Output 1:

Ticket Number	Short Description	Status	Due Date	Department
TCKT001	Network connectivity issue	Open	6/20/2023	IT
TCKT002	Email delivery problem	In Progress	6/18/2023	IT
TCKT003	Application error	Closed	6/17/2023	Development
TCKT004	Printer not working	Open	6/25/2023	Operations
TCKT005	Website loading slow	Open	6/21/2023	Web Development
TCKT006	Login authentication failure	In Progress	6/19/2023	IT
TCKT007	Data backup issue	Open	6/23/2023	IT
TCKT008	Software installation problem	Closed	6/17/2023	IT
TCKT009	File permissions error	Open	6/22/2023	IT
TCKT010	Database connection failure	In Progress	6/20/2023	Database Administration

Figure 10.29: *Sample 1 output after combining HTML table and CSS from GPT*

Sample Output 2:

Ticket Number	Short Description	Status	Due Date	Department
TCKT001	Network connectivity issue	Open	6/20/2023	IT
TCKT002	Email delivery problem	In Progress	6/18/2023	IT
TCKT003	Application error	Closed	6/17/2023	Development
TCKT004	Printer not working	Open	6/25/2023	Operations
TCKT005	Website loading slow	Open	6/21/2023	Web Development
TCKT006	Login authentication failure	In Progress	6/19/2023	IT
TCKT007	Data backup issue	Open	6/23/2023	IT
TCKT008	Software installation problem	Closed	6/17/2023	IT
TCKT009	File permissions error	Open	6/22/2023	IT
TCKT010	Database connection failure	In Progress	6/20/2023	Database Administration

Figure 10.30: *Sample 2 output after combining HTML table and CSS from GPT*

Here is another unique way to use GPT with your data.

We will be extracting the entire HTML body of a table from a webpage, then pass that HTML to the GPT and ask it for relevant information.

Follow the succeeding steps:

1. Launch a new or attach to an existing webpage that has a table similar to the following. https://www.w3schools.com/html/tryit.asp?filename=tryhtml_table_intro

2. Use the **"`Get details of element on web page`"** Action to capture the UI element where it shows as **"`Body`"**, as shown in *Figure* 10.31.

   This depends on the webpage. You may even use any other HTML tags to capture the UI element depending on where the content is, for example, within a <div> tag.

Following is a figure of the **"`Body`"** element when hovered by the mouse via the UI element picker of the **"`Get details of element on web page`"** Action.

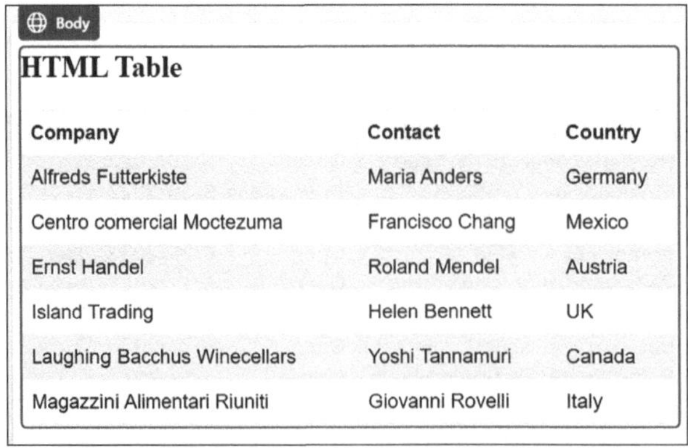

HTML Table

Company	Contact	Country
Alfreds Futterkiste	Maria Anders	Germany
Centro comercial Moctezuma	Francisco Chang	Mexico
Ernst Handel	Roland Mendel	Austria
Island Trading	Helen Bennett	UK
Laughing Bacchus Winecellars	Yoshi Tannamuri	Canada
Magazzini Alimentari Riuniti	Giovanni Rovelli	Italy

Figure 10.31: *Capture the UI element of the Body*

3. In the Action, get the **"Html"** of the UI element. The output variable is **%AttributeValue%**.

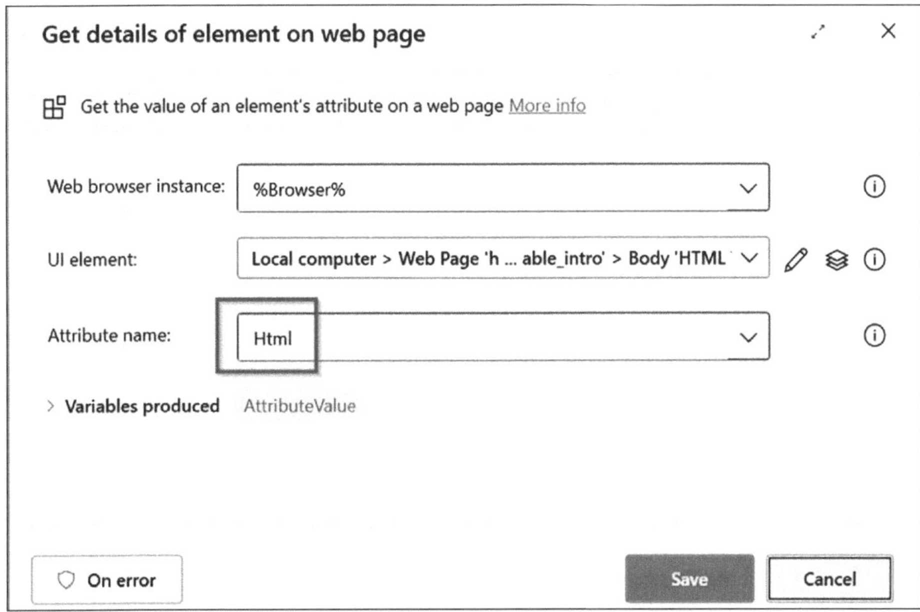

Figure 10.32: *Getting the Html of the Body*

4. Add the **"Create text with GPT"** Action and pass the following instructions. Notice how we are asking the GPT to extract only a part of the entire table with a certain condition. Also, we are asking for the output separated by a comma.

Instructions:

From the below HTML, provide the company and contract name that belong to Canada. Give the output separated by comma.
%AttributeValue%

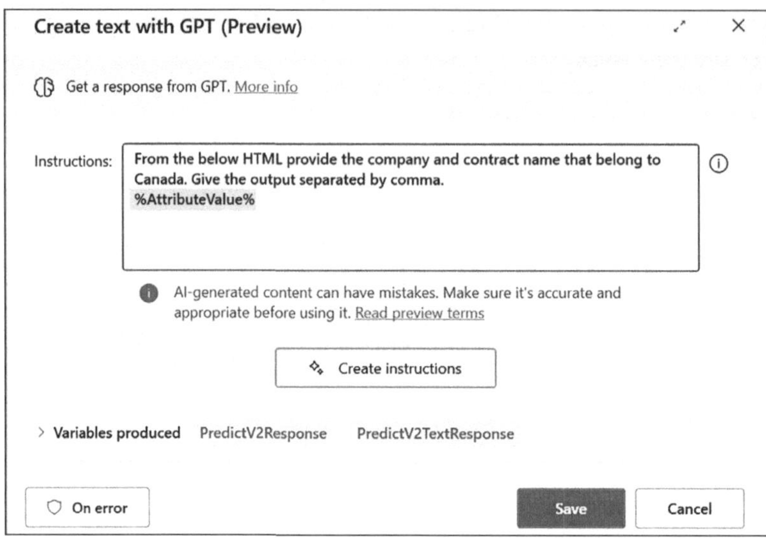

Figure 10.33: *Passing instructions to the GPT action*

5. Add a display message box for **`%PredictV2TextResponse%`** as part of **`"Responsible AI"`** and run the Flow.

Following is the **`%AttributeValue%`** variable populated after running the Flow containing the HTML of the **"Body"**.

Figure 10.34: *Output variable with the Html of the Body*

Following is the entire Flow along with its output extracted by the GPT.

Out of the table of multiple records, GPT has extracted the details only for Canada as prompted, and the company and contract are separated by a comma. Try an example of the other way round too, that is, retrieving a country from a company or contact.

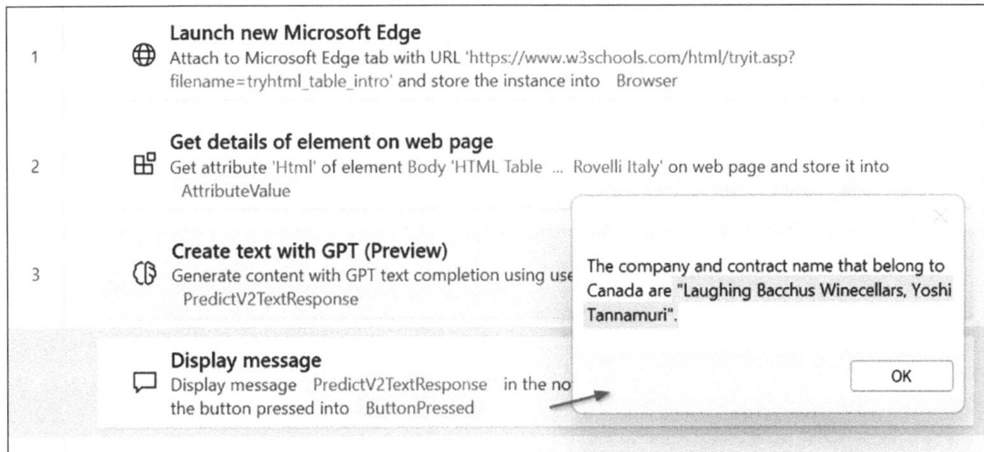

Figure 10.35: *Output after running the Flow*

Copilot Features

Copilot is a generative AI chatbot from Microsoft. It is an "AI companion" available across a vast majority of Microsoft products and services. Likewise, Copilot is available in PAD too. It is not directly used to achieve Intelligent Automation as in the previous sections, but it is a feature within the PAD tool itself that makes use of generative AI. As a companion, you can take help from the Copilot at various sections of the tool, and we will see where all it can be utilized.

These various sections and their usages are as follows:

- **From the Main Console:**

  Copilot is available starting from the main Console of the PAD tool. This section is used to ask questions in the provided box about the PAD Flows. Some sample questions are as shown in the following figure. It can give answers listing the steps to build a Flow and, at times, point to the documentation of the topic in question.

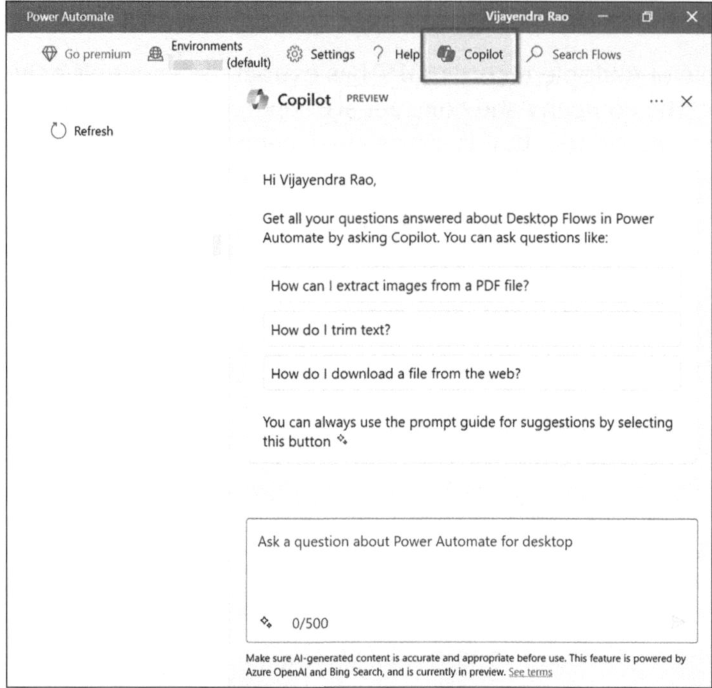

Figure 10.36: *Copilot on the main console*

Look for the **"Prompts"** button on the box provided to pull up a **"Prompt guide"**, as shown in the following figure. Either ask your own questions or use any of the pre-built prompts.

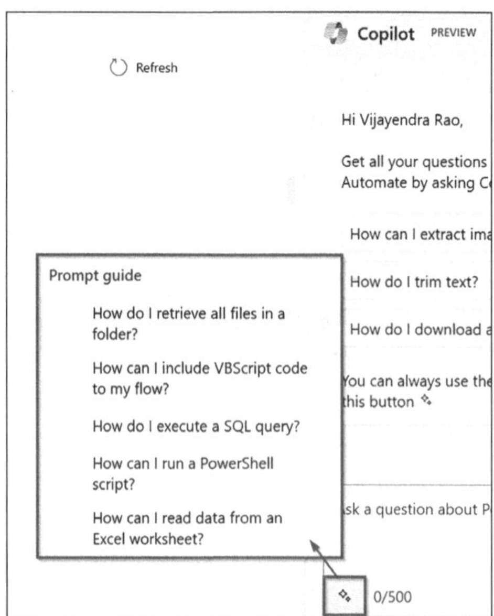

Figure 10.37: *The Prompts button and Prompt guide*

- **From the Flow designer:**

  The same is available from within the Flow designer, as marked in the following figure.

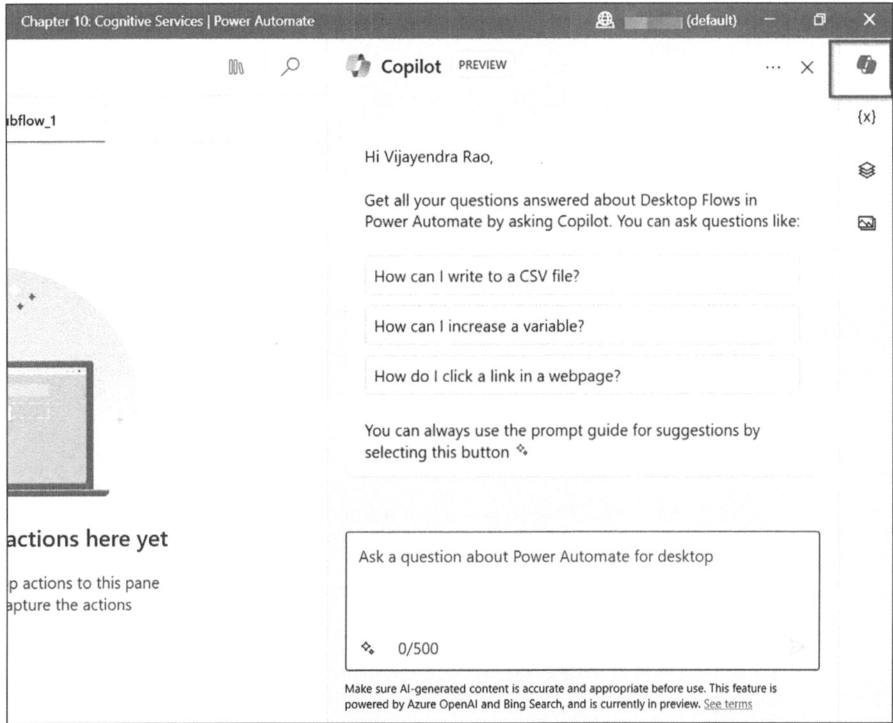

***Figure 10.38:** Copilot from the Flow designer*

- **From the Flow properties:**

  In the main Console, visit the Flow properties using the ellipsis button next to each Flow name or by right-clicking it and then selecting properties.

  Copilot will read the developed Flow and generate a description out of it, using the **"`Let Copilot create a description`"** button, as shown in the following figure.

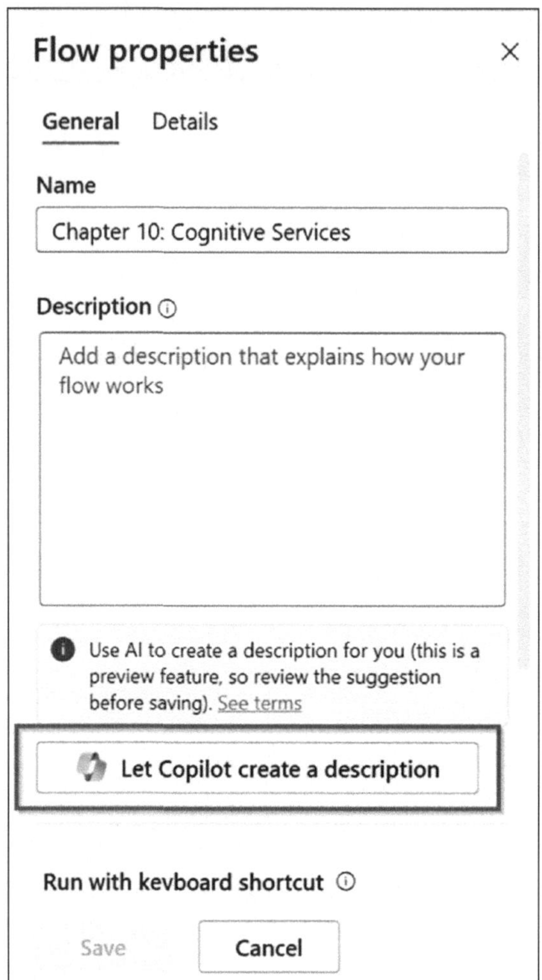

Figure 10.39: *Copilot from the Flow properties*

Following is the Flow description for the IBM Cognitive Services we used in this chapter.

It has precisely made sense out of the Actions we used for building this Flow (*Figures* 10.11 and 10.12).

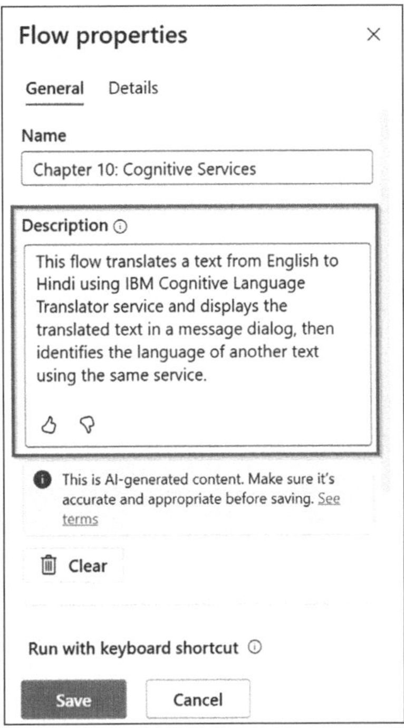

Figure 10.40: *Output of the Flow description via Copilot*

- **For generating SQL statements:**

  This is the Copilot icon to look for on the Actions that have the Copilot capability in them (marked by the arrow in the following figure).

  Use the **"`Generate script with Copilot`"** button to create SQL statements.

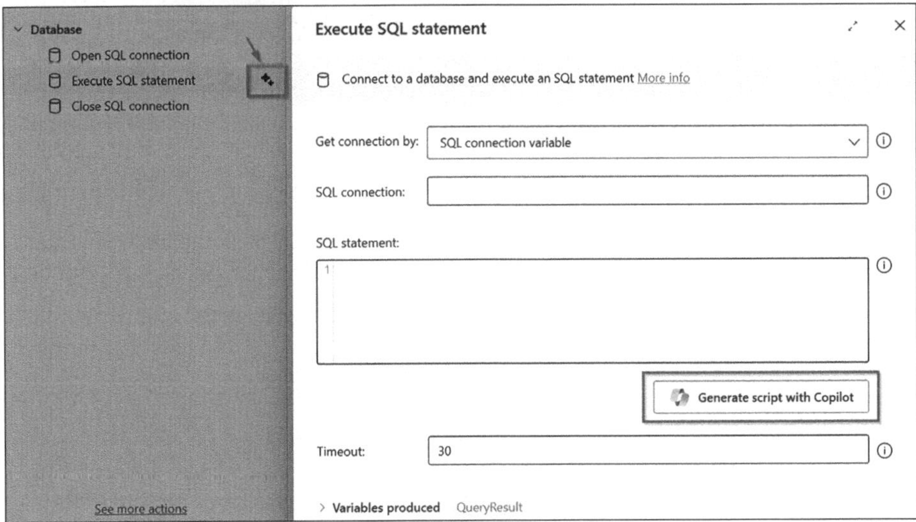

Figure 10.41: *Copilot for generating SQL statements*

Following is a sample prompt and the generated SQL statement by the Copilot. Once the statement appears to be fine, click the **"`Use this script`"** button, **"`Save`"** the Action, and get the results in the output variable, for example, **`QueryResult`** in the preceding figure, when the Flow is executed.

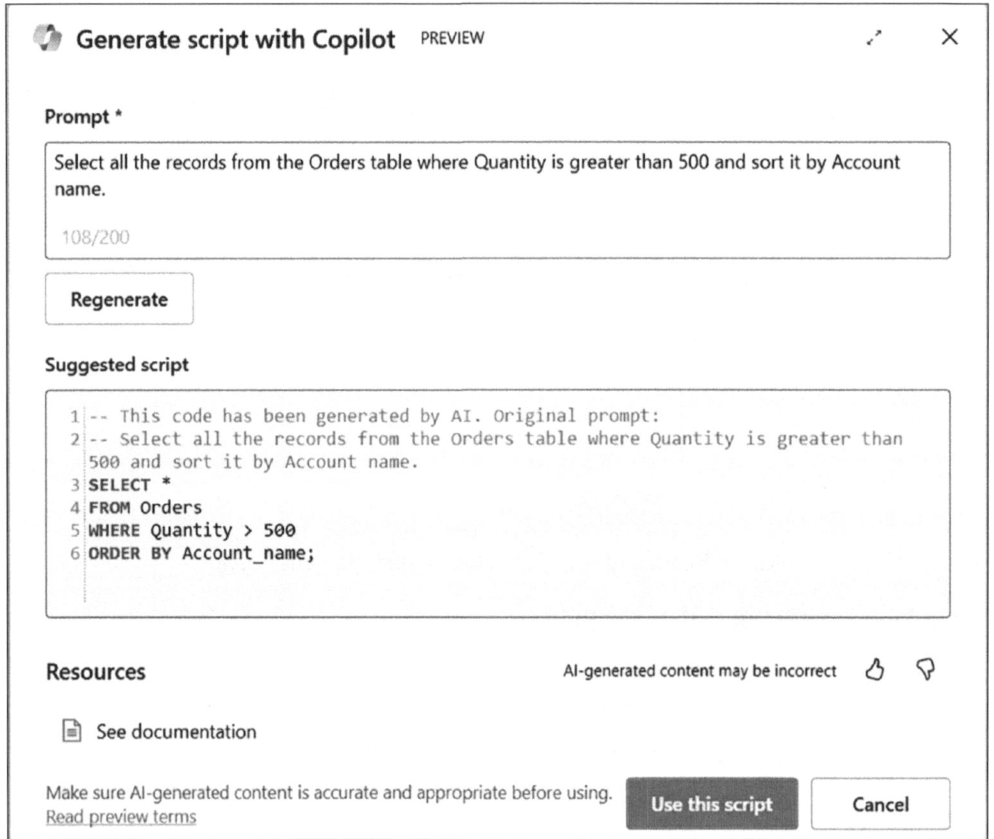

Figure 10.42: *SQL statement generated by Copilot*

- **From the Scripting Actions:**

  Except **"`Run .NET script`"**, every other Action has the ability to generate scripts via Copilot.

  Following is a sample for asking Copilot to generate a DOS command to get the Windows version on the machine where the bot will run.

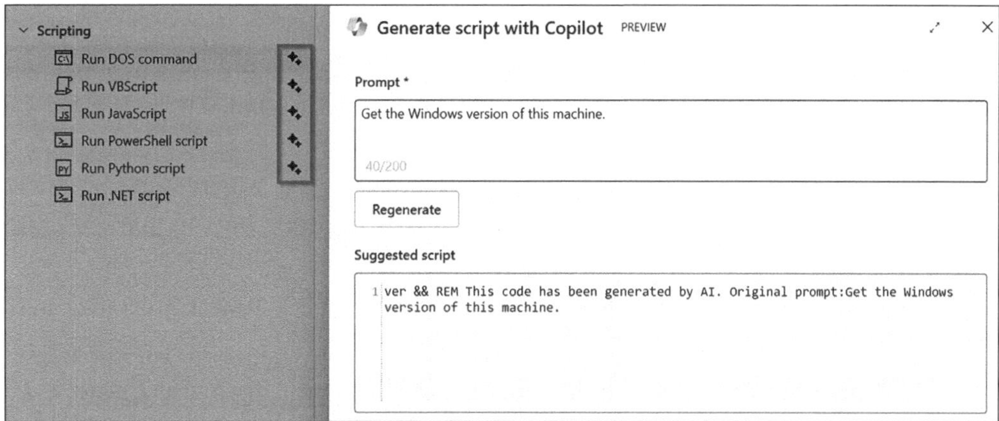

Figure 10.43: *Copilot for generating a DOS command*

The following figure uses the Copilot of the **"Run VBScript"** Action to generate a script for copying and pasting data between Excel files among two different sheets.

If necessary, modify the content as per requirements and call the **"Run VBScript"** Action in the Flow.

Copilot has even generated the comments for the various lines of code.

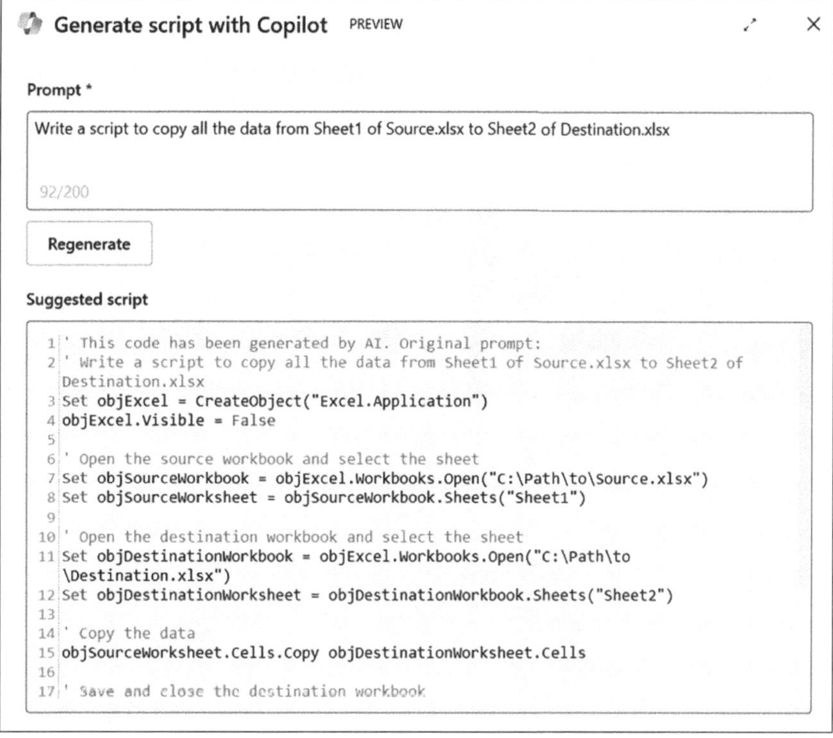

Figure 10.44: *Copilot for generating a VBScript*

- **Using Windows Copilot:**

  Enable the Power Automate plugin for Windows Copilot and instruct it to make use of Desktop Flow automation to work with Emails, Excel, PDFs, and File operations.

  Refer to the bottom right-hand corner marked in the following figure for the Copilot in Windows button. Then click the **"Plugins"** button marked on the top-right.

  This will show a list of plugins, and you need to enable Power Automate in it.

  This is still a Preview feature and not yet available for everyone. The subsequent link gives information on its current availability, the pre-requisites, and examples of actions that can be performed via this feature.

  Bookmark the following link and keep a watch on it because Copilot will keep on extending in all the forthcoming updates:

  https://learn.microsoft.com/en-us/power-automate/desktop-flows/win-copilot-plug-in

Figure 10.45: *The Windows Copilot and the plugins section*

For building bots, there are certainly a lot of productivity gains using Copilot, such as effort saving due to the code generation, ease of bot development with the AI companion on your side, increased help especially for Citizen Developers, reduced turn-around time of a bot, assistance via direct links to the Microsoft official documentation, and so on.

Wherever the AI features of Desktop Flows do not serve your purpose, make use of the **"AI hub"** of the Power Platform on the Cloud portal. This approach to building Intelligent Automation bots is via the **"AI models"** of the Power Platform available from the Cloud portal. Refer to the tab marked on the left-hand side of the following figure. If not available, use the **"More"** or **"Discover all"** buttons.

Here you can create new custom AI models or use the pre-built ones. Then use these models in the Cloud Flows where you would call the Desktop Flows. Just to reiterate as an example, make use of the **"Document processing"** model by building a Cloud Flow that will read an email as soon as it arrives with a specific subject and a specific type of attachment, download the attachment, extract values from the attachment using this AI model, call and pass these extracted values to the Desktop Flow which inserts them into any website or application, creates an Excel report of it, sends an email, and so on.

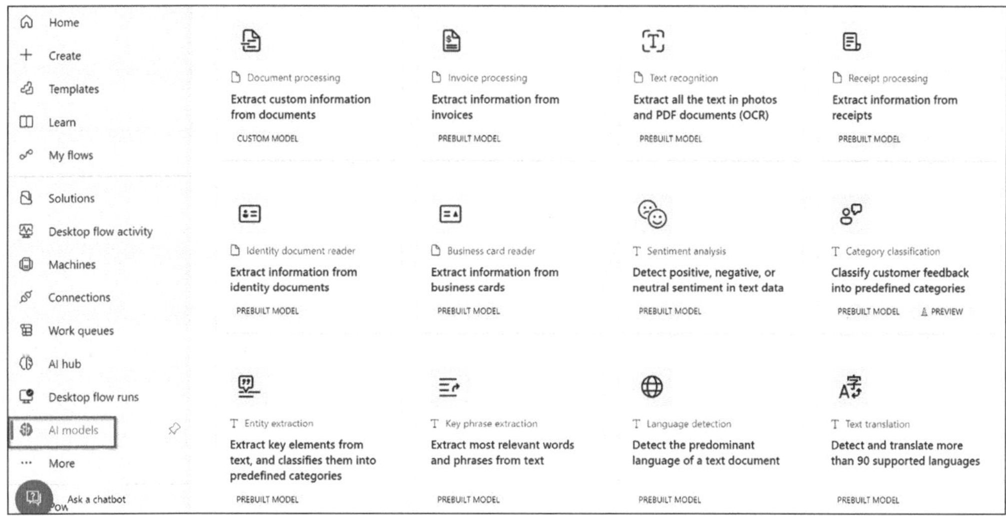

Figure 10.46: *AI models on the Cloud portal*

As seen as a note in all the AI-generated Actions, you need to ensure to verify the accuracy and correctness of the AI content before implementing them in your automation scenarios.

Suggested Actions

Suggested Actions is a feature of the PAD tool to help us expedite in our bot development. It is an AI capability where PAD suggests what the next Action should be based on the current Flow Actions. It analyzes our Flow Actions and gives a predictive list of upcoming Actions that a developer might intend to add in their next step.

For example, as in *Figure* 10.47, when you launch an Excel, the first thing you would want to do is either read data from the sheet, set a particular sheet as an active sheet, or even write to it. This list of Suggested Actions is pulled up from the marked plus button in the figure.

It is currently in Preview and expected to be improving in the future as it is an AI feature. You can also make use of the thumbs up and thumbs down icons and submit feedback on this functionality.

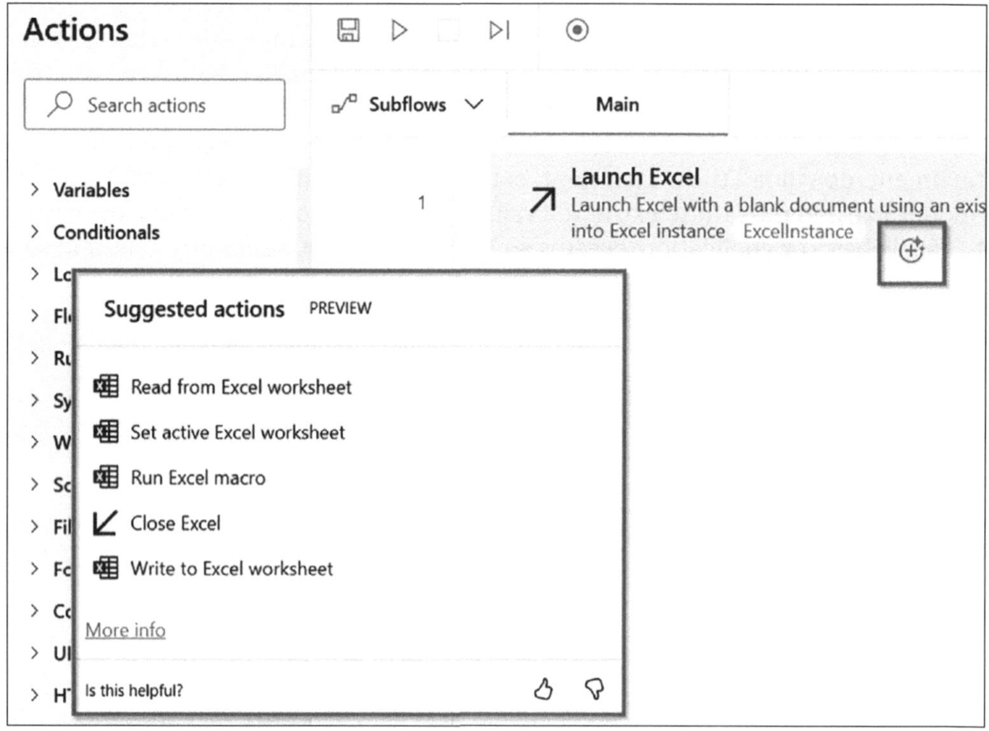

Figure 10.47: *List of suggested actions*

Practically following through all the features explained in this chapter and performing them on the PAD tool are in itself exercises for this chapter.

Conclusion

In this chapter, we looked at how to use the Cognitive Services Actions available in PAD, how to make use of generative AI with the help of several GPT scenarios, and how to use GPT with the data in your Flows – all of these to achieve Intelligent Automation via PAD. We also looked at Copilot, the AI companion from Microsoft, and its various implementations inside the PAD tool. Finally, we looked at the AI capability of Suggested Actions to assist us in our Flow development.

In the next chapter, we are going to look at several development best practices to build more efficient, reliable, and scalable automation solutions.

CHAPTER 11
Development Best Practices

Introduction

Development best practices are a "must have" in any RPA automation, or in any other development project for that matter. The best practices help in enhancing the Flow readability and maintainability, thereby making it easier for the bot development team to collaborate with each other. Not only that, but they also help in activities such as promoting reusability, optimizing performance, reducing execution time, improving efficiency, protecting sensitive data, and even enhancing the user experience. They simplify the development, code review, and testing phases of a bot development lifecycle, allowing a smoother execution of an automation project. One by one, we will be going through a varied list of development best practices in this chapter. You can add these to a spreadsheet and use it as a **development best practice checklist** during the development or even as a **code review checklist** after the development is complete, so that in either case the Flow adheres to the standards.

Structure

In this chapter, we will discuss the following topics:

- Flow Naming Convention
- Variable Naming Convention
- UI Elements Naming Convention
- Separate Desktop Flows
- Subflows
- Custom Actions
- Repetitive or Duplicate Flow Actions
- Header Comments
- Wait Actions

- Static Wait Variables
- Timeouts
- Logging
- Retention Policy for Logs
- Retention Policy for Files
- Reporting Mechanism
- Config File
- Hard Coding in Flow
- Keystrokes/Send Keys
- Error Handling
- Retry Attempts
- Comments and Regions
- Test the Selectors
- Credentials and Sensitive Variables
- Work Queues
- Use of Scripting Actions
- Ensuring Applications/Screens are Open Before Accessing
- Closing All Instances
- Use of Bot IDs
- Screen Resolution
- Verification for Infinite Loop Logic
- Removal of Deprecated Actions
- Handle "Preview" Actions or Features
- Cleaning Up of Flow

Flow Naming Convention

This is the Flow name that shows up on the main Console of PAD. This best practice is about having a meaningful and readable naming convention for the Flow name.

You can create your own naming convention and define them across your development team. Here are some sample formats you can choose from, depending on the scope of your automation.

- **Simple Format:**
  `[Customer Name]_[Bot Name]`

Example:
`HorizonHealthcare_Invoice Processing`
`InnovateLogistics_Employee Onboarding`

- **Medium Format:**
  `[BU Name]_[Bot Name]` where BU stands for Business Unit

  Example:
  `Finance_Invoice Processing`

  `HR_Employee Onboarding`

- **Detailed Format:**
  `[Customer Name]_[BU Name]_[Bot Name]`

  Example:
  `HorizonHealthcare_Finance_Invoice Processing`

  `InnovateLogistics_HR_Employee Onboarding`

  You can even suffix a version number as _v1, as applicable.

  If the main Desktop Flow is built specifically for Work Queue operations, then these names can include the text as **`WQDispatcher`** and **`WQPerformer`**.

Variable Naming Convention

In programming, there have been several different variable naming conventions that vary depending on the language or coding style being used. Example: Camel case, Pascal case, Hungarian notation, and so on. Also, be noted that some notations might have a hyphen in them, but a PAD variable cannot have a hyphen in it.

Any of those can be used while naming variables in Power Automate Desktop too, thus giving meaning and structure to the Flow and its variables.

Generally, adding a data type prefix to a meaningful variable name is considered to be more understandable.

Example:

1. **`strFirstName`**: It denotes a first name of the Text/String data type. A prefix of *txt* is generally used for a text box; hence, *str* can be used here.
2. **`numClaimIdRowCounter`**: A row counter that is used to iterate through a list of Claim IDs and is a number (PAD has **`Number`** and not **`Integer`** as a data type, but **`num`** or **`int`** both can be used if they are understandable to the development team).

   You can even have an underscore symbol in the variable names to give distinction, such as **`intHours_Worked`** or **`int_HoursWorked`**.

In the case of Input or Output PAD variables, you may prefix it with something like **`IN`** or **`OUT`**, such as **`INstrFirstName`**. Since they are used outside of the Desktop Flow, they can be capitalized.

Define your own prefixes, but here is a direction on variable prefixes based on their type.

PAD Data type	Prefix	Comments
Text	str	**`txt`** is not used as a prefix to avoid confusion with a text box UI element.
Number	num or int	Can be modified as **`dec`** for Decimals.
Boolean	bool	**`flg`** can be used to denote a Flag.
Custom Object	custObj	
List	list	**`lst`** is not used as a prefix to avoid confusion with a list box UI element.
Datatable	dtbl	

Table 11.1: *Sample variable data type prefixes*

These are just guidelines. No matter which case or notation you use, standardize it across your development team. Try not to unnecessarily add verbose and reduce their readability. Be noted that at times clients and citizen developers can also come across the variables you use in the Flow, so it should be understandable and clear to them too.

UI Elements Naming Convention

Just like the variables, the UI elements or controls of a web page, window, or screen can be referred to by a naming convention.

A general convention used is in the format of **`[Control Type]`** as a prefix followed by **`[Control Description]`**.

Example: **`txtCustomerID`**, **`btnSubmit`**, **`wndContosoInvoicing`** for a text box, button, and window, respectively.

A different variation of this is as follows:

`Textbox - Customer ID`, **`Button - Submit`**, **`Combobox - Status`**

Another more detailed format is to also include the screen name:

Example: **`AddCustomerDetails_txtCustomerID`**, **`UpdCustomerDetails_btnSubmit`**

Following is a list of generally used prefixes based on the UI element type:

UI element or Control	Prefix
Textbox	txt
Listbox	lst
Combobox	cmb
Checkbox	chk
Option button	opt
Form	frm
Menu	mnu
Label	lbl
Image	img
DatePicker	dtp
Window	wnd
Button	btn
Link	lnk

Table 11.2: *Sample UI element prefixes*

As always, use any convention, but the idea should be to make it readable, understandable, and developer-friendly.

Separate Desktop Flows

Wherever possible, separate Desktop Flows can be used, thus allowing re-usability. They can then be called via the **"`Run desktop flow`"** Action at appropriate places. This best practice is about splitting a large Flow into smaller Flows that handle a specific task within a larger process and also can be called from other Desktop Flows. Be noted about the licensing plans while doing so. For example, if you have a "per bot" license, then it would be an added cost to have separate Flows, but this is largely done in enterprise-level automation where licensing is not an obstacle.

Subflows

Modularize your Flow by moving all sets of Actions that are used repeatedly into a Subflow, and have appropriate names for them.

Have high-level steps in the Main Flow and reusable steps and Actions in Subflows.

Separate each of the Subflow modules to initialize variables, read config files, interact with an external application, and so on.

For example, populating a Form has to be called again and again and therefore, can go into a Subflow.

Identifying all such repetitive sets of activities before even starting to build a Flow is a sign of a good practice.

Having an uncluttered Main Flow and structured Subflows increases readability for other developers too. Also, if a Subflow is built in a customized way, then it can be reused in other Desktop Flows by right-clicking the Subflow tab to copy and then paste them into another Desktop Flow.

Newer versions of PAD have the ability to include spaces in the Subflow names, which was not possible earlier. Thus, a clear and understandable Subflow name can be as: **`Read Config file`**, **`Generate Summary Report`**, **`Upload Invoice`**, and so forth.

Of course, when licensing is a problem for having separate Desktop Flows, then Subflows are always an option for re-usability.

Custom Actions

Custom Actions are about developing a PAD Action using the steps referred to in the next chapter and then using that Action across all Flows. They are a great way of re-usability when you want a PAD Action to be reutilized across multiple Desktop Flows.

Repetitive or Duplicate Flow Actions

Remove or replace any Flow Actions that are repeating or duplicate. Make sure that the same Flow Actions are not written twice at different places of the Flow, and are replaced by other Subflows or Desktop Flows. There is no point to add the same Flow Actions at multiple places for obvious reasons when they can be written once and called from anywhere.

Header Comments

Header comments should be used at the beginning of Main Flow and Subflows. These provide a concise and clear overview of the Flow/Subflow's functionality, making it easy to understand its role and how to use it effectively.

This is made possible with the help of the **"`Comment`"** Action with a format such as the following. Feel free to add additional details, if necessary, such as date, version control, and so on.

```
----------------------------------------------------------------------
Purpose: Describe what the Flow/Subflow does
Inputs: What inputs are passed to this Flow/Subflow
Outputs: What does the Flow/Subflow return, or what output does it produce
----------------------------------------------------------------------
```

Fill in the **"`Comment`"** Action, as described in *Figure* 11.1, and place it as the very first Action of the Main Flow and every Subflow.

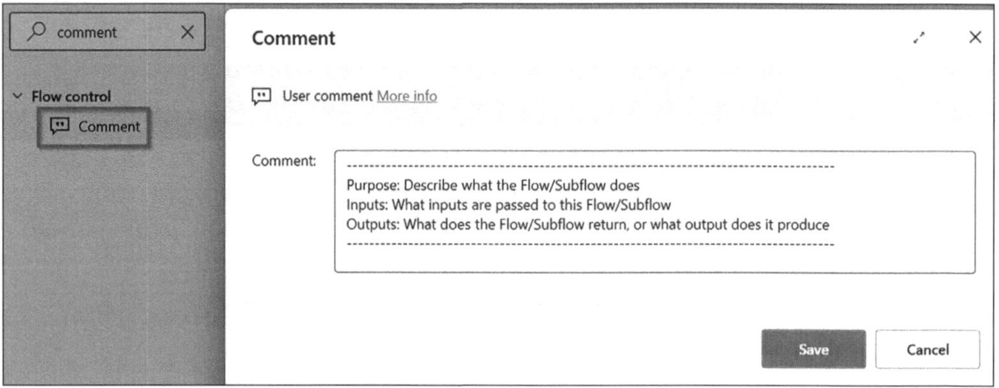

Figure 11.1: *Comment Action with header information*

Wait Actions

Use the available Wait Actions wherever possible instead of a fixed or static wait of specific seconds. This is because of several reasons, such as the external application or web page could be slow or may not have opened yet, and the bot is trying to access the next screen. Some examples are:

1. **`Wait for window`**
2. **`Wait for image`**
3. **`Wait for web page/window content`**
4. **`Wait for text on screen (OCR)`**

Do not forget settings such as the **"`Wait for page to load`"** setting in the Launch browser Actions or **"`Delay between keystrokes`"** in the **"`Send keys`"** Action.

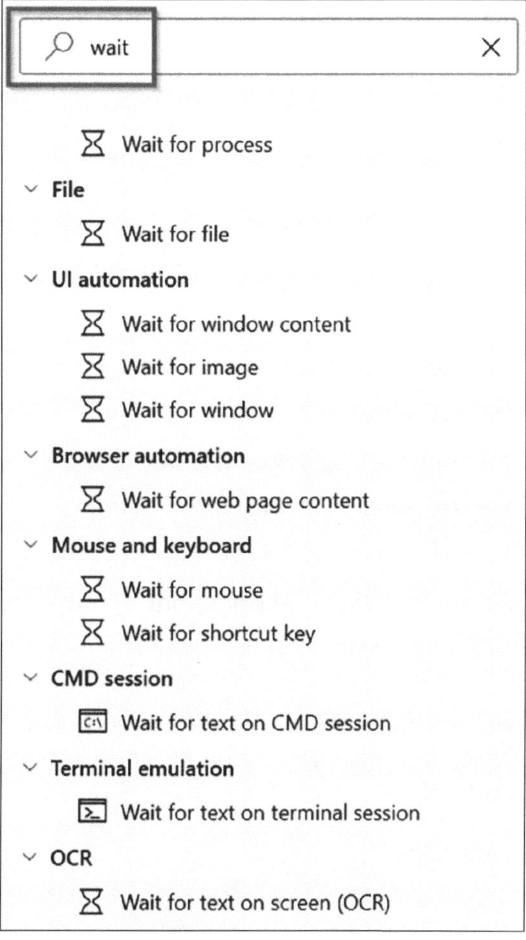

Figure 11.2: *Wait actions*

Static Wait Variables

If your Flow needs to have static Wait Actions, then add different Wait variables and use them all over the Flow.

Example:

1. Small Wait of 1 second
2. Medium Wait of 3 seconds
3. Large Wait of 5 seconds

Feel free to modify the seconds and even add Extra Small or Extra Large depending on the scenario of your automation.

This will help you during debugging or troubleshooting when a particular application is not behaving as expected. Changing the time in a single Wait variable will be far easier than changing it in all places of the Flow, or even at certain places it will be easier to remove a Small Wait and replace it with a Medium Wait variable.

Timeouts

Use the timeout parameter wherever available and as applicable.

Some examples are:

1. **"Timeout on webpage load"** in Launch Browser Actions
2. **"Fail with timeout error"** in Wait for window/web page content
3. **"Connection timeout"** in **"Invoke web service"**
4. **"Fail with timeout error"** in **"Wait for file"**
5. **"Fail with timeout error"** in **"Wait for text on screen (OCR)"**

Note that these are *not* about **"Wait"** Actions, but about timeouts to determine if a particular operation does not complete within the specified time value. These are necessary so that the Actions containing the timeout parameter do not wait indefinitely.

Figure 11.3 contains two settings where timeouts are shown. Navigate the Flow to an appropriate line of Action in case an Action reaches a timeout and still does not produce the desired result.

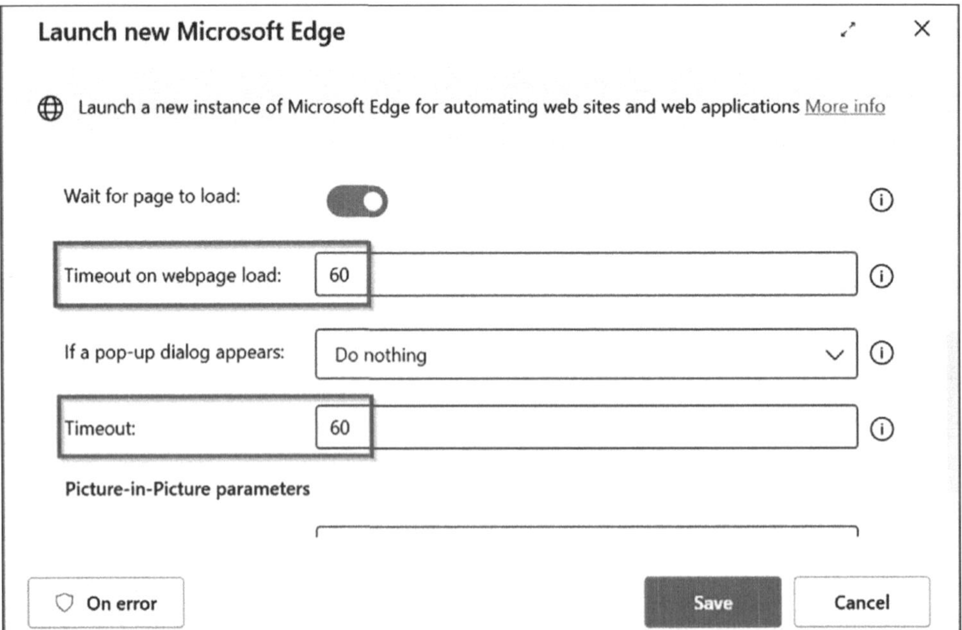

Figure 11.3: *Timeout settings*

Logging

Include logging as a "must have" best practice in your Flows with the features as described in the "*Logging*" section of "*Chapter 9: Leveling Up Your Automation Workflows*".

Some of them are as follows:

1. Using the **"`Log message`"** Action
2. Building your own logging mechanism with your own set of fields
3. Having a separate Subflow for logging
4. Writing the execution steps of the Flow in the logs
5. Splitting the log file into chunks for long running processes

All of these are explained in the aforementioned chapter.

Retention Policy for Logs

Retention policy for log files describe how long to keep the logs and how to dispose them when it is time.

Log files generated by the Flow should follow a retention policy given by the customer or end user for whom the automation is being built.

For example, all log files beyond 60 days should be deleted. This deletion can either happen automatically by the bot or manually, depending on what has been agreed upon.

They can either be archived to a different location or deleted.

Note that this deletion could be done in the same Flow or via a separate Flow depending upon the licensing you have.

Retention Policy for Files

This is the same as the logs, but a retention policy for the files downloaded or generated by the bot.

If the Flow generates certain files, such as Daily Excel reports, downloads PDFs for reading, and so on, then the end user needs to be asked if they require a retention policy. If yes, enquire whether they should be deleted after a specific number of days or immediately after being processed by the bot, and whether to be done by the bot or manually.

The files can also be subject to archival for later reference or can be deleted, as agreed upon with the end user.

The same concept of whether to use a separate Flow or not (as explained in the previous section) applies to the deletion of files too.

Reporting Mechanism

Have a reporting mechanism in the Flow where a final summarized report for each run will explain the status of what happened with each record of that run.

This will help during troubleshooting as well as give details to the end user with the status of each case.

A simple example is in the following format, but can be expanded as necessary.

```
Invoice ID | Status | Comments
12345      | Success| Invoice file 12345.PDF uploaded successfully
78901      | Failed | Invoice file 78901.PDF not found
```

Reports can be in a spreadsheet where they look neat.

A separate Subflow should handle the reporting mechanism in the Flow with a flag/ bool variable that determines whether the Flow will send the report as an email or not if the end user wants to disable it for some time. Also, separate flags can be used to determine whom to send the reports to; for example, the Support team needs the report but the end user does not.

These flags should be config-driven via the config files mentioned in the next section.

Again, this reporting mechanism can be in a separate Flow or as a Subflow depending on the licensing plan you are on.

Config File

In simple words, a config file is a file that contains key-value pairs that define the initial settings or preferences for the automation. The automation should be config-driven for ease and maintainability.

There are several popular formats for configuration files, such as Text files, JSON, XML, and Excel spreadsheets, but you need to choose the format that is easy to maintain and also easy to read the values using the available Actions of Power Automate Desktop.

Also, consider if the business end user or customer is going to change inputs in the config file; for example, turn `GenerateReport` to FALSE in the following figure. A JSON or XML would be complicated for some to understand, and an Excel would be preferred.

	A	B
1	Setting	Value
2	InputFilePath	C:\Invoices\InputFile.xlsx
3	GenerateReport	TRUE
4	SendEmailTo	john@email.com; jane@email.com
5	CompressOutputBeforeSending	FALSE

Figure 11.4: *Sample config format*

Where you have less settings, you could also make use of the Windows Environment Variables. There are ready-made Actions in PAD (**"`Get/Set Windows environment variable`"**) to read and write the values of these variables. This may at first require you to manually create these variables on every machine where the bot will run, and therefore you could use these when there are minimal bot machines. Remember to *not* store passwords in config files or in Windows environment variables.

Some organizations even have their configurations on an online portal and read them via APIs from the bot, or on a SharePoint list, or even on a database table.

If an Excel is chosen, ensure that it is not locked for its next use by the bot. This best practice does not necessarily say about using Excel, but about having a config file for your Desktop Flows. So, no matter which of the many methods you choose, they should be easily accessible to the Flow from all machines where it is running and to the users who are going to interact with the bot.

Hard Coding in Flow

No hard coding should be used in the Flow for file paths, URLs, email addresses, and so on. All of these should be config-driven. You can have a minimum of them, for example, you have planned to use a Windows environment variable called *ConfigPath* which in turn holds the path to the config file. Then the word "ConfigPath" can be hard coded inside a PAD variable so that the Flow reads the value of this variable to get to the config file.

Even the wait variables mentioned in the aforementioned "*Static Wait Variables*" section can be configured in the config file and then read into the bot variables.

Keystrokes/Send Keys

Keystrokes should generally be used when other available options do not work.

For example, if you want to insert a Pivot Table in an Excel, there is no direct Action available yet. A general tendency is to send keystrokes to each of the menus in Excel and then insert the Pivot, which also requires appropriate Wait Actions and correct focus on the right window at all times. This has a low reliability rate, and even the slightest change may cause the bot to stall. Also, there are chances that it may run fine at some times and not at the others.

Instead, in this example, you could use a VBScript called by the **"Run VBScript"** Action, which will not use any keystrokes and will always be reliable.

It is equally true that there are several situations where everything else fails or nothing else is available. In such instances, it becomes mandatory that you use Send keys. But the main idea is to first find out for reliable alternatives and use keystrokes only when necessary.

Error Handling

Just like logging, having a robust and efficient error handling mechanism is a "must have" best practice while building Flows for obvious reasons.

This best practice is about using all the error handling features as explained in "*Chapter 9: Leveling Up Your Automation Workflows*", some of which are as follows:

1. Using Action-level exception handling where applicable.
2. Using Block-level exception handling as necessary.
3. Writing errors to a log file as they arise.
4. Using the **"Get last error"** Action for the line number, Error description, Action name, Subflow name, and so on.
5. Mechanism to report the errors to the Support team or the end user.
6. Retry logic
7. Error on timeout

Retry Attempts

Retry attempts should be made in valid scenarios of the Flow. A retry attempt implies re-attempting to process the same exception record the specified number of times either via a loop-like logic or via the **"Retry policy"** option of the action-level error handling.

Business Exceptions should not be retried as it will give the same result each time (example, trying to process Age < 18 for adult patients). They should be properly logged and moved on to the next record.

System Exceptions can be retried for a configurable number of times without going into an infinite loop, generally three times. Minimum Flow Actions should be included in the error handler of such Exceptions to ensure that those Actions themselves do not cause further exceptions.

If a retry attempt is not possible for certain System Exceptions, then they should not be tried. A smooth exit of the Flow with a possible notification should occur in case of System Exceptions.

Comments and Regions

This best practice implies the usage of Comments and Regions to make the Flows more readable, maintainable, structured, and logical.

- **Comments:** As in any programming language, comments in PAD are used to write a note of text about what is happening with the subsequent Actions.

  In the following example, the comment is marked by an arrow and gives details about the Action following it.

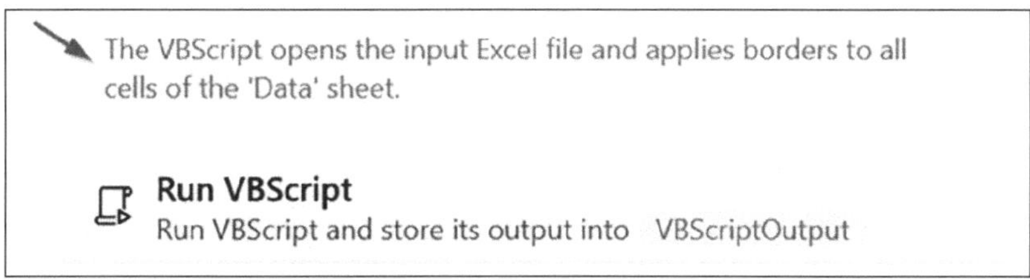

Figure 11.5: *Sample comment*

- **Regions:** They organize your Actions into logical groups that can be collapsed or expanded in the Flow designer. They make your Flows more readable and maintainable by hiding unnecessary details and highlighting important steps. They can be renamed, expanded, collapsed, or deleted as needed for developer friendliness and readability.

  For this purpose, the **"`Region`"** Action is used from the **"`Flow Control`"** group of Actions. In the following example, the start of the region is indicated by an arrow and has its own end of region. The text in the region name explains what steps are performed within that region, giving a clear picture of its set of Actions. This is just an example, and it makes more sense to add such types of Regions for blocks that have a large number of Actions.

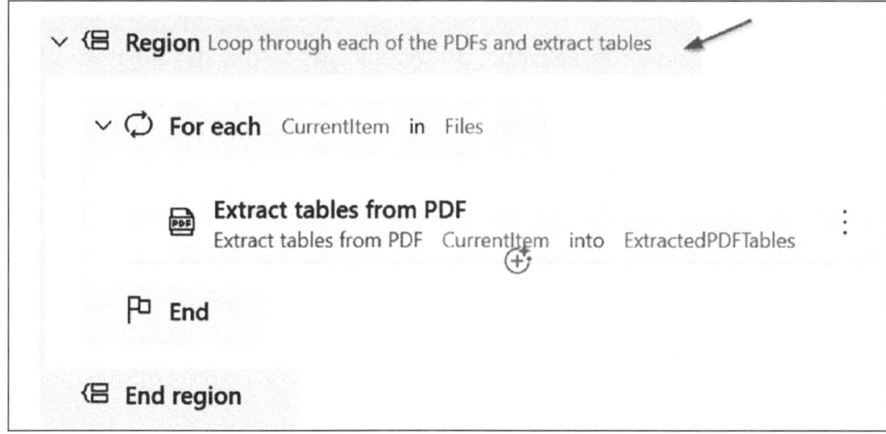

Figure 11.6: *Sample region*

Test the Selectors

During development itself, testing the Selectors before finalizing one is a good practice for bots having UI-based interactions. It is a way of validating a Selector to verify whether an UI element matches the criteria of the Selector or not. This is done with the help of the **"Test"** button on the Selector window, as shown in *Figure* 11.7, and also as explained in "*Chapter* 5: *Building Blocks of a Desktop Flow*". The small dropdown arrow next to the button is capable of testing all selectors at once too.

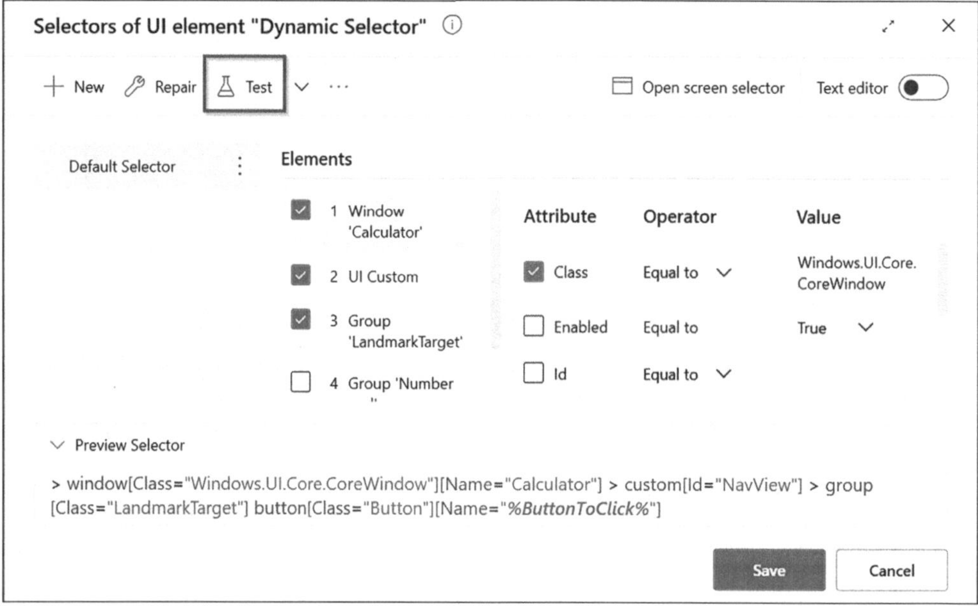

***Figure* 11.7**: *Testing the selector*

Credentials and Sensitive Variables

Credentials, such as passwords, secrets, API tokens, and so on, should always be stored in a secured manner, and as of this writing, PAD does not have a free in-built Credential Manager specific to Desktop Flows, although it has an Action for an external system (CyberArk) to retrieve passwords.

Therefore, it becomes a necessity to use our own credential storage system, and those are done by bot developers by making use of any of the following options.

- Azure Key Vault
- Windows Credentials Manager (using PowerShell or any other script to read/write credentials here)
- CyberArk (Action available in PAD)

Or any other third-party application or website that is accessible from PAD.

Be noted that one or more of these options may require a premium license or a paid external service.

There is a **"Credentials"** tab on the Cloud portal, which can be utilized only to create desktop "connections", as of now. Since this is an important topic, let us expect from Microsoft soon that this tab will be capable of storing the credentials, secrets, and tokens used within the Desktop Flows and easily readable via the PAD Actions.

Other best practices pertaining to this topic are as follows:

- Use of the **"Cryptography"** set of Actions to encrypt and decrypt a text wherever applicable.

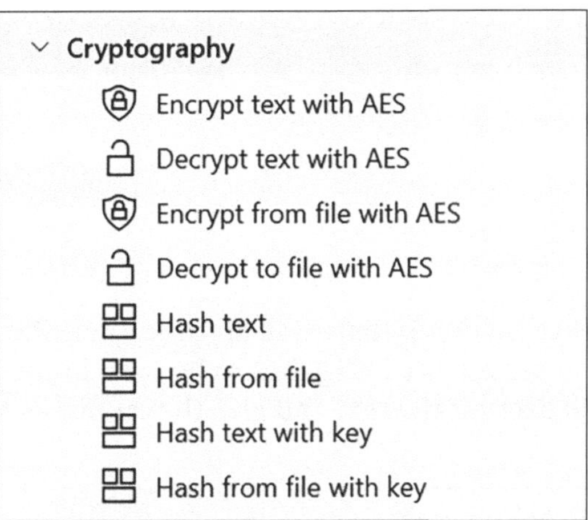

Figure 11.8: *Cryptography set of actions*

The following Action is used to create an encrypted text by using the Advanced Encryption Standard (AES), an algorithm widely used to secure data.

Pass the text that needs to be encrypted along with a key (ABCD in this example), and the **EncryptedText** output variable gives the encrypted format of the input. Be noted that the key still needs to be stored in a secure way via any of the options mentioned in the **"Credentials"** section.

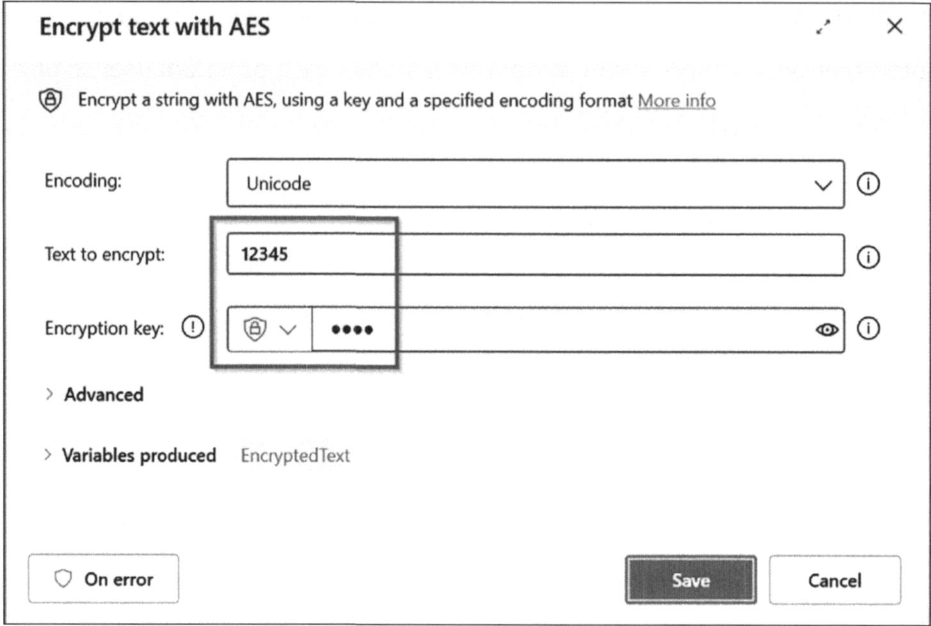

Figure 11.9: *The Encrypt text with AES action*

When the reverse has to be done, that is, decrypt it, then the same **`EncryptedText`** variable, along with the same key (ABCD), has to be used in the **"`Decrypt text with AES`"** Action, which will decrypt the text and give the output as **`12345`**, as shown in the previous figure.

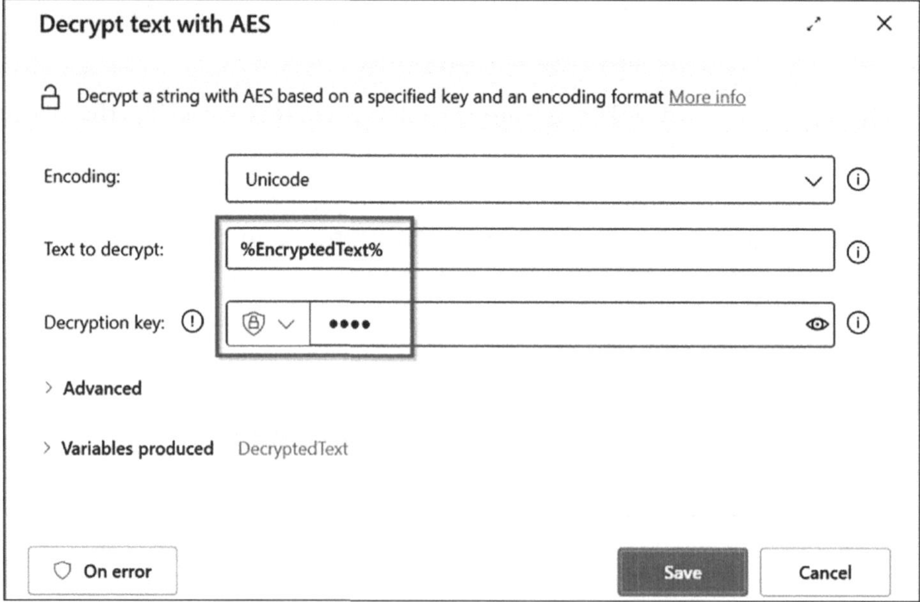

Figure 11.10: *The Decrypt text with AES action*

Refer to the **"Advanced"** section of these Actions for the **"Salting"** approach via the **"Use salt"** toggle. In simple terms, salting is a technique used to enhance or strengthen the security of stored passwords and any sensitive data. If you enable salting in the encrypt Action, it will generate a *Salt* variable, and then the same has to be used in the decrypt Action too.

Likewise, in place of a text, contents of files can also be encrypted using the **"Encrypt from file with AES"** Action and then use its corresponding decrypt Action.

- Also, it is a good practice for marking passwords, tokens, and more as Sensitive variables in the **"Variables"** pane, so their values will not be stored in the run history logs in the portal when the Desktop Flows are run from the Console or from the Cloud Flows.

There is a lot more to read about the behavior of sensitive variables and is given in its following documentation link, which is also shared in "*Chapter 4: Essential Elements of a Desktop Flow*":

https://learn.microsoft.com/en-us/power-automate/desktop-flows/manage-variables#sensitive-variables

Another point that you should be aware of is when calling Desktop Flows from Cloud Flows.

In the following example, an Outlook connector passes some input to the Desktop Flow connector. Enabling the **"Secure Inputs"** and **"Secure Outputs"** settings will prevent these values from showing in the logs. In this case, any input that is going to the Desktop Flows will not be shown in the logs. Likewise, apply these settings as required while interacting with Desktop Flows from the Cloud.

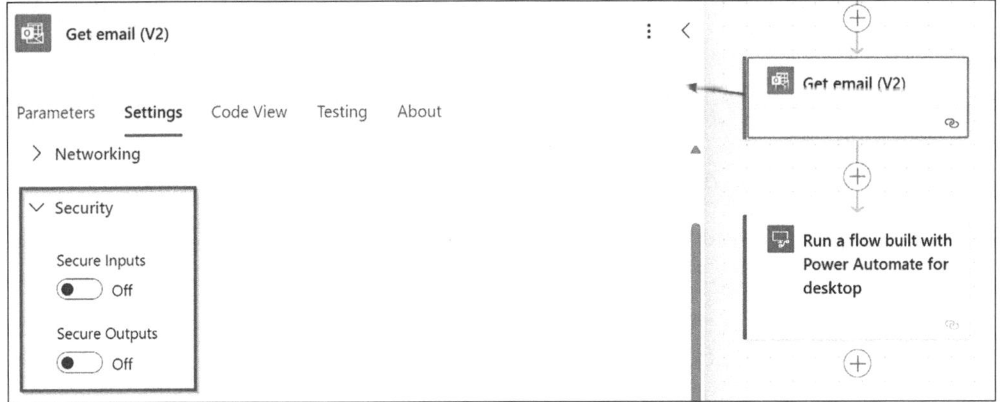

Figure 11.11: *Securing inputs and outputs in Cloud Flows*

Work Queues

This best practice is about making use of Work Queues wherever possible.

This is because they are a great way for several uses such as:

- Workload management
- To prioritize work by completing high-priority items first
- To give a status to a processing record so as to know from where to continue in case of a failure
- Defer processing a record at a later stage
- To understand how much "work" is completed and how much is remaining
- Which cases have a failure and what those failures are
- For reporting purposes and to give a centralized view to all users

When used, have the concept of *Dispatcher* and *Performer* with the right naming convention for them.

Use of Scripting Actions

Wherever possible, make use of the in-built scripting Actions, such as Run VBScript, Run PowerShell script, and others, instead of having external scripting files such as .vbs (VBScript), .py (Python), .ps1 (PowerShell), and so on.

This avoids the need to maintain external files unnecessarily in each of the environments.

For instance, if a macro can be replaced by the **"`Run VBScript`"** Action within the PAD Flow itself, then there is no need to maintain the .xlsm macro file. Be noted that VBA (used for writing macros) is different than VBScript, so one should be aware of the languages for making this conversion or at least be able to look up on the web as to how to convert the code.

Ensuring Applications/Screens are Open Before Accessing

This best practice is about making sure that the desired application or their screens are opened or not before accessing them.

This could be either via the **"`If process`"** or **"`Wait for process`"** Actions, or by checking if an UI element exists on a window or a web page, or waiting for a window itself, or even waiting for a web page to load.

The idea is to make sure the application, the screen, the page, or the window is available before accessing it.

The Flow should take care of logics such as, if some other part of the Flow has closed Outlook, then it won't be available to send emails unless it is launched again.

Closing All Instances

This best practice is about the closure of all open instances, such as Excel, Browser, SQL connection instances, and so on. These are to be done at appropriate places of the Flow and should not be kept open unnecessarily for a long time if they are not going to be used in the Flow.

Use of Bot IDs

This practice is about using dedicated Bot IDs or bot accounts for website logins, API calls that have usernames, and so on.

No person's ID or account should be used at these places. The reasons for doing so could be that it might cause challenges if a person whose ID is being used leaves the organization and is disabled. Using a Bot ID also helps in traceability and auditing. These Bot accounts can be given access rights on a need-to-have level-wise basis, meaning access is provided to a Bot account only for what it is supposed to do and not for anything else. For example, a Bot ID can have access to create invoice entries but not approve them.

Screen Resolution

Keep the same screen resolution of all the machines in all environments where the automation is going to be built, as well as where it is going to be run. Consider machines in multiple environments, such as DEV, TEST, and PROD environments.

Use the resolution-related Actions as explained in the "*Automating Your Workstation*" topic of "*Chapter 8: Beyond Conventional Automation Techniques and Strategies*". Also refer to the two approaches for setting the screen resolution in unattended mode under the same topic.

Verification for Infinite Loop Logic

This best practice is about verifying the Flow logic that has the potential to go into an infinite loop. An infinite loop is a sequence of Actions in a Flow that repeats endlessly without terminating. It occurs when the loop's exit condition is never met or if there is no exit condition defined at all. This best practice is about adding an exit strategy at the correct places of the Flow wherever loop-like structures are used.

Removal of Deprecated Actions

There might be a possibility that you are developing the Flow in a PAD version that is going to be lower than the one in the final Production environment. This best practice is about the removal of any Action or feature used in the current developed version and known to be deprecated in the upcoming PAD versions.

If any Action is about to be deprecated in future PAD versions, there is a note in the tool itself, or in the Microsoft release notes, or in the product updates, or in their documentation. Such Actions or features should be changed to accommodate the newer versions.

A good example of this is the use of the **"Specific time zone"** parameter of **"Get current date and time"** that is soon going to be deprecated. This can be replaced by the other options in the dropdown.

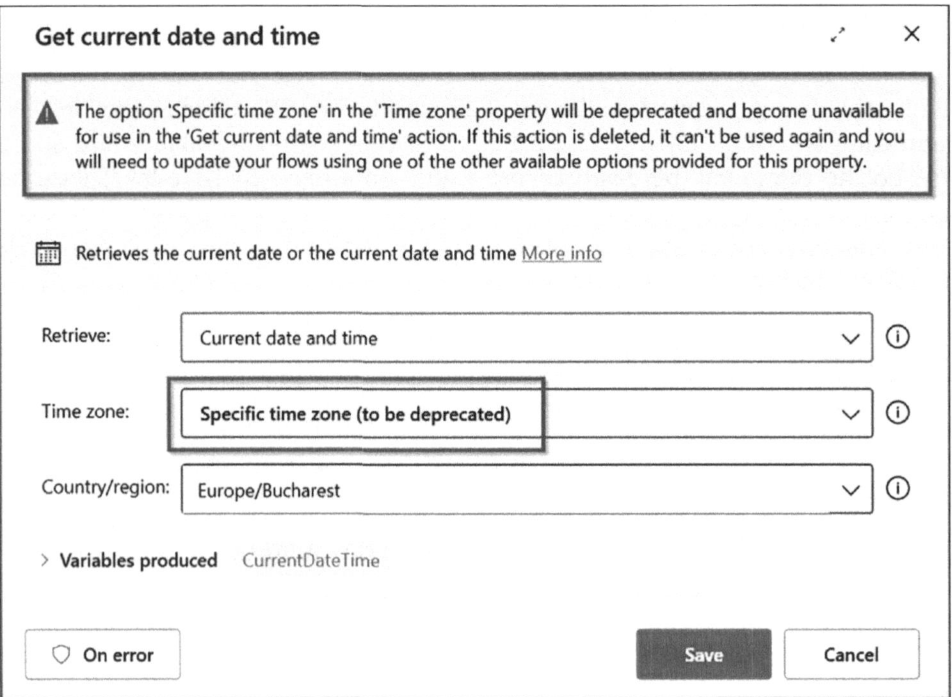

Figure 11.12: *A sample deprecated feature*

Handle "Preview" Actions or Features

You might come across several Actions and features that are currently in Preview, such as the one in the following figure.

Any Action or feature that is currently in Preview is not meant to be used in Production. They can only be used for "live" bot runs when they are released for general availability.

This best practice talks about the importance of ensuring that when a Preview feature or Action used in the DEV bot goes into PROD, it should not remain in Preview mode. Preview features are not supposed to be used in Production. Either you will have to wait for it to come out of Preview (which is a very long time) or use any other alternative approach that is not in Preview.

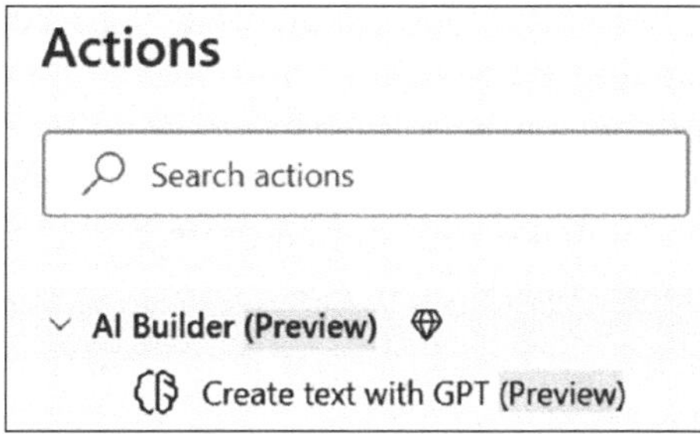

Figure 11.13: *A sample Preview action*

This is not only about Actions but also about features of the tool, such as the one in *Figure* 11.14. For example, creating Power Fx enabled Flows are in Preview and cannot be productionized.

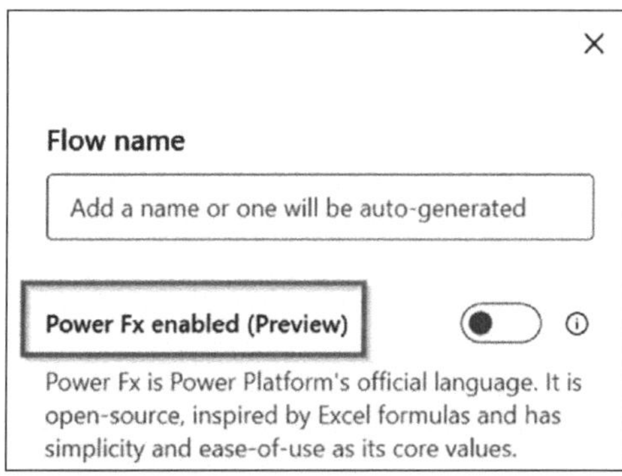

Figure 11.14: *A sample Preview feature*

Cleaning Up of Flow

This applies to the removal of any disabled Actions, unused variables, unwanted UI elements, and so on to keep it clean, readable, and developer-friendly.

This concludes the list of development best practices. You might come across additional ones as you progress in your automation journey. Organizations have stitched together their own error handling mechanism, logging, config files, Subflows, use of Work Queues, and more. They have also created their own PAD framework.

Some final words about best practices are that they should serve as a good guideline. Yes, it is possible that not all best practices can be followed at all times. Use the majority of the ones that work most suitably as per your situation. Implementing the maximum possible ones can go a long way in developing high-quality automation.

Conclusion

These PAD development best practices ensure that your bots are efficient, reliable, and maintainable. By following standardized approaches, developers can create bots that are easier to understand and modify. They can reduce errors and simplify the troubleshooting further, leading to more robust and resilient automation solutions. Having a modular design can make your bots more scalable and flexible, allowing you to adapt to changing business needs.

In the next chapter, "*Extending the Landscape of Your Desktop Flows*", we will see the different ways of extending the reach of your Desktop Flows. It will further give you information on licensing and certification topics.

CHAPTER 12
Extending the Landscape of Your Desktop Flows

Introduction

In this chapter, we will delve into the topics that extend the horizons of your PAD implementations. We will see what Hosted RPA is, how the Picture-in-Picture feature works and its benefits, what are Custom Actions and a direction on how to create and manage them, and how to use the Power Fx low-code language in Desktop Flows. Additionally, we will go through the crucial aspects of Licensing and Certification.

Structure

We will be looking at the following topics in this chapter:

- Hosted RPA
- Picture-in-Picture
- Custom Actions
- Power Fx
- Licensing
- Certification

Hosted RPA

Just like machines and machine groups, Microsoft provides a facility to create Hosted machines and Hosted machine groups, but with a major difference that these machines are hosted and managed by Microsoft. In other words, Microsoft will host virtual machines on an Azure infrastructure which can then be used to run attended and unattended RPA automation without you getting involved in the setup. This innovative method of deploying your PAD bots on hosted machines removes the burden on any company to handle the setup and management of virtual machines required to run the bots. Imagine the lengthy process it would take for manually setting up an RPA infrastructure starting from its inception from requesting a machine till its final readiness.

- **Hosted machines** can be used for attended and unattended bots. They are typically used by bot developers to **develop** and **test** their bots, whereas end users **run** the bots on these machines.
- **Hosted machine groups** can be used for **running** unattended automation in the Production environment. Since they are groups of machines, these can automatically adjust the workloads during unattended automation in the Production environment. Thus, the main advantage of Hosted machine groups is their ability to automatically distribute bots across various groups, thereby balancing the workload of the bots.

They are created via the **"`Machines`"** tab of the Cloud portal.

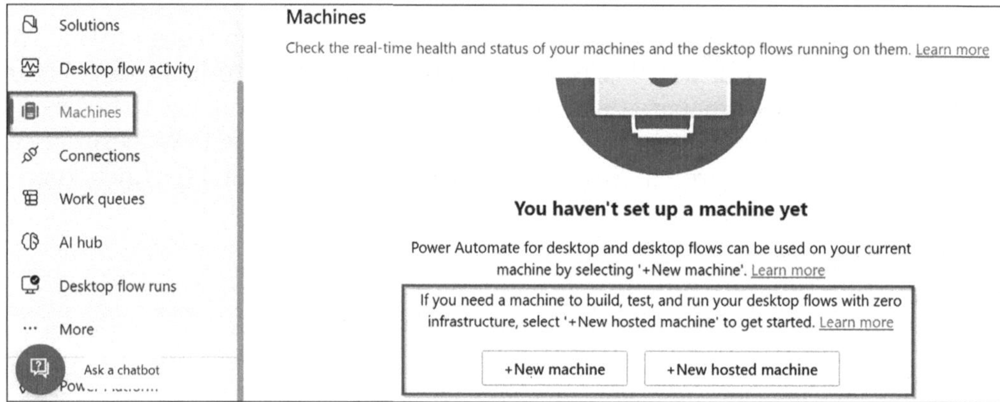

Figure 12.1: *Create hosted machines*

Either Microsoft will provide a *vanilla* virtual machine image that will have default settings and without any customizations, or you can personalize your own hosted machine by providing your own Windows image with all the applications and software installed on that machine needed for your automation.

You need to know the prerequisites, limitations, how they are created and accessed, how to use custom virtual machine images from the Azure Compute Gallery, how to restart them if needed, what permissions are necessary, and so on. Therefore, an extended reading on these topics is needed, and they can be done via the following links. The licensing required for this is mentioned under the "*Licensing*" topic of this chapter.

Overview:

https://learn.microsoft.com/en-us/power-automate/desktop-flows/hosted-rpa-overview

Hosted machines:

https://learn.microsoft.com/en-us/power-automate/desktop-flows/hosted-machines

Hosted machine groups:

https://learn.microsoft.com/en-us/power-automate/desktop-flows/hosted-machine-groups

Picture-in-Picture

Many a times in attended automation, it becomes challenging when a user wants to continue working with their daily tasks on their machine while the bot is running on the same machine. If the bot is running in the background, there are chances of it getting interrupted by the user's activities on that machine. This would generally happen when the bot tries to launch an application, send mouse clicks and keystrokes, focus on a window, perform any kind of UI-based interaction, and so on. The bot could stall or give unwanted results if the user also, at the same time, tries to type something, click using the mouse, or switch the window focus, thus obstructing the running of the bot. This can be circumvented with a feature in PAD called Picture-in-Picture (PIP).

In PIP, the bot launches and starts in an isolated copy of the local machine, separating it from the user's desktop. The difference between a hosted machine and PIP is that the hosted machine is a separate remote virtual machine, whereas the one in PIP is the image of the same local machine from which the automation is started.

The following figure is an output of a bot that launches the Contoso application and displays the ID present on the **"`Accounts`"** tab, all inside the PIP window, when run from the local machine. Notice how identical the two are, marked as **"`Local Desktop`"** and **"`PIP window`"**.

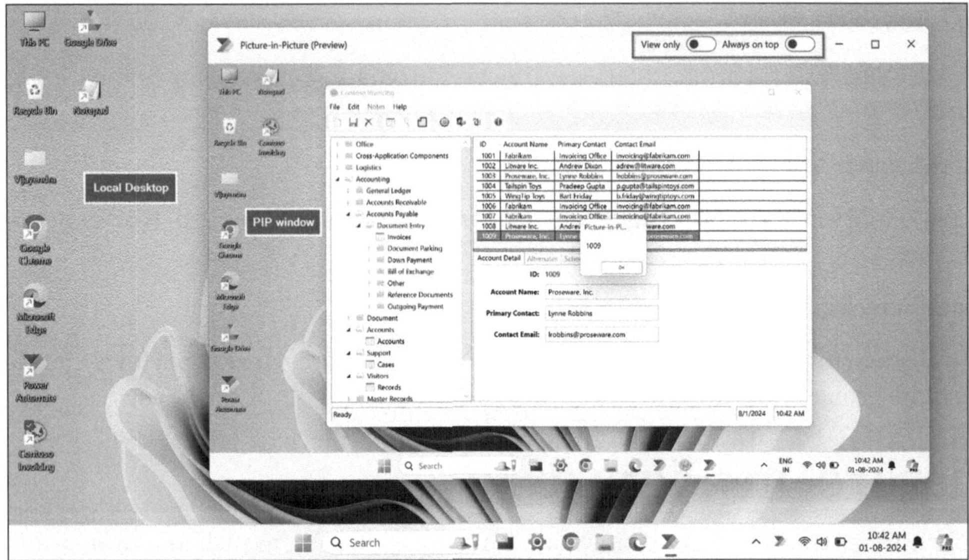

Figure 12.2: *Flow output in PIP window*

Using PIP, anyone can continue their work on the local machine while the automation is running, as well as open the PIP window and watch what is happening in the automation or "attend" to it to click a button or a pop-up, all from the user's desktop.

On the top of *Figure* 12.2, there are marked toggles for **`"View only"`**, which locks the PIP window to avoid any accidental inputs, and the **`"Always on top"`** option to keep the PIP window always on top of other windows.

Let us see the different ways of running a Flow in PIP mode.

1. **From the main Console:**

   Select a Flow from the list on the main Console and then the dropdown next to the **`"Run"`** button, as marked in *Figure* 12.3, to see the **`"Run in Picture-in-Picture"`** menu option.

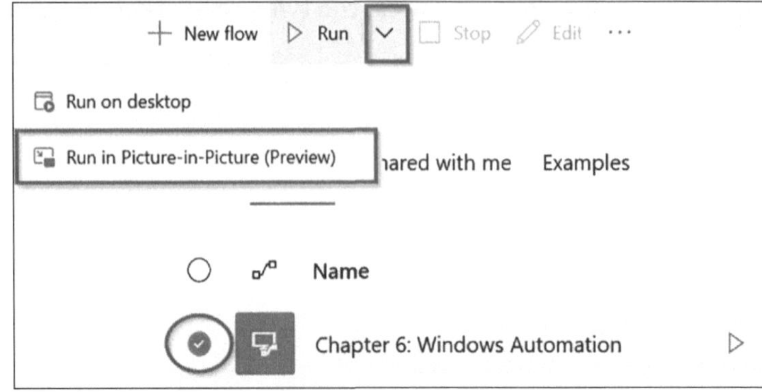

Figure 12.3: *PIP from the main console*

2. **From the "`More actions`" ellipsis menu:**

   Either use the ellipsis menu or right-click a Flow and use the menu options, as shown in *Figure 12.4*.

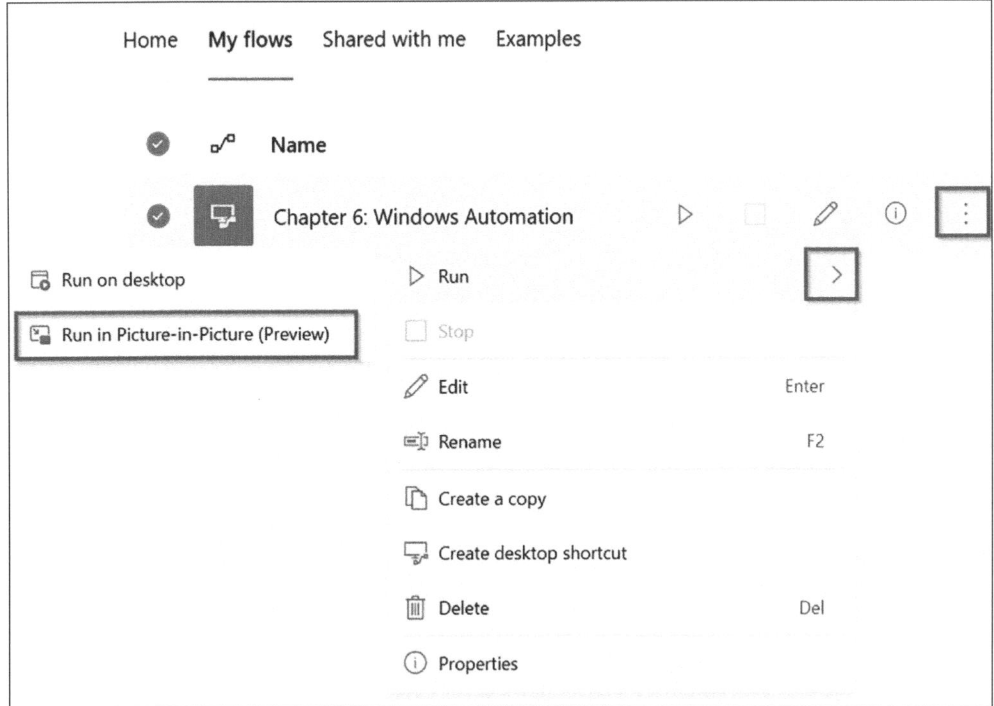

***Figure 12.4**: PIP from the more actions ellipsis*

3. **From the Flow properties:**

   Via the **"`Properties`"** menu item of *Figure 12.4*, go to the **"`General`"** tab of the Flow properties and enable the toggle shown to run the selected Flow always in PIP mode by default, which takes effect when run from the Console.

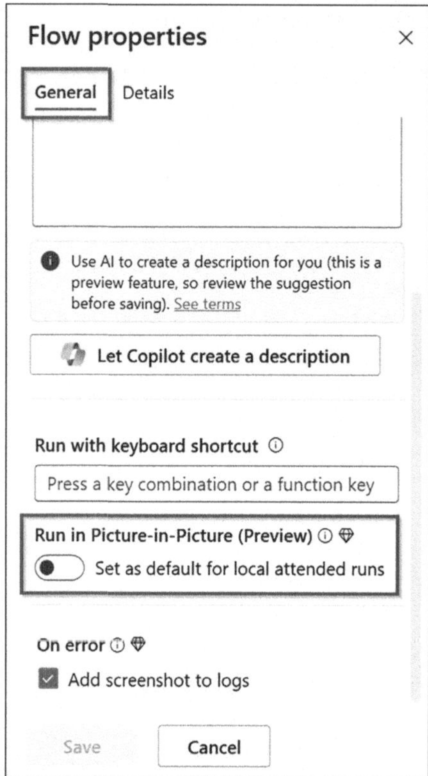

Figure 12.5: *PIP from the Flow properties*

4. **From the Flow designer:**

   You can also debug the Flow from the **"Debug"** menu of the Flow designer.

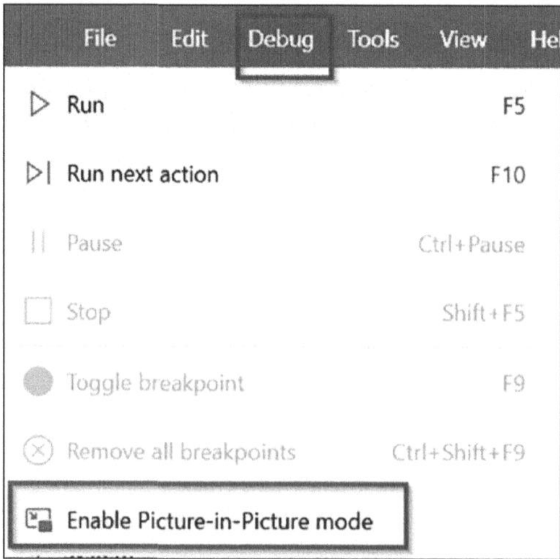

Figure 12.6: *PIP from the Flow designer*

The Picture-in-Picture feature is in Preview currently and is also a premium feature. It has certain limitations that you need to know of, along with how this feature is enabled, how it can be run from the Cloud Flows, what are the prerequisites, and any other known issues; all of these are listed in the following link:

https://learn.microsoft.com/en-us/power-automate/desktop-flows/run-desktop-flows-pip

Custom Actions

We have been using the in-built list of Actions from the **"Actions"** pane of the Flow designer to build any Flows. But what if you would like to build your own **"Action"** and make it available in the **"Actions"** pane so that you or anyone in your development team or organization can make use of it? This is what Custom Actions are used for, to build your own customized Action and then include them in your Desktop Flows. Once dropped onto the Workspace from the **"Actions"** pane, they can then be used similar to the other pre-built Actions. Thus, it behaves as a reusable component and, once built, can be centrally managed and shared across other Desktop Flows.

Custom Actions are built using the Power Automate Desktop Actions Software Development Kit (SDK), which offers methodologies for developers to build these Actions with the C#.NET language.

They involve a series of steps and procedures. Once built, they are added to the **"Actions"** pane via the **"Assets Library"** button located on the Flow designer.

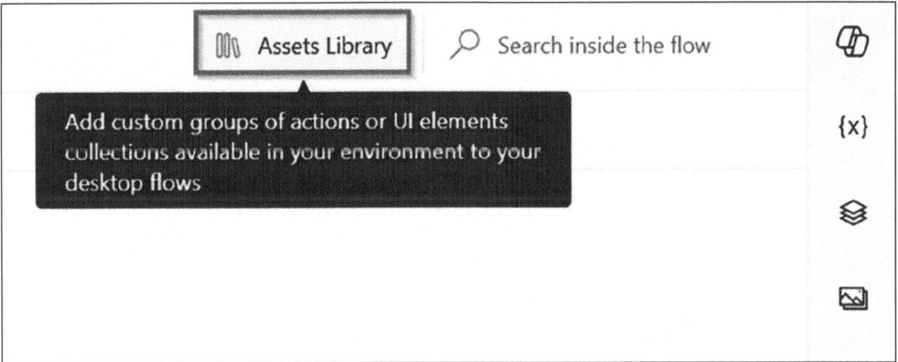

Figure 12.7: *Add custom actions from the Flow designer*

How they are built, deployed, used, and updated, what installations have to be made, what are the prerequisites, known limitations – all of these are walked through as a comprehensive guide in the various sections of the following article. Custom Actions are also a premium feature:

https://learn.microsoft.com/en-us/power-automate/desktop-flows/custom-actions

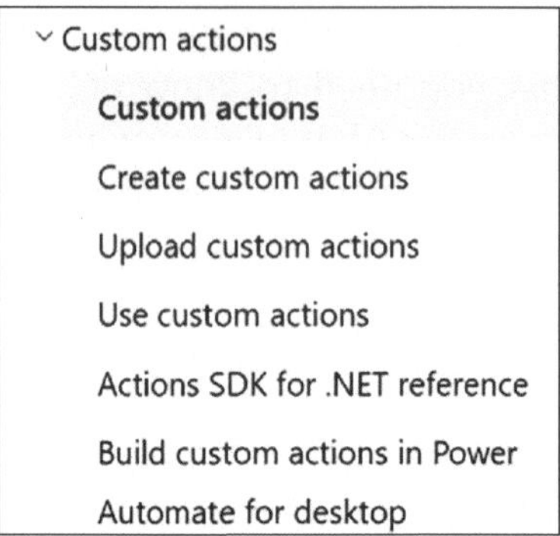

Figure 12.8: *Learning articles for custom actions*

The last section in *Figure* 12.8 shows a Custom Action for writing log messages to the specified file.

Power Fx

Power Fx is the low-code language that is used across the Microsoft Power Platform and is similar to Excel-like formulas. They have been widely used in Power Apps, and now they are introduced in Power Automate Desktop too.

Let's straight away head on to its practical usage on the PAD tool.

When you create a new Flow, the tool will ask you whether to create a Power Fx-enabled Flow via the toggle, as shown in *Figure* 12.9. As mentioned on the toggle, this feature is in Preview as of this writing.

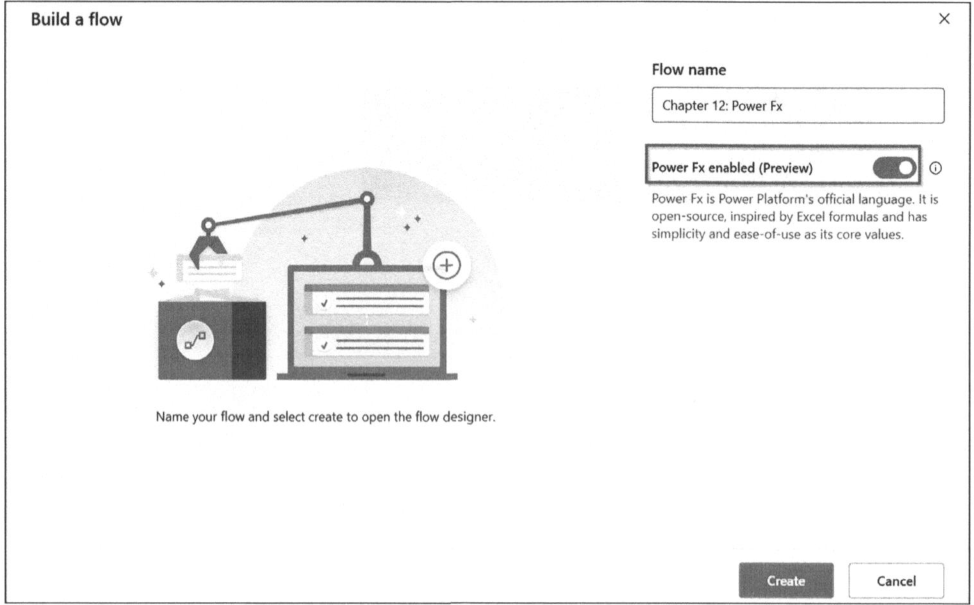

Figure 12.9: *Creating Power Fx-enabled Flows*

Once the Flow is created, it will be denoted in the Flow designer by a notification text, as marked in *Figure* 12.10. This will tell you that you can create Flows in this designer only using the Power Fx language. There is no detailed documentation specifically on how to use Power Fx in PAD as of this writing. But the **"Learn more"** link will take you to an overview of Power Fx and how they are used in Power Apps. Let us hope that Microsoft points the link to PAD related usage of Power Fx in the near future.

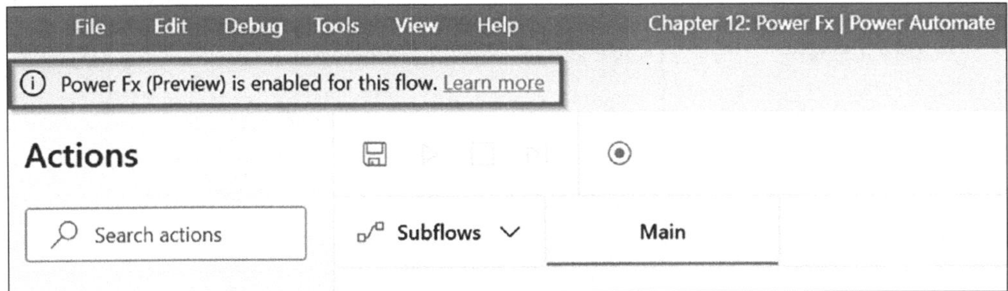

***Figure* 12.10:** *Power Fx enabled Flow*

Set a variable called **`InvoiceAmount`** with a value such as **`$2000`** for this example, and we will use a display message box to print a message such as **`Your total amount is $2000`**.

In Flows **without** Power Fx, you would use the following notation in the message box:

```
Your total amount is %InvoiceAmount%
```

Using Power Fx, the notation is as follows:

```
="Your total amount is " & InvoiceAmount
```

It begins with an "equal to" sign just like Excel formulas, and the text to be shown is in double quotes followed by an ampersand to concatenate the **`InvoiceAmount`** variable. The prefix and suffix of a percent sign for a PAD variable are not used. As shown in *Figure* 12.11, the color of the hard-coded text is also different from the variable, as PAD knows this as a Power Fx-enabled Flow.

Display message

Displays a message box More info

Message box title: Power Fx

Message to display: ="Your total amount is " & InvoiceAmount

Message box icon: None

Message box buttons: OK

On error Save Cancel

Figure 12.11: *Power Fx notation*

If you try to use the conventional notation of **`Your total amount is %InvoiceAmount%`** in a Power Fx- enabled Flow, then you would get incorrect results, as shown in *Figure* 12.12.

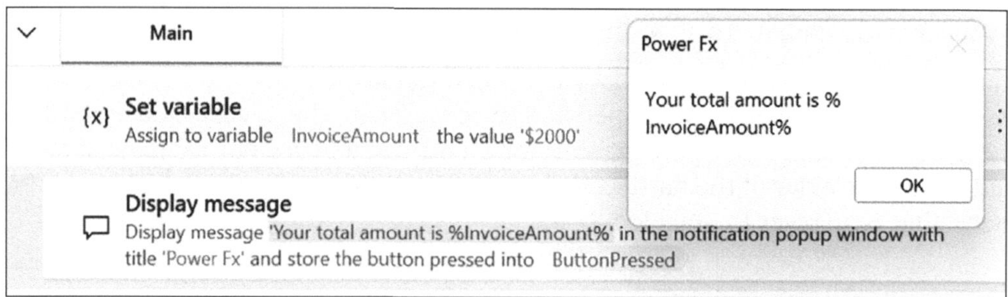

Figure 12.12: *Incorrect output using wrong notation*

When you type an "equal to" sign and start typing a few characters of any existing list of Power Fx functions, the tool shows up a list of functions matching those characters with a tooltip text help of that function, as shown in *Figure* 12.13. Furthermore, as you use the chosen function, it will also start to show the different parameters needed for that function.

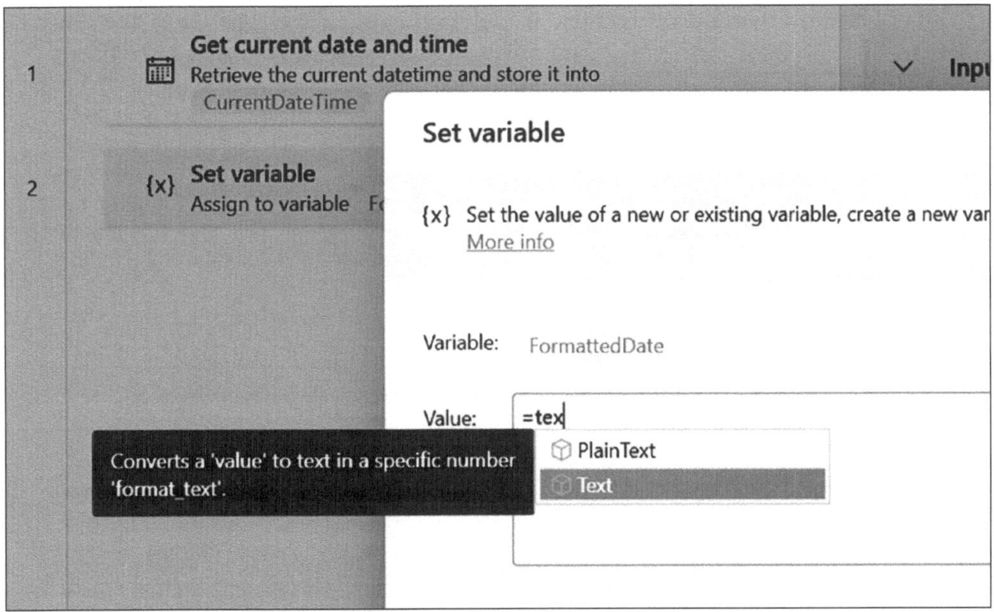

Figure 12.13: *Power Fx function on equal to sign*

You could also make use of the Power Fx functions button, as shown in *Figure* 12.14, next to the variable picker, to bring up the list of available functions.

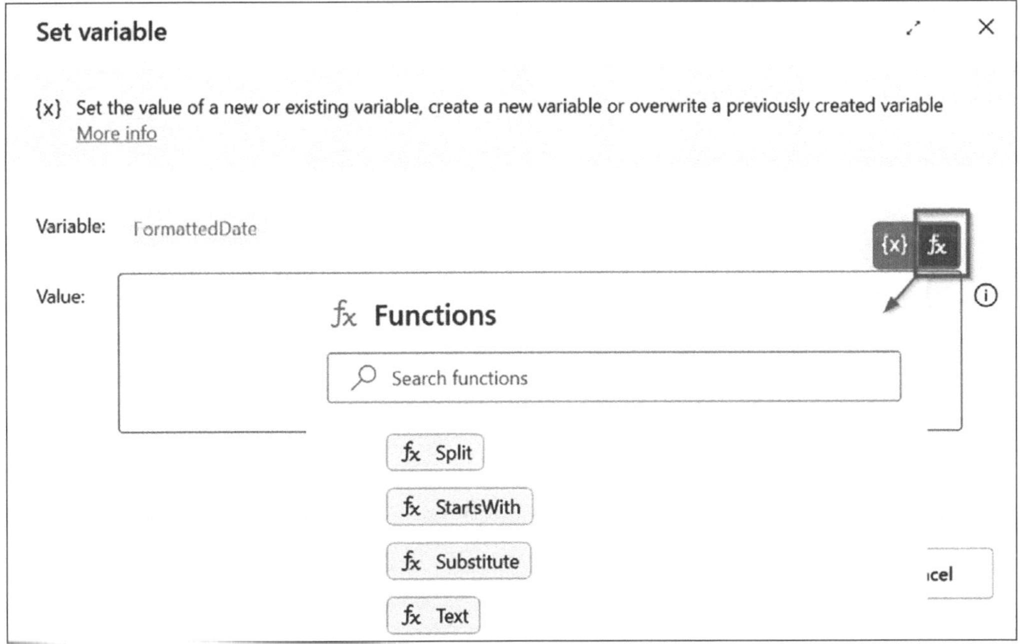

Figure 12.14: *Power Fx function picker*

Get the current date and time and use it in a **"Set variable"** with a **"Text"** function similar to the following, and check the output of the **FormattedDate** variable.

```
=Text(CurrentDateTime,"dd/MM/yyyy")
```

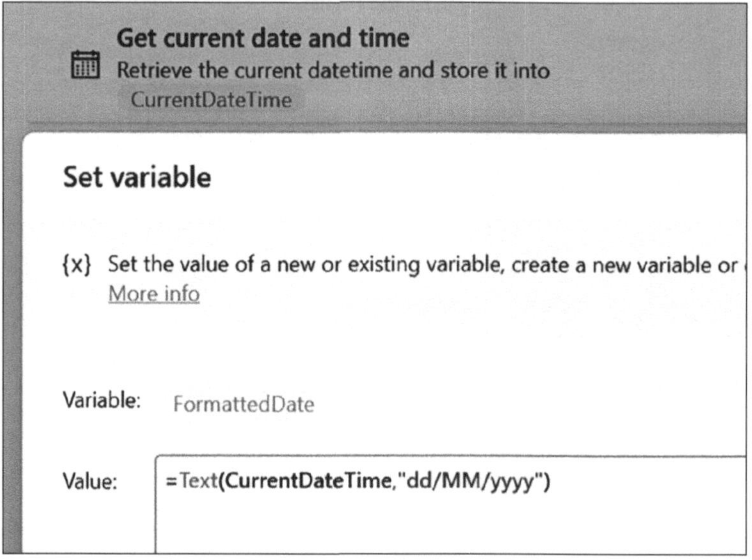

Figure 12.15: *Sample usage of Power Fx function*

This time do not use the **"Get current date and time"** Action and here is another usage of two functions together, that is, the **Text** and the **Today** function.

```
=Text(Today(),"dd/MM/yyyy")
```

String Interpolation in Power Fx

String interpolation (not a feature of PAD) is a concept that allows developers to inject variables or expressions directly into a normal text or string. It makes creating and formatting strings easier and more readable. They have been used in programming languages, are already available in Power Apps, and now in Power Automate Desktop too.

In *Figure 12.16*, **strFirstName** and **strLastName** are two different variables initialized with values via the **"Set variable"** Action.

The interpolated format of the string used here is:

```
=$"Welcome, {strFirstName} {strLastName}. Today is a nice day!"
```

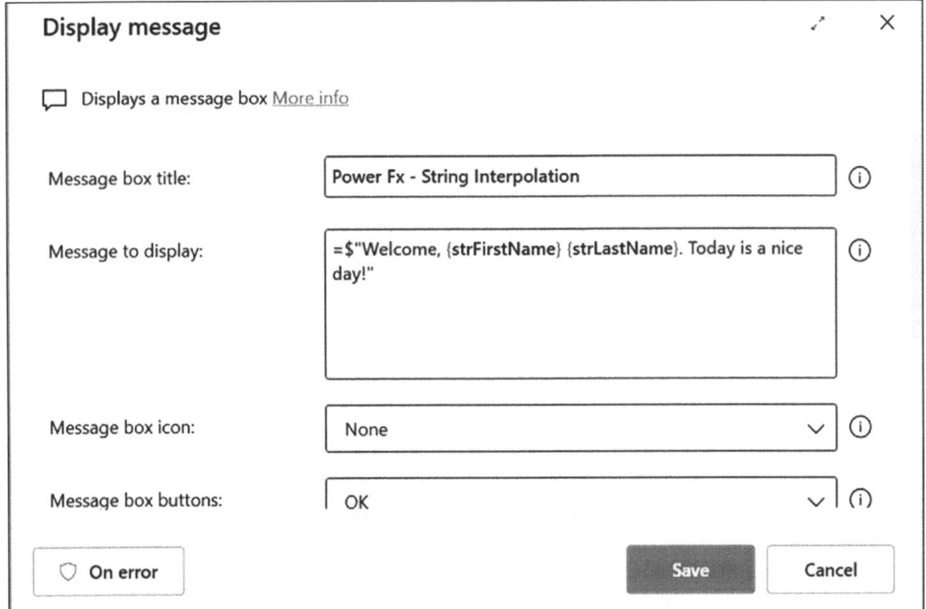

***Figure 12.16:** Sample usage of interpolated string in Power Fx*

Following is the output of the string interpolation after initializing the variables:

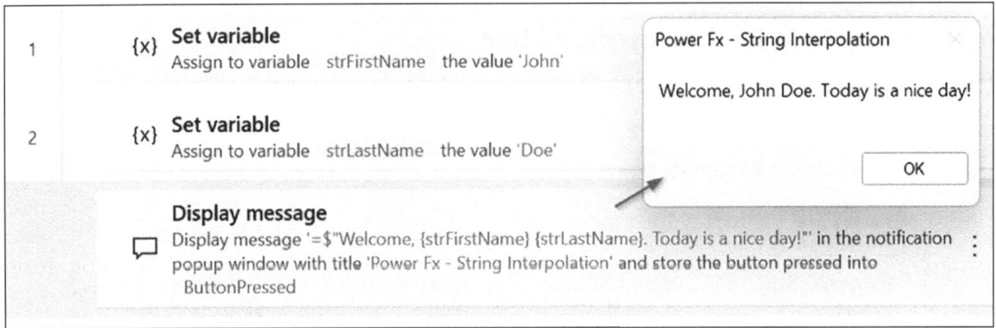

***Figure 12.17:** Output using string interpolation*

Some key points to note about string interpolation are:

- Interpolated strings begin with a **"$"** sign, as in *Figure 12.16*. The **"="** sign at the start is the Power Fx notation.
- Curly braces **{}** are used to evaluate and embed a variable or expression.
- Both normal text or interpolated strings can be used anywhere within that line of text. In the aforementioned example, the textual wordings and the variables are used in continuous sequence within the same line of text without any **"&"** operator or quotes inside the string.
- They are applicable only for Power Fx-enabled Desktop Flows.

Licensing

Either when you use any of the existing PAD features or when you extend the landscape of your automation towards other areas of the tool, knowing what licensing is needed for which features of the tool becomes necessary.

The licensing of Power Automate and its multiple plans have changed a couple of times in the past, and there may even be possibilities of changing in the future.

Therefore, bookmark the following pricing page and refer to the various plans available as of this writing, which gives a short description of each of the plans (*Figure 12.18*). Notice the "user/month" and "bot/month" below the amount under the plan names to indicate which plan is per user and which one is per bot. Also refer to the highlighted sections for plans having the unattended and attended options. The "*Power Automate Hosted Process*" plan is for the "*Hosted RPA*" topic we went through in this chapter:

https://www.microsoft.com/en-us/power-platform/products/power-automate/pricing

The aforementioned link is for USD. To change the currency, refer to the wordings **"`en-in`"** in the following link that refers to the currency in INR:

https://www.microsoft.com/**en-in**/power-platform/products/power-automate/pricing

The following link is for the currency in GBP:

https://www.microsoft.com/**en-gb**/power-platform/products/power-automate/pricing

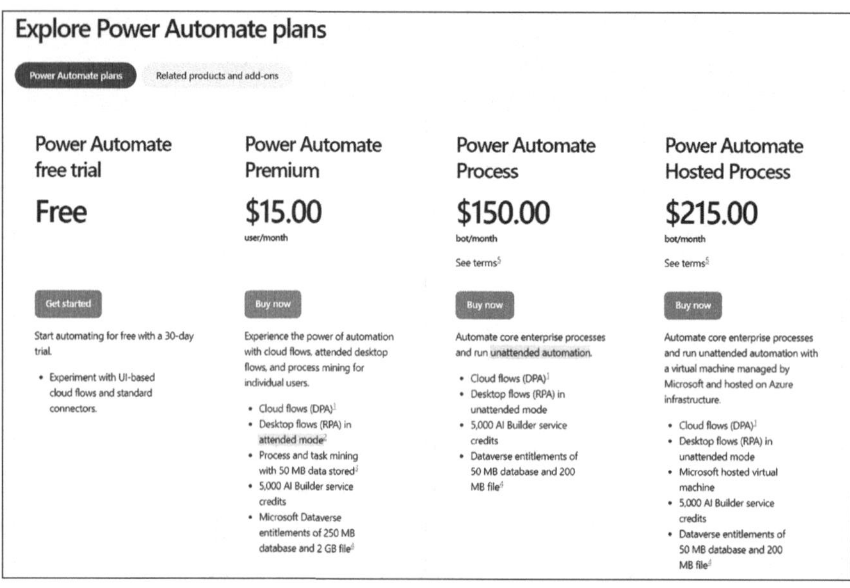

Figure 12.18: *Power Automate pricing plans*

Scroll down on the web page to get a comparison chart of which features are available in each plan.

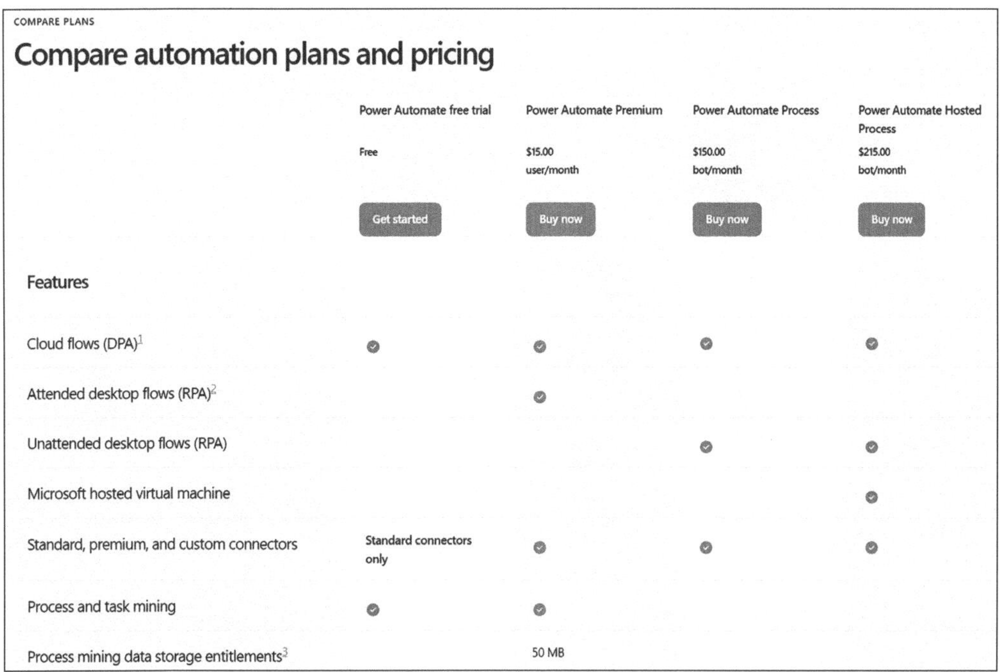

COMPARE PLANS

Compare automation plans and pricing

	Power Automate free trial	Power Automate Premium	Power Automate Process	Power Automate Hosted Process
	Free	$15.00 user/month	$150.00 bot/month	$215.00 bot/month
	Get started	Buy now	Buy now	Buy now
Features				
Cloud flows (DPA)[1]	✓	✓	✓	✓
Attended desktop flows (RPA)[2]		✓		
Unattended desktop flows (RPA)			✓	✓
Microsoft hosted virtual machine				✓
Standard, premium, and custom connectors	Standard connectors only	✓	✓	✓
Process and task mining	✓	✓		
Process mining data storage entitlements[3]		50 MB		

Figure 12.19: *Power Automate pricing table of comparison*

Scrolling down will take you to downloading a guide, which will give comprehensive details on the licensing.

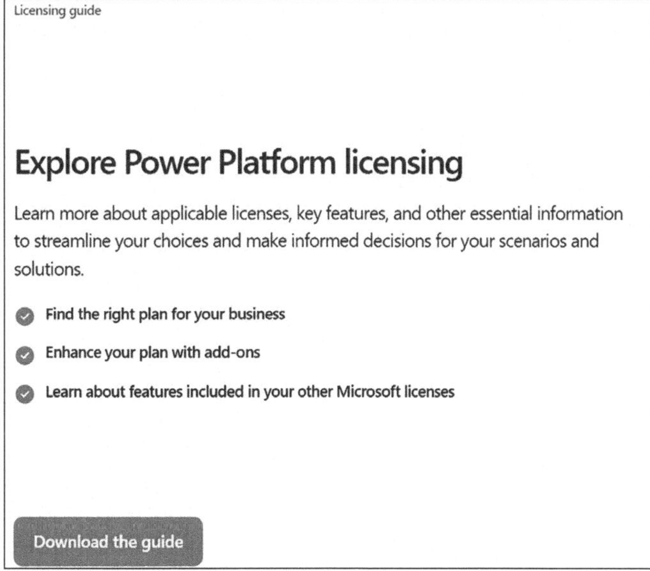

Figure 12.20: *Download the licensing guide*

The Platform also provides certain add-ons that you should be aware of and is available from the marked button, as shown in *Figure* 12.21.

For example, your AI Builder credits have elapsed and you want to buy more as an add-on.

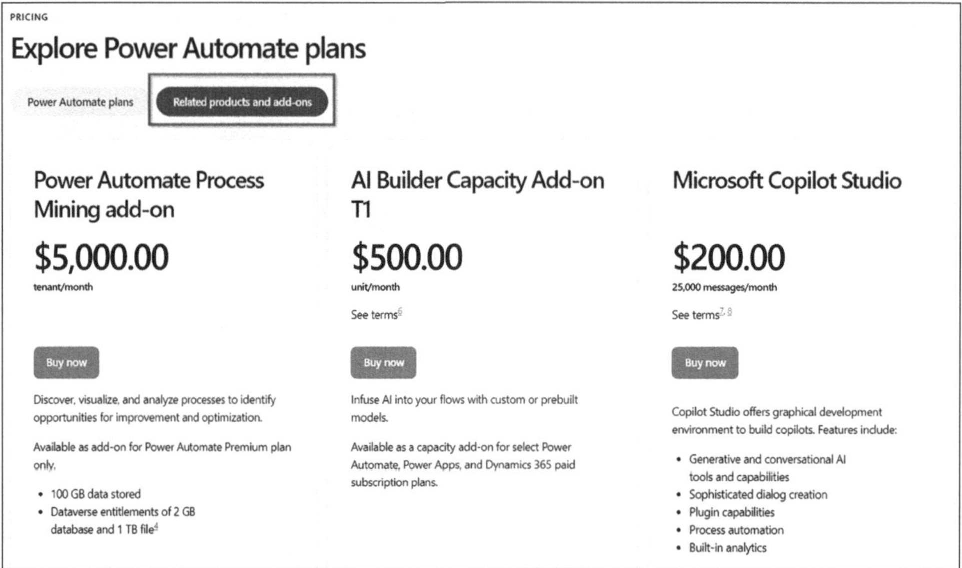

Figure 12.21: *Add-on information*

Another thing that you should be aware of is the premium features list for RPA. You can find more information at:

https://learn.microsoft.com/en-us/power-automate/desktop-flows/premium-features

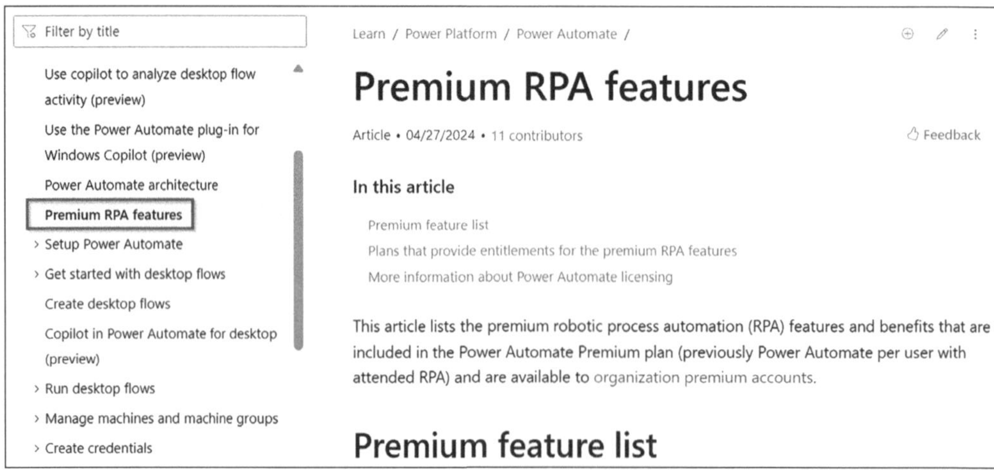

Figure 12.22: RPA *premium features list page*

With the varied amount of information available for several features, it becomes necessary to get a clear understanding of the license types in comparison with the scale of the automation you want to achieve. Also, if you already have other types of licenses, for example, coming from M365, there may be a possibility that you may already be having access to certain premium features. Therefore, it is recommended to get in touch with a Microsoft licensing specialist and discuss the licensing requirements showing your existing landscape and the future scope of your automation.

Certification

It is not just about extending the landscape of the Flows, but also about expanding *your* knowledge on Power Automate Desktop in itself and in conjunction with other areas of the Power Platform.

As of now, there is no dedicated certification fully for PAD, but a major part of the **PL-500 exam** has Desktop Flows in its scope. Hence, by completing this exam, you will extend your knowledge not only in Desktop Flows but also to other areas of the Power Platform. After completing this exam, you will be certified as a **Power Automate RPA Developer Associate**. For all the current and future aspirants of Power Automate Desktop, this is a *go-to* certificate.

You can explore the topics, scope, exam details, learning modules, resources, study guide, as well as schedule the exam, all from the same page:

https://learn.microsoft.com/en-us/credentials/certifications/power-automate-rpa-developer-associate

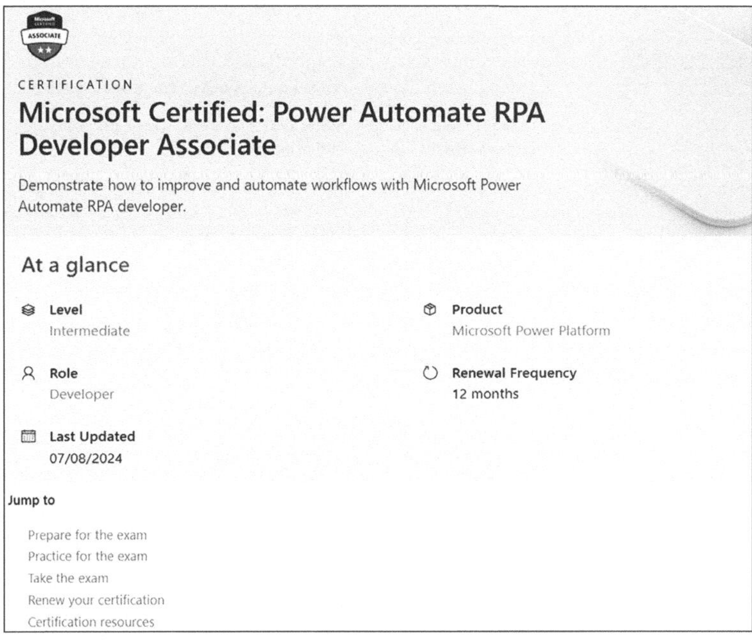

Figure 12.23: *PL-500 certification page*

Conclusion

In conclusion, this chapter has provided you with the essential knowledge to elevate your PAD projects to newer heights. By incorporating Hosted RPA, you can ease the activities of your IT team, use Picture-in-Picture to greatly assist you while the user and the bot work at the same time, learn how Custom Actions can help in achieving greater flexibility, and learn a new way of building Flows using Power Fx as the low-code language of the Platform. This chapter has also pointed out where to look for information on Licensing and Certification, which benefits you in cost management and in being proficient.

Links and Resources

Here you will find key links to Microsoft resources to do a further deep dive in your Power Automate Desktop journey and will provide information on how to stay abreast with the latest of what is going on in the PAD world.

- **Alphabetical list of all Actions in PAD:**

  Here you will find the list of all the Actions available in the **"Actions"** pane in PAD:

  https://learn.microsoft.com/en-us/power-automate/desktop-flows/actions-reference

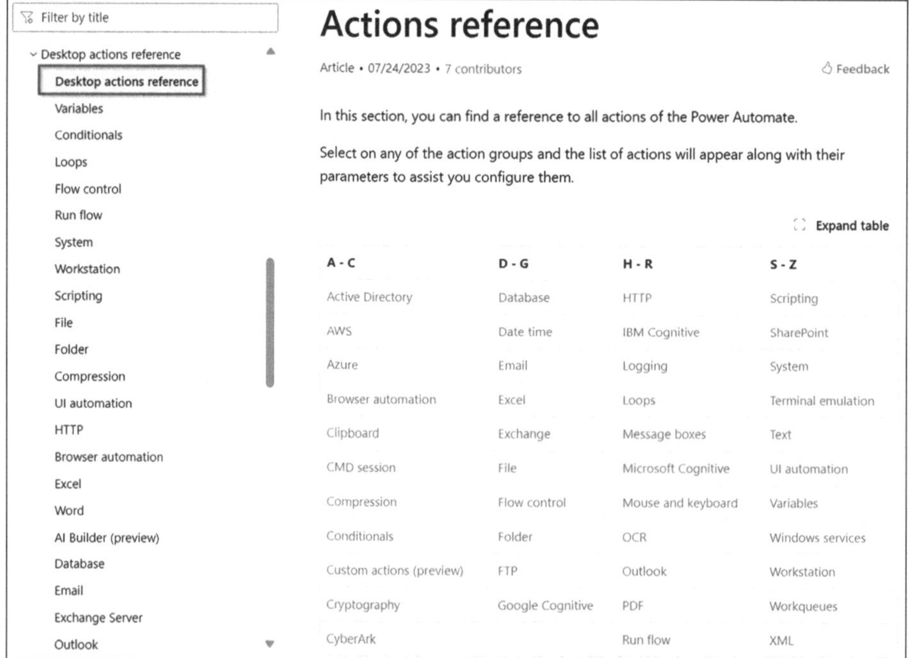

Figure 12.24: *Alphabetical list of PAD actions*

- **PAD learning modules:**

  Using the **"`Learn`"** submenu from the **"`Help`"** menu of the main Console, it will take you to different learning modules from Microsoft specifically for Power Automate Desktop.

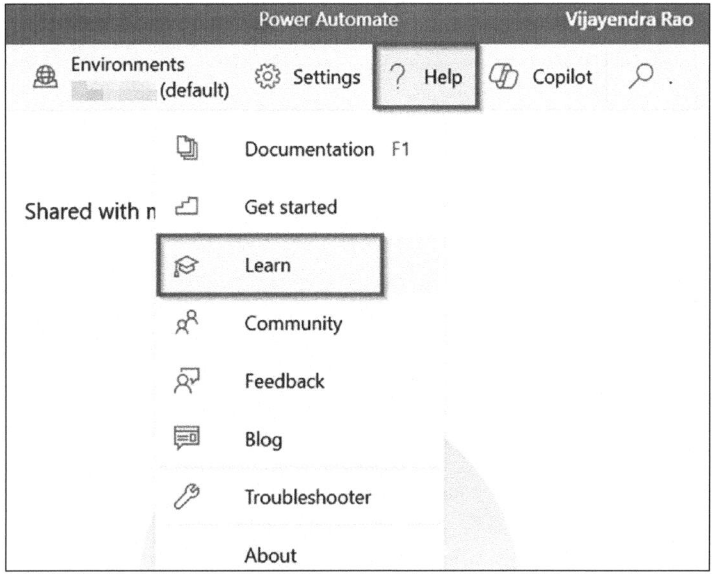

***Figure 12.25:** Learn section from console*

Going through the menu will do a direct search and give the list of available modules for Power Automate Desktop.

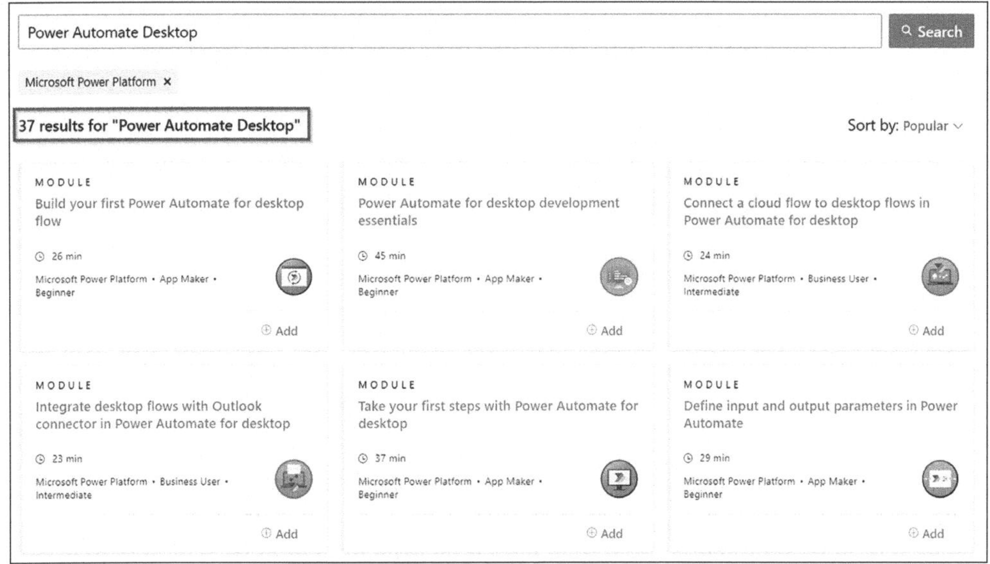

***Figure 12.26:** Learning modules for PAD*

- **Dig deeper:**

  A deep dive for further exploration and a continued journey is required on the current as well as all the upcoming features of the PAD tool, and this is done via the **"Documentation"** section of the **"Help"** menu.

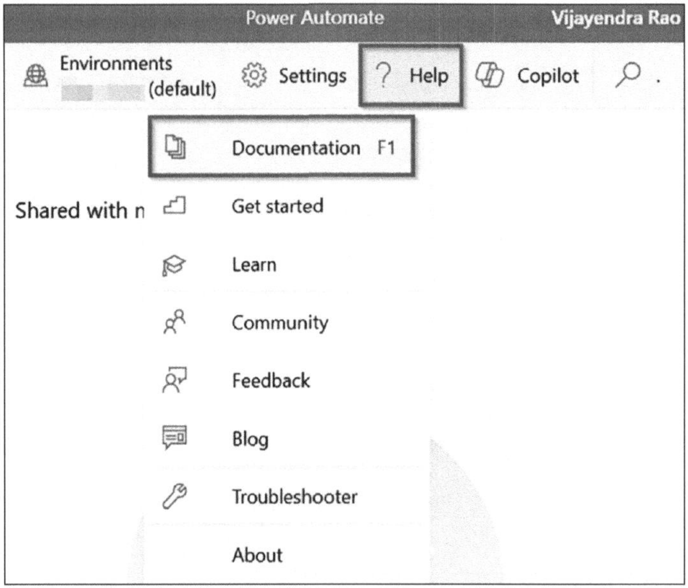

Figure 12.27: *Documentation section from console*

Use the left-hand navigation to search for the desired topic.

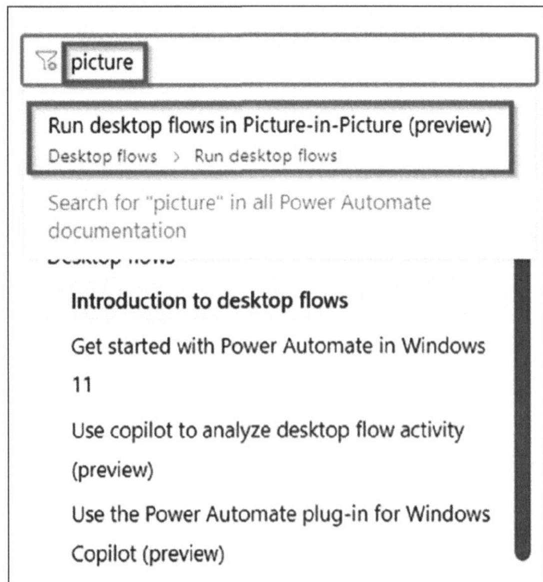

Figure 12.28: *Search topics in Documentation*

- **PAD product updates:**

  A strong recommendation is to keep a watch on these monthly updates, read the new features, and practice them on the tool. That way you will stay updated with the latest happenings in the world of Power Automate Desktop.

  This is done through the Microsoft Power Automate blog:

  https://www.microsoft.com/en-us/power-platform/blog/power-automate

  Make use of the filters and tags for the month-wise updates to see what went into the tool in each month and what is coming up in the next version.

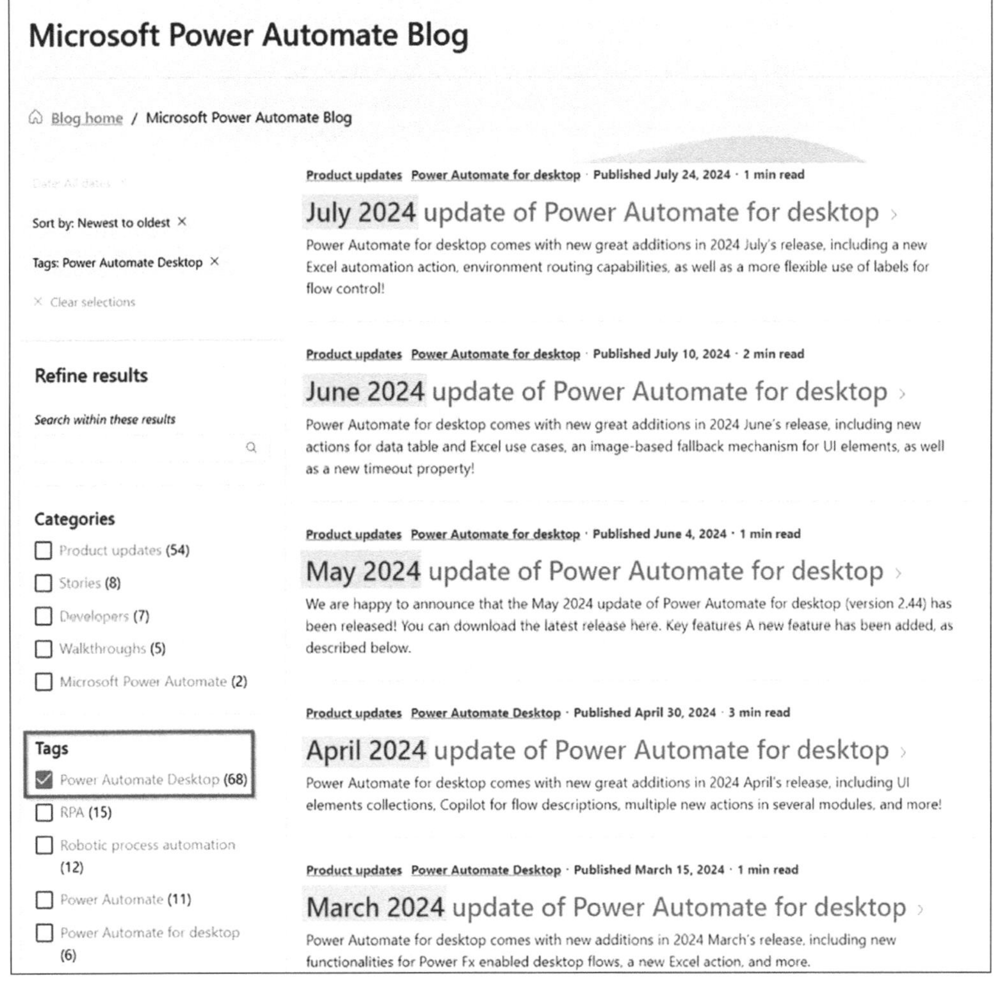

Figure 12.29: *Month-wise product updates*

- **Automation-in-a-day (AuIAD):**

  Earlier called RPA-in-a-day, this is a free instructor-led workshop from

Microsoft and its training partners where you will get practical hands-on training on Cloud Flows, AI Builder, and Desktop Flows, among other features of the Platform.

Visit the **"`Automation in a Day`"** section in the following link and refer to the workshop contents and how to register:

https://www.microsoft.com/en-us/power-platform/instructor-led-training

Automation in a Day

This beginner-level one-day course is designed for you to learn automation using Power Automate and Power Automate Desktop.

While possibilities are limitless, your time is not. No matter if you're a business expert or IT developer, you'll learn to digitize business processes, connect all your applications to share data in real time, and automate and optimize your business processes.

At the end of the day, attendees will understand how to:

- Use Power Automate capabilities such as desktop flows to automate a business process.
- Take advantage of form-processing models developed in AI Builder.
- Use Cloud flows to orchestrate the execution of desktop flows.

The workshop assets are split into two parts:

1. Instructor content includes presentation decks, demo scripts, and train-the-trainer materials.

Download English instructor content >

2. Attendee content includes modules and hands-on labs in the Online Workshop learning path on Microsoft Learn. Other languages are available on Microsoft Learn; select the language identifier on the bottom left of the Microsoft Learn page. Not all languages are available.

Figure 12.30: *Automation in a day workshop details*

- **Community forum:**

  A single place for all the talented people in PAD from all over the world. A single post can help you get going if you are stuck.

  Try to be active on the forum by reading questions and answering them. This is sure to increase your knowledge, not to mention the different ranks and recognition you will get in doing so, such as Solution Sage, Super User, scheduled calls with the PAD product team, and so on. Also, you would make contacts with PAD enthusiasts on the forum from all around the globe.

This is done through the **"Community"** section in the **"Help"** menu.

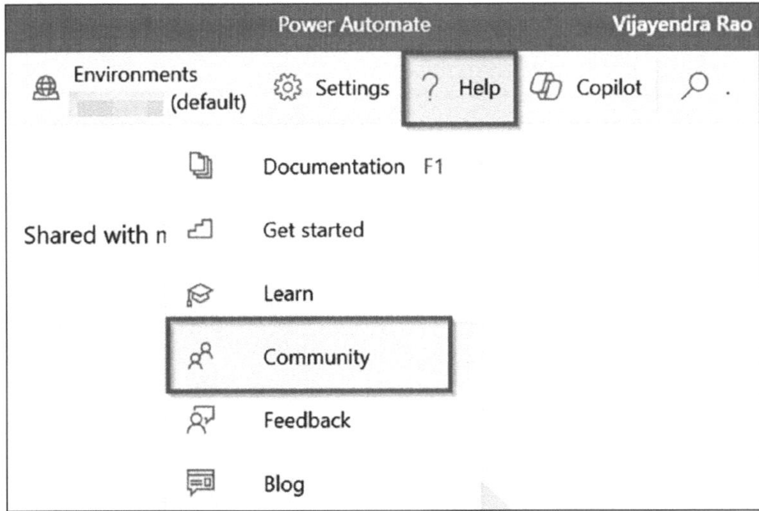

Figure 12.31: *Community section from console*

This menu will take you to a specific section on the community dedicated to Power Automate Desktop questions and answers.

As a thumb rule-
If you know an answer, post it.
If you do not know, find out and post it.

That is the way to share as well as learn at the same time.
This *finding* could be either from the posts of fellow forum members, or yourself researching through various learning resources or practically trying out the tool.

One of the best ways of increasing your PAD knowledge is to:
Be active on the forum
Share what you know
Ask what you don't

Happy automation!

Index

P